Launching Democracy in South Africa

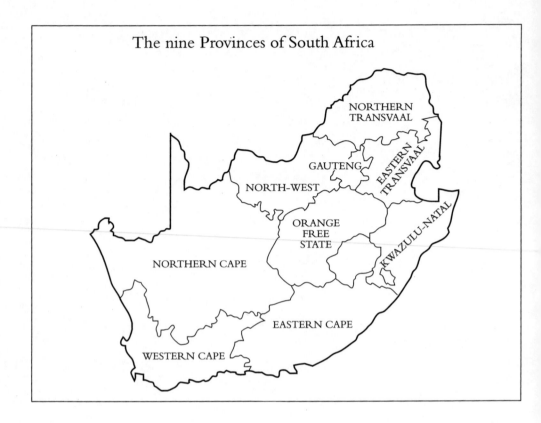

The nine Provinces of South Africa

NORTHERN TRANSVAAL

GAUTENG

EASTERN TRANSVAAL

NORTH-WEST

ORANGE FREE STATE

KWAZULU-NATAL

NORTHERN CAPE

EASTERN CAPE

WESTERN CAPE

Launching Democracy in South Africa

The First Open Election, April 1994

Edited by
R.W. Johnson & Lawrence Schlemmer

Yale University Press
New Haven and London 1996

Set in Bembo by Best-set Typesetter Ltd, Hong Kong
Printed and bound in Great Britain by
Biddles Ltd, Guildford and Kings Lynn

Library of Congress Cataloging-in-Publication Data

Launching democracy in South Africa: the first open election, April 1994/
edited by R.W. Johnson and Lawrence Schlemmer.
Includes index.
ISBN 0–300–06391–1 (hb)
1. Elections – South Africa.   2. South Africa. Parliament – Elections, 1994.
3. South Africa – Politics and government – 1989–1994.
4. Democracy – South Africa.   I. Johnson, R.W.
(Richard William)   II. Schlemmer, Lawrence.
JQ1994.L38   1996
324.968'064 – dco
95–6564
CIP

A catalogue record for this book is available from the British Library

Contents

Foreword

VERY FEW, IF ANY, open elections in Africa have attracted as much international and local interest as the South African election held in April 1994. It was this unprecedented interest that prompted the Institute for Multi-Party Democracy (MPD) to commission a comprehensive study of the election. The objective of this study was to record and document the attitudes of voters, the level of support the various parties enjoyed before the election and the problems and opportunities that the election presented to the entire South African population. The results of this study yielded very interesting information which is now being published in book form for the benefit of present and future scholars and observers of the South African sociopolitical scene.

The Institute is indebted to Professors Bill Johnson, Lawrence Schlemmer, Mervyn Frost and Paulus Zulu, who led this study and co-ordinated a team of South African experts in the various provinces where the study was conducted. We are also indebted to numerous South African and overseas donors who demonstrated their confidence in the integrity and credibility of our Institute and agreed to support the proposal for study.

Finally, we must state that the views expressed in this book are those of the contributors and not necessarily those of the Institute for Multi-Party Democracy.

Dr Oscar D. Dhlomo
Executive Chairman
Institute for Multi-Party Democracy

Acknowledgements

WE SHOULD LIKE TO thank a number of people and institutions for their support, without which this book could not have been written. Most of all we are indebted to the Institute for Multi-Party Democracy and its Director, Dr Oscar Dhlomo, who gave us time and resources with which to carry out a pilot project for the ultimate Launching Democracy project, and then housed us throughout its duration. All the MPD staff made us welcome, swapped information with us and were generous and helpful colleagues. Apart from Dr Dhlomo himself we would like to thank Brian Abbott for his painstaking financial supervision and hard-working help, Richard Mkolo, Joe Matuna, Kerry Moon, Mdu Ndlovu, Sifiso Mhlongo, Eric Apelgren, Khetiwe Maphumulo, Ethel Siko, Thandi Mkhize and Phindile Nyawose. We are also grateful to the project's co-sponsor, the Human Sciences Research Council of South Africa, and its staff who gave us invaluable assistance on many occasions.

Particular thanks should go to Mrs Niri Naidu, who was the project's anchor person throughout, and to Mrs Daphne Bower, her opposite number at the HSRC. Mervyn Frost and Paulus Zulu both stood in for Bill Johnson as National Co-ordinator of the project when he was away, and offered us a great deal of helpful advice and support throughout.

We should like to express our thanks to those who generously funded the Launching Democracy project – US, AID, the Westminster Foundation, the Anglo-American and De Beers Chairman's Fund, the Human Sciences Research Council, the Canadian and Portuguese governments, NAMPAK Ltd, De Beers and Afrox. We should also like to extend our personal thanks to Dennis Wendel, Di Warwick, Tracy Jarvis and Michael Spicer, all of whom showed a shrewd and sympathetic understanding of what we were trying to do and gave us invaluable support.

The survey research for the project was carried out in Natal by Data Research Africa (where we are particularly grateful to Aki Stavrou), and in the rural areas by the HSRC (Natal) under the supervision of Edmund

Pillay, to whom our thanks go equally. Bill Hunt at Research International weighted the data and did some interesting secondary analysis of it: co-operation with him was always a pleasure. In Cape Town we were indebted to Franz Badenhorst and Ernest Markwood whose firm, Market and Opinion Surveys, carried out the Western Cape surveys. In Pretoria we depended on the HSRC opinion survey unit, MarkData, both for the national and PWV surveys. Our special thanks here go to Murray van der Merwe. When it came to press conferencing the survey data the help of Myrna Kaplan was frequently indispensable and Myrna gave the project her help at many other points as well. Modern South Africa has found much use for 'facilitators' who make things possible for other people. Myrna was this project's greatest facilitator.

We are indebted to an army of observers and monitors across the country. It is impossible to thank all of them but special mention should be made of the outstanding contribution made by Mark Shaw and Graeme Gotz and by Hennie Kotze whose Centre for International and Comparative Politics hosted the Western Cape part of the project.

In the Western Cape we were lucky to have the help of a particularly keen and able group of observers, to whom our special thanks go: Chris Cupido, Mahomed Salih Davids, Thembinkosi Domo, Envir Fraser, Esme Gauche, Riedewaan Haywood, Yazir Henry, Larna Houston, Ekshaan Jawoodeen, Bekithemba Langalibele, Kenneth Lukoko, Monwabisi Maqetuka, Sandi Mbatsha, Shadrack Mbatsha, Andile Mfeya, Ellen Mngqibisa, Malixoli Ngoma, Gondiso Ngwenga, Philiup Piki, Dawood Sadien, Ebrahim Sadien, Nkosnathi Sohaba, Sikhuteli Tshaka, Mabotsholi Tabile, Vivienne Smith and Alistair Willemse.

Finally, we are indebted to many others for their kindness and hospitality, notably Fr Alphonso Mooney, Graham and Santi McIntosh, Jannie and Annie Gagiano, Marita and Andre du Toit, Hermann and Annette Giliomee, Monica Bott and Sholto Cross.

R.W. Johnson
Lawrence Schlemmer

Contributors

Chris de Kock is Chief Research Specialist at the Human Sciences Research Council's division for Sociopolitical Monitoring and Analysis, with particular interests in intergroup conflict and political violence. He has published widely on matters pertaining to South African political sociology, most recently as co-editor of *The Prospects for a Free, Democratic Election: Inhibiting and Facilitating Factors in Voting Intention* (1993).

Mervyn Frost is Professor of Politics at the University of Natal, Durban; he is a past president of the South African Political Studies Association, and co-editor of its official journal *Politikon*. He has published widely on political ethics, international relations and political change in South Africa, and is the author of *Towards a Normative Theory* and a co-editor of *International Relations: A Debate on Methodology*, as well as contributing frequently to the South African press. He has been an active contributor to the MPD's Political Leadership Programme, which brings together cadres of all political parties for education in the theory and practice of democracy.

Hermann Giliomee is Professor of Political Studies at the University of Cape Town and has authored many books and articles on South African problems. These include a history of Afrikaner political thought (with Andre du Toit) and a history of the British occupation of the Cape Colony. He co-edited *The Shaping of South African Society, 1652–1820*, co-authored (with H. Adam) *Ethnic Power Mobilized*, and recently co-edited (with S. Hauptfleisch and Lawrence Schlemmer) *The Bold Experiment: The Prospects for the Consolidation of Democracy in South Africa*.

Graeme Gotz was co-ordinator for Gauteng Observer Reports section of the Launching Democracy project. He is a researcher at the Centre for Policy Studies, Johannesburg.

Wilmot James is the Executive Director of the Institute for Democracy in South Africa (IDASA) and Honorary Professor of Sociology at the University of Cape Town. He is author of *Our Precious Metal: African Labour in South Africa's Gold Industry* (1992) and co-editor of *Crossing Borders: Mine Migrancy in a Democratic South Africa* (1995).

R.W. Johnson was National Co-ordinator of the Launching Democracy project at the Institute for Multi-Party Democracy. He is the author of over 200 publications and has written widely on British and French politics as well as on South Africa, which he has also frequently covered for the (London) *Times*. His books include *How Long Will South Africa Survive?* (1977), *The Politics of Recession, The Long March of the French Left* and *Heroes and Villains* (1990). An Emeritus Fellow of Magdalen College, Oxford, he is Director of the Helen Suzman Foundation in Johannesburg.

Alexander Johnston is an Associate Professor in the Department of Politics, University of Natal, Durban. Professor Johnston has written widely about the problems of divided societies, with special reference to South Africa and Northern Ireland, and was the editor of *Constitution Making in the New South Africa* (London, 1993). He is a frequent broadcaster on South African questions for the BBC.

Robert Mattes is manager of the IDASA Public Opinion Service in Cape Town. He has written and researched in the areas of voting behaviour and executive–legislature relations. He worked as a political analyst for the Independent Electoral Commission in the South African election and co-ordinated the work of the Western Cape section of the Launching Democracy project.

Lawrence Schlemmer is a former Vice-President of the Human Sciences Research Council, Dean of the Faculty of Social Sciences at the University of Natal and has been president of both the Association for Sociology of Southern Africa and the Institute of Race Relations. He is a special adviser to the Ministry of Arts, Culture, Science and Technology in the new Government of National Unity and holds chairs at Pretoria and Witwatersrand universities. His more than 300 publications and reports include *Change, Reform and Economic Growth* (with E. Webster), *From Apartheid to Nation Building* (with H. Giliomee), *The South African Election, 1987* (with D. J. Van Vuuren) and *The Bold Experiment: South Africa's New Democracy* (with H. Giliomee and S. Hauptfleisch).

Mark Shaw is a Research Officer at the Institute for Defence Policy at Midrand, near Johannesburg. He has published widely on South African social and political questions and acted as consultant for the Observer Reports section of the Launching Democracy project in Gauteng.

Paulus Zulu is Associate Professor at the Centre for Social and Development Studies at the University of Natal, Durban of which he is also a Deputy Vice-Chancellor. He has published widely on a variety of South African social and political themes and during the 1994 South African election worked as a political analyst for the Independent Electoral Commission.

Parties and Organisations

Africa Muslim Party (AMP)
African Christian Democratic Party (ACDP)
African Democratic Movement (ADM)
African Moderates Congress Party (AMCP)
African National Congress (ANC)
Afrikaner Broederbond
Afrikaner Weerstandsbweging (AWB: Afrikaner Resistance Movement)
ANC Youth League (ANCYL)
Azanian People's Liberation Army (APLA)
Azanian People's Organisation (AZAPO)
Black Consciousness (BC)
Concerned South Africans Group (COSAG)
Congress of South African Students (COSAS)
Congress of South African Trade Unions (COSATU)
Congress of Traditional Leaders of South Africa (CONTRALESA)
Conservative Party (CP)
Constitution-making body (CMB)
Convention for a Democratic South Africa (CODESA)
Democratic Party (DP)
Dikwankwetla Party of South Africa (DPSA)
Election Administration Directorate (EAD)
Federal Party (FP)
Freedom Alliance (FA)
Freedom Front (FF)
Green Party (GRP)
Independent Electoral Commission (IEC)
Inkatha Freedom Party (IFP)
Interim Constitution (IC)
Islamic Party (IP)
Keep it Straight and Simple Party (KISS)

Labour Party (LP)
Luso–South African Party (Luso)
Merit Party (MP)
Minority Front (MF)
Multi–Party Negotiating Forum (MPNF)
National Party (NP)
Non–governmental organisation (NGO)
Pan Africanist Congress of Azania (PAC)
Pan Africanist Students Organisation (PASO)
Patriotic Front (PF)
Right Party (RP)
self–defence units (SDUs)
South African Broadcasting Corporation (SABC)
South African Communist Party (SACP)
South African Defence Force (SADF)
South African National Civics' Organisation (SANCO)
South African Police (SAP)
South African Women's Party (SAWP)
South-West Africa People's Organisation (SWAPO)
Sport Organisation for Collective Contributions and Equal Rights (SOCCER)
Transitional Executive Council (TEC)
Umkhonto We Sizwe (MK)
United Democratic Front (UDF)
United People's Front (UPF)
Volksfront (VF)
Wes-Kaap Federaliste Party (WKFP)
Women's Right Peace Party (WRPP)
Workers' International to Rebuild the Fourth International (South Africa) (WI)
Workers' List Party (WLP)
Ximoko Progressive Party (XPP)

ONE

Introduction: the Transition to Democracy

R.W. Johnson and Lawrence Schlemmer

SOUTH AFRICA'S FIRST DEMOCRATIC election on 27 April 1994 was an event many thought would never take place. Ever since the massacres at Sharpeville and Langa of 21 March 1960 had brought to a close the era of peaceful protest, it had seemed that the forces of Afrikaner and African nationalism were intent on all-out violent confrontation. As the confrontation wore on, decade after decade, the rest of the world changed in ways which served to heighten and highlight the struggle even further. For as colonialism ended throughout the Third World, South Africa remained the last great and un-decolonised settler state, an increasing affront and bitter reminder to anti-colonial sentiment everywhere. Similarly, as institutionalised racism was abolished elsewhere, the struggle also took on a world historical significance as the supreme instance of white oppression of blacks and of racism more generally. The increasingly insurrectionary mood of South Africa's voteless masses in the 1980s further inflamed opinion, so that the South African issue featured high on the agenda of almost every international agency or forum. Trade sanctions, a disinvestment campaign, sporting, cultural and diplomatic boycotts, and an ongoing urban guerrilla offensive all increased the pressure on the regime but, to the despair of the international community, all attempts to mediate and to warn of the racial holocaust ahead were brushed aside.

The major Western states – particularly Britain and America – were clearly the only group with the economic and military leverage sufficient to force a solution. They were overwhelmingly South Africa's most important partners in trade and investment; they were still the originative focus of South Africa's cultural and educational patrimony; they were diplomatically crucial in the Commonwealth and the UN; and, if the worst came to the very worst, they had the naval power necessary to blockade Pretoria into submission. Technically this would have been possible at any time.

1

But the West shied away from such action. It did not like the regime in Pretoria and, more particularly, it could not afford to be thought to side with a regime which practised institutionalised racism and sought to deny citizenship to the bulk of its population. But the West disliked such gross interventionism in principle; it feared damage to its economic interests; and it believed that the two sides were so irreconcilable that such a prematurely forced solution would not produce a lasting deal between them. Without such a voluntarily sought compact, no compromise would hold and the country would soon dissolve into fractious and uncontrollable ethnic strife. In addition, in exile the African National Congress (ANC) had become ever more closely entwined with the South African Communist Party (SACP) and was heavily reliant on support from the Communist bloc. The movement talked the language of Marxism and more or less automatically took the Soviet line in international affairs – siding with the USSR over the invasion of Czechoslovakia in 1968, for example. Thus, while the West did not wish to endorse Pretoria's view of the movement as essentially Communist – to do so would only encourage further intransigence on Pretoria's behalf – in practice it quietly held the same reservations. In the context of the Cold War an ANC victory in South Africa might well take the country into the Soviet orbit, a quite intolerable loss to the Western camp.[1]

South Africa lived for a whole generation in the space created by this stand-off.[2] Inexorably, pressure on the West over the South African issue grew both from the Third World and from its own domestic public opinion. Western countries in turn responded by a progressive tightening of their economic and diplomatic pressure on Pretoria. Within South Africa these pressures hastened the pace of 'reform', that is, an ad hoc set of measures designed to cope with the large and increasingly sophisticated black proletariat.

Most important of all was the concession of trade union rights to Africans, following the growing industrial unrest of the 1970s and the subsequent Wiehahn Commission. Dr H.F. Verwoerd had always defended his absolutist view of apartheid with the claim that the system was like a wall: every brick was important. If you started discarding this or that brick the wall would ultimately fall. This turned out to be true. With the growth of a powerful black trade union movement, South Africa had effectively accepted a new social contract: in its urban heartland there would henceforth be a permanent, organised opposition with the right to demand full industrial and economic citizenship. As T.H. Marshall would have predicted, this led on quite ineluctably to insistent and ultimately successful demands for full political citizenship.[3] Ironically, both the key contenders in the South African struggle failed to see this. On the one hand, the P.W. Botha government (and Wiehahn himself) seem to have believed that union recognition would allow the movement to be incorporated and controlled. The ANC–SACP, on the other hand, denounced early attempts at unionisation as inevitably serving the interests of capital. For the SACP had defined South Africa as a fascist state and it followed that no true trade unions could exist under fascism. Not until the Congress of South African Trade Unions (COSATU) was founded in 1985 did the unions come within the broader Congress movement – immediately becoming the main organisational backbone first of the United Democratic Front (UDF) and then of the ANC itself.[4]

The year of 1985 was, indeed, crucial in every respect. The COSATU president, Elijah Barayi, launched a bitter attack on Chief Buthelezi at the COSATU founding congress in Durban: with this the implicit opposition between the UDF and Buthelezi's Inkatha movement took a new turn. Predictably, an Inkatha trade union federation, UWUSA, was soon formed to oppose COSATU. Bitter fighting between the two sides became entrenched, particularly in the killing fields of KwaZulu-Natal. By the time of the 1994 election more than 10,000 had died in this conflict.

But 1985 was, too, the year of President P.W. Botha's abortive 'Rubicon' speech – also in Durban. Botha's original speech, which had included such radical steps as the abolition of the Group Areas Act, had met with strong resistance from the leader of the conservative Transvaal National Party, F.W. de Klerk, leading Botha to scrap his speech and deliver a bitter chauvinist tirade instead. The shock effect among the major Western states (with whose embassies the original draft of the speech had been cleared) was considerable: in effect, many simply gave up on Botha. In the financial markets the effect was catastrophic. The major Western banks, led by Chase Manhattan, called in their loans. These could not be paid and a strenuous new repayment schedule had to be devised. The rand collapsed, bankrupting those who had borrowed abroad, accelerating capital flight and producing high, persistent inflation.

The abrupt withdrawal of Western economic support represented by the 1985 loan crisis was, in effect, the crucial Western vote of no confidence which Pretoria had always feared. Ironically, the anti-apartheid movement had, at that stage, failed to realise the crucial significance of international credit and had concentrated its efforts on trade sanctions instead. No anti-apartheid activists lobbied for the bank withdrawal of 1985 – the banks acted out of purely commercial considerations. It was, none the less, the crucial blow, the dolorous stroke. For South Africa has throughout most of its history depended on a constant inflow of foreign capital. When that inflow stops – as in the 1930s – economic growth judders to a halt. The gold boom of 1979–81 had seen the South African economy race ahead, but the onset of grave civil unrest in 1983–5 saw foreign investment dry up and go into reverse. In part this was a reflection of the active disinvestment campaign waged by the anti-apartheid movement, but it also reflected a commercial judgement on deteriorating economic prospects. This left South Africa dependent on loan finance for its continuing capital inflows. Once the 1985 crisis kicked this crutch away – and credits from the International Monetary Fund (IMF) were quickly cut off too – it was really just a matter of time before Pretoria gave way.

But P.W. Botha, the very picture of cantankerous stubborness, clung on for a further four years. It was a peculiar period, a true autumn of the patriarch. The economy stagnated and so did the country, for stalemate had been reached on every front. The insurrectionary protest of the UDF had been effectively silenced by the state of emergency but no one doubted that the forces the UDF represented would burst forth once more the moment they were given the chance. Botha tried, unsuccessfully, to coax Buthelezi into negotiations but received from him the same response offered by the exiled ANC, by the Commonwealth, by Western ambassadors and by every other would-be mediator: first he must lift the emergency, unban all the banned parties and release their leaders. Only then could true negotiation begin. To which Botha monotonously replied: It's unthinkable to negotiate with the ANC, they just want to take power and they're Communists.[5]

Ironically, the Soviets themselves had been debating whether or not to ditch the ANC.[6] By the early 1980s, after twenty years of guerrilla struggle, the movement seemed to have got nowhere at all. Voices were raised in Moscow suggesting that it would be better to accept reality: the ANC were hopeless and there could be considerable benefits in making peace with the P.W. Botha regime. The protagonists of this view argued that the USSR had complete control over the SACP and that this in turn meant that the ANC was their virtual puppet. The Botha regime would doubtless pay a good price for having the dogs called off. Others argued that, however great Soviet influence over the ANC was, the fact remained that African nationalism had a life of its own in South Africa, just as it had elsewhere in Africa. The debate raged. Like so many debates, it was never really settled, merely overtaken by events.

For the even greater irony was that in the same fateful year of 1985 fundamental change had begun in Moscow itself with the accession to power of Mikhail Gorbachev. At first there was scepticism in the West as to the reality of the changes, a scepticism felt most keenly on the political extremes. On the one hand Reaganite conservatives refused to believe that *glasnost* and *perestroika* were more than a cunning new Soviet ploy, but on the other so did many radicals. Thus the ANC, SACP and their sister movement, the South-West Africa People's Organisation (SWAPO), remained ideologically fixed to their old verities, apparently unaware that the changes in the USSR were cutting the ground from beneath their feet. As late as 1988 the SACP was holding up East Germany as a model for future South African development – just a year before the Berlin Wall came down and the entire East German state vanished like the Cheshire cat. In Namibia, SWAPO remained so stuck in its old intransigent mode that in the end the Western powers and the USSR simply got together on their own.

For the Western chancelleries had realised that it no longer mattered if SWAPO or the ANC were partially or wholly under Communist influence. With China embracing capitalism on an undreamt-of scale and with the implosion of Communism in its Soviet and East European heartland, Communists in the Third World were now no more than historical curiosities. Even should they come to power they could do nothing without the back-up of the former Communist bloc. In practice they would have little choice but to come to terms with capitalism and with a liberal international economic order. De Klerk too was quick to understand that it no longer greatly mattered whether or not the SACP controlled the ANC: the Communists were now toothless tigers and the 'Communist menace' no longer existed. Negotiation was now possible on terms never possible before.

And negotiation there would have to be, for the other effect of the collapse of Communism was to greatly increase Western pressure on Pretoria, this time not to push for this or that stay of execution or piecemeal reform, but with a full-scale settlement in mind. For the wondrous realisation had dawned that in the new post-Cold War climate it would now be possible to solve a whole series of hitherto insoluble international problems. A definitive arms control treaty? Easy. US–Soviet co-operation in space? Of course. Freedom for the Baltic states? The reunification of Germany? A West Bank state at last? A definitive Middle East settlement? All could be arranged. But the earliest and some of the most striking cases came in Africa. The second Cold War had started in the Ogaden, in the Horn of Africa, where a US-backed Somalia had faced a Soviet-backed Ethiopia. Both sides now withdrew their support from their clients – with dramatic results. In Ethiopia the Mengistu regime fell and the country fragmented, with a new Eritrean state brought to birth, while in Somalia the Barre regime simply disintegrated, leaving no government of any kind in Mogadishu. In south-western Africa an even more comprehensive settlement was attempted: both the Cubans and South Africans were made to retreat from Angola, where a truce and, somewhat too ambitiously, an election were arranged. In Namibia a settlement was simply imposed: South Africa accepted defeat and SWAPO were, willy-nilly, shoe-horned into an election in January 1990 – which they won.

President de Klerk assumed office as the Namibian settlement reached its climax. Its lessons could hardly be lost on him: if he did not move speedily a settlement might be virtually imposed on him. Indeed, foreign pressure was already overwhelming: the British Prime Minister Margaret Thatcher alone stood between South Africa and comprehensive sanctions and she made it plain that she too required an immediate settlement to get her off the hook. There is little serious doubt that the crucial deal between de Klerk and the Anglo-American powers was struck as soon as the 1989 election was out of the way – perhaps even before. Certainly, the major terms of de Klerk's epoch-making speech of 2 February 1990 were known in London and Washington as early as October 1989 – and perhaps sooner.[7] It seems certain that the 2 February speech was in fact a draft negotiated with London and Washington, just as the Rubicon speech had been in 1985. This time, however, there was to be no last-minute welshing on the deal – that could now only lead to an internationally dictated solution, quite publicly imposed. This de Klerk had to avoid. For him to enter the negotiations with the ANC on equal terms – and thus for the ultimate settlement to enjoy legitimacy – it was essential that the dimension of foreign pressure be kept discreet. And there was no doubt that de Klerk, once launched on his new path, embraced it with sincerity.

If these were the principal factors leading up to the famous speech of 2 February 1990, announcing the end of apartheid, the unbanning of proscribed organisations and the complete liberalisation of political life, it was immediately apparent that the speech itself had produced a whole new set of dynamics. Mandela was released, the proscribed organisations unbanned, the emergency lifted, exiles welcomed back and the whole legislative edifice of apartheid abolished in short order. Change was so fast that many, on both sides, could hardly believe it. Among many supporters of the National Party (NP) there was the quiet conviction that the whole thing was an immensely clever tactic by de Klerk and that he would, with the same cleverness, avoid any actual transfer of power. Many ANC supporters held the same dark suspicion, often fearing that once they were flushed out into the open the government would simply pounce on them, lock them up and throw away the key. Only gradually did the general realisation dawn that de Klerk had opened the flood gates to change and that, with all that white water thundering through, neither he nor anyone else could now reverse or even control the consequences.

One of the oddities of the transition to democracy in South Africa is that many of the leading actors had read (at least summaries of) the famous O'Donnell/Schmitter/Whitehead volumes on *Transitions from Authoritarian Rule*.[8] It is instructive to note, however, that while the South African transition accorded well with this model in some respects, in others it departed quite sharply.

In their concluding volume O'Donnell and Schmitter point out that liberalisation and democratisation often proceed independently and at different speeds.[9] South Africa was, indeed, a case of what they term 'liberalised authoritarianism': by the early 1980s not only was it possible to hear all manner of anti-apartheid protest from the stage, the pulpit and, increasingly, the street, but a whole alternative left subculture flourished vigorously and unabashedly. Long before the advent of de Klerk, the

ANC line on the academic and cultural boycott was observed as virtual law by most universities and the generality of producers, directors, actors and musicians, while in the campus bookshops it was possible to buy the works of Che Guevara, Regis Debray and other theorists of guerrilla war, not to mention a whole host of less 'applied' left literature. Similarly, a whole host of ANC-oriented non-governmental organisations (NGOs) grew up and received large-scale foreign funding ('Viking gold' as it was known, for a great deal came from Scandinavia) – a situation tolerated by the state even though the manifest aim of many such NGOs was to undermine it. For those whose benchmark was intellectual and cultural freedom there was considerable poignancy in their situation. Behind they saw the dismal authoritarianism of Verwoerd, ahead the possible authoritarianism of the ANC–SACP alliance. 'Long live the interregnum' became their silent cry.

This liberalisation, occurring in the context of the continued ban on the ANC, the Pan Africanist Congress of Azania (PAC) and SACP and the detention or exile of most of their leadership, created a space for black organisation at the same time as it was disallowed. In the resultant vacuum such black leadership as did exist – in the trade unions, the churches and among the educated elite – achieved a heightened, not to say exaggerated, significance as surrogates for the absent ANC. Later, indeed, the World Bank suggested that real wages had risen by 18 per cent over a market-determined norm as a result of trade union pressure. Without doubt COSATU was able to achieve many of these gains largely because it was seen as a surrogate: with political militancy denied, black industrial militancy acquired a unique legitimacy. The heritage of this situation was seen in the months following the April 1994 election when, with the ANC now in power, the hitherto leading trade union, student and religious elites had to reassess their position. Both the unions and student activists made a concerted push for further gains and Archbishop Tutu, by criticising high parliamentary salaries, was able to trigger a formal review of these salaries, to the annoyance of many within the ANC elite.

Ultimately, write Schmitter and O'Donnell, there comes the crucial moment when the authoritarian ruler announces a major extension of rights – and is believed:[10] a fair enough description of 2 February 1990. As the transition begins, the question is whether the ruling regime can retain control of its agenda and timing or whether these will be imposed by a mobilised opposition, and the answer depends centrally on whether the regime retains the cohesion, capacity and disposition to apply repression.

There is little doubt in the South African case that the regime retained sufficient cohesion and capacity in a physical sense throughout the transition. Indeed, the whole discussion of the loyalty and professionalism of the armed forces which bulks so large in the literature of transition seems fairly well redundant in the South African case. Despite recurrent rumours and allegations of a 'third force' within the security forces, the professionalism of the armed services was generally exemplary. The government was never seriously challenged by soldiers in its reform policies and was even able to sack large numbers of generals and senior police officers without any come-back. In the end both the armed forces and the police transferred their loyalties smoothly to the new government. Even when Generals Viljoen and Groenewald emerged to lead the right-wing Freedom Front (FF) they never so much as hinted at independent action by the armed forces. O'Donnell and Schmitter are doubtless right to talk of the threat of a military coup hanging like a Damoclean sword over most transitions,[11] but this was not the case in South Africa.

Despite this there is no question but that the agenda and timing of the transition progressively slipped from the hands of the government and were increasingly imposed by the ANC. At the outset President de Klerk could announce that Mr Mandela would spend an extra few days in jail simply for the sake of prison technicalities, but no sooner was Mr Mandela free than such seigneurial treatment became unimaginable. By the end it was not de Klerk but Joe Slovo, the Communist leader, who announced the crucial decision on a power-sharing government and the election date itself. Moreover, de Klerk's National Party (NP) had to surrender on many of the constitutional promises it had made to its followers, notably over federalism.

The initiative slipped from de Klerk to the ANC for several reasons. One was that the NP always knew it had to have a settlement ready to take to the electorate in 1994, for its five-year mandate ended then. In that sense the ANC, which was unbothered by such considerations, could always exert pressure simply by delay. Second, the NP was constrained by the knowledge that at the end of the process it wanted to be in a coalition government with the ANC, and that the ANC, if the polls were to be believed, would be able to dispense with the NP if it wanted to. So the NP had to develop a co-operative relationship with the ANC, even make it *want* to work with the NP. The best way to achieve that was by refusing confrontation and going the extra mile to achieve a compromise acceptable to the ANC. Finally, if there was a sword of Damocles in the South African case, it was the threat not of a military coup but of a general lapse into anarchy.

This frequently seemed close. The transition period witnessed continuous bloodshed between the Inkatha Freedom Party (IFP) and the ANC; several major massacres – of IFP supporters at Zonke Zizwe, of ANC supporters at Boipatong and again at Bisho, and later of Zulu royalists in the streets of Johannesburg; the assassination of Chris Hani and a wave of reactive disturbances; several major terrorist attacks by the PAC's Azanian People's Liberation Army (APLA) and a reprisal South African Defence Force (SADF) raid into the Transkei; strikes, marches and direct action tactics as part of an ANC mass mobilisation campaign lasting over half a year; endless threats (and sometimes acts) of violence by the far right; and staggeringly high levels of crime and interpersonal violence. In 1993 there were over 20,000 murders in South Africa and across the whole province of KwaZulu-Natal the murder rate was double that of New York City.[12] As O'Donnell and Schmitter observe,[13] the 'popular upsurge' implicit in mass mobilisation was enough to frighten even ANC moderates (who played little part in the mass mobilisation campaign), but in the end all parties came to worry that the damage to society might be so deep that recovery would be impossible, whatever the political outcome.

It was this worry, rather than fear of a military coup, which hung over all the negotiators and which underlay the implicit pact between the ANC and NP throughout the negotiations. As O'Donnell and Schmitter would have predicted,[14] this political understanding was the work of a tiny (and all-male) oligarchy. At the middle and lower levels of the political hierarchy, far more absolute attitudes and rhetoric continued to hold sway. In the end – the very end – this understanding was broadened to include the IFP leadership as well. For this consciousness of the fragility of the social order led to the further realisation that none of the three major contenders could afford to impose their will unilaterally. In a purely technical sense the NP retained this military ability throughout, but the whole meaning of 2 February 1990 was that the costs of such repression had become too high. Within KwaZulu-Natal the IFP retained a similar last-resort military supremacy but knew that any attempt to use it would imply unacceptable costs at every level. The ANC, for its part, enjoyed a country-wide numerical supremacy which, provided mere numbers were allowed to count, meant it was bound to be the heavy ultimate winner. But it, too, knew that a simple assertion of majoritarianism would burden the nascent new regime with a major rebellion in KwaZulu-Natal and the non-cooperation (at the least) of key whites in the civil service and security forces. This realisation was, naturally, weakest among ANC militants, but the leadership's willingness to exercise this relative restraint met a sympathetic echo at the mass level of ANC voters.

O'Donnell and Schmitter write of the conditions under which such stand-offs occur: 'No social or political group is sufficiently dominant to impose its "ideal project", and what typically emerges is a second-best solution which none of the actors wanted or identified with completely but which all of them can agree to and share in.'[15] This was eminently true in the South African case and helps explain the paradox that the three main parties hammered out an essentially liberal democratic constitution although none of them much believed in it. The NP had, after all, spent its whole period in power up until 1990 attempting to resist international pressure for such a constitution. The IFP, in its governance of KwaZulu, had shown itself to be a party of conservative chiefly oligarchs. KwaZulu was a de facto one-party state and almost all MPs were elected unopposed or on a derisory turnout. The ANC, for its part, had for a generation espoused the language of populist Marxism and had always taken as its goal a revolutionary (and thus presumably single-party) seizure of power. Indeed, until 1990 it had spoken of exercising 'people's power' in terms tainted by long abuse in the Eastern bloc. None of these three parties was much acquainted with grass-roots democracy and all of them had shown a willingness to use violence to further their political ends. Yet the common ground between these somewhat unlikely partners in democracy turned out to be the classic discourse of liberal constitutionalism.

In terms of the interim constitution a 400-member constituent assembly was to be elected on a proportional basis – 200 members from the nine new regions the country was divided into, and 200 elected from a national list. This assembly, together with a Senate indirectly elected from the regions, would also act as the country's parliament for the next five years. Originally, a single ballot was proposed which would then be counted for both sections of this national ballot and also towards the simultaneous election of nine regional assemblies. At the point when the new institutions were first unveiled the IFP was boycotting the talks, but as part of the deal done to tempt the IFP into the electoral process it was agreed that there would be two ballots, one regional and one national. This still left a situation where the national ballot was counted twice, once for the regional list of candidates for the national assembly, and once for the national list.

It was apparent when the election date of 27 April 1994 was announced that this deadline would be under enormous pressure, especially since it had been decided that the running of the election would be taken away from the Ministry of Home Affairs and placed instead in the hands of an Independent Electoral Commission (IEC). Even though there was to be no voters' roll – voters could vote at the polling station of their choice – voters would need to produce identity papers in order to acquire a temporary voting card and it was clear that many million's of people lacked such papers. An enormous job of voter education – there was widespread confusion over the sheer mechanics of voting – had to be done at speed and in a country racked with political violence. The IEC had the awesome, indeed impossible, job of trying to ensure a free and fair campaign throughout the country, despite the fact that power had long since become territorialised, with many areas under single-party control constituting 'no-go' areas to all other parties. An enormous job of policing, monitoring and election observation had to be mounted, with large numbers of foreign monitors, observers, journalists and politicians pouring into the country to assist – and complicate – the task. For the election was not just an election: it was a circus, a great event attracting international celebrities.[16] It meant liberation for many, and not just within South Africa. It was a historic appointment with destiny and yet it was also a catastrophic mess, one which frequently threatened to provide a violent showdown. It was, indeed, very nearly all things to all men.

So huge were the logistical tasks ahead and so great the confusion and disorganisation on every side that many felt at the outset that the 27 April date could not be maintained. Quite quickly, however, it became clear that the date now had a symbolic reality all its own and that any attempt to change or postpone it might well lead to violence. With that the date was effectively set in concrete.

The election was, in the classic sense used by O'Donnell and Schmitter, a 'founding election', from which a new polity emerged. It is worth pointing out how bad the record of 'first democratic elections' is. A colloquium held by the Department of History at the University of Durban-Westville shortly before the elections examined the historical experience of such elections in Brazil (1945), India (1947), Ireland (1921), Nigeria (1960), Russia (1918), Lesotho (1965), Zimbabwe (1980) and Kenya (1961). No fewer than five of these eight cases were marked by civil wars – and it would be possible to regard Mau Mau in Kenya as a sixth case. Separatism and partition actually occurred in three cases and were live issues in three more. In three cases democracy was largely expropriated by a single or overwhelmingly dominant party, while in four more cases democracy regressed to autocracy or military rule – in one case (Russia) so completely that there had to be a second 'founding election' seventy years later. In three of the four African cases the election amounted to little more than an 'ethnic census', resulting in little consideration of issues and an extremely weak sense both of democratic accountability and the legitimacy of opposition. In almost every case democracy led to the enrichment of a narrow elite, with a concomitant prominence of corruption and clientelism. The fact that most ordinary people could relate to authority only by means of clientelistic relationships with powerful patrons effectively undermined the possibility of an independent civil society; indeed it substantially undermined the whole notion of citizenship.

Many of these dangers were apparent as South Africa approached its founding election. The possibility of separatism and partition was particularly apparent in KwaZulu-Natal, in the demands for a *Boerestaat*, and potentially even in the Western Cape too. There was endless talk of a possible civil war and the country's two most populous regions were both racked by high levels of political violence. Opinion polls made it clear that the election would largely have the character of an ethnic census. Political power was highly territorialised and private systems of justice flourished. Clientelism was strong, the notion of an independent citizenry weak.

But South Africa enjoyed three critical advantages. First, it already had a long history (eighty-four years) as an independent state, which meant that its boundaries and political unity were almost universally accepted. This history of independence was not so long that a collapse back into the pre-1910 component parts (or some reshuffle of them) was unthinkable, but it was long enough to make partition a far more difficult proposition than in, for example, India or Nigeria. Second, South Africa had long experience of a functioning partial democracy: of the cases above the nearest comparison is the Republic of Ireland – the sole case where a competitive political democracy has endured without interruption since the founding election. While all the constituents of the 'liberation movement' (ANC, PAC, SACP and the Azanian People's Organisation (AZAPO)) talked the language of revolution, even within the liberation movement powerful tendencies had always existed whose true aim was merely incorporation into the whites-only capitalist democracy they saw dangled before them. Finally, South Africa's attempt to launch democracy was attended by unprecedented international interest and involvement. A regression from democracy there would strike a death blow to hopes for democracy in Africa, indeed of hopes for Africa *tout court*. Should the new South Africa implode or fail disastrously, there would be direct consequences in the ghettos of Chicago and Los Angeles, for black people in Britain, in the Caribbean and elsewhere. This international interest in the success of South African democracy is not so strong as the international dimension which has virtually guaranteed the emergent democracies of Spain, Greece and Portugal, but it is a considerable factor none the less.

In fact South Africa's founding election took place peacefully and, despite enormous confusion, successfully. The whole world greeted with euphoria the televisual image of long lines of Africans, so long disenfranchised, waiting patiently to vote; lines, moreover, in which white and black and coloured and Indian waited happily with one another.[17] Within South Africa this euphoria was magnified by the inauguration of President Mandela: the symbolism of the South African Air Force (SAAF) jets flying past in salute to a man imprisoned for twenty-seven years by a regime of which the SAAF was an intrinsic part was lost on no one – and brought a tear to many an eye. President Mandela's clear generosity of spirit and his emphasis on national unity further increased this euphoria in the early months of the new regime: by late August 1994 whites gave Mandela a 60 per cent approval rating (compared to 38 per cent the previous November), while among Indians he scored 69 per cent, among coloureds 70 per cent, and among Africans 92 per cent.[18] Thus majorities of every group applauded the new dispensation and many South Africans even developed a certain boastfulness about their new popularity.

This euphoria was, in a sense, misleading. Ahead lay the need to consolidate the new democracy, a long and arduous task. In many cases, particularly in Africa, we have seen democracy fail quite quickly in the face of a regression to autocracy. But Schmitter warns[19] that other dangers exist, notably *hybridisation*, that is, the development of a hybrid regime which combines elements of autocracy and democracy, and *non-consoli-*

dation, that is, a democracy which persists only by default. In such a situation, no specific, reliable and generally acceptable set of rules ever quite gels; political actors continue to break the rules if they can, and democracy is a matter of continuous ad hoc and *ad hominem* rulings and actions so that the operation of the polity never achieves the sacrosanct predictability that characterises mature democracies. It is an open question whether South Africa will be able to escape such dangers and gradually consolidate a fully democratic order.

The answer to this question lies in the future. Whatever happens, South Africa's first democratic election will enjoy a peculiar importance, if only (one fervently hopes) as a benchmark against which its future democratic elections must be viewed. Such future elections will deserve the same committed study, observation and public information service that the Launching Democracy project provided in this founding election. If democracy in South Africa is to be consolidated and strengthened it is essential that a similar effort should be mounted in subsequent elections – particularly since such future elections will not attract the same commitment of international observers and resources as did the first democratic election. For, however important the success of democracy in South Africa may be internationally, the launch has been made and we are on our own now.

The election was inevitably fought in highly charged and partisan spirit. In an attempt to provide a non-partisan public information service the Launching Democracy project was set up by the (non-partisan) Institute for Multi-Party Democracy and the South African Human Sciences Research Council. The project established an observer network in the three most populous regions – the Western Cape, the PWV (the Pretoria-Witwatersrand-Vereeniging triangle), now rechristened Gauteng, and Natal, which changed its name to KwaZulu-Natal in the middle of our study.[20] It was clear throughout our study that a special importance attached to KwaZulu-Natal (KZN) where, alone, two rival African nationalisms, roughly of equal strength, confronted one another. The enormously greater scale of political violence in KZN, the IFP's election boycott which threatened to wreck the whole electoral process, and the clear potential in KZN for armed confrontation and attempted secession all meant that we had to concentrate particular attention on that region: if the election was going to fail, it would fail there. Happily, the opposite occurred, but our study was left with a KZN bias in certain respects – a bias which was certainly also warranted by the crucial dramas which unfolded there over the election count and the results. We were, though sad that limits to our resources meant that we were unable to give similarly close attention to all regions.

We attempted to compensate for this by carrying out not just two opinion surveys in each of our three 'critical' regions but also two national opinion surveys covering all regions. Similarly, we drew on a variety of post-election surveys to provide a picture of the new South Africa some way into its first year of 'liberation'.

The information generated by these surveys was made available freely and equally to all the political parties – a service of particular value to the smaller parties, which were not normally able to afford to commission their own polls. In addition the results were handed on to voter education and monitoring organisations, to academic institutions concerned with electoral research and to the media and general public. The present volume draws essentially on the information generated by the Launching Democracy project, and its authors are all people whose participation in the project helped make it a resounding success.

Notes

1 See C. Legum, *The Western Crisis over Southern Africa: South Africa, Rhodesia, Namibia* (New York: African, 1979) and also James Barber, *The Uneasy Relationship: Britain and South Africa* (London: Routledge, 1983). For the international relations of South Africa as it neared the crunch, see R.W. Johnson, 'The politics of international intervention', in H. Giliomee and J. Gagiano (eds), *The Elusive Search for Peace: South Africa, Israel, Northern Ireland* (Cape Town: Oxford University Press in association with IDASA, 1990).

2 For a fuller consideration of the ironies and dynamics of that period, see R.W. Johnson, *How Long Will South Africa Survive?* (London: Macmillan, 1977).

3 See T.H. Marshall, *Citizenship and Social Class*, ed. T. Bottomore (London: Pluto, 1992).

4 See S. Friedman, *Building Tomorrow Today: African Workers in Trade Unions 1970– 1984* (Johannesburg: Ravan Press, 1987) and J. Baskin, *Striking Back: A History of COSATU* (Johannesburg: Ravan Press, 1991).

5 Dr F. Van Zyl Slabbert was granted a private audience with Botha in this period and tried to argue the cause of negotiation. Dr Slabbert gloomily recounted to one of the authors how every argument he made met with this reply.

6 Private communication from Professor Irina Filatova.

7 Private communication.

8 G. O'Donnell, P. Schmitter and L. Whitehead (eds), *Transitions from Authoritarian Rule: Prospects for Democracy* (4 vols, Baltimore: Johns Hopkins University Press, 1986). All citations below are drawn from G. O'Donnell and P. Schmitter, *Tentative Conclusions about Uncertain Democracies*, vol. 4 of *Transitions from Authoritarian Rule*. See also P. Schmitter, 'What kinds of democracy are emerging in South America, Central America, Southern Europe and Eastern Europe?' (1991 draft), Centre for Latin American Studies, Stanford University.

9 O'Donnell and Schmitter, *Tentative Conclusions about Uncertain Democracies*, p. 6.

10 Ibid., p. 10.

11 Ibid., p. 23.

12 *Natal Mercury*, 31 Aug. 1994.

13 O'Donnell and Schmitter, *Tentative Conclusions about Uncertain Democracies*, p. 54.

14 Ibid., p. 70.

15 Ibid., p. 38.

16 P. Schmitter, 'Exploring the prospects of "transitoly"', *Prospects: South Africa in the Nineties* (Human Sciences Research Council, Pretoria), 2.1 (1993).

17 See also R.W. Johnson, 'A bloody route to the ballot box', *Times Higher Education Supplement*, 7 Jan. 1994; 'Weder frei noch fair', *Neuen Zurcher Zeitung Folio* (Zurich), Apr. 1994; and 'Here for the crunch', *London Review of Books*, 28 Apr. 1994.

18 These terms will be used throughout the book for the sake of convenience. This does not, of course, imply acceptance of the racial classification system which originally produced these terms. The figures come from the Markinor survey cited in *Business Day*, 30 Aug. 1994.

19 P. Schmitter, 'Dangers and dilemmas of democracy', *Journal of Democracy* (Apr. 1994), pp. 59–61.

20 We have used the term Kwa Zulu-Natal (abbreviating to KZN) throughout the text, for the sake of consistency. When reference is made solely to KwaZulu, this denotes the former Zulu bantustan within KZN. We have used Natal either to refer to the province as a whole in the period before KwaZulu was carved out of it, or in contexts where comparison is made between the bantustan part of the province (KwaZulu) and the area remaining under white rule until 1994 (Natal).

Several other provinces have changed their names: the North West Transvaal is now just the North West; Northern Transvaal has become the Northern Province; the PWV has become Gauteng; the Orange Free State has become simply the Free State; and the Eastern Transvaal has become Mpuma-langa. Some of these changes have taken place too recently to be reflected in this book.

TWO

Preparing for Democracy in an Authoritarian State

Mervyn Frost

BETWEEN 1990 AND 1994 South Africa witnessed a remarkable bargaining process which transformed the old apartheid order and laid the ground rules for a democratic political practice. This was achieved, moreover, without submerging the country in revolution or anarchy. In the process of seeking constitutional change the key parties themselves changed, as did their *modus operandi*. These changes, though, were not complete, for in some ways these parties remained what they were. In the 'new South Africa', the old and new are mixed in intriguing ways.

This process meant that the politics of 'the Struggle', previously the dominant form of politics, had to give way to the politics of negotiation, culminating in the establishment of the Interim Constitution (IC) under the terms of which South Africa's first democratic election was held in April 1994. It is important to notice how the two forms of politics coincided during the run-up to the election.

A Brief Set of Definitions

Politics may take many forms. In general, politics is talk and action directed at changing (or maintaining) the general rules of association governing some social entity. Where people operate according to well settled rules and feel no need to challenge or change them, there is no politics. Where the general rules of association are challenged, politics may proceed in an ad hoc way. However, where within a given association there is an ongoing need for new rules/laws governing the association (that is, where there is an ongoing need for politics), those involved may set up permanent institutions within which such politics is carried out. A democratic constitution is a typical example of such a framework for politics. The idea of rules governing rule-making is at the heart of constitutional government. I define normal politics as that which takes

16

place within an accepted constitution and contrast it with the ad hoc politics which precedes the establishment of a constitution.

Those engaged in politics make use of power, which I define as people acting in concert to achieve a specified goal. Such a definition is very present to the minds of South Africans who saw the National Party and the Afrikaner Broederbond carry through immensely ambitious feats of social engineering in pursuit of their political objectives. Politics in South Africa has not been just a matter of 'business as usual' or 'minding the shop'. But, of course, power is not necessarily about such root and branch action and, importantly, it is not necessarily political. Thus it is important to notice that power (people acting in concert) may be used for political purposes (changing the rules of association) or it may be used for other purposes (for example, raising funds for a worthy cause). Not all power is political.

Power and Politics at the Height of the Struggle

Since its inception as a Union in 1910 the basic rules of association in South Africa have favoured whites at the expense of Africans.[1] The original constitution and those that followed sought to exclude Africans from participating in the practice of law-making. These constitutions created frameworks within which whites could practise normal democratic politics, but the framework itself and the policies of the government sought to depoliticise Africans – that is, to prevent them taking part in the consideration and enactment of the basic laws of association governing the people of the country. In the forty-six years of NP government following the Second World War government sought to depoliticise Africans by banning their major parties, the ANC, the PAC and the SACP, by banning political literature (including certain newspapers, journals and books), and by harassing, banning and imprisoning key leaders. It sought to provide Africans with alternative frameworks – the infamous bantustans – where, alone, they could practice 'normal' politics.

The great scheme of separate development envisaged by Verwoerd failed comprehensively, for the majority of Africans in South Africa rejected the concept and refused to confer legitimacy on the homeland system. Internationally the little 'states' failed to gain recognition by the UN or by any foreign states. Demographic movements undermined the grand apartheid scheme which set complete physical separation of ethnic groups as a goal. It became increasingly apparent that the flood of Africans to the urban areas in white South Africa was unstoppable. Social and economic integration could not be unscrambled.

In the wake of the failure of the grand plan the NP government set out on a different tack. It attempted a set of reforms aimed at liberalising the economy and doing away with petty apartheid, in the hope that the coloureds and Indians could be politically co-opted, while the majority of Africans could be kept politically apathetic. Major landmarks during this phase were the establishment of the Coloured Representative Council, the liberalisation of employment practices and trade union rights, the establishment of the President's Council, the putting in place of structures for the election of black town councils and finally the enactment of a new constitution for South Africa (in 1983) which established a tricameral system of government with separate legislative chambers for whites, coloureds and Indians. During this phase the government sought to mollify African political demands purely by paying attention to quality of life issues.

None of these measures succeeded in suppressing African politics. Black South Africans persisted in their discussion of the failings of the constitution and in acting against it, although African politics within South Africa was, perforce, largely clandestine. The extraconstitutional and ad hoc politics of the majority went through different phases. In the 1970s there was a strong Black Consciousness (BC) movement which was vigorously repressed by government policy. This movement was strongest within schools and universities and laid the basis for the 1976 school uprisings in Soweto. The most memorable single act of repression by the state of this phase was the murder of the BC leader, Steve Biko, while in detention. Government repression against the movement was so successful that by the end of the decade it had ceased to be a force to reckon with.

The exclusion of the African majority from the tricameral government galvanized an African political response, with the new political dynamism finding expression in a new formation, the United Democratic Front. This was a loose federation of many large and small non-governmental organisations from South Africa's civil society. Member groups ranged from church associations, street committees, trade unions and professional associations (set up by lawyers, teachers, doctors and academics). The UDF was highly successful in orchestrating opposition to the new tricameral system. Its activities dovetailed with three other sources of power directed against the structures of apartheid: the trade union movement, the international anti-apartheid campaign in all its complexity, and the less successful efforts of the armed wing of the African National Congress, Umkhonto We Sizwe (known as MK). Taken together these forms of power proved formidable. The whole effort was commonly referred to by those participating in it as 'the Struggle'.

The Struggle, although complex, was a single-purpose activity. It aimed to achieve the overthrow of the 'apartheid regime'. That is, it aimed to destroy the power of the National Party, reincorporate the puppet states set up by the NP government, and to transform the South African constitutional structure from one which enshrined white minority rule to one which established a single united democratic South Africa based on universal adult suffrage.

It is essential to highlight certain features of the Struggle, for they are crucial to a proper understanding of subsequent developments. First, those involved talked of it in military language. The aim was to defeat the enemy. This involved delegitimising the government of the day and the constitutional order on which it was based, undermining its military capability through guerrilla warfare, weakening the economy through concerted action by trade unions, bringing international pressure to bear through sanctions, and building up pressure on the government by using stay-aways, boycotts, mass action and school boycotts. All of these were to be directed at making areas of the country ungovernable. In the period after 1983 the tempo, intensity and sophistication of these forms of opposition increased dramatically.

Second, the strategies mentioned above were articulated in terms of the rhetoric of Marxism–Leninism. This rhetoric was influential in the struggle because it provided an explanation for the daily experience of the majority, which was one of poverty. It told a simple story explaining why some were rich while others were poor. Built into the simple tale was the assurance that history was moving towards the moment of liberation (the revolution) and that after the revolution there was a better world to come.

Third, those in this struggle understood it as dovetailing nicely with the bipolarity which dominated world politics. The fight in South Africa was not only directed against apartheid, but also against capitalism. Many activists saw themselves on the side of the Communist Eastern bloc in its battle with the capitalist West. This perception was supported by the military training and military hardware which were provided to the revolutionaries by the Soviet Union and other Eastern bloc countries – most notably East Germany.

Fourth, these forms of power were not directed at extracting concessions from the government. The aim was victory. At the height of this struggle (1983–5) there were no bargaining forums within which both the UDF/ANC and the government could make deals of one kind or another. There were no such forums because neither side intended bargaining.

On the opposite side to this struggle was the South African government. It was not an autarchic power which could do as it wished, for it was locked into a world community which was economically, politically and technologically interdependent. By the 1980s, if not before, it had become useless for the government to try to 'sell' apartheid, even in a sanitised form, to this audience. The only justification which would carry any weight in the wider world was that which linked internal events in South Africa, if not into the Cold War struggle of democracy versus Communism (a problematic formulation in South Africa's case), at least with the global struggle between the capitalist West led by the USA and the Communist East led by the USSR. This was, accordingly, the line taken by Pretoria. It found itself lucky in that a series of events in the wider southern African region linked well into such an interpretation.

In 1976 the Soviet Union through its Cuban proxy scored a victory over the West by installing the People's Movement for the Liberation of Angola (MPLA) government in power in Angola, defeating the parties supported by the USA and South Africa. In Mozambique the Front for the Liberation of Mozambique (Frelimo) sought, with the aid of the Eastern bloc, to transform that society in a socialist direction. These developments made it possible for Pretoria to portray itself as beleaguered by a Communist onslaught on its borders, a threat closely linked to the internal threat posed by the ANC, SACP and PAC. For these organisations too, Pretoria argued, articulated a Marxist revolutionary project and received aid, training and weapons from Eastern bloc countries. All this was summed up in the claim that South Africa faced a 'total onslaught'. This rhetoric ran usefully parallel to Ronald Reagan's crusade against the 'evil empire'.

Pretoria responded to the 'total onslaught' with its 'total strategy', a comprehensive policy which led to South Africa becoming thoroughly militarised,[2] with a sophisticated National Security Management System (NSMS) put in place. All politics was made subservient to an overriding military goal – the defeat, or at the very least the containment, of the Communist revolutionary threat. Here, as with the African organisations engaged in the Struggle, what was being sought was not some form of political accommodation, but victory over the enemy.

In summary then, in the run-up to the post-1990 phase of South African politics there was a long period during which little or no politics took place between the two principal antagonists, the majority African group and the ruling white minority. Instead they engaged in a zero-sum quasi-military struggle.

From War to Politics

The end of the Cold War had profound implications for both the South African government and the ANC (and the many other organisations involved in the Struggle). For after 1986 it was no longer plausible for either the government or the anti-apartheid forces to portray themselves as occupying key positions in the global bipolar battle between the USSR and the USA and their respective allies. With the USSR turned towards reform and actively seeking rapprochement with the USA, these two powers were certainly not about to confront each other through proxies in southern Africa. Indeed, they were visibly co-operating in seeking an end to the war in Angola and in bringing about independence in Namibia. The effect of these developments on the parties was not symmetrical. The government, now unable to appeal to a wider crusade against Communism, stood out starkly as merely a minority government seeking to maintain the status quo in the face of majority opinion at home and an international consensus abroad. In the long run this was clearly an untenable position both in terms of ethics and power, especially since anti-apartheid groups worldwide, sensing their opportunity, redoubled their pressure. The government realistically had no option but to turn to reform.

In like manner the anti-apartheid forces had to change their rhetoric and practice. The states both in Africa and abroad which had supported the military struggle against apartheid were no longer prepared to do so. Non-violent forms of protest, spectacularly successful in bringing down Communist regimes in Central and Eastern Europe, were now widely seen as models to be followed by other countries seeking to democratise. In its quest for international support, the ANC had to modify its language and practice from an anti-capitalist revolutionary discourse to one which stressed democratisation and which played down violence as a method of liberation. For the ANC was crucially reliant on international support and was in no position to ignore a coalition which included all the major actors in world politics. If this coalition demanded that it turn to negotiation instead of violence, it had to obey.

Finally and most importantly, the end of the bipolar world had the dramatic effect on the antagonists in South Africe of forcing them both to profess the same political goals – they both had to declare themselves in favour of democratisation and as being opposed to violence. This had major implications for their day-to-day political practice, as I shall show below.

To summarise, during the Struggle politics for both 'the regime' and 'the progressive forces' was in essence a single-purpose, totalising and militaristic activity. The aim was victory, pure and simple, and the major problems were about strategy and tactics. What mattered in this type of politics was mobilising one's political troops and maintaining discipline in the battle. Not surprisingly all this was highly dramatic and commanded a lot of international attention – but the resulting confrontation was essentially a stalemate. When bipolarity ended, the antagonists had to abandon their totalist warring approaches, Internationally the practice of total ideological confrontation was replaced with a practice permeated with a single rhetoric, namely that of liberal democracy.[3] The major blocs facing one another in South Africa had to confront this reality and become competitors striving for the same goal – the establishment of a liberal democracy in South Africa.

Thus, although de Klerk's speech of 2 February 1990 dramatised the new turn, for some time a more gradual process of erosion had been under way, undermining the old totalist confrontation. Ever since the 1985 debt crisis the South African government had been under crippling financial pressure. It managed to renegotiate the outstanding debt, but at a premium which weighed heavily on the South African economy. Raising new loans became increasingly difficult and the calls for the international community to increase economic sanctions grew in number and strength. It was now apparent to the international community that the state of emergency was a device for maintaining minority rule and nothing more. The 'stick' of international economic and political pressure was reinforced by the 'carrot' of the recognition which flowed to Pretoria for the role it played in bringing about an end to Cuban involvement in Angola and in ushering in an independent Namibia. The path of negotiation, it seemed, might have considerable benefits as well as costs.

For its part the ANC too was under great pressure to move away from its strategy of armed struggle, for under the state of emergency the government's security forces within South Africa were steadily destroying its military capacity and its organisational infrastructure. Whereas in 1985 it had seemed that the revolutionary forces within the country might be strong enough to destroy the state, by 1990 it was quite clear that this was not a realisable option. Externally the military campaign was hamstrung by the reluctance of the front line states to continue housing and supporting ANC bases and by the termination of support from the Eastern bloc countries.

The New Politics after 1990

At this moment chance played a decisive role in South Africa's history. President P. W. Botha, who had masterminded the 'total strategy', fell ill and was replaced by President F. W. de Klerk who, it turned out, had the willingness and the ability to move away from militaristic politics. Under mounting international pressure he made his famous address to parliament on 2 February 1990 in which he announced the unbanning of the ANC, PAC and the SACP and the release of key political prisoners including Nelson Mandela. The initiative for this swerve towards negotiations appears to have come from a letter written by Mandela in 1988 from prison in which he proposed to the government the start of a process of negotiation. A similar willingness to negotiate was indicated by the ANC in its Harare Declaration of August 1989 in which it specified preconditions to be met before negotiations could begin.

The release of Mandela and the unbanning of the organisations captured the imagination of the world and radically changed the nature of South African politics. Here, it seemed, a modern political miracle might be possible: a resolution of the apartheid problem without a bloody revolution. It was a spark of light on a dark continent.

Where the years of the Struggle had been grim years of detentions, torture and assassinations without an end in sight, the four years after 1990 were years of heightened emotion, expectation and hope. Where the previous decade had been dominated by the government's technocratic planners working in secret and by the progressive movement's vanguard of revolutionaries plotting in secret, there now suddenly emerged a country in which everybody talked politics all the time. Suddenly the full range of political voices was to be heard. All this took place in the glare of the ever-present international media. The two national leaders were heroes at home and abroad – jointly winning the Nobel Peace Prize and many other awards. In the new politics interest now focused not, as before, on how much damage could be done to the enemy, but on what it was possible for the parties to agree to as common ground.

Political Power in the New Politics

The final agreement on the Interim Constitution which was reached at the end of 1993 was the culmination of a host of subordinate agreements along the way which laid the basis for the IC. Throughout the process, though, the key negotiators still depended on their ability to mobilise power and it was in this dimension that traces of the old practice lingered on. For the majority there was thus still a single goal – the establishment of an inclusive democracy. This was a theme around which the disenfranchised could easily mobilise both internal and international opinion. Mass mobilisation neatly reinforced their claim for a democracy, for the very act of mobilising demonstrated the democratic principle of majority support.

For the minority white government life was not so simple. In the post-1990 period this group too was committed to reform, but precisely what form it should take was not clear. There was no specific democratic constitutional arrangement in favour of which all the members of the minority could be mobilised, for any suggested movement away from the status quo seemed fraught with problems. The most pressing of these was, of course, the prospect of unconstrained majority rule. In general the members of this group were fearful of the consequences of democratisation and were primarily interested in safeguarding their jobs and property. It seemed to them that the best safeguards would involve complicated constitutional devices best understood by constitutional lawyers. For the most part they were happy to leave the process in the hands of 'constitutional experts'. The apathy which they had learned under the old technocratic rulers persisted into the new period. Since it is difficult to mobilise people around the fine print of constitutional texts this group was, by and large, both apathetic and anxious. The extremists who tried frantically to rally white opinion against the coming of democratic rule failed to achieve any corresponding mobilisation on the white side. Most whites (and coloureds and Indians) supported de Klerk silently and even apathetically, content to leave constitutional negotiations to the political leader.[4]

The change in political rhetoric during the three years of negotiation was remarkable. Previously politics had been heavily ideological as each side had sought to discredit the political creed of its opponent in a comprehensive way (at its crudest it was 'Communism' versus 'Capitalism'). But in the post-1990 politics the antagonists no longer presented opposed views but both spoke glowingly of 'democracy', 'rights', 'constitutionalism' and 'the rule of law'. Each sought to gain credit for itself (and to discredit the opponent) *by the same measures*. Most notably, President de Klerk rammed through the abolition of all the major apartheid Acts, so that the NP even tried to share with the ANC the credit for 'ending apartheid'. Locally and internationally credit was given for action which advanced democracy and disapprobation was accorded to those who caused violence or instability. Both Mr de Klerk and Mr Mandela now had political power which rested on their ability to make progress at the negotiating table. Broadly speaking each had two means by which he (and his party) could better the other. First, they could show themselves to be more democratic than the other. This could be done either by arguing that the package of principles which they were putting forward was in some ways more democratic than that offered by the opponent; or it could be done by showing that their party had more support than the other party. Second, they could show that the opposing party was still involved in using violent means to get its way. This amounted to claiming that the antagonist was talking democracy while practising violence. Throughout the negotiation phase this second strategy was used by each of the three major political groups, the ANC, the NP and the Inkatha Freedom Party.

The NP and the IFP claimed throughout the period that the ANC was still engaged in a clandestine armed struggle. They pointed to the creation of self-defence units (SDUs) in KwaZulu-Natal and to the sophisticated gun–running programme used to arm the SDUs with cheap weapons acquired through the informal arms market in Mozambique. The ANC, for its part, claimed that the IFP had self-protection units which were trained and armed by elements within the South African Defence Force (SADF). Furthermore the ANC claimed that the government was implicated in the setting up of a Third Force which specialised in random violence, assassinations and the general destabilisation of African communities. This is not the place to attempt a proper evaluation of these claims and counterclaims, but the scale of political violence during this period seems to suggest that some (or all) of the claims were probably true. Between 1990 and 1993 over 10,000 people were killed in circumstances which might broadly be termed 'political'. With the eclipse of all-out confrontation, the only legitimate excuse for violence during this period was that it was done 'in self-defence'. All the key actors made great use of this excuse, for the public rhetoric of the period was for democracy and against violence, but it goes without saying that this did not provide an adequate explanation for the killing of over 10,000 people.

The Phases of Negotiation

It would be tedious to recount the details of the negotiation process which started in 1990 with the release of Mandela and ended in 1993 with agreement on an Interim Constitution.[5] Instead I offer here a broad outline of four key phases on the road to the IC. These were 'talks about talks', 'the CODESA round', 'breakdown' and 'guided multiparty talks', It must be stressed, however, that each phase should be seen as but a moment in a larger game, this larger game being one in which the two chief protagonists (the ANC and NP) at no time had any real option but to go forward to a negotiated settlement. Neither had the resources to wage the old struggle any further and the international pressures on both were intense. Throughout the process it was clear (to this writer at least) that any breakdown would be temporary.

Talks about Preconditions for Talks

In the first phase after the release of Nelson Mandela, a phase lasting until the end of 1991, the focus was on bringing the political exiles home, negotiating the release of political prisoners and building up the political organisations of the parties which had been banned. The ANC, PAC and SACP were not to be drawn into talks before the exiled leadership had returned and the imprisoned leadership had been released. In July 1991 the ANC held its first national conference since its unbanning, the most important outcome of which was the election of a leadership cadre.

During this phase the NP leadership was basking in the benefits which de Klerk's initiative had brought to the country. It may well have thought that the haggling about preconditions for negotiations would continue indefinitely and thus not greatly disturb the status quo. The NP's main contention at this stage was that negotiations could not begin until the liberation movements had renounced violence and disbanded their military operations. A compromise was reached on the suspension of violence in the Groote Schuur Minute and an accommodation on the release of political prisoners was agreed in the Pretoria Minute.

CODESA

The next phase began in October 1991 when the ANC national executive committee indicated its approval of an all-party conference. A tentative beginning was made when the parties assembled near Jan Smuts airport, Johannesburg, to agree the form of such a conference. The PAC insisted that it be held outside South Africa, and when this demand was not conceded it walked out. The others agreed to establish the Convention for a Democratic South Africa, better known as CODESA I, which met at the World Trade Centre in Kempton Park on 20 and 21 December 1991 under the chairmanship of two judges, Piet Schabort and Ismail Mohammed.

The CODESA plenary set up five working groups to deal with different aspects of the negotiating process. The first was to consider how to establish a free political climate; the second, constitutional principles and a constitution-making body; the third, transitional government; the fourth, reincorporation of the independent homelands (Transkei, Venda, Bophuthatswana and Ciskei); and the fifth, the time frames for the transformation process. All nineteen parties to CODESA were represented on each of the committees and the overall process was overseen by a daily management committee, with the back-up provided by a secretariat. The first five months of 1992 were taken up with these negotiations.

We need not examine what happened in each of the working groups.[6] But there is a general point to be made, which is that to outsiders the proceedings at the World Trade Centre appeared to be extremely complicated, the pronouncements coming from there did not seem to cohere in any obvious way, and it was not at all clear whether the whole exercise was not an expensive and not very significant show. The nightly news on television was a bewildering spectacle for most. The dramatic question which cropped up with monotonous regularity was whether the talks were 'on track' or not. What 'track' they might be on was anybody's guess.

In the middle of this period the white Conservative Party (CP), which was not a participant in CODESA, won a by-election in Potchefstroom, defeating the NP. White militancy had been growing apace and there was now a real fear of a right-wing backlash against the whole negotiation process. Where the workings of the committees at CODESA seemed to be technical and removed from the daily experience of ordinary South Africans, the spectre of the white right seemed very real and worrying to many. It clearly worried the government, who called a referendum (the last ever whites-only electoral consultation) on whether negotiations should go ahead or not. This returned a 68.5 per cent vote in favour of continuing with negotiations. But once again it was not at all clear where these were leading. One possible interpretation is that the government itself was not sure and was not particularly worried as long as they dragged on a long time. It is quite plausible to suppose that it wanted the kudos that went with having negotiations in progress without the discomfort of actually having to change anything in a radical way.

At the next plenary session, now known as CODESA II, the talks broke down on an the issue of what percentage votes would be required to ratify the final constitution. The breakdown was confirmed when the ANC suspended its involvement in negotiations following the Boipatong massacre in June 1992, when ANC squatters were murdered by IFP-supporting hostel dwellers, allegedly with the support of the police. The rupture in negotiations may well have been sought by those within the ANC who saw that the CODESA proceedings were not producing quick results and believed that talk needed to be backed by a demonstration of power. Here again it is plausible to argue that this outcome (the breaking-off of talks) was not uncongenial to the government. For the conservative elements were hardly keen on bringing talks to a conclusion: they would have preferred either that negotiations should drag on interminably, or that they should break down in such a way that the blame could be put on the ANC.

Breakdown

These events led on to the third stage of the process, a breakdown in the formal negotiation process combined with a programme of rolling mass action by the ANC and its allies. This started on 16 June 1992. A series of stay-aways, boycotts, meetings and marches were planned and executed through July and August and culminated in September when the Ciskei military in Bisho opened fire on ANC marchers led by 'Red' Ronnie Kasrils, killing twenty-eight people. The upshot of 'rolling mass action' was indeterminate – for it produced nothing on the scale of the marches in Eastern Europe which had brought Communist regimes to an end. The South African social and economic fabric was intact and even at the peak of mass action it had not been necessary to bring the full military muscle of the SADF to bear. Despairing of bringing down the state, mass action activists took aim instead at the Bophuthatswana, KwaZulu and Ciskei mini-states – but even these survived intact.

What these events did bring about, though, was a firm response from the international community which brought considerable pressure to bear on the internal parties in South Africa to get back to negotiations. One form this took was an invitation of all the parties to New York to address the Security Council to the United Nations on 19 July. This pressure, together with the internal stalemate and the imperatives imposed by a weakening economy, once again brought the parties back to negotiations. This time, though, the negotiating structure was to be significantly different.

The Multi-Party Negotiating Forum

The final phase was started when Cyril Ramaphosa of the ANC together with the NP Minister Roelf Meyer brokered a summit between de Klerk and Mandela on 26 September 1992, where a Record of Understanding was agreed. This paved the way for a resumption of multiparty negotiations. But it was clear that this time it would be the two major parties who were masterminding the process – indeed, the Record of Understanding led the IFP to withdraw in anger from the negotiations. A further major element of consensus between the two parties emerged in November when Joe Slovo of the SACP suggested the idea of 'sunset clauses' in an Interim Constitution. These would include a guaranteed role in government for certain minority parties during the transitional period, together with guarantees about job security for presently serving civil servants. In April the Multi-Party Negotiating Forum (MPNF) got going. This time the white right was represented together with all the other major parties. The procedure followed by the MPNF was to devolve specific problems to technical committees which were charged to produce possible solutions for consideration by the MPNF. Where deadlock appeared imminent the practice evolved whereby the major parties would retreat into secret bilateral discussions, the most important of these being, of course, those between the NP and the ANC. The IFP complained bitterly that the process was being steered by the NP and ANC.

These negotiations produced concessions from both the ANC and the NP on the path to be followed towards a new constitution. The ANC agreed to be bound by constitutional principles negotiated by the MPNF, a concession which made it possible for the NP to agree to the establishment of an elected constitution-making body (CMB): until then the NP had always resisted the ANC demand for a constituent assembly. The ANC agreed that the CMB would be bound by an Interim Constitution, and that this CMB would also serve as an interim government.

Other key issues dealt with in this phase were, first, the establishment of transitional arrangements to ensure that the NP government did not use its superior resources to rig the first election. The solution arrived at was the establishment of the Transitional Executive Council (TEC) – a broadly representative body with the power to make authoritative rulings on any matter required for the 'levelling of the playing fields' prior to the election.[7] Finally, the MPNF agreed upon the structure of an Independent Electoral Commission (IEC) to oversee the first election.

During these negotiations the public were once again never quite sure about the details of the deals being made. For the public the issue was, as always, whether the talks would break down or not. These fears reached fever pitch in a dramatic finale in which the MPNF struggled to reach agreement on the IC and TEC to put to a special session of parliament which convened on 22 November 1993. The date was met and the deal struck.

Core Difficulties in Constitution-Building

What makes politics so difficult in the absence of a stable constitution is the awkward interplay between three things which are well illustrated in the process outlined above. In the first place, under such circumstances, politics can only take place if there is a certain level of trust between those engaging in political discourse (that is, if they confer on one another a certain legitimate standing).

Second, the outcome of political negotiations is dependent on the power of the participants. But assembling such power requires the active delegitimising of the opponent's stance. Thus the government frequently sought to portray the ANC as still fundamentally a Communist organisation which was not firm in its renunciation of violence. Similarly the ANC questioned the bona fides of the government. Such attempts to demonise the opponent had the effect of undermining the trust requirement mentioned in the previous paragraph.

Third, the complexity of the constitutional package to be negotiated produced its own problems, especially when it came to bringing power to bear on the opponent. Through the many phases it took to negotiate the Interim Constitution, which stretched from the Groote Schuur Minute, the Pretoria Minute, CODESA I. CODESA II, the Record of Understanding, the Multi-Party Negotiating Forum, the setting up of the TEC, the IEC and finally the Interim Constitution, the question endlessly presented to the public by the media was 'Are the negotiations on or off?' It was presented as a stark either/or. In presenting the matter in this way the media had correctly perceived that the threat of veto against the whole process was the major form of power which each party brought to the negotiating table. Thus intricate negotiations about a complex set of constitutional issues were threatened at each point by the crudest form of political power. Threatening the use of such power in these circumstances was akin to threatening the use of cannon to influence a chess match.[8]

Under these circumstances the major parties had neither the time nor the capacity to educate their followers about the details of the deals being struck around the negotiating table. Crucially, the major parties (ANC, NP and IFP) needed political power in the negotiating phase and the only power at their disposal was the crude one of complete veto and breakdown. *What South Africa did not have during this phase was a nuanced and normal democratic political practice. The practice of political power was still premised on threats of mass action, violence and counterviolence. In many ways it was still a militarised and polarised political culture.*

This manifested itself as follows. For most whites, supporting the ANC was still understood as something akin to supporting the enemy. Similarly ANC supporters presented blacks who supported the NP as in some sense stooges of 'the Regime'. Superimposed on this was the territorial principle which dominated African politics. This persisted from the days of the Struggle when allowing an agent of an opposing party into one's area was seen as tantamount to allowing enemy agents into the ranks of one's army.

Thus during this negotiation phase the negotiators themselves were deeply involved in preparing a democratic framework for the South African polity, but the wider public were largely excluded from the subtleties of the debate and were kept, as it were, in readiness merely as reserve armies to be used to threaten the disruption of the whole negotiating process. The people of South Africa were still soldiers in the struggle. There was no normal politics.

The constitution finally settled on was a long and unwieldy document of 251 clauses; with its accompanying schedules, it ran to 222 pages in length. It was, without doubt, overlong and cumbersome and contained many clauses which could not possibly be enforced – for example, the right of a child to freedom from abuse or neglect, and its right to nutrition and parental care. Many lawyers shook their heads at the immensity of the task of judicial redefinition and reformulation which seemed likely in the face of such a document, while other voices could almost immediately be heard suggesting that the final constitution, which would emerge from the constituent assembly elected in 1994, would be a very different document. Almost immediately after the election the resignation of the Finance Minister, Derek Keys, led to a swift amendment to the constitution so that his successor could be chosen on a non-party basis and from outside the ranks of MPs. Such speedy *ad hominem* amendment suggested a fairly cavalier attitude to the long work of constitution-making and inevitably doubt persisted as to how seriously one had to take such an overdetailed document which would anyway soon be replaced.

The clauses of the constitution which had the most immediate and powerful bearing on the country's life – and which could potentially exercise influence far into the future – were those creating a new electoral system for the 400-seat constituent assembly/parliament. This was to be along strictly proportional lines both within the regions, which had 200 seats shared between them pro rata to their population, and nationally, where parties presented national lists for the further 200 seats at stake. In addition, the nine new regional assemblies were all to be chosen on the basis of strict proportionality with regionwide lists. Thus neither at regional nor at national level would any politician have a constituency, and enormous power was thus conferred on the party bosses who drew up the lists at regional and national levels. Proponents of this system pointed to the fact that it had been used in Namibia, and surprisingly little comment was made on the fact that South Africa, with a population forty times the size of Namibia's, would enter its new democratic age with an electoral system no other country of its size in the world had ever considered.

The degree to which the new electoral system was a political bosses' charter was further emphasised by the clause which determined that any MPs who lost the confidence of their party (that is, their party's leadership) could by the party's decision alone be excluded from parliament. There were to be no floor-crossers or back-bench rebels, by law. When this clause was added to the fact that the party bosses already held power of political life and death over their MPs – because they decided on the names on their lists and their order – the result was a push towards an extreme centralisation of power liable to negate most, if not all, of the federal influences within the rest of the constitution. This situation was yet further reinforced by the strange fact that voters were originally intended to have only one vote, to be counted for all lists. After enormous protest from the IFP and the Democratic Party (DP) this was changed to two votes – one for the constituent assembly, one for the regional assembly. The oddity remained that the voter was presented with three lists: one for election to the regional assembly of the region the voter was in; a second for that region's slate of MPs to the constituent assembly (which doubles as the national parliament); and a third for a nationwide list of MPs to the constituent assembly. Yet a voter had only two votes for these three contests: one was cast for the regional assembly election, but his second vote was counted both for the national and regional lists for the constituent assembly. Voters were not only powerless to choose between candidates on their party's list but if they voted for the national list presented to them by their parties, they could not prevent their vote also being counted for a regional list – and vice versa.

This extraordinary situation was yet further reinforced by the decision that no names of candidates should appear on the ballot paper at all, only the party's name and logo and the face of the party leader, so that most voters had no idea of which candidates they were voting for other than of the *presidentiable* who was thus taken to personify the party. Certainly, when it came to names half-way down a party's 200-long national list, it would have been rare to find voters who even knew whom they had voted for. The arguments in favour of such a system were that strict proportionality was vital to a country in which minority fears were so strong; that most voters anyway thought in terms of party; and that this tight central control would prevent the emergence of regionalist and tribal divisions.

Many believed that two other reasons were important. First, the SACP had decided to run its candidates on the ANC list and the method chosen not only allowed them to do so in anonymity – there was no indication of who on the ANC list belonged to the SACP – but also enabled a number of white and Indian radicals to be placed in electable positions down the ANC list where they could be coat-tailed in by Mandela. Given the fact that no white or Indian area gave the ANC a majority, a constituency-based system would have presented such politicians with the potentially awkward task of getting elected for African areas whose language they often could not speak. Second, the NP had its own long tradition of political bossism and the system chosen consolidated de Klerk's hold on the party, making life all but impossible for right-wing dissenters within the NP. Certainly the electoral system reflected a degree of dominance over the country's political life by two national elites which would have been unthinkable in any country with a settled experience of a constituency-based democracy.

From Soldiers to Citizens?

On 3 June 1993 the negotiating council (MPNF) chose 27 April 1994 as the date for the election. Everything that followed was, in a sense, part of the election campaign. However, while electioneering did take place, the main focus of public attention was on the parties who rejected the Interim Constitution and thus the election. The really burning question was, would these parties join the process or would they seek to wreck it? The most important of the outsiders was the IFP, followed by the white right-wing groupings, the most important of which was the Afrikaaner Volksfront (VF).[9] Both the IFP and the white right posed the threat of some form of civil war if the ANC and the government went ahead with the election. Thus during the period July 1993 to March 1994 public attention was not focused on electioneering within a settled constitutional framework so much as on the very real possibility of major disruptions of a military nature.

Democrats hoped that during the 'election' campaign the majority of South African citizens would change from being participants in extra-constitutional politics to being participants in normal politics – that they would participate in and allow the politics of multiparty democracy. Yet for most South Africans this transformation did not take place, because of the persistence of territorial politics. The politics of territory was inherited from the Struggle: control over territory had been a key aim of the liberation movements in that period. One component of this had been a policy aimed at making areas 'ungovernable' by delegitimising normal policing and administration. For example, rent boycotts resulted in some administrative functions simply falling away. Similarly, in place of normal policing, alternative security structures were established in many places through the creation of self-defence units. These measures taken together reinforced the practice of territorial politics which meant that if a person lived in an area designated as IFP, for example, that was the party he or she had to support. The borders of party-political territory were very precise, known to all and policed by a large implicit (or explicit) threat of violence against anyone who infringed those borders. This territoriality flowed over easily into the election period, ensuring that it was not generally possible for parties to canvass in areas where another party had been traditionally dominant.

In KwaZulu-Natal this problem was made particularly acute by the fact that the IFP did not agree to participate in the election at all until nine days before the event. Prior to this it had adamantly opposed the Interim Constitution and the election, arguing that these had been arranged by and ANC–NP deal from which the IFP had been excluded. The IFP objected, moreover, to the way in which this deal had established a unitary state instead of a federal one and had set up decision-making mechanisms for a cabinet and Constituent Assembly which would discriminate against the IFP. Thus for the duration of the election campaign it was almost impossible for other parties to canvass for support in IFP areas.

For most of the election campaign, then, the main issue was not competition between parties with different policies. The burning question was whether the election would be able to go ahead at all. Here again the political rhetoric and practice of the parties (especially in KwaZulu-Natal) was militaristic and antipathetic towards democracy.

Conclusion

Although there was a multiparty election on 27 April 1994 which was declared 'free and fair' by the IEC and many international observer groups, the political culture within which it took place was far from democratic and the election was not preceded by multiparty politics of a normal kind. In the early phases of negotiations the power of the major parties still depended on mass mobilisation and/or clandestine violence. However, even when these motifs began to fade, the principle of territoriality guaranteed that the parties remained unable to canvass support freely among the newly enfranchised electorate. Until almost the very end of the campaign the threat of a military conflict was always in the air, with the possibility of a violent conflict between the ANC along with the NP on one side, against the white right and/or the IFP on the other.[10]

What haunted the negotiation process and the election campaign was the possibility, feared by all parties, that the whole negotiated edifice might crumble and place the political actors back in a new version of the old struggle. The fear of this necessitated that all parties retain, until the election itself, the patterns of power built up in the non-democratic past

– but the retention of these patterns could only serve to compromise South Africa's advance into a democratic future.

Notes

1 I use the term African to refer to the majority of South Africans who are not white, Indian or coloured. The term 'black' is too wide, and the term 'Bantu' is not correct politically.

2 See Jacklyn Cock and Laurie Nathan (eds), *War and Society* (Cape Town: David Philip, 1989).

3 This reality was made manifest in the highly influential article by Francis Fukuyama, 'The end of history', *The National Interest*, 16 (Summer 1989).

4 The very anxiety of the minority provided the point around which the National Party government could mobilise support. For example, in the referendum of whites in March 1992 in which it sought a mandate to continue with negotiations, it presented the 'yes' option as being better than a negative response, which would signal a return to the laager. No particular positive vision was offered, merely the thought that going forward to some unknown destination was better than going back.

5 The complex public aspects of this process are reasonably well known, but there were many secret deals which were made along the way of which the details have not yet come to light.

6 The story of what happened in each is well recounted in Steven Friedman (ed.), *The Long Journey: South Africa's Quest for a Negotiated Settlement* (Johannesburg: Ravan Press, 1993). The synopsis given here draws heavily on this work.

7 The TEC started operating in December 1993 and created subcouncils to deal with the following specialist areas: regional and local government; traditional authorities; law, order, stability and security; defence; finance; foreign affairs; status of women; intelligence.

8 Constitutional government is designed among other things to avoid this problem. It allows disagreements over specific matters to be dealt with in a way which does not threaten the whole system of co-operation within which the dispute is situated.

9 The Azanian People's Organisation, which refused to participate in the elections, was not of great significance.

10 These outsider groups were for a time united in the (so-called) Concerned South Africans Group (COSAG).

THREE

Movements in South African Mass Opinion and Party Support to 1993

Chris de Kock

EVERY POLITICAL ANALYST DREAMS of testing theories of sociopolitical change in rapidly changing societies by means of empirical monitoring conducted over a period of time. South African political analysts are no different and felt this need especially in the 1970s and 1980s when much in South Africa's sociopolitical environment seemed set for far-reaching changes. Unfortunately these analysts had neither the time nor the resources to conduct such analyses at the time, and, more importantly, didn't realise that the great moment of rapid change (1990–94) was to dawn so soon.

Despite this situation, several South African sociopolitical analysts – sometimes unaware of each other's work, and often with goals other than monitoring sociopolitical change and testing hypotheses – were able to repeat certain questions in their studies pertinent to sociopolitical change over a period of time. In this way they inadvertently succeeded in capturing very important information on change. The research of Booysen and Fleetwood, of Rhoodie and Ehlers and of Kotzé is especially significant.[1] Booysen and Fleetwood's study focused on students at the Rand Afrikaans University in 1989 and 1991, whereas the studies by Rhoodie and Ehlers and Kotzé concentrated on South African decision-makers (mostly white elites) in the period from 1990 to 1993. These studies, however, cannot be regarded as representative of the South African public at large and they cover only a short time period, thus limiting their relevance to the issue at hand.

In addition to these studies, the Human Sciences Research Council, in its surveys among the general public over the last decade, has repeated a range of questions relating to key aspects of change. This has resulted in an extensive data base of responses over time derived from comparable questions and samples. By its very nature, such a data base can provide a valuable source of information for the monitoring of sociopolitical trends.

In particular, an analysis of the data by means of graphic representations of these responses, a description of the responses and the possible correlation between various keynote factors, is likely to yield significant results. Such analysis forms the basis of this chapter.

The exercise had its methodological problems. For instance the positions and roles of the four population groups – whites as the wielders of power, Africans as the subordinate group mobilised for resistance and coloureds and Indians as marginalised groups – meant that the questions put to one group were not always relevant to the others. For this reason the decision was made to treat the various population groups separately for the purposes of this analysis, especially since the legacy of apartheid is that population group (race) remains a major explanatory variable. Coloureds and Indians will not be considered here at all, since the surveys conducted among these two groups were unfortunately not sufficiently comparable to be included.

Research Design

The various surveys from which the data have been extracted are listed in table 3.1 (see the Appendix of Tables at the end of this chapter), where reference is made to certain surveys which were scheduled to be repeated at regular intervals – 'omnibus' and 'monitor' surveys. Both telephone and door-to-door surveys were used to obtain the data. The figures in the Appendix of Figures reflecting political party and leadership support (figures 3.24–3.30 and 3.41–3.48) also include data from omnibus surveys, which are the same as monitor surveys in that both are conducted door-to-door. The surveys conducted among the whites were invariably countrywide, whereas those conducted among the Africans generally covered the five metropoles, with the exception of the omnibus surveys reflected in figures 3.41–3.48.

The question as to whether trends identified in the door-to-door surveys might be any different from those obtained in the telephone surveys was investigated. The results revealed that although the depth of responses might vary, there was no significant difference in the direction of trends (upward, downward or consistent) over time between the two types of fieldwork, even among the African surveys where only the upper socioeconomic sector is accessible in telephone surveys. In all the figures presented, however, telephone and door-to-door surveys are clearly identified, either by using different types of lines in line graphs, or by footnotes to histograms. In this article the concern is with broad trends rather than with the precise configuration of results.

Some Sociopolitical Trends among Whites

Sense of security or insecurity

Figures 3.1–3.3 reflect the sense of security or insecurity prevailing among the white population since the mid-1980s. Figure 3.1 shows that, although the sense of insecurity fluctuated between October 1987 and July 1993, the proportion of whites feeling insecure grew steadily. This growth was particularly marked after the outbreak of violence in August 1990; after December 1992 when whites became the targets of alleged attacks by the Azanian People's Liberation Army (APLA) – the armed wing of the Pan Africanist Congress; after the assassination of Chris Hani in April 1993; and during the run-up to the April 1994 election

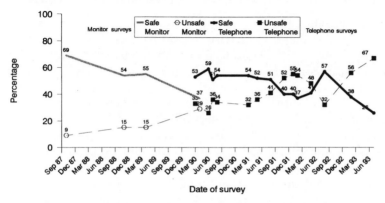

Figure 3.1   How safe do you feel in South Africa today?

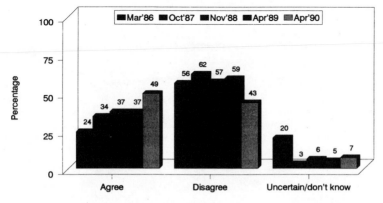

Figure 3.2   Fear for own and/or family's safety in South Africa

which marked the end of white political control. Figure 3.2 confirms the trend of growing white insecurity during the latter half of the 1980s. Figure 3.3 indicates that, especially from the end of 1992, whites seriously began believing that the government had no control over political violence: this perception increased by 26 percentage points between August 1992 and July 1993.

There is a logical correlation between the sense of security or insecurity (figure 3.1) and perceptions of government's ability to control political violence (figure 3.3). This is reflected in the following statistics: 72 per cent of whites who recorded feeling secure in the 1993 surveys believed that the government was in control of the violence, while 52 per cent who felt insecure believed the opposite. Analysis of the 1987 and 1990 data sets reveals an identical correlation.

Satisfaction or dissatisfaction with the general political situation

The trend of white satisfaction with the general political situation (figure 3.4) is virtually identical to that of the whites' sense of security or insecurity (figure 3.1). Dissatisfaction with the general political situation increased markedly between March 1984 and March 1986 with the outbreak and escalation of unrest, between February 1993 and July 1993 when attacks on whites increased, after Chris Hani's assassination and in the period preceding the 1994 election.

Both the 1987 and 1993 survey results show a positive correlation between a sense of insecurity (figure 3.1) and dissatisfaction with the general political situation (figure 3.4). Thus 67 per cent and 92 per cent of white respondents who respectively felt secure and insecure in the 1993 surveys were dissatisfied with the general political situation.

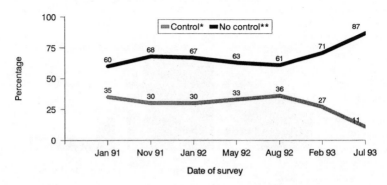

Figure 3.3   In your view, what measure of control does the government have over the violence that is occurring in South Africa at the present time?

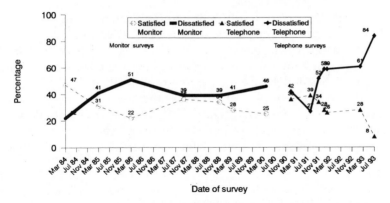

Figure 3.4   How satisfied are you with the general political situation in South Africa at present?

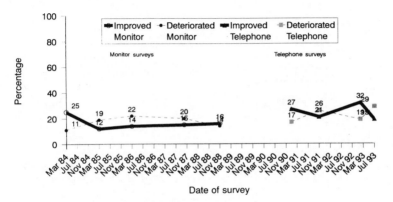

Figure 3.5   Has your present attitude towards Africans improved or deteriorated in the past year?

Attitudes towards Africans

The proportion of whites who felt that their attitudes towards Africans had deteriorated over the past year likewise fluctuated with events, yet remained strikingly low, with negative attitudes towards Africans peaking at 29 per cent in July 1993 (figure 3.5). The deterioration in white attitudes prior to July 1993 might again be attributable to 'APLA attacks' and the events following the assassination of Chris Hani.

The trend of responses to the question *Do whites and Africans have enough common values to create a future democratic South Africa?* (figure 3.6) corroborates the trend in figure 3.5. Between October 1987 and May 1989 the 'yes' response was between 32 per cent and 38 per cent and the 'no' response between 51 per cent and 57 per cent. In August 1992, 59 per cent of the research group gave a 'yes' response and only a third believed that there were insufficient common interests and values. With attacks on whites increasing between August 1992 and February 1993 this situation was reversed: almost two-thirds of respondents felt that there were insufficient common interests and values, while less than a third felt that there were enough common interests and values.

In both the 1987 and the 1993 surveys there was a positive correlation between a sense of insecurity (figure 3.1) and a negative attitude towards Africans (figure 3.5). Only 15 per cent of those who felt secure in 1993 were negative towards Africans, while 35 per cent of those who felt insecure had a negative attitude.

Changing attitudes towards negotiation

Figure 3.7 shows that by the late 1980s the majority of whites were in favour of negotiations between the South African government and the

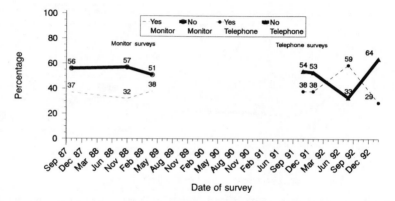

Figure 3.6   Do Whites and Africans have enough common values to create a future democratic South Africa?

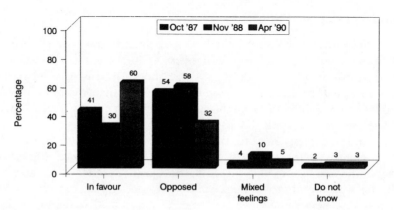

Figure 3.7   To what extent are you in favour of the South African government negotiating with the ANC on the political future of South Africa?

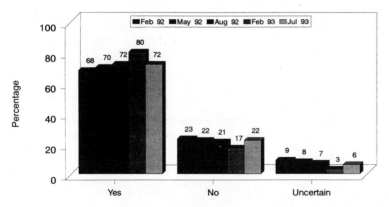

Figure 3.8   Do you personally support the negotiations between the government and the various political parties and organisations on the future of South Africa?

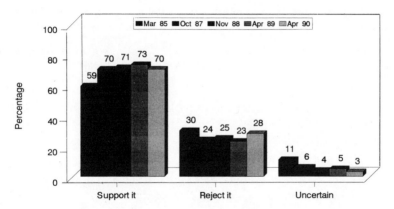

Figure 3.9   When you consider the government's reform policy, are you inclined to support or reject this policy?

ANC. Support for reform also increased (figure 3.9). As multiparty negotiations gained momentum after February 1992, so white support for the process (figure 3.8) grew, reaching 80 per cent in February 1993. However, there was a marked decline in support for negotiations between February and July 1993.

The number of people who believed that reform was being implemented too rapidly decreased between March 1985 and April 1989 (figure 3.10). The April 1989 and April 1990 surveys indicated a sharp rise in the number of whites who felt that reform was proceeding too quickly. This was probably the result of the rapid pace of reform following F. W. de Klerk's historic initiative in February 1990. Although whites adjusted to the accelerated rate over the next two years, by February 1993 nearly a third of the respondents still felt that the tempo of change was too rapid.

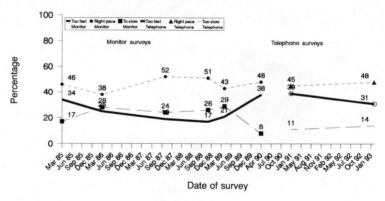

Figure 3.10 How do you personally feel about the pace at which reform plans are being implemented?

The 1987 surveys among whites revealed a negative correlation between a sense of insecurity and

- support for negotiations with the ANC: 44 per cent of those who felt secure favoured negotiations with the ANC, as opposed to 32 per cent of those who felt insecure;

- support for the government's reform policy: 77 per cent of those who felt secure favoured this policy, compared to 44 per cent of those who felt insecure;

- a perception that the government's pace of reform was appropriate or too slow: 82 per cent of those who felt secure believed the pace was correct or too slow, as opposed to 54 per cent of those who felt insecure;

- the perception that a mixed government (African, white, coloured and Indian) would be a good thing: 65 per cent of those who felt secure believed it would be a good thing, as opposed to 40 per cent of those who felt insecure.

The 1993 surveys likewise showed an inverse relation between a sense of insecurity and support for multiparty negotiations: 80 per cent of those who felt secure supported multiparty negotiations as opposed to 69 per cent who felt insecure.

Hopes of a peaceful future for South Africa

Figure 3.11 shows that the proportion of whites who saw little hope of a peaceful future for South Africa rose from 32 per cent in January 1991 to 42 per cent in August 1992. Between August 1992 and July 1993 this figure increased by a further 24 percentage points, from 42 per cent to 66

per cent. As in the case of other trends, the attacks on whites after
December 1992 and the events following Hani's assassination in April
1993 had a significant impact on the public's perceptions of security.

As one might expect, those who felt insecure (figure 3.1) had less hope
of a peaceful future than those who felt secure (figure 3.11). Respectively
45 per cent and 16 per cent of those who felt secure and insecure in 1993
had hopes of a peaceful future for the country.

Mistrust of the ANC and of an African-dominated government

Despite the fact that white acceptance of the need to negotiate with the
ANC was increasing (see above) together with the growing realisation
that the ANC enjoyed majority support among Africans (especially after

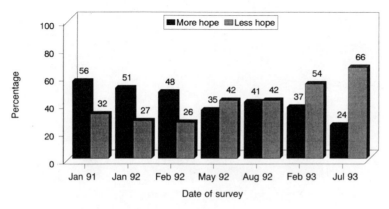

Figure 3.11   Do you now have more or less hope for a peaceful future for
South Africa than a year ago?

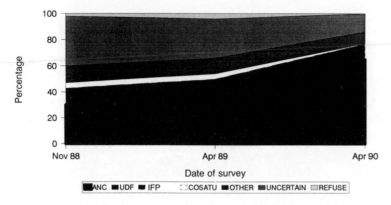

Figure 3.12   In your view, which one organisation enjoys the greatest
support among Africans?

February 1990 – figure 3.12) and that Africans had to become part of the political system (figures 3.13 and 3.14), there was no parallel trend in the level of confidence in the ANC and/or an African-dominated government prior to the election (figures 3.15, 3.16 and 3.17). Thus 83 per cent and 80 per cent respectively of white respondents in the February 1992 and July 1993 surveys still did not trust the ANC and were not at all or only slightly sure that their pensions would be safe under a new government, which of necessity would be African dominated.

The 1990 white surveys revealed a strong positive correlation between a sense of insecurity (figure 3.1) and a mistrust of ANC promises that it would not allow a black domination of whites (figure 3.16). Respectively 54 per cent and 87 per cent of those who felt secure and insecure indicated that they did not trust the ANC's promises at all.

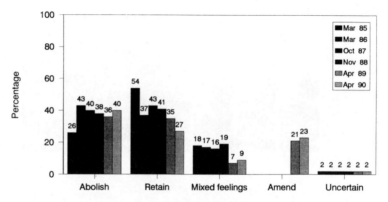

Figure 3.13   What should be done about the policy that prevents Africans from having seats in the current parliament?

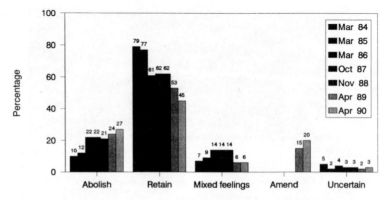

Figure 3.14   What should be done about the policy that makes provision for separate parliamentary representation for whites, coloureds and Indians?

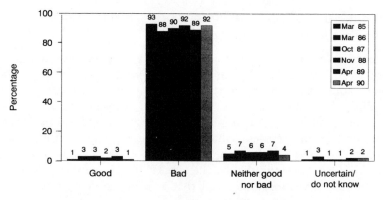

Figure 3.15   Views of the future under an African majority government

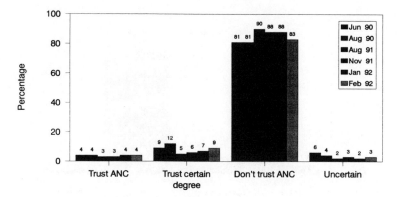

Figure 3.16   To what extent do you trust the ANC's promise that it will not tolerate African domination over whites?

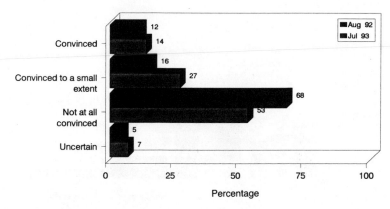

Figure 3.17   To what extent are you convinced that your pension/savings will be safe under a new government?

Intentions to emigrate, perceptions of a *volkstaat* and white domination

One option for the whites who felt insecure was to leave the country. Figure 3.18 shows a rise in the number of whites who were *considering* leaving South Africa (from 15 per cent in January 1991 to 21 per cent in July 1993) but the emigration option was *acceptable* to only a small proportion even among economically privileged white South Africans.

Another option for these whites was to attempt to secure a *volkstaat*, that is, a homeland in which they could live under a white government. Figure 3.19 shows clearly that by the late 1980s (November 1988 to April 1990) whites increasingly believed that a future under a white government in an independent country was not viable. During the period of multiparty negotiations this particular aspect was not monitored in the

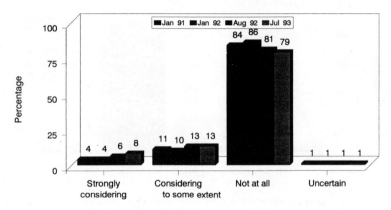

Figure 3.18   To what extent are you considering emigrating in the next three years?

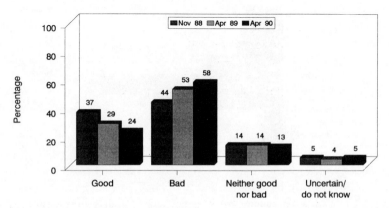

Figure 3.19   Future under a white government in own independent country

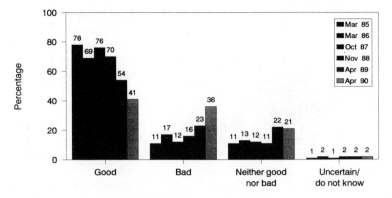

Figure 3.20   Future under a white government

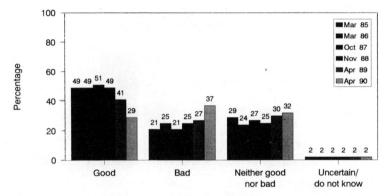

Figure 3.21   Future under a government consisting of whites, coloureds and Indians

surveys mentioned above, but an independent countrywide survey in July 1993[2] contained the question *How do you feel about demarcating an area for Afrikaners and other whites in which they might enjoy self-determination?* This survey showed that 18 per cent of white respondents believed in a *volkstaat* so fervently that they would have been prepared to move there. Among these respondents 12 per cent were willing to move provided their standard of living remained the same but only 6 per cent were willing to move even if it meant lowering their standard of living.

Figures 3.20, 3.21, 3.22 and 3.23 show that by the second half of the 1980s a growing proportion of whites realized that the days of white domination were over (figure 3.20); that the days of the Tricameral Parliament were numbered (figure 3.21); that Africans would have to be involved in political decision-making (figure 3.22); and that the best long-term method of combating political instability would be the political

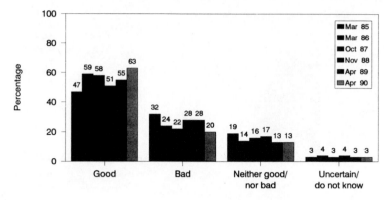

Figure 3.22   Future under a government consisting of whites, coloureds, Indians and Africans

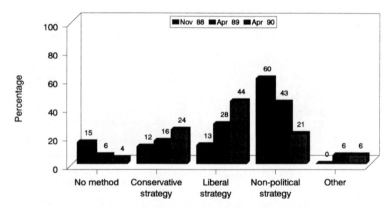

Figure 3.23   What do you think is the best method to prevent or reduce political instability in the long run?

strategy of accommodating Africans in political decision-making (figure 3.23). In fact, the number of supporters of a liberal political strategy increased by 238 per cent between November 1988 and April 1990, while the proportion of whites who supported a conservative political strategy increased by 100 per cent during the same period. The number of exponents of non-political strategies (such as economic development and security action) declined sharply.

Sociopolitical trends and party support

As indicated, the trends above clearly show that the whites' sense of insecurity grew steadily during the decade surveyed. In addition, their perception that the government had no control over political violence and their dissatisfaction with the political situation also increased, while hopes of a peaceful future faded. Whites also increasingly realised that the solution to South Africa's problems was a political one; that Africans had to be involved in political decision-making; and that the maintenance of white domination, even in a white homeland (*volkstaat*), offered no solution. Finally, more and more whites accepted that the ANC represented the majority of African people and that negotiations with the ANC were unavoidable. None the less their mistrust of the ANC did not diminish before the election.

Did these trends in any way influence white support of political parties and political leadership as shown in figures 3.24 to 3.30? These figures reveal that for most of the period between March 1984 and July 1993 the National Party managed to attract over 50 per cent of white support (figure 3.24). However, despite short-term fluctuations, white support for the NP showed a declining trend, which became noticeably stronger after the August 1992 survey. This analysis so far reveals a clear decline in whites' sense of security and in their perception that the government could control political violence, particularly during the latter part of 1992 and early 1993. The decline in NP support over the same period can probably be associated with the sharp rise in insecurity and dissatisfaction with the general political situation as a result of the attacks on whites and the aftermath of Hani's assassination.

The reason for this decline in support, however, could be interpreted in another way. It is also possible that their movement from the NP *especially* to the parties to the right of the NP (tables 3.3, 3.4 and 3.5) influenced their views of security, control over violence, etc. Qualitative research, however, tends to support the first possibility, namely that as people felt increasingly insecure, doubted the government's ability to control the violence and became more dissatisfied with the political situation, they were inclined to move away from the NP towards the right-wing parties in particular.

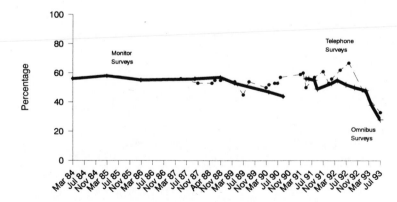

Figure 3.24   Support for the NP

The post–August 1992 decline in NP support may have been reflected in minor increases in support for parties to the left and right (figures 3.25 and 3.26), but substantially greater increases in 'unsure' and 'support no party' responses occurred (figure 3.27), as well as increased white support for the IFP (table 3.2). None the less it is interesting that the NP government was able to regain its lost white support in the latter half of 1993 and early 1994. Support for the NP party leader F. W. de Klerk following his inauguration as president in 1989 mirrors the pattern of NP support but at a slightly higher level (figure 3.28).

The right-wing parties virtually never managed to exceed 30 per cent of white support and the CP leader, Dr A.P. Treurnicht, always ran behind his party. After May 1987 right-wing support among whites remained virtually constant at 25 per cent. Greater fluctuations became noticeable in 1992, possibly attributable to the strain and conflict in right-wing circles and white perceptions of a deteriorating security situation.

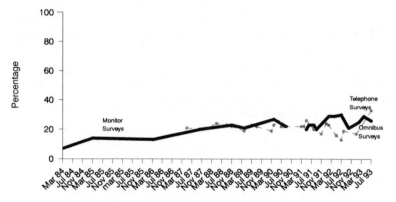

Figure 3.25   Support for the right-wing (mainly CP)

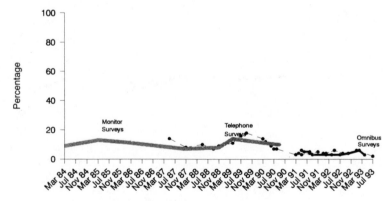

Figure 3.26   Support for the left-wing (mainly DP)

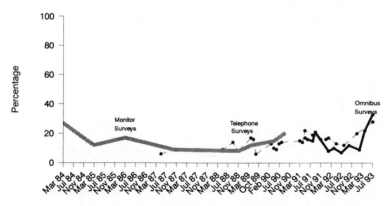

Figure 3.27   Support for any political party: uncertain/do not know/none

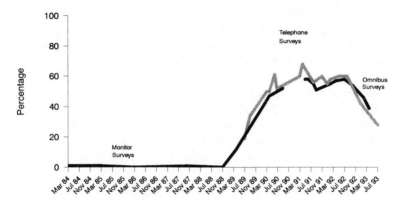

Figure 3.28   Support for de Klerk as leader for South Africa

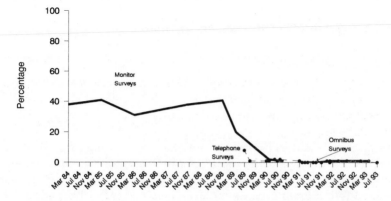

Figure 3.29   Support for P. W. Botha as leader for South Africa

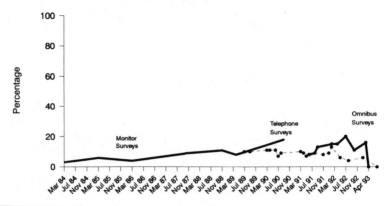

Figure 3.30   Support for A. P. Treurnicht as leader for South Africa

White support for parties to the left, in effect the Democratic Party (DP), peaked in 1989. After de Klerk's initiative in February 1990, it dropped to a very low level. The rise in DP support during the period 1987 to 1989 may be attributable to a growing feeling among whites that African political accommodation was the only solution and to growing insecurity and dissatisfaction with the political situation.

In this context it is important to note that none of the surveys indicated more than 2 per cent white support for the ANC – a finding that accords with white mistrust of the ANC noted above. Indeed, for most of the period covered by this analysis (1984–93) there was no noteworthy white support for any African party, except for a brief spell in early 1993 (see table 3.2) when an appreciable proportion of whites indicated support for the IFP, reaching as high as 15 per cent in July 1993.

In conclusion, the trends in sociopolitical change among whites seem to show that although whites feared and rejected the prospects of a political accommodation of the African majority, rationality prevailed.

Some Sociopolitical Trends among Africans

Perceptions of negotiation and violence as political instruments

Figures 3.31 to 3.34 reflect African perceptions of violence and multiparty negotiations in the period March 1986 to July 1993. The figures clearly indicate that, with some fluctuations, there was a growing realisation among Africans during the late 1980s and early 1990s that violence as a political strategy had its limitations and that, in the long term, negotiation would secure them a better deal. Occasionally African support for the violence option strengthened and support for the negotiation option weakened (see the response on violence between July 1991 and July 1992 in figure 3.31 and the 'yes' response for August 1992 in figure 3.34).

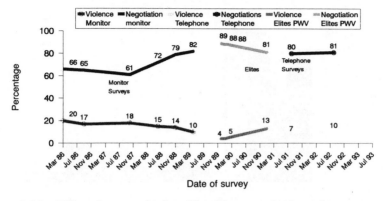

Figure 3.31   What do you think will achieve more for Africans in South Africa in the long run: violence or negotiation?

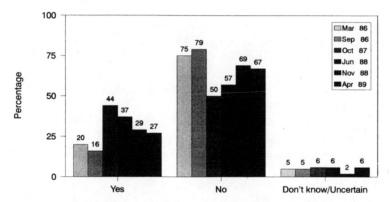

Figure 3.32   Have Africans gained anything from the unrest up to now?

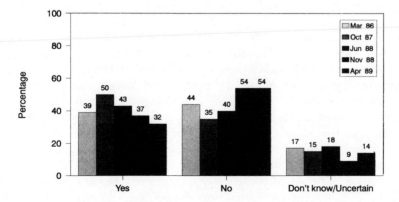

Figure 3.33   Will Africans gain anything from the unrest in the future?

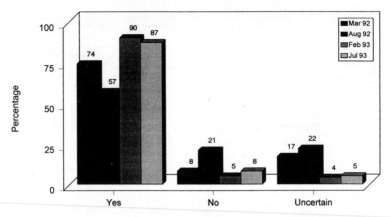

Figure 3.34 Do you personally support the negotiations between the government and the various political parties and organisations on the future of South Africa?

For example, in a survey in August 1992 following the Boipatong and Bisho massacres, 57 per cent of African respondents supported negotiations between the government and political parties, as opposed to 74 per cent and 90 per cent respectively in the preceding (March 1992) and following (February 1993) surveys.

African perceptions of whether unrest had been helpful to their cause in the past (figure 3.32) most probably influenced their view of the usefulness of unrest in the future (figure 3.33), and hence their support for negotiations. In the 1987 surveys it was found that respectively 48 per cent and 8 per cent of those who believed that unrest had been effective in the past felt that negotiation would achieve better results than violence in the future and that future unrest would achieve nothing. By contrast, 73 per cent and 62 per cent of those who thought that unrest had secured no gains in the past believed that negotiation would be more effective than violence in the future and that unrest would be ineffectual. This correlation was confirmed by the 1991 surveys.

This finding may explain the increase in African support for negotiations during the early 1990s (figure 3.34). Until 1989 the violent struggle against apartheid or the white-dominated government had proved to be effective and could be viewed as a useful political instrument in the future. However, a power struggle developed after 1987, mainly between Inkatha and the UDF–COSATU alliance which, despite the fact that many analysts regarded it as part and parcel of the anti-apartheid struggle, did not secure any advantages for Africans; indeed, most of the victims were African. This could explain the decline from 44 per cent in October 1987 to 27 per cent in April 1989 (figure 3.32) in the proportion of Africans who believed that violence was effective. After February 1990 violence spread to the Witwatersrand and, since the victims were again

African, there was an increasing rejection of violence and acceptance of the need for negotiation (figure 3.34).

The 1987 surveys also established a positive correlation between a sense of insecurity among Africans and the perception that violence would achieve more than negotiations. Respectively 14 per cent and 23 per cent of those who felt secure and those who felt insecure believed that violence would achieve more than negotiations. This finding might explain the periodic decline in support for negotiations following dramatic episodes of violence such as those at Boipatong and Bisho (figure 3.34, August 1992).

Sense of security or insecurity

Figures 3.35 and 3.36 are based on survey data reflecting the sense of security/insecurity among Africans between March 1986 and July 1993. Unfortunately the period July 1989 to July 1991 was relatively poorly

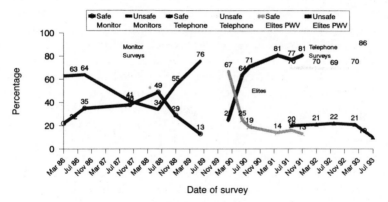

Figure 3.35   How safe do you feel in your community?

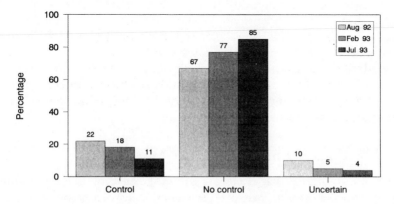

Figure 3.36   In your view, what measure of control does the government have over the violence that is occurring in South Africa at the present time?

covered by the two types of surveys referred to up to now. Respondents in surveys conducted in this period generally were African respondents with Std 10 and higher qualifications and were largely confined to the highly industrialised area of the PWV. However, since this period was marked by events of historical importance – de Klerk's watershed speech, the release of political leaders, the unbanning of organisations and the outbreak of violence – the responses from the African elite surveys have been included in figure 3.35 to cast light on sense of security at this time, but the interpretation of the relevant figures needs to be approached cautiously.

Figure 3.35 shows that after the national state of emergency in June 1986 the sense of insecurity declined from 63–64 per cent in mid-1986 to 34 per cent in July 1988. After July 1988 it escalated sharply from 34 per cent to 76 per cent in July 1989 possibly because of the Inkatha–UDF/COSATU conflict in KwaZulu-Natal. De Klerk's historic 1990 speech, the release of political leaders and the unbanning of organisations triggered a popular passion for peace, and in an African elite survey in February/March 1990 in the PWV 67 per cent of respondents believed that enduring peace and security had dawned. The perceptions of the masses are not likely to have differed much from those of the elite. By June 1990, when rumours of the impending outburst of violence in August 1990 were already circulating – as revealed in the evidence to the Tokoza Committee of the Goldstone Commission – the sense of security had declined from 67 per cent to 25 per cent. Throughout 1991 and 1992 the level of insecurity remained between 70 per cent and 80 per cent, and then increased by a further 16 per cent between late 1992 and July 1993. This increase in a sense of insecurity corresponds strongly with that among whites (figure 3.1 and the observations above), although the sense of insecurity among Africans was consistently higher than that among whites. This is ascribable to the fact that the actual violence occurred in African areas and that up to the end of 1992 whites experienced it largely on television. It was not until after December 1992 that whites were directly affected by incidents of violence, and these were still far fewer in number than the incidents affecting Africans. Figure 3.36 basically corroborates figure 3.35 and indicates that, as the sense of insecurity increased, fewer and fewer Africans believed the government could control the violence. Thus only 9 per cent of those who felt insecure in 1993 believed the government could control the violence, while 25 per cent of those who felt secure believed that it could.

Hopes of a peaceful future for South Africa

Figure 3.37 indicates that despite a growing sense of insecurity among Africans, they – unlike whites – remained consistently optimistic that South Africa had a peaceful future. The number of people who were less optimistic increased between March 1992 and August 1992, these dates corresponding with Boipatong and Bisho.

The hope for a peaceful future seems to have consistently influenced African support for multiparty negotiations as shown in the 1993 surveys, which revealed a positive correlation between the hope of a peaceful future and support for multiparty negotiations. Of respondents who were optimistic of a peaceful future, 91 per cent supported multiparty negotiations, in contrast to 83 per cent of those who were less optimistic.

Satisfaction or dissatisfaction with the general political situation

Largely because of their position in the South African social structure and because of the state of emergency, on average 71 per cent of Africans were dissatisfied with the political situation in 1986 and 1987 (figure 3.38). A single African elite survey in the PWV, which is not reflected in

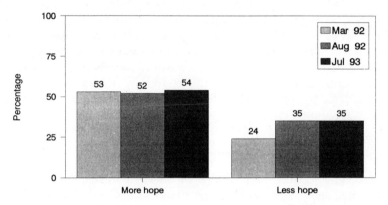

Figure 3.37   Do you have more or less hope for a peaceful future for South Africa?

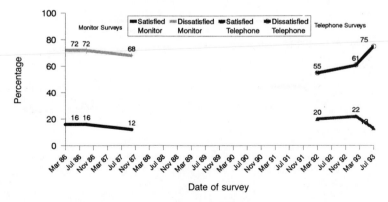

Figure 3.38   How satisfied are you with the general political situation in South Africa at present?

figure 3.38, revealed a sharp drop in dissatisfaction after February 1990 but a rise again in the latter half of 1990 as violence escalated. By March 1992 respectively 55 per cent and 20 per cent of respondents were dissatisfied and satisfied with the political situation. Fifteen months later in July 1993 these proportions were respectively 75 per cent and 13 per cent. The increase in political dissatisfaction among Africans can clearly be linked to escalating political violence, a sense of insecurity and frustration about the fact that the new South Africa had not yet arrived.

In the 1987, 1992 and 1993 surveys a strong correlation was evident between a sense of insecurity and dissatisfaction with the political situation. In 1992 respectively 78 per cent and 51 per cent of those who felt insecure and secure were dissatisfied with the political situation.

Attitudes towards whites

Figure 3.39 shows that in spite of high levels of African frustration in the mid-1980s, attitudes towards whites were improving. Even in the midst of the 1991–2 violence, the Boipatong and Bisho incidents and crises in negotiations, more positive attitudes were evident. As among whites, attitudes deteriorated again in 1993, possibly because of extreme right-wing reactions to the APLA incidents (during this period there were several attacks by whites on Africans) and the fact that Chris Hani's assassin was white.

Sociopolitical trends and party support

The preceding sections indicate that up to 1993 and especially after 1987 Africans had less confidence in the usefulness of political violence and were more inclined to support negotiations. As already suggested, the

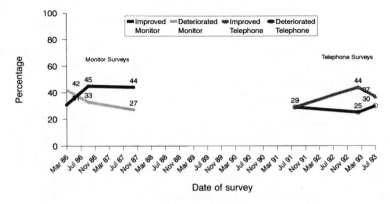

Figure 3.39   Has your present attitude towards whites improved or deteriorated in the past year?

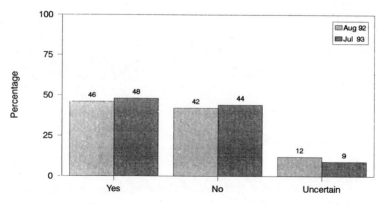

Figure 3.40   Do Africans and whites have enough common values to create a future democratic South Africa?

decrease in support for political violence can possibly be ascribed to the escalation of political violence between the IFP (formerly Inkatha) and the ANC (formerly the UDF–COSATU alliance). From time to time there were flare-ups in support of the political violence option, usually following violent incidents such as Boipatong and Bisho. In highly unsafe situations it can perhaps be expected that people will support the utility of political violence as a means of self-defence.

As with the whites there was a sharp increase in perceived insecurity, except that levels were far higher among the Africans, probably because they were much closer to the violence. Africans also experienced a rise in political dissatisfaction and the perception that the government did not have control over the violence. In contrast with whites, Africans were consistently optimistic that peace would be established in South Africa. This popular hope for peace was doubtless one of the driving forces behind the negotiation process.

Did these trends influence African party and leadership support in any way? Figures 3.41 and 3.42 reveal that Africans were not inclined to indicate support for the ANC while the organisation was banned. It was against the law to belong to or support the ANC and it was easier for respondents to claim they were uncertain (figure 3.42) or supported the United Democratic Front (figure 3.41). The figures indicating support for the UDF and the ANC until January 1990 should in fact be added together. It is also interesting to note that the UDF disappeared or became part of the ANC after February 1990. Following the unbanning of the ANC, African respondents started to reveal their true patterns of support and at the same time had high expectations that the ANC could find solutions to the South African impasse. These expectations and the support from the UDF led to a virtual doubling of support for the ANC between February 1990 and May 1990.

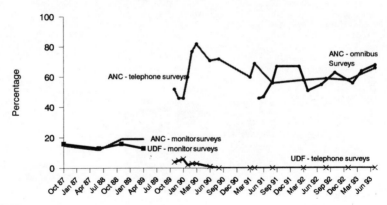

Figure 3.41   ANC & UDF support

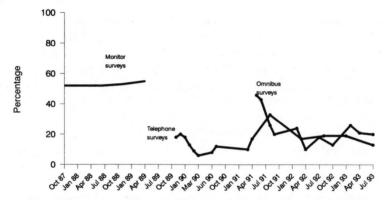

Figure 3.42   Support for political party: uncertain/do not know/none

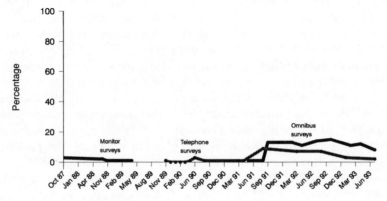

Figure 3.43   Support for the IFP

The violence that erupted in August 1990 reduced support for the ANC, which dipped below 60 per cent in 1991 and 1992. In spite of this, both the omnibus and telephone survey results indicated that support for the ANC increased after mid-1991.

As in the case of whites (tables 3.3, 3.4 and 3.5), an analysis was done to establish the relation, if any, between some of the preceding trends and party support. These trends related to feelings of security or insecurity, satisfaction with the political situation and support for a political party, as measured in the 1987, 1991 and 1993 surveys. Possibly because of the very high levels of support for the ANC and the very low levels of support for the other parties, no statistically significant correlations were found.

Figure 3.43 reveals that the IFP gained more African support after the middle of 1991, but returned virtually to its former low levels of support in mid-1993. This decreased support can perhaps be ascribed on the one hand to the fact that, as the April 1994 election approached, many IFP supporters believed that their party was not going to participate in the election. They therefore indicated in surveys that they did not support any party or were unsure. It can be safely assumed that when the IFP re-entered the election, these supporters voted for this party.[3] On the other hand its threatened boycott meant that the party had acquired a 'spoiler' image.

From September 1991 to July 1993 there was a discrepancy between the trend in omnibus results on IFP support (the first three points on the omnibus survey 'line' were also telephonic surveys) and those of telephone surveys (figure 3.43). The omnibus level was on average six percentage points higher than the telephone survey level and by June 1993 the omnibus reflected support at 10 per cent compared to 3 per cent in the telephone surveys. This discrepancy can be explained methodologically: telephone surveys do not reach people at the lower socioeconomic levels and rural Africans, especially in KwaZulu-Natal, and therefore the omnibus survey, which showed a 10 per cent level of IFP support by June 1993 – and higher levels before that date – can be regarded as the more valid reflection of IFP support. Against this background it came as no surprise when the IFP secured 11 per cent of voter support in the election.

Figure 3.45 shows that the NP had the support of some 10–12 per cent of African respondents shortly before and after the historic events of February 1990, but that the party lost support after mid-1991. The lower levels of support could have been the result of a growing African perception (figure 3.36) that the government did not prevent violence and in fact might even have been responsible for it.

Figure 3.44 reveals that the PAC was never able to break through the 5 per cent support barrier among Africans. The explanation could be that the party is basically racist and anti-white, while very few Africans are in fact anti-white. The patterns of support for leaders (figures 3.46, 3.47

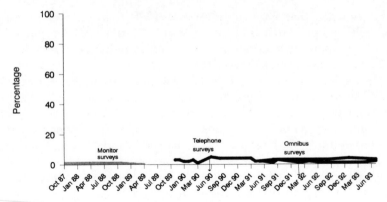

Figure 3.44   Support for the PAC

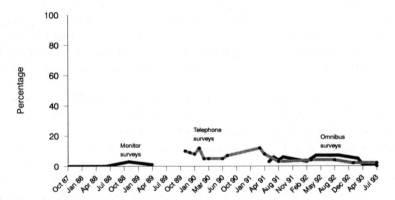

Figure 3.45   Support for the NP

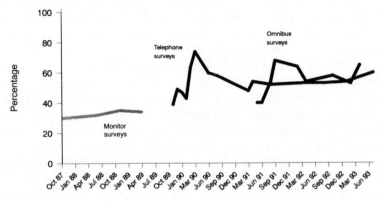

Figure 3.46   Support for Mandela as leader for South Africa

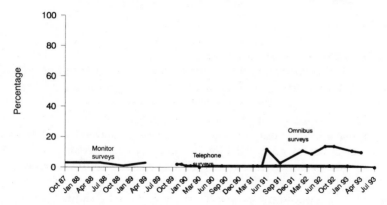

Figure 3.47   Support for Buthelezi as leader for South Africa

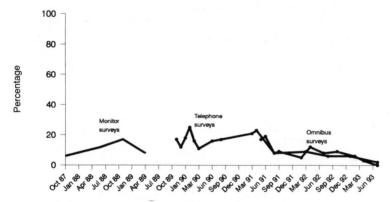

Figure 3.48   NP leader as leader for South Africa

and 3.48) largely mirror the patterns of support for political parties –
thus Mandela's support rose and then declined around August 1990
(figure 3.46).

Figure 3.47 indicates that as regards support for Buthelezi there was a
greater difference between the levels obtained in telephone surveys and
those of the omnibus than was the case with support for the IFP (figure
3.43). The explanation could be that support for Buthelezi was even
stronger than support for his party in rural areas.

National Party leaders' support stood at approximately 25 per cent just
after the historic turning point in February 1990 – more than twice that
obtained by the party itself. Almost all of the support was for F. W. de
Klerk, who at that stage, because of his bold initiatives, was highly
regarded by many Africans. As that regard decreased, the support for the
party also decreased.

Conclusion

What message is conveyed by the sociopolitical trends of the past decade? These trends show that a government – especially a government that does not have the support of the majority – suffers a double loss of legitimacy and acceptance of its right to govern if it cannot ensure order, safety and peace. A government's legitimacy in a democracy is not derived only from popular support, but also from the image of authority it can project. The Government of National Unity – and any subsequent government – will at all times have to ensure an optimal balance between freedom and order. If not, they may find that the other components of their legitimacy, namely upholding principles such as human rights, equality and freedom, will be impossible to achieve and that their popular support will become eroded. The government therefore has to bear in mind that order without freedom (a dictatorship, for example), while obviously highly undesirable, is possible; but that freedom without order is impossible, for freedom without order would result in a Hobbesian 'war of all against all', in which only the strongest is free.

Appendix of Tables

Table 3.1 Summary of the research designs of the survey data (all probability samples)

Survey date and type	Target population	Realised (effective) sample size
Africans		
Mar. 1986 Monitor	Africans 18 years and older in African townships of the PWV, Durban-Pinetown, PE–Uitenhage, Bloemfontein and Greater Cape Town metropolitan areas	1,338
Sept. 1986 Monitor	Africans 18 years and older in African townships of the PWV, Durban-Pinetown, PE–Uitenhage, Bloemfontein and Greater Cape Town metropolitan areas	1,459
Oct. 1987 Monitor	Africans 18 years and older in African townships of the PWV, Durban-Pinetown, PE–Uitenhage, Bloemfontein and Greater Cape Town metropolitan areas	1,467
June 1988 Monitor	Africans 18 years and older in African townships of the PWV, Durban-Pinetown, PE–Uitenhage, Bloemfontein and Greater Cape Town metropolitan areas	1,788
Nov. 1988 Monitor	Africans 18 years and older in African townships of the PWV, Durban-	1,809

Table 3.1   *Continued*

Survey date and type	Target population	Realised (effective) sample size
	Pinetown, PE-Uitenhage, Bloemfontein and Greater Cape Town metropolitan areas	
Apr. 1989 Monitor	Africans 18 years and older in African townships of the PWV, Durban-Pinetown, PE-Uitenhage, Bloemfontein and Greater Cape Town metropolitan areas	1,804
4–13 Dec. 1989 Telephone	Adult African elites★ (persons with matric and higher) 18 years and older in African townships of the PWV	849
22–30 Jan. 1990 Telephone	Adult African elites★ (persons with matric and higher) 18 years and older in African townships of the PWV	763
26 Feb.–3 Mar. 1990 Telephone	Adult African elites★ (persons with matric and higher) 18 years and older in African townships of the PWV	785
4–13 June 1990 Telephone	Adult African elites★ (persons with matric and higher) 18 years and older in African townships of the PWV	1,013
8–14 Aug. 1990 Telephone	Adult African elites★ (persons with matric and higher) 18 years and older in African townships of the PWV, Durban-Pinetown, PE-Uitenhage, Bloemfontein and Greater Cape Town metropolitan areas	1,018
18–19 Jan. 1991 Telephone	Africans 18 years and older in African townships of the PWV	427
Apr. 1991 Telephone, Omnibus	Telephone interviews with Asians, coloureds, Africans and whites from urban areas with respondents 18 years and older★★	907
May 1991 Telephone, Omnibus	Telephone interviews with Asians, coloureds, Africans and whites from urban areas with respondents 18 years and older★★	916
June 1991 Telephone, Omnibus	Telephone interviews with Asians, coloureds, Africans and whites from urban areas with respondents 18 years and older★★	731

Table 3.1 *Continued*

Survey date and type	Target population	Realised (effective) sample size
5–9 Aug. 1991 Telephone	Africans 18 years and older in African townships of the PWV, Durban-Pinetown, PE-Uitenhage, Bloemfontein and Greater Cape Town metropolitan areas	1,205
8–9 Nov. 1991 Telephone	Adult African elites★ (persons with matric and higher) 18 years and older in African townships of the PWV	550
Feb. 1992 Omnibus	Personal interviews with Asians, coloureds, Africans and whites from urban and rural areas with respondents 18 years and older★★★	1,092
2–5 Mar. 1992 Telephone	Africans 18 years and older in African townships of the PWV, Durban-Pinetown, PE-Uitenhage, Bloemfontein and Greater Cape Town metropolitan areas	1,267
Apr. 1992 Omnibus	Personal interviews with Asians, coloureds, Africans and whites from urban and rural areas with respondents 18 years and older★★★	1,098
July 1992 Omnibus	Personal interviews with Asians, coloureds, Africans and whites from urban and rural areas with respondents 18 years and older★★★	1,100
17–20 Aug. 1992 Telephone	Africans 18 years and older in African townships of the PWV, Durban-Pinetown, PE-Uitenhage, Bloemfontein and Greater Cape Town metropolitan areas	1,302
Oct. 1992 Omnibus	Personal interviews with Asians, coloureds, Africans and whites from urban and rural areas with respondents 18 years and older★★★	1,072
22–25 Feb. 1993 Telephone	Africans 18 years and older in African townships of the PWV, Durban-Pinetown, PE-Uitenhage, Bloemfontein and Greater Cape Town metropolitan areas	1,246

Table 3.1   *Continued*

Survey date and type	Target population	Realised (effective) sample size
Feb. 1993 Omnibus	Personal interviews with Asians, coloureds, Africans and whites from urban and rural areas with respondents 18 years and older★★★	1,100
Apr. 1993 Omnibus	Personal interviews with Asians, coloureds, Africans and whites from urban and rural areas with respondents 18 years and older★★★	1,114
21–24 July 1993 Telephone	Africans 18 years and older in African townships of the PWV, Durban-Pinetown, PE-Uitenhage, Bloemfontein and Greater Cape Town metropolitan areas	1,229
July 1993 Omnibus	Personal interviews with Asians, coloureds, Africans and whites from urban and rural areas with respondents 18 years and older★★★	1,085

Whites

Mar. 1984 Monitor	Whites 18 years and older in urban areas countrywide	1,024
Mar. 1985 Monitor	Whites 18 years and older in urban areas countrywide	1,108
Mar. 1986 Monitor	Whites 18 years and older in urban areas countrywide	1,067
Oct. 1987 Monitor	Whites 18 years and older in urban areas countrywide	1,013
Nov. 1988 Monitor	Whites 18 years and older in urban areas countrywide	1,077
Apr. 1989 Monitor	Whites 18 years and older in urban areas countrywide	1,068
Apr. 1990 Telephone	Whites 18 years and older in urban areas countrywide	1,287
18–20 Apr. 1990 Telephone	Adult white South Africans in households with telephones	1,287
28 May–4 June 1990 Telephone	Adult white South Africans in households with telephones	1,058

Table 3.1   *Continued*

Survey date and type	Target population	Realised (effective) sample size
8–14 Aug. 1990 Telephone	Adult white South Africans in households with telephones	1,014
9–14 Jan. 1991 Telephone, Omnibus	Adult white South Africans in households with telephones	1,012
Apr. 1991 Telephone, Omnibus	Telephone interviews with Asians, coloureds, Africans and whites from urban areas with respondents 18 years and older★★★	440
May 1991 Telephone, Omnibus	Telephone interviews with Asians, coloureds, Africans and whites from urban areas with respondents 18 years and older★★★	415
June 1991 Telephone	Telephone interviews with Asians, coloureds, Africans and whites from urban areas with respondents 18 years and older★★★	423
5–9 Aug. 1991 Telephone	Adult white South Africans in households with telephones	1,435
11–13 Nov. 1991 Telephone	Adult white South Africans in households with telephones	779
13–16 Jan. 1992 Telephone	Adult white South Africans in households with telephones	1,476
21–22 Feb. 1992 Telephone	Adult white South Africans in households with telephones	1,836
Feb. 1992 Omnibus	Personal interviews with Asians, coloureds, Africans and whites from urban and rural areas with respondents 18 years and older★★★	399
Apr. 1992 Omnibus	Personal interviews with Asians, coloureds, Africans and whites from urban and rural areas with respondents 18 years and older★★★	381
25–29 May 1992 Telephone	Adult white South Africans in households with telephones	1,584
July 1992 Omnibus	Personal interviews with Asians, coloureds, Africans and whites from urban and rural areas with respondents 18 years and older★★★	400

Table 3.1 *Continued*

Survey date and type	Target population	Realised (effective) sample size
11–13 Aug. 1992 Telephone	Adult white South Africans in households with telephones	1,466
Oct. 1992 Omnibus	Personal interviews with Asians, coloureds, Africans and whites from urban and rural areas with respondents 18 years and older★★★	383
16–18 Feb. 1993 Telephone	Adult white South Africans in households with telephones	1,029
Feb. 1993 Omnibus	Personal interviews with Asians, coloureds, Africans and whites from urban and rural areas with respondents 18 years and older★★★	400
Apr. 1993 Omnibus	Personal interviews with Asians, coloureds, Africans and whites from urban and rural areas with respondents 18 years and older★★★	382
26–29 July 1993 Telephone	Adult white South Africans in households with telephones	1,033
July 1993 Omnibus	Personal interviews with Asians, coloureds, Africans and whites from urban and rural areas with respondents 18 years and older★★★	379

★ The reader should take into account that these telephone surveys were done among adult (18 years and older) African people. Furthermore, that they had matric or higher educational qualifications and lived in the PWV (Pretoria-Witwatersrand-Vereeniging) area (with the exception of the survey done from 8 to 14 August 1990). These surveys are not strictly comparable to the other telephone surveys done among Africans. They are even less comparable to omnibus and monitor surveys. In this contribution the surveys are clearly identified as elite surveys. They are used to 'fill in' the very important and meaningful period of 1990–1. It may be accepted that, although there may be depth differences between the elite and mass tendencies, there will not be directional differences.

★★ The omnibus surveys done in April 1991, May 1991 and June 1991 were done by telephone. Although they are comparable to the other telephone surveys among African people, they are less comparable to surveys among Africans in the seven omnibus surveys done between February 1992 and July 1993. Sample sizes indicated are merely the N values for African people in the omnibus sample.

★★★ Although omnibus surveys include all four population groups throughout the country, the N values as indicated are only those for the particular population group under discussion (that is, Africans or white people).

Table 3.2 White support for political parties (per cent)

Date	Traditionally white parties	Traditionally African parties		Unsure/None
	NP+DP+CP	ANC	Inkatha	
Apr. 1991	87.4	0.2	0.0	12.5
Aug. 1991	82.2	0.3	3.0	14.5
Nov. 1991	83.1	0.1	0.6	16.2
Jan. 1992	81.0	0.1	2.0	16.9
Feb. 1992	82.3	0.4	1.0	16.4
May 1992	84.1	0.4	2.0	13.4
Aug. 1992	84.4	0.6	3.0	12.0
Feb. 1993	73.3	0.8	6.8	19.2
July 1993	56.5	1.5	15.0	27.0

Table 3.3 White party support (1987) analysed according to feelings of security/insecurity; perception of the government's control over violence; satisfaction with political situation; and support for negotiations with ANC (per cent)

Explanatory variable	NP	Left of NP	Right of NP	IFP	Uncertain	Other
Feeling of security/insecurity						
Safe	59	11	17	–	–	13
Neither safe nor unsafe	54	7	25	–	–	15
Unsafe	34	10	42	–	–	14
Government's control over violence						
Has control	57	10	20	–	–	13
Has no control	51	9	28	–	–	11
Uncertain/Do not know	62	15	2	–	–	21
Satisfaction with political situation						
Satisfied	78	2	11	–	–	8
Neither satisfied nor dissatisfied	56	7	21	–	–	15
Dissatisfied	35	18	30	–	–	16

Table 3.3 *Continued*

Explanatory variable	NP	Left of NP	Right of NP	IFP	Uncertain	Other
Support for negotiations with ANC						
Support	54	16	13	–	–	17
Reject	57	5	29	–	–	9
Mixed feelings	57	14	14	–	–	16
Uncertain	58	0	5	–	–	37

Table 3.4 White party support (1990) analysed according to feelings of security/insecurity and perception of the government's control over violence (per cent)

Explanatory variable	NP	Left of NP	Right of NP	IFP	Uncertain	Other
Feeling of security/insecurity						
Safe	69	9	11	–	10	1
Neither safe nor unsafe	52	6	21	–	20	1
Unsafe	38	3	39	–	17	2
Government's control over violence						
Has control	68	8	13	–	11	1
Has no control	20	3	58	–	17	2
Uncertain/Do not know	36	4	17	–	43	0

Table 3.5 White party support (1993) analysed according to feelings of security/insecurity; perception of the government's control over violence; satisfaction with political situation; and support for negotiations with the ANC (per cent)

Explanatory variable	NP	Left of NP	Right of NP	IFP	Uncertain	Other
Feeling of security/insecurity						
Safe	50	4	10	10	20	6
Neither safe nor unsafe	40	4	11	15	24	7
Unsafe	25	4	21	17	24	9

Table 3.5   *Continued*

Explanatory variable	NP	Left of NP	Right of NP	IFP	Uncertain	Other
Government's control over violence						
Has control	43	5	13	10	23	6
Has no control	17	2	24	23	22	11
Uncertain/Do not know	27	0	9	0	36	27
Satisfaction with political situation						
Satisfied	69	7	5	8	10	2
Neither satisfied nor dissatisfied	52	5	8	11	21	3
Dissatisfied	27	4	19	16	24	9
Support for negotiations with the ANC						
Yes	40	5	12	13	23	6
No	10	1	32	20	21	17
Uncertain/Do not know	18	0	29	16	35	2

Notes

Throughout the decade discussed here, I worked at the Centre for Socio-political Analysis of the Human Sciences Research Council. I was accordingly either a team member or team leader of the surveys referred to here, and I would like to give special recognition to Dr Nic Rhoodie, Dr Charl Schutte and Dr Mick Couper as fellow team members at different times during the ten-year period. I also thank Diana Ehlers for the analysis of the data through the greater part of the decade and also for this chapter.

1   S. Booysen and J. Fleetwood, 'Political events as agents of political socialization: a case study of change in racial attitudes in South Africa', *South African Journal of Sociology*, 25.3 (Aug. 1994); N.J. Rhoodie and D. Ehlers, 'Political stability scale: comparative analysis of 1991–1993 surveys', *Information Update*, 4.1 (1994); H.J. Kotzé, *Elite-houdings en politieke verandering in Suid-Afrika: Verslag van 'n houdingsopname in 1989–1990* (Stellenbosch: University of Stellenbosch, 1991); H.J. Kotzé, 'Attitudes in transition: towards an elite settlement' and 'Attitudes in transition: elites on economy', *Indicator SA*, 10.2 and 10.3 (1993).
2   L. Schlemmer, 'Who and where are the Volkstaat supporters?', *Information Update*, 4.1 (1994).
3   L. Schlemmer, C.P. de Kock, C. Schutte and D. Ehlers, 'Polls vs. reality: how well did polls predict the election results?', *Information Update*, 4.2 (1994).

FOUR

National Issues and National Opinion

R.W. Johnson and Lawrence Schlemmer

Basic Questions and Uncertainties

WHAT WAS SOUTH AFRICA's first open election about? To some extent the answer is obvious. After centuries of minority domination and decades of more structured apartheid, the election was about liberation from minority rule, or about political freedom. History will record the event as such.

Between these broad parameters of the event, however, there were many nuances in voter behaviour which matched the complexity of South African society. This finer detail complements the stark view that the election was only about black liberation from white or neo-colonial minority rule. The complexities of the event were signalled beforehand and resulted in a surprising degree of confusion and uncertainty in the months and weeks before the election. Many South African and foreign observers viewed the event as a large, historical experiment. The only real certainty was that the ANC would win because it was a large, celebrated and aggressive liberation movement with a famous and charismatic leader in a society about to become liberated from race-based minority rule. How much the ANC would win by, how the other parties would fare and what the commitments of the new voters would be, were all issues of heated debate and intense speculation.

In scores of interviews with journalists in the weeks preceding the election, and in conversations with dozens of businessmen and some politicians, various critical uncertainties were expressed over and over again. Would the ANC obtain a two-thirds majority? Could the powerful and cohesive National Party really be roundly defeated? Why should the PAC, with its appeal to black racial solidarity, not perform extremely well? Was this election not the historical moment when the virtuously non-racial and reformist Democratic Party would reap its reward? Would the Freedom Front not attract a stampede of fearful white Afrikaans voters? And so on.

Popular wisdom was that Buthelezi and the IFP would be trounced everywhere as punishment for their role in the violence and what was seen as petulant brinkmanship over participation in the elections. African traditionalism tended to be written off as a spent force, discredited by its association with apartheid. With only rare exceptions foreign journalists perceived the mass of African voters as radical in their expectations, angry with whites and likely to resent the negotiated pre-election agreement among major parties to share power. The possibility that a majority of voters of mixed blood might support the white-dominated NP seemed far-fetched to the less well-informed journalists who arrived in droves just before the elections.

Pointing to the results of opinion polls as a basis for more informed speculation was often regarded as unconvincing. Opinion polls were seen as the biggest experiment of all. Could one place any trust in polls in a society with so many illiterate people living in either remote and inaccessible places or in townships devastated by violence? Some businessmen were blunter – opinion surveys were naive exercises in futility, mere toys that academics liked to play with.

Amidst the confusion which these enquiries reflected were some very important questions about the election. Was it predominantly a celebration of liberation and freedom, a vote overwhelmed by sentiment and symbolism? Was it about race and racial power – a reaction to the racial structuring of apartheid? Or was it about policy and calculations of interests, benefits and costs? Answers to these questions are critical to an understanding of how easy or difficult it will be to consolidate South Africa's new democracy.

These questions cannot be answered on the basis of the election outcome itself or the myriad interpretations of the outcome which appeared in the media. Quite aside from the irregularities in voting, the inaccuracies of the count and the ineptitude of the Independent Electoral Commission (see chapter 10), the reported outcomes combine categories and classes of voters whose orientations are vital to an understanding of the dynamics of the election. For more specific insights, therefore, we have to rely on the results of pre-election surveys of voter opinion.

The Pre-election Surveys: How Valid a Basis of Information Are They?

As already suggested, many people were sceptical about the validity of pre-election polls in a mass population as unsophisticated and destabilised as that of South Africa. As practitioners, however, we knew that the pre-election polls were very substantially valid, and this degree of validity can now be demonstrated in broad comparisons with the outcome of the election. The polls were conducted as part of a regular series of surveys undertaken by MarkData, the survey research unit of the HSRC.[1]

Table 4.1 and figure 4.1 present the results of MarkData's pre-election polls from October 1992 to February 1994, as compared with the outcome of the election. Despite the irregularities already referred to it can be assumed that the official results of the election are broadly correct. Figure 4.2 shows a comparison between the election outcome and our final pre-election survey in February. These comparisons, taken together, suggest the following:

• All the pre-election polls broadly predicted the eventual pattern of the election outcome, with the ANC in a clear lead, the NP in second place – a fairly long way behind – and the IFP with roughly half the support of the NP;

• The last survey in February appears to have overestimated support for the ANC (69 per cent vs 63 per cent in the election). It is, however, perhaps more accurate to say that this was because the February poll underestimated IFP and NP support. At the time of the last poll the IFP was still boycotting the election. When faced by the question of which party they would vote for, would-be IFP voters were thrown into confusion – a fact which naturally lowered the apparent support for the IFP.

Table 4.1 Surveyed party support levels between October 1992 and February 1994 compared with the election results of April 1994 (per cent)

	Oct. 1992	Feb. 1993	Apr. 1993	July 1993	Oct. 1993★★★	Feb. 1994★★★	Election
ANC	53	55	62	62	70	69	63
NP	28	25	18	17	16	17	20
IFP	13	11	11	10	5	7	11
Right-wing (FF)★	4	6	7	4	5	4	2
DP	1	2	1	2	2	1	2
PAC	1	1	1	2	2	1	1
Other★★	0	0	0	3	0	1	1

★ The support for the FF, which did not exist at the time of the surveys, was estimated by combining all respondents supporting right-wing parties.
★★ In the surveys as published at the time the category 'other' included uncertain and non-applicable responses. These are not included in the table.
★★★ The October 1993 and February 1994 results include all the former independent homelands whereas earlier results excluded Bophuthatswana.

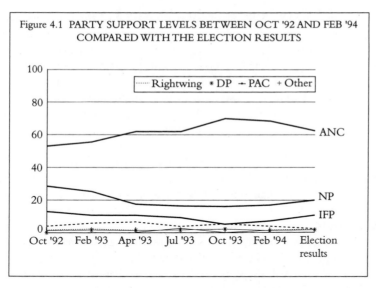

Figure 4.1 PARTY SUPPORT LEVELS BETWEEN OCT '92 AND FEB '94 COMPARED WITH THE ELECTION RESULTS

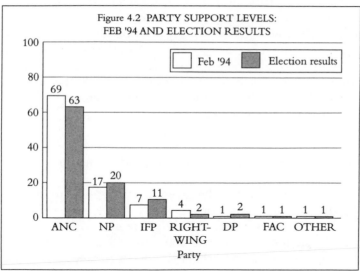

Figure 4.2 PARTY SUPPORT LEVELS: FEB '94 AND ELECTION RESULTS

- Another major reason for the deviation in the February poll result lies simply in trends over time. If the slight trends reflected in the polls are extrapolated from February to the election, the survey results actually came very close to correctly predicting the outcome (see figure 4.1 and table 4.1). What appears to have happened is that support for the National Party dropped from 1992 to October 1993, and then recovered. The same applied to the IFP, with its recovery even more marked when the IFP entered the election after mid-April. It may also have benefited from publicity given to the negotiations between the Zulu king, the government and the ANC over the participation of the IFP. Had we been able to survey opinion after February, this strengthening of the NP and IFP would probably have been evident. The overestimation of right-wing support in the pre-election polls is understandable since the Freedom Front did not exist at the time of the polls and right-wing support consequently had to be estimated from support for right-wing parties which boycotted the election. Clearly not all right-wingers voted in the election, whether out of preference or because of pressure not to vote.

Pre-election polls are like snapshots over time of a moving object. Patterns of support for political parties change, particularly as an election draws near and the campaigns of political parties intensify. Hence it is improbable that pre-election polls undertaken some time before an election will be able to predict the outcome exactly, unless support levels for the political parties remain unusually static. The Electoral Act prohibited the publishing of political poll results after 6 April, three weeks before the election on 26, 27 and 28 April, and for this reason the last survey had to be conducted in February 1994. Broadly speaking, however, the comparisons suggest that the results of the pre-election polls were sufficiently close to the election outcome to suggest considerable validity for the surveys. The Johannesburg *Sunday Times* of 8 May 1994 even suggested that '. . . South Africa may be one of the few countries where opinion polls were more accurate than voting results.' We will, therefore, proceed to base our analysis of the dynamics of voting intention very largely on the results of the pre-election surveys.

A Racially Polarised Electorate in the Run-up to the Elections

In table 4.2 the results already given in table 4.1 are disaggregated according to whether respondents were white, coloured, Indian or African, and the responses of those who made no choice, refused answers or indicated that they would not vote are included. They suggest the following broad patterns for each of the major parties.

The ANC–SACP alliance   African support for the ANC hovered around the 60 per cent mark until February 1993, after which it rose strongly to reach some three-quarters by February 1994. Clearly an impressive mobilisation of African voters was accomplished by activist structures on the ground during this period. Among coloured voters support for the ANC vacillated, reaching a high of one-fifth by late 1993, then dropping sharply, with voters being drawn back towards the NP. Indian support for the ANC was somewhat more consistent, rising by up to one-fifth and remaining there. White support for the ANC never surpassed the 1–2 per cent range.

Table 4.2 Patterns of support for political parties over time (N = 2,100)

	ANC–SACP	PAC	AZAPO	NP	DP	IFP	CP/AWB/ Volksfront	Other answers/No choice/Will not vote
JULY 1992								
White	1	–	–	56	3	2	28	11
Coloured	10	–	–	64	2	1	–	25
Indian	6	–	–	58	1	1	–	34
African	60	2	–	8	–	11	–	18
OCTOBER 1992								
White	–	–	–	50	4	3	21	21
Coloured	12	–	–	61	4	–	–	23
Indian	8	–	–	58	2	–	–	32
African	63	1	1	7	–	15	–	13
FEBRUARY 1993								
White	1	–	–	48	6	5	25	17
Coloured	12	–	–	58	6	–	–	24
Indian	11	1	–	46	4	–	–	40
African	56	1	1	6	–	11	–	26
APRIL 1993								
White	2	1	–	38	3	3	29	24
Coloured	19	–	–	47	2	–	–	30
Indian	24	–	–	36	4	2	–	35
African	65	1	1	1	–	12	–	21

Table 4.2   *Continued*

	ANC–SACP	PAC	AZAPO	NP	DP	IFP	CP/AWB/ Volksfront	Other answers/No choice/Will not vote
JULY 1993								
White	1	–	–	28	4	8	26	33
Coloured	12	–	–	44	2	1	3	38
Indian	17	–	–	39	2	3	1	38
African	68	2	1	–	–	8	1	20
OCTOBER/NOVEMBER 1993								
White	2	–	–	40	5	4	18	31
Coloured	21	–	–	27	3	–	3	46
Indian	18	–	–	48	1	1	1	31
African	72	2	–	1	–	5	–	19
FEBRUARY 1994								
White	1	–	–	44	5	4	17	29
Coloured	10	–	–	43	–	–	1	46
Indian	19	–	–	46	1	1	1	33
African	74	1	–	1	–	7	1	16

The National Party Support for the NP was relatively high among all four racial groups just after the March 1992 referendum which gained massive white support for negotiation. Thereafter support for the NP among whites dropped to half its previous level by July 1993. It subsequently rose among whites and probably continued to rise as the election campaign continued. Whatever white discontent there was with the NP, the party nevertheless consolidated its position as the principal champion of the whites as the electoral crunch drew near.

Among coloured voters, however, support for the NP dropped by over half after July 1992, though far more of the defectors retreated into uncertainty than moved to support other parties. As already indicated, coloured support for the NP recovered sharply by February 1994. Among Indians there was also a fall in support for the NP by mid-1992 but, as with whites, support rose again later. African support for the NP fell steadily from July 1992 and came to rest at some 1 per cent. The fall from the NP's 7–8 per cent level of support among Africans in late 1992 to the October/November 1993 level was by far the biggest element in the NP's decline over the period – and was, indeed, probably the largest movement of opinion during the entire campaign.

The Inkatha Freedom Party Among African voters, support for the IFP was well over 10 per cent until April 1993. This was higher than the IFP score in many other polls essentially because our surveys had an extensive and representative coverage of rural areas, shack areas and hostel residents: many South African polls survey only urban Africans. African support for the IFP declined to roughly half of its earlier level by late 1993 but thereafter showed signs of recovering even before the party ended its election boycott. Among whites support for the IFP rose until July 1993, but appeared to decline again thereafter. The notion that the IFP might replace the NP as the principal pole of resistance to the ANC had only a brief life. As the election drew near, the old ANC–NP polarity reasserted itself, doubtless not helping the IFP's position.

The Democratic Party Support for the DP varied over time but remained at less than 6 per cent among whites and much less among other voters. The coloured and Indian support which had begun to move towards the party in early 1993 (at the same time that the NP was losing ground among these groups) fell back and was virtually obliterated by February 1994.

The Conservative Party, the AWB, the Volksfront and other right-wing parties The right-wing parties tended to have the support of just under 30 per cent of white voters until early 1992, but the later results showed a sharp drop in support, falling at the end to under 20 per cent of whites. Prior to the March 1992 referendum the CP had been gaining strongly from the NP, but the referendum halted that movement and it never recommenced. It is very striking that the CP was unable to capitalise on the NP's declining fortunes. The CP had doubtless been adversely affected by the death of its leader, Dr Treurnicht, and by the continued organisational turmoil on the right, but it is tempting to see in its sharp decline as elections approached a growing sense of resignation among white conservatives that the coming transition, however unwelcome, could not really be resisted.

The PAC and AZAPO   These parties were supported only by Africans, but as primary electoral choices these parties consistently showed support of 3 per cent or less.

No choice   The proportions of respondents unable or unwilling to indicate a choice tended to rise among whites and coloureds, to decline slightly among Indians and to vary between 13 and 26 per cent among Africans. Broadly speaking, these trends over time leave one with the impression that, despite uncentainty among whites and coloureds about the credentials and performance of the NP some months before the election, a shift back to the party occurred as voters made final strategic choices. Meanwhile the ANC consolidated among its major support base, the Africans, as did the IFP, despite uncertainty over its participation. The right-wing fell back among whites and in the end not all right-wingers voted for the surrogate party, the Freedom Front, which entered the campaign only weeks before the election. The other smaller parties, the DP and the PAC, were simply ground out of contention.

The net effect of these trends was a very substantial degree of racial polarisation, seen most clearly in the massive African swing towards the ANC and the more modest but nevertheless substantial swing among 'non-Africans' back to the NP. The largest deviation from these trends in the pre-election polls was found among voters who made no choice.

The lack of precision in the final statistics of the election results, probable imprecision in the estimates of the total voting population and the lack of a voters' roll mean that no one will ever know exactly how many South Africans did not vote. The pre-election polls suggest that the figure may have been quite substantial. Given that the ANC's mobilisation effort was so much more powerful than that of other parties in 1994, it is possible that scope for mobilisation by opposition parties may exist among 1994 non-voters in the future.

Sympathy for and Identification with Political Parties

As already suggested, party choice can be strategic and as such need not reflect broader and more complex reactions to political parties. Accord-

ingly, we asked how 'close' or 'distant' voters felt in relation to each of
the parties. This question, regularly posed in the HSRC–MarkData surveys and included in the two pre-election polls, was intended to identify
sympathy for or rejection of political parties underlying the crystallised
choice for one party over others. In table 4.3 results are given of the
proportions of white, coloured, Indian and African voters who felt 'very
close' or 'close' to each of the parties or alliances which existed in
October 1993 and February 1994.

The results showed what earlier results had suggested, namely strengthening support for the ANC over the six months before the election. The
results also show that the South African Communist Party was certainly
no mere appendage of the ANC in the alliance, since it emerged as the
second most 'popular' political party among Africans and in the electorate
overall. This does not mean that four out of ten Africans were 'Communists' – it probably simply meant that the SACP had a strong image of
commitment to redistribution and the advancement of the interests of the
poor. It drew virtually no sympathy from whites, coloureds or Indians,
however.

The results in table 4.3 speak for themselves. It is worth noting,
however, that sympathy for the DP, the PAC and the right-wing
parties substantially exceeded the level of support they obtained in the
election, confirming the point that many voters voted tactically in the
end for larger parties they thought would have more influence and
count for more in the balance. This instinct not to 'waste one's vote'
was, of course, wholly inappropriate to an electoral system based on
strict proportionality, but was a reflex dinned into voters under the
previous, first-past-the-post system. The result was to draw support
away from smaller parties which probably represented voter sentiments
as well or better than the larger parties. It should be noted that surveys
conducted in 1991 and 1992 showed much higher levels of sympathy
for the PAC – up to 40 per cent among Africans. Although viewed
more favourably by Africans than the final choices would suggest, the
PAC was clearly sliding in the weeks before the election. It is also
clear from these results that the Freedom Front, the only right-
wing grouping to participate in the election, enjoyed more than double
the sympathy among whites than the final choices of party were to
show.

Finally, one must note that patterns of identification with political
parties often exceed the level of primary choice of each party simply
because individuals can have sympathy for more than one party. Some
parties, however, appear to attract considerably more sympathy than the
level of primary choice, indicating a potential for growth under certain
conditions which may be relevant in years to come.

Parties which appeared to have some potential for growth on this basis
were:

Table 4.3 Levels of identification with parties: feelings of being 'close' or 'very close' to particular parties, recorded in October/November 1993 and February 1994 (per cent)

IDENTIFICATION. Close and Very Close

All voters

	Oct/Nov	Feb 94
ANC	53	57
SACP	21	30
NP	21	20
PAC	15	9
IFP	9	2
AZAPO	9	5
DP	6	5
CP	5	5
Volksfront*	5	5
Freedom Alliance	4	5
AWB	4	3

Whites

	Oct/Nov	Feb 94
NP	50	52
Volksfront*	24	28
CP	23	26
IFP	21	27
Freedom Alliance	17	24
AWB	15	18
DP	14	16
ANC	3	1
SACP	1	0
PAC	0	0
AZAPO	0	0

Coloureds

	Oct/Nov	Feb 94
NP	41	45
ANC	28	17
DP	7	3
IFP	1	1
PAC	1	2
SACP	1	2
CP	1	1
AZAPO	1	0
Volksfront*	1	0
Freedom Alliance	1	1
AWB	0	0

Indians

	Oct/Nov 93	Feb 94
NP	50	57
ANC	17	25
SACP	6	4
IFP	4	5
DP	4	8
PAC	1	0
AWB	1	0
Volksfront*	1	0
AZAPO	0	1
CP	0	0
Freedom Alliance	0	1

Africans

	Oct/Nov 93	Feb 94
ANC	75	75
SACP	31	42
PAC	22	12
AZAPO	13	7
NP	7	8
IFP	6	10
DP	3	3
Freedom Alliance	1	1
CP	1	1
AWB	1	1
Volksfront*	1	0

- the SACP among Africans (if it were to stand on its own ticket)
- the PAC and AZAPO among Africans
- the NP among Africans to a limited extent
- the IFP among whites
- the right-wing among whites
- the DP among whites
- the NP among coloureds

It is perhaps of some concern in the light of future harmony in the country that the more extreme parties attracted relatively wide sympathy from voters. The future coherence of the ANC and the NP may be very important for the future of race relations in South Africa.

Leadership

Another variable which interacts with party choice is that of the image and reputation of political leaders. The choice of strict proportionality as the basis for the allocation of seats and especially the choice of monster (200-seat) national lists inevitably 'presidentialised' the electoral race, with great attention focused on list leaders, both regionally and, particularly, nationally. In this respect it was of considerable significance that both the NP and ANC had leaders regarded by the voters as people of presidential timbre. Both men were generally more popular than their parties (see table 4.4), but de Klerk more so than Mandela. While Dr de Beer and Dr Hartzenberg both trailed their parties, Chief Buthelezi was more popular among whites than the IFP and he also retained slightly greater African support than did his party. De Klerk's enormous lead over his party among coloured and Indian voters suggests that he retained support at his party's earlier peak levels among these minority voters.

Table 4.4   Difference (±) in support for leaders over support for their parties, by group, October/November 1993 (per cent)

	Whites	Coloureds	Indians	Africans	All
Mandela	−1	+2	−1	+1	+1
De Klerk	−	+13	+10	+1	+1
Buthelezi	+6	−	−1	+1	+2
De Beer	−2	−1	−1	−	+1
Hartzenberg/Viljoen	−6	−2	−1	−	−2

The National Party's Lost African Vote

The results given in tables 4.1 and 4.2 reflect a decline in NP support from some 28 per cent in 1992 to the election outcome of 20 per cent. This support was lost largely among Africans. A poll conducted by Lawrence Schlemmer in 1991 (by Market and Opinion Surveys of Cape Town, with a sample including 1,600 Africans) presented respondents with a choice between the established political parties, but it also included a further option, namely a party alliance 'led by F. W. de Klerk', a possibility at that stage. Excluding non-responses and people who made no choice, the ANC was selected by 60 per cent of Africans, the NP by 12 per cent and the hypothetical alliance led by de Klerk by 17 per cent. Thus in 1991 the NP had the potential of gaining up to some 29 per cent of the African vote, as compared to some 1 per cent recorded in our November 1993 and February 1994 polls. This enormous slippage of potential support was the key to the entire election.

Until late in 1993 NP strategists entertained high hopes of attracting high levels of support from African voters, hopes partly based on the fact that certain leaders of the powerful African Zionist Independent Church had actually taken out NP membership. The NP government minister Dawie de Villiers, for example, made a claim in late 1992 which, with the wisdom of hindsight, sounds childishly naive: 'We are going to win – I am convinced we will win' (*Citizen*, 8 October 1992). A year later, reality was beginning to dawn but the party strategists still expected to attract a substantial black vote: 'We have set ourselves a very difficult but not impossible task of winning 40 per cent of the overall vote,' said Olaus van Zyl, the executive director of the NP (*Rapport*, 24 October 1993).

By then, however, some 3 to 4 million Africans who had been inclined to support the NP had shifted their allegiance or had decided not to vote. This raises the interesting question of whether or not the earlier support for the NP was a superficial and transient commitment on the part of people who perhaps admired F. W. de Klerk for his bold political reforms but whose deeper commitments had been ANC all along.

This question is not only of importance to the NP; it also has a bearing on the likely quality of South Africa's democracy. The NP was, and seems likely to remain, one of the main sources of opposition and counterbalance in a South African polity which is now clearly a 'dominant party system'. If, aside from IFP support, which we will discuss presently, there were no meaningful basis of opposition support among Africans, South Africa's politics would be very uncomfortably racial in its divisions, with election results a foregone conclusion.

However, this is not necessarily the case. We discuss later in this chapter the problem of freedom of choice and evidence of constraints on it in the election. These factors are undoubtedly very relevant to the NP's loss of support. The 1991–2 Schlemmer/MOS survey referred to above reflects significant variations in political attitudes and commitments among Africans who in the end virtually all voted for the ANC or the IFP.

Party-linked Political Attitudes among Africans

The 1991 survey is particularly useful in looking at variations in political commitments among Africans because the subsample of Africans was relatively large and because it was conducted before the mass convergence of African support on the ANC. In other words, the sample contained a sufficient number of Africans supporting the NP or de Klerk to draw reliable conclusions about the various types of African voter.[2] The broad pattern emerging from the results of the 1991/92 survey can be summarised as follows:

- ANC supporters tended to have relatively strong material demands, had strong needs for changes in national symbolism, were low on religiosity and equally low in terms of their rootedness in family and social networks. They tended to be urban in origin and anti-traditional in outlook.

- NP supporters tended to be relatively more concerned than ANC supporters with law and order, religion, morality and economic growth. They were also more politically tolerant than ANC supporters. They had doubts about the quality of a future black government, were less politically militant than average, and also exhibited less intense levels of partisanship. In many other ways they were similar to ANC supporters, but tended to have a marginally higher socioeconomic status than ANC supporters.

- IFP supporters had some very clear characteristics. They had relatively low expectations as regards welfare and material gains and redistribution. They were anti-socialist, anti-militant, strongly in favour of law and order, economic growth, cultural rights for minorities, morality and religiosity. They had doubts about the capacity of a future black government. They were also very rooted in social or family networks. Like NP supporters, they did not seem to have high ego needs to identify with a party. It is interesting, however, that when it came to issues such as being treated with dignity and respect, their position relative to whites and affirmative action, they had very strong demands. They were predominantly rural in origin, more inclined to be members of the Zionist church, and were older than average.

- PAC supporters tended to follow their party's line in that they appeared to be fairly radical, militant and anti-white and generally 'left' of centre. The results, however, were based on a small sample and have to be treated with caution.

- People who supported no party or a range of smaller parties tended to be
  highly concerned with material welfare, but also with cultural rights for
  minorities and with religion and morality. They were non-militant and
  quite conservative other than in their concern with welfare. Like the IFP
  supporters, they were predominantly rural in origin and were also older
  than average. If mobilised, these non-voters would quite significantly
  strengthen parties other than the ANC – and thus the opposition in the
  new dominant party system in South Africa.

The ANC constituency, being a very large support base, was rather
more varied than that of other parties. In general, ANC supporters tended
to be more 'modern' in outlook than other voters and could be described
as 'social democrat'. The NP or de Klerk supporters tended to be
'Christian democrat' and rather 'respectable' in orientation, although their
economic views tended towards the welfare sentiments of ANC supporters. The IFP supporters, those of smaller homeland-based parties and
those with no party affiliation were the most marginal to the modern
urban political culture. They were regional or rural in orientation and
could be described as traditionally oriented 'conservatives'.

Looking deeper into the results of the earlier survey data at our disposal
suggests that there is a quite considerable degree of *contradiction* in African
attitudes, with the majority of people being radical on some issues and
moderate on others. Using the 1991–2 sample survey as a basis, these
'contradictions' can be quite clearly illustrated. The schematic presenta-
tion in table 4.5 contains the results on a large number of items. They
give some idea of how complex and varied the interplay of political
attitudes among South Africa's new voters is. The picture emerging is one
of mass support for both redistribution and reconciliation, with a great
deal of support for evenly balanced views in between. Broadly speaking,
although expectations of voters were high, they were moderated by a
strong awareness of the need for national reconciliation, peace and economic growth. It would seem, therefore, that no political party with a
fairly representative mass base need feel obliged to pander to extreme
demands and expectations. This fact, however, is balanced by clear evidence that a minority of roughly one-third of new voters are very highly
politicised and quite militant in their views. The latter category of voters
tends to be more prominent in politics, and therefore more visible to
political leadership.

Political parties therefore have difficult choices to make. More importantly, however, the variety visible among the African electorate shows
that they do have choices. It is simply wrong to assume that the 'ethnic
census' voting seen in 1994 adequately represented the rich variety of
opinion within the different party electorates, particularly within the
biggest electorate, that of the ANC. That is, the 'one party dominant
system' may be less inevitable than it looks, and there may be a substantial

Table 4.5   African political attitudes

Radical/progressive views 55% or more endorse:	Moderate/conservative views 55% or more endorse:
• more trade union influence on government • co-determination of workers and managers • rural land redistribution • occupation of vacant land • affirmative action • theft justified by discrimination • wage increases before productivity • influence on government by civics • greater Communist influence • anger at whites • rejection of white role models • black 'entitlement' due to apartheid • majority-based national symbols and nation-building • maximum welfare for the needy	• opposition to mass action • negotiation and compromise • power-sharing between parties • national reconciliation • checks and balances in constitution • individual rights • protection of language and culture of minorities • rights for ethnic groups • need to preserve/retain white skills • non-punitive redistribution • individual self-reliance • job creation before wage considerations • beneficial role of big companies • protection of 'homeland' interests • value of international trade • strict law and order

Evenly-balanced views
Plus-minus 50% endorse/oppose:

• higher taxes on wealth
• merit as basis for advancement
• majority party control of security forces
• lowering educational standards to benefit black pupils
• devolution of central powers/regionalism
• blacks as most important citizens/whites with lower civic status
• respect and admiration for black political leaders
• religion as more important than politics
• state intervention in private sector
• representation in government for traditional chiefs
• nationalisation of private companies
• legitimacy of rent boycotts and stay-aways

Based on national sample of 1,660 Africans. Fieldwork by Market and Opinion Surveys.

body of African opinion opposed to the dominantly 'social democrat' orientation of the ANC. After considering other pre-election findings we will return to the issues of why these alternative types of voters ended up supporting the ANC.

General Feelings about the Election and Intentions to Vote

As we have already suggested, the official election outcome leaves one in some doubt about the percentage turnout. The level of motivation to vote reflected in the pre-election polls is, accordingly, of some interest. We have already referred to the very large number of voters who felt unable to make political choices before the elections. Some of the reasons for this were probably to be found in attitudes towards the election. Respondents in the late 1993 poll were asked to give spontaneous responses to the prospect of the election. These open-ended answers were classified as they appear in table 4.6.

These results make it clear that South Africa's first open election was not exactly a feast of positive anticipation. Among Africans, slightly over 6 out of 10 viewed the election positively, but among coloured, Indian and white voters the proportion was between 3 and 4 out of 10. The election was certainly not a joyous moment of liberation for all South Africans. More seriously in terms of the possible effects on the outcome, the results vary quite widely according to party supported. In table 4.7 summarised results are presented for each category of party supporter.

As we know, some of the parties whose supporters were most negative did not participate. There were also clear differences in responses to the election between supporters of the various parties which did participate,

Table 4.6   Attitudes towards the event of the election according to group: a classification of spontaneous answers, October/November 1993

Percentages	African	Coloured	Indian	White	Total
Positive – unspecific	50	25	29	32	43
Positive – specific reasons	13	10	12	3	11
Negative – unspecific	7	7	13	22	10
Negative – specific reasons	6	5	16	6	6
Indifferent, cynical	3	11	1	5	4
Neutral	6	8	11	10	7
Don't know, unsure Don't know of election Other, refused	16	34	18	22	19

Percentages may not add to 100 due to rounding.

Table 4.7 Attitudes to the election by party preference (summarised), October/November 1993

Percentages	AZAPO	PAC	ANC	DP	NP	IFP	CP	AWB
Positive	82	75	72	59	47	53	18	21
Negative	18	11	11	14	17	16	48	50
Other answers	–	14	17	27	36	31	34	29

Percentages may not add to 100 due to rounding.

Table 4.8 Negative and positive feelings about the election, February 1994

Categories of voters	Feel excited/ Happy %	Worried/ Unhappy %
Africans	70	16
Coloureds	37	37
Indians	35	34
Whites	20	44
Support		
PAC	58	20
ANC	79	10
DP	32	5
NP	36	39
IFP	33	34
CP	1	43
Volksfront	12	59
AWB	17	64
Other	5	55

however. One cannot help noticing that the responses in table 4.7 show a gradient of positive to less positive attitudes from the more progressive to more conservative parties. The correlation between voter enthusiasm for the election and the electoral prospects of their parties was much less close, however; PAC and AZAPO supporters, despite their parties' very restricted electoral support, were most enthusiastic of all about the election, and DP voters were more enthusiastic than NP supporters, despite their party's lesser prospects.

The second survey, using a reworded question, revealed even greater contrasts in mood than the first survey, as table 4.8 shows. The figures in table 4.8 speak for themselves. In results not tabulated, regional perceptions differed strongly: only 17 per cent of whites in the Eastern Cape/Transkei and 26 per cent in the Orange Free State said they were 'worried and unhappy', compared to 57 per cent in the North-West and 65 per cent in the Northern Cape. Given recent controversies in the social sciences in South Africa about the continued relevance of 'ethnicity' as opposed to social class factors, it is worth pointing out how far ethnic factors appeared to swamp material interests in the South African context. Thus the most euphoric group in the population consisted of unemployed Africans seeking work (with over 75 per cent 'excited and happy' about the election), and the most fearful group consisted of unemployed whites, with over 93 per cent 'worried and unhappy'. It is worth pointing out, however, that the small African middle class was considerably more fearful and anxious than other sections of black society; indeed, there were multiple pointers to the fact that many better educated and professionally employed Africans felt bullied by township pressures and concerned lest this was the shape of things to come.

Comparing the results of the two surveys on this issue is made complex by the change in wording of the relevant items, but even so it would seem that ANC supporters became more elated as the campaign progressed, while virtually all the supporters of smaller parties, including the previously very optimistic PAC supporters, became more demoralised. The most important implication of these finding is that, certainly in emotional and symbolic terms, the electoral playing field was not level: it sloped sharply downwards to the left.

In the light of the patterns just reported on, it is important to look at differences in the intention to vote. Results are presented in table 4.9 for both pre-election surveys in order to discern trends in the run-up to the election. In our experience of comparing previous pre-election surveys with election outcomes, only the people who say they will *definitely vote* are reasonably certain to go to the polls in large numbers. It was of some concern, therefore, that the level of motivation to vote was so much

Table 4.9   Intention to vote by group (%)

	African		Coloured		Indian		White		Total	
Year	93	94	93	94	93	94	93	94	93	94
Definitely vote	78	67	51	46	50	49	75	77	73	66
Qualified answers	19	29	33	47	43	47	18	19	21	29
Definitely not	4	4	16	8	7	8	8	5	6	5

Percentages may not add to 100 due to rounding.

Table 4.10   Intention to vote by political party preferred (abridged) (%)

	PAC		ANC		DP		NP		IFP		CP		AWB	
Year	93	94	93	94	93	94	93	94	93	94	93	94	93	94
Definitely vote	84	33	88	80	78	90	79	76	72	36	61	74	50	63

Percentages may not add to 100 due to rounding.

Table 4.11   Reasons for not voting among all respondents who would not definitely vote, according to group, October/November 1993 (per cent)

	African	Coloured	Indian	White	Total
1) Reject participation	–	–	6	14	3
2) Uncertain about political choice	21	31	21	23	24
3) Fear violence/intimidation	17	8	15	7	13
4) No documents	3	1	–	1	2
5) Lack of voter education	12	5	2	2	
6) Indifferent/cynical about outcome	13	23	24	20	8 17
7) Practical/logistic difficulties	2	1	–	5	2
8) Personal reasons	8	8	10	6	7
9) General uncertainty, confusion	16	13	20	15	15
10) Other, diverse	8	10	2	7	9

higher among whites and Africans than it was among coloured and Indian voters.

Once again, there are also differences according to party preference, to be seen in table 4.10. With the exception of the dramatically low positive response of the IFP and the PAC in the second survey, differences in levels of motivation to vote between parties likely to contest the elections were not particularly large. However, some of these differences were both statistically and materially significant and could have affected critical levels of support in the election.

The levels of intention to vote were significantly higher than the levels of enthusiasm for the election, suggesting that many voters would turn out to vote defensively – in other words to attempt to prevent rather than achieve certain outcomes.

In the light of the results appearing above it is of interest to explore the respondents' reasons for not voting. Table 4.11 contains the answers to such a probe among all respondents who indicated that they would not *definitely* vote. The results reflect some significant groups of factors which could have constrained effective political participation. Aside from respondents who rejected the elections in principle (category 1), mainly whites, there appeared to be a high level of uncertainty about formulating choices (categories 2 and 9). The proportions fearing violence and intimidation were not large in overall terms, but could have had important marginal effects on the election.

What these results show is that despite efforts by independent organisations to promote political literacy, political parties had a large task in assisting voters in making appropriate choices. The general election took place within a completely transformed context in South African politics and clearly many voters had not yet worked themselves into the new framework.

Constraints on Freedom of Choice and Other Influences on Voter Behaviour

The figure of 13 per cent of voters who, according to the results in the table 4.11, felt constrained by the threat of violence and intimidation suggests that the free exercise of democratic choice was seriously problematic. In the event and contrary to many expectations, open violence during the election turned out to be a minor factor. Clearly many people who had contributed to a death rate which at times exceeded ten per day before the elections, turned their energies instead to the act of voting and of mobilising others to vote. Tensions also decreased sharply once the IFP and FF entered the campaign. Perhaps above all, a sense settled on the populace that, whatever their feelings, the election was a summation of so much passion and history that it now had to take its course; a mood of both acceptance and expectancy was born which simply made violence less appropriate.

Of far greater consequence to the freeness and fairness of the election were more subtle and less directly coercive factors which affected voters. We were alerted to the relevance of these factors many years prior to the election as the battle for political control of territory unfolded in South Africa's liberation struggle. From the early 1980s onwards the political struggle had shifted from the relatively less strategic protests of Sharpeville in 1961 and Soweto in 1976–7 to a more concerted mobilisation, particularly of youth, to oppose, pressurise and discredit establishment- and apartheid-aligned black leadership. Early examples were youth activist groupings in the Durban townships of Lamontville and Chesterville in the early 1980s. Somewhat later, similar mobilisations took place in the Eastern Cape, where not only agents of apartheid were targeted but also

PAC, AZAPO and Black Consciousness groupings which were mobilised separately from the dominant Charterist movements (that is, those with allegiance to the ANC Freedom Charter).

This new phase of struggle emerged in the strategy of rendering the townships of the Witwatersrand and elsewhere 'ungovernable' after 1984. While hundreds of establishment (and often corrupt) local African councillors were murdered or forced to flee in the process, violence was not the most effective part of the liberation strategy. Rather it was the persuasive, at times aggressively persuasive, actions of so-called street and area committees to convince residents to cease paying rents and service charges and, at regular intervals, to stay away from work and boycott non-African businesses. Of all the strategies against apartheid, this liberatory mobilisation was perhaps the most persuasive and most effective.

Obviously, the local structures and the patterns of deference established in this struggle did not dissolve when South Africa's transition started. Hence, when the election campaign first commenced, we were not surprised to hear and read of numerous complaints by the Democratic Party in particular, but also by AZAPO and the PAC in places like the West Rand, that their canvassers and organisers were quite routinely harassed and at times attacked. Once again, however, the instances of open aggression were perhaps the least significant – it was the continued imposition of a guiding political framework on the rank-and-file local residents which was more pervasive and influential in securing political conformity to party strategy.

One must be very careful, however, to avoid defining this as political intimidation. Quite obviously, majorities of residents were very happy, indeed enthusiastic, about aligning themselves in the way these local structures pushed. In assessing the quality of democracy, however, one is concerned about the freedom of dissent, that is concerned not just with majorities but with minorities and whether or not they were free to articulate and mobilise round their dissenting interests.

We posed a number of questions bearing on constraints on political choice. These items were not all intended as quantitative indices of enforced conformity – they could not be since most residents/voters in areas of political control would willingly conform. We posed some of them to assess the degree to which political minorities might have felt constrained or intimidated. The items and the outline results are presented as a compendium in tables 4.12a and 4.12b. The results are those derived from the February 1994 survey.

A follow-up question was asked after the item in table 4.12 about political groups that controlled local areas. Respondents were asked which party people in such areas would feel they had to vote for. Whites, coloured people and Indians tended to answer in the abstract, most frequently stereotyping the ANC as the source of influence. Since their

Table 4.12a   Factors constraining freedom of choice among voters (questionnaire items paraphrased; results below = % constrained), February 1994

	Africans %	Col. %	Ind. %	White %	W-Cape %	E-Cape %	N-Cape %	OFS %	KZ-Natal %	E-Tvl %	Gauteng %	NW-Tvl %	N-Tvl %
'Within community it will be known how you vote' – yes	28	13	40	19	16	39	17	22	22	27	21	22	32
'Does your area support mainly one party or a few different parties?' – one party	49	17	29	20	21	57	25	23	43	34	35	38	80
'People not supporting dominant party feel frightened/worried'	28	30	57	29	23	19	26	14	44	30	29	30	30
'Will you vote the way you want or feel you have to vote in a particular way?' – particular way	8	10	10	7	6	12	7	9	10	5	9	2	5
'Groups controlling area make sure you have to vote in a particular way'	18	6	6	15	6	26	10	10	29	11	7	7	27
'Feel it is right that certain parties *not* be allowed in areas'	20	8	22	13	9	28	17	10	25	18	11	11	22
'Neighbours are hard on a person who disagrees politically'	24	2	3	7	4	32	13	28	23	10	12	16	21
'Vote with majority to avoid conflict'	9	3	4	2	3	6	4	9	15	4	3	8	8
'Definite/some pressure to vote for party you don't support'	20	1	2	7	5	20	5	6	32	12	7	11	20

Table 4.12b   Factors constraining freedom of choice according to political party supported, February 1994

PAC %	ANC %	DP %	NP %	IFP %	CP %	Volksfront %	AWB	Other	No vote
						'Within community it will be known how you voted' – yes			
18	32	19	21	19	24	34	16	28	7
						'Does your area support mainly one party or a few different parties?' – one party			
4	51	1	21	54	58	18	33	11	22
						'People not supporting dominant party frightened/worried'			
31	27	30	32	36	36	49	15	25	38
						'Will you vote the way you want or feel you have to vote in a particular way?' – particular way			
7	7	10	6	11	4	12	26	21	22
						'Groups controlling area make sure you have to vote in a particular way'			
14	20	22	12	27	12	14	17	14	3
						'Feel it is right certain parties not be allowed in areas'			
11	21	12	13	25	21	31	25	–	9
						'Neighbours are hard on a person who disagrees politically'			
21	25	10	7	31	3	20	17	–	6
						'Vote with majority to avoid conflict'			
1	7	–	3	21	–	–	–	–	8
						'Definite/some pressure to vote for party you don't support'			
1	20	18	5	27	2	13	16	–	6

areas were least likely to be controlled by parties they were omitted and in table 4.13 we present results for Africans only.

The results in table 4.13 may be unfair to the ANC in as much as a very large party has an opportunity of controlling more territory than other parties. Nevertheless, the fact that some 10 per cent of black voters felt that they had to support a particular party which controlled their area must have been of some consequence to the election.

These results indeed provide evidence that community pressures and the fear of violence and intimidation meant that many voters cast a ballot which was less than fully 'free'. Thus 13 per cent of coloureds and 19 per cent of whites but 28 per cent of Africans and an astonishing 40 per cent of Indians (including 47 per cent of Indian men) thought that 'the

Table 4.13   Proportions of African voters by province who considered that various parties controlled their areas and put pressure on people to vote for that party, February 1994

Parties seen to be controlling/ pressurising	W-Cape %	E-Cape %	N-Cape %	OFS %	KZ/ Natal %	E-Tvl %	Gauteng %	N-West %	N-Tvl %	Total %
ANC	–	23	3	5	11	6	4	4	18	10
PAC	–	2	1	–	–	–	–	–	–	–
NP	–	–	–	3	2	–	–	–	1	1
AWB	–	–	–	3	1	–	2	–	3	1
IFP/Freedom Alliance	–	–	–	–	12	–	1	–	–	3
ANC + PAC/ AZAPO	–	–	–	–	–	–	1	–	–	–
ANC + IFP	–	–	–	–	2	–	–	–	–	–
Party I like	2	2	–	–	1	1	1	4	–	1

community will know how I vote.' Indeed, overall only 54 per cent of Africans – barely half – were confident that their vote would not be known by the community. Again, the figures were powerfully differentiated by region and language: 38 per cent of Xhosa-, Swazi- and Ndebele-speakers held such a belief compared to 20 per cent of Zulu-speakers. Community pressures were clearly most pervasive among the Xhosa-speakers of the Eastern Cape/Transkei (where 43 per cent thought their vote would be known by the community and 49 per cent didn't) and, above all, in the Western Cape, where a plurality of 43 per cent to 31 per cent disbelieved the notion of ballot secrecy. Ironically, the notion that one's vote would be unknown to the community was strongest (60 per cent to 17 per cent) among KwaZulu-Natal Africans.

Just how much more heavily community pressures weighed upon African voters than others was apparent when we asked whether the community would be 'hard' on a person who disagreed politically with their neighbours: only 2 per cent of coloureds and 3 per cent of Indians thought this would be the case, compared to 24 per cent of Africans. This figure rose even higher in KwaZulu-Natal (29 per cent), the Orange Free State (32 per cent) and the Eastern Cape/Transkei (38 per cent). But such pressures were felt by some whites too: 7 per cent thought their community would be hard on such a person. These instances of 'community intimidation' among whites were particularly pronounced in the Northern Cape (10 per cent), the Northern Transvaal (19 per cent) and the Eastern Transvaal, where a remarkable 29 per cent said the community would come down hard on such a person.

In order to explore further the phenomenon of community pressure we asked whether 'people in the local area supported mainly one political party' or several different parties. As we would have expected, belief in such local political homogeneity was far lower among coloureds (17 per cent), whites (20 per cent) and Indians (29 per cent) than among Africans, where, staggeringly, over 49 per cent said they lived in one-party areas. Such feelings were particularly pronounced in two areas, the Eastern Cape/Transkei (63 per cent, and 54 per cent among all Xhosa-speakers) and in the Northern Transvaal (80 per cent, and 75 per cent among Tsonga-, Shangaan-, Venda- and Lembede-speakers). No less than 53 per cent of all ANC supporters (and 59 per cent of IFP supporters) said they lived in one-party areas – compared to only 3 per cent of PAC voters.

This de facto habituation of such a huge proportion of the electorate to a local single-party reality is hardly a healthy augury for multiparty democracy, but, surprisingly, when we asked whether people felt happy, cautious or frightened to voice political opinions different from those prevailing locally, we found only small differences between racial groups: 43 per cent of Africans gave 'cautious' and 28 per cent 'frightened' as their responses, but these were actually lower figures than those found in other racial groups, doubtless an index of the acute anxieties currently felt among these minorities. International observers could have found it difficult to discover another electorate which was so generally fearful as South Africa's before the election, with 46 per cent of all groups giving 'cautious' and 29 per cent 'frightened' as responses to the question above. One could not but wonder whether a free and fair election was truly possible in KwaZulu-Natal, where 44 per cent of the electorate gave 'frightened' as a response to the above. Only in the Western Cape did one find a calmer atmosphere, with only 4 per cent of Africans giving 'frightened' as a response – though even there 67 per cent chose 'cautious'.

We then asked whether or not respondents felt they would be 'able to vote in the way you really want': hearteningly, 92 per cent of the whole electorate gave a positive response – though, of course, even 8 per cent (1 voter in 12) admitting to a constrained vote is a high figure and in the Eastern Cape/Transkei the figure reached 14 per cent, worse even than in KwaZulu-Natal (10 per cent). Among better educated (post-Matric) Africans the figure rose to 15 per cent and among African professionals, business people and managers to 17 per cent.

Pursuing this theme of constrained choice from a slightly different angle, we asked respondents whether it was true of their area that it was under the control of political groups 'who will make sure that people vote for a particular party whether they want to or not'. Here KwaZulu-Natal came out worst with 25 per cent of Africans there agreeing that this was so, followed by Northern Transvaal (22 per cent) and Eastern Cape/Transkei (13 per cent). When asked which parties used such local control to exercise these constraints, Africans instanced the ANC in 58 per cent of cases and the IFP in 14 per cent. But here there were striking disparities between regions. In KwaZulu-Natal the IFP was mentioned as exerting such pressures by 39 per cent and the ANC by 38 per cent, while in the PWV the comparable figures were 7 per cent and 40 per cent, with 21 per cent accusing the AWB of exerting such forcible suasion. Elsewhere the ANC was overwhelmingly the party mentioned as being guilty of such pressures, the worst cases being in the Northern Cape (83 per cent), the Eastern Cape/Transkei (81 per cent), the Eastern Transvaal (75 per cent) and the Northern Transvaal (64 per cent). Only in the Northern Cape (18 per cent) and Eastern Cape/Transkei was the PAC accused of exerting such constraint, while the NP and AWB (24 per cent each) were both heavily accused in the Orange Free State alongside the ANC (47 per cent). Similarly, in the Northern Transvaal the NP (5 per cent) and AWB (9 per cent) drew significant mention from Africans in this regard.

Given the apparent and alarming generality of these perceived pressures, it is encouraging to note that large majorities of Africans everywhere believed it was wrong that other parties were not allowed to campaign and seek support in certain areas: overall 67 per cent said such practices were wrong against only 20 per cent who said they were right. The most notably illiberal regions were the Eastern Cape/Transkei and KwaZulu-Natal, where 30 per cent and 27 per cent respectively thought such pressures were legitimate.

As a whole voters find it easier to accept that others are intimidated than to admit that they themselves are intimidated, but in the end, of course, the only acid test of community pressures is to ask whether voters, under such pressure, would stick to the party they supported or, in order to avoid conflict, they would switch to the party favoured by the community. In fact far fewer than we had expected in all communities said they would stick to their guns in such a situation: 90 per cent of whites, 75 per cent of Africans, 70 per cent of Indians and 64 per cent of coloureds – with the minorities who would buckle under such pressures, or who were uncertain whether they would, being probably large enough to swing the election. Within those broad racial categories some groups were far more 'intimidatable' than others: among Africans only 62 per cent in the Eastern Transvaal and 56 per cent in KwaZulu-Natal said they would stick to their chosen party under such pressures. Among whites, coloureds and Indians the more 'intimidatable' were simply the socially more vulnerable groups – women, the lowest paid, least educated and so on.

But, we asked, were voters actually under 'any pressure to vote for a party you do not particularly support?' Only 1 per cent of coloureds said 'yes' or 'yes, to some extent' to this, as did 2 per cent of Indians, 7 per cent of whites but 20 per cent of Africans. Among whites those reporting most such pressures were the most socially vulnerable, the young and the poor. The phenomenon was most pronounced in the Eastern Transvaal (where 24 per cent reported such pressures) and in KwaZulu/Natal (where 25 per cent did). Among Africans too, KwaZulu/Natal had the worst incidence (38 per cent), followed by the Eastern Cape/Transkei (24 per cent) and Western Cape (21 per cent). Only in the Orange Free State (7 per cent) and Northern Cape (9 per cent) was an African less than 10 per cent likely to feel under such pressure – a quite unacceptable situation.

The earlier survey in November 1993 produced results which were in general similar to those discussed above. Two of the items are worth presenting because they reflect particularly telling influences which reinforce the conclusions emerging from table 4.12 and the other results discussed above. One item was a different phrasing of the probe into the constraining effect of neighbour's views; the results are given in tables 4.14 and 4.15.

Obviously the critical categories in table 4.14 are the second and third responses, in which holding divergent opinion was perceived to be difficult or impossible. Here again, the African and coloured voters had

Table 4.14 Perceptions of whether it was easy or difficult to hold opinions different from surrounding people, by group, November 1993

	African	Coloured	Indian	White
Easy – no problem	62	50	66	80
Difficult	14	12	6	3
Impossible	8	4	–	1
All opinions similar	6	5	4	2
Surrounding opinion unknown	11	30	23	14

Table 4.15 Perceptions of whether it is easy or difficult to hold opinions different from surrounding people, according to political party, November 1993

Percentage	AZAPO	PAC	SACP	ANC	DP	NP	IFP	CP	AWB	No choice
Easy – no problem	23	65	40	70	79	77	46	88	49	41
Difficult	–	16	6	12	6	4	19	2	10	16
Impossible	–	9	4	6	–	2	15	–	16	11
All opinions similar	77	11	–	4	7	5	17	–	–	3
Surrounding opinion unknown	–	–	50	7	8	12	4	11	25	29

the greatest problem. While not a majority, over one-fifth of Africans considered that there were social penalties for freedom of conscience. The white voters appeared to live in a climate of the greatest tolerance, which is no more than expected given their protected middle-class lifestyles.

These results may be misleading. We know that the vast majority of Africans supported the ANC, and as we have already cautioned, one would not expect large numbers to have felt constrained among their political compatriots. Therefore it is necessary to consider also the results according to political party, which are given in table 4.15.

These results begin to show the nature of the problem. The proportions saying it is difficult or impossible to hold divergent opinions are the critical ones. In terms of this constraint, with difficult and impossible combined, the parties ranked as follows:

Holding divergent views seen as 'difficult' or 'impossible'

IFP	34%
No choice	27%
AWB	26%
PAC	25%
ANC	18%
SACP	10%
DP/NP	6%
CP	2%

Thus it would seem that the smaller and more marginal parties (IFP, AWB, PAC) experienced the greatest constraint. Given that some of the IFP supporters are white or Indian, and that many others were interviewed in politically homogeneous hostels or traditional rural areas, the constraints on IFP supporters in the townships appear to have been very great. Obviously the pressure could have come from their own party or from an opposing party, but they added up to a substantial constraint, one way or another.

A similar question was whether people felt free to hold whatever opinions they wanted to, or whether they were under pressure to support a particular party. The results according to racial group appear in table 4.16.

Here again whites were in the least constrained position. The same problem of interpretation applies as in the previous results, however, this

Table 4.16   Freedom of opinion, by group, November 1993

Percentage	African	Coloured	Indian	White
Free to hold views	84	89	91	98
Under particular pressure	16	11	9	2

Table 4.17 Freedom of opinion, by party, November 1993

Percentage	AZAPO	PAC	SACP	ANC	DP	NP	IFP	CP	AWB	No choice
Free to hold views	100	86	100	87	90	95	84	99	98	82
Under particular pressure	–	14	–	13	10	5	16	1	2	18

Table 4.18 Does any party control your area and keep other parties out? (November 1993)

Percentage	African	Coloured	Indian	White
Yes	27	8	6	5
To some extent	17	18	14	10
No	56	74	80	86

being that most blacks might hold views which conform with those of the community. Therefore the results according to political party, given in table 4.17.

These results present a generally positive picture, but one should not underestimate the effects of constraints at the margins. IFP, ANC and DP supporters appeared to be under the greatest constraint, a problem applying to between 10 and 20 per cent of voters. In absolute terms, this was a very large number of people. People who gave no political choice also experience significant pressures, which might have been one of the reasons for their lack of commitment.

More pointedly, we also asked respondents whether or not a particular political party controlled their areas, keeping other parties out and in so doing influencing the way people would vote. The results according to race are given in table 4.18. It was interesting to see that perceptions of political hegemony existed even in white areas. It is, of course, most likely in smaller white rural communities. The major problem appeared to exist among blacks, however, among whom up to 4 out of 10 people perceived at least a degree of political hegemony in their local areas.

The seriousness of the problem emerges more clearly if one considers the results according to political party. The proportions perceiving *some extent or more* of political domination among the supporters of the different parties are as follows:

SACP	96%
AWB	51%
IFP	49%
ANC	44%
PAC	44%
DP	37%

Others all lower

Clearly, in some instances respondents were thinking of control by their own parties and in other instances of parties they opposed. The problem is clearly serious either way and the percentages above must be taken as a rough quantitative estimate of limitations on freedom to canvass and attract support.

Thus the results of both the first and the second pre-election surveys strongly suggest that impediments to the exercise of free choice between parties were present right up to the election. While we cannot estimate the effect of these problems on the election outcome in quantitative terms, it is clear that the effect was significant, especially for smaller parties.

Sources of Political Influence

There is an underlying notion concerning democracy that it is most fundamentally based on individual conscience and choice. Against this the reality throughout the world is that collective influences are brought to bear on the process. We attempted a brief exploration of this issue in the South African context by trying to assess the relative importance of various local sources of political influence on voters in the election. Some kinds of influence are politically benign, but when influence is exercised by organisations which purport to control entire areas and which have known methods of coercive or imperative mobilisation, such influences can usurp the democratic process. The results in table 4.19 relate to this question.

Other sources of influence volunteered spontaneously and not included in the table included the media, colleagues, neighbours and, of course, political parties.

White voters, and to a somewhat lesser extent Indian voters, appear to be the most 'self-sufficient' and closest to the pristine notion of individual conscience, although narrow majorities of African and coloured voters also replied spontaneously that they 'decide themselves'. But African and coloured voters clearly felt the pressure of influence from a greater number of sources than did other groups.

Generally, however, the sources of influence were constructive and benign – a normal part of community life. It is however questionable

Table 4.19 Groups influencing voter choice, November 1993

Source of influence – Percentage influenced	African	Coloured	Indian	White
Their church	25	29	11	9
Community elders	24	21	20	7
Trade unions	19	27	7	3
Employers	13	13	4	3
Traditional chiefs	17	–	–	–
Civic association	27	–	–	–
Street committee	25	20	18	2
Spouse	25	31	25	10
Parents	24	29	20	10
Children	21	19	15	4
'Decide myself'*	57	56	75	72

* This last category was a spontaneous addition by respondents not choosing a category above.

whether or not street committees and civic associations, whose influence was clearly prominent, were in the same category as the other sources of influence. Recent consideration by the ANC and the civic associations that the latter should move towards a voluntary membership base and cease to claim automatic representativeness for entire areas might begin to resolve this question. If street committees continue to operate as *some* have in the past, with a tendency to impose conformity to particular strategies on entire areas, they must clearly be regarded as problematic in a democratic context.

Traditional chiefs are another problematic category of influence, since the possibility of imposed conformity arises here as well. However, the degree of influence from this quarter suggested by the results was not great in overall terms, though this influence rose to well over 20 per cent in African rural areas. This too could be as problematic for the democratic process as the urban movements referred to above.

Closing Remarks

In general it would seem that the pre-election surveys not only had substantial validity but also considerable utility in offering early warnings of factors which could cloud the quality and legitimacy of election outcomes in South Africa. We would hope that election administration and monitoring agencies will recall this in future elections.

South Africa's first open general election aroused justifiable excitement and anticipation within South Africa and far beyond its borders. Sadly, however, among the voters themselves only ANC–SACP and to a lesser extent PAC supporters generally shared the positive anticipation and excitement. Among all other political party supporters, substantially less than 40 per cent felt happy and excited over the election. Their election was characterised by worry and anxiety.

While majorities of Africans and whites appeared to be sufficiently determined to have voted, slightly less than half of coloured and Indian potential voters said that they would 'definitely vote'. The effect of lower turnouts among these voters, who felt particularly uncertain and nervous, could have been quite significant for the strength of opposition in the post-election parliament.

The major indictment of the quality and adequacy of the election emerging from our results lies in the strong and consistent evidence of constraints on the exercise of free voting choice, particularly among Africans. Over a dozen different questions were asked in the two surveys about various kinds of pressure to vote in ways which might not have been the voter's conscience-driven and unfettered choice. Taking *a rough average* of the responses across the replies to these items would suggest that broadly one-quarter of Africans, one-fifth of Indians and some 10 to 15 per cent of coloured and white voters might have had their electoral behaviour distorted by factors which cannot be counted as normal in a democracy.

It seems possible that South Africans have become somewhat blasé about the high levels of intimidatory political pressure felt at many levels within their society, but it is worth repeating the fact that in many other countries results such as those we obtained would be felt to disqualify an election from the sobriquet of 'free and fair'. Moreover, our study shows that the problems were not by any means all concentrated, as there is a tendency to assume, in the highly contested areas of the Reef and KwaZulu-Natal. Over and over again, for example, the Eastern Cape/ Transkei, for all that they had a fairly high degree of political (ANC) homogeneity, were shown up as areas where freedom of choice was not easy to exercise. But on many indices the same could be said of, for example, the Northern Cape: indeed, it was harder to find areas where political choice reached acceptably free levels than to do the opposite.

There are issues which civil society in South Africa must work on if its new democracy is to become consolidated. Now that minority domination has passed, that opportunity and that challenge are immediate and urgent. Nevertheless, our remarks on the distortions which the results reveal should not be seen as discrediting a generally successful election. Our pre-election polls reinforce the broad conclusions of the IEC that, by and large, the will of the people prevailed.

Notes

1 Both the national surveys were conducted as part of regular nationwide omnibus survey undertaken by MarkData, the opinion-polling organisation of the HSRC. The basic sample is a stratified probability sample of 2,100 South African adults of 18 years and older, drawn in metropolitan, urban and rural-agricultural areas. Hostels and informal residential (shack) areas are included in the sampling frame. The final stage of selection of a respondent is based on a random selection 'grid', thereby avoiding bias in selection. The sampling frame is based on the enumerator areas of the 1991 population census. The major fieldwork for the first survey was undertaken in October and November of 1993 and in February 1994 for the second survey.

Interviews are conducted on a personal, face-to-face basis with systematic back-checks to ensure consistent coverage. The final sample realised has been weighted to bring it into conformity with the distributions in the census. The second survey covered all territories, but the first excluded one formerly independent 'homeland', Bophuthatswana. In regard to support for political parties, however, data from other surveys conducted for specific purposes were able to be added to the results of the first survey to make estimates for the whole country possible.

The national surveys were conducted in identical fashion to the Markdata Omnibus surveys described and analysed by de Kock (ch. 3), but they were carried out later and consisted of questionnaires designed by Schlemmer and Johnson precisely for this study. Six separate surveys were commissioned – two each in the Western Cape, KwaZulu-Natal and Gauteng. In Gauteng we again used the MarkData organisation but elsewhere we deliberately farmed the work out to other survey organisations in order to achieve greater pluralism and diversity of approach.

2 For full results see H. Schlemmer and I. Hirschfeld (eds), *Founding Democracy and the New Forth African Order* (Pretoria: HSRC, 1994), ch. 4.

FIVE

The Election in the Western Cape

Robert Mattes, Hermann Giliomee and Wilmot James

THE NEWLY DEMARCATED WESTERN CAPE province provided South Africa with one of its most interesting and exciting campaigns and elections of 1994. Three political parties (the African National Congress, the Democratic Party and the National Party) all entertained realistic hopes of either controlling or playing a major role in the new provincial government, since the regional balance of power was truly in doubt right up until – and due to the IEC, long after – polling day. In order to understand the main factors which shaped the way this election was fought and decided, we begin with a survey of the unique 'political world' of the Western Cape that confronted political parties as they began their campaigns, concentrating on the roots of the most important elements of its peculiar political culture. In the following section we examine the campaign itself, focusing on the parties' strategic decisions and behaviour, as well as on the extent to which that campaign was free and fair. In our final section we scrutinise how voters in the province reacted to those campaigns.

The Political World of the Western Cape

It is not altogether clear just how much an examination of Western Cape electoral politics helps one understand South African electoral dynamics in general. To be sure, the diversity of the Western Cape is a microcosm of the country as a whole; it has large proportions of black, white and coloured voters, speakers of three major languages, and adherents of at least two major faiths and a multitude of denominations. Thus the Western Cape is a 'divided' or at least a 'plural society' in itself. Yet the province is also fairly atypical in that the configurations of its divisions are far more heterogeneous than any of South Africa's other eight new provinces in terms of factors such as race, ethnicity and religion. It is no surprise, then, that it is also the most diverse in terms of political culture.

The most important and atypical feature of Western Cape politics is the fact that it has not revolved primarily around the 'white–black' conflict that has been such a predominant feature in the rest of the country. Along with the Northern Cape, it is the only province which did not have within its present borders a large indigenous black population or home-land, and therefore does not have a majority of black citizens.[1] Rather, the majority (just under 60 per cent) are 'coloured', a term that histori-cally has been fraught with political and ideological difficulties. It is certainly true that this is an identity that has been 'constructed' by four decades of apartheid and a preceding two centuries of enforced segre-gation and slavery. Yet it is also true that the vast majority of coloured citizens of the Western Cape bristle at the heretofore politically correct term of 'so-called coloured', or indeed at any placement of quotation marks around the word (a lesson learned all too late in the campaign by the ANC). While the term was used to lump together a wide range of people solely because of roughly similar skin colour,[2] the common inter-national perception of this group as only a 'mixed race', catch-all category is mistaken. Members of the coloured community, especially in the Cape Town area, largely descend from three specific groups, Malaysian slaves, Khoi-San tribes and Europeans. Yet, if for no other reason than decades of common oppression, the coloured community is a reality to anyone living in the Western Cape.

The black community of the Western Cape (20 to 25 per cent of the population) consists of people who have lived steadily in the urban Cape Town townships and a few scattered rural townships for the past few decades. It also consists of more recent migrants from rural areas in the old Transkei and Ciskei bantustans who have come seeking work in Cape Town. Over the past fifteen years, between 800,000 and a million migrants have swelled the old townships, started sprawling new townships and 'squatter camps' on the sand flats outside the city, and have accom-plished as much as any other social dynamic in demonstrating the futility of apartheid and 'influx control'.[3]

Uniquely in South Africa, this region has, moreover, had historical experience of a non-racial franchise. Afrikaners and coloureds first received the vote in 1853 under the Cape colony's non-racial constitu-tion. The Afrikaner Bond, founded in 1880, directed its mobilising efforts mainly at white, Dutch-speaking Afrikaners (in the pre-industrial era, 'Afrikaner' was used as often to refer to people born in the region as to any specific ethnic group). Yet it also rejected efforts to impose a formal ban on 'brown' Afrikaners. Indeed, its leader 'Onse Jan' Hofmeyr on occasion said that there were Afrikaners whom he wanted out of the organisation and coloureds whom he wanted in.[4]

The National Party initially continued in this tradition. Founded in 1915 as a vehicle for Afrikaner nationalism, the NP of the Cape province vigorously campaigned for coloured support, calling on brown and white

Afrikaners to stand together against British immigrants taking away their jobs. In 1919 the prominent Western Cape nationalist J. H. H. de Waal hit out against imperialist politicians who 'set the Coloured population against their fellow-Afrikaners who speak the same language, have the same love for South Africa, have mostly the same history and interests, are hoodwinked by the same friends . . . and find themselves in virtually all respects in the same position'.[5] Indeed, coloured votes helped bring the NP to power in 1924. During that campaign, General Hertzog had promised that the NP would draw white and coloured people together as 'civilised' people against the 'natives'. Once in government, however, it emphasised rehabilitating 'poor whites' and in the process openly discriminated against coloured people, who subsequently defected from the NP in the 1929 election. It was in the aftermath of this election that the NP moved to reduce the strategic importance of coloured voters by enfranchising white women but not coloured women (as it had earlier promised).

Key cleavages

Black and coloured South Africans share a long, common history of racial oppression and political repression. Blacks living in the Western Cape endured the typical pains of apartheid: influx control raids; forced repatriation to their assigned bantustans; repeated government bulldozings of sprouting shanty communities; and government detention, imprisonment and banning of activists and political organisations. After the National Party won uncontested power in 1948, it repeatedly tried to disenfranchise coloured voters, finally removing them from the common voters' roll in 1956. Coloured people were also the target of forced removals from 'white' areas throughout the province, the most notorious instance being Cape Town's District Six where tens of thousands were forcibly removed to new suburbs miles outside the city. In fact, by the time the Group Areas Act was abolished, one in six coloured citizens had been forcibly removed.[6] However, it is interesting to note the differing circumstances of coloured victims of repression who were more than once the victims of larger power struggles. When the Afrikaner–English conflict dominated national politics, the NP disenfranchised coloureds not so much on the grounds of race or colour, but because they allied with English-speaking, pro-empire parties. Later, coloureds were forced to operate within apartheid structures less because the NP considered them a political threat than because it was convinced that only through apartheid could Afrikaner nationalists continue to control the state and exert white hegemony over blacks.

Indeed, despite similar histories of oppression, the general social characteristics of black and coloured citizens of the Western Cape illuminate sharp cleavages between them which constitute crucial parts of any satisfactory explanation of electoral politics in this province. Tables 5.1 through 5.8 display provincial figures for several fundamentally important characteristics and reveal a significant amount of social and economic 'distance' between black and coloured people.

Needless to say, the social and cultural patterns revealed in tables 5.1 to 5.8 are not necessarily 'natural' and were certainly shaped by the enforced segregation of 'separate development'. Black and coloured South Africans lived in separate areas and went to separate hospitals, schools and

Table 5.1   Residential status (%)

Type of residential area	Total	White	Black	Coloured
Urban	61.9	69.0	57.0	61.3
Rural	31.3	31.0	12.9	38.6
Squatter	6.8	0.0	29.9	0.0

Source: Institute for Multi-Party Democracy/Market & Opinion Surveys, Feb. 1994, N = 2,500.

Table 5.2   Housing situation (%)

Type of dwelling	Total	White	Black	Coloured
Formal house	73.5	74.3	57.8	79.4
Flat (in building)	7.0	13.3	2.3	6.6
Flat (on property)	1.3	1.4	0.4	1.6
Townhouse	6.6	8.2	2.2	7.8
Shack	7.4	0.0	29.9	1.1
Hostel	1.3	0.0	5.9	0.0

Source: MPD/M&O Survey, Feb. 1994, N = 2,500.

Table 5.3   Migration patterns (%)

Area lived in longest before the age of 18	Total	White	Black	Coloured
Large town/City/Township	59.1	63.6	41.5	64.5
Small town/Township	25.9	22.8	27.3	28.4
Black rural area	8.2	0.1	35.5	0.3
White farm	6.8	13.4	0.7	6.7

Source: MPD/M&O Survey, Feb. 1994, N = 2,500.

Table 5.4   Education (% and cumulative %)

Years of education	Total		White		Black		Coloured	
None	3.0		0.0		6.6		3.0	
Sub A/Sub B	2.2	(5.2)	0.5	(0.5)	4.8	(11.4)	2.2	(5.2)
Standard 1–5	14.7	(19.9)	0.5	(1.0)	16.0	(27.4)	14.7	(19.9)
Standard 6–9	40.0	(59.9)	17.7	(18.7)	45.5	(72.9)	40.0	(59.9)
Matric	19.0	(78.9)	35.2	(53.9)	14.7	(87.6)	19.0	(78.9)
Diploma	15.1	(94.0)	29.2	(83.1)	9.5	(97.1)	15.1	(94.0)
Bachelors/Honours	5.2	(99.2)	14.3	(97.4)	2.2	(99.3)	5.2	(99.2)
Masters/Ph.D.	0.7	(99.9)	2.9	(100.3)	0.4	(99.7)	0.7	(99.9)

Source: MPD/M&O Survey, Feb. 1994, N = 2,500.

Table 5.5   Employment (%)

Work status	Total	White	Black	Coloured
Full-time	37.3	40.2	30.6	38.9
Part-time	4.6	5.2	6.6	3.6
Self-employed	4.7	9.9	6.7	2.4
Informal	6.6	1.8	6.6	7.9
Housewife	11.5	14.2	2.9	13.9
Unemployed	18.5	4.7	25.9	20.6

Source: MPD/M&O Survey, Feb. 1994, N = 2,500.

Table 5.6   Income (% and cumulative %)

Joint household income	Total		White		Black		Coloured	
None	2.9		1.0		7.3		1.8	
1–999	24.2	(27.1)	5.4	(6.4)	48.8	(56.1)	21.2	(23.0)
1,000–1,999	17.3	(44.4)	9.3	(15.7)	24.6	(80.7)	17.4	(40.4)
2,000–2,999	7.1	(51.5)	7.0	(22.7)	4.6	(85.3)	8.2	(48.6)
3,000–3,999	6.2	(57.7)	11.2	(33.9)	2.2	(87.5)	5.9	(54.5)
4,000–4,999	2.7	(60.4)	5.3	(39.2)	0.7	(88.2)	2.4	(56.9)
5,000–5,999	4.2	(64.6)	12.3	(51.5)	0.4	(88.6)	2.8	(59.7)
7,500–9,000	2.1	(66.7)	6.8	(58.3)	0.3	(88.9)	1.2	(60.9)
10,000–14,999	1.5	(68.2)	5.1	(63.4)	0.0	(88.9)	0.8	(61.7)
15,000–19,999	0.4	(68.6)	2.0	(65.4)	0.0	(88.9)	0.0	(61.7)
Over 20,000	0.7	(69.3)	2.0	(67.4)	0.0	(88.9)	0.6	(62.3)
Won't say/ Uncertain	29.5		29.5		11.3		36.6	

Source: MPD/M&O Survey, Feb. 1994, N = 2,500.

Table 5.7   Religion (%)

Denomination	Total	White	Black	Coloured
Anglican	13.7	7.3	8.4	18.1
Catholic	7.3	7.4	7.0	7.3
Dutch Reformed	18.9	38.0	0.6	19.4
Islam/Muslim	3.9	0.0	0.0	6.8
Methodist	9.5	12.0	20.0	4.5

Source: MPD/M&O Survey, Feb. 1994, N = 2,500.

Table 5.8   Language (%)

	Total	White	Black	Coloured
Afrikaans	57.4	49.3	1.2	82.6
English	20.2	50.1	0.2	20.2
Xhosa	21.4	0.0	95.2	0.0

Source: MPD/M&O Survey, Feb. 1994, N = 2,500.

universities. Yet separate development left coloured people in a peculiar situation that is fundamental to an understanding of provincial political dynamics. While coloured citizens were oppressed by apartheid, they were also relatively advantaged in relation to black people, not least because the western part of the old Cape Province was traditionally defined in labour legislation as a 'coloured preference hiring area'. Thus, tables 5.1 through 5.6 reveal a black community with a large proportion of shack dwellers, most of whom are recent migrants from rural bantustans. In comparison, the coloured community is relatively better educated, better housed, more employed, and more prosperous. Furthermore, while whites occupy better houses and better-paying jobs, the housing and employment figures (especially the proportions in the 'housewife' category) suggest a much greater *class* affinity between white and coloured people in the province.

White Afrikaner political culture in the Cape has been dominated by a secure and confident ethnic establishment which has traditionally been willing to seek allies beyond defined ethnic and racial boundaries when political exigencies demanded it. This differed sharply from the northern provinces where the NP developed as a precarious alliance between insecure workers, struggling farmers and a small professional class. In the Cape, by contrast, wealthy farmers, university professors, professionals and businessmen found each other in a union of the heart, mind and interest. They created an elite ethnic establishment from the overlapping memberships of the leadership positions in major finance and insurance companies, publishing houses, universities and churches.

This influence has extended beyond defined white Afrikaner boundaries. One of the striking characteristics of the coloured community is the fact that it lacks any major cultural 'markers' of its own (such as language, religion or other symbols) and shares more in common with the dominant social group.[7] Thus the predominance of Afrikaans and the large membership in the Dutch Reformed Church revealed in tables 5.7 and 5.8 also suggest a significant *cultural* affinity between coloureds and whites. In rural areas, the Dutch Reformed Mission Church, the largest church in the coloured community, is often financially supported by its white counterpart. Nasionale Pers, the Afrikaans press conglomerate, has succeeded in inculcating a common Afrikaans identity as its publications have become increasingly dependent on a growing coloured readership: one-third of the NP-supporting Afrikaans-language daily newspaper *Die Burger*'s 90,000 weekday readers are coloured, and one-quarter of the weekend *Rapport*'s 400,000 readers now buy the 'coloured' *Metro* edition.[8] During the 1994 campaign, the ANC often accused the NP of using *swart gevaar* ('black threat') tactics to drive insecure coloured people into the Nationalist camp. Yet when asked whether coloured people feared blacks, community leader, intellectual and DP candidate Richard van der Ross suggested that 'It is rather a feeling that there is not enough which is common between brown and black people. Although they share certain things there exists a great gap when it comes to culture, religion, language and attitudes toward family life.'[9] It was such factors that led the Cape National Party leader Dawie de Villiers to predict as early as May 1991 that coloured people would support his party because of their 'deeper affinity' with whites.[10]

The Tricameral System

A series of government reforms in the 1980s attempting to modernise apartheid had provided the coloured community with significant advances. In 1983, the government imposed a new constitution and instituted a very limited form of 'power-sharing' among the officially demarcated white, coloured and Indian race groups. The impetus for these reforms came about in the late 1970s when the NP under P. W. Botha came to believe that they had to concentrate on the defence of middle-class interests and values against a perceived 'black power' onslaught. In this endeavour, the help of coloured people was now deemed to be indispensable. As one NP propaganda sheet put it, the idea was to 'gather in with the whites the Coloureds as a bloc of 2.5 million people in order to broaden our power base and avoid handing them over to a "black power" situation'.[11] Such ideas, however, ultimately threatened to split the party. Significantly, it was the Cape NP that concluded that party unity at all costs had become unaffordable and that it was better that the conservatives under Treurnicht should go their own way, which they duly did in March 1982. Support for the NP among coloureds gathered momentum from the moment the party split became irrevocable. For moderate coloured people there was no surer sign that the political tide had turned than Botha's willingness to sacrifice party unity in his attempt to accommodate coloured people.

The most important element of this new dispensation was a tricameral national parliament officially operating on the principle of concurrent majorities and a division between 'own' and 'general' affairs.[12] In addition, the government also created elected township councils, or Black Local Authorities, to create a limited form of self-government among urbanised blacks.[13] To be sure, the Tricameral system hardly granted coloured citizens full democratic citizenship. At the same time, however, these were not the same powerless 'toy telephone' structures previously created by the National Party for Coloured and Bantu Affairs. Locally elected coloured authorities were able to obtain real, albeit limited powers because they now had an important access point through their members of parliament and, at times, cabinet members, who took up their plight at the national level. And because most of these local structures were also dominated by the Labour Party (LP) (who controlled the coloured House of Representatives), LP MPs had an interest in increasing local community powers in order to augment party patronage and support. Indeed, the NP government also had an interest in giving these structures more say in the running of their 'own affairs' in order to gain some form of legitimacy for the system, as well as to advance the social and economic development of the coloured community (successive NP governments believed this would have a peaceful rather than a politicising effect).[14]

From 1984 to 1989, available funds for development programmes in coloured communities doubled. At the same time, elected coloured leaders close to their communities allocated these increased resources somewhat better than the distant white bureaucrats who had previously administered them.[15] Several different indicators reveal the relative embourgeoisement of coloured South Africans during this period, especially in comparison with blacks. One important 'own affair' constitutionally transferred to the coloured House of Representatives was housing, and it embarked on an ambitious housing and urban upgrading initiative in the late 1980s.[16] Indeed, under the Tricameral system, over 100,000 houses were built (60,000 in the Cape Town area). In another 'own affair', education, the number of coloured children in secondary school increased by one-third, and the number of successful graduates doubled.[17] Finally, the fertility rate in the coloured community declined from 6 children per female in 1960 to 2.9 in the late 1980s.[18]

All in all, between 1975 and 1991 the mean income of the lowest three quintiles of black households decreased substantially (the lowest two by 40 per cent). In contrast, the lowest two quintiles of coloured households decreased very slightly, and the top three quintiles grew strongly (by some 20 per cent). In 1969, whites earned eleven times as much as coloureds (who in turn earned 20 per cent more than blacks). By 1988, whites earned only three times as much as coloureds (who now earned twice as much as blacks). Not only was economic growth among coloureds much stronger than among blacks, it was also much broader and more even. Indeed, while most blacks did much worse during the 1975 to 1991 period, the income of the top 20 per cent *increased* by 40 per cent; among blacks the GINI coefficient of income inequality increased from 0.47 to 0.62 while among coloureds it remained virtually unchanged (0.51 to 0.52).[19]

The United Democratic Front

Yet the imposition of the Tricameral parliament had other important, enduring legacies for Western Cape politics. In 1983, the United Democratic Front was created to organise and lead popular opposition to the new constitution. Ideologically linked to the then-banned ANC's Freedom Charter, the UDF was a multiracial confederation of affiliated labour, church, student and civic organisations, and had strong roots in the Western Cape.[20] Its apparently successful boycott of black and coloured local elections, and Indian and coloured parliamentary elections in 1983–4, offered a bright hope for creating a non-racial, internal opposition to the government's reform programmes. In 1983 electoral turnout for five Cape Town area coloured Management Committees ranged between 2 per cent and 12 per cent (though it was much higher in rural areas above the city, extending to as much as 29 per cent in Worcester); and only 12 per cent of 50,000 registered voters in black townships turned out for elections for local authorities.[21] Table 5.9 shows turnout patterns for the 1984 parliamentary elections for the House of Representatives.

The effect of the UDF boycott can be seen in table 5.10, which reveals that coloured turnout in 1984 was significantly lower than previous votes for the powerless Coloured Representative Council (CRC). Indeed, during these previous campaigns the victorious LP had pledged to 'wreck' the CRC should they become the majority party.[22]

However, from its inception, the Western Cape UDF was ultimately unable to bridge tensions between coloured and black affiliates, or even between groups representing black townships and black squatter camps. Such tensions could be seen even as early as 1982 when black civic organisations withdrew from the Cape Areas Housing Action Committee (CAHAC) and formed the Western Cape Civics Association (WCCA) due to conflict over language, the dominance of coloured activists, and

Table 5.9   Coloured turnout in 1984 parliamentary elections

	Percentage of registered voters
Cape Province	29.5
Cape Peninsula	(11.1)
Western Cape rural	(35.4)
Natal	26.9
Orange Free State	61.4
Transvaal	43.4
National	32.5

Source: Gerd Behrens, 'The other two Houses: the first five years of the Houses of Representatives and Delegates', Ph.D. diss., University of Cape Town, 1989, pp. 108–10.

Table 5.10   Coloured turnout over time (Coloured Representative Council, 1968 and 1975, and Tricameral Parliament, 1984)

	Percentage of registered voters	Percentage of eligible voters	Percentage of registered voters (Cape Province)
1968	49.1	35.7	46.1
1975	48.3	25.3	45.7
1984	32.5	19.7	29.5

Source: Behrens, 'The other two Houses', pp. 120, 330.

differing political needs. These same tensions also hindered attempts to create united student organisations in the region.[23]

In fact, black participation in the Western Cape UDF was initially quite limited due to the weakness of political organisation in the townships. Yet while the UDF attempted to create one regional structure bridging 'group area' boundaries, different concerns and organisational methods led to a split and the creation of one structure for black townships (supporting more militant actions) and one for coloured areas (which were seen as more conservative and wary of militancy). Veteran black township leaders also mistrusted the newer, better educated, largely coloured (or, sometimes, white) UDF elite.[24]

While the regional UDF had shied away from confrontationist measures out of concern for the more conservative coloured townships in 1983–4, the detention, in early 1985, of most of the national leadership and the countrywide escalation of township protests led to a swing towards more black township-centred forms of direct confrontation, featuring school and consumer boycotts and attempts to advance civics as alternative local governing structures. Many of these campaigns were accompanied by a great deal of coercion and intimidation, something which alienated many coloured supporters. In addition, UDF plans to oppose forced removals of blacks never received substantial support from its rank-and-file membership, further widening the divide between younger, more radical black township groups and the regional UDF.[25]

Moreover, the extended national state of emergency from 1986 to 1989 and the government's counter-revolutionary programme under the National Security Management System devastated the UDF and many of its affiliates through detentions, bannings and restrictions.[26] It never recovered in coloured areas. In fact, while it should not be overestimated, there was a significant trend towards greater coloured participation in the system throughout the latter half of the decade as turnout for local elections in places like Athlone and Kensington went from 1.8 per cent and 12 per cent in 1983 to 13 per cent and 31 per cent in 1988 respectively.[27]

Increasing protests and rent boycotts deeply politicised some parts of the coloured and much of the black community in the Western Cape. In contrast to the slight increases in participation in coloured local elections, local black councils and councillors became targets of repeated physical attacks and intimidation. Councillors were seen as illegitimate puppets of the apartheid state, with the result that 37 per cent of the council seats in the Cape were vacant by 1990.[28] This emphasised the increasing role of black civic organisations in negotiations with provincial and local state bodies. And alongside the civics, the Congress of South African Trade Unions and structures related to the militant Umkhonto We Sizwe (MK) also gained ever-increasing influence in the townships as they filled the space vacated by the repressed UDF.[29]

One fundamentally important consequence of the rise and decline of the UDF concerned the increasingly differential political organisations of black and coloured areas, especially in the different ways that citizens received information and persuasion about politics. These patterns are illustrated in tables 5.11 through 5.13. Coloured citizens have come to look primarily to the mass media for their political information; they place their greatest trust in the information provided by television (47 per cent), the family (34 per cent), radio (32 per cent) and friends (23 per cent). They look essentially *inwards* to family (22 per cent) and to friends (20 per cent) for explicit cues about how to vote. In contrast, blacks are much less incorporated into the mainstream mass media of television and newspapers than either white or coloured people. They get significantly more political information, and information they trust, from community sources such as political meetings and civic organisations. They look

Table 5.11   Information flows (%)

Where do you get most of your information about politics?	Total	White	Black	Coloured
Television	75.7	81.1	54.4	82.1
Newspapers	53.5	63.0	34.5	57.1
Radio	39.5	38.9	41.7	38.8
Political meetings	10.4	3.0	28.3	6.1
Community organisations	5.6	0.4	17.9	2.7
Family	6.9	5.6	10.1	6.1
Friends	9.6	11.7	9.4	8.9
Magazines	8.7	9.6	6.4	9.3

Source: MPD/M&O Survey, Feb. 1994, N = 2,500.

Table 5.12   Influence patterns (%)

Do the following encourage you to vote for a certain party?	Total	White	Black	Coloured
Politicians	26.3	24.1	57.9	14.5
Friends/Colleagues	24.7	15.1	40.8	21.8
Family	23.4	15.1	39.6	20.1
Civics	14.9	0.4	47.5	7.2
Area/Street committees	13.3	2.0	37.4	7.9
Trade unions	12.1	1.6	35.3	6.6
Churches	10.7	3.8	26.0	7.1
Ministers	10.5	3.5	23.9	7.9
Elders	8.8	2.7	24.6	4.7

Source: MPD/M&O Survey, Feb. 1994, N = 2,500.

essentially *outwards* to the community for explicit cues about how to vote: politicians (58 per cent), civics (48 per cent), friends (41 per cent), family (40 per cent), street committees (37 per cent) and trade unions (35 per cent). And when it comes to information and influence patterns, as with the data reported in tables 5.1 through 5.8, one can see far greater similarity between coloured and white voters than between coloureds and blacks.

Another important cleavage was the differing orientation of community organisations. As one analyst recently remarked, for blacks 'the civic was local but the struggle was national. Local urban struggles were first and foremost a mechanism for defining nationhood.'[30] Yet while

Table 5.13   Trust in sources of information

% 'trustworthy'	Total	White	Black	Coloured
Political meetings	23.2	9.6	60.9	13.2
Television	47.9	40.2	58.2	46.7
Community organisations	19.3	11.2	48.7	10.6
Radio	36.0	35.6	46.5	32.0
Family	37.1	38.5	38.5	33.7
Newspapers	23.8	16.6	35.1	20.3
Friends/Colleagues	26.5	29.3	29.3	22.7
Magazines	15.1	10.3	27.9	11.8
Other meetings	10.1	5.9	25.5	5.5
Respected people in community	23.1	22.4	22.4	19.1

Source: MPD/M&O Survey, Feb. 1994, N = 2,500.

Afrikaner nationalism was also characterised by its willingness to sacrifice local interests at the altar of apartheid, the NP always put heavy emphasis on the local party branch as the foundation of its organisational structure. At election time it was the local branch together with other local community structures which mobilised party support. Significantly, qualitative ethnographic research conducted by our MPD fieldworkers during the campaign indicated that coloured NP supporters tended to consider the local or regional battle against the ANC as more important than the national battle. ANC supporters, in contrast, focused on the national battle to the detriment of local organisation and mobilisation.

The role of community organisations and trade unions becomes all the more important when combined with other information provided by our field researchers. One of the ANC's clear advantages in black townships was its tight integration with a wide variety of community structures, especially civics, street committees and self-defence units. This enabled the ANC to be seen to 'deliver the goods' to local residents in terms of confronting authorities over issues such as housing and services. More importantly, this meant that these organisations generally provided the same, reinforcing political messages to black voters. Thus the ANC stood at the top of an apex supported by a web of community structures which acted as informational 'gatekeepers' to black voters. Consequently, black voters were much less likely to be cross-pressured from the political messages they received from the outside world.

Unbanning and after

Because the UDF had generally been seen as a front to demand the return of the liberation movements rather than as a political party in itself, it quickly lost its political relevance once the ANC was unbanned in 1990, and it officially disbanded within a year. However, a glorified interpretation of the UDF's successes in the Western Cape left a powerful impression on the ANC's strategic thinking. Along with a set of simplistic assumptions about 'the unity of the oppressed', 'progressive' political leaders in the Western Cape assumed that the non-racial, activist organisational abilities and strength apparently evidenced through the UDF would automatically translate into mass electoral support for the ANC. Thus the ANC never really believed in the possibility of strong coloured support for the NP until the very end of the campaign, and for many this realisation occurred only once the results were announced.

Yet the merger of UDF structures with the unbanned ANC in the Western Cape was not an easy one. As the ANC began to revive its internal structures, tensions quickly emerged between the largely coloured UDF leadership and structures and the largely black returning exiles and political prisoners. As Allan Boesak noted in 1991, 'For many people, the UDF was an organisation that they had built. In the beginning, the ANC was perceived as an organisation that had come back from exile.' Many UDF activists were sidelined by local black electorates who selected black leaders. Indeed, until late 1993 the Western Cape ANC leadership was dominated by an 'Africanist' grouping headed by the regional secretary Tony Yengeni, and many coloured activists became disenchanted with its leadership.[31]

Nationally, most UDF-affiliated organisations concerned with local development tended to move towards a national civic federation (eventually called the South African National Civics' Organisation, SANCO).[32] In the Western Cape, however, a 1991 attempt to merge the four existing civic umbrella associations, CAHAC (in coloured areas), WCCA, the Western Cape Hostel Dwellers Association and the Western Cape United Squatters Association (which all served black areas) under the SANCO initiative failed due to the historical differences among these organisations and their constituencies. CAHAC remained outside of this structure and eventually joined an alternative and opposing umbrella organisation called the Western Cape Community Organisation (WECCO) in 1993. This organisation was originally headed by Joe Marks, a former vice-president of the UDF, who had left the ANC and defected to the Democratic Party because of the ANC's alleged maltreatment of CAHAC following its decision to stay out of SANCO.[33]

At the level of mass opinion, polls as early as 1991 began sending very negative messages to the ANC about its coloured support. At times the ANC rejected these findings, dismissing them as either government propaganda or methodologically flawed.[34] Yet by late 1991 some in the ANC began to take these problems seriously. Perhaps the frankest admission was made by Mandela himself during the ANC's July 1991 inaugural national conference as he warned that the party could not afford to be content with its low levels of support among non-blacks. In a stunning departure from the concept of non-racialism, he argued that 'The ordinary man, no matter to what population group he belongs, must look to our structures and see that "I, as a coloured man, am represented. I have got Allan Boesak there whom I trust." And an Indian must also be able to say: "There is Kathadra – I am represented."' Yet as Heribert Adam and Kogila Moodley pointed out, the ANC was ill-prepared for such a course of action because its coloured and Indian members generally rejected a role as ethnic representatives.[35]

None the less, Mandela hammered at this theme repeatedly. At the October 1991 ANC Western Cape congress, he argued that the regional predominance of coloureds was not reflected in party leadership or membership and warned that the NP was taking support away from the ANC.[36] Pointing to the polls, he told the regional congress that until they could prove otherwise, they would have to accept coloured NP support as fact. The regional organisation's response was to elect Allan Boesak as chairman, the Muslim leader, Ebrahim Rasool, and Jakes Gerwel, rector of the University of the Western Cape, to top posts.[37] Yet such a move was not uncontroversial, for Boesak had been locked in a bitter struggle with old movement stalwarts such as Trevor Manuel, who argued that Boesak had never accepted the movement's discipline. In fact, Boesak had still not become an official ANC member by the time of its inaugural conference. Boesak responded that the ANC had failed to win coloured support and that its rhetoric praising the SACP and MK was doomed to failure with this electorate.[38] He claimed that these new elections would soothe fears about African domination of the ANC, arguing that 'In the interim period we have almost got to have affirmative actions. . . . We must not only say we are non-racial, we must be seen to be non-racial.' Ironically, following his election, while Boesak did acknowledge the party's problems in attracting coloured support, he also publicly stated that Mandela took 'dubious' polls about coloured support too seriously.[39]

Beyond these moves, initial ANC overtures to the coloured community were weak. Early ANC campaigns were driven from the 'top down' and ignored the local, largely coloured, former-UDF structures. They focused on the charisma of the national ANC, its leaders and its policies. Couched largely in terms of redistribution, they were aimed at mobilising poorer black communities and ignored coloured interests.[40] In fact, in a March 1992 tour of coloured areas in the region, Mandela conceded that the party had been 'preoccupied with Africans and had neglected the coloured people', promising that an ANC government would legalise Muslim weddings.[41] In August of that year, he told a Western Cape audience that 'If you look at the power structure of the ANC you will see it is still run as an organisation fighting for the rights of one ethnic group and not of the whole community. . . . While we say we are non-racialist, the structures don't reflect other sections of the community.'[42] Two months later, internal ANC documents had come to admit that its coloured support was unacceptably low and Mandela continued his pleas to Western Cape leaders to make the organisation more attractive to coloured voters.[43] Yet by April 1993 the polls had not shown much improvement and Allan Boesak bemoaned the 'high-handed' manner in which the ANC had re-established itself in the Western Cape and ignored existing structures.[44] By mid-1993, the ANC claimed to have formed 125 branches in the province and to be in the process of opening another 65 (each with a minimum of 100 members per branch).[45] However, while branches in black townships generally had memberships of around 1,000, those in coloured areas had no more than 150 to 200 members and generally extended no further than the activist community elite.[46]

Another important factor during this crucial period of realignment was the absence of any coloured political party as a credible alternative to the ANC. While the Labour Party had pursued a strategy of resistance and boycotts during the 1970s, its 1983 decision to co-operate and join the Tricameral parliament destroyed its legitimacy in the eyes of many progressives. And for those who accepted its claim that participation was a short-term goal aimed at achieving non-racial representation, the party was undercut and marginalised by F. W. de Klerk's 1990 initiatives. By mid-1991, the NP and LP's transitional and constitutional proposals were virtually indistinguishable.[47] In fact, due to increasing conflicts with party leader Allan Hendrickse, LP MPs began in 1991 to defect to the National Party and the Democratic Party (the same was even true of the opposition in the House of Representatives, the United Democratic Party). By October 1991, the NP held 16 out of the 20 Cape peninsula seats, and by February 1992 they actually controlled a majority in the House of Representatives. In 1993, Hendrickse attempted to form an LP alliance with the ANC, a move opposed by many of the LP's remaining members. In any case, the ANC itself rejected the proposal because of lingering resentments over the LP's participation in the Tricameral system.[48]

Besides attracting LP MPs, the NP also began to open branches and hold rallies in coloured areas. By mid-1991, it had created eight branches in five weeks in Mitchell's Plain, each with more members than the previous *sole* LP local branch.[49] In October, the former LP Finance Minister Reverend Andrew Julies was elected as vice-chairman of the Cape NP. In 1992, de Klerk's first attempt to campaign in a coloured area (Mitchell's Plain) was halted by stone-throwing, ANC-aligned crowds. However, the NP's March 1993 rally in the more controlled Goodwood Showgrounds drew about 10,000 people, mostly coloured. By July, the NP claimed to have around 1,000 branches throughout the Western Cape. Eight months later, the Cape NP leader Dawie de Villiers estimated that 45 per cent of the regional party membership was coloured, absorbed into 545 branches.[50]

The DP also began to make tangible inroads into these communities. Its recruitment efforts in black communities were the object of intimidation and intolerance, often from ANC youth.[51] Yet in October 1991 key coloured leaders such as Richard van der Ross (former rector of the University of the Western Cape) and Norman Daniels (trade unionist and former Cape Town city councillor) were elected onto the party's national council. In September 1992, several prominent members of the Labour Party joined the DP. New branches opened in coloured areas on the Cape flats, and by July 1993 the number of DP Western Cape branches had gone from 14 to 66, growing at two per week. In October 1993, its provincial leader, Hennie Bester, claimed that the DP was the fastest growing party in the province, signing up 1,500 new members each month.[52] By January 1994, DP officials claimed that it was gaining 2,000 to 2,500 members a month in the Western Cape.[53]

However, by August 1993 the DP had begun to encounter serious problems. One regional organiser, who claimed to have been personally responsible for setting up 44 of the 49 new DP branches in coloured areas, defected to the ANC (Joe Marks said he was sacked for 'absconding'). And in September and October the DP began to get intense competition from the Inkatha Freedom Party. A relative newcomer to provincial politics, the IFP targeted recent DP converts and succeeded in enticing many of these people to defect. Virtually the entire branch executive of Blue Downs defected to the IFP, citing white paternalism, and took 500 to 1,000 members with them. Chairman Patrick Damons called the DP 'a party for the upper classes. . . . All they want from coloured people is their votes' and pointed to the fact that most senior posts in the Western Cape DP were filled by whites. He said the party gave priority treatment to Joe Marks ('a form of paternalism') but not to other coloured officials. Claiming that the IFP had assured him that coloureds would be allowed to forge their own political programme within the party, Damons predicted that at least five other Cape Town coloured branches would soon cross over to the IFP, taking with them between 3,500 and 4,000 members.[54]

In fact, by mid-1993, the IFP claimed to have opened 20 new branches in the Western Cape (with membership of at least 100 each) bringing its regional membership close to 10,000 in 50 branches.[55] One IFP official attributed the party's regional successes to its simple message: 'Let the Capies rule the Cape.' By October, they had raised their figures to 13,000 members and 54 branches, to which DP regional organiser Stuart McLoughlin responded, 'There are a lot of exaggerated claims being made. We have found no evidence of even half the support the IFP is claiming.'[56]

One other potential contender for support in the Western Cape was the PAC. With a history of activist support in the Cape Town townships, the PAC was widely seen to have a great deal of potential growth, especially in the large shack communities. Indeed, in 1993, with growing black alienation following the assassination of Chris Hani and a series of ANC negotiating reversals on power-sharing, federalism and allowing the Multi-Party Negotiating Forum to write principles which would bind the Constituent Assembly, PAC prospects appeared to brighten. The year could have been profitably used to build support for the organisation. In fact, a PAC rally in Khayelitsha in June 1993 drew double the attendance (10,000) of a simultaneous ANC–Boesak rally (5,000) in Guguletu.[57]

But such events were rare. At precisely the moment when it could conceivably have capitalised on mass disillusionment with the ANC and built an active support base, the PAC was boycotting the entire negotiations and electoral process. In fact, our MPD community research demonstrated that the PAC never managed to re-establish a serious grass-roots organisational presence in the black community following its unbanning, certainly not one to compete with the ANC. By July 1993, it claimed to have 50 branches in the province,[58] yet our field research indicates that virtually all of these branches were empty shells operating out of people's houses, many operating within an 'underground', bunker mentality.

Campaign Decision-Making

The African National Congress's campaign

As early as June 1993, ANC reviews of commercially sponsored research revealed that its leaders, as opposed to government leaders, were not well trusted or believed by coloured voters.[59] From its own commissioned surveys of February–March and July–August 1993, ANC strategists drew several important lessons for the regional campaign.[60] First of all, the surveys revealed that its support among black voters nationally was solid to overwhelming, and they also estimated black support for the ANC in the Cape Town townships to be between 80 per cent and 93 per cent. ANC support among blacks was weakest among female, rural and less educated voters. However, the surveys also revealed that the NP had done a good job in showing itself to be a reformed multiracial party. Second, there were large numbers of undecided voters, even among blacks, and especially among coloured voters in the Western Cape. Third, there were significant problems in the coloured community, especially in the Western Cape. The main problem seemed to be that the ANC's coloured leaders, whether regional or national, were neither well known nor well trusted among that community. Also, coloured voters tended to associate the ANC with mismanagement and political violence, and were very concerned about its links with Communism. Another negative finding was that the ANC's coloured support base was generally male, educated, urban, and white-collar – not a common profile in that community. The findings also suggested that there would be a high level of coloured abstention on election day.

The surveys also gave strategists information about how to address these problems. The key issues most frequently cited by both black and coloured voters were jobs, political violence and housing. When it came to personalities, it was clear that no other ANC leader came close to Mandela in terms of stature among undecided voters. In fact, Mandela's face was better known than the party's logo. Another important finding which impressed party strategists was that voters, especially blacks, claimed that they formed the bulk of their political opinions on the basis of what they learned from the media.

One direct consequence of the ANC's growing understanding of its problems in the coloured community was the November 1993 selection of Allan Boesak, an otherwise weak and vulnerable candidate, as its standard-bearer in the Western Cape. Yet while the provincial ANC selected Boesak to woo coloured voters (he beat Lerumo Kalako and Tony Yengeni for the position of list leader), it did so under a great deal of internal doubt that his past might provide the NP with a tempting target. Boesak's divorce of his first wife, his leaving the church, and his marriage to a white woman were clear drawbacks to coloured voters. ANC activists thought he was self-important and lacked a clear grip on the issues. In the same elections, Lerumo Kalako ousted the more radical Tony Yengeni as regional secretary, and Chris Nissen was elected as regional deputy secretary, moves which were seen in ANC circles as a positive step towards attracting coloured votes.[61]

The information from the ANC surveys also translated into several specific strategic decisions about how to run the campaign.[62] The polls told campaign planners that Mandela should personify the campaign. He was, therefore, widely used in print advertisements, road shows and rallies. Mandela was used especially heavily in the Western Cape in a direct response to de Klerk's widespread popularity among coloured voters (in fact, the Western Cape received the most visits by the ANC leader).[63] On the other hand, ANC leaders such as Winnie Mandela and Peter Mokaba were deliberately kept out of the Western Cape as far as possible because of their highly negative impact among coloured voters.[64]

More importantly, poll-based conclusions influenced the tone of the ANC campaign. Research findings that people were becoming more optimistic as the election neared meant, according to pollster Stanley Greenberg, that 'an unrelentingly negative campaign might backfire and put the ANC out of synch with the mood of the country.' He warned the ANC of the 'tendency for parties to play out the past rather than the new context that they are in; to get caught up in their personal histories and personal struggles'.[65] Thus, at least until the last few weeks, negative ads focusing on apartheid in general or specific events such as Sharpeville or District Six were relatively absent. According to Ken Modise of Applied Marketing and Communications, a division of Hunt Lescaris which handled ANC advertising, 'it would be patronising to tell black South Africans that they've had a bad life under apartheid. They don't need to be reminded.' At the same time, ANC media adviser Joel Netshitenzhe added that 'We have to acknowledge the National Party has been successful in presenting itself as a transformed multiracial party. FW is not PW. So rather than going back to the evils of apartheid, we have to show that, even now, under the new transformed FW, policies still discriminate against black people.' This translated into an important campaign effort to emphasise that *current* NP policies were racist, had bankrupted the country and had plunged it into violence. One of the main ways in which this was conveyed was by using Mandela himself as the most effective and credible way to attack the NP, and specifically de Klerk. Right from the start of the campaign in November, Mandela launched into vicious attacks on de Klerk as a 'man who does not care about black lives'.[66]

The ANC campaign was also characterised by a heavy emphasis on assuring voters that it was able to assume the responsibilities of government. As Modise noted, 'everybody knows the ANC was a highly effective liberation movement. But will it be an effective government? . . . we had to be serious, to show people that we had the wherewithal to govern.'[67] Thus strategists decided that the election should be fought as a contest of issues and their ability to change society rather than as a 'freedom election'.[68] Greenberg had warned of the potential pitfall of popular mass-based parties who 'tend to think that an election is only about mobilisation and not about persuasion', and whose belief that they hold the moral high ground 'can lead to empty dogma'.[69] As one national ANC MP remarked, candidates were told by campaign officials to avoid negative attacks because the research showed that it made people stop listening.[70]

Significantly, a positive, performance-based campaign was not a foregone conclusion. There were strong pressures in the organisation for bringing the legacy of the past forty years into the campaign and to 'wave the bloody shirt'. As one ANC strategist argued in 1993, 'Emotions are crucial and apartheid must be deployed as an emotional issue – the NP–apartheid connection has to be stressed.'[71] In fact, in early 1993 (before it had begun its extensive polling operation), the ANC Elections Commission had declared that the election could 'be described as a continuation of the contest between apartheid and democracy . . . this election is the liberating event to black communities. It is not about setting up government.'[72] As one campaign official concluded, without Stanley Greenberg (President Clinton's Pollster, hired by the ANC to guide its campaign) and media adviser Frank Greer the ANC would have run a negative campaign based on history and apartheid.[73]

Indeed, the emotions of the past forty years often bubbled to the surface, despite the pollsters' warnings. One notable example was an early February speech in Pochefstroom, where Mandela said that coloured and Indian people who voted for the NP were 'traitors to the revolution'.[74] Indeed, as the campaign wore on, advisers publicly called for the ANC to redirect its Western Cape strategy to focus on NP weaknesses.[75] In the last three weeks of the campaign, the ANC directly attacked the unsuitability for government of Hernus Kriel, NP candidate for premiership, as well as the NP's responsibility for violence and its connection to racism and corruption.

In fact, regional campaign officials had wanted for quite a while to run a separate campaign in the Western Cape aimed at addressing what they saw to be the racism of the coloured community and the NP campaign, as well as to allow them to lay fertile ground in which a positive campaign would take root. These officials pointed out that Greenberg's decision to run a positive campaign was based on focus groups which identified the themes of peace, forgetting the past and reassurances of a better life as key. Yet, they pointed out, in the Western Cape coloured communities the same studies highlighted fears of the ANC. The regional campaign fought a long battle with the national directors over negative ads and leaflets, as well as autonomy over its advertising. One problem was that the ANC was never able to resolve the question of how to run a positive campaign nationally and a negative one regionally. Yet Greenberg also told the Western Cape officials that they would have had to run a negative campaign for eighteen months in order to lay fertile ground. Eventually the regional officials simply ignored national instructions, as much as a way to placate and to galvanise its activists as to convert any voters.[76]

Survey findings also translated into an enormous emphasis on a media-dominated campaign. Yet the Multi–Party Negotiating Forum had agreed to ban television advertising (and only permit radio advertising beginning on 28 March), a decision prompted largely by ANC fears that the NP would have benefited greatly from sponsored television advertising.[77] This meant much more emphasis on newspapers and hard–to–control face-to-face contacts. As Frank Greer observed, 'Newspapers here really set the tone. People pay more attention to print advertising here than in any other country I've worked in.'[78]

This tied in with the ANC's decision to emphasise issues and its competence to govern. The campaign proceeded with a series of print advertisements filled with thick text about party policy stances, which were ultimately intended to send a deeper, much more important message. 'What was being communicated', according to Greer, was 'that they as a party have thought about solutions to South Africa's problems and that they have been willing to present that in a plan.' 'Even if you don't read or can't read the details,' added Greenberg, 'you get the message: the ANC has a plan: it's serious.'[79] Also closely tied to its decision to invest a great deal of resources in a media campaign was the ANC's decision to invest a large amount of energy in a series of 'people's forums'. Here, Mandela or some other top leader would arrive at a meeting organised by local branches with a specific theme (workers, women, squatters, farmers, etc.). These forums gave the ANC greater control over face-to-face contacts as well as providing a photogenic vehicle which would both attract television news (thus providing free airtime and advertising) as well good images and copy for full-page print advertisements. Thus the intended audience was not those in attendance (who were there presumably *because* they already supported the ANC), but those reached through television news and print advertisements stimulated by the events.

Borrowed directly from Bill Clinton's bus campaigns, the media opportunities afforded by the forums were important in order to communicate their real symbolic message of the ANC's accountability, representativeness and accessibility, and rebuild its image as a 'parliament of the people', badly dented during the negotiations process. Rather than making set speeches, the leaders responded to questions from audience representatives who addressed the leaders from podiums of equal height to dramatise an egalitarian atmosphere.[80] These forums were also integrated with the ANC's decision to focus on Mandela. By the end of November, Mandela was already attending three forums a day, stressing the theme, 'Your problem is my problem. Your solution is my solution.'[81] In the Western Cape, COSATU ran a series of 'court forums' in the common areas of public housing complexes in coloured neighbourhoods.

Yet regardless of these strategies, the ANC faced a series of difficulties in attracting coloured votes, some of them self-imposed and some of them structural. One major problem identified by the political scientist Tom Lodge was that ANC rhetoric revealed a 'cultural condescension toward the people it was suppose to attract' by using the term 'so-called coloureds'.[82] And, in contrast to Mandela, who used the Labour Party as a useful ally in multiparty talks, Boesak never could bring himself to accept the LP as a regional ally rather than an 'enemy'. He refused to work with them, arguing that they lacked credibility.[83] Large elements of the ANC regional leadership also suffered from a reluctance, amounting almost to hostility, to think seriously about ethnicity. In a post-election reflection on the provincial campaign, for example, one ANC leader (now a cabinet minister) reaffirmed his belief that there were no such things as ethnic interests, but only class interests.[84] Lodge also notes that ANC campaigners often 'cajoled and threatened their coloured audiences, accusing them of ingratitude and racism'. Allan Boesak declared that coloured people who voted for the NP acted against God's will. And another major ANC coloured leader, Franklin Sonn, threatened one crowd: 'We must not make the same mistake as the brown community in Namibia. When they asked for houses, Nujoma asked: For whom did they vote?'[85] Yet another disaster was Mandela's previously mentioned 'traitor' speech, which was intensely criticised and produced a major backlash.[86]

Another problem was the ANC's inability to establish viable local structures in coloured areas; most were driven by head office. Already in November 1993 one regional strategist admitted that they were 'thinking of suspending the establishment of more branches. Maybe we will just have working groups who have a presence in most places.'[87] The campaign quickly became heavily dependent on activists from the Cape Town head office or Shell House in Johannesburg, who would make sorties to coloured suburbs and rural towns. These activists were generally much too inclined to speak English, the mother tongue of fewer than one-fifth of coloureds.

An even more insurmountable problem was the differing class and cultural interests presented by the black and coloured communities (as revealed by the data reported in tables 5.1 through 5.8). These differences made it difficult to run a common, undifferentiated campaign in both communities. As one regional party strategist observed, while the majority of voters were coloured, the majority of party members were black. This was a difficult balance to maintain and the ANC had a difficult time targeting each community.[88] Nowhere were these differing interests highlighted more than on the issues of housing and affirmative action. ANC canvassers reported that affirmative action and the increasing encroachment of black squatter settlements next to coloured areas made campaigning in those areas very difficult.[89] As one regional organiser admitted after the campaign, it was difficult to explain that affirmative action did not mean replacement of coloured jobs by African jobs.[90] In fact, according to key Western Cape campaign officials, ANC strategy meetings often became very tense because some officials thought that the party was bending over backwards to work with coloured people rather than Africans.[91]

Mandela was repeatedly forced to reassure coloured crowds that their communities had also been the subject of repression, that they had nothing to fear from affirmative action, and, indeed, that they would benefit from it in the form of job opportunities and government contracts for small businesses. These efforts, however, were undercut by private employers who openly stated their preference for Xhosa-speakers. Mandela also argued that coloured people would benefit from housing programmes and pledged to protect houses already earmarked for coloured residents against seizures by black squatters.[92] But this could not undo the harm done by the squatter invasion of a House of Representatives (that is, coloured) housing complex in Delft, which sparked a major political storm. The ANC charged that the NP inspired the event in order to capitalise on coloured fears, and Chris Nissen worried that 'It could create so much division and confusion it will drive people straight into the arms of the Nats.' Boesak personally went to the scene to try to persuade the squatters to leave, and national leaders Walter Sisulu, Steve Tshwete,

Cheryl Carolus and Pallo Jordan flew in from Johannesburg to defuse the problem,[93] though the damage had probably already been done.

In March, the ANC received results of a new regional party survey that showed coloured support had actually decreased slightly since December 1993. According to one provincial campaign official, the national campaign directors then turned down a Cape request to double its organisational size, because they had concluded that the province was a lost cause.[94] Sensing defeat, the regional ANC quickly revamped its Western Cape election strategy, bringing in Mandela and its most popular officials for tours in coloured areas, as well as stepping up door–to–door canvassing in those areas.[95] The ANC also persuaded the prominent coloured leader Franklin Sonn to resign his seat on the South African Broadcasting Corporation (SABC) board and campaign full-time for the party, aiming at more conservative sections of the coloured community. They also opted for full saturation coverage in the Western Cape media, buying three to four full-page advertisements a day, mostly featuring endorsements by prominent coloured and Muslim figures.[96] The tenor of ANC attacks also became shrill. Sonn called on 'all God-fearing, decent and principled people' to help 'in saving this region from the disaster of a Kriel-led National Party government'.[97] In a late trip to the province, Cyril Ramaphosa urged supporters 'to take on the Nats and to expose them for what they are – the same racists of the past who shouted "swart gevaar"'.[98] Boesak stressed that coloureds would remain second-class citizens under the NP despite being the majority in the region. He contrasted an NP-dominated 'island of doom' with an ANC-led 'country of hope'. Under the NP, he argued, 'we'll still be sitting in "hotnotsland" with Baas F. W. and Baas Hernus Kriel and you'll remain the same hotnot [Hottentot] you were before the election.'[99]

Thus, while the NP distributed its infamous 'comic book' suggesting black racism against coloureds, the ANC distributed leaflets containing a cartoon showing Hernus Kriel welcoming right-wingers, Third Force members, the AWB and volkstaaters into the Western Cape while local residents ran in panic. The text said that he would give jobs to civil Co-operation Bureau (CCB) agents and hit squad generals, and that the AWB would flock to the Cape.[100] ANC activists also circulated copies of an old Afrikaans weekly containing alleged statements by the President's wife, Marike de Klerk, that coloured people were 'leftovers' and 'non-people' and a 'negative group'. And in the final week of the campaign, an unsourced poster widely seen on Cape Town streets read: 'Your vote is your secret, but not before God. Don't vote National Party.'

The National Party's campaign

The NP began its campaign with a daunting task and low morale. In November 1993, its chief provincial strategist, Melt Hamman, MP for Ceres, bemoaned that

The party is at its lowest ebb. . . . Dawie de Villiers just told me that all the attempts to attract black leaders as allies have failed. The task is now to get black support at the grass-roots level. But the task is complicated by the fact that the party and the government are seen as inextricably linked to each other. When the NP held a meeting with some squatter leaders they asked: 'Who is governing the country? Why are ANC-aligned organisations like SANCO and POPCRU [Prison Officers and Police Civil Rights Union] allowed to call the shots?'

According to him, the NP's 'first prize' in the Western Cape was to get at least 55 per cent of the provincial vote, and second, to draw enough provincial support to achieve de Klerk's 'first prize' of getting 40 per cent nationally. He calculated that the second task required 25 per cent black support and 60 per cent white and coloured support in the Western Cape.[101]

At the organisational level, the NP's plan was to bring coloureds and 'uncontaminated' black leaders into the party structures, as well as to link up with potentially well-disposed organisations tired of the disruption and violence which accompanied ANC campaigns (such as Zionist churches and squatter leaders). Yet the party also had to accommodate several ineffectual politicians presently in its ranks, especially former Tricameral parliamentarians. In addition, its new black candidates such as the squatter leaders Mali Hoza and Johnson Ngxobongwana were long suspected of collusion with the security and intelligence forces in local township conflicts. Hamman admitted that 'We have to take our chances with them, but there is the danger of losing blacks supporting other squatter leaders if we draw those two to our bosom.'[102]

On the mass level, party-sponsored research helped NP campaign stategists draw the following lessons.[103] First of all, it was clear that President de Klerk's popularity far exceeded that of his party among all groups. Then, it was evident that there was a clear basis of support in the Western Cape, especially among coloured voters, but the NP also knew it had to overcome a strong tendency towards abstentionism among the coloured electorate. Yet the NP also remained serious about obtaining a large slice of the black vote nationally. Internal surveys indicated a willingness among many blacks to support the party; many believed that the ANC had made too many promises and were now doubting their ability to deliver. The largest potential area for attracting black support to the NP was among women and rural people. However, a key problem was that only one-quarter of black voters believed the NP's claims that it had changed itself.

From this information, campaign strategists drew the following implications.[104] Most importantly, the NP decided (as with the ANC) to focus the campaign around their presidential candidate (the campaign theme was 'Vote F. W. de Klerk, Vote NP'). The party continued a tactic it had

adopted during its 1992 referendum campaign and eschewed its traditional 'town-hall' meetings. Rather, it used de Klerk in 'American-style'
rallies and media roadshows. In other parts of the country these were
largely focused on black rural areas. In the Western Cape, however, few
blacks actually lived on the land. Thus most of de Klerk's time was spent
in the coloured community. He was used heavily in the Western Cape,
especially from January to March, going on a number of successful and
enthusiastic roadshows in coloured Cape flats suburbs. As with the ANC's
people's forums, the roadshows were also a vehicle which would attract
free television news coverage by creating one publicity event after another and creating an image of widespread support and goodwill. Significantly, Hernus Kriel never shared the platform with de Klerk when the
President campaigned in the province (in contrast with other parties'
practices). Indeed, de Klerk dominated the Western Cape campaign to
the exclusion of Kriel.[105]

Like the ANC, the NP also devoted a great deal of resources to a
media campaign, especially radio (featuring an advertising emphasis on
black women).[106] Because the NP was never able to organise effectively
in black areas in the Western Cape, advertising was immensely important
and bore the brunt of the party's attempt to change its image among black
voters. Nationally, media events put de Klerk in the company of traditional leaders and cheering black supporters, and a late, intensive print
advertising campaign featured endorsements from ordinary black members
and was intended to reassure blacks that there were indeed black NP
supporters. As Eldad Louw of Saatchi and Saatchi put it, the purpose was
to show them that 'they are not alone, that there are others who feel the
same way as they do'.[107]

The NP also decided that it did not want the election to be a
retrospective referendum either on apartheid or on the constitution-
making process, and that it had to convince voters that the election was
about the future and not the past. This meant demonstrating that apartheid was already over, that freedom had already been delivered by the
NP, and that the NP had truly changed. Prior to the campaign, the NP
was usually hesitant to make blanket apologies for apartheid, and usually
wanted to link this with cautions not to dwell on the past. Once the
campaign began, however, de Klerk made sincere and frequent apologies.

The main aim was to force a choice about which party would be most
trustworthy to run the government. This meant painting a stark choice
between a new, competent and trustworthy NP and an old, dangerous
ANC that could not govern. The NP highlighted the ANC's role in
violence, sanctions and strikes which affected the economy, education
and medical care. They also stressed the ANC's relationship with Communism and atheism. They would then contrast these things to their
own role in building roads, clinics and schools, stressing their ability
to maintain prosperity, stability, security and the place of Afrikaans.[108]

Significantly, in contrast to the ANC's difficulties in devising a common set of messages which would attract both black and coloured voters, NP strategists felt that they could direct the same messages at both white and coloured voters because the profiles of these communities resembled one another so much.

The Western Cape party was keen to give the campaign a specific regional flavour which transcended the white and coloured communities. Kriel was targeted towards lower-income groups to whom he was presented as an outgoing Minister of Police and a man not soft on crime. He repeatedly committed the party to protecting personal security and painted the ANC as promoting violence and intimidation. Press advertisements featured pictures of Table Mountain and 'Cape Coon' marches. They proclaimed 'Let's keep it [the Cape] peaceful. Let's keep it NP country.' In an open letter to coloured voters, de Klerk waxed nostalgic about a range of regional traditions (like rugby and 'snoek runs'), concluding that 'The ANC and its communist allies are a danger to the things that are so dear to us. That's why we must stop them.'

However, while surveys helped shape NP strategy, other developments on the ground often interfered with their plans. First of all (as will be seen in the next section), the NP was never able to organise publicly or campaign in the black Western Cape townships.[109] And while surveys might have told the NP to apologise as much as possible to blacks for the pains of apartheid in order to demonstrate its sincerity, de Klerk's apologies seemed to be most frequent and most heartfelt in front of coloured audiences.[110] Another major problem, one frequently highlighted by the ANC, was that while the racial nature of the NP's potential electorate might have shifted, the composition of its party leadership had not. Indeed, the NP reserved 60 per cent of its most likely winning positions for former MPs and other old-guard loyalists on its nine regional lists. In the end, 60 per cent of NP National Assembly candidates were white and of the top ten candidates in the Western Cape lists for national and provincial assemblies, only the second and third members were not white.[111] The final Cape Town rally was a good example of the dual nature of the party. The wildly enthusiastic, almost exclusively coloured crowd of 10,000 infused the event with jokes, songs and rhythms quite unlike the staid and purposeful NP meetings of old; yet the speakers (de Klerk, Kriel and the Cape NP leader, Dawie de Villiers) remained all white.

Winning a large share of the coloured vote was of the utmost importance to the NP. Canvassers focused almost all their efforts on coloured voters, virtually ignoring white areas.[112] The local branches were the lynchpin of the process, and were assigned the tasks of scouting the environment, directing canvassing and voter education, launching youth and women actions, co-ordinating transport, and arranging road shows for visiting party leaders. Two months before the election day, the ANC admitted that they were not only up against the *swart gevaar* (black peril) but a well-organised NP as well.[113]

Yet the party was still concerned late in the campaign about the volatility of coloured support and the probability of low turnout (expecting about 60 per cent compared to 70 per cent for whites and 60 per cent for blacks in Western Cape).[114] The paramount importance of this task translated into some decidedly nasty campaign tactics in the province (which contrasted sharply with an otherwise subtle and well-thought-out campaign). Martinus van Schalkwyk slammed Mandela's 'traitor' speech as a 'subtle threat' from a party that was actually a black party which favoured Xhosa-speakers.[115] Rallies featured increasing assertions that the ANC was a 'Xhosa and Communist party' alien to regional traditions. They emphasised that the NP was rapidly becoming a brown party geared to protect Western values.[116] Posters reading 'Stop the comrades!' were visible throughout coloured neighbourhoods.

The NP quickly responded to the Delft squatter invasion by placing an ad in Afrikaans newspapers warning that 'Your home is not safe under the ANC. The ANC is not yet part of the government and already its supporters are taking houses which belong to legitimate owners.'[117] At meetings in coloured rural towns, the NP minister, Abe Williams, warned audiences that affirmative action would mean that blacks received jobs first and that coloureds would now take a back seat to black people.[118]

The NP also played on growing fears in the coloured community of Mitchell's Plain stemming from a string of child murders, reputedly carried about by a black abductor. A late March NP advertisement showing a clearly darkened identikit version of the so-called 'station strangler' read 'Can you imaging the Cape Strangler having the vote? The ANC and the DP can,' referring to both those parties' support for prisoners' right to vote. Perhaps its ugliest move was the infamous NP 'comic book' (actually a photo magazine, of which 80,000 copies were printed). Its theme was a coloured family debating how to vote, and it presented a dismal picture of life under an ANC government, with young black thugs preventing elderly women from going to church. In the most memorable section of its thoroughly negative and racist strain was a frame in which the family dog mused that the radical phrase: 'Kill a Boer, kill a farmer' could become 'Kill a farmer, kill a coloured.' The Independent Electoral Commission, seized of the case by an ANC complaint, delivered an interdict on the NP and confiscated all remaining copies (only, however, after 70,000 copies had been distributed).[119]

The Democratic Party's campaign

The DP clearly understood that its best hope lay in the Western Cape. Yet its early boasts that it would win the Western Cape were later downgraded to statements that they would hold the balance of provincial power. Still, it expected to come out of the election as an influential regional actor. It led the drive for the double ballot, and in February 1993 the local DP leader, Hennie Bester, declared that its adoption 'virtually assured' that the DP would be one of the two largest parties in the Western Cape.[120] He then told the press that in the event of a hung parliament, he would bargain with the NP and ANC separately for at least two cabinet seats among the police, trade and industry, and economic development portfolios, as well as sounding out which party was willing to push for greater provincial powers. He added that it was impossible to predict which way their support would go.[121]

By the end of March 1994, the party's 'tracking research' (based apparently on canvassing reports rather than systematic surveys) told it that it had the firm support of 15 to 20 per cent of coloured voters, with an additional 30 per cent of that group up for grabs. Its opinion polls also found that 6 per cent of blacks were not prepared to vote for either the ANC or PAC and therefore could be ripe for persuasion if only the DP could gain access to them.[122] Party strategists remained optimistic about their chances right up until the election, pointing to soft support for the ANC and NP and the large amount of undecided votes. Indeed, they were buoyed by late poll findings prominently featured in the *Sunday Times* purporting to find a doubling of DP support in the Western Cape. Even the ANC and NP became concerned about a late DP surge. While they had always urged voters to focus on a choice between them and not to 'waste' their vote on the 'irrelevant' DP,[123] they nevertheless both launched intense attacks on the DP in late March following the publication of the new polls.[124] One NP ad showing a young woman read: 'Could you look her in the eye and tell her you're giving her rapist the vote? The DP can.' Remarkably, the ad singled out the DP even to the exclusion of the ANC, where an ad the previous week showing the 'station strangler' had been targeted on both the DP and ANC.[125] Another late advertisement claimed that the DP was content to be a 'minor opposition party, however weak and ineffectual'.[126] In fact the DP was hoping for much more than that and the party's poor final election results gave quite a traumatic shock to many top leaders.[127]

The party's most important strategic decision was to steer an unmistakably centrist course between the ANC and the NP. This was best exemplified by an ad with the DP logo positioned clearly in the middle, with text on the left saying 'If the left get in, there'll be nothing right,' and text to its right reading 'If the right get in, there'll be nothing left.' Such a decision, however, was not always obvious. Since the de Klerk reforms, several DP MPs from its 'progressive' wing had strongly urged the party to move to the left and possibly even form an alliance with the ANC. Indeed, just prior to the start of constitutional negotiations in late 1991, the DP was willing to attend the 'Patriotic Front' conference – until they were 'disinvited' by one of the conference co-convenors, the

Azanian People's Organisation (a unilateral move which got AZAPO thrown out of the PF). At the same time, several MPs led by Tony Leon openly suggested that the party disband and join with more liberal members of the NP to form a new party with a new name under the leadership of F. W. de Klerk. The party ultimately decided to maintain the centre course, which resulted in five MPs bolting and representing the ANC in the final year of parliament. De Beer and the DP began to take a decidedly strong anti-ANC tack at their party congress in late 1993.

One important constraint on the DP campaign was the limited size of its budget (R11 million), which was only slightly bigger than the ANC's budget for posters alone. Its Western Cape campaign focused on 'leadership visits' for most of the early going, rather than the roadshows of the ANC and NP. Once they did begin, DP roadshows consisted of personal and rented vans and pick-up trucks with small loudspeakers. Rather than large venue events, the party concentrated on personal contacts and small group canvassing.[128]

The DP's advertising campaign targeted middle-class people who would not vote ANC yet were anxious about the alternative of voting NP to create a strong opposition. Advertising consultant Carolyn Wibberly of Jupiter Drawing Room Agency said the goal was to make those people reconsider the DP as a credible opponent to the ANC.[129] In sharp contrast to both the ANC and the NP, the DP's national leader, Zach de Beer, was clearly kept in the background.[130] Key themes explained that proportional representation eliminated the idea of a wasted vote, emphasised its success at constitutional talks, and portrayed both the NP and the ANC as corrupt yet in bed with each other. They emphasised that they alone could be entrusted with providing effective opposition to an ANC-led government and with protecting South Africans from the 'abuse of power'. The campaign was intentionally strident (one controversial poster read 'We never killed anybody, only apartheid') in order to break – what journalist Mark Gevisser called – its 'namby-pamby image'.[131]

Yet their advertising campaign was far from consistent. In response to an alarming February decline in support (a recent *Argus* poll had given it 3 per cent nationally, with virtually no black support), the DP shifted its advertising campaign to focus on its 'progressive' image and on Helen Suzman; it was apparently aimed at black and coloured voters old enough to remember the Progressive Federal Party's stands against apartheid, as well as to make the point that small parties could still make a difference.[132] In the last two weeks, the party again shifted its focus to law and order. Utilising images of Tony Leon being chased off the campus at the University of the Western Cape, the new theme focused on what voters now cited as the most important problem, crime and violence. In speeches and ads, it pointed to the ANC's vilification of the police, as well as the government's release of 10,000 prisoners from overcrowded jails. The DP came out in favour of an enlarged police force.[133] As election day neared, yet another new theme took advantage of growing perceptions of an overwhelming ANC victory and emphasised that every DP vote simultaneously decreased the size of the ANC majority.[134]

The Freedom Front's campaign

With the combination of its late start and the relatively liberal culture of white politics in the Cape, one would not have expected much of a Freedom Front campaign in the province. Yet once organised, the FF received a wave of calls from English-speaking voters who were so impressed with Constand Viljoen's television appearances and its party advertising that they initiated canvassing and leaflet drops in Cape Town's southern suburbs.[135] Significantly, officials in the regional party observed that they received many enquiries from coloured voters and felt that they could have attracted significant support from conservative elements in the coloured community, linking up with the separatist Cape Republic Organisation. They claim, however, that this was vetoed by national headquarters. National constitutional negotiators had agreed to count the provincial FF vote as a referendum on Afrikaner self-determination and a *volkstaat*, and de Klerk had warned Viljoen that if he campaigned among coloureds (or Indians) the FF's total vote would not be counted towards that goal.

The Pan Africanist Congress's campaign

The PAC ran an ill-starred campaign. Late out of the blocks, it was underfinanced, understaffed and hopelessly disorganised. The campaign had virtually no administrative support, with no visible, formal offices in the townships and a provincial headquarters in shambles. Its Western Cape campaign was also significantly hobbled, once it began, by police investigation and detention of key local leaders in relation to the late December massacre at the Heidelberg Tavern in Cape Town.

Our MPD field researchers also reported that the PAC's decision in early 1994 to suspend the armed struggle alienated many of its young, activist supporters. Followed quickly by meetings in support of a double ballot between Clarence Makwetu and, first, Zach de Beer and the DP, and second, Chief Buthelezi and the IFP (Makwetu even held hands with Buthelezi!), these actions cost the PAC leadership dearly among its activist supporters. Makwetu and Benny Alexander were seen as too moderate and to have acted without proper consultation. Yet it was precisely such activists who might have been counted on to organise and mobilise those township residents predisposed to vote for the PAC and get them to the polls on election day (the February MPD/M&O poll did show around 13 per cent black support for the PAC). The *coup de grâce* was the late defection of key squatter and youth leaders (such as Jeffrey Nongwe), who deserted the PAC candidate list for the ANC.

A free and fair election?

While events in KwaZulu-Natal grabbed most of the headlines concerning the fairness and freeness of the 1994 elections, developments in the Western Cape merit a closer inspection. First of all, popular attitudes in the province did not lay a firm basis for any real optimism about a free and fair campaign. The MPD/M&O survey first posed a fairly abstract question asking people whether any particular party should be prevented from holding meetings and seeking support in 'their' area. Of blacks, 14 per cent thought it was right to do so (as did 5 per cent of whites and coloureds), yet 70 per cent thought it was wrong. However, a sterner test consisting of a widely used 'content-controlled' measure first asked people for the party to which they were most opposed (table 5.14) and then asked them whether they would allow members of that party to exercise a range of civil liberties and civil rights.[136] Tables 5.15 and 5.16

Table 5.14   Least-liked political party (%)

Least-liked party	Total	White	Black	Coloured
ANC	26.4	26.2	1.6	36.3
Conservative Party	22.2	6.8	24.6	26.8
Democratic Party	1.6	0.0	5.0	0.8
Inkatha Freedom Party	14.3	2.0	43.4	7.3
National Party	5.9	0.7	17.5	3.1
Pan Africanist Congress	19.9	60.9	2.9	11.8

Table 5.15   Attitudinal intolerance towards the 'least-liked group': civil liberties

% who would not allow a member of their least-liked group to . . .	Total	White	Black	Coloured
Give a speech in your area that criticises your party	46.1	31.4	61.0	45.5
Visit people to enrol support for that party	36.2	23.5	51.2	35.0
Hold a public protest in your town	43.5	50.8	51.0	41.0

Source: MPD/M&O Survey, Feb. 1994, N = 2,500.

Table 5.16   Attitudinal intolerance towards the 'least-liked group': civil rights

% who would not allow a member of their least-liked group to . . .	Total	White	Black	Coloured
Teach in a school in your area	46.2	56.2	42.1	44.2
Be associated with your friends	34.7	33.8	38.4	33.6
Live in your neighbourhood	30.1	26.3	34.2	29.9
Operate a business in your neighbourhood	31.2	19.7	39.3	32.2

Source: MPD/M&O Survey, Feb. 1994, N = 2,500.

reveal a wide range of attitudinal intolerance from people in the Western Cape towards their 'least liked group'.

Significantly, most people's least-liked group was not a fringe political movement (such as the AWB) but a mainstream political party: black voters were most opposed to the IFP, the CP and the NP (in that order); coloureds (significantly) to the ANC, the CP and the PAC; and whites to the PAC and ANC.[137] We also found important differences between racial groups with regard to voters' willingness to allow members of their least-liked groups to canvass for support or to criticise their favourite parties in their neighbourhoods. Black voters were much more likely to say they would not allow these activities, all of them crucial to a free and fair election campaign. Yet we need to be cautious about overinterpreting these results since political differences seem to explain as much as race. In our two surveys, 54 per cent and 65 per cent of those who intended to vote for the DP were *willing* to allow their opponents to speak and canvass. Respectively, and surprisingly, this was also true of 72 per cent on each occasion of those planning to vote IFP (virtually all IFP supporters in the province were white). Indeed, NP (30 per cent and 39 per cent) and ANC (30 per cent and 42 per cent) voters were relatively similar. PAC and CP supporters were the most intolerant.

Interestingly, racial differences were much less significant for the final measure of civil liberties (the willingness to allow your least-liked group to protest in your own area) – whites and blacks were equally intolerant. And racial differences were less pronounced across four items measuring the enjoyment of civil rights and other social freedoms. In this case, whites were more likely than blacks to say they would not allow a member of their least-liked group to teach in a neighbourhood school. With regard to political preferences, the small group of IFP supporters were far more likely to be tolerant of opponents associating with their friends and living and operating businesses in their areas (with scores ranging from 72 per cent to 83 per cent). DP supporters were consistently tolerant across the entire range of items. CP voters (and, to a lesser extent, PAC supporters) were consistently the most intolerant.

Probably the most important conclusion is that with the exception of these very small numbers of IFP and DP voters, nowhere did we witness high degrees of attitudinal tolerance in the Western Cape. Voters across the province were relatively intolerant, though levels were generally higher in the black community, especially among PAC voters. While some might question the generalisability of these responses since they were collected against the backdrop of an intensive campaign for a 'founding election', they were largely consistent with those measured four years ago in the Cape Town area.[138] The relevance of these responses is reflected in the ability of the PAC and AZAPO student organisations (PASO and AZASM) to launch a sustained campaign in 1993 aimed at driving white teachers and professionals from Cape Town townships. It was during this campaign that the much-pubicised murder took place of Amy Biehl, a white American exchange student, by black youths.

Furthermore, other questions revealed that these attitudes were not merely contextual or hypothetical. Tables 5.17 through 5.19 report responses to a series of more specific questions concerning perceived political freedom during the campaign. First, a significant portion of blacks said it was difficult or impossible to disagree with the electoral messages coming from important and trusted community sources (ranging from 40 per cent to 27 per cent depending on the source). Second, a significant fraction (13.8 per cent) of black voters felt undue pressure on

Table 5.17 Pressure from various sources (results given only for those sources chosen as a source of influence by over 20 per cent)

% saying it is difficult or impossible to disagree with these sources about politics	Total	White	Black	Coloured
Politicians	35.6	15.6	38.5	–
Friends/Colleagues	30.1	–	27.3	19.2
Family	23.9	–	33.6	18.0
Civics	–	–	30.0	–
Area/Street committees	–	–	37.7	–
Trade unions	–	–	36.4	–
Churches	–	–	40.3	–
Ministers	–	–	33.0	–
Elders	–	–	31.1	–

Source: MPD/M&O Survey, Feb. 1994, N = 2,500.

Table 5.18　Pressure to support a party you don't support? (%)

	Total	White	Black	Coloured
Yes, a lot	2.9	0.7	7.6	1.9
Yes, to some extent	4.8	3.1	6.2	4.9
No	84.9	95.0	77.3	84.1
Don't know	4.7	0.7	5.0	6.0
Refuse to answer	2.7	0.5	3.8	3.0

Source: MPD/M&O Survey, Feb. 1994, N = 2,500.

Table 5.19　Treatment of dissident opinion (%)

If a person supports a different political party from neighbours, how would they treat him/her?	Total	White	Black	Coloured
Tough treatment	8.5	6.4	11.4	8.2
Toleration	62.0	80.8	60.6	55.7
Don't know	29.5	12.8	28.1	36.1

Source: MPD/M&O Survey, Feb. 1994, N = 2,500.

them to vote for a party which they did not support. Finally, relatively low proportions of black (60 per cent) as well as coloured (58 per cent) citizens could say with confidence that people expressing dissident political opinions would be tolerated by their neighbours (most of the remaining respondents were uncertain about the fate of such people, although, significantly, 11 per cent and 8 per cent of these two groups felt that such people would be ill-treated).

What were the behavioural consequences of such attitudes with respect to the 1994 election and campaign? Table 5.20 reports available data from the Western Cape IEC for a four-week period during the height of the campaign to indicate how far parties were able to organise and have their messages heard (which could be conceived as a measure of the freedom of electoral speech). In general, about 85 per cent of all scheduled campaign events proceeded peacefully in the Western Cape (and the collected data reported here are not significantly different from IEC experience before or after this period). The ANC attracted somewhat more disruptions and obstructions of their rallies and meetings than the NP (most of these occurred at large, open-air rallies in coloured Cape Town suburbs). For such a small party, the DP attracted a great deal of attention. It was harassed and chased off the campus of the University of the Western Cape (UWC) twice. Following the first incident involving a DP Youth information table on campus, the UWC student representative council launched a 'mass action' campaign against the DP; it led 3,000 students in a march on an IEC tribunal called to adjudicate the conflict, and various peace monitors had to form a human chain in order to allow DP officials to leave the premises through the crowd. The second time, students prevented Tony Leon from delivering a scheduled speech despite protestations from UWC's electoral officer, Colin Bundy, from the senior ANC member, Kader Asmal, and the rector, Jakes Gerwel. This did not prevent the students from subsequently – and literally – chasing Leon off the campus.

Yet while around four-fifths of all scheduled campaign events proceeded 'without incident', it is significant to note that the probability of such an event passing off peacefully fell dramatically once the supporters of opposing parties were present. In fact, of those events recorded by the IEC where opponents are known to have been present, only around one-half went off peacefully. Again, the most raucous and contested events were NP and ANC open-air rallies in coloured urban areas around Cape Town where appearances by de Klerk and Mandela attracted large crowds as well as significant numbers of protesters and hecklers.

Yet the data in table 5.20 fail to reveal several important points. Because IEC monitors could not report on events which were never held, or never scheduled, this data set suffers from a severe 'positivity bias'. In other words, the data do not speak about 'the dog that didn't bark'. More to the point, the IEC simply had no evidence of the NP or DP being able to hold a rally of any kind in a black township anywhere in the province. Neither were the NP and DP able to organise or campaign publicly in black townships in the Western Cape. NP officials did arrange clandestine township meetings through community and squatter leaders, advertising them only by word of mouth due to fears

Table 5.20   Campaign events, Western Cape Province, 21 March to 4 April 1994 (no. and %)

	Minor obstruction	Major obstruction	Minor disruption	Major disruption	Without incident
ANC	19	1	13	4	155 (83%)
NP	7	1	5	5	70 (90%)
DP	3	0	2	2	20 (80%)
PAC	0	0	0	0	10 (100%)
All parties	34 (9%)	2 (0.05%)	20 (5%)	16 (4%)	318 (85%)

Source: IEC Western Cape (Information Analysis Department, Monitoring Directorate).

about security. On other occasions, they transported people out of the townships to attend meetings in other areas. But they had absolutely no organisational structure in the townships, and were forced to operate out of headquarters in urban Cape Town. DP organisers worked 'under-ground' and mostly on a one-to-one basis. They refused to send cam-paigners into the townships for fear of their lives. In one situation, a DP official was forced to flee his area and take up residence with party members elsewhere out of fear for his life. Indeed, during one trip into a small squatter camp outside the Cape peninsula town of Noordehoek, DP officials were knifed and the DP list leader, Hennie Bester, had to be spirited out of the area.

Thus places like Khayelitsha, Nyanga, Crossroads, Langa and Guguletu were, to all intents and purposes, 'no go' areas for these parties. The consequences of this were fairly stark: what this meant was that two out of the three largest political parties in the province were denied personal access to almost one-quarter of the provincial electorate. Furthermore, the ANC claimed that it was systematically denied access to major wine and fruit farms employing large numbers of coloured and black workers (around 200,000 in total). IEC investigations did find that there were indeed several problems, though these seemed to be more random than systematic. In fact, many farmers initiated voter education programmes, if for no other reason than their assumption that their labourers were all likely to vote NP. Yet another problem uncovered by the IEC as well as by our MPD research was the use of gangs in coloured areas by both the NP and the ANC in order to harass political opponents intimidating canvassers and tearing down campaign signs.

In addition, the increasingly nasty campaign (especially charges of racism) fed a climate of heightening inter-racial hostility in Cape Town. Racially based fears increased and race relations became extremely fragile. MPD field researchers recorded a significant increase in vulgar racist talk and graffiti in coloured towns during the final weeks of the campaign. To demonstrate the ease with which just one incident could turn these fears into overt hostilities, one needs only to look to the gang rape in late March of a coloured woman on a commuter train, allegedly by black youths, an incident which resulted within minutes in hundreds of coloured people lining the tracks and stoning all trains bound for the black townships.

Voter Reactions to the Campaign

Now that we have examined the prevailing political culture of the province and detailed the political parties' campaigns, the next question is how the region's voters reacted to those campaigns. Table 5.21 displays the final election results in the Western Cape.[139] How can we best

Table 5.21   Provincial election results of major parties by group (%)

	Total	White	Black	Coloured
NP	53.3	72.7	1.6	68.7
ANC	33.0	3.5	80.2	24.6
DP	6.6	12.5	0.6	5.3
FF	2.1	7.0	0.0	0.0
IFP	0.6	3.9	0.1	0.2
PAC	0.1	0.0	5.8	0.3

account for the patterns? Two questions seem most relevant. First, while the voting patterns appear to be the result of a 'racial census', as proclaimed by a wide range of post-election literature (at least for black and white voters), is there evidence that race or ethnicity were the driving motivations behind individual votes; or did race play a more mediated and indirect role, merely by shaping voters' cultural and socioeconomic locations in society and thereby influencing their world-views and specific attitudes, which were themselves much more direct influences on the vote?

Second, how can we explain the apparent paradox of the coloured vote: how is it that formerly oppressed people voted in large numbers for the political party which was directly responsible for immeasurable harm to their social and economic well-being in the past? To be sure, this is not a unique phenomenon. The former military dictator of Chile, Augosto Pinochet, received considerable support from the very people he harmed, and former Communists have been returned to seats, or even to power in some East European legislatures despite the repressive record of the previous Communist regimes. None the less, the fact that the large majority of coloureds were swimming against the twin tides of 'liberation' and colour requires some further elaboration.

We will turn for evidence to two surveys done for the MPD by Market & Opinion Surveys, one in November–December 1993 (N = 3,432) and the second in February 1994 (N = 2,500). We shall also draw on a smaller survey (N = 400) conducted by the South African Broadcasting Corporation (SABC) during the period 12–16 March.

A racial census?

South Africa qualifies as the most divided society in the world if only because it was historically the only one in which citizens' legal status was statutorily defined by race.[140] And as table 5.21 shows, at least for black

Table 5.22   Racial bases of provincial party support (%)

	NP	ANC	DP	FF	IFP	PAC
White	32.3	3.1	50.8	100.0	90.9	0.0
Black	0.5	51.5	1.6	0.0	0.0	84.6
Coloured	67.1	45.8	47.5	0.0	9.1	15.4

and white voters, the election indeed appears to have been a census: that is, a registration of birth and identity rather than an exercise in choice. Yet if the importance of race emanated from the role given to it by apartheid, one might have expected the election to pit the coloured and black victims of apartheid equally against their former white oppressors. This did not occur. Moreover, the 'racial census' model has two other deficiencies. First, coloureds (like Indian voters in Natal) did not cast their votes monolithically for one party, as did blacks and whites, and as the 'racial census' model would suggest. Second, viewed from the perspective of party support bases (table 5.22), the three largest parties did not derive an overwhelming proportion of their support from any single racial group (though the three smallest certainly did).

A cultural explanation

Needless to say, the role of race or ethnicity is a highly mixed and complex one. Race obviously plays a central role in determining a whole range of citizen opportunities, constraints and behaviours. Yet it does not determine everything. As we saw earlier (see tables 5.1 through 5.8), far more cultural affinities appear to have developed between coloured and white voters than between coloured and black. From this perspective, one might expect to explain the election along these cultural lines. If this occurred, one would expect to find similarities in voting behaviour along linguistic or religious lines which cut across racial lines.

However, looking to a question on party preference from the February MPD/M&O survey,[141] NP performance among coloured Afrikaans-speakers (51 per cent) differed little from that among coloured English-speakers (46 per cent). For the ANC, there was virtually no difference (20 per cent and 19 per cent).[142] Moreover, although the NP did well among coloured adherents of the family of Dutch Reformed churches, it did not perform significantly better than its overall performance in the coloured community. For instance, it was the preferred party of 52 per cent of the coloured sister church of the Dutch Reformed Church, the Dutch Reformed Mission Church. Yet it was preferred by 50 per cent of all coloured voters. Indeed it did slightly better among coloured Catholics (54 per cent) and much better among New Apostolics

(63 per cent) and Lutherans (77 per cent)[143] than it did among the mainstream Dutch Reformed Church adherents. Such data do not support the notion, beloved of press commentators, of white and brown Afrikaners bound together by their common Calvinist heritage.

Yet when questions were posed in a different manner, it appears that some aspects of cultural identity clearly did make a difference. The SABC survey of early March asked coloured people whether they felt closer to whites or to blacks. Of those who felt closer to whites, 81 per cent supported the NP and 5 per cent the ANC. Among those who felt closer to neither group, the margin was still 50 per cent NP to 11 per cent ANC. Only among those who felt closer to blacks did the ANC come out ahead (48 per cent to 31 per cent).[144]

Class

Another approach to these voting patterns might argue that the effect of race on the vote was indirect rather than direct. Through its determining effect on social location under apartheid, race shaped the larger class structures, economic incentives and life chances which themselves might more directly relate to voting behaviour (see tables 5.1 through 5.16). Significantly, the MPD data revealed a strong relationship between preferred party and joint monthly household income (table 5.24). While these relationships remained within each race group, they did so with varying strengths and with differing directions. For example, while the income–party relationship among the Western Cape public as a whole was strong and linear, as it also was among white voters as a group, among black and coloured voters it tended to be curvilinear and slightly weaker (especially for blacks).

We also saw (table 5.25) a significant and moderate relationship between employment status and party preference for provincial voters, especially for the NP and ANC. In the black community, ANC support was fairly stable, wavering by only six percentage points between the unemployed (77 per cent) and fully employed (71 per cent). Among

Table 5.23 Coloureds: which group do you feel closer to? (%)

	Support ANC	Support NP
To whites	5	81
To blacks	31	48
To neither	11	50

Source: SABC Survey, 12–16 Mar. 1994, N = 400.

Table 5.24   Joint monthly household income and party support (%)

	R0 to R199	R200 to R999	R1,000 to R2,000	R3,000 to R4,000	R5,000+
All voters					
ANC	59	42	29	21	19
DP	3	3	4	11	12
NP	22	31	45	50	58
PAC	6	8	5	2	–
White voters					
ANC	33	9	3	4	5
DP	17	25	14	14	13
NP	50	56	58	63	69
Black voters					
ANC	84	73	72	73	100
NP	–	2	1	–	–
PAC	11	17	17	13	–
Coloured voters					
ANC	24	16	15	27	39
DP	4	3	4	9	9
NP	52	55	62	45	40
PAC	–	–	1	2	–

Source: MPD/M&O Survey, Feb. 1994, N = 2,500.

Table 5.25   Party preference by employment status (%)

	Unemployed	Informal sector	Part-time	Full-time	Housewife*	Other**
All voters						
ANC	34	26	36	29	9	31
DP	3	6	8	6	6	7
NP	40	45	35	40	55	40
PAC	5	5	6	3	–	5
White voters						
ANC	8	10	3	3	4	7
DP	20	20	18	10	15	17
NP	50	60	58	63	61	63
Coloured voters						
ANC	17	14	19	26	6	22
DP	3	6	7	6	3	4
NP	58	57	54	43	55	50
PAC	1	1	2	–	–	–

  * Refers to housewives not looking for work. Those seeking work were categorised as
    unemployed.
 ** Military service, students, pensioners.
Source: MPD/M&O Survey, Feb. 1994, N = 2,500.

whites, however, the NP experienced a significant drop-off among the unemployed, while the DP lags considerably among the fully employed. Among coloured voters, the NP turned out to be the party of the unemployed and underemployed, with the ANC doing its best among fully employed workers. The NP's huge advantage among white and coloured housewives (a group not easily categorised along normal employment scales) should be noted.

Informational networks

In a society as starkly divided as South Africa, race has also historically determined a person's social location. As we saw in tables 5.11 to 5.13 citizens of different races were confronted with very different persuasion and information networks, which in turn meant that they were confronted with different sets of informational flows. When one combined this with the different economic positions of the black, coloured and white communities, it translated into very different overall 'world-views', as well as different specific attitudes. Importantly, information, ideology and opinion should all be much more directly related to the voting decision, if only because they are closer to the vote in both time and space than forces such as race or class.

Fascinating patterns emerge when we look at the interaction of information sources, race and party preference. As table 5.26 demonstrates, there were significant trends among the entire public. The ANC and PAC did much better among people whose primary source of information was from community organisations and political meetings. The NP did much better among people who looked to the mass media, or to their family and friends.

Things do change once we break the figures down by racial group. The pattern seems to disappear among blacks; ANC support is fairly

Table 5.26   Source of most political information by party preference (%)

	ANC	DP	NP	PAC
Television	25	6	47	2
Newspapers	27	7	47	2
Radio	30	6	44	3
Magazines	28	7	33	1
Political meetings	66	5	11	10
Community organisations	61	2	6	19
Friends and colleagues	31	6	45	2
Family	31	6	46	3
Respected people in community	21	7	46	9

Table 5.27   Source of most political information by party preference and racial group

	White voters			Black voters			Coloured voters		
	ANC	DP	NP	ANC	NP	PAC	ANC	DP	NP
Television	4	14	64	76	2	13	20	5	53
Newspapers	5	13	63	80	1	10	23	6	52
Radio	4	16	64	80	1	12	19	5	56
Magazines	6	17	57	85	–	6	21	7	33
Political meetings	14	14	43	79	2	15	54	11	24
Community organisations	–	–	–	67	–	26	53	6	22
Friends and colleagues	9	12	54	82	2	10	22	7	59
Family	4	26	52	79	4	9	9	1	74
Respected people in community	0	14	57	50	–	33	19	6	58

invariant across different sources of political information, though PAC support does rise significantly in several cases once we move away from the mass media and turn to community-based sources. Yet here we need to remember several things. First, black South Africans are often tuned into separate media: for example, blacks tune into and trust 'black' channels such as TV-2/CCV much more than the 'white' TV-1, and the same would apply for radio. Second, their overall levels of exposure to the mass media are much lower than for whites or coloureds. And third, political meetings and community organisations are often more trusted sources of information than the mass media (see table 5.13).

Among whites, NP support was significantly higher among those who depended on the mass media. But the most interesting patterns emerged in the coloured community, which tended to reflect many of the provincial patterns; the ANC was much stronger among coloured voters who depended on community-based sources for their political information and the NP was much stronger among those who turned to the mass media. The key factor was, as we noted earlier, that relatively few coloureds depended on or trusted community organisations for their information – and this was perhaps the main 'cultural' factor which accounted for the political differentiation of the two groups.

Swart gevaar? Expectations of the future

One popular explanation of the NP's margin of support among coloured voters was their successful manipulation of the *swart gevaar* (black peril), as exemplified by some of the tactics discussed in our account of the NP campaign. Indeed, anxiety and fear were unevenly distributed throughout the public, depending on the lifestyle and life-chances of particular individuals and groups. We can glean some evidence about voters' fears about the future from the February MPD survey, which attempted to gauge people's expectations of life after the elections by posing a series of semantic differentials 'insecure–secure', 'violent–peaceful', etc.). When we examined the results by race, we saw clear and stark differences across all items. Whites were much more certain about a decline in their quality of life in the future, almost fatalistically so. Answers to these items doubtless reflected worries about and fear of nationalisation, seizure of property, high taxes, and redistribution of income.

Black voters were, by far, the most optimistic about their future. Significantly, however, coloured voters were no more certain about a decline in their conditions and society than blacks. Some items even showed coloured people to be slightly less anxious than blacks. However, this pattern was not as counterintuitive as it might have first seemed, for coloureds were also much more likely to be found in the 'don't know/ uncertain' column. That is, while coloureds were no more likely than blacks to hold pessimistic views of the future, far more coloureds were simply uncertain about the future.

These patterns were reflected in an examination of anxiety by party support. Here, another unmistakably clear pattern emerges. PAC and ANC supporters were by far the most optimistic, with DP voters the most pessimistic. Interestingly, NP voters were consistently the most uncertain.

Yet race did not totally shape perceptions of the future, and therefore did not wholly shape voting behaviour. First of all, economics certainly played a key role. For example, between 17 per cent and 24 per cent of coloureds in the lowest economic group were pessimistic compared to 5–8 per cent of those in the highest group. Second, among whites, ANC supporters were consistently the most optimistic across the whole range of scenarios we presented. DP voters were most pessimistic on half our questions, NP supporters on the other half. Among blacks, ANC supporters were a bit more optimistic than PAC supporters. Among coloured voters, ANC supporters were consistently the most optimistic and the least uncertain. DP and NP supporters were about equally pessimistic, but NP supporters were generally far more uncertain.

When viewed from the perspective of party success among optimistic and pessimistic voters, ANC support did not differ in any systematic fashion among black voters, though the PAC consistently did best (often a 10 to 12 point improvement) among pessimistic blacks. Among white voters the ANC consistently did better (c. 9–10 per cent support) among the more optimistic, as did the DP (though the pattern there was more mixed). Strikingly, among pessimistic whites the NP fared anywhere between 2 and 10 points worse than average.

The effect of pessimism/optimism about the future on party preference was greatest in the coloured community. In the coloured community the ANC consistently fared best among optimists (with between 33 per cent and 36 per cent support) and worst among the uncertain (8 to 12 per cent support). The NP fared best among the pessimistic (51 to 57 per cent) but, surprisingly, also did worst among the uncertain (44 to 48 per cent). This, however, can be explained by an important point. Those coloured voters who were uncertain about their future were also much more likely to be unsure about which party to support: their uncertainty was general. However, other MPD questions, as well as much of the evidence discussed below, strongly indicates that the NP eventually picked up by far the greatest share of the undecided vote.[145]

Policies and issues

The study of political sociology in other polities suggests that voter attitudes to the policies, leaders and candidates of political parties tend, in a general sense, to be secondary phenomena. That is, voters tend to have previously established 'identifications' with political parties, usually based on socialisation or evaluations of past party performance. Attitudes to that party's policies, leaders or candidates then tend either to confirm or undermine those previous identifications, but seldom themselves explain those identifications. Of course, if negative feelings about policies or leaders are strong enough they may cause voters to 'defect' from their natural party to vote for another party, if only for that specific election. For only among truly 'independent' voters, or those with very weak partisan identification, do issues and candidates generally play a more central role in affecting the vote.[146]

Our data suggested definite differences by racial group in what people might be looking for in terms of choosing a party (see table 5.28). When asked about values, blacks principally cited positions on equality and rights, whites emphasised stability and ability to govern, and the concerns of coloured voters centred around equality and stability. PAC supporters alone showed concern for the issue of land. Coloured voters' preferences seemed to be a function of party rather than race; that is, coloured ANC voters had the same value preferences as blacks, while the more numerous coloured NP supporters had the same preferences as whites.

Table 5.28 Reasons for supporting a particular political party (%)

	White	Black	Coloured	White			Black		Coloured	
				ANC	DP	NP	ANC	PAC	ANC	NP
Stands for democracy	7	8	8	1	21	5	9	4	18	6
Stands for equality	10	21	14	5	5	9	24	8	22	13
Fights for stability and peace	19	7	12	9	18	20	8	1	9	15
Fights for people's rights	3	18	7	5	4	3	18	14	12	6
See to the future of my group	8	4	2	5	7	6	3	1	3	2
Will govern well	12	2	7	14	1	15	2	0	8	7
General policy	11	8	6	18	9	12	8	7	8	6
Economic policy	10	2	2	14	19	8	2	2	2	2
Will provide jobs	1	3	8	5	0	0	5	0	6	10
Honesty and trustworthiness	10	1	8	14	12	11	1	2	3	12
Will get our land back	2	5	0	0	0	0	1	31	0	0

Source: MPD/M&O Survey, Feb. 1994, N = 2,500.

Table 5.29 Which of your party's policies do you like best? (%)

	White	Black	Coloured	White			Black		Coloured	
				ANC	DP	NP	ANC	PAC	ANC	NP
Democracy	13	1	8	19	15	2	0		9	9
Equal rights/ opportunities	20	16	25	21	22	17	11		32	28
Peace and stability	13	5	11	4	16	4	7		3	14
Economic	14	8	7	22	16	8	7		13	6
Jobs	4	24	10	3	4		25	25	13	12
Education	2	25	4	1	3		26	25	9	4
Housing	1	23	6	1	1		25	18	9	6
Group interests				4	5	1	0		1	1

When people were asked which specific policies of their parties they liked best (table 5.29), blacks put a clear emphasis on concrete things they wanted such as jobs, education and housing. High unemployment guaranteed that coloureds, too, laid emphasis on jobs, but otherwise coloureds shared the whites' focus on equality of rights and opportunities and general economic policy. On the whole, however, differentiation by issue preference was weak, confirming the fact that the election revolved more around general values and a gut decision on party identification than on specific policy issues.

In many countries pollsters have found that voters often care more about a party's managerial competence than about its attitude on this or that policy. Here we found the NP enjoyed a significant advantage over the ANC. Even in our first survey (table 5.30) the NP was thought more competent by a small majority of all Western Cape voters, and by a clearer proportion of coloured voters – this even before the campaign had begun. This perception strengthened noticeably during the campaign so that the final SABC poll found coloured voters giving the NP a preference over the ANC of 37 per cent against 20 per cent as the party best able to manage the issues they thought important (table 5.31).

The SABC survey found that most of the issues they tested had relatively little independent impact on party support. Thus the parties received support from similar proportions of people in all the respondent groups on a wide range of questions.[147] But some issues – notably those centring on group identity and economic benefits – produced responses which correlated better with voting intention. The SABC pollster Craig Charney concluded that the NP had managed to move the contest on to

Table 5.30   Which parties best on issues? (%)

	Total		Coloured	
	ANC	NP	ANC	NP
Enforcing law and order	23	32	14	43
Creating a climate of peace	24	31	16	41
Being capable rulers	23	33	16	42
Promoting education	29	28	20	36
Promoting health care	26	30	17	40

Source: MPD/M&O Survey, Nov.–Dec. 1993, N = 3,432.

Table 5.31   Which party can best deal with the most important issue? (%)

	Total	White	Black	Coloured
NP	37	30	3	52
ANC	20	3	73	12

Source: SABC Survey, 12–16 Mar. 1994, N = 400.

Table 5.32 All voters: 'By putting Africans into jobs, the ANC will threaten the job security of those who now hold jobs'

	Support ANC	Support NP
Agree	14	57
Disagree	32	38

Source: SABC Survey, 12–16 Mar. 1994, N = 400.

Table 5.33 Does the ANC–SACP alliance make you uncomfortable? (%)

	Support ANC	Support NP
Yes	8	56
No	54	29

Source: SABC Survey, 12–16 Mar. 1994, N = 400.

a terrain that most benefited itself. The key issues (identity, Communism and affirmative action) were the ones where the NP was the strongest. Half of all whites agreed that the ANC's policies of affirmative action threatened their jobs. Of coloureds, 40 per cent also agreed with this proposition (with 43 per cent disagreeing); among blacks, 17 per cent agreed and 64 per cent disagreed. Of the entire SABC sample, 57 per cent said that the ANC–SACP alliance made them uncomfortable (including 78 per cent of whites and 61 per cent of coloureds).

The NP, we have seen, capitalised heavily on the shock caused to the coloured community by the squatter invasion of Delft. The indications are that this was effective. When voters were asked whether they were worried that such incidents would increase under the future governments, 68 per cent said 'yes' (including 58 per cent of coloureds). Of those coloureds who said they were worried, the NP was supported by 66 per cent, the ANC by 7 per cent.

Leaders and candidates

Party leaders can, in all political systems, pull or push voters away from their 'natural' party homes, an effect generally magnified among independent voters. Typically, this 'leadership effect' increases in presidential systems. Although South Africa does not have a directly elected presidency, its politics have become steadily more presidentialised since 1983;

in 1994 the two major parties certainly fought the campaign in heavily presidential style and it was a major disadvantage to the smaller parties that their leaders were not generally admitted into the same frame as Mandela and de Klerk. (In this respect, the minor parties had reason to complain of the SABC's decision to stage a presidential debate featuring only de Klerk and Mandela.)

In the Western Cape, at least, the leadership factor worked heavily in favour of de Klerk and the NP. De Klerk solidified the partisan choice of those already predisposed to support the NP, as well as pulling voters away from the DP and winning a substantial share of the undecided. This emerged strongly from our February 1994 survey in which we asked people to rate parties on a ten-rung ladder, allowing us to group together those with a generally high opinion of a party or a general preference for it, and those who said they would actually vote for it. We also asked voters to state their preferred leader. Even between the two big parties, the NP had a small advantage: of those who had a general preference for the ANC, 95 per cent said they would vote for it, while among those with a general preference for the NP, those who intended to translate this into an actual vote rose to 98 per cent. But only 75 per cent of those who generally preferred the DP said they would vote for it – and 20 per cent said they would vote for the NP. The reason was de Klerk. Of the 45 per cent of DP supporters whose preferred leader was Zach de Beer, 5 per cent said they would 'cross the floor' to vote NP. But even among this group – and it was a terrible weakness for the DP that less than half its voters preferred the leader the party presented them with – only 72 per cent intended to vote DP, with a large number still uncertain. It seems likely that many of these uncertain DP voters actually defected to the NP in the end. No less than 28 per cent of DP supporters openly preferred de Klerk as leader and among this group only 47 per cent intended to vote NP with 28 per cent intending to defect to the NP; again, one suspects the final numbers were better than this for the NP.

Among coloured voters, de Klerk was an even more decisive factor. While Western Cape voters as a whole preferred de Klerk over Mandela by a 43 per cent to 25 per cent margin, among coloureds this margin rose to 53 per cent against 17 per cent. In addition, the popular weakness of both the NP and ANC candidates for provincial premier did nothing to counter the gravitational pull of the national-level leaders. The SABC poll found that the provincial candidates had little appeal to regional voters: only 12 per cent thought Kriel would make a good premier (indeed, only 18 per cent even of NP supporters said Kriel would make a good premier), and 21 per cent thought Boesak would (including 65 per cent of ANC supporters). This figure was not as favourable for Boesak as it might appear: he had been picked as leader because of his presumed ability to swing coloured opinion, but in fact he benefited more from the apparently knee-jerk loyalties of black ANC voters – and he was thus far more popular among blacks than coloureds. Indeed, a majority of coloureds as well as of whites viewed Boesak unfavourably – and majorities of all racial groups viewed Kriel unfavourably. Neither Kriel nor Boesak had much appeal among uncommitted voters. The DP list leader, Hennie Bester, had never been heard of by 45 per cent – and was disliked by most of those who knew of him.[148]

Ultimately, the NP was able to develop a strong, favourable image among the Western Cape electorate, stronger even among coloured voters than white. By March, the SABC found that 61 per cent of the public had a positive image of the NP (including 74 per cent of coloured voters). Perhaps most important, 55 per cent of all voters felt the NP had changed (including 59 per cent of coloureds). Such positive images even outweighed the very negative ratings given the NP's past economic performance. Of all voters, 43 per cent agreed that the NP had 'ruined' the economy (even 27 per cent of NP supporters agreed); yet 43 per cent of coloureds disagreed.

The DP failed because it settled on a range of issues which failed to differentiate among voters, or did not appear salient to their needs. The SABC found that only 25 per cent of the voters agreed with the key DP claim that 'Neither the ANC nor the NP will protect your freedom,' with these essentially negative opinions spread among all race groups. The DP suffered badly by having a largely invisible leader; de Beer's image was simply not competitive with that of de Klerk or Mandela. The DP was also hobbled by an image of an ethnic or class-oriented party. Presented with the statement that 'The DP has run Cape Town for years, but they have only done things for whites,' 63 per cent of blacks, 38 per cent of coloureds and even 25 per cent of whites agreed. Ultimately, only 33 per cent of coloureds and 10 per cent of blacks had a positive view of the DP.

The PAC faced many similar problems. Few people cared about its central issue (land). Its national and regional leadership was weak. The SABC found that even 43 per cent of blacks (and 56 per cent of the whole electorate) agreed that the PAC was racist against whites. Moreover, it was underfunded, badly organised and lacked the activist support which might have capitalsed on its modest attitudinal support. However, campaign surveys did detect some possible signs of future optimism for the PAC, most notably a succession of survey findings showing them to be the second-choice party of around 25 per cent of blacks.

After the election some depicted the Western Cape result as aberrant, the result of the deployment of unscrupulous *swart gevaar* tactics by the NP on an unsophiticated coloured electorate. Despite what we have said about the NP's campaign it must be stressed that this was an inadequate appreciation. Rather, the NP ran a highly professional campaign, which by March had clearly worked. Among those who were still uncommitted in early March, 44 per cent gave very high ratings (8 or more out of 10) to de Klerk, while only 22 per cent did so for Mandela. Among the uncommitted, the NP was rated favourably by 55 per cent, the ANC by 36 per cent and the PAC by only 14 per cent. And on those campaign issues identified by Charney as key to the vote, the NP was picking up the lion's share of the undecided: 59 per cent were uncomfortable with the SACP–ANC alliance, 37 per cent were concerned about the effect of affirmative action on job-holders, only 28 per cent felt the NP had not changed, and only 12 per cent of uncommitted coloured voters said they felt closer to blacks than whites. In contrast, the ANC was never able to shed its negative image among the white or coloured communities. By March, amazingly, the ANC's image was actually worse among coloureds than among whites; while 42 per cent of whites viewed it favourably (and 46 per cent unfavourably), only 33 per cent of coloureds had a positive view of the ANC (with 4 per cent negative).

Far from simply relying on crude *swart gevaar* tactics, the NP skilfully elicited feelings which emphasised identity, cleverly promoted its leadership, and hit hard at ANC policies (especially redistribution and Communism). Yet the NP had to overcome large disadvantages. Only 37 per cent of the public thought the NP was the best party on the issues and it was widely judged to have ruined the economy in the past. But modern campaigns are won by parties that succeed in shifting the battle on to the terrain where they are strongest and this was that the NP managed to do, shifting the campaign towards its strongest issues. Even among those who said the NP had ruined the economy, 49 per cent still felt that affirmative action threatened job-holders, and 40 per cent were still uneasy about the ANC's link with the SACP. Of coloureds who said the NP had ruined the economy, 74 per cent still felt that coloured people were closer to whites or that coloureds formed a distinct community, both of which attitudes translated into NP support.[149] In the final analysis, the NP articulated a set of policies that addressed the immanent concerns of coloured voters.

In contrast, the ANC never adapted well to campaigning in the coloured community. It took a long time to get over its initial ideological predisposition against ethnic politics, and tended too easily to assume that what went down well in Khayelitsha would also go down well in Mitchell's Plain. Moreover, the ANC was never able to articulate an effective vision of where coloured people fitted into its major policy proposals, which were clearly aimed mainly at helping blacks. Thus when ANC speakers held forth on their Reconstruction and Development Programme they generally felt it sufficient just to add on a sort of 'you too can benefit' clause for coloureds. It was bad enough that it tried to direct a single campaign at two diverse constituencies, but actually more still was required. If it was going to do what was required to win in the Western Cape, it would have had to run a regional campaign different in tenor from its national campaign. This never looked like happening.

The ANC was also hobbled by a problematic regional leadership. After the elections, one ANC source said that they 'always knew Dr. Boesak and his history was a risk, but we thought his assets would outweigh his liabilities. . . . Indications are that we polled about thirty per cent of the coloured votes in the Mitchell's Plain district and about nine per cent of the rural votes. Those were Dr Boesak's supposed strong areas.'[150] Yet the problem went beyond Boesak. The leadership in the coloured community is thin and dominated by preachers, academics and teachers, who have some appeal to the intelligentsia and professional middle classes, but have little rapport with the working class or rural people. And the ANC's coloured support draws perhaps too heavily on this narrow – and atypical – educated elite. Thus, when the ANC campaign appeared to be heading for defeat in late February, it could do little better than haul out Franklin Sonn and a few other educationalists who were respected within their field but relatively unknown in working-class areas such as Mannenberg and Mitchell's Plain. Sonn pulled the normally conservative Cape Teachers Professional Association, the largest body of coloured teachers, into the ANC camp. But that was as far as it went. Instead of persuading people with appeals that addressed their concerns, anxieties and needs, he berated people for lacking proper historical consciousness and forgetting the days of apartheid. This was not really an answer to the contemporary anxieties of the coloured working class facing tough competition from blacks over jobs and housing. The ANC leadership often confused present-day social, cultural and economic insecurity and uncertainty with a pre-modern, racist form of fear and ignorance. They assumed that ordinary coloured voters supported the NP only because they were unenlightened and poorly informed, and to that extent simply failed to take their concerns seriously. In any event, as we saw earlier, coloured people were getting their political information from the media, especially television, and from family and friends, not from what the ANC overconfidently termed 'respected community leaders'. Again, this was a somewhat unthinking translation of a political idiom from a black context (where it worked) into a quite different coloured context. Within the coloured community the days when the teacher and the preacher enjoyed a special respect and their words carried an automatic moral authority are long passed.

A final paradox

There is a final – and perhaps temporary – paradox to the coloured vote. Essentially, the coloured community in 1994 was called upon to make a choice between three parties which, for all that they made much of their multiracial character and appeal, were actually white-led (in the case of the NP and DP) or clearly dominated by black interests (in the case of the ANC). In the end, coloureds decided by a large majority that they felt more comfortable with the former than the latter, but in so doing they, like the Indians of KwaZulu-Natal, transformed the NP into a party with an electorate which is now about half non-white. Yet there was relatively little reflection of this reality in the NP itself and one cannot help but wonder if, by the time another election hoves into view, the coloured majority of the Western Cape may flex its muscles in order to secure a party and a premier which are more closely its own. Should such a trend develop, one would doubtless witness the exquisite spectacle of the NP campaigning passionately against such 'separate development' in politics.

Notes

This chapter is the result of a larger research project sponsored by the Institute for Multi-Party Democracy and co-ordinated by Hennie Kotze, Jannie Gagiano, Hermann Giliomee, Wilmot James and Robert Mattes. We would also like to thank Anneke Greyling for her invaluable technical expertise and assistance.

1   We recognise the long-standing historical and anthropological arguments about whether Xhosa-speaking Africans were 'naturally' absent from the Cape when white settlers first arrived, or whether they were 'cyclically' absent and henceforth prevented from returning. We do not offer an answer to this debate.

2   Official race classifications subdivided the coloured group into Cape Coloured, Malay, Griqua, and Other Coloured.

3   These migration patterns forced the government to accept the presense of large informally settled black populations in 'white' South Africa (e.g. Crossroads), and forced them to build new townships (e.g. Khayelitsha), as well as to grant leasehold rights to established township dwellers (e.g. Nyanga, Guguletu and Langa). See William Cobbett, Daryl Glaser, Doug Hindson and Mark Swilling, 'A critical analysis of the South African state and reform strategies in the 1980s', in P. Frankel et al. (eds), *State, Resistance and Change in South Africa* (Johannesburg: Southern, 1988), p. 23.

4   T. R. H. Davenport, *The Afrikaner Bond* (Cape Town: Oxford University Press, 1966), p. 120.

5   *The Clarion*, 3 May 1919.

6   Gerd Behrens, 'The other two Houses: the first five years of the Houses of Representatives and Delegates,' Ph.D. diss., University of Cape Town, 1989, p. 238.

7   Ibid., p. 11.

8   Hermann Giliomee, 'The National Party campaign for a liberation election', in Andrew Reynolds (ed.), *Election '94 South Africa: The Campaigns, Results and Future Prospects* (Cape Town: David Philip, 1994), p. 54.

9   *Die Burger*, 22 Feb. 1994, p. 13.

10 De Villiers quoted in *South*, 8 May 1991.

11 Cited in Alf Ries and Ebba Dommisse, *Broedertwis* (Cape Town: Tafelberg, 1982), p. 112.

12 In actuality, the absence of required coalitions in the cabinet, and built-in white majorities in the President's Council and Electoral College (which selected the powerful State President) meant that the leadership of the majority party in the white chamber would always retain final and unmistakable control over 'general affairs' decisions, as well as over the very definition of 'own' and 'general' affairs.

13 This constitution was part of a broad set of reforms which received their initial impetus from the B. J. Vorster government in the late 1970s. These reforms came

to include the legalisation of black trade unions, the granting of citizenship to urbanised blacks, and the abolition of pass laws permitting the free movement of labour.

14   Robert Cameron, 'An analysis of the structure and functioning of Coloured and Indian Local Authorities since the introduction of the Tricameral system', *Politikon: The South African Jouranl of Political Science*, 18.1 (1991); Johann Groenewald, 'Relative deprivation: a component of transformed political awareness in Cape Town, 1976–1983', *Politikon* 15.2 (1988), p. 33; and Giliomee, 'The National Party's campaign', p. 50.

15   Behrens, 'The other two Houses', pp. 207, 209.

16   Cameron, 'An analysis of the structure and functioning of Coloured and Indian Local Authorities', pp. 38–40. In fact, the Department of Local Government in the House of Representatives often removed housing schemes from the white Cape Town City Council (which, ironically, had been resisting any co-operation with these structures because of their opposition to apartheid).

17   Giliomee, 'The National Party's campaign', p. 51.

18   Hermann Giliomee, 'Great white hope', *Indicator SA*, 11.2 (1994), p. 13.

19   Mike McGrath, 'Disparate circumstances', *Indicator SA*, 11.3 (1994), pp. 49–50; and Rory Riordan, 'The Christian Democratic Alliance', *Monitor* (June 1991), p. 10.

20   Its official birthplace was in Mitchell's Plain, a large coloured township outside of Cape Town, which housed people who had been forcibly removed from District Six. Of the original 565 UDF affiliates, 358 came from the Western Cape. See Tom Lodge and Bill Nasson, *All Here and Now: Black Politics in South Africa in the 1980s* (Cape Town: David Philip, 1991), p. 51.

21   Ibid., p. 61; and Jeremy Seeking, 'The United Democratic Front in Cape Town, 1983–1986', Centre for African Studies, University of Cape Town, pp. 8–9, 13.

22   Behrens, 'The other two Houses', p. 330.

23   Seekings, 'The United Democratic Front in Cape Town', pp. 1–4; and Colin Bundy, ' "Action, comrades, action!!" The politics of youth-student resistance in the Western Cape, 1985', in Mary Simons and Wilmot James (eds), *The Angry Divide* (Cape Town: David Philip, 1989).

24   Seekings, 'The United Democratic Front in Cape Town', pp. 1–10.

25   Ibid., pp. 16–17.

26   Mark Swilling and Johannes Rantete, 'Organization and strategies of the major resistance movements in the negotiation era', in Robin Lee and Lawrence Schlemmer (eds), *Transition to Democracy* (Cape Town: Oxford University Press, 1991), p. 202.

27   Cameron, 'An analysis of the structure and functioning of Coloured and Indian Local Authorities', pp. 40–41. It should be noted that a 1987 survey in Athlone (funded by the Cape Town City Council) found that only 10.5% of the suburb supported the system while 67% wanted a non-racial local authority (p. 43). Indeed, less than one-fifth of eligible coloured voters went to the polls in the next (1989) parliamentary election. See Rupert Taylor, 'The South African election of 1989', in *South African Review 5* (Braamfontein: Ravan, 1989), p. 65.

28   Chris Heymans and Roland White, 'Playing politics without the power: the state of black local government in the South Africa of the 1980/90s', *Politikon*, 18.1 (1991), pp. 6–9.

29   Jeremy Seekings, 'From boycotts to voting? The extra-parliamentary opposition in transition', *Die Suid-Afrikaan* 43 (1993), pp. 32–3; and Seekings, 'The United Democratic Front in Cape Town', pp. 17–21, 23.

30   David Christianson, 'Local government the loser', *Indicator SA*, 11.4 (1994), p. 28.

31   Tom Lodge, 'The African National Congress and its allies', in Reynolds (ed.), *Election '94 South Africa*, pp. 39–40; and Boesak quoted in Mike Robertson and Norman West, 'Come on in, folks', *Sunday Times*, 13 Oct. 1991, p. 23.

32   Seekings, 'From boycotts to voting', p. 33; Swilling and Rantete, 'Organizations and strategies of the major resistance movements', p. 203.

33 Anneke Greyling and Hennie Kotze, *Political Organizations in South Africa, A–Z* (Cape Town: Tafelberg, 1994), pp. 122–3; and Lodge, 'The African National Congress and its allies', pp. 39–40.

34 For example, as Mandela announced plans for a March 1992 tour of Western Cape coloured communities, the ANC played down HSRC findings of a 54% to 7% NP lead over the ANC for support among coloureds, claiming that its findings were regularly inconsistent with other independent survey agencies and that it was concerned with producing results that overplayed government support and underplayed the ANC's. See 'ANC, CP reject "support" survey', and Anthony Johnson, 'Nelson in bid for coloured support', *Cape Times*, 14 Feb. 1992, p. 5.

35 See Heribert Adam and Kogila Moodley, *The Negotiated Revolution* (Parklands: Jonathan Ball, 1993), pp. 73–5 (Mandela quote on p. 74). As Adam and Moodley pointed out, 'Were Mandela's views followed literally, the ANC would embrace the National Party policy of group representation, paradoxically at the very moment when the old racist party had forsworn any reference to race or ethnicity in its constitutional blueprints' (p. 74).

36 Robertson and West, 'Come on in, folks', p. 23.

37 Ibid.

38 R. W. Johnson, 'Durban '91: what really happened at the ANC congress', *Weekend Argus*, 20 July 1991, p. 16.

39 Robertson and West, 'Come on in, folks'.

40 Riordan, 'The Christian Democratic Alliance', p. 11; and Cheryl Hendricks, 'Ethnic consciousness and potential voting behaviour', Centre for Development Studies, Bellville, 1993, p. 31.

41 Mandela cited in *Weekend Argus*, 21 Mar. 1992; and Kurt Swart, 'Mandela's tough tour of W. Cape to boost support', *Sunday Times/Cape Metro*, 22 Mar. 1992, p. 1.

42 Mandela quoted in 'FW violence: "ample evidence" – Mandela', *Cape Times*, 18 Aug. 1992, p. 2.

43 'Local ANC preparing for poll', *Cape Times*, 19 Oct. 1992, p. 2.

44 Nazeem Howa, '"High-handed" ANC made allies into aliens', *Sunday Times*, 11 Apr. 1993.

45 Frans Esterhuyse, 'Buthelezi explains his hard line', *Weekly Mail*, 17–18 July 1993, p. 14; and Norman West, 'Political parties gear up to win your vote', *Sunday Times/ Cape Metro*, 18 July 1993, p. 2.

46 Malthew Eldridge, 'In retrospect: a collection of interviews with strategists and candidates from the African National Congress's 1994 Western Cape campaign', paper, University of Cape Town, 1994.

47 Riordan, 'The Christian Democratic Alliance', p. 9.

48 Eventually, as a member of the Patriotic Front, it managed to get several people on to, albeit low, positions on ANC lists. Greyling and Kotze, *Political Organizations in South Africa*, pp. 185–9.

49 Hendricks, 'Ethnic consciousness and potential voting behaviour', p. 9; Gaye Davis, 'Coloureds ready to forgive the past NP wrongs', *Weekly Mail*, 30 May to 6 June 1991, p. 12.

50 Robertson and West, 'Come on in, folks', p. 23; Frans Esterhuyse, 'Buthelezi explains his hard line', p. 14; Norman West, 'Political parties gear up to win your vote', p. 2; Giliomee, 'The National Party campaign,' p. 54; and personal interview by Hermann Giliomee with Carel Greyling, Cape Town, 19 Nov. 1993.

51 Michael Morris, 'The dangers of crossing over', *Argus*, 23 Nov. 1991, p. 23.

52 Michael Morris, 'DP in intensive bid for support', *Argus*, 24 Oct. 1991, p. 10; John McLennan, 'New centrist party with DP at core?', *Saturday/Sunday Argus*, 5–6 Sept. 1992, p. 23; Gavin Evans and Philippa Garson, 'Blushing bride enters Soweto', *Weekly Mail*, 11–17 Sept. 1992, p. 17; 'Fired-up DP aims high', *Sunday Times*, 15 Nov. 1992, p. 2; Chris Whitfield, 'While the cynics smile, the DP is pushing ahead', *Cape Times*, 17 Nov. 1992, p. 6; Nazeem Howa, 'Parties move into gear for election', *Cape Times/Cape Metro*, 13 June 1993, p. 4; Esterhuyse, 'Buthelezi

explains his hard line', p. 14; West, 'Political parties gear up to win your vote', p. 2; and 'Party's growth faster in W. Cape', *Cape Times*, 4 Oct. 1993, p. 5.

53 Pippa Green, 'The boundaries of the possible', *Leadership*, 12.3 (1993), p. 21.

54 Michael Morris, 'IFP, DP in tussle for votes on Cape flats', *Argus*, 6 Oct. 1993, p. 6; and Chris Louw, 'Crisis after crisis wracks the DP', *Weekly Mail*, 1–7 Oct. 1993, p. 5.

55 Esterhuyse, 'Buthelezi explains his hard line', p. 14; and West, 'Political parties gear up to win your vote', p. 2.

56 Louw, 'Crisis after crisis wracks the DP', p. 5; Morris, 'IFP, DP in tussle for votes on Cape flats', p. 6.

57 'Support up, say PAC', *Cape Times*, 21 June 1993, p. 2.

58 Esterhuyse, 'Buthelezi explains his hard line', p. 14; and West, 'Political parties gear up to win your vote', p. 2.

59 Ayesha Ismail, 'ANC surveys fresh image for election', *Sunday Times/Cape Metro*, 20 June 1993, p. 9.

60 These lessons are taken from interviews with participants in the ANC polling efforts, as well as from Edyth Bulbring, 'The image markers', *Sunday Times*, 20 Feb. 1994, p. 25; Mark Gevisser, 'Clinton's men on the ANC campaign trail', *Weekly Mail*, 25 Feb.–3 Mar. 1994, p. 10; Chris Baseman, 'NP facing uphill battle in Cape's black townships', *Cape Times*, 25 Apr. 1994, p. 10; and Lodge, 'The ANC and its allies', pp. 28–9.

61 Boesak cited in Dennis Cruywagen, 'Watch Nats, not DP – Boesak', *Weekend Argus*, 27–8 Nov. 1993, p. 17; Anthony Johnson, 'ANC "dove" Kalako ousts Yengeni', *Cape Times*, 19 Nov. 1993, p. 1; and Mondli Waka Makhanya, 'How the West (Cape) was won', *Weekly Mail*, 8–14 Apr. 1994, p. 19.

62 This information is based on conversations with participants of the ANC polling process, as well as Ismail, 'ANC surveys fresh image for election', p. 9; Bulbring, 'The image makers', p. 25; and Lodge, 'The ANC and its allies', pp. 28–9.

63 Eldridge, 'In retrospect'.

64 Frans Esterhuyse and Tyrone Seale, 'Kriel Western Cape PM?' *Weekend Argus*, 8–9 Jan. 1994, p. 3; Nazeem Howa, 'ANC, NP pin poll hopes on leaders', *Sunday Times/Cape Metro*, 23 Jan. 1993, p. 1; and Chris Bateman and Barry Streek, 'ANC: is the tide turning enough in its favour?', *Cape Times*, 26 Apr. 1994, p. 8 (Winnie Mandela did get in an appearance late in the campaign in Cloetesville, a coloured neighborhood, and delivered virtually all of her speech in Xhosa).

65 Gevisser, 'Clinton's men on the ANC campaign trial', p. 10.

66 Farouk Chothia, 'Mandela's many faces', *Weekly Mail*, 19–25 Nov. 1993.

67 Mark Gevisser, 'Under the pig's hat, a careful strategy', *Weekly Mail*, 15–21 Apr. 1994, p. 6.

68 Andrew MacDonald, 'On the campaign trial: Mandela's drawing on Clinton's best', *Work in Progress*, 88 (1993), p. 15.

69 Gevisser, 'Clinton's men on the ANC campaign trail', p. 10.

70 In Eldridge, 'In retrospect',

71 Quoted in Hein Marais, 'Will the ANC win?', *Work in Progress*, 88 (1993), p. 12.

72 ANC, 'From apartheid to peace, development and democracy', International Solidarity Conference, Jan. 1993.

73 In Eldridge, 'In retrospect',

74 David Breier, 'Mandela does a turnabout on controversial "turncoat" speech', *Weekend Argus*, 5–6 Feb. 1994, p. 17.

75 See Richard Calland, 'Nats use fear to reach for power in the Western Cape', *Weekend Argus*, 23–4 Apr. 1993, p. 30. Calland commented that research from previous British campaigns showed that positive, issue-oriented advertising only solidifies the support of those already predisposed to support a party, rather than converting voters.

76 In Eldridge, 'In retrospect'.

77 Lodge, 'The ANC and its allies', p. 27.

78 Gevisser, 'Clinton's men on the ANC campaign trail', p. 10.
79 Ibid.
80 Shaun Johnson, 'Mandela will fire a big shot today', *Weekend Argus*, 6–7 Nov. 1993, p. 15; Anton Harber, 'Experienced trio lead shrewd ANC campaign', *Weekly Mail*, 26 Nov.–2 Dec. 1993, p. 14; Gevisser, 'Under the pig's hat, a careful strategy', p. 6; and Lodge, 'The ANC and its allies', pp. 29–30.
81 Harber, 'Experienced trio lead shrewd ANC campaign', p. 14; and Chothia, 'Mandela's many faces'.
82 Lodge, 'The ANC and its allies', p. 40.
83 Farouk Chothia, 'Top leader battle for power in the provinces', *Weekly Mail*, 30 Dec. 1993–6 Jan. 1994, p. 6.
84 In Eldridge, 'In retrospect'.
85 Cited in Lodge, 'The ANC and its allies', p. 40.
86 Breier, 'Mandela does a turnabout on controversial "turncoat" speech', p. 17.
87 Personal interview by Hermann Giliomee with Willie Hofmeyr, Cape Town, 19 Nov. 1993.
88 In Eldrige, 'In retrospect'.
89 Farouk Chothia, 'Battle for Indian hearts and minds', *Weekly Mail*, 29 Oct.–4 Nov. 1993, p. 8.
90 In Eldridge, 'In Retrospect'.
91 In ibid.
92 Anthony Johnson, 'Spin doctors in onslaught on coloured voters', *Cape Times*, 23 Feb. 1994, p. 16, and 'ANC plans to build a million houses', *Cape Times*, 14 Feb. 1994, p. 1; and Mondli Waka Makhanya, 'In the coloured Cape flats, Mandela's just a "Kaffir"', *Weekly Mail*, 25–30 Mar. 1994, p. 16.
93 Gaye Davis, 'Hidden hand behind Cape housing conflict?' *Weekly Mail*, 29 Oct.– 4 Nov. 1993; Vuyo Bavuma, 'Sisulu flies in to defuse house crisis', *Weekend Argus*, 30–1 Oct. 1993, p. 4, and 'Mandela lashes NP for fanning violence with advert', *Weekend Argus*, 30–1 Oct. 1993, p. 20; Roger Friedman, 'NP "using housing crisis to exploit fears"', *Argus*, 1 Nov. 1993, p. 4.
94 In Eldridge, 'In retrospect'.
95 Norman West, 'New ANC tactics to beat Nats', *Sunday Times/Cape Metro*, 17 Apr. 1994, p. 4.
96 Daniel Silke and Robert Schrire, 'The mass media and the South African election', in Reynolds (ed.), *Election '94 South Africa*, p. 135.
97 Quoted in 'Technikon rector quits SABC post', *Argus*, 31 Mar. 1994, p. 6.
98 Quoted in Norman West, 'Nat lead has ANC worried', *Sunday Times/Cape Metro*, 27 Mar. 1994. p. 6.
99 *Cape Times*, 1 Mar. 1994, p. 6.
100 Jean Le May, 'Dirty tricks election', *Weekend Argus*, 16–17 Apr. 1994, p. 5. The CCB was a government death squad carrying out hits against dissidents in the 1980s.
101 Personal interview by Hermann Giliomee with Melt Hamman, Cape Town, 19 Nov. 1993.
102 Ibid.
103 Sources include Norman West, 'The Nats change colour and pin their hopes on the bones', *Sunday Times*, 14 Mar. 1993, p. 1, and 'Sun rises on a new look NP', *Sunday Times*, 2 May 1993, p. 4; Anthony Johnson, 'New symbols, but will they ease memories of NP's past?', *Cape Times*, 5 May 1993, p. 6; Kaizer Nyatsumba, 'Hit the road – FW on a drive for black votes', *Weekend Argus*, 29–30 Jan. 1994, p. 8; 'Election "choice between NP, ANC" – De Villiers', *Weekend Argus*, 19–20 Feb. 1994, p. 5; Bulbring, 'The image makers', p. 25; Gevisser, 'Under the pig's hat, a careful strategy', p. 6; and Silke and Schrire, 'The mass media', p. 135.
104 Subsequent passages are based on personal interview by Hermann Giliomee with Melt Hamman, Cape Town, 19 Nov. 1993; *Weekend Argus*, 'Election "choice between NP, ANC" – De Villiers', p. 5; Bulbring, 'The image makers', p. 5; West, 'The Nats change colour and pin their hopes on the bones', p. 1; Gevisser, 'Under

the pig's hat, a careful strategy', p. 6; West, 'Sun rises on a new look NP', p. 4; Anthony Johnson, 'New symbols, but will they ease memories of NP's past?', *Cape Times*, 5 May 1993, p. 6; and Giliomee, 'The National Party's campaign', p. 56; and Silke and Schrire, 'The mass media', p. 135.

105   Tos Wentzel, 'FW the video star!', *Weekend Argus*, 18–19 Dec. 1993, p. 17; Barry Streek, 'FW to focus on W. Cape', *Cape Times*, 13 Jan. 1994, p. 2; Ray Hartley, 'FW's roadshow of surprises', *Sunday Times*, 23 Jan. 1994, p. 4; Nyatsumba, 'Hit the road – FW on a drive for black votes', p. 8; Johnson, 'Spin doctors in onslaught on coloured voters', p. 16; John MacLennan, 'Nats could defeat ANC on Cape flats', *Weekend Arugs*, 26–7 Feb. 1994, p. 6; Anthony Johnson, 'Nats looking to voters who will opt for "the devil I already know"', *Cape Times*, 22 Apr. 1994, p. 8; and Norman West, 'Hot contest in the Western Cape', *Sunday Times/Cape Metro*, 20 Mar. 1994, p. 8.

106   Key figures in the NP campaign were Olaus van Zyl and Chris Fismer (personal assistant to de Klerk). The NP also used media and campaign advisers from the British advertising agency Lowe Bell, which had formerly worked for Margaret Thatcher. Optimum Marketing Communications, a division of Saatchi and Saatchi, handled campaign advertising; see Bulbring, 'The image makers', p. 25. The NP campaign budget was estimated at around R30 to R40 million; see Giliomee, 'The National Party's campaign', p. 58.

107   Gevisser, 'Under the pig's hat, a careful strategy', p. 6.

108   See Norman West, 'FW fires the first salvo of NP election campaign', *Sunday Times/Cape Metro*, 28 Mar. 1993, p. 1; Edyth Bulbring, 'FW on a roll as he dishes up "New" NP', *Sunday Times*, 20 June 1993, p. 2; Philip van Niekerk, 'Blackening the white name of the NP', *Weekly Mail*, 25 June–1 July 1993, p. 15; Wentzel, 'FW the video star!', p. 17; Barry Streek, 'FW to focus on W. Cape', *Cape Times*, 13 Jan. 1994, p. 2; Hartley, 'FW's roadshow of surprises', p. 4; Nyatsumba, 'Hit the road – FW on a drive for black votes', p. 8; and 'ANC hits "new Nats" with election poster power', *Weekend Argus*, 5–6 Feb. 1994, p. 17.

109   Nyatsumba, 'Hit the road – FW on a drive for black votes', p. 8.

110   Giliomee, 'The National Party's campaign', p. 56.

111   Donald Simpson, 'An embarrassment of pale faces', *Weekend Argus*, 16–17 Apr. 1994, p. 18; Giliomee, 'The National Party's campaign', pp. 55–6 (NP officials did point out that with 55 per cent of the Western Cape vote, one-third of their winning candidates would be non-white).

112   Giliomee, 'The National Party's campaign', p. 65.

113   *Argus*, 22 Feb. 1994, p. 4.

114   Johnson, 'Nats looking to voters who will opt for "the devil I already know"', p. 8 (NP Western Cape officials predicted 50–55% NP, 33–35% ANC, 5–7% DP, 3–5% PAC and 2–3% FF).

115   Van Schalkwyk cited in Giliomee, 'The National Party's campaign', p. 63.

116   *Rapport*, 20 Mar. 1994, p. 13.

117   Davis, 'Hidden hand behind Cape housing conflict?'; Bavuma, 'Sisulu flies in to defuse house crisis', p. 4, and 'Mandela lashes NP for fanning violence with advert', p. 20; and Friedman, 'NP "using housing crisis to exploit fears"', p. 4.

118   'Coloureds will be losers – Williams', *Cape Times*, 9 Mar. 1994, p. 2; Barry Streek, 'Coloured vote could secure Overberg for NP', *Cape Times*, 15 Mar. 1994, p. 8.

119   Gevisser, 'Under the pig's hat, a careful strategy', p. 6.

120   'Double voting helps', *Cape Times*, 18 Feb. 1994, p. 2.

121   David Breier, 'DP to make "deals" with Nats, ANC in W. Cape', *Weekend Argus*, 12–13 Feb. 1994, p. 6.

122   Anthony Johnson, 'Cautious DP ready for a late charge at the polls', *Cape Times*, 20 Apr. 1994, p. 10.

123   Wentzel, 'FW the video star!' p. 17; Dennis Cruywagen, 'Watch Nats, not DP – Boesak', *Weekend Argus*, 27–8 Nov. 1993, p. 17; Dennis Cruywagen and Tos Wentzel, 'Head to head', *Argus*, 29 Nov. 1993, p. 1; 'Election "choice between

NP, ANC" – De Villiers', *Weekend Argus*, 19–20 Feb. 1994, p. 5; Daniel Silke, 'DP has to carve a new role to take on NP, ANC', *Weekend Argus*, 2–3 Apr. 1994, p. 16.

124 Cruywagen, 'Watch Nats, not DP – Boesak', p. 17; Cruywagen and Wentzel, 'Head to head', p. 1; 'Election "Choice Between NP, ANC" – De Villiers', p. 5; Silke, 'DP has to carve a new role to take on NP, ANC', p. 16; and Silke and Schrire, 'The mass media', p. 135.

125 David Breier, 'Nats hit low to keep the Cape from DP, ANC', *Weekend Argus*, 9–10 Apr. 1994, p. 16.

126 Silke and Schrire, 'The mass media', p. 135.

127 Johnson, 'Cautious DP ready for a late charge at the polls', p. 10; and Farouk Chothia, Chris Louw and Mondli Waka Makhanya, 'Defections and debacles hit bruised DP', *Weekly Mail*, 10–16 June 1994, p. 5.

128 Norman West, 'Hot contest in Western Cape', *Sunday Time/Cape Metro*, 10 Mar. 1994, p. 8; Anthony Johnson, 'DP leaders take to the road in Pied Piper style', *Cape Times*, 16 Mar. 1994, p. 5.

129 Bulbring, 'The image makers', p. 20.

130 Ibid.

131 Gevisser, 'Under the pig's hat, a careful strategy', p. 6.

132 David Breier, 'DP pins hope on Suzman legend', *Weekend Argus*, 26 Feb. 1994, p. 12.

133 Ray Hartley, 'DP seeks security crackdown', *Sunday Times*, 17 Apr. 1994, p. 7. One DP ad showed a pig wearing a policeman's cap with a caption reading: 'This is what the Left call them. This is how the Nats treat them. No wonder there's no respect for law and order.'

134 Brian Pottinger, 'Watchdog yapping at the heels of giants', *Sunday Times*, 17 Apr. 1994, p. 6.

135 Anthony Johnson, 'Freedom Front seeks balance of power in W. Cape', *Cape Times*, 25 Apr. 1994, p. 10.

136 This conceptualisation and operationalisation of tolerance was first used in John Sullivan, John Piereson and George Marcus, 'An alternative conceptualization of political tolerance: illusionary increases, 1950s–1970s', *American Political Science Review*, 73.3 (1979).

137 'Target group' distribution also differed significantly by party preference: those who intended to vote for the ANC were most opposed to the CP and the IFP; NP voters were most opposed to the PAC and the CP; PAC voters were most opposed to the IFP and the NP; IFP voters were most opposed to the PAC; and all people intending to vote for the CP were most opposed to the ANC.

138 Amanda Gouws, 'A study of political tolerance in the context of South Africa', Ph.D. diss., University of Illinois, Urbana-Champaign, 1992.

139 The breakdowns by racial group in table 5.21 were created by multiplying the MPD's election projections by a factor of difference between the total MPD projections and the actual results (the MPD had projected the NP with 52.2%, ANC 34.5%, DP 6.3%, PAC 4.2%, Right-wing 1.6%, IFP 1.8%). See J. Gagiano et al., *Launching Democracy: Second Western Cape Survey on Issues Relevant to a Free and Fair Election, February 1994* (Durban: Institute for Multi-Party Democracy, 1994); Andrew Reynolds, 'The results', in Reynolds (ed.), *Election '94 South Africa*, p. 204; and Independent Electoral Commission Provincial Count, Western Cape Election Administration Directorate.

140 Timothy Sisk, 'A South African social contract? Institutional choice in a divided society', Ph.D. diss., George Washington University, 1992, ch. 1.

141 The MPD/M&O survey asked two questions. First, they asked people to rank the political parties on a ladder, their most preferred parties at the top and the least preferred parties towards the bottom. Second, they asked people how they would actually vote. In this section, we shall use the first (most preferred party) question. This is because the vote question failed to obtain answers from 30% of the

respondents, who said they did not know, would not vote, or that their vote was confidential. Because many of these people did indicate a most preferred party, the first question garnered a higher proportion of answers than the second. Also, the most preferred party seems to be a strong indicator of voting intentions. Of those who selected a party in this question, 97% also indicated in the other question that they would vote for it.

142 The only place where language does matter is among whites, where the CP was preferred by 8% of Afrikaans-speakers and 1% of English. For the DP, it was 5% and 22%, and for the NP it was 66% and 56%. Xhosa-speakers were virtually coterminous with blacks (95%).

143 Among whites, while the NP figures were relatively similar across a number of churches, its strongest performance was undoubtedly among the Dutch Reformed Church (76%). Among blacks, the strongest ANC preference was among Apostolics (80%) and the Methodist South Africa Church (81%).

144 Crary Charney, 'Western Cape survey highlights', SABC press release, 24 Mar. 1994.

145 For instance, while the NP was the most preferred party of 36% and the ANC 28% in the February survey, the MPD analysts were able to project on the basis of other questions that the NP would get 52% of the final vote and the ANC 35%. See Gagiano et al., *Launching Democracy: Second Western Cape Survey.*

146 See Angus Campbell, Philip Converse, Warren Miller and Donald Stokes, *The American Voter* (New York: John Wiley, 1960); V.O. Key, *The Responsible Electorate* (New York: Vintage, 1966); and Morris Fiorina, *Retrospective Voting in American National Elections* (New Haven: Yale University Press, 1981).

147 Charney, 'Western Cape survey highlights'.

148 Ibid.

149 Ibid., p. 10.

150 'Growing pressure for ANC to dump Boesak', *Sunday Times/Cape Metro*, 15 May 1994, p. 1.

SIX

The Political World of KwaZulu-Natal

Alexander Johnston

The Dynamics of Politics in KwaZulu-Natal

IN THE MONTHS PRECEDING the April 1994 election, the politics of KwaZulu-Natal (KZN) came to occupy an apparently disproportionate place in the painfully constructed national framework of transition. Two reasons for this stand out. First, the violence which corrupted the nego-tiation process was endemic in KZN to an extent not matched elsewhere. Second, the most formidable obstacle to the transition process was based in KZN. This was the constellation of forces formed by Chief Buthelezi, the Inkatha Freedom Party, the Zulu monarchy and the KwaZulu gov-ernment. The IFP's foothold in African popular politics gave a tenuous and partial credibility to the rejectionist front formed with the white right and the Ciskei and Bophuthatswana homelands, the Freedom Alliance (FA). So threatening were the portents of low-level civil war in KZN and the obstructionism of the FA that the fate of negotiated transition seemed to rest on the outcome of events and developments in KZN. Whether a negotiated settlement would be crowned with inclusiveness or unravel altogether in the chaos of secessionist violence would be decided here.[1]

Behind both these reasons for KZN's singularity lies the question of competition for African votes. KwaZulu was the only homeland where existing political forces were not susceptible to being co-opted or over-whelmed by the ANC. In some of the independent homelands, leaders helped deliver the territory and population to the ANC (as in Venda and Transkei). In others, the ANC waged a campaign of destabilisation against patronage regimes with no effective popular base (as in Ciskei and Bophuthatswana). In the non-independent homelands, Africans with no prior commitment to the ANC could be mobilised through a variety of strategies. These included enthusiasm for the 'Uhuru' moment, and the ANC's skilful handling of local traditions, issues and notables, whose presence on ANC election lists could deliver votes. In KZN, however, Inkatha[2] was a genuine rival to the ANC for Africans' allegiance. Ethnic mobilisation and manipulation of devolved powers and resources by effective leadership were the bases for nation- and state-building which made KwaZulu and Inkatha focuses of allegiance.[3]

If it is competition for the political allegiance of Africans which makes KZN distinctive in national politics, some explanation of Inkatha's success as a challenger to the ANC is called for. Three salient factors should be noted at this point. First, the potential for ethnic mobilisation in black politics is greater in KZN than in other parts of the country. The nineteenth-century Zulu kingdom offers a mythological resource to contemporary political entrepreneurs which is unmatched elsewhere in South Africa. The sheer vigour of its projects of state-, nation- and empire-building, and the extent to which these exploits are regarded as crucial in shaping South African history, have ensured that here, as nowhere else, pre-colonial social formations and resistance to colonialism obtrude directly into current political conflict.[4]

Second, the geopolitics of KZN differ in one crucial respect from those of other regions. KwaZulu was the only homeland whose territory impinged significantly on the borders of white cities and their satellite black townships. Indeed, Durban and Pietermaritzburg were surrounded by areas administered by KwaZulu. As a result, a major point of conflict between Inkatha and the United Democratic Front in the 1980s was the threatened incorporation of African townships into KwaZulu. Given Inkatha's control of the KwaZulu administration then, the proximity of KwaZulu to Natal's major African areas allowed it to challenge the ANC (and, before 1990, its surrogates) in urban areas. In addition, this geographical factor ensured that Inkatha featured in the consciousness and calculations of white business and political elites in Natal in a way no other black political movement in the rest of South Africa could match.

The third factor has to do with the dynamics of white politics in Natal. Natal has no sizeable and concentrated Afrikaner population, and as a result the National Party has had no natural constituency there. Natal's ambivalence about the Union, rejection of the Republic and durable identification with its own colonial origins and English ethos have contributed to a sense of separateness from the wider white polity. This has made itself felt in many ways, from the aggrieved claim that Natal was starved of its true share of central government disbursements because its citizens would not vote for the National Party,[5] through the desire for more provincial autonomy, to vaguely federalist and even residually secessionist sentiments. The mutually reinforcing alienation between Natal and the central government disposed white elites in Natal to consider separate negotiations with black political forces. They found a more than willing partner in Chief Buthelezi, who saw that such arrangements would give him invaluable political space in which to resist the government's pressure to take independence for KwaZulu on the one hand, and in which to prosecute Inkatha's rivalry with the ANC on the other.

This coincidence of interests was reinforced by Buthelezi's firm rejection of sanctions and armed struggle as legitimate ways of bringing about political change in South Africa. The rapprochement bore fruit in the Buthelezi Commission and the KwaZulu–Natal Indaba extensively publicised negotiating initiatives which, though weakened by the absence of the National Party government and the ANC, did much to legitimise the idea of negotiations between black and white representatives.[6] They also served as a warning to both the nationalists and the liberation movements that excessive immobilism on their parts would open the way to initiatives which they could not control. Less highly publicised, but perhaps even more important, were initiatives which brought together certain aspects of provincial and homelands administration in the KwaZulu–Natal Joint Executive Authority.[7]

The interaction of these three factors allowed Inkatha to transcend the stereotype of homeland patronage politics, creating a political movement which shared concerns with white business and political elites and had a foothold in the urban African politics of 'white' South Africa. This does not mean that patronage was an insignificant part of Inkatha's mobilisation strategies. On the contrary, the KwaZulu government's role as a conduit for central state expenditure, and as a major employer, offered considerable resources of patronage to whoever controlled it. Patronage offered a material return for the ethnic identities propagated by Inkatha, and ethnicity clothed patronage in the mantle of popular politics.

This self-reinforcing relationship between ethnicity and patronage established Buthelezi's claims to be a popular leader and Inkatha's to be a mass movement. It was on the basis of this credibility that another self-reinforcing relationship was grounded, one in which Buthelezi and his movement could play the role of broker between black and white interests. Buthelezi appeared to channel black aspirations within limits compatible with white vested interests. On the other hand, for conservative blacks he appeared to offer liberation from apartheid without either the trauma of armed struggle and sanctions, or the self-mutilating strategies of strikes and educational boycotts. What is more, his conception of liberation did not threaten to sweep away the established practices, prerogatives and relationships of traditional culture in a general revolutionary upheaval. In this way, it was his claim to be a popular leader which validated his leverage in white circles, and this supposed leverage which validated his claim to rival the ANC with an alternative liberation strategy.

Buthelezi and Inkatha after 1990

President de Klerk's reforms of February 1990 had both positive and negative effects for Inkatha. Like other parties, Inkatha could now take part freely in negotiations and Buthelezi could join his voice to the chorus of those who claimed credit for setting the conditions which the release of Nelson Mandela and the unbanning of liberation movements now fulfilled. What is more, he could claim that the Buthelezi Commission and the Indaba were pioneering and agenda-setting precedents for negotiations whose spirit others were now emulating. The negotiations were underpinned by the tacit admission that no party could impose its preferred solutions on the others. This meant that alliances and understandings would be necessary. Inkatha, with a foot in both white and black politics, would be well placed to exploit this situation.

These encouraging prospects were offset by some formidable problems, which stemmed from the two principal features of the reforms, the freeing of political activity and the repeal of the major apartheid laws. The unbanning of the ANC threatened Inkatha's positions of influence in both white and black politics. First, by legalising the ANC, de Klerk forced a revolution in official white attitudes to it and an equally revolutionary task of transformation on the movement itself. The world of Communist and Afro-Asian solidarity which sustained the ANC for so long was crumbling visibly by the day and the government's 'total onslaught'/'total strategy' rhetoric of counterinsurgency was swiftly ended. These developments undermined the logic of Buthelezi's appeal to whites. The effect was strengthened as the ANC began in earnest the task of transforming itself from a revolutionary underground movement into a responsible political party. It began to speak the language of pluralism and compromise in politics, and in economic policy it progressively abandoned *dirigiste* designs on the commanding heights of the economy in favour of responsible fiscal management and a strong role for the private sector in plans for reconstruction and development.

These effects should not be misinterpreted. Whites did not learn to trust and give their support to the ANC because it was apparently changing its character. Buthelezi, both in the policies he espoused and the character of his movement, remained the acceptable face of black aspirations for most whites. That was, however, not the point. The issue for white political parties and for individual white voters was not to choose the black political party whose policies were most compatible with white interests. White votes cannot make the difference between black political parties as South African politics is configured at present, certainly at national level. The issue for whites has been to put what pressure they could on the party which will represent the majority of blacks, to control and confine their aspirations and expectations, thus limiting the damage to white interests.

This refocusing of white attention away from the IFP and towards the ANC was a setback for Buthelezi's hopes that his history of restraint in opposition, his moderation in policies and frequently expressed sensitivity to the fears and potentially destructive powers of whites would win him a pivotal position in the transition process. Much of Buthelezi's subsequent bitterness and intransigence can be traced to the belief that despite his own best efforts on behalf of whites, he was abandoned as a result of a cynical calculation of the balance of political forces.[8]

Second, the unbanning of the ANC threatened to drive a wedge into Inkatha's position in black politics. Buthelezi was acutely aware that the ANC's new status and the general freeing of political activity did not only mean a seat at the negotiating table for his principal antagonist. These things also meant a new freedom for the ANC to practise its various forms of 'mass action': strikes, stay-aways, boycotts, demonstrations and occupations. The ANC made it quite clear that its agreement first to suspend and then later to abandon the armed struggle did not cover these kinds of direct action pressure tactics.

Mass action served many functions for the ANC and its alliance partners, of which three in particular impinged on the IFP's aspirations:

- It put pressure on the government by weakening its negotiating position and establishing the ANC as the most significant black political force;

- It was a weapon of destabilisation against 'illegitimate political structures', including bantustans (or at least those which had not declared for the ANC), and a way of forcing the issue of 'free political activity' in them;

- It was a way of mobilising by participation and, through shows of strength, of inhibiting allegiance to other parties and intimidating their supporters.

These functions and their effects had a significant impact on the balance of power between Inkatha and the ANC. Buthelezi was deeply concerned from the first that the negotiations should be taking place in the context of mass action and, like the nationalist government, he always insisted on having the term 'intimidation' attached to accords, codes of practice and joint statements of intent on the subject of violence. Although successful at the rhetorical level, this tactic had no substantive effect, defeated as much by the difficulty of defining 'intimidation' (let alone policing it) as by the ANC's insistence on the legitimacy of 'mass action'.

The ANC's resort to mass action fuelled Buthelezi's disillusion with negotiations, confirming his view that they were only the fig leaf of a power struggle which was taking place on the streets and in the townships. In Natal's townships this power struggle had been prosecuted since the mid-1980s. The ANC's surrogates used intimidation to enforce mass action. Inkatha's countermeasures of using vigilantes, supported by the security forces, to break strikes and boycotts had been camouflaged by the states of emergency of the 1980s. These tactics were more difficult to deploy under the new, freer and more visible political conditions. The repeal of the state of emergency[9] also meant greater freedom to investigate and write about covert government actions. Extensive media publicity about Inkatha's links with South African security forces was another problem Buthelezi had to deal with after 1990.

It was not only the new, more open conditions of political activity which posed problems for Inkatha. The repeal of apartheid legislation raised the question of the reintegration of the homelands into South Africa. Since an insistence on the territorial integrity of South Africa had been a key feature of Buthelezi's refusal to take independence for KwaZulu, the question of reintegration should not, on the face of it, have been too threatening a development. In practice, however, it was. First, if KwaZulu was reintegrated without Inkatha developing into a national political movement, a bankable asset would be lost without corresponding gain. Second, the homeland base was essential to the reproduction of Inkatha's support. The claim that KwaZulu stood in direct lineage from the Zulu kingdom, and the patronage that devolved institutions of government offered, were both central to Inkatha's strategies of mobilisation. As a result, it was paramount that a wide measure of autonomy be guaranteed for KwaZulu as the basis for reincorporation.

Strategy and tactics

In order to address this balance sheet of challenges and opportunities, Inkatha relaunched itself as the Inkatha Freedom Party, seeking to attract support from all South Africans and specifically geared to the new multi-racial electoral politics. The place of the new party in the politics of negotiation and electioneering as they evolved over the following three years can usefully be discussed under the following headings: constitutional negotiations and the place of elections in the process; the relationship between the centre and the regions; ethnicity and the monarchy; the search for allies; and the war on the ground in KZN.

The IFP's attitude to negotiations was conditioned throughout by a preference for a 'Lancaster House' model, from which a new dispensation would emerge.[10] This envisaged negotiations taking place unaffected not only by armed struggle, but by all forms of political struggle. These negotiations would be undertaken by parties with demonstrable existing support and an established position. Negotiations between these interested parties would produce a new constitution which, if ratified by a referendum, would lead the way towards elections, a new assembly and a new government. These bodies would not be able to alter the constitution except by whatever special majority the constitution itself specified, in line with constitutional practice elsewhere in the world. In other words, the IFP wanted no test of popular support before the constitution was finalised, and elections would be exclusively for the purpose of choosing a new government, having no effect on constitution-making. This contrasted sharply with the ANC's goal of transitional constitutional arrangements and an early election for a constituent assembly, which would be a constitution-making body reflecting the popular support enjoyed by each party.

Although the ANC had to compromise by accepting quite strict limitations on the constitution-making body's freedom of action, the IFP was never properly reconciled to the timing and purpose of elections. Even at the last moment, the IFP's attempts to bargain terms for joining the election represented an attempt to salvage something of its original position by entrenching as much as possible before a test of popular will.

The IFP was also at odds with the ANC and the government over the structure of negotiations and the way decisions were taken. By the second half of 1992, it was generally recognised that the negotiation process was being driven by bilateral agenda-setting and secret deals between the ANC and the government. The so-called Record of Understanding of September 1992, which ended the formal suspension of talks caused by the failure of CODESA II (May) and the Boipatong massacre (June), is generally taken as the point at which this development complete. But the Record of Understanding contained two provisions which ran directly counter to IFP positions. These were the fencing-off of hostels, which were the focus of violence on the Witwatersrand, and a ban on the carrying of 'cultural weapons' by Zulu demonstrators.

To have his party marginalised in this way confirmed Buthelezi's suspicions that henceforth multilateral negotiations would merely rubber-stamp decisions made by the ANC/government axis. The IFP briefly (April–June 1993) rejoined the next round of multilateral talks, but when the decision-making formula of 'sufficient consensus' was interpreted to mean consensus between the government and the ANC, especially in setting the date of the first non-racial elections, the IFP walked out for good.

The IFP's first strategic concern, then, was to take issue on normative and procedural grounds with its opponents' consensus on the meaning, pace and mechanics of the negotiations. The second was a question of the content of the negotiations. The most important issue here was the division of power between the centre and the regions in the new South African political system. There was no mistaking the vehemence and consistency with which the general principle of regional autonomy was pursued by the IFP, but the form in which this principle might eventually be expressed was shrouded in ambiguity. All IFP representatives, right up to the highest, were quite capable of switching from detailed discussions of federal principle (like original powers of taxation) to thinly veiled secessionist threats at a moment's notice.

The party's most complete statement on the matter – the Constitution of KZN, a document presented to the KwaZulu Legislative Assembly with the avowed intention of placing it before the region's electorate in a referendum[11] – is deeply confederal in both tone and substance. The issue was muddied further by the Zulu monarch's declaration of a 'sovereign Zulu kingdom' within the 1838 boundaries of Zulu territory, an intervention which was historically problematic and constitutionally vague.[12]

It is difficult to say with authority whether all this reflected genuine confusion of discourse, crude negotiating tactics in which secession was threatened to extract democratic federal principles, or a long-term strategy of using federalism as a stalking-horse for independence. This uncertainty was compounded by the third of the IFP's strategic concerns, the assertion of Zulu ethnicity and the prerogatives of the Zulu monarchy. It was often unclear whether strong regional powers were being sought in the name of democracy or of ethnic self-determination. Since there is no necessary connection between the two, this was an important source of ambiguity.

Capitalising on ethnicity had always been an essential part of Inkatha's mobilising strategies, and the new political conditions of the 1990s tended to encourage its further exploitation. The IFP redoubled its long-standing charges that the ANC is Xhosa-dominated, now that the leaders in question were visible and accessible. When the violence on the Witwatersrand took on an ethnic cast and victims were targeted by dress or language, the IFP claimed the role of protector of Zulus in alien territory, turning hostels inhabited by Zulu migrant workers into fortresses and Trojan horses. ANC demands that the 'bantustan structures' of the KwaZulu government be dismantled were interpreted by the IFP as threats to 'annihilate' the Zulu people.[13] Charges of 'ethnic cleansing' on the part of ANC-aligned groups became an everyday part of IFP discourse.

Ethnic concerns became vital to the IFP's negotiation strategies because they gave the party a stronger case against marginalisation. A political party considered purely as a secular compact of interests on the basis of ideology, patronage and policy programme can expect no special treatment if it attracts only a small minority of voters. But it is not prudent to dismiss, purely on the grounds of numbers, a party which represents a sacred compact of blood, kin, history, culture and claims to self-determination. By taking up issues like the cause of the Zulu hostel dwellers, demanding the right for Zulus to carry 'cultural weapons', and holding party political rallies in a 'traditional' cultural format,[14] Buthelezi and the IFP served a warning that to treat the IFP merely as a minority political party was to marginalise a nation.

This was effective enough as far as it went, but since many people who spoke Zulu and adhered to Zulu customs supported the ANC, language and culture on their own were problematic bases for politicised ethnic identity. It was through the monarchy that Buthelezi and the IFP tried to establish the sacred compact between nation and political party.

Beginning in May 1992, when Buthelezi refused to attend the multiparty negotiating forum, CODESA II, because the Zulu King was not granted status as an independent negotiator, the monarchy became the IFP's central preoccupation. This situation was not without its problems and ironies. Buthelezi's position as 'traditional prime minister' to the royal house – a status he resorted to more and more in the later stages of negotiation – is not universally recognised and relations between the two men have not always been good. In 1979, Buthelezi arraigned the young King Goodwill in front of the KwaZulu Legislative Assembly, accusing him of conspiracy to found an opposition party and threatening to cut his stipend. Whatever the differences between the two men and whatever the King privately felt about the circumscribed and co-opted role he had been forced to play since the 1979 confrontation, both shared enough concerns about the future to act in concert. Neither could look forward with equanimity to the formal reintegration of KwaZulu into a South African unitary state under ANC rule, so Buthelezi became the King's champion in negotiations and the monarchy became the IFP's most important electoral asset.

Despite Inkatha's markedly ethnic provenance, throughout its existence Buthelezi consistently sought to construct alliances and understandings with other black and white political parties. It is not surprising, then, that the fourth element of the IFP's post-1990 strategies was a continuation of this policy. The IFP and the National Party had concerns in common, including strong regional powers and the protection of minorities. They had collaborated in the past, too, though more often at the level of covert counterinsurgency than at that of open political alliance. Despite these incentives, it was difficult for them to act together in the post-1990 political environment. The central problem was that the NP could not sacrifice its delicate adversarial partnership with the ANC – which was essential for the transition to take place at all – in the interests of an alliance with a regional force which was engaged in a murderous civil war with the ANC.

By the 1990s, Inkatha/IFP was clearly incapable of co-operating with any party to the left of the NP (it had thoroughly alienated the Democratic Party for instance), and its best hope of alliance politics now lay on the right. A shared commitment to ethnic self-determination and an implacable hostility to the ANC were enough to make the IFP and the white right reasonably compatible. The principle of self-determination even raised the partnership somewhat above the level of pure opportunism, although this could not be said for both parties' links with the 'independent' bantustans, Ciskei and Bophuthatswana. By mid-1992 these four disparate forces had joined together to oppose the emerging ANC/ National Party consensus on transitional arrangements. The rejectionist front which they formed was known first as the Concerned South Africans Group (COSAG) and from mid-1993 as the Freedom Alliance. As the ANC and National Party brought the negotiations to a successful conclusion towards the end of 1993, the Freedom Alliance's strategy crystallised around opposition to the holding of elections within the transitional framework which the negotiations produced.

The IFP and the white right were by far the most important components of the Freedom Alliance. But despite the veneer of shared concerns, the fantasy of a 'Boer and Zulu' axis of warrior peoples (which became a staple of right-wing leaders' rhetoric) was an improbable one. Despite its Zulu ethnocentrism, the IFP did have a genuine commitment to multi-racial and equal citizenship. It could not hope to rule KZN with its influential white and Indian minorities, in any other way. The same could not be said for the white right, whose components differed only in the degree to which they rationalised and camouflaged their racism. Such a basic clash of values would have made co-existence difficult in the future even if the two sides helped each other win self-determination. In addition, the certainty of competing territorial claims in Northern Natal between Afrikaner and Zulu underlined the incongruity of the partnership.

The failure of right-wing paramilitary forces to save the government of Chief Lucas Mangope in March 1994 exposed the hollow basis of the Freedom Alliance. There is no doubt that right-wing whites (and 'Third Force' elements in the security forces) could and did help irregular black forces in localised campaigns of raid and reprisal on ANC-supporting elements in many parts of South Africa after 1990. But the overthrow of Mangope showed that the white right wing could not act decisively to forestall a coup against its black allies, even under the relatively favourable strategic circumstances provided by Bophuthatswana's proximity to right-wing strongholds in the Western Transvaal. In particular, after Mangope's fall it was hard to believe that any act of secessionist defiance in KwaZulu could be brought to a successful conclusion by the assistance of a by-now divided and demoralised white right.

The fifth and last of the IFP's strategic concerns after 1990 was to prosecute the war against the ANC in Natal and KwaZulu. Political competition between the IFP and the ANC is widely believed by observers and participants to be central to the violence in KZN.[15] While each side routinely blames the other, however, no authoritative, non-partisan account exists ascribing to either side a coherent strategy of war-making, sanctioned and planned at high leadership levels. There are good grounds for this caution, given that much of the research conducted into the violence in KZN suggests the importance of localised conflicts, reflecting a condition of anomie rather than politically directed strategy.[16]

Since 1990, perpetrators of political violence have not been able to make the most common claim of moral justification, that they are denied alternative forms of political expression. Partly for this reason, political violence in South Africa has been covert, largely ˌanonymous and as a result very difficult to interpret. The paradigm of political violence in which guerrilla groups claim responsibility through the media or otherwise make the significance of actions explicit through precise political timing and targeting of victims by no means always holds in South Africa, especially in KZN. Often the political allegiance of victims is unknown, or is disputed, both sides claiming the dead for 'their' side. Poor records of arrest and conviction and an understandable tendency to be non-committal on the part of most independent monitors, who are the main sources of data on violence, compound the difficulties of interpretation.

In any case, political competition between the IFP and the ANC in KZN is inextricably mixed with other dimensions of conflict: crime, tribal and factional disputes and intergenerational tensions are fertile sources of violence. Participants in these struggles often show keen opportunism in approaching one or other of the main parties for help, and are met with matching eagerness to exploit tensions. Central to this kind of relationship is the phenomenon of 'warlordism', in which powerful local figures act as brokers for the interests of squatters, hostel dwellers or other marginalised groups, attaching themselves to one or the other political party in the process, but not always placing themselves under their control. Individuals or cliques of this sort tend to have their own conceptions of what it means to 'belong to' or be associated with the ANC or the IFP. The general impression of localised conflict is reinforced by the fact that peace pacts between ANC- and IFP-supporting groups seem to hold in some areas and not in others.

These observations on the nature of conflict in KZN do not by any means absolve the ANC and the IFP from charges of pursuing deliberate strategies of violence. There is ample evidence to suggest that political violence in the region became much more systematically organised and pursued, especially after about mid-1992. The proportion of casualties suffered in incidents of communal violence involving crowds armed with stabbing weapons or crude firearms decreased. The targeting of victims and the tactics employed in assassinations increasingly indicated that those now involved were armed, trained and organised along military lines, suggesting that Umkhonto We Sizwe units and 'hit squads' drawn from the KwaZulu Police were being regularly used by the respective sides. In addition, regional leaders on both sides came much closer to issuing direct threats of violence and of acknowledging that 'their' troops were involved, although always of course in self-defence.

Perhaps most significant of all, the escalating death toll in the first four months of 1994, which directly paralleled the acute political tensions over whether the IFP would participate in the election or not, seems to indicate the direct link between political competition and violence. Even more so, the dramatic decline in violence once the IFP agreed to participate suggests a degree of central control over the level of operations in the field.

These arguments are not conclusive, however. Even since the election there have been many deaths in violent clashes. It is possible that these incidents are merely being redefined by observers, without the ANC/IFP tag which would have been routinely attached before 27 April 1994, or that localised factional disputes are again becoming more prominent.

The role of the IFP and ANC in channelling, exploiting, and sometimes containing the violence in KZN cannot be denied. Clearly there were also times when the level of violence was being affected by high-level commands. But the idea that the multidimensional constellation of local conflicts, which has accounted for the bulk of the casualties in KZN, has been initiated and orchestrated by one or both sides cannot be sustained on the available evidence.

The ANC in KwaZulu-Natal

That KZN loomed so large in national politics in the months leading up to the election was due to the singularity of the IFP, with its fusion of traditional and modern agendas and confusion of federal, confederal and secessionist politics. While the burden of explaining regional politics should appropriately fall on this phenomenon, it is also important to discuss the condition of the ANC in KZN.

In 1990, the newly unbanned ANC faced the same tasks in KZN as it did over the whole of South Africa.[17] These included integrating exile, underground, ex-prisoner, trade union and community activists into a coherent movement and establishing an organisational infrastructure on which to build a mass membership. At the same time, the ANC had to negotiate with the government, plan for elections and ensure that the regions and grass-roots remained in step with the newly formulated policy programmes of the national leadership.

In KZN, these problems were given an extra dimension by the need to compete with the IFP for Africans' votes. This in turn was part of a wider problem, that of coming to terms with the force of traditional beliefs, customs, authority structures and allegiances in African life. It was necessary for the ANC to negotiate a position of mutual recognition and respect between traditional and modernised forces, in order to establish a popular bridgehead outside the urbanised elite of workers and township dwellers.[18] This had to be done without compromising the sternest imperative of African nationalism in South Africa, the injunction against tribalism. At the same time it was necessary to avoid alienating progressive lobbies (notably women's interests) within the movement.

These issues were overlaid with three questions of internal organisation and political division. The first came to light immediately after the unbanning of the ANC and arose from accusations that there was a 'cabal' which manipulated the organisation's affairs in the region during the underground years. The charges – among other things, of personal corruption and inadequate leadership during the township struggles of the 1980s – were made by a reform group spearheaded by former Robben Island prisoners. They were directed at leaders both of the ANC's surrogate, the UDF, and (in particular) of the Natal Indian Congress (NIC). Although some of the accused successfully went on to influential careers in regional (and even national) politics as individuals, the cabal affair (which carried uncomfortable echoes of historic conflicts between Indians and Africans in Natal) caused bitter recriminations and debilitating infighting. It was one source of bitter disputes over the ANC's election candidate lists in KZN, in which former NIC people did rather badly.

The second question of internal organisation reflected the difficulties of integrating the three KZN regions of the ANC into an effective whole. The three regions are Southern Natal, which includes the Greater Durban area, the largest centre of population; the Natal Midlands, including the provincial capital and second city, Pietermaritzburg; and Northern Natal, which includes the bulk of KwaZulu's territory.

There is always something to be said for decentralisation in the organisation of political parties and allowing local issues and enthusiasms to galvanise mobilisation. On the other hand, the growth of parochial fiefs with wayward policies which are difficult to reconcile with higher levels of leadership can be a danger of allowing too much local initiative. Under the charismatic but dictatorial leadership of the veteran trade unionist and ex-Robben Islander Harry Gwala, the ANC in the Natal Midlands probably made less progress than in any other region in making the transition from underground liberation movement to legitimate political party. Gwala's unreconstructed Stalinism, populist rhetoric and straightforward advocacy of direct paramilitary action in the struggle against the IFP made him extremely popular with the youthful 'comrades' in the ANC. They had been the shock troops of the township struggles of the 1980s, and under Gwala their violent and radical ethos has remained a stronger influence than in other regions.

Gwala's popularity was not confined to his own fief. As the National Executive Council elections in 1991 showed, he was a very popular figure with the rank and file nationally.[19] His close association with other national figures who had a reputation for militancy – the late Chris Hani, Winnie Mandela and Peter Mokaba – helped cement this. Despite an ineffective top-dressing of white defectors from the Democratic Party (parliamentary and local government representatives from Pietermaritzburg in the main), the ANC Midlands region functioned on a diet of raw revolutionary rhetoric, paramilitarism and underground intrigue. The latter caused Gwala to be the subject of an official investigation of the South African Communist Party, facing accusations that he has plotted to murder other prominent Communists in the region.[20]

These factional disputes were paralleled by poor relations between the Midlands region and the national leadership. Gwala was at times bitterly critical of the leadership and his militant rhetoric was often out of step with the requirements of national-level strategy. The leadership responded with procedural objections to Gwala's simultaneous tenure of regional and national offices, which were scarcely concealed efforts to marginalise and neutralise him.

It would be an unjustifiable oversimplification to contrast a 'moderate' Southern Natal region with a 'radical' Midlands. Elements in Southern Natal appreciated the place of direct action and paramilitary tactics along-side and behind the negotiating process. The cabal issue also showed that intrigue was not unknown in the region. On the other hand, the various structures of the ANC alliance in Southern Natal appeared to grasp more thoroughly than their Midlands counterparts the fact that diplomacy and public relations were now as important as street militancy and covert military action.

In some respects, the Northern Natal region has been the most prob-lematic of the ANC's three administrative divisions in KZN. In addition to the standard difficulties of organising in underdeveloped rural areas – including poor infrastructure, low levels of education and political con-sciousness, and collisions with traditional authorities – ANC organisers faced a vigorous campaign of harassment and repression from the IFP and the KwaZulu government. This campaign included systematic denial of facilities under the jurisdiction of the homeland government to the ANC and the intimidation and murder of ANC organisers. The latter was a reciprocal feature of the ANC/IFP conflict everywhere in KZN, of course, but given the question of jurisdiction – including that of the KwaZulu Police – the balance of power in the North was very much in the IFP's favour.

The resulting weakness of the Northern Natal region had interesting side-effects. It is likely that the debilitated condition of these regional structures allowed the coup in late 1993 which saw the regional leader-ship deposed by supporters of ANC national deputy secretary-general, Jacob Zuma. Despite the controversial nature of the takeover – which was the subject of acrimonious exchanges between the three regions and national leadership[21] – it was agreed that the unfavourable circumstances faced by the ANC in Northern Natal justified a disproportionate weight-ing for that area in the selection process to find a candidate for the regional premiership. Partisans of the unsuccessful contenders (Gwala and

Jeff Radebe of the Southern Natal region) claimed that these unusual, perhaps irregular, circumstances formed the basis for Zuma's successful bid for top spot on the regional candidates' list.

The question of Zuma's leadership highlights the third organisational problem faced by the ANC in KZN, the sometimes strained relationship between the Natal regions and the national leadership. Aside from any question of personal qualities, Jacob Zuma represented a considerable asset to the national leadership. There were two reasons for this. First, the presence of at least one official of Zulu origin in leadership circles provided a partial answer to the frequent accusations that the ANC was 'Xhosa-dominated'. Second, Zuma was not merely a 'token Zulu' but identified himself enthusiastically with Zulu culture and the monarchy. This made him a credible emissary in negotiations with the king and the IFP, and a bridge-builder between the ANC and traditional forces in Zulu society.

These qualities carried rather less weight in the Natal regions. Despite the credentials of local birth and upbringing, Zuma had spent virtually all of his political career in exile and he is firmly identified with the exile leadership rather than local activists. There was something proconsular about him, as if he had been sent from a distant capital to pacify rebellious tribesmen. His concern for the pieties of Zulu ethnicity and his ease of manner with leading IFP figures did not find universal favour with the Natal regions. In the eyes of some KwaZulu-Natal activists, Zuma fraternised too much with the enemy and appeased forces which were inimical to their conception of core ANC values. In addition, Zuma's responsibilities in exile included counterespionage work on behalf of ANC intelligence. In order to weed out informers and provocateurs he was vested with powers of interrogation and detention which would not have endeared him to many who were on the receiving end of them.

Zuma's good lines of communication with the IFP and ability to flatter traditional forces in Zulu politics fitted well with the national leadership's preoccupations in coping with the IFP challenge. Faced with the real prospect of a debilitating struggle to preserve the country's territorial integrity, or even a catastrophic war of secession, the ANC's leadership was aware of how important it was to make agreement on the interim constitution and transitional arrangements as inclusive as possible. In the eyes of the leadership, long-term goals of political stability and reconciliation should not be endangered by the urgings of local forces, whose closeness to the bitter struggle with the IFP distorted their vision of national priorities.

Attitudes like this could make ANC activists feel that their life-or-death struggle was being treated like an irritating parochial concern and an unwelcome distraction from the real business of national negotiation and long-term nation-building. Some ANC militants clearly wanted to destabilise the IFP's KwaZulu stronghold by a combination of mass action and armed struggle. They argued that violence was the only language that the IFP understood and that to make concessions was futile, since Buthelezi's appetite for them was infinite. Others appreciated the depth and durability of the IFP's support and grasped the dangers of believing that 'one last push' would solve the IFP problem once and for all. They too were seriously perturbed at the prospect of concessions to the IFP, but realised the need for diplomacy as well as war.

It was the development of the IFP's own strategies which presented an alternative to the ANC other than the equally unenticing prospects of appeasement and war. By tying its fortunes so closely to the monarchy, the IFP unwittingly exposed a flank which the ANC could turn. If the ANC was willing to propitiate the king and accept the importance of the monarchy in a post-apartheid dispensation, it could engage the IFP on its own ground, challenge its monopoly of Zulu ethnicity and make useful political capital out of claims that Buthelezi was debauching the heritage of all Zulus for sectional political advantage and personal advancement. While appeasement of Buthelezi was politically impossible, generous gestures could be made to the king. At worst, this policy would give Buthelezi a face-saving formula with which to join the elections. At best (and more probably in the long term), it would detach the king from Buthelezi, counter the IFP's most negotiable political asset, ethnic mobilisation, and allow for more flexible alignments and freer political activity.

Such a policy would bring its own problems. The Zulu king is not the only traditional leader (or indeed the only monarch) in South Africa. To show favour solely to the Zulu monarchy might offend others, including the Congress of Traditional Leaders of South Africa (CONTRALESA), an influential lobbying group of 'progressive chiefs' aligned to the ANC. On the other hand, if the ANC's courtship was extended to all traditional leaders, this would conflict with the modernised, progressive image of the movement. Lastly, encouraging the independence of the Zulu monarchy might be useful as a ploy in the contest with the IFP, but at the cost of creating a force in regional politics which could be awkward to deal with in the future. In this respect, the language used by the king in declaring a 'sovereign kingdom' and the territorial claims which accompanied this vaguely worded aspiration were enough to set off alarm bells.[22] For this reason, while some elements in the ANC's Natal regions were susceptible to the appeal of tradition, others were more concerned to limit the influence of the monarch.

Such considerations were evident when in May 1992 the ANC had to react to Buthelezi's demand that King Goodwill be accorded full status as a negotiator at CODESA II. By attempting to deal with the matter as one of protocol involving all traditional leaders, the ANC tried to signal its concern for tradition without explicitly favouring the Zulu monarchy. In theory, these considerations still prevailed when, in October 1993, the

Natal regions of the ANC held a huge rally in Durban to celebrate African traditional culture. Its theme was inclusiveness, its name was 'Sonke' (Zulu for 'all of us') and its slogan was 'many cultures, one people'. Despite this, the rally was clearly meant as a signal that the ANC was comfortable with Zulu traditions, and although many monarchs and traditional leaders from around Southern Africa were invited, the invitation to King Goodwill was the symbolically important one. At this stage it was still politically impossible for the king to attend, but the ANC had made an important step towards recognising the monarchy's special importance in the region and defining itself in terms compatible with Zulu traditions.

This policy seemed to have borne fruit when, in December 1993, the king issued a statement in which he criticised those who were holding up the progress towards a negotiated settlement. Some observers interpreted this as evidence of the king's growing detachment from Buthelezi, but a smokescreen of denials and 'clarifications' in the next week diffused the impact of the statement. Although the affair blew over, it began to appear that Buthelezi was having to work harder and harder at keeping the king in line.

The IFP, the ANC and the Approach to the Election

The final phase of the approach to the election in KZN was governed by four factors. The first, early in 1994, was the collapse of Bophuthatswana and the fragmentation of the white right, which left Buthelezi isolated and exposed in the struggle to force the ANC and the government to postpone the election and modify the interim constitution. The second was the escalation of violence in KZN and the response of the interim authorities. The government and the Transitional Executive Council declared a state of emergency on 31 March 1994, signalling their determination to hold the election (at least in those areas they could secure) and demonstrating the allegiance of the security forces to them. The third factor was the growing realisation in the IFP camp that if it did not contest the elections, KwaZulu, its fief and source of patronage would cease to exist and the new region would be ruled by its bitter enemies.

All three of these were powerful factors in pushing the IFP towards acceptance of the election, but probably a fourth was crucial. Because the IFP's demands were made in the name of the king, Buthelezi could portray himself as the selfless champion of the monarchy and the nation, rather than as an obdurate and unscrupulous leader who was willing to risk civil war in order to cling to power at all costs. At the same time, the royal factor made it possible for the ANC (and the government) to accept a formula which looked like gracious acknowledgement of the monarchy, rather than the appeasement of unruly rejectionists.

In fact, until close to the end, Buthelezi tried to link the IFP's agenda to that of the monarchy and insist that the party's concerns be addressed too.[23] These concerns were articulated when, in November 1993, the IFP set six minimum demands which had to be met before the party took part in the election. Among them were the powers (especially financial) of the provinces, the status of provincial constitutions, the inclusion of the principle of self-determination in the constitution and the mechanisms for ratifying the final constitution. Two demands were added later, for the inclusion of the name 'KwaZulu' in the title of the new province and for a double ballot.

By April 1994, some of the demands had been granted in full, some partially and some not at all, while the IFP now began insisting on a postponement of the election and lifting of the state of emergency. At the Skukuza talks on 8 April, the government and ANC offered the king recognition as a constitutional monarch with entrenched powers, prerogatives and rights in KZN, but the offer foundered on Buthelezi's insistence that the IFP's agenda be addressed.[24] A little over a week later, essentially the same offer to the king was accepted along with the vague assurance of international mediation between the parties after the election. The pressures above finally persuaded Buthelezi of the dangers of further intransigence, and the IFP joined the electoral fray at last.

Conclusion

The balance of forces which precipitated the negotiation process in February 1990 was such that for the ANC to achieve its goal of political power through victory in a free election, it had to make many adaptations to entrenched powers and interests. The transitional arrangements, the interim constitution and the reshaping of ANC economic policy reflected this balance sheet of compromise with white power in government, the security forces, the bureaucracy and the economy. After a beginning of stutters and misfires, the ANC played its hand with increasing confidence and assurance in this confrontation. In a sense this was not surprising. The logic of retreating white power in the face of an inexorable black majority and its demands reflected the ANC's core understanding of itself and its adversary.

The political world of KZN defied this logic and the ANC seemed much less sure of itself in adapting to this world than in its contest with white power. A central part of ANC strategy was to disabuse the government of any notion that it could combine with black homelands' interests to contain and even defeat the ANC. If the ANC could achieve this, homelands parties and administrations – including the IFP/KwaZulu constellation – would wither on the vine or be overturned by a combination of shock tactics and subversion.

For reasons outlined above, this did not happen in KZN and the IFP emerged as an independent force. As a result, the ANC had to contemplate adapting to another world, one less predictable and in its way more alien than that of the white minority with which it was successfully engaging. This was the world of tribal chiefs and their control of land tenure, of pre-colonial glories, and of the successful fusion of ethnicity with bantustan institutions and the migrant labour system. When it became clear how costly frontal assault on this world would be, the ANC attempted to come to terms with it obliquely, by propitiating its most central symbol, the monarchy. This was enough to ensure that the election took place in KZN, but not enough to win the region for the ANC. Events since the election have shown, however, that the question of finding a place in the new South African political system for traditional authorities and practices was not settled in April 1994, at least in the political world of KwaZulu-Natal.[25]

Notes

1   Regional (and to a lesser extent national) newspapers were important sources in researching and writing this chapter. In order to keep notes to a minimum, only the most important references to press sources are made in detail. The *Natal Mercury*, the *Daily News*, the *Sunday Tribune* (all Durban) and the *Natal Witness* (Pietermaritzburg) were particularly useful. Discussions with ANC and IFP party activists also yielded useful information. All informants wished to remain anonymous. This condition is hardly surprising, given the tense and violent nature of party competition (and, for that matter, intraparty relations) in this region. In this chapter, as in chapters 7, 10 and throughout the book, the province formerly known simply as Natal is given its new designation, KwaZulu/Natal (KZN). Where KwaZulu is used, it denotes the territory previously under the administration of the KwaZulu homeland government. Where Natal is used, it denotes the remainder of KZN.

2   This movement was formed (or, strictly speaking, re-formed) in 1975 as Inkatha Yenkululeko Yesizwe, a 'Zulu cultural liberation organisation'. It was generally known as 'Inkatha' until August 1990 when it was transformed into the Inkatha Freedom Party, geared to multiracial, electoral politics. References to the movement in this chapter will vary accordingly.

3   The academic literature on Buthelezi and Inkatha is largely critical and sometimes hostile. The most frequently cited source is G. Maré and G. Hamilton, *An Appetite for Power: Buthelezi's Inkatha and South African Politics* (Johannesburg: Ravan Press, 1987). See also by the same authors, 'The Inkatha Freedom Party', in A. Reynolds (ed.), *Election '94 South Africa* (Cape Town: David Philip, 1994), pp. 73–87.

4   See G. Maré, *Brothers Born of Warrior Blood: Politics and Ethnicity in South Africa* (Johannesburg: Ravan Press, 1992), esp. pp. 52–105. See also C. Hamilton, 'An appetite for the past: the re-creation of Shaka and the crisis in popular historical consciousness', *South African Historical Journal*, 22 (1990), pp. 141–57.

5   See for instance *Government Expenditure in Natal/KwaZulu: A Regional Comparison*, issued by the KwaZulu-Natal Joint Executive Authority (March 1993). This document describes the region as 'seriously underdeveloped' and 'grossly underfunded'.

6   On the politics of negotiation in the region generally, and on the Indaba specifically, see K. Roberts and G. Howe (eds), *New Frontiers: The KwaZulu/Natal Debates*, Indicator Project South Africa (Durban: University of Natal, 1987).

7   The Joint Executive Authority was set up in 1986 to facilitate the 'joint and co-ordinated exercise of powers and performance of functions by the provincial government of Natal and the government of KwaZulu' (Roberts and Howe [eds], *New Frontiers*, p. 16). The annual volumes of the South African Institute of Race Relations, *Race Relations Survey* provide useful brief reports on the functioning of the JEA.

8   Buthelezi had grounds for believing whites had betrayed him before, when they voted 'yes' by a large majority in the 1983 referendum on the Tricameral constitution which excluded blacks. Buthelezi campaigned hard against the Tricameral system and it was particularly galling to him that the highest 'yes' percentage was recorded among the whites of Natal. See 'It's either now or never', address to a meeting of the residents of Durban by Mangosuthu Buthelezi, Durban, 22 Oct. 1992 (mimeo), p. 4.

9   The state of emergency was lifted in all parts of the country other than Natal in June 1990, and in Natal from October.

10   A useful summary of the IFP's position on negotiations and transition can be found in D. Madide, 'The IFP vision . . .', *Sunday Tribune*, 10 Nov. 1991. At that time Dennis Madide was an IFP central committee member and KwaZulu Minister of Finance.

11   'The Constitution of the State of KwaZulu/Natal', as adopted by the KwaZulu Legislative Assembly, 1 Dec. 1992 (mimeo). For a critique of the document's confusing terminology and confederal tone see D. van Wyk, 'Federalism and governance', a paper presented at a seminar on 'The Federal Option for Natal/KwaZulu', Durban, 15 July 1993. David van Wyk is Professor of Constitutional Law at the University of South Africa.

12   King Goodwill's announcement (14 Feb. 1994) hinted strongly at secession: 'if the society expressed by the Zulu nation cannot co-exist with other societies in a united South Africa, then it becomes necessary and ineluctable that the society expressed by the Zulu nation exists on its own with its own territorial bases and with its own government. . . . The nation which was exercising its sovereignty over the land is abdicating its power to open the door for new nations to exercise their sovereignty over the land. Under this set of circumstances, I take the position that the sovereignty of the Zulu nation is revived.' Verbatim extracts from South African Press Association wire service, 14 Feb. 1994.

13   The high leadership of the IFP made these charges freely, but more often verbally than on paper. Author's notes of a meeting addressed by Dr Ziba Jiyane under the auspices of the Institute for a Democratic Alternative in South Africa (Durban, 24 Mar. 1994) record a typical instance of a frequent usage. Dr Jiyane, who is now the IFP's secretary-general, was at that time the party's principal media spokesman in the KwaZulu-Natal region.

14   On these and other manifestations of the IFP's ethnic strategies see C. Rickard, 'The power and the danger behind the ethnic wave', *Weekly Mail*, 30 May–6 June 1991.

15   For a discussion of the violence in Natal which centres on the inadequacy of a one-dimensional 'political' interpretation, see R. Taylor and M. Shaw, 'Interpreting the conflict in Natal', *Africa Perspective*, 2.1 (Dec. 1993), pp. 1–14.

16   See for instance D. Hindson and M. Morris, 'Understanding the conflict in Natal', in 'Towards the new Natal', supplement to the *Sunday Tribune*, 14 Oct. 1990. See also A. Minnaar, 'Mayhem in the Midlands: battle for Bruntville', *Indicator SA*, 9.3 (Winter 1992), pp. 60–4. Many articles published in *Indicator* in the last five years point to this conclusion and it is with this publication that serious research into the violence in Natal should begin.

17   See Y. Carrim, 'The ANC as a mass political organisation', in A. M. Johnston et al. (eds), *Constitution Making in the New South Africa* (London: Leicester University Press, 1993).

18   See A. M. Johnston, 'South Africa: the election and the transition process: five contradictions in search of a resolution', *Third World Quarterly*, 15.2 (1994), pp. 187–204.

19   Gwala came eighth in the election with 1,644 votes, the only one of the 50 elected members of the NEC to have a Natal profile.

20   As a result of the investigation, Gwala's membership of the SACP was suspended. The verdict (and indeed the charges themselves) became public knowledge only in May 1994, although the inquiry had been held at least three months earlier. It is likely that the SACP made sure the affair remained secret until after the election in order to avoid damaging the ANC's chances.

21   Natal activists claim that the ousted Northern Natal leader was personally removed from ANC regional and national lists by Nelson Mandela, who vetoed his candidacy for any elected public or ANC office.

22   See note 12 above.

23   For a full list of demands and discussion of progress in negotiations up to mid-February 1994 see A. M. Johnston, 'Trial of strength looms', *Daily News*, 18 Feb. 1994.

24   For a report see 'Royal flush beats ANC ace', *Sunday Times* (Jonannesburg), 10 April 1994.

25   For the immediate aftermath of the election in KwaZulu-Natal see A. M. Johnston, 'Zulu dawn: the election result in Natal/KwaZulu', *Indicator South Africa*, 11.3 (Winter 1994), pp. 23–6, and Johnston, 'IFP enigma', *Democracy in Action* (Cape Town), 8.3 (31 May 1994), pp. 5–6. In the second half of 1994, problems between the royal house and Buthelezi came to a head when the king dismissed Buthelezi from his position as traditional prime minister.

SEVEN

Public Opinion in KwaZulu-Natal

R.W. Johnson and Paulus Zulu

KwaZulu-Natal has, since 1985, witnessed more political violence (and more violence altogether) than any other part of South Africa. One result of this was to make the carrying out of opinion surveys extremely difficult, not only because interviewers ran real risks of physical violence, but because violence and intimidation were such entrenched parts of daily life for many respondents. Moreover, KZN politics are largely *territorial* – there were many ANC areas and IFP areas in which it was difficult to envisage genuinely free political activity and in which individuals would consider it extremely dangerous to profess support for a party other than the one dominant in their area. The fact that such areas could be largely or even wholly peaceful did not lessen the sense of implicit menace felt by their inhabitants.

This situation encouraged in many voters – including large numbers with no direct experience of violence or intimidation themselves – an attitude of fear and distrust. Respondents are prone, in such situations, to refuse to respond, to conceal their preferences, and often to tell the interviewer what they think he or she would like to hear. In general our interviewers were likely to have the classic ANC profile: they were relatively young, urban and educated. No matter how sensitive and careful they were, there was a built-in danger that respondents would give the sort of pro-ANC answers they imagined would please such interviewers.

It also seemed likely that opinion in KZN was changing quite rapidly away from a situation of overwhelming Inkatha dominance to one in which the ANC had large and perhaps even predominant strength. The largest and most thorough opinion survey in KZN prior to the liberalisation of political life in 1990, the so-called 'Project Pineapple' survey carried out for the KwaZulu-Natal Indaba in August 1988,[1] found that only 34% of respondents were spontaneously aware of the ANC, 44% of the ANC's predecessor the UDF, and 66% of Inkatha. Even when these organisations were named by the interviewer, awareness only rose to 61%, 69% and 82% respectively. When asked 'which organisation most blacks should support', Inkatha led by 38% to 6% each for the ANC and UDF, but with 49% saying 'none' or refusing to answer. When respondents were asked who was the best leader, Buthelezi (41%) led Mandela (10%) and Tambo (1%) but 28% said 'none' and 15% refused to answer.

The KwaZulu-Natal Indaba was widely viewed as a pro-Inkatha organisation, which might have prejudiced the above results to some extent. None the less it seemed clear that there was a genuine Inkatha plurality in KZN at that time (1988), especially since Inkatha's lead remained even when response rates rose. Thus only 7% of respondents refused to say which black leaders they would like to see involved in a future government in response to a question where they could name as many as they wanted: 64% wanted Chief Buthelezi involved and only 14% didn't, while only 40% wanted Nelson Mandela involved and 27% didn't. But Buthelezi was tremendously helped by a much higher (78%) spontaneous recognition rate than Mandela (32%). Even when respondents were reminded of leaders' names, total awareness of Buthelezi (93%) remained higher than for Mandela (64%).

Such advantages fell away with the changes of 1990. Even so, when the HSRC averaged its findings for January–July 1992 it found the IFP leading the ANC by 37% to 23%. However, 1992–4 saw enormous further publicity for the ANC and a considerable organisational effort by the ANC in KZN, all of which led to at least anecdotal reports of large ANC gains, particularly in the urban areas. This was the political context in which we conducted two large-scale surveys in KZN,[2] the first in November–December 1993 and the second in February 1994. During this period the political situation continued to deteriorate, with violence and tension at a high level throughout. The Inkatha Freedom Party was at the time of the first survey clearly moving towards an election boycott, and by the time of the second survey the boycott had begun to seem virtually inevitable – it was in fact declared shortly after our fieldwork was completed, and was lifted only shortly before the actual vote. The result was that the second survey took place in conditions of even greater tension and repeated warnings of impending civil war.

The First Survey, November–December 1993

Partisan choice

In our first survey we tested partisan choice both by a direct question asking respondents which party they supported (table 7.1) and by a

Table 7.1   Party choice in response to direct question (rounded %)

	Total	Whites	Indians	Coloureds	Africans
PAC	1	–	–	–	1
ANC–SACP	1	–	–	–	1
ANC	36	2	8	10	45
IFP	23	14	2	1	28
DP	2	9	1	7	1
NP	7	23	27	28	1
CP/VF	1	3	1	–	–
FA	1	2	–	1	–
FA/IFP/NP	–	2	–	–	–
AWB	1	5	–	–	–
No party	3	7	13	2	2
Don't know	6	10	1	–	6
Won't say	18	23	47	51	15

Table 7.2   Party choice in simulated secret ballot (rounded %)

	Total	Whites	Indians	Coloureds	Africans
PAC	–	–	–	–	1
ANC–SACP	3	–	1	2	3
ANC	48	4	27	33	57
IFP	24	19	2	6	28
DP	2	13	4	11	–
NP	13	42	63	45	2
CP/VF	1	3	–	–	–
FA	3	6	1	–	3
AWB	1	6	–	–	–
Other	1	2	1	3	–
Won't say	4	5	1	–	6

simulated secret ballot (table 7.2) in which respondents were asked to select parties in order of preference from a simulated ballot paper, which they could mark and place in a sealed envelope without the interviewer seeing – though respondents knew that we would be able to retrieve the data later. This produced a much higher response rate but still did not amount to a secret ballot since 41% of our sample (23% of whites, 32% of coloureds, 42% of Indians and 45% of Africans) required the interviewer's assistance to fill out the form. Since another 3% either deliberately spoilt their ballot or refused to fill it out, only 56% actually filled out the form in true secret ballot conditions. It will be seen that the ANC had a large advantage in table 7.1 and an even larger one in table 7.2, though we were not in a position to explain this discrepancy. (But see also Chapter 12, p. 345.)

We decided that it would be better to use table 7.1 for purposes of analysis since this question was posed in a manner uniform with other questions in the survey. The ANC's predominance among Africans was based on its overwhelming strength in the urban townships (where it received 84% support), among the better educated (69% of those educated beyond Std 6 supported it) and the 64% support it received among the 18–34 age group. IFP support was inversely related to these variables, though in the rural areas sampled it was running barely ahead of the ANC.

The NP was heavily dependent on the substantial support it achieved among coloureds and, particularly, among Indians: indeed, on the figures the KZN NP had become a predominantly Indian party – though the NP clearly stood in some danger if the large number of Indian non-respondents abstained.

Racial and partisan polarisations were very apparent. Over 80% of whites were unwilling to name the ANC as a first, second or third choice – though 32% mentioned the IFP. Over 95% of Africans were similarly unwilling to choose the DP under any circumstances, though 24% named the NP as a second/third choice, with another 26% naming the PAC and 31% the SACP; 25% of Indians and over 40% of coloureds saw the DP as an acceptable alternative to their first choice, but more striking was the fact that 80% or more of Indians and coloureds named the NP as their first, second or third choice. Of Africans, 66% would not name the IFP under any circumstance, while 37% would not name the ANC under any circumstance.

The key contradiction between tables 7.1 and 7.2 lay, of course, in the relative strengths of the IFP and ANC. If party strengths shown in table 7.1 were re-expressed, excluding the No party/Won't say/Don't know categories (a common enough polling technique), the ANC came out at 51% and the IFP at 32.7%. At that point our 'best guess' was that IFP support was probably around one-third of the electorate; table 7.1 adjusted for abstention suggested 32.7%; the 37% of Africans who would not name the ANC even as third choice seemed likely to be mainly IFP supporters; and (see below) 34% wanted to see the IFP sharing power in government.

The other party with a large 'submerged' vote was the NP: large numbers of whites and Indians who had refused to answer in table 7.1 switched to the NP in table 7.2, thus causing its support almost to double in size from 7% to 13%.

Violence and intimidation

Only African respondents reported substantial political activity in their areas of residence, with 40% mentioning parties going round talking about the election. About a fifth (22%) mentioned ANC activity, 11% the IFP, 3% the PAC, 1% the SACP and 1% the NP. Whites were prone to see greater violence as the inevitable concomitant of the election campaign, but Africans reported by a better than 2:1 margin that violence had actually decreased since campaigning began. This was primarily a reflection of general white pessimism and the growing African euphoria about the election, for on most indicators the amount of violence was actually fairly stable. The irony was that violence and intimidation were largely absent from white areas and less pronounced in Indian and coloured areas than among blacks, so pessimism, including pessimism about violence, was inversely related to its incidence.

By a 5:3 margin Africans felt that violence and intimidation helped the ANC more than the IFP, though the reasons for this were diverse. Nearly half said violence and intimidation merely made people more determined than ever to vote for their own party; only 11% said people would be bullied into supporting a party; and 29% said it made people keener to vote for the party they thought capable of stopping the violence.

Violence and intimidation were overwhelmingly experienced by Africans as pressures within their own community rather than as something stemming from exterior forces such as the police or employers. When respondents were asked whom they would fear most if it became known how they intended to vote, 17% said the IFP, 11% the ANC, 7% 'the opposition party' and 8% said 'the neighbours'. Less than 1% mentioned the South African Police or the KwaZulu Police. Rural Africans were considerably more fearful in general: only a third said they would be frightened of no one (against 58% of urban Africans who said so).

On the other hand, no less than 43% of urban Africans (and 41% of rural Africans) said it was difficult or impossible to live next to neighbours with political views different from their own. Another 21% said there was no problem because their neighbours had always held views similar to their own (that is, leaving the difficult/easy dimension untested), and only 15% said they didn't know their neighbours' views. Only 21% of urban Africans (though 35% of rural Africans) said it was easy to live next to people with differing views.

Slightly over half of the African respondents (52%) agreed that voters would be influenced, at least to some extent, by political groups who controlled local areas. The only group that approved of 'certain political parties not being allowed to seek support in certain areas' were rural Africans (54%), though so did 26% of urban Africans, with intolerance being particularly marked among the younger and less educated. Asked which other influences would be important with them, over half of rural

Africans (though only 31% of urban Africans) mentioned their chief and slightly fewer in both cases mentioned 'the elders of the community'. Just over half of urban Africans (though only 28% of rural Africans) mentioned civics as an influence, and a few per cent less mentioned street or area committees. The influence of the churches, trade unions and employers all came well behind the influence wielded not only by the actors mentioned above but by parents, spouses and children.

There was an even greater disparity between rural and urban Africans over the question of whom they would turn to for protection if violence started in their area: 62% of rural Africans but only 30% of urban Africans said the police. About a tenth (11%) of the former and 13.5% of the latter mentioned Umkhonto We Sizwe (MK), but 12% of urban dwellers also mentioned 'my party'. Only 5% of rural dwellers mentioned their chief, while 8% of urban Africans mentioned street or area committees and another 5% said self-defence units.

The fear of violence was also apparent in African attitudes towards the preferred type of political party activity. While urban, younger Africans heavily favoured mass rallies – the archetypally 'African' political format, preferred by ten times as many Africans as whites – Africans were also more likely than any other group to say that they would 'prefer the parties to do nothing, just to leave people alone', and this preference rose steeply among rural and older Africans. In total, 42% of Africans preferred to avoid face-to-face contact in the way the parties sought their support, opting for TV, radio, newspapers, pamphlets – or nothing at all.

None the less, despite all these deep concerns about violence and intimidation, the determination of all groups of voters to proceed with the election was striking – 64% of the entire sample were of this opinion (though, of course, one could regard this as a low figure given that our sample was over 90% black). Whites were the most likely (at 31%) to believe that there was too much violence for elections to be held, but even among them two-thirds held the contrary opinion – despite this also being the group most convinced that the election would lead to an increase in violence. Over a quarter of rural Africans thought there was too much violence for an election, but nearly twice as many wanted an election all the same. The Indian and coloured communities were the most emphatic of all in their determination that elections must be held.

A liberation election

The survey left no doubt that the approaching election was viewed in a quite special way, with a mood of excitement, even euphoria, apparent among many African (and some Indian and coloured) voters. Inevitably, this mood was enormously advantageous to the ANC and somewhat disabling for all its opponents, who could not counter this diffuse but intense optimism with any more exciting prospect – and to the extent that they took a more pessimistic line it is easy for them to be cast as 'spoilers'.

One of the most striking indices of this mood was found in answers to the question as to whether respondents thought they were better or worse off since the great turning point of 1990. Since that date one survey after another had monotonously recorded majorities among all groups saying they were worse off – which was hardly surprising: whites, Indians and coloureds were fearful of the future and their real incomes were shrinking, while Africans bore the brunt of rising unemployment and increased violence. For the first time, however, Africans now began to say that they were better off (by 41% to 34%), with the small plurality of rural Africans still saying they were worse off countered by a more than 2:1 majority among urban Africans saying they were better off.

This was a remarkable result. Unemployment had continued to mount, real incomes had carried on falling and insecurity stemming from crime and violence had hardly diminished. But respondents (especially ANC respondents – the correlation was clear) were so full of expectations of radical improvement consequent upon the election that their mood had changed to one of excited optimism. So great was this anticipation that it actually caused them retrospectively to revalue upwards their experience of the last three years.

This was borne out by African expectations of life after the elections: large majorities (especially of urban Africans) believed they would be richer, stronger and more secure, that there would be more jobs, that race relations would get better, and so on. There was unanimity among all racial groups only in their expectation of better race relations – with coloureds the most optimistic group of all. But the greater optimism of Africans was striking in almost every respect: a majority of Indians, whites and coloureds gloomily expected the levels of violence to escalate in the wake of an election, but urban Africans believed the opposite by 3:1 and rural Africans by almost 2:1. (The Africans, it turned out, were right.) Most whites and Indians felt that after the election they would become weaker and more insecure, and all the minority groups expected to get poorer or at least no better off. Indians and coloureds were optimistic, however, that a new government would treat all groups in the same way, while a small plurality of whites felt that such a government was bound to favour its own group the most. This was, none the less, a surprisingly optimistic finding, given the near-universal expectation of an ANC-led government and the fact that ANC support was so one-sidedly African, suggesting that the ANC's professions of non-racialism have been largely accepted as genuine by the electorate.

There were, however, some jarring notes. Most whites and a third of Indians and coloureds said they would be afraid to criticise a new government, as did 20% of Africans. The passage of a bill of rights as part of the new constitution appeared to have had little or no popular impact in this respect: confidence in the democratic right to critical dissent was still far from widespread. Moreover, the near-euphoria of African respondents sat somewhat oddly with the fact that 48% of them expected significant numbers of coloureds to leave South Africa in the wake of the election and that 64% said the same of Indians and 81% of whites. More than 60% of the whole sample expected 'a lot' of whites to emigrate. Whether this phenomenon was something other groups wished to see happen, or whether it was simply their comment on how whites might typically behave, was unclear. Among KZN whites themselves, thoughts of emigration seemed virtually universal: 62% of whites said 'a lot' of whites would leave and another 32% said that 'a few' would leave: only 6% said that 'none' would leave. Interestingly, 17% of Africans thought that 'a lot' of Africans would also leave South Africa after the election, though this may have merely reflected hope of an enhanced right to foreign travel in the new era of 'liberation'.

Asked what they understood by the word 'liberation' the consensus reply across racial groups was that it meant 'that apartheid will finally be dead', with the second definition of 'the people shall rule' close behind. Whites were predictably somewhat sceptical about the term but around 80% of Africans ascribed some meaning to it.

A polarised electorate

The electorate was already in a fully polarised state – not just in the racial sense, with virtually no whites supporting the ANC and virtually no Africans supporting the NP or DP, but in the sense that many months in advance of the election the electorate had already achieved a high degree of fixity in its partisan choice. Only 4% of the entire sample said they did not support any political party – with a figure of only 2% among Africans. This would be a startlingly low number even in the electorate of a long-established democracy with frequent occasion for the making and reaffirmation of partisan choice at the polls. Among an electorate with no previous history of such activity it was doubtless only possible because the electorate had, since 1985, been living through a virtual war which had forced everyone to choose sides. Moreover, only 3% of African respondents said their political views had changed in any way in the previous three months – an astonishingly low figure (24% of whites and 20% of coloureds said their views had changed in that period, 4% and 5% respectively having actually changed party, against only 1% of Africans).

Similarly, African voters gave the impression of having made one big choice – of their party – and of then orienting all other attitudes around that. When asked what were their reasons for supporting their particular political party, the most significant reasons among whites, Indians and coloureds were often issue-specific – particularly in relation to law and order. African voters were far more likely than others to say they supported their party because it was 'powerful with a great and inspiring leader', with no performance on issues implied. Africans were also far more leadership oriented when it came to how election candidates should be chosen, with a far greater number than among other groups willing to leave the matter in the hands of the party leadership. A large measure of this disparity derived from rural Africans. However, urban Africans were far less trusting of their leadership and will probably be more demanding on issue performance.

This relegation of issues to a lower plane than party choice was apparent elsewhere too. When asked which party would be best at dealing with various issues, most voters simply said their party would be best at everything. Small differences did appear: the NP generally got its best rating over law and order and in its ability to prevent intimidation, the ANC had high scores on health, education and housing. Interestingly, all the three major parties scored lowest on the attribute of 'being free of corruption in government'. Given the innumerable corruption scandals of the last few years, the NP's downrating was not surprising, but those of the ANC and the IFP were, given that they had little or no record in government, corrupt or otherwise, on which to be assessed.

There was a similarly undiscriminating tendency to rate virtually all issues facing a new government as equally important, though it was notable that respondents across all groups were virtually unanimous in giving top priority to the achievement of peace and harmony between political groups, to achieving greater safety and security and having less crime and violence. The lowest priority was attributed to redistributive issues. Whereas 95% or more of Africans gave priority to the law and order issues above, a smaller number (74%) thought it was important that whites should be forced to share their wealth and opportunities with blacks and another 78% said it was important that whites should henceforth have to respect blacks as the foremost group in South Africa.

Power-sharing and federalism

Large majorities across all races favoured power-sharing, with coloureds (74%) most favourable to the idea, followed by whites (68%), Africans (60%) and Indians (58%). The relative lack of Indian support for the idea came as a surprise. It derived from the hostility to the idea felt by lower-income and older Indians, both of which categories were more hostile to the idea than the normally most radical group of young, urban and better educated Africans. Given that these same groups of Indians tended to support the NP, which has sponsored the idea of power-sharing and has most to gain from it, this hostility could only mean that such Indians were reluctant to see Africans sharing in power at all. Even so, Indians favoured the idea by 2:1 and this was a rare area of broad consensus.

There was far less consensus about which parties should share power – it was as if the general idea of power-sharing was popular without its contents having been greatly scrutinised. Over 40% of the whole sample tended to duck the question and other responses were fragmented between a very large number of possible coalitions. Only 30% of Africans suggested combinations of parties including the ANC and NP. Another 28% of Africans wanted the PAC to be included in such a government, and 34% wanted the IFP included.

To test views about federalism we asked our sample whether they would like the provincial government or the national government to have the greater power. Respondents took the centralist course by 54% to 37%. The responses showed how little success the party elites had had in transmitting their views to the electorate on this, as on virtually all other issues. Despite the party's centralist line, less than two-thirds of the ANC's support was centralist and 28% took a federalist view. Among the pro-federal parties 40% of IFP supporters, 50% of CP/VF/AWB supporters and 54% of NP supporters took a centralist line, while the DP's voters divided only 49%–46% in favour of federalism. Thus the federalist case lost because of the failure of the supporters of pro-federal parties to take their parties' line on the issue. NP and CP supporters were so used to taking a strongly centralist line that they had simply failed to adjust to changed circumstances, while many of the IFP's supporters had probably not heard of or understood their party's view on federalism. The most anti-federal group, oddly, were older and upper-income Indians – despite the fact that in KZN federalism would greatly increase the leverage of just such Indian elites.

Acceptance of the result

All racial groups tended to be optimistic about the chances of the parties they supported: 69% of Africans expected their party to win the largest number of votes in their community, as did 47% of Indians and 43% of coloureds. Not all these expectations were likely to be met. If those who thought their party 'would do very well and be one of the largest parties in the area' are added to the first category, more than 50% of whites were optimists for their party, as were 60% of coloureds, 62% of Indians and 86% of Africans.

When asked how they would behave if their party got fewer votes than expected, only 52% of the sample replied that they would simply accept the result, with whites being the least and coloureds the most accepting. Whites were similarly the most inclined to refuse to accept the result altogether, 15% taking this view, but Africans were the most likely (at 23%) to say they would in that case organise protests of one kind or another.

The quality of democratic choice

Clearly the most worrying finding in the survey was the restriction on democratic choice apparent in a situation where 43% of urban Africans (and 41% of rural Africans) said it was difficult or impossible to live next to a neighbour with political views different from their own. This was hardly propitious to the exercise of a free vote. Our Western Cape study had shown that there 29% of Africans and 13% of coloureds had said they would find it difficult or impossible to live next to politically different neighbours: the situation in KZN was a long way worse. In the urban townships, where only 21% of Africans said it was easy to live next to politically differing neighbours, the situation was particularly difficult. Such a finding also showed how inadequate mere election day monitoring would be, for intimidation of this kind was clearly part of the fabric of day-to-day life – and would be as difficult to monitor as it would be to prevent.

The territorial nature of political power was attested to by the fact that over half of all Africans agreed that voters would be influenced by parties who 'controlled' local areas. Moreover, only 30% of urban Africans felt they could look to the police for protection if violence started: in effect township residents could not look to the normal public agencies to secure their own physical safety and had, perforce, to look instead to political parties or other politically based organisations. Such a situation meant that conditions for free and fair elections could not properly be said to exist, for that can only be achieved when the policing of the townships becomes both non-political and achieves a far higher level of public confidence.

The fact that confidence in the police was twice as high among rural Africans did not, however, necessarily mean that such conditions had been achieved there. This still left a considerable confidence 'gap' and it was clear from the answers to many questions that rural Africans were actually more fearful and worried about many conditions of life than were urban Africans.

None the less, despite the violence, intimidation and the growing likelihood of an IFP boycott, it was clear that people wanted to vote. Among most groups this went without saying, but it was true even for a plurality of IFP supporters: 41% said there was too much violence for an election to be held – but 47% wanted the election to go ahead.

The Second Survey, February 1994

Our first survey suggested that 93.3% of all respondents – including 91.7% of Africans – already had identity documents. These results were strongly queried by voter education workers, who said they were coming up against large numbers of voters without the necessary ID. Some of this apparent discrepancy was doubtless due to the survey's deliberate exclusion of Mozambican refugees and other immigrants, but even so we had the uncomfortable feeling that in the context of the approaching excitement of the election it had become the 'politically correct' thing to do to say that one had ID, or at least to claim that one had applied for it, whatever the truth of the matter. Our scepticism increased when our second survey found that the number of Africans claiming to have ID had actually fallen to 90.2%, with a 5% drop among rural Africans.

Again on this occasion we found that very substantial numbers – 34.6% of the total sample – required assistance to fill in a ballot form, including 3.2% of whites, 16.5% of Indians and 41.6% of Africans. Among both whites and Indians women were twice as likely as men to require assistance, but there was no such gender bias among Africans. The key point was that compared with 20.8% of urban Africans requiring assistance, 53.3% of rural Africans did, with older people particularly needing help. In party terms, the IFP was particularly handicapped: whereas one-third of African supporters of the ANC, NP and PAC required assistance, 52.9% of the IFP's African supporters did. The cumulative evidence for a 'lie factor' – an unfortunate term for the understandable behaviour of vulnerable people often under circumstances of unbearable pressure – should be borne in mind throughout.

Despite the apparent certainty of an IFP election boycott – which would have made voting more hazardous for everyone, given that IFP militants clearly interpreted the boycott as meaning they should actively prevent people from voting – a large majority of Africans were keen to vote. Only 9.6% of Africans said they approved of a boycott, the same percentage as for coloureds and less than for either whites (12.5%) or Indians (15.8%). Of Africans, 22.7% said they did not know or refused to reply, but this still left 67.8% of Africans disapproving of a boycott, including, notably, 90.7% of ANC supporters, 75.1% of PAC, 56.9% of NP and 52.1% of IFP supporters. The IFP had spent the previous four months inveighing against the election but its campaign had had only limited effect. The number of IFP voters saying they would 'definitely vote' was completely static (at 54%) between our two surveys, and even the number of IFP supporters saying they 'would try their best to vote' had fallen only from 12% to 9.7%. On the other hand, the determination of ANC supporters to vote had grown very markedly. Our first survey showed 61% of such voters 'definite' to vote and 30% willing to 'try their best'. These two categories had now moved to 86.7% and 7.4% respectively. DP and NP voters also showed an increasing keenness to vote. Thus the general environment was one of a growing determination to vote, with the result of the IFP boycott campaign being merely to resist that general pressure by holding steady – but not reducing – the willingness of their supporters to vote.

Partisan choice

However, it appeared that IFP support had continued to fall – hardly surprising given the deliberate demobilisation of their electorate – and there were signs of IFP voters moving towards the NP and, to a lesser extent, towards the DP. Tables 7.3 and 7.4 suggest a complex evolution. The ANC had picked up extra support among whites, Indians and coloureds since our first survey due entirely to the shrinkage of the Don't Know/Refusal category, but among Africans ANC support was static. IFP support among the non-African minorities, on the other hand, was virtually static, but nearly a quarter of its African support had shifted away. On the face of it, it might seem that this support had moved towards the NP, but in fact this was not so. What had happened was merely that with the electoral mobilisation of all the other parties

Table 7.3   Party choice by group (%)

	Total	Whites	Indians	Coloureds	Africans
ANC–SACP	36.7	4.4	14.2	23.2	44.1
IFP	18.1	14.8	–	0.9	21.3
NP	13.9	40.5	71.9	37.1	2.1
DP	2.3	19.6	1.9	4.9	0.2
FF	0.8	7.0	0.2	–	0.1
PAC	0.8	–	0.1	–	1.0
Don't know	10.5	6.1	7.1	12.2	11.5
Won't say	8.4	4.8	2.9	8.5	9.6
Won't vote	8.2	1.9	1.2	13.1	9.9

Table 7.4   Party choice by group, with don't knows/refusals/abstainers excluded (%)

	Total	Whites	Indians	Coloureds	Africans
ANC–SACP	50.3	5.0	16.0	35.0	63.9
IFP	24.8	17.0	–	1.4	30.9
NP	19.1	46.4	81.0	56.0	3.0
DP	3.2	22.5	2.1	7.4	0.3
FF	1.1	8.0	0.2	–	0.1
PAC	1.1	–	0.1	–	1.4

increasing and the IFP's failing to move, much the same bloc of African IFP support as before simply constituted a smaller fraction of the total than hitherto. The NP's strong improvement had in fact been achieved with almost no addition of African votes but with dramatically higher scores among the non-African minorities as the heating-up of the electoral battle pushed voters off the fence. That is, it is possible to give a satisfactory explanation of the evolution shown in table 7.5 without recourse to changes in partisan allegiance: it looks very much as if the evolution resulted from relative shifts in the mobilisation of fairly static bodies of party support.

The IFP's white support, we have seen, remained quite steady – and over 80% of it was still determined to vote. But the IFP's African electorate was at sixes and sevens, with nearly half of it still determined to vote, another tenth saying they 'would try their best' to vote, and another third unsure. Only one IFP voter in fourteen was already adamant that they would not vote. When we queried why they might not vote, only half mentioned the possibility of an IFP boycott and the rest gave an assortment of reasons ranging from violence and intimidation to lack of voter education. The confused state of the IFP's African electorate was such that it was difficult to feel that it was psychologically ready for the 'civil war' of which there had been so much talk. This was particularly true if one took account of how largely the IFP electorate consisted of rural women and the elderly – not normally a warlike group.

In order to measure the width of party support bases we asked respondents to place all the parties on a scale of ten, with the most favoured party getting top place and the most disliked party tenth place. In the highly charged atmosphere of KZN, many voters did not like allocating tenth place and retreated into a 'don't know' response. This was particularly true of the way African voters regarded the IFP and ANC. Perhaps the most striking finding was that less than 14% of Africans were willing to put either the IFP or the ANC in tenth place. IFP supporters were the most polarised: 38.4% of them put the ANC in tenth place, while only 21.9% of ANC supporters put the IFP in tenth place.

Table 7.5   Evolution of party strengths (%)

	Nov.–Dec. 1993	Feb. 1994
ANC–SACP	52.0	50.3
IFP	32.7	24.8
NP	9.5	19.1
CP	2.8	1.1
DP	2.2	3.2
PAC	0.8	1.1

Even more striking was the relatively flattering rating given by Africans to the National Party – a sign of just how far the parameters of the South African political system have shifted in four years. No less than 51.1% of the IFP's African supporters ranked the NP in the top five places – and even this was comfortably surpassed by the 59.9% of the ANC's African voters who did so. It was very noticeable that this ability to 'forgive and forget' the NP's past record was far rarer among the ANC's non-African supporters. IFP and ANC voters were far more polarised in their attitude towards the PAC: 46.5% of ANC supporters ranked the PAC in the top three places, but only 17.9% of IFP supporters did so. This sense of overlap was reinforced when we asked voters to say what reasons they had for supporting their respective parties, for much the same issues – law and order, democracy and governmental competence – were cited by supporters of all parties. In fact this was probably less a real sign of convergence than an indication of the relatively small significance of issues and the prevalence of symbolic and expressive voting. No issue attracted really large-scale interest: only 6% mentioned 'more jobs' as an important issue and 3.9% economic policy – this in a country suffering mountainous unemployment after three years of recession.

If issues were relatively unimportant, leadership was crucial: South Africans as a whole seem to be leader fixated. This was apparent in several different ways. Leaders of all parties tended to run ahead of their parties in popularity; within each party electorate, leaders frequently had ratings of almost universal acclaim; and they had virtually no significant intraparty challenger in popularity. The sort of situation common in Europe where a party may be popular but its leader far less so, or in which several alternative leaders share the spotlight, with none of them dominant, seems to belong to a wholly different reality.

Nelson Mandela led the popularity ratings, performing better both among whites and Africans (and the total electorate) than the ANC. Mandela was the favourite leader of a staggering 92.3% of African ANC supporters – by comparison only Slovo and Ramophosa scored even 1%. Mandela also attracted minorities of DP voters among all race groups. Mandela's support was notably male: women of all race groups rated him lower than men.

Buthelezi's showing was even more striking, running far ahead of the IFP, particularly among Africans. His 27.7% score there contrasted with the IFP's 21.3%, again causing one to wonder about 'hidden' IFP support. He was the favoured leader of 89.3% of African IFP supporters and of 73.4% of white ones. Among rural Africans he ran neck and neck with Mandela, and he too attracted minority support from NP and DP voters.

De Klerk was the favoured leader of 87.3% of NP whites and of an astonishing 96.5% of NP Indians and 97.1% of NP coloureds. He ran comfortably ahead of the NP as a whole and attracted quite sizeable minority support among DP and even ANC supporters, especially among Indians.

Other leaders were notably less successful. The DP leader, Zac de Beer, was chosen by only 60.7% of DP whites and fewer of DP Indians and coloureds. Clarence Makwetu, the PAC leader, was favoured by two-thirds of PAC supporters, whereas the leading PAC spokesman Bennie Alexander was favoured by almost a quarter. Most divided of all was the white right, 37.8% of whom mentioned Constand Viljoen, 29% Terreblanche and 12.9% Hartzenberg.

Violence, intimidation and community pressure

Our second survey continued to focus on themes affecting the possibility of a 'free and fair' election. We asked how the incidence of violence and intimidation would affect turnout – the answer being an overall drop of 11.5%. Indian men, higher-income Indians and white women were most likely to be affected. Africans, already subject to far more pressure than other groups, had built their reactions to it into their behaviour. In party terms, the NP, DP and IFP were all more adversely affected than the ANC by a climate of violence, the NP and DP because they are more reliant on the white and Indian groups – liable, under such pressures, to abstain in droves – and the IFP because its African electorate simply seemed far more timorous and bullied. Thus 74.8% of African ANC supporters said that if violence and intimidation were present they would still definitely vote, against only 40.5% of African IFP supporters who said so.

We then asked, 'If violence comes about in your area, which group, organisation or party is most likely to start it?' Perceptions differed markedly, with most voters simply treating the matter as one of partisan loyalty, attributing blame to the party they anyway opposed. None the less, the results were not comforting for the ANC: 23.1% of the whole electorate pointed the finger at them, compared to 27% at the IFP – a far narrower result than the overall distribution of party support in Natal would have suggested. The only other party to be 'blamed' was the AWB – particularly by whites. 'Third Force' explanations of the violence have fastened on the role of the police and right-wing elements acting in conjunction with the IFP, but few voters among any group appeared to blame such elements. Instead, the simply chaotic nature of much of the violence as it is popularly experienced led significant numbers either to blame the IFP and ANC equally, or just 'anybody' or 'nobody'. Similarly, the white, Indian and coloured supporters of the ANC were far less likely to blame the IFP as instigators of violence than their party allegiance would have suggested. In this, as in much else, Indians – even ANC Indians – tended to feel a strong gravitational pull towards a more NP-defined set of political realities (see table 7.6).

Table 7.6   Indian attitudes (%)

	R2,499	R2,500	−34 years	35+ years	Men	Women
ANC 1st place	7.9	22.7	17.0	11.0	16.2	11.5
ANC 10th place	9.6	7.1	8.3	10.1	4.6	13.7
Don't know	37.1	10.2	20.7	28.7	25.0	25.0
NP 1st place	84.4	54.7	72.5	70.8	70.6	72.5
NP 10th place	−	−	−	0.3	0.4	−
Don't know	3.1	3.3	3.6	2.5	3.5	2.6
Reasons for supporting party of choice						
Good economic policy	23.2	11.3	18.1	16.7	19.2	15.6
Law and order	24.8	8.4	14.9	20.3	19.9	15.9
They are democrats	10.0	24.2	18.3	16.8	17.0	17.9
Most capable government	20.0	24.2	25.2	17.9	23.4	19.3
Favourite leader						
Nelson Mandela	6.8	21.8	14.9	11.3	15.7	10.4
F. W. de Klerk	88.3	66.1	76.5	79.9	74.6	81.7

Africans, especially urban Africans, were far more likely than other groups to experience pressure to vote for a particular party. We asked respondents about the source of such pressures, and in almost every category mentioned African respondents reported more pressure. Politicians were most frequently cited as a source of pressure (by over half of urban Africans and nearly 40% of rural ones), followed by friends, colleagues and family members. But civics and street and area committees exercised significant pressure (mentioned by a quarter to a third of urban Africans), as did trade unions on urban males. Chiefs and elders were cited by over a fifth, ministers of religion and teachers by one in seven, and employers by one in ten. All told, one had the impression that Africans, particularly those in an urban context, were subject to a great battery of pressures emanating from many different parts of the social structure, while their non-African counterparts experienced significant (and far less) pressure only from friends, colleagues, family members and politicians. This difference did not derive from differential sources of information – all groups got their information mainly from newspapers and the broadcast media and put their greatest trust in the latter.

We then asked respondents how easy they found it to disagree with these sources of pressure. Most non-Africans found it fairly easy to disagree with almost anyone: even among the famously family-centred Indian community, for example, less than a fifth found it difficult or impossible to disagree with family members. Africans found it far harder to disagree (table 7.7), but the pattern was not wholly what we had expected. While 53.3% of all Africans said they found it difficult or impossible to disagree with politicians (further extraordinary evidence of the power of leadership in this setting), far fewer said the same of friends and family members, despite the fact that they had been so heavily cited as sources of pressure. Chiefs, on the other hand, though mentioned by far fewer respondents, were seen as very difficult indeed to disagree with – not just by rural and IFP Africans but even by urban and ANC Africans. Similarly, the civics and street and area committees drew forbidding numbers who said they would find it difficult or impossible to disagree with them. But rural and less-educated Africans were more likely in general to say they found it hard to disagree with any source of pressure. In part this corresponds with our earlier picture of this group feeling particularly vulnerable, but it may also be that such respondents were simply more deferential.

In our second national survey we found that large numbers of Africans nationwide believed that it would be known in their communities how they voted – though many feared little consequence from this. In KZN we found, to our amazement, that the proportion of Africans reporting such a belief (13%) was far lower than elsewhere, the figure reaching only 16% even among African urban males. This figure was so low that we suspected that many were actually too frightened to admit they were

Table 7.7   Africans only: Impossible/difficult to disagree about politics with . . . (%)

	Urban	Rural	Std 5	Std 6	Men	Women	IFP	ANC
Friends/Colleagues	24.1	31.7	32.6	25.6	24.8	32.3	27.6	21.7
Family members	30.0	37.1	36.3	32.9	34.7	34.3	29.6	30.8
Politicians	53.6	53.1	59.1	47.9	52.4	54.0	56.5	48.4
Street/Area committees	38.6	56.4	57.0	43.6	50.8	49.3	46.0	46.3
Chiefs	49.7	75.0	73.8	58.6	64.7	66.9	74.3	60.4
Civics	31.4	58.6	57.2	41.1	45.7	51.2	47.1	45.2

Table 7.8   Responses of Africans to community pressure (%)

	Urban		Rural			
	Male	Female	Male	Female	ANC	IFP
Community will tolerate dissenters	48.6	32.5	47.7	52.9	52.0	43.9
Community will be tough on dissenters	25.4	31.9	33.4	23.2	33.4	35.1
Will stick to own party under pressure	80.8	64.6	71.0	60.8	87.3	67.3
May vote with majority to avoid conflict	9.2	17.8	8.9	12.8	7.2	22.4
Pressure on me to vote for a party I don't support	8.8	10.6	20.8	24.5	17.3	23.0

frightened. Our suspicion was strengthened when we found that a far larger number of Africans (28%) believed that their community would be tough on someone whose political views differed from those of neighbours (table 7.8). This figure rose to over a third among rural men. Moreover large numbers were unsure how their communities would behave in such an event – in itself a worrying situation – which meant that only a minority were confident of their community's tolerance towards politically different individuals.

To test how strong such tolerance actually was we asked whether respondents thought it right or wrong that a political party might be prevented from holding meetings or seeking support in their area. Indians were by far the most tolerant, with only 2.4% thinking such prohibition right but around one in twelve whites and coloureds thought it right, intolerance being sharply higher among white women and coloured men. Some of this was actually a party effect: intolerance was strikingly higher among white supporters of the far right (30%) and ANC Africans (21.4%). We also asked respondents whether they would like to hear only messages from their own party on TV or radio, or whether they liked to hear other parties as well. Africans were again the least tolerant, with 16.6% (and 29.6% among African IFP voters) saying they wanted to hear their own party only. But the large majority of Africans wanted to hear other parties' messages and to hear debates between the parties.

We then asked respondents to think of the party they most opposed and then to consider whether they would tolerate its members associating with their friends, living or operating a business in their neighbourhood, teaching at a local school, holding a public protest, giving a political speech or canvassing political support in their area. By international standards, tolerance was shockingly low in all communities. Whites were by some way the most tolerant, but even so a bare majority of them would tolerate opponents holding teaching positions or holding protests in their area. None the less, a majority of whites did vote for tolerance in every instance, as did a plurality of Indians (though Indian and white women were always less tolerant than their menfolk). Coloureds were less tolerant, with pluralities against the holding of public protests or the holding of teaching positions by opponents. Pluralities of Africans felt the same on these two issues and also did not wish opponents to visit their areas to enrol support for their parties. But lack of tolerance was at wholly different levels among Africans on every issue − on no issue did those favouring tolerance reach even 40%. Such figures showed only too painfully how difficult life might be in many African communities in Natal for those of dissident political views or even those wishing to exercise free political activity and speech. It was worrying, too, that intolerance among Africans increased markedly − instead of decreasing − at higher educational levels, and also among the younger age group.

But political intolerance has a sociological as well as a moral reality. The terrible strife within African communities in KZN has increased such feelings of intolerance, for people are extremely aware of circumstances which might act as trouble flashpoints and they would generally prefer peace to almost anything. On the other hand, tolerance was at its lowest in rural areas and among IFP supporters: ANC supporters in urban townships were notably more tolerant − a striking fact when one considers that those townships have generally seen more conflict than many rural areas. It makes more sense to see our African respondents as living within a far denser network of community institutions and pressures than their non-African counterparts. The possibility of privatised space and individualistic behaviour is simply less within such a framework than it is within the more atomised and suburban lifestyles of the non-African communities.

It is this crucial difference which accounts for at least some of the high racial polarisation we saw in many of our responses, and for the low levels of African 'tolerance'. In fact it was noticeable that African levels of tolerance rose sharply when the behaviour under consideration did not involve an intrusion into the community networks within which respondents lived. Thus African respondents were likely to adopt fairly tolerant positions when asked about matters of pure principle or, for example, in their preference for multiparty broadcasting and open debate in the media. Levels of tolerance shrank the more the questions posed involved the possible disturbance of the dense community environment. At that time that environment was strongly mobilised for political ends and openly 'deviant' behaviour within it was neither easy nor safe.

Finally, we asked whether respondents were under pressure to vote for a party they didn't support and whether, if their community mainly favoured a party they didn't like, they would consider changing their views to those of the majority in order to avoid conflict. Substantial numbers of Africans – rising to almost a quarter among rural women and IFP supporters – felt this pressure. (It is, though, important to add that we do not know whether IFP supporters felt that pressure from the ANC or whether they were IFP because they had already experienced such pressure from the latter quarter.) A similarly striking number said they might change their vote in order to avoid conflict – and many more were uncertain as to how they might behave. In all a third of KZN Africans said they might change their vote under pressure or didn't know what they would do, figures high enough to change the course of the election and thus undermine the whole notion of free and fair elections in the province.

The Future

Expectations of the post-election future followed the pattern we saw in our first report, with the general gloom among the non-African minorities contradicted by the euphoric views of the African (and particularly the ANC) majority – the feeling of excitement and elation we have come to regard as typical of a 'liberation' or 'uhuru' election. African euphoria was to some extent tempered by party, but while IFP voters were more cautious and less optimistic than their ANC counterparts, they far more nearly shared the general African optimism than they did white pessimism. The greatest African consensus was that the country would become free, democratic and equal, with large minorities worried that violence, disorder and insecurity would continue. None the less, given the strife-torn realities of KZN over the last nine years, it was far more striking how large were the African majorities believing that the post-election world would be dramatically different from present realities. Indian and coloured voters were more cautious than Africans but in general they were closer to sharing African optimism than white pessimism.

One great exception to this lay in the issue of the seizure and occupation of property – a matter of considerable discussion in KZN after the seizure of 799 Indian homes at Cato Crest, Durban, by African squatters. This incident caused considerable trauma in the Indian community and we found that Indians were even more hotly opposed than whites to such occupations. Among ANC supporters the divide was very clear, with Africans more than seven times more likely than their Indian comrades to support or sympathise with such occupations. All told, 19.7% of African respondents said they 'fully supported' the occupations and another 18% expressed sympathy with no critical comment: these were exceptionally high, many would say alarming, figures in support of the outright seizure of property. Among ANC Africans a third 'fully supported' the action and another 18.3% expressed sympathy. Not surprisingly, large majorities of whites, coloureds and (especially) Indians expressed fears that the advent of a black government would see more such occupations, though over half of all Africans (and 70.7% of ANC Africans) said they were not worried by such a prospect.

The unspoken fear lying behind Indian anxieties dates back to the 1949 riots in Natal and the widespread perception that Africans in Natal feel a particularly deep animosity towards Indians. We wondered how far the troubled times had actually provided a basis for such fears by inflaming African hostilities to whites and Indians. We had, in this respect, been struck by the results in our first survey showing a very high level of African expectations of large-scale white, Indian and coloured emigration in the post-election period and so decided to probe attitudes further on this matter. In fact the results were quite reassuring. When asked about their attitude to white emigration, only 17.8% of Africans said 'It's good they're going, we don't want them' – a figure pushed up by the some-what surprising 25% of rural African women who held such an opinion. But almost 5 Africans out of 6 felt it was a pity such whites were going, wanted to persuade them to stay or, at the least, said that it was their own business what they did and no one should interfere. The proportion of Africans who would be glad to see Indians go was lower at 10.9%, peaking at 16.7% among rural men. Given the past history of white oppression and the exploitation of Africans by some Indians, these figures were remarkably low and evidence yet again that inter-racial relations in Natal are actually quite good, whatever the incidence of intra-racial violence.

Something of this inter-racial optimism was also apparent in responses to our question whether all South Africans could form one united nation or whether a future South Africa would contain different nations. A clear majority of whites believed there would be different nations but all other groups – and particularly Indians and coloureds – believed in a 'single nation' future. Among Africans, IFP supporters and rural women were most likely to believe in a 'different nations' future but even so a clear majority of both groups still believed in a single nation. In fact partisan effects were weaker than racial ones: while a 78.1% majority of ANC Africans believed in 'one nation', as did a 56.9% majority of IFP Africans, 68% of white IFP supporters took a 'different nations' view. This 'single nation' view of the IFP African majority was the more striking given that the IFP leadership repeatedly talks of the Zulu nation, the Afrikaner nation, and so forth. The IFP's history is that of an African nationalist party and the bulk of its followers clearly still shared the instincts of African nationalism on this issue.

★

At the time we carried out our second survey Natal seemed about to head into civil war. In fact the late IFP decision to re-enter the election changed everything and guaranteed a far more peaceful outcome than we had feared. The ultimate result in KZN – a clear victory for the IFP on both the national and regional ballots – directly contradicted what our surveys had led us to expect. The question as to how this data should be interpreted in light of the actual result is tackled in this book's twelfth chapter.

Notes

1 Research International South Africa, 'Project Pineapple. Prepared for KwaZulu-Natal Indaba Survey No. 88/871', 29 Aug. 1988 (printout).
2 Both the Natal surveys were carried out by Data Research Africa in conjunction with the Natal section of the HSRC. The stratified random probability sample of 2,500 was, on both occasions, divided so that the HSRC carried out the interviews in the rural areas. The data was weighted by Research International Ltd.

EIGHT

The Election on the Reef: Choice and First-Time Voters in Gauteng (the PWV)

Graeme Gotz and Mark Shaw

The Paradox in the Picture

ONE OF THE MOST intriguing images to emerge from South Africa's first democratic elections was found on an IEC information poster (see p. 213) which stressed the importance of the secret ballot to the newly enfranchised. The image, a simple drawing, depicts an African woman leaning into a voting booth to make her cross, presumably for the first time. Standing beside her, holding on to her dress and eating a fruit, is portrayed a small child who stares out engagingly from the picture.

It is the boy's gaze that makes the image provocative. The woman's face is hidden from view by the sides of the booth: in the act of voting she appears to us as anonymous, devoid of individuality, being but one of countless equivalent voters each indistinguishable from the others at the moment they mark the ballot. It is the child in the illustration that gives the particular act being depicted, and the person performing the act, their humanity. In a strange way he seems to locate this 'voter', providing her with form and character when she can claim none for herself. Through his presence she assumes an identity, a position within a social context in which she is distinguishable as woman, mother, black, working class – that is, as a subject with determinable interests, needs and desires. Unable to vote himself, the boy defines by association the grounds that determine the faceless woman's vote, the place in society from which she speaks.

The image, if considered carefully, presents a paradox: at the instant that democracy is realised the individual voter is both anonymous and definable, a figure without singularity next to a multitude of others, but at the same time locatable as a real subject with a determinable social and political character. It is a paradox which goes to the heart of the democratic process, and it is through its particular terms that this chapter will analyse the elections in the PWV region, now rechristened Gauteng.

YOUR VOTE IS YOUR SECRET

NOBODY WILL KNOW WHO YOU ARE VOTING FOR

ISSUED BY THE INDEPENDENT ELECTORAL COMMISSION VOTER EDUCATION PROGRAMME

The paradox turns on vantage point. From a point of view that regards democracy as a distinct social-historical system engendered and sustained by a clear set of conceptual principles, individual voters are necessarily 'anonymous'. Under democracy, all citizens must be allowed the effective possibility of participating actively in the process of instituting a sovereign and legitimate political arrangement.[1] No one must be excluded from this process for reasons of their place in society. Democracy therefore necessarily implies a state of formal equality between its subjects, wherein each private expression of will is treated as absolutely equivalent with every other. This means that each and every citizen, regardless of ancestry, economic station or racial character, must come to be regarded as a free and rational agent, an independent site of personal initiative and conscious decision-making. They must be seen to be liberated from any inherited structure in which their identity, and therefore their political will, might be fixed to pregiven ends and goals, imprisoned in set social roles.[2]

Democracy has thus been said to rest on the exigency of treating all citizens as free and equal persons.[3] It must be recognised, however, that autonomy and equality are not permanent features of the society governed by this system. In practice, they are realised only in periodic moments of 'undecidability' when the political order opens itself up to any and all possibilities. In these crucial moments, during national elections, society proposes to itself the explicit need to look upon its members as equally free and in doing so effectively de-identifies everyone from that position in society in which they are regarded as superior or inferior, by which their political wills might be known a priori. Thus elections permit choosers the rare opportunity to select between equally valid political alternatives out of sight, as it were, of any person or social force that might impose upon their decisions. Anonymity, graphically illustrated in the figure of the woman whose face cannot be seen, hence encapsulates a principle which is the very core of the democratic project – the principle of a moment of entirely free choice grounded in equality and autonomy.

From the vantage point of democracy as conceptual ideal, then, the woman in the picture is necessarily without features. But from a different point of view, the voter cannot possibly be without identity at the moment that choice is exercised. This is the other side of the paradox. In reality, voters never approach the field of anonymity always already free and equal.[4] They enter the terrain of choice from situations where they are socially embedded in a differentiated societal order which confers on them structures of privilege and disadvantage and hence different interests and aspirations. Individuals inevitably choose from within the horizon of previously constituted identities, using the resources that coalesce in their determined social spaces as the bases for their decisions. Hence, an unemployed and widowed black woman with a small child to care for, and living in Kagiso township on Johannesburg's West Rand, would define herself differently, have quite different needs and expectations, and consequently be inclined to make different choices from, say, a white male manager from the northern suburbs.

The attempt to problematise democracy in this way is not motivated by a desire to engage in abstract speculation. The 'paradox of democracy' presents a problem which became compellingly real in South Africa's first non-racial elections. The problem, simply stated, is this: if subjects' identities are formed within an overdetermining social context, is it not possible that this context might impose certain attributes that would severely constrain these subjects when they come to exercise democratic choice? The democratic ideal holds that in the realm of choice configured by the vote, a contrived realm which temporarily guarantees anonymity, people are momentarily emancipated from the dictates of the social order in which they find themselves situated. They are offered the chance to speak the needs, interests and ideals that attach to their social position in the hope that, through the political power being established, they may one day change this position for something better. The franchise thus holds out a liberating vision for those who exercise it, the possibility of a fundamental reinvention of society and self. But surely this vision would be unavailable to any voter whose social environment so determines their subjective capacities for autonomous thought and action that they are quite unable to feel free and equal at the moment they mark the ballot.

It can be argued that the symbolic benefits of choice can only become accessible if voters have previously enjoyed the capacity for informed and conscious political decision-making. Their environment must be such that they are allowed the space and given the resources to carefully interrogate themselves and the social, political and economic factors determining their consciousness, and thus are empowered to make choices which offer them the best hope for the future. Real democratic choice is a liberating act of self-analysis and expression of personal will behind an effective veil of anonymity. All too often, though, political identities are made to be pure and passive products of circumstance, such that choice becomes no more than a simple reflection of what a society would have the individual be, think and do.

This chapter considers the possibilities for adequate democratic choice during the first all-inclusive election in Gauteng (formerly PWV) region. Through a careful examination of some of the events, processes and campaign practices witnessed during the electoral period, as well as the broader political background against which these took place, it seeks to engage the following key question: given the democratic ideal of free and equal choosers symbolically reinventing themselves and their society during elections, to what degree were first-time voters in Gauteng enabled or constrained to make critical and creative choices?

The discussion proceeds through three sections. As a first step it considers the underlying political milieu of the Reef, asking to what extent it was conducive to critical choice by opening up or closing off the capacity for self-interrogation of potential voters. Second, it presents an analysis of the period of campaigning itself, showing how the form and content of party campaigns brought a new set of pressures, both negative and positive, to bear on political identities. Lastly, it contemplates the effect of the election itself as a distinct political moment rounding off the campaign.

A short note on methodology and the limitations of this work is necessary. This piece does not attempt an analysis of poll data. It starts from the premise that for all the stark clarity of the election results the meaning that the elections held for people in Gauteng was is not immediately transparent in the vote count. To know what first-time voters were 'saying' with their choices one has to look behind the count and analyse the barely visible, often grass-roots, dynamics and processes that shaped the outcome, or, more accurately, shaped the people that made the outcome what it was. This is an ambitious and thorny project indeed. Essentially, it is to try to intuit what went on in the mind of the average first-time voter as she prepared to cast her ballot, using qualitative, often anecdotal, evidence as to how most people seemed to be responding to evolving political processes. Inevitably, therefore, the arguments developed here and the conclusions drawn will be interpretive and speculative. They seemed on the basis of available information to have applied to many voters, but they cannot conclusively be proved to have been valid for all.

The Political World of the Reef

The PWV voter was shaped by an extremely complex political environment. In certain respects, this environment strongly encouraged political identities open to the possibility of fully democratic choice. In others, however, it seemed to provide conditions for an election grounded on anything but the values of liberty and equality in which the vote as an emancipatory act must flourish. To understand this duality, one needs to conceive of Gauteng as both a regional political framework in and of itself, and as a constellation of diverse communities each with their own very particular political dynamics.

A regional political formation

The politics of Gauteng, as a region,[5] can be shown to have been given by its social and economic character. Gauteng is by far the most populous section of South Africa, with over 25 per cent of the country's total population (some 8 million people) squeezed into an area little more than 100km in length. Yet this population is a strangely artificial one. Many millions of the people living in the area are recent or less recent in-migrants whose families have come here in an effort to escape the largely rural and poverty-stricken homelands in which apartheid sought to confine them. Gauteng, in a sense, is the New York of South Africa, a melting pot for people from every corner of the country who have journeyed here seeking a gateway to a new world, a place where there is hope for a job, property and a home, electricity and running water. For the desperate millions who have converged on it, Gauteng is wealthy, cosmopolitan, fast-paced and full of opportunity – for all its problems the only way out of some stagnating rural backwater.

But while it has been a symbol of hope for some relief from apartheid, Gauteng is also very much a symptom of the apartheid disease. First, too rapid urbanisation over past decades has put unbearable strain on a social and economic infrastructure primarily geared towards meeting the needs of a racial minority. In a sense, the sheer number of people who have reached out for the dream has meant that for most it has remained unattainable. The system condemned them to the margins of a relatively undeveloped economy; it refused to incorporate them as anything but labour of lower status in the service of the privileged. For so many to step outside this ascribed place and role, and to demand a better future, was inevitably to invite disappointment in a world not designed to accommodate them. Hence, an estimated 40 to 50 per cent of the economically active population of Gauteng was unemployed or underemployed at the time of the election. Almost 2.5 million people were without formal housing. Some 70 per cent of households did not have direct access to running water. And there was a dire shortage of schools and the most basic health and recreational facilities.[6]

Second, Gauteng reproduces in its socioeconomic make-up the syndrome that was grand apartheid – millions of people forcibly kept separate, and very unequal, in their various groups and areas. The chronic inequalities of this region are impossible to ignore. Here townships such as Alexandra, where 750,000 people are crammed into two square kilometres of slum houses and dusty shacks, and where the constant struggle for resources and space have repeatedly spilled over into brutal violence during the last decade, stand side by side with, but distinctly separate from, white suburbs like Sandton – opulent, spacious and tree-lined. It is in this hard contrast of shackland and parkland that one sees the essence of Gauteng: if it is a gateway to the dream, it is a gateway open only to an already privileged few. Where so many have congregated to seek a better future, most have found only the constant frustration of having to serve the wealth and comfort of others, rather than own it themselves.

On this socioeconomic reality, which appears as the very antithesis of freedom and equality, has arisen a multifaceted political formation. The fact of so many people concentrated in the same place, and all striving for roughly the same thing against the injunctions of an unjust system, has given rise to what, following Hannah Arendt, might be called a 'public sphere'. Briefly, Arendt uses the term 'public sphere' to denote a realm of political activity standing over against the disturbing trends towards routinisation, bureaucratisation and alienation she sees enervating modern society. A public space, for Arendt, is created when individuals extract themselves from their solitary and soulless pursuits and engage in collective, civic actions: 'wherever people come together to establish a common ground, and seek to take the initiative and inject themselves by word and deed into the events going on around them, they have created a public realm, a forum for action that is itself the outcome of action.'[7] This public sphere of plural and communal action, Arendt has argued, is significant because it establishes a so-called 'space of appearance', an arena in which agents can freely express their identities and have these identities affirmed through the building of relations of reciprocity and solidarity.

Gauteng, given the socioeconomic base described, has provided the ideal conditions for the emergence of such a public space. Over the past decade alone, although one could think as far back as the Soweto uprising and even the Sharpeville massacre in 1960, the region has seen countless community-based protests and movements intended to transform its harsh and iniquitous urban environment. The union movement, the civics, street and area committees, people's education, rent and services boycotts – all testify to a space of popular politics in which any person could enjoy the benefits of solidarity and reciprocity that come from investing in collective struggle. Gauteng, by its very nature, gives opportunities to its citizens to establish between them a 'common ground' oppositional to that world which oppresses them, to take the initiative and create a 'forum for civic action' in which they can critically interrogate their social condition and consciously strive to change it.

This public realm, and in this it is different from that which exists in many other parts of South Africa, is also an internally divided one.[8] Repetition and similitude have given way to a multiplicity of divergent interest groups each trying to reshape the social environment in accordance with their own unique perspective. The public terrain in Gauteng is therefore multifarious and highly contested, with movements of every ideological and political complexion appealing to variously located people.[9] So many competing sources of political conviction – tugging the identities of social agents in every conceivable direction – have naturally led to a proliferation in the sites of conflict between variously positioned political identities. A prime example of such conflict was seen in KwaThema during the period of campaigning. Here, a year-old conflict between the PAC Pan Africanist Students Organisation (PASO) and a loose alliance of the Congress of South African Students (COSAS) and the ANC Youth League (ANCYL) erupted into renewed violence, the stated reasons for which seemed trifling.[10] Over ten youths were reportedly killed in the ensuing battles, with PASO strength periodically being boosted by an injection of new members from nearby Thokoza and Katlehong. COSAS and PASO could easily be fraternal organisations, having a common enemy in the apartheid state, which for both was represented on the ground by the 'brutal' Internal Stability Unit (ISU).

At root such conflicts reflect a social formation marked by an over-supply of political attachments as well as an extreme scarcity of resources, wherein identities seem always to be under potential threat from alterna-tive sources of meaning.[11] They are certainly not healthy, but they testify to a flux of meaning by which social agents can choose to occupy, defend and if necessary vacate various political positions which advance their subjective interests. Gauteng citizens, it is implied, could critically engage their world through a variety of strategically constructed and adapted identities, and so by extension (if they were prepared to fight for these associations) could avoid being foisted with a fixed and immutable con-cept of self in society.

As an overarching political space, then, Gauteng seemed to provide conditions highly conducive to democratic choice. Objectively, it fur-nished residents with opportunities to reject social positions and roles imposed on them by the system or people in authority, to conceive themselves in ever new and better social and economic circumstances, and to become immersed in a realm of struggle which afforded multiple sources of identification by which to pursue greater personal freedom and equality.

However, the fact that Gauteng residents had these symbolic resources available to them should not lead us to conclude that they then had immediate access to democratic choice. If the political identity and demo-cratic capacity received by Gauteng voter is to be fully understood, one also needs to have regard for the sociopolitical formation they encoun-tered at a more grass-roots level. The region also needs to be viewed as a cluster of self-contained, self-identifying communities, where local poli-tics brought an altogether more negative set of compulsions to bear on the newly enfranchised. An examination of political realities, events and processes in a particular part of the Reef – the so-called West Rand – is instructive in this regard.[12] One township in particular, that of Bekkersdal, presents in the starkest terms the logical consequences of a particular type of politics seen, to varying degrees, in virtually every community during the run-up to the elections.

Local politics on the Reef: territory and the stifling of political contestation

The 'West Rand' is shorthand for a diverse collection of residential, industrial and mining areas situated to the west of Johannesburg. These areas range in physical character from the fairly typical black townships of Kagiso and Bekkersdal, through to the rapidly expanding informal settlements of Swanieville and Luna Sands (as well as a host of smaller, emergent and as yet unnamed site and service settlements), the town of Munsieville (where separate white and black areas face each other across a narrow stretch of road), and the uniformally white magisterial districts of Randfontein, Roodepoort and Krugersdorp.

The area is affected by much the same geopolitical realities as the rest of Gauteng. Interestingly, though, the townships here give the impression of a politics harder than elsewhere in the region. Though not much further from the metropolitan centre than many other townships, and not much worse off in socioeconomic terms (parts of it have almost 100 per cent tarred roads, electricity and sewerage removal), a place like Bekkersdal conveys the appearance of a deeper and more intractable poverty. It is dull and smoky, with no appearance of any natural inclination towards development. It simply exists, a site nowhere in particular, surrounded by marshes and old mines. Many of its residents are forced to find employment in the conservative town of Westonaria, which in turn connects to the far right-wing mining and farming districts of the Western Transvaal. But for all its lack of appeal it has been the protracted focus of the most intensely violent contestation. It has a history steeped in bloodshed which seems to taint the entire West Rand in much the same way as Thokoza and Katlehong do for the East Rand.

The causes and the course of violence in Bekkersdal are interesting for the purposes of this study. Until 1990, the Azanian People's Organisation was unquestionably the dominant organisation in the township. On the unbanning of the ANC, party activists from the Kagiso area sought to establish a presence in the vicinity by introducing members to a new squatter settlement, now known as Mandela Park, adjacent to the township proper. The settlement was then not aligned to any political party but the efforts of the emergent ANC clearly antagonised the established AZAPO grouping. Tensions between the parties steadily increased and eventually erupted in open warfare. At this point AZAPO, searching for ways to increase its power *vis-à-vis* its opponent, called upon armed IFP supporters from the East Rand to defend itself against ANC attacks.

But the move only brought a new dynamic to the conflict. The IFP soon set its sights on another part of Bekkersdal, the so-called X-section squatter camp on the northern edge of the township, as a political base for itself as new settlers began to move into the area. AZAPO, in turn, began to suspect that the deaths of some of its members could be attributed to the activities of its supposed allies, and animosity between the community and these new intruders rapidly developed. By the start of the election campaign the conflict between AZAPO and the ANC had been completely supplanted, and these former enemies had united against Inkatha.[13]

In January and February 1994, Bekkersdal captured media attention with an escalating spiral of violence which saw scores killed and between

5,000 and 8,000 people forced to flee their homes. A cruel spin was given to this conflict by the designation of hard no-go areas between rigidly defined zones of control 'belonging' to the various parties. Schooling in the area ground to a halt as the local high school found itself in no man's land separating AZAPO and IFP turf. The map clearly demarcates the political territories claimed by the various organisations operative in the area in mid-February. Remarkably, the hostel was regarded as neutral.

Significantly, the Bekkersdal violence has had spillover effects in a number of adjacent informal settlements. In mid-January, a large number of squatters were forcibly removed by white landowners from farms in the Nooidgedacht area. While the incident itself made headline news, subsequent events were to compound the squatter's ordeal. Allocated a spot in the Swanieville camp not far from Bekkersdal, the squatters were soon accused by IFP organisers in the area of being ANC sympathisers. Meetings were called in a bid to address the issue, but the IFP remained convinced that the new arrivals would boost the presence of the ANC in the area and so upset the fine balance of power. Tensions escalated and eventually erupted with the stabbing to death of the local civic's secretary, closely followed in turn by the murder of an IFP leader. At around the same time, at the Luna Sands squatter camp adjacent to

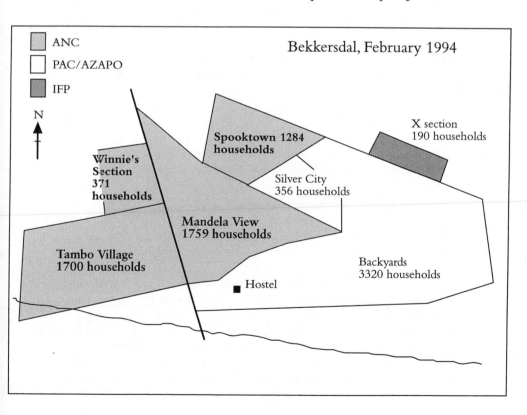

ANC

PAC/AZAPO

IFP

N

Bekkersdal, February 1994

X section
190 households

Spooktown 1284
households

Winnie's
Section
371
households

Silver City
356 households

Mandela View
1759 households

Tambo Village
1700 households

Backyards
3320 households

Hostel

Swanieville, some 250 ANC households, in an apparently precautionary move, simply emigrated *en masse* after a number of attacks on residents were attributed to the IFP. Interestingly, their destination was Swanieville itself, which is only some hundred metres distant from Luna Sands, though separated by a five-kilometre journey around an intervening swamp area. And at a new site and service settlement on the edge of Kagiso a number of IFP families set up shacks in what seemed to herald a pre-emptive land grab by Inkatha in an effort to gain political control of the area. It was rumoured that a large number of IFP families were moving into the vicinity in anticipation of the land being formally opened. This feared invasion was apparently prevented when irate Kagiso residents who had paid for stands in the settlement protested through a mass march. The police decided that it was wise to remove those who had settled illegally.[14]

Now it can be argued that a single logic underpinned all this, from warfare in Bekkersdal to land invasion near Kagiso. The logic is captured in the concept of 'territory'. The struggle to secure and maintain political territory was the backdrop against which a fair proportion of the election-eering in Gauteng occurred.

From very early in the campaign it became apparent that certain parties' access to specific communities was going to be severely con-strained by what was taken for granted to be the pervasive presence of other organisations in these areas. Evidence suggested that those parties which had historically used community-based organs of civil society – organs whose web-like structure encompassed every part of a township – to advance their struggle against apartheid easily claimed the strongest presence at a local level, regardless of their ideology or national policy orientation. In the eyes of most township residents, civic associations, and their appendages the area, block and street committees, were not politi-cally neutral bodies. It was clearly understood that their leadership and membership were aligned to a particular political party, and therefore that their efforts on behalf of residents (involving everything from advice on access to resources through to crime control and mediation in domestic strife) were being undertaken by that party itself. The civics and street committees effectively stood as proxy for a definite set of party political interests and, as such, seemed to imbue entire areas under their control with a clear party-political identity.

This imbrication of territory and party identity can be seen from two angles. From the point of view of the party activists working in the civic, it amounts to a claiming of the right to speak for all people living in an area, a claim justified *post facto* in the light of all the struggles and sacrifices undertaken by them and their colleagues on behalf of the community. Jonny Steinberg, writing on grass-roots conceptions of democracy in Attridgeville township outside Pretoria, lucidly picks up on this dimen-sion. He traces how leaders in the Attridgeville/Saulsville Residents

Organisation (ASRO) began to conceive of their structure as the embodied 'voice of the people', the only true reflection of the composite will of the community: 'What emerges is the notion of a single voice resonating from the community, but only insofar as the latter is represented by its authentic leadership – which in turn is gauged by looking back to the moment when the community constituted itself qua political entity; i.e., in the struggles which marked the birth and growing hegemonic position of ASRO.'[15] For Steinberg the result is a deliberately constructed myth of 'unicity', an assumption by the leaders of the civic that the residents of an entire township could and did wish to speak in chorus and, by extension, that each would indeed hear in the utterances of the civic their own personal voice.

A classic example of this claiming of turf – the assertion of the right to exercise exclusive control over a township on behalf of its residents, who are regarded as comprising a homogeneous mass – was seen in Kagiso on the West Rand during the election campaign. Here two different civics each demanded the allegiance of a separate section of the population. In March, the two structures, one ANC-aligned and the other with PAC orientations, entered into independent negotiations with the Electricity Supply Commission (Eskom) for the electrification of the township. The effect was to symbolically divide Kagiso in half as each structure presented different proposals to Eskom, both hoping to get credit for successful electrification. Friction between the two civics intensified as the election approached, and by mid-April sporadic clashes between groups of youthful supporters seemed to have become an accepted norm. Campaigning by each group in the area claimed by the other had become all but impossible. Electioneering posters belonging to the opposition were torn down as soon as they were put up, and so by election day PAC and ANC posters had come to be regarded as crude signposts demarcating the boundaries of the respective party's territory. Local political figures made it apparent that each organisation was quite convinced that the people residing in its area would vote for it.[16]

From another angle, individual residents experienced this insistence on homogeneity in their area as a real force. From the point of view of the voters themselves, there was an inescapable expectation that they conform to the political character of the locality in which they lived. At the very least, even if they did not actually go so far as to internalise and echo its ideological hailings, they were obliged to acquiesce in the face of what publicly appeared to be a single unified political community over which one party held a monopoly of power. To speak a different language from that sanctioned by the prevailing power, or worse, to speak openly against that power, was potentially to incur the wrath of their neighbours, 'represented' by the ever-present and ever-watchful grass-roots activist. To be dissentient against the prevailing party ideology was tantamount to being anti-community.

For people in most parts of the Reef, then, living in a particular area meant learning what was ordained as permissible to say, and, even if one disagreed substantively with the weight of community consensus, learning to be silent when confronted with it. The fear of being identified as different within the community at large was by no means an insubstantial one.

First, it was a fear given weight by a deep-seated culture of anxiety and uncertainty prevalent on the Reef from well before the start of the election campaign. Gauteng had been engulfed by a tidal wave of political violence from mid-1990, during which time the spectre of Bekkersdal had also become that of Katlehong, Thokoza, Alexandra, Sharpeville and other places.[17] This spiral of violence, which was overlaid throughout by the stresses and strains of constitutional negotiations, had crystallised in the minds of many township residents an image of a force supposedly radically opposed to democracy. The IFP 'hostel dweller' had become the eternal 'other', the perceived source of virtually all conflict that had, or might potentially, beset a community.[18]

The self-justifying symbolic construction of a violent IFP, and in turn the pervasive culture of fear, was reinforced during the period of campaigning by a number of incidents – none more important than the violence in Johannesburg on 28 March 1994, a month before the election. Here, a huge Zulu gathering in the centre of town, aimed at protesting the exclusion of Zulu interests in what was then regarded as an inequitable constitutional dispensation, turned ugly when marchers were fired on by snipers in front of the city library, and they in turn laid siege to the ANC headquarters, Shell House. Though the ANC seemed as much at fault for the violence as Inkatha, and though a substantial number of the over forty people who died on the day were Zulu-speakers, blame was instinctively laid at the door of the marching hostel residents.[19] A wave of fear spread across the Reef in the wake of the march and townships braced themselves for what was thought to be imminent civil war launched from the hostels.[20] In Kagiso, for example, rumours started to circulate in mid-April that IFP leaders Themba Khoza and Humphrey Ndlovo were paying regular visits to Kagiso hostel. People became convinced that they were planning a huge attack close to the election, and passionate pleas were made to the township youth not to taunt Inkatha members.[21]

For the average township resident, there could be no worse fate than being labelled a sympathiser of Inkatha, or of the white 'regime parties' which supposedly supported or turned a blind eye to its violent excesses. To be identified with the 'other' would be to become the embodiment of all that was outside and threatening towards the community. In a set of structured interviews conducted by Launching Democracy researchers in Gauteng, the question 'Do you think the community would be angry if you voted for a party that is not supported in your area?' evoked, among others, the following responses:

- Yes, because then I will be part of the enemy. All the people in my street are ANC. (Unemployed 40-year-old, Kagiso)

- Yes, the IFP. People in Kagiso have a serious hatred for the IFP and the NP so they will be angry. (30-year-old single parent, Tembisa)

- Yes, because I will be betraying the people. (18-year-old student, Kagiso)

- Like Inkatha? Yes, the community would be rightfully angry because those people are murderers. (35-year-old worker, Meadowlands)

- Ya! Most would exclude me from community issues and in fact might burn me because I support whites. (Hawker, 32 years old, Mamelodi West)[22]

Second, the fear of being regarded as different was made real by the physical enforcement of consensus by party activists on the ground. It was well known that anyone who did dare raise their voice in support of 'another party' would be quickly muscled into silence. As the election campaign gathered pace, and parties who had never before tried to elbow for space in the townships began to assert their presence here, this clear prohibition on elements considered antithetical to that which had been established as the community identity became brutally apparent. Whenever community consensus appeared to be threatened, intimidation was considered necessary to reassert it. In Kagiso, the chair of the ANC branch was formally charged with threatening to kill the National Party organiser for the West Rand: the matter was one of the very first taken up by the Investigations Division of the IEC. But this was by no means the only example:

- By mid-march the Democratic Party's postering team had begun refusing to enter Soweto after posters were repeatedly torn down and their lives threatened.

- The house of a DP member and organiser was reportedly firebombed in Meadowlands, and when DP posters were placed in the window of a Spaza shop here, the owner was told by youths that he would be killed and his business burnt.

- Also in Meadowlands, AZAPO members were informed that they would be 'dealt with' if they pursued their anti-election campaign. Closer to the election a public meeting at which AZAPO tried to explain its stance was hijacked by ANC members. Permission for other parties to use the community hall in the township, which had been claimed by the ANC as a base for its campaigning, was repeatedly denied on the pretext that 'it might cause trouble.'

- In Mamelodi, a local resident known to be a candidate of the NP's regional lists became the target of harassment from street committee members. Her car tyres were slashed, she was threatened with death and she was forced to stop all personal campaign activities. In Tembisa, another member of the NP was forced to withdraw her candidature when veiled threats were made on the lives of her children.

- In Mamelodi, the National Party felt compelled to start using bullet-proofed minibuses mounted with loudspeakers after their campaign cars were repeatedly stoned. Pamphlets distributed were routinely collected and burnt at a central point.

- The DP 'battle-bus' was stoned and spray-painted in ANC colours in KwaThema.

- In a similar vein, a visit to Zamdele township in the Vaal by the PAC deputy president, Johnson Mlambo, was hastily abandoned after shots were fired at the entourage.[23]

It was argued above that Gauteng provided conditions for a politics which was tailored explicitly towards transforming the lives of the region's inhabitants. An arena of permanent and vigorous political struggle was developed which seemed to present ideal opportunities for the formation of democratic subjects yearning for the benefits of choice. Now it is seen that this 'public realm', while internally dynamic, often had an oppressive effect at its margins. Even as the politically active sought to open up a space for struggle out of which they could contest apartheid's racial code, they systematically closed down other avenues and sites of contestation. Claiming for themselves exclusive jurisdiction over defined territory, demanding that the diversity of township life be redefined according to a new code of their own making, they permanently occupied the arena of local politics. All willing comers were welcome to join them in this space, but no one could pursue political projects outside of it because it totalised everything. Hence, even while it gave access to freedom and equality, the ground of political struggle in Gauteng made these principles its own exclusive property, denying them to any who tried to define themselves differently and establish alternate 'spaces of appearance'.

The political world of the Reef, then, was such that it moulded citizens' identities into two distinct yet strangely coterminous forms: it conferred the capacity for critical and creative choice by encouraging aspirations for personal freedom and social equality, yet at the very same time, at a different level, it seemed in certain areas to close this off, to give the conditions by which individual wills were always anchored fast to exclusionary party-political interests prevalent within a particular territory.

But now which of these bases for identity, it might be asked, deter-mined what voters did in the voting booth? Did the faceless woman from the IEC poster unthinkingly vote ANC simply because 'all the people in her street are ANC,' or because even to consider voting for another party would have been to associate herself with 'murderers' and 'oppressive whites', and might have aroused the righteous anger of the community directed against herself or even her child? Or did she vote ANC, or perhaps another party, only after careful consideration, and for the deliberate reason that this option best corresponded to her definition of herself and her aspirations for the future – that it seemed to offer her the best chance to remake her life and that of her son? Unfortunately, this question – as to whether voters' choices are a simple reflection of or a critical reaction against their social situation – cannot yet be answered unequivocally. We must first become cognisant of the effect of another set of political processes.

The Effect of Campaigning

It has been argued thus far that individuals receive their personal identities in a definable social context, and it is from within the horizon of these received identities that they enunciate their private political will. But in no modern democracy are the private interests, needs and ideals of voting subjects spoken directly into the public domain. They are always first channelled through the representational activity of organised political entities; individual wills must attach to party programmes if there is to be any political speaking at all. Now clearly no political party can wholly disregard the received conceptions of self and society already present in its defined constituency, but it is important to realise that there is not necessarily a direct congruence between people's lived experience and a party's own corporate identity.[24]

Parties appropriate and redepict their supporters' individual political wills by seeking to define a constituency with common interests and desires. In doing so they inevitably map a new identity on to the existing terrain of identifications. If we could fully understand how voters carried their social situation with them into the voting booth, surely we would then be aware of the effect of this new source of identity. We must carefully consider how the form and content of parties' election campaigns in Gauteng fed into and reinforced, or offset and nullified, the structure of possibilities and constraints that made up the political world of the Reef.

Modes of campaigning

Of all the political parties competing in Gauteng only the ANC was able to develop methods of campaigning which presented a substantially new image of itself to the electorate. The rest, mostly out of necessity, resorted to tactics which simply replicated the manner in which township residents had traditionally perceived them.

There were aspects, of course, of the ANC's campaign in Gauteng which were far from commendable. In many townships youthful street-level activists took it upon themselves to ensure that the fabric of community consensus was as seamless as possible. Grass-roots campaigners compiled exceptionally detailed 'street sheets' of confirmed support among households in their areas. Families identified as uninterested in the election, undecided on who they should support or harbouring sympathies for other parties were targeted for visits by more senior activists. There is evidence that these house visits often involved harsh psychological tactics: it was first suggested to the family that they should feel acutely ashamed at not having previously engaged in political struggles which were for the good of the country and community; the ideals of the ANC were then presented in a way which made disagreement inconceivable; and finally, a local activist was assigned to oversee the 'further political development' of the household.[25]

There were also numerous reports of hard-sell campaign tactics being employed to win new territory for the ANC. Swanieville, which, it has already been noted, was also home to a company of hard-core IFP supporters, was inundated with promises of jobs and sanitation facilities should people vote ANC. In Kagiso, a highly successful feeding scheme run by the American Methodist Evangelical Church was temporarily closed shortly before the election after church elders were repeatedly requested by the ANC to inform recipients that 'the food came from Mandela.' The elders argued that should the church be seen as favouring any one party, it would be under risk of attack from others such as the PAC.[26]

These tactics almost certainly aggravated the existing set of constraints on democratic choice identified above. However, much of official ANC strategy was such that it could only have had the opposite effect of opening people's minds to the political possibilities presented by the election. A substantial part of the ANC's energies on the ground were directed towards furnishing the electorate with the requisite confidence and skills to participate effectively in the democratic process.[27] In almost every township, in schools, churches, hospitals, shebeens and community halls, and at every meeting and rally, the ANC conducted voter education and organised mock elections to ensure that potential supporters felt comfortable with the procedure of voting. At times the communication of technical information was accompanied by hard political crusading for the ANC or against competitors, but very often trainers chose not to push their party explicitly.[28] However, even when the name of the party was clearly foregrounded, voter education, by its very nature, must have imparted to people some conception of the singular and private character of the vote. Merely to have said 'your vote is your secret' was to elevate individuals who heard it to a state of self-esteem from within which personal interests and aspirations could be regarded as inviolable.

ANC voter education was closely married to a strategy of People's Forums and community mass meetings involving high profile speakers. People's Forums entailed ANC national and regional leaders, sometimes Nelson Mandela himself, but in Gauteng most often Tokyo Sexwale, confronting an audience given the liberty to ask questions on any topic or issue of concern. In theory, no prepared speeches were allowed to be delivered – the forum was entirely open to the floor. Most other ANC rallies comprised, in roughly equal parts, an address, question time and some form of voter education, but always the basic flavour of the People's Forum *stricto senso* was replicated. Where voter education was provided it was done in a way which provided for maximum audience participation – often through the teaching of catchy chants ('one ballot, two ballot . . . vote ANC!' was chanted again and again at the ANC's final mass rally of the campaign period to allay confusion about the separate national and regional votes). And when speakers of the likes of Tokyo Sexwale addressed a gathering, hard rhetoric took a back seat to a pure charisma, an infectious, earthy humour and heartfelt assurances that an ANC government would be attentive and responsive to people's needs. Together, these mass meetings and People's Forums gave the overwhelming impression that the ANC wanted to talk with and listen to ordinary people, rather than simply proselytise them in a calculated effort to win power. Their very format seemed to hold out a promise of citizens able to be reconnected to a public terrain clearly open and susceptible to change, the prospect of people actively and critically engaged in the shaping of future social and political developments, wherever these might affect them.

Deprived of the space to campaign normally and above board in the townships, parties like the DP and NP resorted to a variety of creative strategies to get their message across. Unfortunately, the very innovativeness of the methods gave them the appearance of extravagant publicity stunts, somehow forced and unnatural and decidedly out of touch with the hard realities of life in the townships. The Democratic Party campaign focused almost exclusively around the hype generated by its campaign bus. Dubbed the 'battle-bus', this open-topped double-decker toured most townships on the Reef, blaring loud music and campaign slogans and scattering pamphlets. At the height of the campaign a DP organiser enthused to the media that the bus was reaching approximately twenty-five people every minute, but people on the ground appeared to regard the vehicle simply as a rude interruption of normal daily activity. At best, most people seemed largely uninterested; at worst, they expressed annoyance at the littering of their streets with unwanted campaign media. Only children were amused at the clown costumes and carnival appearance of the entourage.[29]

The National Party, in its turn, at times made a concerted effort to establish a real presence at a grass-roots level. But its methods often made it even more unwelcome than usual in most townships. Township residents were heard to express anger at reports of campaign tactics which they regarded as nothing short of political bribery. In Attridgeville early in the campaign, the National Party was rumoured to have approached pensioners with a scheme by which they could apparently receive a reduction in rent if they took an NP membership card to the local authority. Local government officials knew nothing of the proposal.[30] In Soweto a food scheme by an apparently non-political agency issued identity cards to its recipients which had a remarkable likeness to the NP logo. In Orlando West, residents were offered R1 for every poster they put up in the township. A local NP organiser admitted that his office had begun to be regarded as an 'employment agency' by many residents. And in virtually every community, rumours circulated that the NP was prepared to pay people R10 for every new member they recruited.[31]

Even when it tried less suspect strategies, however, the NP seemed to fare no better in convincing first-time voters that it was a party for the people. In Soweto, an automatic telephone dialling system was activated to reach households with telephones – a recorded message was played and voters were asked to indicate their support for the party by pushing a button. And in a number of townships a variety of pamphlets were dropped by helicopter. The responses of residents in Kagiso to one such drop, at two o'clock in the morning on the Sunday just before the election, encapsulate the attitudes of the vast majority of people to these methods. 'The NP campaigns from the air,' one person remarked cynically, 'whilst we the people are down here on the ground.' 'It is unacceptable that the NP chooses to stalk us during the night. Is the NP a night party? Some of us want light, not darkness!' said another. The pamphlets were in Setswana, a language predominant in Kagiso, but they contained glaring spelling and grammatical errors.[33]

For most ordinary people, then, the campaign strategies of parties other than the ANC seemed to have the effect only of reinforcing their traditional image as elitist, whites-only interest groups distantly removed from everyday life in the townships. Their methods were popularly perceived as disempowering in that they trivialised real concerns behind a façade of false jollity, or treated people as fools and children who would give away their precious vote to any who could provide temporary material or comic relief. Now one could argue that the effect of these campaigns was to confirm the impression of a political realm always radically divorced from, and insensitive to, personal needs and interests on the ground, and as such could only have further subdued a politically marginalised population already subject to great anxiety, uncertainty and despondency. But this would be to misread the fascinating reversal behind a statement like 'Is the NP a night party? Some of us want light, not darkness.' This sentiment surely communicates a profound sense of frustration and anger, underpinned by a firm demand for personal recognition, respect and opportunity. What it suggests is that NP campaigning on the Reef, far from closing off people's perception of what the then imminent election might make possible, may have opened their eyes to the circumstances of their lives and focused their sight on a future in which these lives might be altered. In effect, the 'disempowering' practices of the NP and DP became a prism by which people's received image of themselves as powerless could be inverted.

Campaign practices in this election were therefore not neutral, contentless vehicles by which the 'meaningful' message was delivered to the populace. The way in which parties chose to speak to the people, the portrait of the first-time voter tacit within their terms of address, had a profound effect on political identities. In the case of the ANC's People's Forums and mass meetings, campaigning brought to bear a new set of identifications to which addressees responded gratefully and positively. It offered them the chance to redefine themselves as individuals worth listening to in a political context, as confident and capable political actors, and as people with real concerns which any future polity would have to address. In the case of DP and NP campaigning most people seemed to respond critically and creatively to what they perceived to be a fundamentally negative portrait of themselves as new voters. Evidence suggests that many turned the image they saw in upon itself, and in the process focused an interpretation of themselves as political beings having been too long disempowered, and therefore as subjects craving real democratic choice. Interestingly, if one considers the content of the various parties' campaigns, and how these were received by the communities under discussion, one see precisely the same self-liberating processes at work.

The campaign message: content and reception

It would seem that while many people had a soft spot in their hearts for the PAC as 'the other liberation movement', the organisation's campaign message did not meet with a positive response from Gauteng residents. People interviewed suggested that the single campaign promise of 'The land first . . . everything else will follow' was inappropriate for a constituency which hoped to reap the fruits of a modernising economy now working on its behalf. 'Many people still remember the poverty and hardship of life in the rural areas. They came to the towns and cities to get away from that; they have no interest in going back to being peasants even if they could own the land they worked. Today most people want houses, jobs and education, not land. We cannot farm in Johannesburg,' one informant stated bluntly.

A backward-looking message was also the downfall of the Democratic Party. Its campaign themes swivelled around the idea that the party upheld the classic liberal value of freedom from excessive government power. The DP, potential supporters were urged to appreciate, had a decades-long tradition of effective opposition in defence of citizens' rights. It would continue to perform this function in the new government. The campaign took great pains to recall the party's historical contribution towards fighting apartheid from within; it sought to emphasise the party's unwavering commitment to long-held principles; and it called attention to the victories achieved at multiparty negotiations (judicial independence, powers of the provinces, etc.). This legacy was then presented as proof that the party was 'battle hardened' and 'vigilant enough' to ensure that the new government did not abuse its power. The all-important concept here was that the Democratic Party could be trusted for the future given its track record of the past. Given its credentials it would be the ideal opposition, the strong, quality counterweight to government excess.

Despite the intrinsic potency of its message, the Democratic Party campaign exuded a fundamental negativism. At the very moment which seemed to offer hope for a new beginning, reconciliation and reconstruction, it appealed to a past role which most people could not help but associate with misery, and attempted to define a role for the future which seemed nothing but antagonistic. For those who suffered so long under a system of rule which the DP admitted it was integrally involved in for decades, there was little comfort in the claim that the party could be trusted because of its history of opposing injustice. And by positioning itself in a watchdog role standing against the new government, the party necessarily erected an image of the individual citizen always at least potentially threatened by government action. For many first-time voters interviewed, who saw themselves as historically marginalised from the political process and who now, for the first time, could anticipate a government working for them, this was not a happy idea.

By contrast, the National Party campaign sought to create the impression of a political entity which was positive, dynamic and forward looking. It appealed to people of a more traditional morality, and those who had become frustrated with violence, intimidation and social and economic uncertainty, but its frame of reference was always what was possible in the future, rather than what was discouraging about the past. Cleverly, it steered well clear of issues that might have reminded the voter of the National Party's past policies or projected a negative image. Law and order, protection of cultural minorities, community standards, all elements of NP discourse in the early 1990s and all potentially potent electoral themes, hardly appeared in the campaign message.

The conceptual linchpin of the campaign was the notion that the National Party was no longer the party it had once been. The 'new National Party' was one which had broken the shackles of the past, confessed its wrongdoings and was now looking to the future. The key refrain that the party was a new one, besides being the single most effective jingle in the party's repertoire, also provided the basis for comparison with other contenders for the vote. None of the other parties had broken with its own past, it was pointed out – the ANC was still steeped in discredited Communist ideology, the PAC could only echo racist sentiments, and the DP remained elitist, removed from the people's struggles and sufferings. Ergo, only the National Party could be entrusted with the responsibility for building the future.

Coupled to the idea that the National Party had reinvented itself was the message that they were 'builders' of a new society. Here the detail of what exactly was to be constructed was less important than the possibilities the idea of 'building' offered in the way of juxtaposing the party identity with that of the ANC. The ANC, the campaign delighted in stressing, was an organisation of 'breakers' – it represented a past of violence, intimidation, the burning of schools, disruption of the economy and the unruliness of youth. And it promised to bring a future of economic ruin through nationalisation, labour unrest, racially based affirmative action, etc. By contrast, the National Party had experience of government and could thus confidently offer a future of foreign investment, a growing economy, labour policies that would bring harmony and job opportunities for all, social development programmes that would guarantee access to housing and affordable health care, equal opportunities through decent education, and a safe and peaceful community life free of crime and violence. The NP was thus the party that could bring political forcefulness to, and the reinvigoration of, an old tired polity which had till then not worked for the people.

Unfortunately, for all the care taken to efface its own past, people in the townships steadfastly refused to forget what the NP had done to them. 'The NP are like jackals in a sheep's skin,' sneered a twenty-four-year-old student from Meadowlands (inverting an NP newspaper advert which portrayed the 'Communist ANC' as a fierce-looking jackal in a sheepskin disguise). 'They oppressed us for forty years, I will never believe them or forgive them.' These sentiments were repeated in virtually every interview conducted in the townships. The more the National Party disseminated platitudes about its own transformation, and its own renewed ability to transform the country, the more clearly most people seemed to remember their own experiences of apartheid, and the more eager they were to picture themselves outside of and unencumbered by the NP's vision for the furture.

The campaign of the African National Congress turned on an invocation to voters to project a radical improvement in their lives through the liberating vision of the party. It was a highly effective appeal organised around three core slogans: 'A better life for all', 'Working together for Jobs, Peace and Freedom' and 'We have a plan.'

The first slogan, 'A better life for all', was one heavy with allusion to past sufferings and struggles. While it would seem, at first glance, to have looked to the future, its central concern was with the legacy of apartheid.

The party's manifesto booklet opened with the idea that the proximity of the day when all could vote for a government of their choice was a 'tribute to the efforts and sacrifices of millions of people'. The ANC's vision of a non-racial and democratic future was one firmly rooted in years of brutal racial oppression: 'Our children and grandchildren should never again know the violence and the suffering, the shame and the pain many of us endured. They should enjoy their childhood secure in family life, and grow up with equal opportunities to live life to the full.'

Upon these poignant reminders of past injustices, the second slogan served to construct a more positive vision. 'Working together' was a clever prefix. It alluded to the principle of non-racialism, while inviting images of peace, reconciliation and collective endeavour organised around clear common interests and goals. It symbolically broke the feelings of alienation, isolation and segregation that were the essence of apartheid. 'Jobs, Peace and Freedom' was a catchy troika of ideas, suggesting at once:

- Real material improvement (it incorporated the detailed promises for housing, electrification, education and health care that are the backbone of the Reconstruction and Development Programme);

- An end to conflict, a concern uppermost in the minds of many voters even if they were not residents of strife-torn areas. For many, as has been indicated, the recent transition had been synonymous with violence, such that any final settlement to be endorsed through the franchise had to contain the firm promise of an end to constant fear and uncertainty;

- Personal liberation. The concept of freedom was always given positive inflection in the campaign message. Rather than attach it to notions of protection from the abuse of power, it was consistently used to suggest both the long-awaited fruits of struggle, and more importantly, the possibility of a radical break with the past.

The third key slogan in the ANC's campaign, 'We have a plan', crystallised vague hopes for the future into faith that workable alternatives to past policies could bring about real change. The slogan, supported by pages of policy objectives, sought to inspire trust and confidence through the image of a well-conceived practical programme of action, and it had the effect of inviting popular participation in this grand project of social reconstruction through the attempt to sound as inclusive as possible. The incorporative terms 'we' and 'our' were prevalent throughout the ANC's campaign, suggesting commonality of interest and purpose, and the possibility of individual contribution towards the shared ideal of remaking the country.

It was suggested above that the way in which parties speak to their constituencies has a real effect on the capacity of ordinary people to perceive their position within society and to envisage the transformation of this society. This effect, it can be argued, is compounded by the way in which parties allow people to speak politically, by marketing a particular vision of society which supporters can buy into. Even if the vision on offer is an expedient and highly contrived one (as many election platforms are wont to be), and even if voters' investment in it is temporary (lasting only until the election is over), its representation of a particular political identity almost certainly impacts upon the capacities for self-definition of people who receive it. The content of party campaigns affords a template from which people can take interpretations of their own individual experiences and on to which they can project their personal aspirations and ideals for the future.

In South Africa's first democratic elections this template always seemed to provide identifications orientated around the key symbolic referent of change. Each of the parties sought to define itself, and by extension those who 'saw themselves' more clearly through this definition, in terms provided by the dialectic of past versus future. They each posited, in various ways using various codes, a version of the past relevant for the present, on the basis of which the future could be projected. It makes no difference in which of these versions voters saw themselves most accurately portrayed. What is important is that through the prism of *any one* of the competing parties, voters could sharply define the person their existence had made them to be, and how they wanted to make themselves in the future. As such, party campaigning in Gauteng could have been an important catalyst for the emergence of real political reflection. It had the potential to encourage voters to ask the all-important questions: 'Who am I?', 'What has history and society legislated for me?', 'Do I like who I am – do I approve of this social law as it has been laid down for me?', 'Who do I want to be?', 'How must society change so that I might be made anew?'

Political campaigning, then, had the potential effect of fundamentally loosening the constraints placed on voters by the traditional closure of local political spaces. This is by no means to suggest that it did in fact do so, only that campaigning seemed to provide the opportunity, as well as the vital symbolic resources, for people to interrogate their existence and invest a desire for transformation. Could the process of voting, the election itself as the all-important end to the feverish campaign period, have brought to bear an overdetermining set of compulsions which augmented, or alternatively entirely subverted, this effect?

The Vote: Three Choices in One

There are three factors to consider when reflecting upon the election in Gauteng. First, this was the moment of greatest risk, when any festering conflict between those opposed to and those committed to the democratic process, as well as between old political adversaries contesting the vote, could have come to a head. The sites where people had to gather to cast their votes inevitably became the focal points of much fear and anxiety. Second, this was the moment of truth, when people had finally to associate themselves unequivocally with one or other of the contending parties, and hence when the tension between discretionary and determined political convictions would have been most sharply felt. Third, it was the moment of change, the threshold between the dissolution of the old order and the establishment of the new, when social and political forms and practices were either to be carried over or left behind.

In essence, there were three choices embodied in the vote of any Gauteng resident: a choice to come to the polls and expose oneself to potential danger, or to remain safely at home; a choice between options on the ballot paper which voters perceived to be more or less available depending on their political circumstances; and the 'choice' (to some extent dependent on how the other two were exercised) of either remaining subject to the fear, uncertainty, passivity and expected submission to authority imposed by apartheid, or embracing a new sense of openness in political relations and emancipating oneself with society. The election, therefore, as a distinct political moment, crystallised all pressures and all possibilities into a final overdetermining compulsion. It allowed some people to make truly self-reflective and creative political decisions for the first time, while for others it only hardened constraints. Did the majority find it liberatory or oppressive?

In the context of a less than tranquil period of campaigning, perhaps the cardinal choice was the decision to vote at all. Voter education studies undertaken in 1992 suggested that at that stage fear, despondency and a general cynicism about the value of voting would keep many away from the polls.[33] Independent surveys since then have seemed to show that as the elections approached the determination to vote has gradually but steadily increased.[34] A week before the election, however, there again seemed every indication that large numbers of potential voters might stay away from the polls. In a number of informal interviews in the Orlando West and Dube sections of Soweto, soon after the Zulu March on 28 March, residents registered new lows in morale and interest in the election. It was a common refrain that despite a desire to vote, campaign activities and the polling stations would be avoided at all costs. April 27 was to be the start of civil war in South Africa, with inevitable violence at the polls and widespread looting and anarchy to follow.[35]

For observers of the electoral process in Gauteng, there was therefore something remarkable about the sudden and fundamental change of mood just days before the election. The IFP's surprise entry into the election race spread a wave of relief across the townships. The sudden dissipation of the 'other' seemed to precipitate the instant relaxation of local-level political codes set in place to counter its ever-present imaginary threat.[36] Suddenly, the Democratic Party was allowed to distribute pamphlets in Meadowlands, unhindered by the guardians of ANC consensus. Tensions dropped palpably in Alexandra and, though the no-go border between the separate ANC and IFP communities here remained firmly in place,[37] there was for the first time a real sense that co-operation needed to replace mutual suspicion and distrust.[38]

For many people, this new feeling of openness and tolerance, the sense that fear and uncertainty were suddenly dissipating, seemed only to deepen as the great event arrived. Apathy and antagonism gave way to a profound desire to participate personally in the process of voting, and to ensure that others, even erstwhile political enemies, were able to do the same. Surprisingly, neither the spate of right-wing bombings on the Reef nor the daunting prospect of standing in agonisingly long queues caused by administrative chaos seemed to deter voters. In fact they appeared to steel people's resolve. Coming as a last-ditch effort to halt the progress towards full democracy, the bombings had an effect quite the opposite of what was intended. From people spoken to informally at the polls, it seems they inspired a righteous anger at what in essence was a savage intrusion of the past at the very moment that the past finally seemed to have been usurped. They crystallised a feeling of revulsion at everything that apartheid oppression had meant and they seemed to signal that this was indeed the end of white rule: that whites were driven to such desperate measures meant that they were finally vulnerable. Likewise, the fact that the queues were so long, that thousands of people seemed *happy* to stand for hours in the blazing sun, became symbolic of the tremendous importance of the event and instilled even in the most fearful and apathetic of people a fervour to partake in the 'moment of final emancipation'. In Attridgeville near Pretoria, young white security force members did the unthinkable and stood in line with the people they had formerly been responsible for oppressing. Reports suggested that this, more than anything, signalled to residents that old practices were finally on their way out and that they had everything to gain from participating actively in the election. In the end an estimated 89 per cent of potential voters in Gauteng went to the polls.[39]

Interestingly, though, the fact that people made their way to the voting stations did not necessarily indicate that they had invested in the widespread feelings of relief and the new sense of possibility that the election spontaneously seemed to precipitate. In Kagiso on the second day of the poll, a woman was asked by researchers how she was feeling about her vote. 'I was told I must come here,' she replied nervously. 'They said if I did not vote I would be fined R2,000 or put in jail.' Asked who 'they' were the woman looked around furtively and hurried away.[40] And in Mamelodi near Pretoria, the Bloed Street bombing seemed to put a profound damper on the willingness of the elderly in the township to exercise their franchise. It was reported that it was only through the efforts of youth in the street committees, urging people to let nothing stand in the way of their right to vote, that many of the aged picked up enough courage to leave their homes. It is quite probable that a counterfear, that they might become known in the community as cowards not prepared to do their civic duty, and not a last-minute fortitude, got many of these people to the polls.[41] On the whole, Gauteng voters seemed able to escape such negativity, and most came to polling stations willingly and expectantly. But there were certainly some whose 'first choice' was driven not by any considered assessment of their self and society, but by a socially imposed compound of fear, uncertainty and passive submission to the enforcers of consensus. For some the perilous hour of choice appeared only to reinforce constraints.

To what extent did this same compound impose upon voters 'second choice', that between the available options? Did most people in Gauteng, in spite of the protective veil of anonymity, end up voting PAC or ANC for the simple reason that these parties' dominance at a local level prevented full access to the images of self and society afforded by other parties? Or did they, at the moment of the election, somehow find the space to break with the force of consensus? Once again, the answer is necessarily an equivocal one, but there is weighty evidence to suggest that even where the web of imposed public consent was strong, residents successfully resisted this political pressure by quietly transferring their support to parties which had no overt community presence.

In Naledi on the western edge of Soweto, where no other parties ventured to challenge the dominance of the ANC during campaigning, an active young member of the street committees had a radical change of heart as the election arrived. Though she would not tell researchers where she had put her cross, she was firm that the ANC had not got her vote: she had become totally disillusioned with the behaviour of the youth and had realised that the organisation completely lacked direction for the future.[42] And at the Nasrec counting station, where the process of reconciling and counting ballots was long and tedious, male members of the IFP quickly became bored and, during subsequent days, decided to send women members of the party to act as electoral agents on their behalf. These women openly admitted to counting officers that they had in fact voted ANC, against the instructions of their husbands.[43]

Evidence besides the merely anecdotal can also be advanced. After the election, these authors got sight of an original provincial batch tally form from a polling station in Soweto, supposedly an ANC stronghold throughout. Of the 3,000 people whose votes were recorded here, 760 clearly felt something similar to the young street committee member above – they had all voted NP. And perhaps most importantly, there are clear indications that many first-time voters used the double ballot creatively by casting their separate votes for two distinct parties. In Gauteng the ANC lost approximately 68,000 of its 2,486,938 national votes in the regional tally, and the IFP shed 20,000 of 173,903. By contrast, a total of 246,000 votes were gained by smaller parties in the regional ballot: the PAC was boosted by 9,000 to 61,512, the African Moderates Congress by 5,400 to 12,888 and the African Christian Democratic Party by 5,000 to 25,542. Most interestingly, the Democratic Party and the right-wing Freedom Front jointly gained approximately 100,000 each in the provincial count. Since the FF increment could only have come from the National Party, and since the NP only lost 158,000 provincial votes to other parties, substantial numbers of ANC and IFP voters must have given their second votes to either the DP or the NP (some 40,000 DP votes are otherwise unaccounted for).[44]

None of this could lead one to conclude that first-time voters felt no coercion, that all constraints simply evaporated as they stood waiting to vote. But certainly it would seem equally untenable to argue that the majority were able to conceive of no option but that which was imposed upon them, and therefore that the veil of anonymity which the polling supposedly afforded was torn from the start. In the exhilaration of the long-awaited moment of choice, not a few seemed to find the power to make entirely autonomous decisions.

However, even if the final set of choices visible to township residents was indeed quite limited, it does not necessarily follow that most residents were therefore utterly unable to enjoy any of the symbolic benefits of democratic choice. Just because a fifty-year-old worker from Naledi township in Soweto – all of whose friends were ANC sympathisers, who had to deal with ANC-organised civics and street committees on a daily basis, and whose fellow factory workers were organised by an ANC-leaning COSATU union – ended up supporting the ANC at the polls, it does not necessarily mean that she had her vote decided for her. She may yet have carefully interrogated her existence, consciously and critically defined her aspirations for the future and then accessed a moment of real choosing in which she was entirely unconstrained by the determination of her own identity, even though she seemed simply to reiterate the political convictions her society had marked out for her. How so?

The election was a moment of risk and of decision-making. But there seemed to be something else besides in the poll which made it a unique *moment of possibility* for voters whose capacity for critical choice had previously been closed off. Certainly the election days brought a palpable sense of feverish excitement and optimism which very few could ignore, but this does not quite capture it. The intangible factor, the third 'choice' that voters made, only really becomes apparent when we consider the political culture that crystallised out in the election's aftermath.

In April 1994, just before the election, researchers at the Centre for Conflict Analysis at the HSRC came to the following conclusion in a review of Gauteng conflict: 'Conflict figures are unlikely to go down after the elections since the underlying dynamics of political violence in Gauteng will not have been eliminated or even substantially addressed merely because the elections have occurred. It would be fairly safe to predict that violence and conflict in Gauteng will continue for a considerable period after the elections.'[45] In mid-May, however, some two weeks after the final results of the poll had been released, researchers visited Bekkersdal to find that in this former well-spring of violence a real and lasting peace was already starting to develop. Residents were still cautious, of course, in heralding a complete end to the conflict. After so many years of bloodshed many found it difficult to conceive of a life without any fear of attack. But there was a real feeling that something had changed and that, if only everyone remained committed to it, this change could be permanent. Indeed, a veritable sea-change in political culture seemed to sweep across Gauteng in the wake of the elections. Apart from some minor skirmishes between ANC self-defence units and hostel residents in Thokoza in July, levels of political violence in the region dropped suddenly to virtually zero. Widespread violence had not resurfaced at the time of this chapter's writing and seemed unlikely to do so in the near future.

The HSRC conclusion sits uneasily with the reality of post-election politics in Gauteng, and yet its prediction was entirely plausible given what was seen during the period of the election. There was every indication that the steady escalation in the political stakes, the brinkmanship of certain parties, the persistence of no-go areas, and other contributing factors were going to make for a violent election and an even more violent aftermath. Everything suggested that the underlying dynamics of conflict would indeed be perpetuated. The fact that they were not can mean only one thing: something interrupted the self-sustaining logic of violence. This something can only have been the election itself.

Claude Lefort has said that in democratic elections, 'The substance of society dissolves into number.'[46] The term 'dissolves' suggests here that during elections society of a certain 'hard form' suddenly becomes malleable and changeable. A measure of indeterminacy is introduced so that there would now seem to be the potential for a radical recreation of the social form. Elections, this suggests, carry a symbolic significance over and above their formal processes, in that they concretely afford the possibility for society to radically break with its past. The election, as the moment which first-time voters suddenly recognised as the hour of emancipation, would seem to have brought exactly this regenerative effect. It seemed to suggest to people that through this event they could redefine their lives – that because all the old markers of certainty were suddenly now unfixed, they themselves could step outside received social places and roles without fear of repercussion. The remarkable cordiality and peacefulness of the election days themselves, as well as the pervasive feeling of catharsis that followed – the sense that somehow society had reinvented itself in a way which meant the end of antagonism, suspicion and fear – *only makes sense* if we perceive large numbers of voters to have made a more fundamental 'choice' than simply coming to the polls and selecting one or other party.

Between Territory and Autonomy – the Issue Decided?

Were voters pure and passive products of their social situation, compelled to mark the ballot paper in a particular way by the daunting constraints imposed by their communal context? Or did they instead carry their social situation into the ballot box in an eminently critical and creative manner by shrugging off the determinism of their society and history and choosing autonomously? There is no final answer to this question. It has been posed in numerous forms in established democracies all over the world, and argued through to no greater clarity than has been achieved here. No analyst can discern with any ultimate certainty what average voters feel and think as they enter the voting booth for the first time. At best he can provide an overview of the political forces which could have shaped their capacity to choose and then look for evidence, even if circumstantial and anecdotal, which might just suggest how they responded to these. The constraints and pressures on voters were clear, but voting is ultimately an existential and individual act.

But is this to say that no conclusion at all can be offered? If all the evidence were to be weighed, an answer to the question would, on balance, probably have to be a positive one. The discussion has shown that local dynamics in many Gauteng townships, even where the logic of territory was not taken to the extreme of no-go areas, reinforced by a variety of campaign practices, were certainly cause for real concern. There were indeed voters who found no opportunity to escape the burden of pervasive fear, uncertainty and enforced submission to community consensus. But against this must be set the following considerations:

- The political culture of challenge and contestation so long prevalent on the Reef probably gave the conditions for many voters to refuse absolute submission to those who would totalise local social spaces;

- The form and content of campaigning in Gauteng was such that it surely could not have further closed off the possibilities for self-reflective political choice. Even where party messages and campaign tactics were dismissed with disdain, rather than carefully considered, they must have provided opportunities for interrogation of self and society;

- A vast majority of Gauteng voters left their fears behind and went to the polls, even though some may have felt coerced even in this choice;

- There is evidence that many voters made choices which were not sanctioned by their communities, not least of which is the indication that the double ballot was used creatively by many;

- The fact that the politics of antagonism and conflict did not reassert itself in the aftermath of the poll suggests that many people regarded the election as an opportunity to break with the past, to reinvent themselves and their society. Whereas the campaign was largely a process of positioning people on opposing sides, the election seemed to be a fundamental act of consensus-building. In it most people apparently saw the opportunity to institute a political arrangement based on a new trust rather than old antagonisms.

Once again, were most voters in this region so constrained by their environment that the liberatory potential of the act of voting was lost to them? The answer would seem to be a qualified no. Certainly, our woman in the IEC poster had her vote determined for her to some extent. Yes, she was probably more severely constrained by her place in society than voters would normally be in established democracies. But on the evidence there seems every likelihood that she was able to take some advantage of her moment of anonymity.

Notes

The information included in this chapter is drawn from the research of 26 field observers, conducted during the period January to May 1994 on 23 distinct geographical areas in the PWV: Garankuwa, Mamelodi, Attridgeville, Midrand/Ivory Park, Alexandra, Tembisa, KwaThema, Edenvale/Modderfontein, Reiger Park, Benoni/Boksburg/Brakpan, Thokoza/Katlehong, Ratanda, Sharpeville/Sebokeng/Evaton (the Vaal), Lenasia, Johannesburg Southern Suburbs, Johannesburg Central, Orlando West, Diepkloof, Pimville/Klipsruit, Meadowlands, Naledi, Bekkersdal and Kagiso. The field observers who participated in this project were Andile Mngxitama, Keith Nxumalo, Gareth Smith, Simon Mapadimeng, Gersh Kgamedi, Hassan Khoza, Meganathan Vythilingan, Simon Mamabola, Chris Landsberg, Lisa Klein, Stephanie Allais, Calvin Kekana, Nicki Spurr, Sello Molefe, Claire Tucker, Jackie Dugard, Phandelani Liphosa, Marc Flior, Darren Leishmann, Adrian Barratt, Ike Hloka, Vaneshri Chetty and Michael Van Huysteen (three others preferred to have their names withheld for professional reasons). These observers' individual reports have been compiled into five volumes which are lodged at the Human Sciences Research Council (Pretoria) and the Institute for Multi-Party Democracy (Durban). References in this chapter to the reports will follow the notation LD PWV Observer Reports, volume no., page no.
    Many thanks are due to the following for helpful commentary and criticism on drafts of this chapter: Laurence Pretorius, Professor of Sociology at the University of South Africa, Dr Rupert Taylor and Stephen Louw of the Political Studies Department, University of the Witwatersrand, Richard Humphries at Centre for Policy Studies, and participants in the Postgraduate Students Seminar Series, Arts Faculty, Wits University.

  1 Democracy, by definition, is a system in which citizens 'discover themselves to be equally responsible for the exercise of public authority'. Claude Lefort, 'Reversi-

bility', *Telos*, 63 (Spring 1985), p. 109. See also Cornelius Castoriadis, *Philosophy, Politics, Autonomy* (Oxford and New York: Oxford University Press, 1991), p. 142.

2 Castoriadis, *Philosophy, Politics, Autonomy*, p. 164: 'Autonomy does not consist in acting according to a law discovered in an immutable Reason and given once and for all. It is the unlimited self-questioning about the law and its foundations as well as the capacity, in light of this interrogation, to make, to do, and to institute. . . . [It is to] make one's own laws, knowing that one is doing so.'

3 Chantall Mouffe, 'Citizenship and political identity', *October*, 61 (1992), p. 31.

4 In truth, this fact is a precept integral to democracy rather than an 'unfortunate reality'. Logically, if individuals were always already free and equal there simply would be no basis for choice: identical subjects, all unencumbered by any prior location within a social system, all expected to contribute through their own personal decisions to the formation and reformation of political power, would have no grounds for developing differential notions of what is socially right, just or good. Each would want of the political power being installed almost exactly the same thing. And if it could be established beforehand that any one individual speaks for all others in asserting her particular interests, needs or ideals, then what point the democratic project that seeks to apprehend the will of the people as a whole? Democracy requires the possibility of multiple and competing political interests, which in turn depends on a dispersal of social experiences, meanings, values and concerns. This in its turn rests on persons being variously positioned within a differentiated societal order.

5 Gauteng was yet to be constituted as a regional political entity *per se*; the new interim constitution which established it as a distinct province came into effect only at the end of the election period. 'Regional political formation' is therefore used in a loose sense to refer to a general framework or context of politics of a sort subtly different from that seen in KwaZulu-Natal, the Western Cape or elsewhere.

6 South African Institute for Race Relations, *The Township Annual* (Johannesburg: SAIRR, 1993).

7 Phillip Hansen, *Hannah Arendt: Politics, History and Citizenship* (Cambridge: Polity Press, 1993), p. 65.

8 We would argue that a 'public realm' of some sort is to be found almost everywhere in South Africa. Even in the deepest rural areas people gather to partake in forms of collective action in burial societies, churches, women's groupings, tribal courts, etc. This activity, however, mostly has the function of ensuring the stability and self-perpetuation of primordial social forms. The question of the legitimacy of the tradition that frames the collective action being engaged in is hardly ever posed. Only rarely, under conditions such as that which prevail in Gauteng, is the foundation laid for reflective interrogation of a received socioeconomic and political complex *from a variety of different viewpoints*.

9 As anecdotal evidence for this fact one could list the various youth organisations active in the Thokoza area at the start of the election campaign (the Congress of South African Students, the ANC Youth League, Azanian Students Movement and Azanian Youth Organisation, Pan Africanist Students Organisation and Azanian National Youth Unity, the IFP Youth Brigade) or note that Alexandra had as many as six civic organisations, each representing a different interest group in the population (the Alex Civic Organisation (ACO), the Alex Civic Association (from which the ANC-aligned ACO broke away in the mid-1980s), the Alex Land and Property Owners Association, the East Bank Residents Association, the Reconstruction Area Residents Association (IFP-aligned) and the Hostel Residents Committees in the IFP dominated hostels). (LD PWV Observer Reports, vol. 1, pp. 39–47, p. 81.)

10 LD PWV Observer Reports, vol. 4, p. 153. War between the two organisations broke out on 25 March after two rape suspects were apprehended by members of the community. One of the suspects later died of injuries sustained during the arrest. It

was later discovered that the two were members of PASO, whose supporters then swore to retaliate for what was interpreted as an affront to the movement's dignity.

11　Investment in a particular set of political ideals is a way to accumulate knowledge, power, status and sometimes even wealth. Continued access to these resources requires that the corporate identity with which one has become associated, and within which one seeks to distinguish oneself, be actively, sometimes fanatically, defended against any other which might displace and supersede it. The result is a multiplication of antagonisms between small political fiefdoms which objectively would seem to have much the same interests and goals.

12　It is important that this case study be seen as illustrative of developments across Gauteng during the election period. A truer portrait of Gauteng politics would of course be obtained if we could provide details of all the communities researched from January to May 1994, but the sheer volume of information obtained makes this impossible. The study is by no means exclusive, however. Where it is considered important and applicable, similar dynamics and processes in many of these communities will be cross-referenced.

13　This history is taken from an unpublished Peace Action discussion paper entitled 'A working document: violence in Bekkersdal'. As this document is at pains to stress, it is a highly contested history. AZAPO, the IFP and the ANC would each highlight, and give differing emphases to, different factors and events in the unfolding of conflict in the township.

14　LD PWV Observer Reports, vol. 2, pp. 61–2; vol. 3, p. 70.

15　J. Steinberg, 'A place for civics in a liberal-democratic polity? Contemporary civic discourse on democracy and representation', paper, History Workshop on Democracy: Popular Precedents, Practice and Culture, University of the Witwatersrand, 13–15 July 1994, pp. 16–17.

16　LD PWV Observer Reports, vol. 4, pp. 133–5.

17　The Thokoza-Katlehong-Vosloorus complex (Katorus) is the classic case of open conflict between territorially placed political interests, separated by hard no-go areas. In August 1990, it was the fountainhead for violence which seemed to spread inexorably outwards across the Reef. Some sources estimate that almost 3,000 deaths have been reported over the past four years in this particular part of Gauteng. Alexandra erupted in violence in 1991–2 when attacks launched from the IFP hostels displaced close to 4,000 people. Vacant homes adjacent to the hostel were appropriated by hostel residents and the area now constitutes a separate section, known as the Reconstruction Area (RCA), within the largely ANC-supporting Greater Alex. The two areas are divided by clearly demarcated no man's land, and the respective forces in each have developed a ruthless gang-territory mentality. During the election campaign any person who dared to cross the 'border' was at risk of being killed. On 28 February a coloured man visiting the area was pulled off London Road into the RCA. His body was later found near the hostels. The killing was apparently in retaliation for an incident on 17 February when youths locked a passing Zulu man in an outside toilet after having told him that he was IFP and must therefore die. The man was saved only by the swift reaction of the Internal Stability Unit. (LD PWV Observer Reports, vol. 2, p. 45.)

18　The concept of the 'other' is used here to refer to an artificially contrived symbol of wrong or evil assigned to a real body deliberately located outside the self or society, which then retroactively orientates understanding of, and conveniently explains away, a malaise internal to the self or social order. The concept is drawn from Slavoj Zizek, who shows how the Jew became a convenient 'other' for the self-constitution and justification of the Nazi regime; see *For They Know Not What They Do: Enjoyment as a Political Factor* (London: Verso, 1991), p. 18. In Gauteng, the often complex and multidimensional nature of violence was all too often uncritically reduced to just such a construct which explained everything and automatically vindicated those who used it: the Third Force was to blame.

19　This is not to suggest that the marchers were blameless. The day's violence started and ended in the townships around Johannesburg, touching large numbers of people personally in their homes and on their way to and from work. A woman was almost raped by a gang of men dressed in traditional Zulu garb while waiting for a train to work at a Soweto station; on the morning of 28 March commuters were attacked while waiting for taxis in Meadowlands and in the evening a man was shot dead while passing the Meadowlands hostel; six people died when they were thrown off trains in and around Benoni – these, and many other reported incidents, could not possibly have been attributed to the ANC. LD PWV Observer Reports, vol. 4.

20 According to high-profile Inkatha spokespeople, interviewed a few days after the march, the hostel residents returned home shellshocked – they had expected none of the violence that had occurred. The feeling in the hostels was one of utter dismay and despair, not anger. There was no inclination to launch large-scale attacks on surrounding townships.

21 There were numerous similar instances during the election campaign, both before and after the Johannesburg violence, when Inkatha was tagged as a source of imminent violence, purely on the basis of rumour and prejudice. In Duduza on the East Rand the IFP-supporting hostel was razed by ANC self-defence units. When hostel residents fled to nearby KwaThema, the community threatened to lay seige to the KwaThema hostel where they had taken refuge. In Soweto, a leadership dispute in the Merafi Taxi Association turned ugly when one of the factions aligned itself to the IFP in Merafi Hostel. As friction increased, notices were sent out identifying certain taxis (by numberplate and physical description) as belonging to Inkatha. 'Dangerous taxis that may not be used. These taxis belong to IFP members. . . . They kill you, watch for your life. The only life that God borrowed you; IFP people are bloodthirsty for that,' was the terse message which headed the notice. In Attridgeville, an impromptu celebratory march by a handful of Inkatha supporters, on the announcement that the IFP would indeed contest the election, was called off when residents coldly told the marchers, 'Do not provoke us.' LD PWV Observer Reports, various.

22 Over two-thirds of respondents in the 35 interviews conducted gave similar replies.

23 LD PWV Observer Reports, various.

24 Leerom Medevoi et al., analysing the 1990 Nicaraguan elections, have drawn a critical distinction between representation as mere proxy and representation as portraiture. The speaking of citizens through the agency of political parties might appear as a case of proxy, the standing in of the latter for the former in a relation of passive reflection. But, they argue, this conceals the fact that representation pivots on the need for portraiture, the co-ordination of a multitude of dispersed voices in a unified discursive schema. Leerom Medevoi, Shankar Raman and Benjamin Robinson, 'Can the subaltern vote?', *Socialist Review*, 20.3 (July–Sept. 1990), p. 145.

25 LD PWV Observer Reports, vol. 3, pp. 16–17.

26 Ibid., vol. 4, p. 136.

27 Pilot studies conducted by the Centre for Development Studies and the Media Research and Training Unit at Rhodes University in late 1993 indicated a profound unease among many first-time voters as regards their enfranchisement. Besides a widespread uncertainty as to the mechanics of voting, certain psychological and attitudinal constraints on the will and capacity of would-be voters to involve themselves in the democratic process were identified. Many were recorded to have felt anxious, even fearful, about participating in activities which seemed fundamentally alien to their everyday experience; others immediately associated politics with ever-increasing intimidation and violence and hence tended to want to distance themselves as much as possible from the proceedings of national elections; and quite a few refused to connect the idea of voting with the possibility of realising future hopes and aspirations or with solving social problems impacting on the quality of their lives. A large number of non-aligned voter education projects set out to address this situation, including Matla Trust, the Independent Mediation Services of Southern Africa (IMSSA), the Black Sash and the IEC itself, among others. It could convincingly be argued, however, that none was as effective as the ANC in reaching people in their communities.

28 Their efforts seemed in any case to garner votes for the ANC: why would people not support that party which took the time and trouble to allay some of the suspicions, fears and uncertainties around what was a new and complicated process? New-found confidence and enthusiasm was easily commuted into sympathy for those who had resolved political insecurities.

29 LD PWV Observer Reports, vol. 4, p. 53.

30 Ibid., vol. 2, p. 60.

31 Ibid., p. 19.

32 Ibid., vol. 4, p. 135.

33 Susan Booysen, 'Democracy, liberation and the vote in South Africa's first democratic election: the Matla Trust Voter Education Survey', paper, History Workshop on Democracy, University of the Witwatersrand, 13–15 July 1994, p. 11.

34 The Matla Trust Voter Education Survey put the commitment to vote at around 83% in August 1993. This tallied with HSRC poll data for November/December and for March 1994.

35 LD PWV Observer Reports, vol. 5, pp. 50–1.

36 This 'relaxation of codes' was just as apparent in sites and centres of IFP control. Pre-election polls suggested that a large number of IFP supporters wanted to participate in the election. An official party boycott would have made this impossible as no polling stations would have been designated in the hostels or recognised IFP territory. The physical act of travelling to and lining up at a polling station in an ANC area would have indicated clear support for the electoral process and would have exposed those who dared to oppose official policy to severe penalties. The entry of the IFP therefore reduced substantially the chances of widespread violence and intimidation in Inkatha areas themselves.

37 See note 17 above.

38 Greater Alex residents willingly offered their services to a hastily designated polling station in the formerly off-limits Reconstruction Area, and in turn IFP personnel from the RCA ventured into Greater Alex to get temporary voter cards and to be trained as peace monitors for the days of polling. LD PWV Observer Reports, vol. 4, p. 131.

39 Booysen, 'Democracy, liberation and the vote', p. 21.

40 LD PWV Observer Reports, vol. 5, p. 75.

41 Ibid., p. 84.

42 Ibid., pp. 23–4.

43 Ibid., p. 95.

44 Election Administration Directorate (IEC), *Republic of South Africa 1994 General Election: National and Provincial Results by Province/District*, 26 May 1994. See also the appendix to the present volume.

45 Anthea Ki and Anthony Minnaar, 'Figuring out the problem: overview of PWV conflict from 1990–1993', Conflict Supplement, 1 (April), *Indicator South Africa*, 11.2 (1994), p. 28.

46 Claude Lefort, *Democracy and Political Theory* (Cambridge: Polity Press, 1988), p. 9.

NINE

Political Attitudes in South Africa's Economic Heartland

R.W. Johnson and Lawrence Schlemmer

THE NEW PROVINCE OF Gauteng, previously referred to as the Pretoria/ Witwatersrand/Vereeniging (PWV) region, is the economic hub of South Africa and is also the most powerful centre of communications, media and popular culture. Political trends and styles in Gauteng inevitably exert great influence on the rest of the country.

Second only to KwaZulu-Natal, Gauteng has been a centre of violent political conflict – it and to a lesser extent the Eastern Transvaal were the only regions outside KZN in which serious and sustained conflict between ANC and IFP supporters occurred. Parts of the East Rand, namely Katlehong, Thokoza and Vosloorus, were virtually no-go areas because of the tensions between IFP hostel-dwellers and ANC-aligned residents, activists and self-defence units. The Witwatersrand/ Vaal Triangle region in the 1970s and 1980s was the area in which popular resistance to apartheid was the most intense and sustained. The rolling wave of protest and civil disobedience in the final decade of apartheid started in the Vaal Triangle in 1984 and quickly spread to the Witwatersrand.

Hence politics in South Africa cannot be properly understood without understanding the politics of Gauteng. For this reason Gauteng was an obvious choice as one of the areas in which the *Launching Democracy* pre-election study was to be conducted. Two Gauteng surveys were conducted by means of personal interviews among 2,328 and 2,419 voters or potential voters during November and December 1993 and February and early March 1994 respectively. Fieldwork was undertaken by MarkData, the opinion survey centre of the Human Sciences Research Council.[1] In the chapter which follows the two surveys will be referred to as the 1993 and 1994 surveys.

Motivation to Vote

As the election drew near there was considerable enthusiasm about voting. The results of a question on voting intentions in the second survey are presented in table 9.1. Looking at the motivation to vote over the period before the election, comparisons between the 1993 and 1994 survey results point to some distinct trends. Among Africans the proportion saying they would *definitely* vote increased from some 79 per cent to 84 per cent between November and February. The proportion among Indians rose from 50 per cent to 65 per cent. Coloured motivation remained constant, but determination to vote among whites dropped slightly from 80 per cent to 76 per cent.

Comparing motivation to vote among supporters of different political parties shows that the determination to vote among ANC supporters rose to virtual saturation point, from 86 to 96 per cent. The enthusiasm to vote of supporters of other parties also increased slightly, except among IFP and Conservative Party supporters, where the declines in the proportions definitely intending to vote were 84 to 73 per cent and 78 to 72 per cent respectively. These declines were undoubtedly due to the fact that by February 1994 both these parties had indicated that they were going to boycott the elections. Intentions to vote among right-wing organisations other than the CP were even lower by February 1994, as table 9.1 shows.

It is impossible to say whether or not right-wing motivation to vote increased, stayed the same or declined after February since any further opinion polls were prohibited by law for six weeks prior to the election. One can only speculate from the results of the election (see pp. 301–6), and the crudeness of the election result makes precise calculations impossible. Broadly speaking, however, our results tend to show that there was burgeoning enthusiasm for the elections among ANC supporters in par-

Table 9.1 Intentions to vote in the election according to race and party (%)

	Afr. %	Col. %	Ind. %	Wh. %	ANC %	PAC %	DP %	NP %	IFP %	FA %	CP %	AWB %	VF %	Other %
Definitely vote	84	77	65	76	96	90	93	88	73	45	72	55	42	93
Try best to vote	3	8	10	6	1	4	3	5	–	30	4	27	4	3
Not sure	8	7	19	11	3	6	4	5	9	24	8	18	22	2
Definitely not vote	4	5	5	6	–	–	–	1	9	–	16	–	28	1
Refusal	1	3	1	1	–	–	–	1	9	–	–	–	4	

Notes: Afr. = Africans; Col = Coloureds; Ind = Indians; Wh = Whites in this and subsequent tables.
In this and subsequent tables where percentages do not sum to 100 it is due to rounding.

ticular, which was not matched among supporters of other political parties.

Prior to the election, there was some concern that marginal populations, such as shack area residents and occupants of single men's hostels, would be less likely to vote than others. We examined our data in this light. The differences were not sufficient to suggest that the election would be handicapped in any particular area, although it seems likely that the Vaal Triangle had the largest turnout in the province. Among types of residence the single-quarter hostels appeared to be most enthusiastic about voting, with 94 per cent definitely intending to vote. Even in shack areas there was an 85 per cent level of determination to vote. The latter areas, however, had a relatively low rate of possession of identity documents at 76 per cent. This could have been due to large numbers of foreign work-seekers in these areas and hence there was no reason to believe that the citizens in such areas had a low participation rate.

We asked respondents who did not say that they would 'definitely vote' what their reasons for this would be. The pattern of results according to racial group are given in table 9.2. These results reflect the general confusion that existed among a minority of voters, seen in the first row of answers in the table. This was not something that voter education could have addressed because it is generally associated with lack of interest in politics. The relatively high figure for fear and intimidation among coloured voters (31 per cent) might well have carried through to influence the election outcome to some degree.

Among African voters the fear/intimidation factor was highest among probable non-voters in the Vaal Triangle (30 per cent), followed by the East Rand (16 per cent) and with the Central Witwatersrand and far East Rand lowest of all. We must remember, however, that the East Rand results certainly underestimated the problem there.

Table 9.2   Reasons for not definitely voting, by race, 1994 survey

Reason	Africans %	Coloureds %	Indians %	Whites %
Don't know/Uncertain	37	24	43	45
Disinterest	14	12	16	7
Religious reasons	4	1	6	4
Support no party/policies	2	4	7	5
No ID	7	–	1	1
Afraid/Intimidated	12	31	12	10
Refuse to answer	23	29	10	24
Practical reasons	1	–	4	5

Even though there was very little violence or disruption in the election, the results above show clearly that small but significant minorities of voters were fearful in their anticipation of the election. Here again, however, it is impossible to say to what extent the outcome was affected by this marginal fear factor.

Political Party Choice

As we have pointed out in chapter 4 on the national opinion surveys, good pre-election polls can provide insights into voter behaviour which the aggregated data of the official outcome obscure. In particular, the election results cannot show trends among the different racial groups – and, unfortunate though it may be, the continuing primacy of racial cleavages means that this is a vital thing to know: only the pre-election surveys can provide such insights. Nevertheless, the validity of the pre-election surveys has to be established by comparison with the overall results of the election outcome. In chapter 4 we were able to demonstrate how close the pre-election polls were to the final outcome. A difficulty arose, however, with the results of the second Gauteng survey, which produced results on party support sharply at variance with those of the first survey.

Particularly among African voters a *fear factor* entered the political consciousness, which made it difficult to compare the results with those of the previous survey. Most notably, the supporters of the largest party, the ANC–SACP alliance, appeared to become very cautious about disclosing their party choice. This was probably due in very large measure to the IFP–ANC violence and to a spread of fear of some form of victimisation by opponents of the ANC. Needless to say, this same fear may have been present among IFP supporters, but it was more difficult to discern in the results.

Among ANC supporters this fear appeared to result in a substantial proportion of African voters referring to 'another party' or refusing to divulge voting choice when asked. We were able to identify this by correlating party choice obtained from a simulated 'ballot' question with the rating of the popularity of parties in another question. It was quite clear from this comparison that the vast majority of the 'other party' supporters were ANC adherents.

In table 9.3 we present the results of the 1993 and 1994 surveys as the answers were given to interviewers or indicated on the ballot, followed by the 1994 results 'reallocated' in terms of popularity ratings of parties in order to reclassify the 'other party' category. Some of the parties referred to in the table did not stand for election. It simply reflects voter sentiments, so adjusted as to be strictly comparable for the two survey periods. These results would suggest that the ANC–SACP

Table 9.3 Patterns of political party choice for the sample as a whole (all voters together) for November 1993 and February 1994, with the evasive answers in the latter results reallocated according to ratings of party popularity

Political Party	Nov. 1993 (%)	Feb. 1994 (%)	Feb. 1994 (corrected %)
ANC–SACP	46.2	23.9	38.6
PAC	1.2	1.1	1.6
NP	15.8	18.3	18.6
IFP	2.3	1.1	1.1
DP	2.2	2.4	2.4
CP	6.9	2.8	2.8
AWB	2.2	1.0	1.0
VF	2.3	2.4	2.4
Freedom Alliance	1.9	0.8	0.8
'Other party'	–	15.5	2.0
Uncertain	6.3	8.0	8.0
Not vote	2.6	4.0	4.0
Refuse	10.1	18.6	16.6

Table 9.4 Party support by race, November 1993 and February 1994 (%)

Party	Africans Nov. '93	Feb. '94	Coloureds Nov. '93	Feb. '94	Indians Nov. '93	Feb. '94	Whites Nov. '93	Feb. '94
ANC–SACP	81.2	68.1	36.5	40.0	28.8	17.4	2.0	1.0
PAC	2.2	3.0	–	–	–	–	–	–
NP	0.4	1.8	43.5	23.8	31.2	31.8	33.2	39.4
IFP	1.3	0.3	2.4	–	0.6	1.0	3.5	2.2
DP	0.1	0.1	6.9	3.3	1.3	2.6	4.7	5.3
CP	–	–	–	–	–	–	16.6	6.7
AWB	–	–	–	–	–	–	5.2	2.4
VF	–	–	–	–	–	–	5.5	5.8
FA	–	0.1	–	–	–	–	4.5	1.8
Other	–	–	–	1.0	–	1.0	–	–
Uncertain	5.3	8.0	2.0	7.5	3.3	28.7	8.1	7.3
No vote	3.3	4.6	1.0	5.5	–	3.6	1.8	3.2
Refuse	5.9	14.0	7.6	19.0	34.8	14.9	14.9	24.5

alliance dropped somewhat in relative support, as did the IFP and the right-wing parties, while the National Party regained support which it lost during 1993, emerging in quite a strong second position.

In table 9.4 the same comparisons are given for the races separately, with the estimates for February reallocated on the basis of party ratings to eliminate the evasive 'other party' support category. These results suggest that in the last weeks before the election, the ANC's popularity dropped slightly among Africans. The NP lost support among coloured people but strengthened among whites. The IFP lost support among all groups and the right-wing parties also lost ground. All these trends, however, were imprecise because of the increase in the refusal factor. This was probably due to increasing tension and anxiety among voters as the election drew nearer. There were ways of correcting for this in the overall estimates, however, once again by correlating the results for party choice with those of the popularity ratings of parties.

Allowing for the effects of the higher refusal and non-response rates, one could, however, make the following generalisations about the last period of the election campaign:

- The NP gained among whites, Indians and slightly among Africans;
- The NP probably lost support among coloureds;
- The ANC appeared to gain strongly among coloureds;
- The right-wing parties lost support among whites.

In table 9.5 we present a recalculation of party support in which the results already given are compared with results in which the non-response categories have been reallocated on the basis of the non-responding voters' ratings of party popularity. The final column was an estimate of what the election outcome would be *if* all the parties listed were to have stood for election and *if* there was an equal propensity to vote among all party supporters. The people who said that they would not vote were eliminated for obvious reasons, and the 'uncertains' were eliminated because, on the one hand, they had a lower propensity to vote (36 per cent would definitely vote compared with the average of 81 per cent) and, on the other, the minority who did vote would be inclined to distribute their support across the parties roughly in proportion to popularity, and hence not affect the results.

The final column in table 9.5 was not usable as an estimate of an election outcome simply because there were variations in the inclination to vote between parties and because the IFP, the CP, the AWB, the Afrikaner Volksfront and the Freedom Alliance were boycotting the election, the IFP re-entering the campaign a few days before the election.

The right-wing Freedom Front under General Constand Viljoen also registered to enter the election at the last moment and probably attracted the votes of FA and right-wing supporters who had said that they were determined to vote. We reallocated these voters to the Freedom Front

Table 9.5   Estimated party support, non-responses reallocated according to party popularity, February–March 1994 (%)

	Party choice with 'other' party reallocated to most popular party	Party choice with refusals reallocated	Party choice with non-voters and uncertains eliminated
ANC–SACP	38.6	46.1	52.5
PAC	1.6	2.6	3.0
NP	18.6	22.6	25.7
IFP	1.1	1.8	2.0
DP	2.4	3.2	3.6
CP	2.8	3.8	4.3
AWB	1.0	1.5	1.7
VF	2.4	3.4	3.9
FA	0.8	0.8	0.9
Other	–	2.0	2.3
Refusal	18.6	–	–
No vote	4.0	4.0	–
Uncertain	8.0	8.0	–

and we weighted all party choices according to the level of determination to vote and the level of possession of ID documents. This provided a basis for a *tentative* estimate of an election outcome, which we present in table 9.6. A poll by the same organisation which conducted the two pre-election surveys, with the same sample size, provides a comparison for July 1993.

Hence table 9.6, allowing for the uncertainties and the elaborate correction factors, suggests that the NP, despite its losses among the small coloured community, lost support in 1993 but later consolidated its position and could have strengthened further. The ANC rose in popularity and then dropped in relative strength, but still seemed likely to be able to obtain an absolute majority. In terms of the ranking of parties the pattern of results in the pre-election forecast and that of the official outcome are identical. The ANC, however, did slightly better than we predicted and the DP and PAC turned out worse results than we would have expected. The IFP improved on the pre-election forecast, but this was to be expected since the IFP was still officially boycotting the election when our last survey was conducted.

However, taking statistical error into account as well as the lack of coverage in both surveys of two East Rand townships due to violence, not to mention the possible imprecision of the final outcome of the

Table 9.6   Estimated election outcomes in Gauteng (%)

	Mark Data estimate July 1993	Estimate Nov–Dec 1993	Estimate Feb–March 1994	Actual outcome
ANC-SACP	64	71	54	59
PAC	2	2	3	1
NP	17	14	29	28
DP	2	3	5	3
IFP	8	5	2	4
FF (1993: CP, FA, VF)	7	5	5	4
Other	–	–	2	1

Table 9.7   Percentage of voters giving popularity-ratings of 8 out of 10 or more to:

Partisan Identification	ANC/ SACP	PAC	NP	IFP	DP	CP	AWB	VF
SACP	–	66	5	–	6	–	–	–
ANC	–	68	21	1	26	–	–	–
PAC	52	–	5	3	1	3	–	–
NP	25	16	–	42	55	37	36	8
IFP	1	5	31	–	29	41	28	78
DP	11	4	34	51	–	10	10	8
CP	3	5	28	9	7	–	63	80
AWB	–	2	12	10	4	53	–	58

election, the final pre-election survey and the final outcome of the election were a reasonable fit. The results of the surveys, on this basis, certainly appear to be sufficiently valid to offer representative insights as regards other aspects of the responses of voters.

Support for Alternative Parties – A Floating Vote?

As we have seen from the results of the national surveys reported in chapter 4 there was a convergence of African support towards the ANC which tended to obscure underlying differences in political attitudes and commitments. The same phenomenon occurred in Gauteng. The ANC was able to mobilise support on a symbolic basis, which outstripped the extent of support it would have obtained had voters made their choices strictly according to values and socioeconomic interests. In the light of this phenomenon, inevitable in any 'liberation' election, it is of interest to look at how voters viewed alternative parties. As the symbolic appeal of their first democratic choices fades in the years ahead, some of these alternative choices could come to the fore as a floating vote or even as opposition to the parties sharing power in the first democratic government.

In the second survey we used a rating scale in the form of a 'ladder' to tap the popularity of all parties, not only the respondents' first choice of party. Results drawn from these popularity ratings are presented in table 9.8. The results show that the PAC and to a much lesser extent the NP were second choices among ANC supporters, while the ANC was the dominant second choice among PAC supporters. Among NP supporters second choices were spread across a range of parties with the DP, the IFP and the CP almost equal and the ANC slightly lower. Among IFP supporters the DP and the NP were the dominant second choices. For CP supporters the AWB was slightly ahead of the NP and the IFP as second choices. AWB supporters favoured the CP over the NP and IFP

Table 9.8   Major reason for supporting a party (items paraphrased), 1993 survey (%)

	Africans	Coloureds	Indians	Whites
Party protects my language and culture	21	10	19	43
Powerful party with great and inspiring leader	32	15	31	13
Party supports religious teaching and morality	12	19	9	22
Party tough and strong in order to restore law and order	21	38	27	13
Party will work to improve lives, jobs and living conditions	4	11	4	2
Uncertain/Don't know	9	8	10	7

as second choices and VF supporters dominantly favour the IFP and the CP after their own party.

These results, however, did no more than confirm the common view that the parties, relative to each other, were positioned across the spectrum from left to right as follows: PAC, SACP, ANC, DP, NP, IFP, CP, AWB, VF. Other than this they showed that the PAC and to a lesser extent the NP have some scope for growth by drawing support away from the ANC, but, by the same token, the ANC could make inroads into NP and DP support.

Given the very considerable popularity which the PAC enjoyed among ANC supporters, it was not surprising that the ANC's accommodation of a dominantly non-African party like the NP in the government of national unity at central and provincial level was not universally popular among the ANC's constituency. The PAC may have done very badly in the election but the results in table 9.8 show that its 'Africanist' outlook had wide appeal among African voters.

What the results in table 9.8 also imply is that the ANC's support base covered a wide spectrum, with sympathies extending to the left and right of the party's core position. If the ANC, as the currently dominant party in our politics, were to lose its symbolic grip on its supporters, an extremely fluid situation would develop in the new South African polity.

The Basis of Party Choice

If, as we have argued, the ANC was able to mobilise opinion beyond the admittedly very large core of support for its political policy position, on what basis did this occur? We have referred to the symbolic attractions of the party in the first liberation election. What was the basis of this symbolism? In the first survey we posed a question on reasons for supporting a party, and on the basis of qualitative interviews prior to the survey gave five alternatives for respondents to choose from. The results are given in table 9.8.

It was noteworthy that motivations relating to socioeconomic interests – living conditions and jobs – obtained such a relatively low response. Law and order, charismatic qualities of the party and leader, ethnic and group protection and moral standards all emerged more prominently in the minds of respondents. Political response patterns based on issues and interests had yet to emerge strongly. Voter motivations appeared to be a mix of symbolism and concern about physical and group security not normally associated with the critical and conditional support for parties in a democratic marketplace. For African voters, the charismatic factor appeared to be the single most important motivation.

Voter Literacy

We turn now to a consideration of the quality of the election in Gauteng in terms of voter preparedness and other factors which could have prejudiced the quality of the outcome. We begin with voter literacy. Of very great consequence to the effectiveness of the election was the extent to which voter education programmes and broadcasts had been able to establish basic knowledge and confidence about voting within a relatively short time. We employed one major index of voter competence by way of the final question in the interview schedule which was presented to respondents in the form of a simulated ballot. Pictures and logos of political parties were not included, however, though they were present on the real ballot paper on election day.

We recorded all cases where the respondent could not complete the simulated ballot on his or her own and needed assistance from the interviewer. We were aware that the absence of logos and pictures of the party leaders on our ballot paper would exaggerate the numbers likely to find difficulties with the real ballot, but our results nevertheless provide an approximate index of the social groups most likely to have been at a disadvantage. A selection of findings, in particular reflecting areas of greater than average need for assistance by the interviewer, is presented in table 9.9.

As soon as we had these results to hand we circulated them to political parties and all voter education bodies, suggesting that they give special attention to the categories identified in the short time left before the election. It is worth noting that the popular assumption that only Africans needed assistance in voting was demolished by these figures. In the light of the results in table 9.9 it was not surprising that voting officers were very frequently called upon to give assistance to voters in the polling booths. One presiding officer known to the authors as a reliable source told us that he personally marked the ballot papers in approximately 1,400 instances. Overseas election observers, speaking frankly and confidentially, gave us the same impression.

This type of assistance does not necessarily mean that the results were skewed. Given the fact, however, that the personnel of the IEC were disproportionately drawn from a pro-ANC world of NGOs (a fact which the IFP and right-wing election boycott had made quite inevitable), this was not an entirely happy situation. Inevitably, the non-ANC parties believed that IEC officials had sometimes used their position of assistance in a manner favourable to the ANC. We encountered no evidence that this was so, though the very existence of such allegations makes it essential that the personnel of any future IEC is chosen in such a manner as to make such allegations impossible.

Table 9.9   Respondents requiring assistance in completing a simulated ballot

Social category	Percentage requiring assistance
Africans	23
Coloureds	11
Indians	6
Whites	15
ANC	15
PAC	12
DP	16
NP	17
CP	6
AWB	19
VF	24
Rural blacks	29
Hostel dwellers	35
Backyard dwellers	35
Urban squatters	32
Central Witwatersrand Africans	26
Far East Rand Africans	24
West Rand Africans	29
Pretoria Africans	26
Africans 55 years plus	34
Swazi/Ndebele-speakers	36
Shangaan/Venda	29
Blacks, Std 3 or less	36
Coloureds – West Rand	26
Whites – Pretoria	30
Flats, boarding houses – whites	25
Coloureds 55+ years	30
Unemployed coloureds	24
Portuguese-speakers	38
Coloureds, Std 4/5	24

Political Intolerance

Before the elections there was a great deal of news coverage of political meetings in Gauteng being disrupted by the followers of opposing parties. Opinions varied as to the scope of this manifest political intolerance. Some maintained that small groups of township youth were responsible and that they were a minority in otherwise tolerant communities. Others felt that political intolerance was widespread, and that the political climate particularly in African townships and in some smaller white urban centres made free electioneering impossible. We explored this issue in the survey as the most important focus of the investigation.

First we asked respondents whether they felt it was right or wrong for people in a community to prevent any particular political party from holding meetings. The overall results according to the racial group of the respondent and political party supported are given in table 9.10. The results represented a marked improvement on those obtained in the first survey in which 27 per cent of Africans, 21 per cent of coloureds, 7 per cent of Indians and 18 per cent of whites felt that preventing opposing parties from seeking support was 'right'. Hence voter education may have had some effect.

The results in the second survey suggest that overtly intolerant orientations were present only in small minorities. These minorities were nevertheless substantial, accounting for hundreds of thousands of people. Contrary to many stereotypes, this overtly intolerant group may have been largest among whites. The intolerance encountered among whites was concentrated in right-wing movements and parties: the AVF, the CP and the AWB. One might have expected the AWB's intolerance to exceed that of the CP and the AVF but the latter reflected the highest proportions of intolerance. The most tolerant of political support groups appeared to be those who chose the Freedom Alliance (the temporary IFP–right-wing negotiating coalition), the IFP, the NP and the DP. The results for IFP supporters suggest that the pockets of militant and intolerant IFP-supporting hostel residents were a minority within that constituency. The ANC and PAC supporters were marginally less tolerant than the NP, DP and IFP pattern, but the intolerant minorities in these parties represented less than one-fifth of the support groups. While these results cannot be conclusive, they suggest that the disruptive elements in all party support groups were atypical of supporters in general.

Table 9.10 Respondents believing that it is right or wrong to prevent less popular parties holding meetings in the local area, by race and party

	Afr.	Col.	Ind.	Wh.	ANC	PAC	DP	NP	IFP	FA	CP	VF	AWB	Other
Right	15	11	3	20	18	16	12	12	10	7	36	38	27	12
Uncertain	5	5	19	7	2	14	11	10	–	–	9	4	10	4
Wrong	79	81	77	69	80	70	78	77	90	93	48	58	63	82

Refusals to answer/No information make up the balance.

If one considers the results by racial group according to subregions within Gauteng it would seem that the following categories of people had higher levels of intolerance than average, being more likely to believe that it was *right to prevent* meetings:

Africans (Central Witwatersrand)	22%
Coloureds (West Rand)	27%
(Pretoria)	23%
Whites (Rural)	37%
(West Rand)	42%
(Pretoria)	29%
(Flats, boarding houses)	34%
White immigrants	66%
White unemployed	31%
Africans – Std 10/Matric	41%
Whites <R500 pm	33%
R2,500–3,499 pm	36%

In similar vein we posed questions about the kinds of action to be allowed to the parties to which respondents were 'most opposed'. A range of actions was presented for consideration, as reflected in table 9.12. The pattern of results in the table is rather complex. It is clear, however, that when specific situations were presented to voters, much of the tolerant sentiment reflected in the answers to the previous, more general question disintegrated.

Among Africans, consistently greater proportions would disallow, rather than allow, specific activities by a party they most oppose. Coloured people appeared to have been most tolerant when faced with specific issues, followed by Indians. Whites, while more tolerant than Africans, nevertheless wanted to curtail opportunities of opposition parties in education and as regards the right of protest. Clearly there seemed to be a conviction among most whites that children should be protected from opposing political influences and also that local order should not be disturbed by protests and demonstrations.

As one might perhaps expect, DP supporters had the most consistently tolerant sentiments. The National Party's supporters tended to hold views close to the average among minorities, although they were as concerned as whites as a group about preventing the politicisation of education and protests. Among right-wing groupings, the prevailing attitude was one of intolerance, although the Afrikaner Volksfront's views were softer than those in other right-wing parties. The supporters of the IFP and the Freedom Alliance tended to blend both tolerance and intolerance.

The most significant finding related perhaps to whether or not majorities were inclined to allow the supporters of the most disliked parties to live in the local area. A denial of this right is obviously at the basis of the control of political territory and the enforced political homogenisation

Table 9.11 Tolerance in neighbourhood of party most strongly opposed: views on what such a party should be allowed to do or not, according to race and political party supported (only clearly positive and negative options included), 1994 survey (%)

	Afr.	Col.	Ind.	Wh.	ANC	PAC	DP	NP	IFP	FA	CP	VF	AWB	Other
Proportions of people who would *allow* most opposed party members to:														
live in area	40	52	35	58	43	43	75	63	54	75	25	37	19	33
associate with friends	38	48	34	46	43	48	63	48	54	44	15	44	–	28
operated business	41	59	36	61	46	48	73	67	80	74	33	67	27	34
teach at school	41	43	30	26	44	54	59	35	36	20	11	16	–	34
canvass support	33	45	28	50	36	46	65	53	85	64	22	62	18	25
make critical speech	24	41	31	45	29	25	60	44	63	67	19	46	27	16
hold a public protest	33	50	35	28	38	48	53	36	32	–	6	17	10	27
Proportions of people who would *not allow* party members to:														
live in area	50	13	23	28	49	56	20	23	21	13	61	59	53	59
associate with friends	51	15	21	33	49	52	32	31	32	56	62	41	63	63
operate a business	48	9	21	23	46	51	13	20	20	26	42	23	53	60
teach at school	48	21	30	57	47	46	22	50	55	68	87	72	90	59
canvass support	59	18	27	34	59	54	25	31	7	28	54	33	63	69
make critical speech	68	24	23	39	66	75	19	42	37	18	76	40	55	79
hold a public protest	59	17	27	59	57	52	32	54	59	93	94	79	71	67

which characterises so much of South Africa. It was, in fact, only among the supporters of the DP, the NP, the IFP and the Freedom Alliance that respect for individual dissent appears to have been a majority sentiment. Between 5 and 6 out of 10 supporters of the ANC, the PAC, the right-wing parties and the very small parties grouped together under 'other' would have excluded their major political enemies from their neighbourhoods.

Taking the results in more detail we found that among Africans the right of political opponents to live in an area was *denied* by greater than average proportions by those living in hostels (65 per cent), in Pretoria (58 per cent), and on the West Rand and Vereeniging (55 per cent). Those living in the larger core townships of the Central Witwatersrand were more tolerant.

We followed the probes analysed above with a question on why the respondents felt that it was necessary to prevent parties from operating in their local areas. The results according to race are presented in table 9.12. They show precisely why violent political competition undermines democracy. Given the propensity of certain parties to accompany their gatherings and meetings with marches, uniforms, aggressive chants and the like, voters were understandably fearful of the consequences.

The argument that the intrusion of other parties into an area may cause violence is the sole democratically acceptable response in 9.12 – and even that argument is sometimes dubious, for something will depend on the respondent's own attitude and the reason may occasionally be a cover for less respectable motives. Clearly, none of the other responses have any justification in a democratic society. The responses in table 9.12 are proportions of proportions and therefore reflect very tiny minorities. Intolerance, however, was not a minority phenomenon, as we have seen, and this gave the replies greater relevance.

However, in order to understand our findings in a proper context one must have recourse to the concept of *community mobilisation*, a phenomenon not uncommon in Third World settings. By this we mean a

Table 9.12   Reasons for preventing political parties from operating in neighbourhood, according to race, 1994 survey (%)

	Africans	Coloureds	Indians	Whites
Cause violence	57	30	20	53
Cause confusion	10	–	–	9
My democratic right	8	–	–	7
Oppose party	15	15	20	14
Don't know	10	55	60	17

condition under which community members are mobilised by means of multiple pressures within an extremely dense environment, that density being both physical (as in the crowded confines of a squatter camp, township or *favella*) and social (with a closely surrounding network of street, area and party committees, church and trade union groups, civic associations, relatives, and so on). Individuals are subjected to such massive and continuous pressures to take one particular direction that they are both coerced into taking it and yet are also happy to take it; in some sense the decision is also voluntary. Indeed, such individuals are rather in the position of members of (say) the British, US or Soviet armies facing the Nazis: they fight the Wehrmacht both because they dislike fascism and also because they are commanded to and are distinctly scared of their sergeant-majors. The political choices of members of a mobilised community work in much the same way: it becomes extremely difficult to say whether they acted voluntarily or were coerced and indeed the individuals might not be sure themselves. Hence in South Africa we frequently found voters who told us 'I vote for the IFP because I live in an IFP area' or 'Of course I vote ANC. My whole township is ANC and everybody in it.' Community mobilisation is thus often the other side of the territorialisation of politics.

It must be understood that when we put questions as to how voters would greet members of the party they most disliked entering their areas to organise, speak, canvass, teach in the schools, work in local jobs, etc., we were asking this question of people who were very unequally situated. In the leafy and low-density white suburbs this amounted to asking whether residents would take strong objection to what went on at some remove; in a township or squatter camp the suggestion conjured up notions of intimate intrusions into a densely packed social and physical environment which would almost certainly lead to violence and disruption, there being no available physical or social space for such troublesome outsiders. Yet when we asked whether people agreed *in principle* with the prevention of free speech and free political organisation, and whether voters preferred only to see their party on TV or a proper debate between different parties, our African and coloured voters were predominantly 'liberal' in their responses. That is, if the question was posed in a way which did not threaten intrusion into their over-dense local environment, they were as willing to be tolerant and liberal as the next man. This was a reality we met over and over again throughout our study.

We broadened the issue of political tolerance by asking a question on the role of opposition. Respondents were asked whether they felt it was best for a country if opposition parties were weak and without influence, strong enough to influence government or strong enough in combination to impose their views on government. The results are presented in table 9.13 according to racial group and to political party supported. The

Table 9.13   Amount of influence opposition parties should enjoy in society, according to race and party, 1994 survey (%)

Best if opposition is:	Afr.	Col.	Ind.	Wh.	ANC	PAC	DP	NP	IFP	FA	CP	VF	AWB	Other
Weak	46	16	14	9	47	39	5	1	—	5	13	8	36	50
Strong enough to influence government	27	54	24	27	36	25	49	30	27	30	12	11	—	22
Collectively strong enough to force government	14	10	25	54	11	23	42	46	59	64	65	81	37	18
Uncertain	12	19	37	11	5	13	5	12	14	—	11	—	27	10

Table 9.14   Views on the inclusion in government of parties which do not win the election, according to race and party, 1994 survey (%)

Good government best served by:	Afr.	Col.	Ind.	Wh.	ANC	PAC	DP	NP	IFP	FA	CP	VF	AWB	Other
One party able to govern on own	28	8	13	12	22	26	7	11	7	12	9	25	36	39
Winning party includes other parties in government	52	52	44	32	60	61	28	42	44	33	10	11	18	16
Largest party not strong enough to govern on own	14	26	13	48	16	9	51	42	50	55	62	57	27	13
Don't know	6	12	30	8	2	4	14	5	—	—	9	7	27	3

pattern of replies was probably based on a blend of political values and anticipation of how well parties were likely to perform in the election. A preference for an opposition sufficiently powerful to collectively impose its views on government was characteristic of the parties not likely to emerge with a majority, with the exception of the PAC supporters, who, despite the small size of the party, were attracted to powerful majoritarianism. The largest contrast in the results was between the African ANC supporters and minority group voters.

Related to the views as regards the relative strength of opposition were views on the degree to which opposition parties should be included in government. The results of this probe appear in table 9.14. They are remarkable in reflecting relatively few proponents of outright majoritarianism. In fact it was among the AWB supporters that the sentiment was most prominent; one can be certain that their context and that of the Afrikaner Volksfront was not that of a multiracial South Africa but rather of a *Volkstaat*. Majoritarian sentiments in the context of a unitary state were at their highest among Africans and supporters of the ANC and the PAC, but even here the level did not even rise to one-third.

The major division in views was between the voluntary (or perhaps co-optive) power-sharing model and the enforced coalition model in terms of which the largest party cannot legislate without including smaller parties in government. The power-sharing model attracted very large proportions of Africans, coloured people and Indians, as well as supporters of the ANC, the PAC and small parties. The enforced coalition model attracted the DP, the IFP, the Freedom Alliance and the right-wing parties (excluding the AWB). As one might expect from the co-operative stance of the NP in the negotiations and in the Transitional Executive Council, its supporters were more or less equally divided between the co-operative and the enforced coalition models. It is apparent that, with the exception of the PAC, the smaller parties tended to favour the obligatory coalition model, perhaps as a reaction to minority anxieties.

The broad pattern emerging among South Africa's new voters, the Africans, was that while they were divided on the issue of the strength of opposition, they favoured accommodation between political parties. Thus their sentiments tended to favour 'corporatism' rather more strongly than liberal democracy. All the permutations notwithstanding, one of the positive indications of democratic tolerance in this study was a lower than expected incidence of principled majoritarianism. This sentiment, moreover, tended to be associated with a low standard of education and with rural African traditional communities. It is, therefore, also likely to be a declining trend.

Constraints on Freedom of Conscience and Choice

The results on political intolerance in the previous section show up the limitations of South Africa's political culture as far as the sustainability of democracy is concerned. One might expect the substantial political intolerance we have recorded to be reflected in voters' felt constraints on their freedom of choice as voters. To assess this we asked certain questions to probe the extent to which pressures in the social environment constrained respondents' freedom to exercise their private political preferences. The items covered:

- pressure on people to vote for parties they would not otherwise support;
- whether or not neighbours were tough on dissenting political opinion;
- the extent to which people found it difficult or impossible to disagree with sources of political influence;
- whether or not people would resist majority pressure and maintain their own preference.

For ease of reference, indicators from these results are all combined in table 9.16.

There are some disquieting trends in the table. Clearly coloured people were under great pressure to conform to the expectation that they would vote for a particular party – this seems to have been particularly true in Pretoria and the West Rand – and it seems that many coloureds were inclined to vote with the majority to avoid conflict. Among Africans a particular problem appeared to be constraints on political dissent in the local neighbourhood. Neighbours were seen to be tough on political dissenters in a small but substantial minority of perceptions. A scan of other survey data would suggest the following areas and categories where this was a particular problem among Africans, that is where there was a higher than average incidence of neighbours being tough on political dissent:

Africans overall	20%
Hostels	33%
Pretoria/Vereeniging	25%
Traditional communities	37%
Std 10	38%

One can understand the pressure to conform in hostels and in traditional circumstances. The results for Pretoria and Vereeniging tie in with a consistent pattern in other probes to suggest that these were areas in which political conformity featured a great deal, not only as regards Africans but for coloured people and whites as well. The most distressing feature, however, was the fact that Africans with Std 10 perceived this problem more than average. We had encountered evidence of this in other regional surveys too: namely that better-educated people often felt more intimidated than others. That is not to to say that the pressures on them were necessarily greater than on others, but rather that they felt – and were – frustrated by the constraints to a greater degree and were thus less inclined to accept community consensus as normal and natural.

In the first (November–December 1993) survey fewer questions were posed on the topic of freedom of choice but the results broadly confirm the fact that the social climate in Gauteng was certainly not ideal as regards individual freedom of conscience. Changes in the phrasing of

Table 9.15   Constraints on freedom of choice experienced by respondents, according to race and party, 1994 survey (%)

	Afr.	Col.	Ind.	Wh.	ANC	PAC	DP	NP	IFP	FA	CP	VF	AWB	Other
					Pressure to vote for a party not supported									
Yes	3	14	1	5	4	2	13	2	—	12	—	4	—	2
					Neighbours tough on dissenting individuals									
Yes	20	8	4	9	17	28	8	10	28	13	10	10	10	15
					Will vote with majority if community favours a party									
Yes	5	16	5	—	5	2	—	1	—	—	3	—	—	5
					Difficult or impossible to disagree politically with									
Church	38	28	24	18	36	38	5	20	4	20	30	3	—	41
Trade union	32	52	25	12	31	30	11	14	12	—	29	—	—	36
Political leaders	46	59	26	19	45	4	17	23	7	43	27	3	10	49
Street committees	35	30	23	11	32	31	6	12	20	7	16		10	42
Civics	34	50	25	12	35	34	10	15	16	30	22	—	—	37
Chiefs★	40	—	—	—	—	—	—	—	—	—	—	—	—	—
Elders★	74	—	—	—	—	—	—	—	—	—	—	—	—	—
Employees	28	30	19	12	28	32	2	15	2	20	19	—	10	31
Teachers, etc.	37	25	18	13	35	22	5	14	7	20	18	—	10	43

★ Rural-traditional Africans only.

items made direct comparison with the second survey's results difficult but the broad pattern gave at least as much cause for concern.

In this context respondents were asked how easy or difficult it is to live next to people with differing political views. The following proportions felt that it was 'easy':

Africans	43%
Coloureds	39%
Indians	32%
Whites	78%

Only among whites does the proportion rise to a majority. The right of individuals to hold divergent views appears to be tenuous in other communities. In the same context, people were asked whom they would most fear if it were to be known how they voted. Here the results were more reassuring: 65 per cent of Africans and 72 per cent of Indians spontaneously said 'nobody'. Among coloureds and whites the proportions fearing nobody were much lower at 41 and 50 per cent. Among both these groups around one-third of people feared the ANC or a future ANC government.

We also enquired whether or not political groups and organisations controlled local areas and influenced the way people would vote. Some 10 per cent of Africans, 15 per cent of Indians, 18 per cent of whites and 31 per cent of coloureds perceived this to be true of their areas at least to some extent. When probed as to the identity of these groups, the ANC, the NP and right-wing parties were most frequently mentioned. Influence, canvassing and mobilisation are obviously normal and healthy in any democracy. The problem, however, might lie in the issue of 'control' of local areas; political territoriality can make people political captives of a local hegemony. Fortunately the proportions perceiving this problem were not large, except in the case of coloured people.

Broad comparisons with the results obtained in the national surveys reveal one trend which appears to be very significant, namely that the small coloured minority in Gauteng felt particularly threatened and constrained. For example, whereas only 1 per cent of coloured people nationally felt pressure on them to vote for a party they did not support, in Gauteng this answer was given by 14 per cent. Only 2 per cent of coloured people nationally felt that their neighbours were tough on political dissent, while the proportion in Gauteng was 8 per cent. Nationally, only 3 per cent of coloured voters said they would vote with the majority to avoid conflict, but in Gauteng the proportion was 16 per cent. Reference to other answers given suggested that pockets of fairly radical mobilisation in coloured communities had the effect of making substantial minorities of coloured people very fearful and cautious.

Among Africans a trend was less clearly discernible but, if anything, African voters in Gauteng felt somewhat less constrained by community pressures than did Africans elsewhere. This is what one would expect in a province of far greater social heterogeneity than applies in the country as a whole.

Uncritical Thinking

Democracy thrives on critical thinking, so we attempted to measure this in two ways. First we asked respondents whether they found various sources of information trustworthy or not. In table 9.16 the proportions

Table 9.16   Percentage of respondents finding diverse sources of information completely trustworthy, 1994 survey

Source	Africans	Coloureds	Indians	Whites
Press	25	28	12	12
Magazines	22	20	8	8
Radio	63	27	22	28
TV	71	39	27	37
Political meetings	44	18	9	9
Community meetings	22	5	6	3
Community leaders	38	16	34	17

finding various sources completely trustworthy are presented. There was a consistently greater acceptance among Africans and to a lesser extent coloureds of the dependability of information. With regard to television this reached the point of gullibility. While this pattern was undoubtedly a function of education and certainly not of racial group, it does illustrate a brittle area for democracy.

As it happens, however, any image of a slavish adherence to messages from a politically agreeable source was counteracted by the fact that only 12 per cent of Africans, 5 per cent of coloured people, 1 per cent of Indians and 5 per cent of whites were 'most interested' in hearing messages from their own political party. Only in the AWB did this tendency reach majority proportions.

The Future

To understand perceptions of the future among voters one must recognise the very different ways the election was perceived. Our other surveys have shown that most ANC- and PAC-supporting Africans anticipated the election with joy and excitement, while only minorities of whites, coloured people, Indians and IFP supporters shared this elated mood. These different emotional entrances to the new South Africa affected perceptions of the future. Results which appear in table 9.17 tell the story. The downward gradient of expectations from Africans to whites was almost dramatic in its consistency. African IFP supporters, on the other hand, had a contradictory mix of almost wild optimism and crippling fears.

In the first survey a different question was asked about the future but it tended to yield the same broad pattern of results, as table 9.18 shows.

Table 9.17   Endorsement of words describing the new South Africa, 1994 survey (%)

	African	Coloured	Indian	White	African IFP
'Secure'	69	25	33	21	9
'Honest'	69	40	28	14	9
'Abundant'	64	43	25	24	42
'Equal'	76	42	48	23	9
'Not violent'	54	30	16	15	81
'Free'	81	38	46	26	81
'Democratic'	82	47	58	38	52
'Orderly'	71	29	21	20	9

Table 9.18 Anticipations of the future among different race groups, 1993 survey

Percentages expecting:	Africans	Coloureds	Indians	Whites
Improvement in personal wealth	45	14	6	4
Influence and security for own group	71	23	17	11
Less violence	51	22	13	16
Freedom to criticise new government	72	45	39	34
Improved race relations	65	31	38	27
More employment	65	51	27	20
Impartial treatment of different party supporters	81	64	46	28
Non-discrimination against minorities	84	63	45	20

Table 9.19 Expectations of performance by race and party, 1994 survey (%)

Party will:	Afr.	Col.	Ind.	Wh.	ANC	PAC	DP	NP	IFP	African IFP	CP	VF	AWB	Other
win most votes	67	35	30	13	79	40	1	23	11	71	12	27	8	68
be one of the largest	21	25	27	47	18	48	39	64	13	29	36	18	11	29

Thus Africans were generally optimistic and whites deeply pessimistic, with Indians and coloureds in between. As one perused the responses of the whites, it made one wonder how former President de Klerk managed so successfully to initiate the beginning of a process of democratisation in South Africa. Given their fears, other factors were very powerful in inducing whites to give such overwhelming support to de Klerk in the 1992 referendum. One such factor might have been the expectation that parties representing minorities would do very well in the election. We explored this in both pre-election surveys in Gauteng, and relevant results from the second survey are presented in table 9.19. The implications of this table are dramatic. Some 40 per cent of PAC supporters, 23 per cent of NP supporters, 27 per cent of AWB supporters and no less than 71 per cent of African IFP supporters expected their parties to be able to wield the power to address their fears and realise their hopes.

Between the first and second Gauteng surveys, however, while expectations remained constant among Africans, the proportions of whites, coloureds and Indians expecting their party to win the elections declined as follows:

Whites	23 to 13 per cent
Coloureds	52 to 35 per cent
Indians	36 to 30 per cent

We suspect that the period from November 1993 to March 1994 was a brief segment of a longer period of declining optimism among minorities. There was probably a period up to mid-1992 when majorities of NP-supporting whites, coloureds and Indians expected their party to win the elections outright. This leads to the ironic conclusion that naive optimism among minority voters, induced by unrealistic bullishness among their political leaders, may have been quite an important factor facilitating the transition to democracy in a deeply divided society.

Before the election many people expected that the reactions of certain types of voters to defeat in the contest would become a source of instability in the country, a possibility we explored in the first Gauteng survey. The results are presented in table 9.20. The supporters of the parties given in the table were unrealistic about the election outcome to a lesser or greater degree. Hence powerful surprises awaited them. The anticipated reactions among PAC, DP and NP supporters did not suggest significant popular reaction as a result. In the case of supporters of the IFP, the CP and particularly the AWB (who would probably have voted for the Freedom Front) there was an indication in the results that signifi-

Table 9.20 Expectations and reactions to lack of success among minor party supporters, 1993 survey

	PAC	NP	IFP	DP	CP	AWB
Proportions expecting party to win largest number of votes or to do very well	89	68	54	30	53	61
Perceived reactions of supporters if result is disappointing:						
– accept result	75	68	50	63	40	22
– criticise result	14	11	11	14	23	–
– peaceful protest	7	7	8	14	8	6
– angry protest	–	2	11		7	28
– rejection of government	4	3	8	2	14	33
– uncertain/other	–	10	13	6	8	11

cant minorities might react aggressively to the election outcome. We should add, however, that because the parties were small, the subsamples on which they were based were small, and the results were tentative. In general, however, the results left us with the impression that the election outcome would not be contested on a large scale – which was indeed the case.

The degree of potential dissent that the results in table 9.20 revealed was none the less a danger sign of sorts. In the election and afterwards, certain of the dangers have been averted by various developments. First, the fact that the IFP did obtain a majority in KwaZulu-Natal probably avoided an increase in violent contestation by IFP activists in that province. Second, the fact that the ANC has been quite generous (some would say strategically co-optive) in agreeing to the establishment of an Afrikaner *Volkstaatraad* undoubtedly ameliorated some of the right-wing frustration that table 9.20 reveals. Whether or not minority dissent could emerge to disrupt South African politics in the future was not a question which our pre-election surveys could really answer, however. Further research would have to be conducted in much greater depth to shed light on this possibility.

Overview

In many ways the results of our pre-election surveys in Gauteng simply confirmed the patterns which emerged in the national surveys. No dramatically different patterns emerged for Gauteng which set it aside from other areas. Broadly, however, the results reflected the fact that Gauteng is a more complex political environment than all other provinces save for Kwazulu-Natal and the Western Cape. The fact that the ANC's majority in Gauteng was slightly smaller than in the country as a whole partially just reflects the fact that population minorities are proportionately larger in Gauteng than elsewhere in the country.

The results of probes into political intolerance and constraints on freedom of choice show that there may be a slightly more mature political culture in the African areas than exists elsewhere in the country, particularly in large townships like Soweto. At the same time, however, minorities, particularly coloureds, seemed to experience a greater degree of political duress and constraint than the national surveys revealed.

The remarks on the greater political maturity of Gauteng should not detract from the fact, however, that as with the national surveys the general pattern of results for Gauteng revealed what can only be described as unacceptable pressures on voters to conform to community pressures and activist dictates on both the right and the left. These problems were found to characterise certain white areas to an even greater extent than African areas. Furthermore, while majorities of all voters supported reconciliation and co-operation in government – a corporatist type of response – attitudes to the principle of opposition in a democracy were very much divided. As with the rest of the country, the battle for a truly liberal democracy has not yet been won in the country's economic powerhouse.

Note

1   The samples of 2,328 and 2,419 people were both stratified probability samples based on a sampling frame constructed from the 1991 census. Census enumerator areas, within strata defined by subregions, were the units selected in the first stage of sampling. At the second stage, dwellings within the selected enumerator areas were selected randomly. Within dwellings, households were randomly selected, and finally, within households, a respondent was selected using the randomly based Kish/Politz grid system.

   All types of residential areas were covered, including formal housing and apartment areas, shack areas, backyard shacks, backyard rooms and servants' quarters, smallholdings and farms. Where maps of enumerator areas were not available, aerial photographs were used as a basis of selection (e.g. in informal shack areas).

   Certain places could not be covered due to internal political violence of crisis proportions. Hence in both samples Katelehong and Thokoza townships had to be omitted for fear of placing fieldworkers' lives in jeopardy. Some 80 interviews in each of the samples could not be conducted in Katelehong and Thokosa. Other similar areas adjacent to these townships were well covered (e.g. Vosloorus) and weighted up to compensate for the missing areas. Nevertheless, we must record that the results for the near East Rand are distorted by these unavoidable omissions. Furthermore, interviewing could also not proceed in one small area, Delmas, due to an outbreak of typhoid fever there.

TEN

The Election, the Count and the
Drama in KwaZulu-Natal (KZN)

R.W. Johnson

On 26 April the polling stations opened for 'special votes' – voting by the aged and infirm and those unable to cast a vote on 27–8 April (for example, police and members of the armed forces on election duty). It was immediately apparent, however, that the IEC had far from mastered the logistics of the situation. Almost everywhere there were reports of polling stations failing to open, of ballot papers lacking the IFP sticker, of a shortage of invisible ink and the ultraviolet (UV) lights which verified whether someone had voted. In general it tended to be only polling stations in the former white areas where things went according to plan. The atmosphere was, however, peaceful and cheerful. That evening the black American IEC commissioner, Gay McDougall, appeared on television to promise that the IEC had learned from the first day's mishaps and that by the next day the election operation would be 'a well-oiled machine'.

Long before polling stations opened on 27 April – *the* day – long lines of all races waited patiently for what many felt to be nothing less than their own rendezvous with history. As journalists moved up and down the lines interviewing voters, many spoke in extremely moving terms of how they saw the event. Some spoke of the day as the fulfilment of hard struggle, others as something they had never thought they would see, a day to tell their grandchildren about one day. Whites were as cheerful as blacks and generally seemed to enjoy the sense of common citizenship symbolised by waiting in line with other races. For the era of apartheid – of detentions and house arrests, of sanctions and boycotts, of international exclusion and internal confrontation – had long since become as burdensome to whites as it had to other races. To almost everybody the election seemed to signal the end of a long agony and the birth of a new and hopeful era.

The early morning television cameras fastened on the figure of Mr Mandela casting his ballot at the strife-torn squatter camp of Bhambayi, near Durban – the historic site of Mahatma Gandhi's printing press and settlement. Ms McDougall, who drew criticism in some quarters for her keen appreciation of photo-opportunities that would play well with black American audiences at home, shepherded Mr Mandela through the functions of voting so closely that she had actually to be cautioned by an IEC official for intruding on the privacy of his vote. Mr Mandela, wreathed in smiles, re-enacted his vote again outside the polling station to the joy of his ecstatic supporters.

As the day wore on, however, it became clear that the logistical failures of the previous day had merely been replayed on a far larger scale. Many polling stations failed to operate at all, others rapidly ran out of ballot papers, others lacked stickers, or lights, and so on. As reports of confusion spread, the IEC came to be the butt of much public criticism and ridicule. This criticism was further amplified as it became clear that whole sections of the IEC were in a state of collapse.

Thus, for example, the all-important IEC Investigations and Prosecutions Department, charged with investigating complaints of intimidation and electoral irregularities, simply fell apart during the election. Of the 3,558 complaints laid before it, only 52 went to court. According to one insider, this was mainly because the department's lawyers were simply too frightened of offending the major parties, but it was also because the department was hopelessly administered, a fact put down by many to affirmative action appointments. As the pressure mounted in election week, the department's staff gradually stopped working and sat round watching TV instead. In the following days they simply abandoned the office for other pursuits, and the department – including the head of the department – vanished like the Cheshire cat. The staff only reassembled to hold an election party; those few who wanted to carry on working had to attach themselves to other departments. The promised legal report on electoral irregularities was never prepared. Once the election results were declared all investigation of complaints ceased on the grounds that it was pointless to pursue problems which could not, in any case, make any difference to the results, now regarded as set in concrete. It is difficult, in light of this attitude, to see why the department was set up in the first place.

A good part of the IEC's problems were due to the simple fact that at least two years' preparatory work were required to ensure the election went smoothly – and the IEC had only a fraction of that. Given the expansion of the franchise, one major task was to identify sites for new polling stations. The Ministry for Home Affairs began to do this in March 1993 but was ordered to stop in November on the grounds that Home Affairs could not be trusted to run the election. Instead, the IEC was to run it as 'a people's election'. What this meant was the last-minute drafting in of politically correct folk without experience, including a large number of affirmative action appointees, some of whom were to prove wholly or partially unable to do their jobs. When election pressures mounted, so did the frustration of the more competent IEC employees, who, inevitably, began to go over the heads of those whose incompetence they believed to be blocking things. Given that there had, at the outset, been a lively distrust between black and white IEC employees, that all the affirmative action appointees were black and many of the complainants white, this inevitably caused great ill-feeling: one insider estimated that 60 per cent of the IEC's time was spent on internal wrangles.

These tensions were dramatically displayed when, on 1 May, the IEC announced that it was investigating five of its own officials for the concealment of ballot materials. One of the officials had turned away monitors from his warehouse on 28 April – and the warehouse was now found to contain 5,499,000 ballot papers. Another warehouse in Pretoria was found to contain 5.4 million ballots, as well as UV lights and ink. Three of the officials under investigation had been seconded to the IEC from the Department of Home Affairs, which immediately led to accusations of sabotage – rebutted by an indignant Home Affairs spokesman who pointed out that all ballot materials had been placed where they were on the order of IEC officials and that all those in charge were IEC appointees.[1] Publicly at least, the case was never resolved. The problem was, of course, that these and other cases of vanished ballot papers produced the possibility of the large-scale 'manufacture' of votes.

The general confusion within the IEC led some to realise that it would not be difficult to steal from the organisation. Others, seeing what was happening, joined in, and a virtual epidemic of theft developed. Employees took money, furniture, cellular phones, stationery, vehicles, computers – and whatever else they could lay their hands on. Stories circulated of theft on a hilarious scale, of a convoy of twenty-four IEC vehicles starting out from one town and only fourteen reaching their destination, with the ten missing ones later found in the private possession of an IEC transport director who, it emerged, had a criminal record for car theft. In the end, despite the recovery of many stolen vehicles and the writing off of many more, ninety-eight were still missing. In one sense this was quite good: during the UN-supervised election in Namibia in 1990 some 400 vehicles vanished. All told, 45 per cent of all IEC computers were stolen, including 80 per cent of all laptops.[2] Stories of theft and incompetence within the IEC had already largely eroded public sympathy for the organisation when, in its post-election budget, the new government levied an extra 5 per cent on income tax for those earning over R50,000 in order to 'pay for the costs of transition'. In fact this involved a deliberate sleight of hand, with the government appropriating three-quarters of the tax yield as general revenue: the levy raised R4 billion, while the costs of the IEC amounted to just under R1 billion.

By March 1994 the IEC had worked out sites for 6,500–7,000 polling stations, which it considered to be quite adequate. In the dying weeks of the campaign, however, the ANC woke up to the fact that its hopes of a two-thirds majority depended on maximising its vote in its heartland, the Eastern Cape, especially the Transkei. Accordingly, the IEC came under great pressure from the Holomisa regime in the Transkei to set up another 1,000 polling stations there on account of the difficult terrain. In the end the Transkei got its way: the Eastern Cape was originally scheduled to have 850 polling stations but ended up with 2,600 – well over a quarter of the national total. Similar pressures resulted in the single township of Soweto having no fewer than 135 polling stations. In the end there were 8,493 fixed polling stations, another 950 mobile stations, 1,040 special voting stations (on 26 April, in hospitals, prisons, etc.) and 187 stations abroad – a total of 10,670 stations. In principle each of these had to be counted separately but the IEC, wisely despairing of organising so many different counts, grouped into just 670 counting stations these 10,500-odd 'voting streams'. With twenty-six IEC officials detailed to each voting station and thousands of others required at the 670 counting stations, this meant that the IEC had to train and deploy nearly 300,000 people – a colossal, indeed impossible task, even before the countervailing demands for affirmative action appointments were met.

Similar emergency measures were necessary with temporary voters' cards. The Department of Home Affairs had maintained that most people had identity documents and that not more than 500,000 temporary cards would be needed.[3] This was an excusable mistake: the Launching Democracy project was keen to assist in identifying those who needed documents, passing on data to voter education units in various parts of the country. We repeatedly found 98 per cent or more of all respondents claiming they had ID, whereas voter educators on the ground continually told us that this was a long way from the truth. We could only conclude that saying one did have ID had become the politically correct answer and that many cowed and intimidated voters told interviewers what they thought they wanted to hear about this, as about other things. Luckily, the American organisation SAFE (the South Africa Free Elections Fund) carried out detailed investigations in several areas and, realising the urgency of the situation, established 1,500 temporary voter card teams (working with the IEC). All told, 3.5 million cards were issued.[4] Undoubtedly, unknown but large numbers were issued to under-age voters, sometimes in conditions of acute duress. This was a potent source of electoral fraud, but there was no doubt that SAFE's energetic endeavours were vital.

None of these efforts prevented a considerable mess on election day. By 1 p.m. on 27 April, no less than 30 per cent of the polling stations in Gauteng were either functioning ineffectively or not at all. In Northern Transvaal and KZN the figure was 25 per cent, in the Eastern Cape and Eastern Transvaal 20 per cent, in the Orange Free State 13 per cent, in the Western Cape 6 per cent, and the North-West 5 per cent: only the Northern Cape had a 100 per cent record. In general the most difficult regions throughout the election were KZN, Northern Transvaal and the Eastern Cape, but whereas the latter two were one-horse races, KZN was the most bitterly contested of all the provinces. All the problems of the election – and of the IEC – were seen in particularly stark form there, and in the end the question of how free and fair the election had been tended to centre on KZN. It is for this reason that this section concentrates particularly on the election and the count in the region.

The Election

The IFP's decision to enter the election transformed that election and, more than any other single act, was responsible for the calm, even euphoric, spirit in which the election took place. The effect was particularly great in KZN, but it also created huge problems for the IEC there. Eighty million ballot papers had already been printed, without the IFP on them. The solution now was to print IFP stickers which had to be affixed to the bottom of the ballot paper – thus occasioning a problem for the NP, the previous bottom of the list, who had already spent a good deal of money advertising this fact, money which the IEC now had to pay in compensation to the NP. Eighty million IFP stickers now had to be printed and distributed to over 10,000 (often very remote) polling stations in six days: a virtual impossibility. The early shortage of ballot papers caused another 9.3 million extra papers to be printed – this time with the IFP printed on them. But this was easy compared to the problems of setting up an extra 549 polling stations in KwaZulu in the same six days.

In the run-up to the election, with the IFP boycott still very much in force, the IEC had found itself effectively unable to operate in almost all of KwaZulu. When, for example, IEC monitors were sent to inspect schools in Ndwedwe and Port Shepstone in order to get them set up as polling stations, the schools were immediately burned down. It was hard to see how the election could work in KwaZulu unless KwaZulu civil servants and teachers – the homeland's largest group of educated blacks – would play a part, and this most were simply too scared to do. The IEC's Electoral Administration Department (EAD) refused to accept defeat and instead began making plans for 'election raids' into KwaZulu, bussing in student helpers from the University of Natal and the University of Durban-Westville and, in order to avoid drawing IFP wrath upon buildings nominated as polling stations, to use mobile polling stations instead. Understandably, at this stage many IEC staff tended to regard KwaZulu as 'enemy territory', a tendency doubtless reinforced by the fact that the IEC staff were themselves overwhelmingly of ANC provenance. The IFP, for its part, simply equated the IEC with the ANC and saw resistance to it as little less than their patriotic duty.

At this stage, indeed, it was difficult for election planning to be divorced from the more general war psychosis into which KZN had been plunged by the IFP boycott and the state of emergency there. South African Defence Force units had been stealthily moved into the province and were tensely preparing for an armed showdown. Many local ANC activists, anticipating that the SADF would come under ANC control on the morrow of the election, were quite gleeful at the thought of IFP resistance to the ANC victory in KZN made inevitable by the IFP boycott. It would, clearly, be the SADF's task to quell such resistance and enforce acceptance for the newly elected government. Such an operation would surely entail the reduction of the IFP by military means, permanently diminishing the party's role in the province and perhaps smashing it altogether. After nine years of bitter warfare with the IFP it was hardly surprising that many local ANC activists were quite ready to cheer on the SADF in such a campaign. Umkhonto We Sizwe units marched and paraded quite openly in the Durban townships while in Umfolozi the IFP, equally openly, ran a military training camp.

Steve Collins, the director of the Institute for Democratic Alternatives in South Africa in KZN who, shortly before the election, was switched from his post as IEC director of monitoring to run the EAD, was actually meeting with all three services of the SADF three times every day at this point.[5] He found the army quite unwilling to play any role in providing election security, its commanders wanting to keep their troops fresh for military action in the week before and the four weeks after the election. It seemed clear that the IFP's military organisation was also being brought to combat readiness and army raids on IFP camps turned up not only the usual small arms and rifles but Claymore mines and heavy weaponry.[6] The navy, for its part, was preparing to maintain a presence off the Zululand coast in case of trouble. Collins, by no means sure that his election role would not end in large-scale bloodshed, pressed the navy to have hospital ships at the ready.[7]

But Collins's greatest fear was of the effect of bringing the National Peace Keeping Force (NPKF) into KZN. The NPKF, the result of a hasty integration of Umkhonto We Sizwe (MK) guerrillas into the SADF, had performed badly from the outset. Its training camp was racked by mutinies, heavy drinking and the resignation of white officers. When it was moved into the East Rand townships it performed outstandingly badly, simply cracking under pressure and shooting several journalists, killing one. Even the local ANC leadership furiously demanded that the NPKF be withdrawn – which it was. Then, however, the NPKF was ordered into KZN, despite the frantic urgings of the IEC and the Human Rights Commission, who both warned of the explosive consequences – for the IFP regarded the NPKF as simply 'the ANC army'. In the end the NPKF was withdrawn before it ever saw action and was soon after disbanded altogether.

Collins, with his long experience of KZN's procrustean realities, also dissented from the EAD's notion of 'election raids' into KwaZulu. Both the University of Natal and the University of Durban-Westville had long been campuses where, in effect, only one party (the ANC) was allowed to organise. To bus in student helpers from what the IFP regarded as virtual ANC bases was bound to be highly provocative, especially since the ANC had quite normally achieved political penetration in KZN by the bussing in of youthful activists from outside to organise in IFP areas. Such a tactic might, literally, end in a massacre. Moreover, what was the point of sending in mobile polling stations if the local population didn't know where they were going to be and were, in any case, too scared to vote? Had not the chairman of the IEC, Judge Kriegler, himself been humiliated and booed down when he went to Ulundi to address the Zulu chiefs in caucus?

That had, indeed, been a disastrous meeting. Kriegler had tried to insist that the election would go ahead in KwaZulu, but the chiefs (especially Gideon Zulu)[8] had barracked him: let them come into our areas, they had said, and you will see what will happen, let them just try. The more Kriegler had insisted, the more the chiefs had laughed. Kriegler retired, personally humiliated and, with the somewhat petulant note he tended to employ under pressure, told the government that it was not his job to make KwaZulu behave. In effect, Kriegler then washed his hands of KZN and it was left to Danie Schutte, the Minister for Home Affairs, to set up a working party of representatives of the IEC and the South African and KwaZulu governments. It was to this committee that Collins now turned, arguing that they may as well face facts: there was little chance, as thing stood, of holding a free and fair election in KZN. Reluctantly, the working party accepted this thesis and Collins badgered its every member into signing his report saying so. The report provoked considerable consternation within the IEC and the various teams of international observers, all of whom were intent on declaring the election free and fair, come almost what may.

With the IFP's last-minute entry, the IEC faced an impossible task: it had to train no fewer than 14,300 new election officials and workers and set up 549 new polling stations in KwaZulu.[9] The South African Police (SAP) and SADF protested that they could only provide security for 600 polling stations in KZN. The IEC wanted 1,200: in the end around 1,000 were set up, though these were supplemented by roving mobile stations. KwaZulu civil servants were now plentifully available as election officials, monitors and workers, but their training was a farce: huge numbers were shepherded together to receive rapid instruction *en masse*. The sessions were far too brief and the audiences so big that many at the back could not even hear what was being said at the front.[10]

The IEC's last-minute frenzy of activity was parallelled by a furious burst of IFP organisational activity as the party sought desperately to make up lost ground. At just this point the author had occasion to drive from the Mozambique border to Durban – all the way down through Zululand. At village after village excited gatherings of Inkatha warriors and ululating women were in evidence as the traditional induna structure sprang to life, the countryside alive with passion. There was no sign of activity by any other party. For while the IFP with its late entry had certainly handicapped itself, ANC supporters had generally been too scared to venture into rural KwaZulu while the IFP boycott lasted and also lacked time to make much impact there once the boycott was lifted. Later, critical voices within the ANC also alleged that its local leadership had simply been too urban to take the rural vote seriously enough. Others pointed out bitterly that one result of the IFP's late entry was to prevent the IEC from creating its own structure within KwaZulu and thus it was forced to depend heavily on the (presumptively pro-IFP) KwaZulu civil service to run the election there.

As the last weekend before the election dawned Collins asked whether all the equipment – ballot boxes, ink, UV lights, seals, ballot papers, stickers, tally forms and so on – had arrived. Yes, he was told, the containers were all there. But no one had bothered to open them to check the contents; those charged with operating the various election equipment warehouses round the province had no stores experience; and no arrangements had been made to transport either equipment or officials to the polling stations round KZN. The situation was actually far worse than Collins suspected. The IEC was heavily staffed and led by appointees with virtually no experience of management or administration. Many were not even sufficiently well equipped to realise how far they were falling short of the massive logistical task now only days away.

The business community had supplied a considerable number of personnel to the IEC – bank tellers and accountants to help with the count, for example. As a result of the trickle-back of information from such recruits, some businessmen grasped early on what a shambles the IEC was. On Saturday (23 April) Bobby Godsell, a director of the giant Anglo-American Corporation, phoned Terry Rosenberg, chief executive of one of Durban's biggest firms, the McCarthy Group.[11] Anglo, he said, was involved in the election in every region. KZN looked as if it was going to be a mess. Would Rosenberg help? Rosenberg agreed and went straight to the IEC's headquarters at 88 Field Street, Durban, where he was met by Charles Nupen, one of the three IEC commissioners assigned to KZN.[12] Nupen wrote out a letter formally appointing Rosenberg to take charge of the IEC headquarters and thus of the IEC operation in KZN. The chief executive whom Rosenberg thus superseded, a black lawyer called Thabani Jali, had run such a loose ship that many of the staff were unaware even of his name.

Rosenberg found that he had inherited complete chaos. Information from monitors all over KZN flowed into the monitoring division on the nineteenth floor and was being fed down to EAD on the ninth floor. But it wasn't getting there and EAD was trying to run the election completely blind. The pieces of paper detailing information and requests for action were to be found littering the ninth floor, in garbage cans and strewn across desks. There was no filing system, no one could say which piece of information had gone to whom or which requests had been dealt with. Inevitably, with even the nineteenth and ninth floors unable to communicate with one another, the IEC's ability to service its operation out in the field was virtually nil. Rosenberg spent the rest of the day establishing a new management structure.

The next day, Sunday, Rosenberg cast his eye over the physical arrangements for the election and realised that there had been drastic underprovision of ballot papers, IFP stickers, ballot box seals, lighting for polling stations without electricity, and of transport to ship the needed items to polling stations. Worse still, the warehouses in the five subregions of Natal were all in a chaotic state: no one could say how much or what they had received, how much they had handed out and to whom, or how much they had left and who was now short of what. Moreover, as Tuesday's special voting showed, polling stations only signalled when they were short, never when they had an unnecessary surplus of materials, so the only way to be safe was to go for overkill. The situation lent itself to fraud: by claiming that ballot papers were short an election official might acquire a surplus of papers which in turn could then be filled in to the satisfaction of one or another party. On one occasion Rosenberg took a call from a warehouse official claiming to have no ballot papers and a simultaneous call from a monitor in the same warehouse who was looking at 150,000 ballot papers as he spoke.

On Tuesday night Rosenberg met with IEC commissioners Charles Nupen and Dikgang Moseneke (the deputy chairman of the IEC). To be safe, he told them, he needed six million extra ballot papers (two for each voter). The problem was that 27 April was a public holiday, but Rosenberg got hold of the McCarthy Group's own printers and also drafted in another forty McCarthy staff to strengthen the management structure – by this stage he was getting only around two hours sleep a night. The next job was to call in the South African Air Force to get the ballot papers to the polling stations. The air force was quite indispensable, setting up an emergency air base at Newcastle to complement its other fields, calculating at great speed the weight and volume of papers to be lifted and expressing them to remote rural polling stations via a fleet of Dakotas and Puma and Alouette helicopters. Despite such efforts, election day was a complete shambles in much of KZN. Scores, perhaps hundreds, of polling stations failed to open, patient voters waited in long queues all day, often in vain, and shortages of materials developed everywhere.

Moreover, by Wednesday evening an absolute shortage had appeared both of the invisible ink with which to mark voters' hands and the UV lights necessary to recognise the ink marks. Without these materials the election could not proceed. After a frantic search Rosenberg located a supplier for the ink but then found he needed 4,000 one-litre containers in which to transport the ink. Scores of phone calls later Rosenberg discovered a director of Barlow Rand who might be able to help. He had him pulled out of a dinner party late in the evening and managed to acquire a private plane from the Sappi paper company, which flew the containers down. The UV lights were an even greater problem. In the end Rosenberg tracked down a possible supplier in Singapore and was wondering about trying to charter a special Concorde flight to bring them in when a UN official from Jamaica said she had seen such lights in use at the Lesotho election the previous year. By now it was after midnight but Rosenberg got a somewhat indignant Lesotho cabinet minister out of bed and from him obtained the name of the Chief Election Officer of Lesotho. Ultimately 1,500 UV lights were shipped to Maseru airport, which, however, had strict rules about not opening until 7 a.m. So a SAAF Dakota arrived to circle the airport at 6.30 a.m., flew in at 7 o'clock sharp, loaded the lights while still on the runway and flew straight on to Ubombo to distribute the lights to polling stations in Northern Natal. But, once again, such heroics were not necessarily enough: many of the electrically powered UV lights were delivered to rural polling stations without electricity, while the battery-powered ones all too often ended up in towns.

The first day of (special) voting had been a catastrophe in many parts of Northern Natal – very few polling stations had opened at all and many old and ill people waited all day to vote, in vain. On the following day things were virtually the same. Even on Thursday, the last scheduled voting day, things were nearly as bad. Many polling stations didn't open at all and of those that did, many did so only at 10 a.m. – and very few indeed were open after 4.30 p.m. The fact was that many of the IEC staff of ANC provenance felt they were risking their lives by being out in the Zululand countryside at all – and no power on earth was going to keep them there in the hours of darkness. Polling stations which did stay open after dark were often reliant on battery power and their batteries often failed them. The result was sufficient to drive IFP organisers (for it was their voters mainly at stake) to furies of frustration. The IFP organiser for north-western Natal, Dave Durham, spoke indignantly of the difficulties he faced:

By Wednesday I had spoken to Judge Kriegler's personal secretary to tell him there was absolutely no way that we could get through the election. All the old people who came on Tuesday either slept in the *veld* or went home and then came back the next day. Then on Wednesday most of them still couldn't vote and so they came back on Thursday. On the day we finally got some of the polling stations going in the afternoon, but I would say about 80 per cent of our polling stations shut about 4.30 p.m. The IEC people were just so scared of Zulus. . . . For example we had one polling station in the township next to Dundee and the station closed down because the batteries ran out. We said, look, there's electricity only a few hundred yards away, can't we just run a cable there? They said, only if we could give them a personal assurance that the electricians would be safe. I mean, hell, the township's small and it borders Dundee, but these guys were petrified.

We knew that things weren't right from the IEC side when we arrived at a polling station and found they had run out of ballot papers or stickers, and we would radio through to the IEC to tell them. The IEC would come back and say that polling station doesn't exist. We'd say, well it's listed in the newspaper, the name is there, there are paid IEC employees operating it, and you tell us it doesn't exist. They just wouldn't help us. But what it was, you see, was that all polling stations were numbered and somehow they'd got the numbers mixed up.

There were many places where polling stations never opened, for example Sgwetheche on the edge of the Tugela River valley. We tried for two days to get a polling station operative there. People climbed all the way up the valley to get to the polling station – there was one crowd of people who had walked for two days to vote, sleeping overnight at a kraal on the way. And then when they arrived, the station wasn't working. We finally got it going on the second day but then it turned out the station wasn't equipped to issue temporary voting cards. On the Friday they still hadn't voted so we loaded them all on to a lorry and drove them 20 km to a polling station that was working. But you can imagine how few people lasted all the way through that saga and managed to vote in the end. Then on the Friday it rained and that was the end of the election in rural areas.[13]

By this time, however, IEC monitors were reporting the existence of many 'pirate' polling stations or, as the EAD always called them, 'informal voting stations'. The term covered two phenomena. First, there were confusions of the kind mentioned above by Durham, and there were also cases where IEC officials were supposed to set up a polling station in a particular building but found, on inspection, a much more suitable building close by and used it. In both cases the station would not correspond exactly with IEC data. But far more often the term referred to stations run by KwaZulu civil servants and apparently set up at the instigation of the KwaZulu administration. IEC (and ANC) reports singled out the figure of one of Buthelezi's secretaries, Christa Claasen-Williams, who, it was claimed, had effectively displaced the IEC's District Election Officer at Mhlabathini (Buthelezi's own home district) and become DEO herself, with her husband installed as Counting Officer. This, it was not unreasonably claimed, placed the election there under

IFP control. Moreover, the IEC monitors reported that Ms Claasen-Williams was also provisioning KwaZulu officials with ballot boxes, papers, stickers and other materials to set up other polling stations.[14] Receiving these reports back in Durban, Steve Collins raised the matter with the commissioners. Surely the IEC should act immediately to prevent more votes being cast in such stations: it could seize these pirate stations, shut them down and lay charges against those operating them.

Meanwhile, however, Buthelezi had communicated to the IEC in no uncertain terms his furious concern at the voting shambles in KwaZulu. Once again, the whole process hung in the balance: it seemed only too possible that he might pull out of the election or refuse to accept the result. This would be the greatest disaster of all. Buthelezi made it clear that, of the three KZN commissioners, he would deal only with Dikgang Moseneke. In part this reflected Moseneke's position as the second most powerful man on the IEC after Kriegler, but it was also a political question. Buthelezi refused to have anything to do with McDougall, whom he regarded, not without reason, as an ANC sympathiser. Nupen, though an independent mediator by profession, also had far more links with COSATU and the ANC than with the IFP. Moseneke, on the other hand, could not be suspected of ANC sympathies: he had until recently been a leading light in the PAC, with whom Buthelezi maintained fraternal relations.

Moseneke flew to Ulundi together with the Minister for Home Affairs, Danie Schutte. It was a crucial meeting and there is no doubt that Moseneke deserves particular credit for the fact that the IFP stayed in the election. In effect this meeting led to the extension of voting by an extra day and the allaying of Buthelezi's worst fears by the immediate printing of an extra 2 million ballot papers – this time with no need for IFP ballot stickers.

However, this crucial summit between Moseneke and Buthelezi (Schutte's presence there is forgotten in most accounts) quickly produced a mythology of its own, that Moseneke had agreed to the continuation of 'pirate' voting stations as a quid pro quo for keeping Buthelezi in the election. This was completely untrue, but the story was widely believed even in the KZN section of the IEC, for the fact was that after this meeting the whole issue of 'pirate' voting stations dropped away and those within the IEC who tried to raise it received no response. From that they concluded that it had been agreed that, given that there were so many non-performing IEC stations, the summit had accepted that it was better to have 'informal' stations than none at all. What this implied, so the story went, was a sort of 'equal right to cheat'. For while there was grave doubt about the partisan (IFP) loyalties of many of the KwaZulu officials who manned many of the so-called 'informal' stations, it was equally undeniable that many of the IEC officials in charge of the 'formal' voting stations were ANC activists. Indeed, when such activists were named as district election officers or counting officers, they were given power to appoint their subordinate officials. Generally it followed as night follows day that these jobs too were given to fellow activists, frequently to family members, for all such officials drew useful salaries. Steve Collins worked out that some such families collectively made as much as R20,000 or even R30,000 from the election. Given this situation, it was argued, Moseneke had had to placate Buthelezi by allowing the 'pirate' stations to continue.

The Moseneke–Buthelezi summit was, indeed, almost as crucial to the election as Buthelezi's decision to enter the hustings in the first place. For the bottom line was fearsome: the possibility of an Angolan-style rejection of the result and a consequent unilateral declaration of independence of the whole area north of the Tugela. Despite the pre-emptive military preparations to crush just such a rebellion, the IEC (and behind it the Transitional Executive Council) knew that such an outcome would mean that the new South Africa would be born amidst blood, tears and bitterness. It was all very well massing armour, aircraft and men to go to war against grass-hut villages, but such an action would run counter to the whole spirit of liberation and would anyway poison the wells of the future. Moreover, the more thinking spirits within the IEC had always seen the election as essentially a way of completing the process, imperfectly achieved at CODESA, of including everyone in. In was simply vital that the FF, PAC and IFP (not to mention the smaller parties) should be in at the birth of the new nation so that they would feel and be part of it when the election was over.

Seen against this background, it was not difficult to conclude that even a corrupt deal to keep Buthelezi in would have been worth it. The rumour of a deal was, in fact, wholly untrue.[15] But the myth grew and flowered, especially when, on the day after the summit, two SAAF helicopters were withdrawn from the IEC and placed instead at Ulundi's disposal for the distribution of election materials. Those within the KZN IEC who had been getting reports of 'pirate' stations were horrified that Buthelezi should now apparently be given assistance to make such stations work. Steve Collins, who was getting almost hourly reports of 'informal stations', queried this new deployment but was told that it stemmed from a direct instruction by the TEC's National Security Committee. This could only mean that the ANC, too, had agreed to it.

In the wake of this supposed Moseneke–Buthelezi deal the temperature rose within the KwaZulu-Natal IEC, especially when the next day saw reports of 'informal stations' mushrooming everywhere. Collins again approached the commissioners. Surely, he asked, we should stop such stations: we have helicopters, we can pounce on them from the air and close them down. The commissioners vetoed such action but instructed instead that all ballot boxes from 'informal' stations should be marked and counted separately. Yet a moment's reflection would have shown that the IEC had no power to implement such an instruction. Many normal IEC polling stations were routinely shambolic enough not to keep proper records of their ballot boxes, so that in many cases it became quite impossible to establish which boxes came from where. But in any case, the IEC was in no position to enforce its decision because many rural polling stations (such as Mhlabathini) were not on the phone anyway. Since this was particularly true of 'informal' stations, it followed that the IEC instructions could not be relayed to the places that mattered. Once counting started this error showed up in the fact that it was impossible to effect a reconciliation of the ballot boxes with the written records of the polling stations.

By this time complaints were raining in from all sides. There seems to have been widespread voting – and even more attempted voting – by under-age youths: there was a near-riot in Ndwedwe when a stop was put to this. All too often the UV lights didn't work and this led to deliberate multiple voting in some instances. A particular problem was the thousands of Transkeians who came flooding into KZN to vote. For conditions in the Transkei were often even more chaotic than in KZN and it was often easy, monitors reported, for voters there to vote without the invisible ink being used, allowing them to come and vote a second time in KZN. And, IEC officials were convinced, there was a good deal of cheating in the 'informal' voting stations. There were frequent problems over identity documents. Despite all the efforts at voter education many voters roled up without the necessary voter's card or ID documents. In the KwaZulu voting stations temporary voters' cards were issued merely on the basis of a photograph and a KwaZulu official stamp – too slender a basis to engender much confidence. At other polling stations (including the one where the author voted) some voters rolled up with birth certificates and demanded (and got) voters' cards, only for it to be discovered later that the same certificates reappeared more than once with different names tippexed in and out. There were also many makeshift measures: frequently there weren't enough ballot boxes and in that case votes were (with IEC permission) decanted into mail sacks and the old boxes reused. After the election 150 unused ballot boxes and huge numbers of unused ballot papers were recovered from Empangeni, although officials there had denied their existence throughout the election. Some believed that these items had been hidden rather than mislaid.

Although the IFP claimed that many of its older voters had been so discouraged by their inability to vote on the Tuesday or Wednesday that they had lost heart and failed to vote as a result, there was otherwise little complaint by Friday that voters who wanted to had not been able to vote. From this point on, the complaint was more often that too many votes had been cast, not too few.

The Count

It had been decided that there ought to be a counting station for every 30,000 voters. In practice there seemed a better prospect of assembling the necessary expertise if much larger counting centres were used, grouping a number of counting stations in one place. The same decision was made in the other large metropolitan centres. In the case of the Durban metropolitan area (the Durban Functional Region or DFR), with its estimated population of 3 to 4 million, there were expected to be some 1.8 million voters casting 3.6 million ballots, which implied 63 counting stations with no fewer than 28 of these grouped in the Durban Expo Centre (DEC). The DEC was to become the epicentre of the contested count in KZN and, eventually, became the tense focus of both national and international attention as the counting process dragged traumatically on.

Tony Wilson, a lawyer working at Deloittes's Durban office, had been asked to join the IEC effort on the Friday before the election, when it belatedly became clear to the EAD officials that they were hopelessly unprepared for the count.[16] Wilson, who was given the job of organising the 63 counting stations of the DFR, found that while the IEC had hired 60 counting officers, mainly from the banks, nobody knew much about the elaborate procedures necessary to count votes: the matching of the tally slips from polling stations, the reconciliation of numbered ballot boxes, the verification procedures, the actual mechanics of the count, and so on. Such training as there had been was pretty perfunctory. Moreover, nobody had yet even worked out which buildings would serve as counting stations – Wilson spent much of the weekend scouting out likely venues.

To his even greater consternation, Wilson worked out that in total he would need 7,500 counters and that, with just six days to go to the count, not one of these had been recruited or trained. Accordingly, he had notices put up at the University of Natal and the University of Durban-Westville, calling for recruits from the university faculties to act as supervisors and student recruits to act as counters. Wilson believed that it would be impossible to hire so many people in such a short time but he had not taken into account the extent to which the election was now widely viewed as a financial opportunity: word had spread far and wide that one could earn R250 a day and more, even as a humble counter. The result was huge numbers of willing recruits at both universities, and scenes of virtual riot as volunteers jostled the recruiters and one another.

Word spread wider still and soon school pupils and unemployed workers joined the scrum, all claiming to be students. A particularly difficult situation developed at the University of Durban-Westville, often a scene of subterranean tension between African and Indian students. The recruiters, themselves mostly bank clerks, were virtually all Indian, as indeed are many of the UDW faculty. African students, seeing Indian recruiters recruiting only other Indians as supervisors, bitterly accused the IEC of reserving only lowly jobs for Africans. This led, inevitably, to a minor riot. But even when counters had been recruited they could not be assigned to counting stations (since venues hadn't yet been selected), and since the IEC hadn't thought to provide identity badges for counters, there was no immediate way of identifying who was a legitimate counter and who was not. To Wilson's amazement the 7,500 were duly recruited by Tuesday and some emergency training sessions were organised, ready for the count to begin on Thursday.

Fifteen hundred counters had been told to turn up at the DEC for the first shift on Thursday. Some counters, realising that the extension of a third day of voting on Thursday meant that there could be no count on that day, didn't bother to turn up. But many more did. To his horror, Wilson found himself facing a crowd of over 3,000, all insisting they were counters and wanting employment. Since there was no way of identifying *bona fide* counters, Wilson could only tell the crowd that no counting would be done that day – he had only heard this himself the previous midnight – and to tell them instead to go to their various counting stations so that some further training sessions could take place. Making and enforcing this announcement was a difficult and unpleasant task and it was with horror that Wilson learnt that Radio Zulu was still announcing that there were vacancies for counters. None the less, when the counters had gone to their respective counting stations it emerged that there were gaps at a number of them, so more counters were hastily recruited from the crowd in the street to fill the gaps.

As voting ended, Steve Collins started moving ballot boxes to Durban for the count. Concerned about security for the boxes, he asked if there was a safe place where he could store them. He was told that there was no such place but that 1,200 guard monitors would be trained to look after the boxes. The 1,200 were duly recruited and trained but at the last moment it was decided that this was too risky a procedure: instead the boxes destined for the DEC (which is close to the beach) could be stored at the nearby Coast of Dreams depot under lock and key. Thus 1,200 duly trained guard monitors turned up only to be told that they had no jobs after all. They became extremely angry, rioted, stormed and occupied buildings and held officials as hostages in pursuit of their claims. In the end they were dealt with only by resort to the riot police, the Internal Stability Unit (ISU), which constantly patrolled the area with Nyala armoured vehicles. Luckily, the ISU contained what Collins called 'Rambo-style anti-terrorist units', specially trained by the Israelis to deal with hostage dramas. Collins distributed cellular phones to this unit so that they could be contacted easily to deal with such cases: indeed, many officials felt that the whole electoral process depended quite heavily on the introduction of the cellular phone. On Friday, Tony Wilson, attempting to negotiate with the angry crowds outside the DEC, was three times taken hostage.

As the ballot boxes were brought into the DEC, trouble erupted there too as the ANC and IFP launched bitter objections against one another; each had its own long list of alleged electoral irregularities, intimidation and downright cheating by the other side in the areas which it controlled. The IEC decided to set up a committee of party representatives with the idea that, while the verification of boxes was ultimately an IEC decision, much was to be gained if a prior consensus could be achieved. This was undoubtedly a good idea, but it strengthened the feeling inside the DEC that the people really in control were the various party representatives – who were typically far more articulate, forceful and, of course, politically powerful than the IEC officials. Given that the two biggest parties had been at war with one another for years and hated one another with a passion, this was a recipe for a great deal of difficulty within the DEC. And, of course, there was much for the parties to object to: by no means all the required paperwork relating to the ballot boxes had been carried out. Some ballot boxes had ballot papers lying flat and unfolded inside them, an impossibility if voters had cast their ballots in the normal way. Other ballot boxes had grass in them or traces of food, both of which were taken as evidence of tampering: some imagined scenes in which boxes were opened in fields or in kitchens, with votes for the 'wrong' party extracted and replaced with ballots manufactured from the many ballot papers that had gone missing.

Throughout KZN the tension over the count was heightened by several factors. The concern within the IEC over 'pirate' voting stations had been thoroughly communicated to the ANC, who made much of it and generally refused to trust any polling station where KwaZulu government officials had been in charge. In particular, the ANC objected strongly to any votes being counted at Mhlabathini, arguing that a fair count was impossible in this Inkatha epicentre. In the end they succeeded in their objection and votes from the Mhlabathini region were transported for counting elsewhere. The IFP had similar feelings about polling stations manned by ANC sympathisers, and had many stories of stations without IFP stickers, or where IFP stickers were affixed to the ballot paper only after a vote had been cast. In general the IFP was extremely conscious of the handicaps it had suffered as a result of its own late entry, was well aware that the IEC was heavily staffed with ANC supporters, and was almost morbidly suspicious that its handicap would be exploited. The ANC, for its part, had clearly had something of a shock as reports flooded in of heavy IFP voting in rural areas. Moreover, because the delays at the DEC were worse than elsewhere, word tended to leak in from quicker counting stations elsewhere in KZN of large IFP votes. The ANC response, according to Dave Durham, the IFP organiser, was to question the vote wherever possible:

When we started the count in Dundee, the ANC were very optimistic. But as the votes came in the count began to go 3:1 against them – despite the fact that 5,000 votes were declared invalid because they lacked the stamp of the presiding officer, a fact about which we felt bitterly since she was the wife of a known ANC member. Then suddenly in came a whole lot of senior ANC people and they objected to this and that and generally to everything. They brought the count to a grinding halt, which was clearly their intention. The same pattern was repeated all the way down to Maritzburg and Durban.[17]

The tension was sharpest at the Durban Exhibition Centre. No counting at all took place on Saturday because of a furious party stand-off occasioned by the fact that the ballot boxes could not be reconciled. The presiding officer of every polling station was supposed to fill in papers certifying the number and origin of each box, the number of ballot papers in it, their serial numbers and tally slips to allow checking. In addition, all the boxes had to be sealed. In fact many such officers were barely trained, and had failed to do some or all of these things. Some boxes were not sealed at all and were merely pegged shut with a twig; some votes arrived in canvas sacks and not in boxes at all. The parties, particularly the IFP and ANC, were adamant that they would not allow counting to proceed until all the boxes had been satisfactorily reconciled.

This log-jam was to lead Judge Kriegler to another of his famous *malentendus*. Announcing that the formal requirement for ballot box reconciliation prior to counting was being dropped, Kriegler said: 'Getting the count done is more important – people want to have the results . . . the election is about national reconciliation, not ballot reconciliation.' Kriegler added that in any case, reconciliation 'served no particular purpose' as a security check in the absence of voters' rolls – a clear non-sequitur – and went on to criticise the Electoral Act which had laid down the reconciliation procedures as 'a very strange document'.[18] This enraged IEC staff even more than his famous declaration that he himself would not vote since none of the parties had done enough to deserve his confidence: an almost incredible lapse in sensitivity for the head of a commission charged with creating maximal conditions for one and all to vote. So infuriated were the IEC staff in KZN by the 'reconciliation' quip that an instant order was sent out to all IEC staff in the field that they must ignore Kriegler and do their utmost to reconcile the ballot boxes.

All Saturday long the parties quarrelled and no counting was done. The implications of such a deadlock for peace in KZN were greatly alarming, particularly to the local business community. Guy Harris, a finance officer for the South African Sugar Association seconded to the monitoring section, was so alarmed that the Durban stand-off might capsize the whole election that he rushed down to the DEC at 7 a.m. on Sunday and tried desperately to get the count started. He took a sample of boxes and their accompanying documentation and showed that a full reconciliation of the boxes was simply impossible: if the parties waited for that, they would wait forever. He phoned Terry Rosenberg, who came down to the DEC equally eager to see the count start, and he then phoned the IEC commissioners in Johannesburg, getting Gay McDougall out of bed. Harris kept up the pressure all morning. The ANC representatives talked on their cellular phones to ANC headquarters in Shell House and to Mandela; on their cellular phones the NP talked to de Klerk; and on theirs the IEC officials talked to Kriegler. One of the ANC representatives demanded to know what business it was of Harris's to push so hard for a count. Harris replied that, for a start, the sugar industry had major foreign exchange exposure and that if the markets, when they opened on Monday, saw the electoral process in crisis, the rand would plummet and there would be heavy losses. This cut no ice: 'Well, let the markets go to hell then,' came the reply.[19]

In the end Harris's arguments won the day. All the boxes in dispute were isolated and at 2 p.m. on Sunday counting of the other boxes began. This delay meant that the DEC lagged well behind the other, smaller counting stations in rural KZN. As these began to declare their results the IFP took an early lead, a fact trumpeted by banner headlines in the *Natal Mercury*. This had explosive effect. Among the ANC representatives at the DEC it was an article of faith that the IFP could not win except by cheating. Rumours spread of colossal IFP majorities being 'manufactured' in rural areas, and for the first time the ANC leadership in Durban began to face the humiliating possibility that they might go down to defeat while their ANC peers were winning almost everywhere else. Within the DEC the pressure cooker atmosphere sharply worsened.

The pressure was greatest on the man in charge of the count, Tony Wilson. Like many of the IEC staff, he had now had no sleep for three nights. Inside he faced the endless squabbling of the party representatives, outside (and often inside as well) he faced furious crowds demanding money and employment. These latter invaded the IEC headquarters, took hostages, threatened to take the IEC commissioners hostage or to burn the building down if they didn't get their way – and they had to be cleared from the building by riot police. At this point Wilson, who had come to count votes but who had instead found himself being taken hostage or riding on Nyalas to rescue hostages, turned to Commissioner Gay McDougall and demanded help. The situation was now way out of hand, with angry would-be vote counters invading the DEC, demanding their jobs. They were in an extremely angry mood, physically threatening officials and some even talking of burning down the building. At one point Terry Rosenberg, hearing a shot, rushed downstairs to find, in a room spattered with blood, an IEC official with his shoulder shattered by a short-range pistol shot from an enraged would-be vote counter.

Several hundred would-be counters were toyi-toying in the street, while in the counting hall (intended for 250) 300 counters were already at work. It was decided to invite the protestors into the building to negotiate, but only the counting room was big enough to hold them, so the 300 were asked to step outside to let the protestors enter – a dangerous thing to do, not only because it meant meeting with ballot papers and boxes all strewn around, but because the people who were supposed to be outside were now inside, and those supposed to be inside were now outside. As rumour spread among the 300 that they might now lose their jobs, discontent began to rise – while, inside, the 200 were not getting their way and began toyi-toying and threatening the life and limb of those who thwarted them. At this point Tony Wilson simply collapsed under the strain and had to be rushed to hospital. The whole counting process in the most contested province now stood on the point of collapse too, with the likely consequences for the whole country almost too appalling for rational contemplation.

The situation was saved by Bheki Sibeiya, a personnel manager at South African Breweries, who had been running monitoring in KZN. Sibeiya now moved over, together with his management team, to run the count. Very much against the wishes of the lawyers who proliferated (to almost universal dislike) within the IEC structure, Sibeiya struck a deal with the disappointed surplus counting workers, offering them R300 each for the time they had wasted and the fact that they had been falsely promised jobs. Most of them took the R300 – and then refused to leave the Exhibition Centre, still demanding 'their' jobs. Sibeiya then took the public address microphone and announced that the building had to be evacuated in orderly fashion, that everyone should stay calm and walk, not run, to the exits. He did not specifically mention a bomb threat but the implication was clear to all. Everyone, including the protestors, filed out. Sibeiya then readmitted only those he wanted inside. Thanks to this brilliant ploy the counting process was able to resume.[20]

A few hours after this fake bomb threat, however, there was a real bomb threat: the bomb, the caller said, had been placed inside the building and would explode at 10 p.m. Sibeiya was loath to disturb the count or to evacuate the centre into the mass of angry ejectees still swirling in the street outside: anything might happen, with physical violence against counting officials a real possibility. He suspected, indeed, that the threat was a revenge hoax by one of those ejected. The bomb call came at 8 p.m. and Sibeiya had timed the previous evacuation at under half an hour, so he knew he had some time in hand. So, telling almost no one inside the DEC, he called the bomb squad and told the election workers that a routine security check was being conducted, but that they should ignore it and continue with their work. The bomb squad swept through the building with no one suspecting that they were the bomb squad, and pronounced it clear. Accordingly, Sibeiya ignored the threat –

though he admitted that the last few minutes before 10 p.m. were almost unbearably tense. The witching hour passed without incident. Twice within a few hours Sibeiya's calm resourcefulness had saved the day.

The counting continued. When he took over, Sibeiya had no knowledge of counting procedures and had to sit down and read everything from scratch. Faced by the demand that boxes be reconciled before being counted, he ordered counting to begin and said reconciliation could be done afterwards. But now another crisis erupted, sparked by the National Election Observers' Network (NEON). NEON, drawn largely from NGOs, had worked in an entirely voluntary capacity, but many of its members, as they saw the useful amounts of money being earned by election workers (and also listened to rumours of stolen computers, furniture and vehicles within the IEC), began to use direct action tactics to press their claim that they too should be rewarded. This produced trouble right round the country, with difficult and often violent scenes in Johannesburg, Cape Town and elsewhere. NEON's internal structure broke down and the leadership lost control of its bitterly clamant rank and file.

In Durban Sibeiya offered a deal of a token R150 each to members of the local branch, KNEON. This was rejected out of hand. KNEON activists invaded the IEC Durban offices, took Sibeiya hostage and said they would not allow the IEC vice-chairman, Dikgang Moseneke, to leave, that he was now their hostage too. Moseneke was determined not to yield to this disgraceful behaviour: 'These guys believe that if you get somebody by the balls then their hearts and minds will follow. But let me tell you they could tear my balls off but my heart and mind would not follow.' In fact Sibeiya bore the brunt and was held hostage by KNEON on four separate occasions. By the last occasion KNEON had become so physically threatening that Sibeiya actually feared for his life. Luckily, he was rescued by the ISU anti-terrorist squad. Moseneke's tough line held and KNEON were defeated. The IEC was much criticised for affirmative action appointments which put hopelessly ill-qualified black people in positions they could not handle, but it is worth noting that in the toughest spot in the whole election the situation was saved – repeatedly – by two black men, Moseneke and Sibeiya.

In the end all the votes had been counted save for those in 112 disputed ballot boxes (though half-a-dozen boxes had been rejected outright as almost certainly bogus). Then the votes in the disputed boxes were counted, but since the ANC still vehemently objected against their validity, they were left in limbo and not added into the cumulative totals. The IFP was clearly ahead whether or not the disputed votes were counted in, but since the disputed votes were heavily IFP, the effect of including these votes would be to push the IFP just across the 50 per cent line in the provincial (though not the national) contest in KZN. Apart from the symbolic importance of the 50 per cent figure, these last votes would make the difference as to whether or not the IFP had a majority in the regional assembly.

By this stage the count had been completed everywhere else in the country and only the deadlock over the count in the DEC was holding up the declaration of the national result. The whole election now hung on the crisis inside the DEC: if the election in Natal – a region including almost a quarter of the national electorate – was declared invalid (or even regarded as such by the biggest party), then the validity of the entire election would be undermined. This meant that the issue of the disputed boxes was debated not merely by the parties' representatives in Durban but by the various party high commands in Johannesburg. Suspicion grew that the parties were actually bargaining about what the result should be, and as the deadlock continued and rumours flew, public scepticism about the fairness of the count began to surface. Judge Kriegler fed this impression by yet another indicretion, arguing that people should not be too squeamish about a bit of horse-trading by the parties. This was widely taken to mean that the parties were horse-trading votes, while in fact the bargaining was merely about which ballot boxes the parties would agree to regard as valid.

In the end the ANC representatives at the DEC went into private caucus and then, to the general amazement, emerged to say that they would accept the validity of the 112 disputed ballot boxes and thus of the final result. Although the ANC comfortably ran ahead in the DEC count in both the national and provincial races, both its relative lead over the IFP and its absolute number of votes were far below its expectations. In order to overturn the IFP's lead built up elsewhere in KZN the ANC had needed to do far better in the Durban region, so acceptance of these figures also meant accepting IFP victory in KZN as a whole. The ANC's volte-face meant swallowing a bitter pill. It was undoubtedly the result of a direct instruction from Mandela himself, for both he and de Klerk were on the phone repeatedly to their representatives in Durban. In effect Mandela enforced acceptance of Buthelezi's victory in KZN because not to do so would have greatly damaged the legitimacy of the entire electoral process, and thus of his own party's sweeping national victory.

There were several remarkable features in these results of the count at the DEC, shown in table 10.1, not least the fact that 114,629 more votes were counted in the national than in the regional contest. This was an impossible discrepancy. Voters filing through the polling station were given both ballot papers in immediate succession; few, if any, would have got all the way to casting a national ballot and then refused to cast a regional vote. The table suggests that one voter in six of those counted at the DEC behaved that way, something all poll-watchers would concur to be impossible. In other words, at least one (and possibly both) of the vote totals above is likely to be incorrect, the cause of the discrepancy being simply that too many ballot boxes were disqualified in the regional ballot

Table 10.1   The count at the Durban Exhibition Centre

Party	National		Regional	
	Votes	%	Votes	%
ANC	342,799	48.49	280,647	47.38
IFP	117,301	16.59	152,324	25.72
NP	195,368	27.64	100,410	16.95
DP	27,398	3.88	28,322	4.78
Minority Front	2,235	0.32	8,402	1.42
FF	4,905	0.69	3,585	0.61
PAC	4,833	0.68	4,882	0.83
ACDP	4,735	0.67	5,471	0.92
Africa Muslim Party	2,810	0.40	5,451	0.92
Others*	4,515	0.64	2,776	0.47
Total	706,899	100.00	592,270	100.00

* Nine at national level, three at provincial level.

or too few disqualified in the national ballot. It is difficult to avoid the impression that more boxes were disqualified in the regional count simply because that was the one which local politicians cared about most: the figures in the national ballot section could not much alter the ANC's overwhelming victory in the country as a whole, but the figures in the regional ballot would decide the key question as to whether Inkatha would rule KZN with a clear majority or not. It is important to remember that, because the DEC was the last counting station to declare, the local party representatives knew exactly how these figures would affect the balance of forces in the region and the country.

A further oddity was that it had been decided to release the results only by region, but in fact results were counted by polling station and then by counting station – the latter unit being chosen so as to avoid an exact correspondence with magisterial district. The principle in all this was to avoid allowing the parties or the public to know exactly how particular communities voted for fear of possible intimidation or reprisals as a result. So the newspapers printed only the results for the nine regions and this is all that most South Africans knew of their own election. The same sort of thinking had led to the maintenance of the ban, inherited from the previous regime, on the publication of opinion polls in the last month before the election. All that this means is that politicians continue to carry out private opinion polls so that they can see how opinion is moving, and can behave according to those movements, while the electorate is kept in ignorance.

Some while later it was possible, by special application, to obtain the results by counting station and a tiny handful of people obtained these. But the parties at the count were, of course, insistent to know details of polling station results. At the DEC Tony Wilson tried to withhold these since to release them would be to make a mockery of all other attempts at secrecy. To his amazement he was instructed to give the parties what they wanted. He was extremely nervous as he did this that they would notice that if they put together the polling station tallies, the counting station tallies and the regional tallies, they would realise that they did not always add up, for inexplicable and irremediable discrepancies had crept in. To his astonished relief none of them appeared to notice.[21] It was not until August that the IFP complained aloud of these discrepancies, by which time no one much was listening.

The IEC had decided that results must be declared as they were verified, despite the pressures this was bound to produce at counts round the country: the alternative, of suppressing results until they could all be announced together, would probably not have worked – results would have leaked. But, given the long and agonising delays that developed, there might have been a major crisis had no news at all been available. As it was, the IEC's reporting of the results was extremely erratic and had to be endlessly corrected. On one occasion the IEC reported 744,039 spoilt papers in Gauteng – about a third of the total votes counted in the region at that point. This produced panicky phone calls from foreign investment bankers who worried that the ruling out of so many votes would lead to violence. It was, it turned out, merely a typing error, though it was difficult to see how 744,039 could have been a typing error for the right figure (33,915).[22] On Tuesday morning (3 May) the IEC total votes counted shot up by nearly 3 million. This included some 2.5 million votes cast in the Western Cape, home to only 2.4 million extra voters. Twenty minutes later the IEC subtracted 2.75 million votes from its tallies.[23]

Incidents such as these merely increased the distrust of the IEC and the amount of ridicule levelled at it. With all the parties denouncing its deficiencies and the media more and more critical as time wore on, nerves within the IEC became taut. Judge Kriegler lost his temper with foreign journalists, while IEC commissioner Zac Yacoob launched an ill-judged attack on the media for its 'jeers and criticisms'. There had been mistakes, said Yacoob, but they were due to many factors, 'including the legacy of apartheid'.[24] Such speeches only led to further ridicule. The IEC's loss of credibility was a bad blow: for the election to succeed there needed to be widespread acceptance of the authoritative fairness and competence of the IEC. Once this reputation was lost, the propriety of the electoral process as a whole inevitably came into question. There were, in the case of the IEC, many extenuating circumstances but – strangely, for a body headed by a judge – it adopted an approach to several major decisions which can only be described as injudicious. As Tim Cohen of *Business Day* commented, it took a

> cavalier attitude . . . towards its own agreed procedures, not to mention the legislative requirements. On the first day of voting, it gradually became clear that a 'special directive' had been issued which would allow officials simply to write in the Inkatha Freedom Party voting space in direct contravention of the agreement arrived at with Inkatha. . . . But more policy-making on the hoof followed. First, Thursday was made a public holiday. Second, 9.3 million more ballot papers were distributed. Next, voting was extended in several former homelands. And then the process of reconciliation was scrapped. . . . How could these extraordinary adaptations be justified? Why did these problems arise in the first place? Who was to blame? Questions arose quick and fast, only to be replaced by others without the original ones being adequately answered. At Gallagher Estate (the central IEC HQ in Johannesburg) a mood of cynicism developed as the IEC spokesmen became more vague and journalists more frustrated. Worst of all, a new justification for failure was being bandied about. This was the 'This is Africa' retort – the 'what do you expect, you are not living in Europe' logic that erodes any demand for adequacy and precision.[25]

Certainly, the decision to allow write-in votes for the IFP on ballots which had no IFP stickers thoroughly muddied the water. If the idea had been to placate the IFP, it did not work, for the IFP furiously rejected the idea of write-in votes, not only because this would then remove all urgency from the need to get stickers put on ballot papers, but because a large proportion of its electorate would be unable or unwilling to write in their party, either through illiteracy or general nervousness of their vote being traced. However, the IEC thereafter faced the quandary of whether or not write-in votes should be counted, as well as whether votes from suspect/unreconciled boxes should. All of which gave the counting process a highly undesirable degree of latitude and allowed the political parties to see the count as susceptible to political bargaining. When word of such bargaining leaked, the damage to the IEC's credibility was disastrous.

Moreover, as the final count was being put together in Johannesburg, a further, almost surreal incident occurred, with the discovery that computer fraud had been committed on the main IEC computer dealing with the national count. The truth was that security at IEC headquarters had been lamentable, with all too many people roaming the building with access to files and computers. It passed without comment that one computer room was always full of (mainly white) enthusiasts playing computer games; only later did the thought occur that some of these people might have been hackers, breaking into networks to get access to confidential documents and to the count itself. For a while nobody paid much attention: the IEC had followed Canadian voting models and had bought a software package alleged to be proof against tampering. However, confidential documents began to be stolen off computers. On Tuesday morning, 3 May, one of the Canadian election observers ran a check and quickly discovered that the election computer had been tampered with: as the faxed tallies came in from around the country, whatever votes the ANC received, the totals achieved by the NP, the IFP and FF would have an automatic multiplier added to them so as to maintain a constant ratio with the ANC. Some, though not all, of the counting station results had also been altered – but not sufficiently to match the alterations in the totals. If this had been malicious interference (and those who investigated thought it was by a 4:2 majority), it had either been interrupted or not very expert.[26] The motive for such tampering was obvious: by this method the ANC could never attain the crucial two-thirds majority which would enable it to write its own constitution at will. Once the electrifying news of the presumed fraud was known, the IEC computer was shut down and the count handled manually. Hordes of pin-striped young accountants from Deloittes moved in, set up a book-keeping audit of the count and sorted out the mess. 'They brought in a bunch of grey-suited men who looked like they all had the same father,'[27] said one African IEC staffer of this final and symbolic rescue by white expertise.

The computer fraud episode, coming on top of the long drawn-out trauma of the count at the DEC, together with the multiple reports of electoral fraud and intimidation both in KZN and elsewhere, made it inevitable that no sooner was the count completed than its credibility was called into question. Had it really all been free and fair? Wasn't the result all just a bit too convenient: the ANC just missing a two-thirds majority, the NP just scraping over 20 per cent and thus gaining one of the deputy presidencies, the IFP just attaining the respectability of a 10 per cent plus score and scraping into power in KZN by the narrowest possible margin? Suspicions grew and festered and the fact that the international observer missions speedily pronounced the election free and fair made no impact whatsoever: had they not come to South Africa merely to consecrate the transition? Did anyone doubt that they would have said the same thing whatever happened? Was not international relief at the end of apartheid so great that it would have been virtually sacrilegious to find fault with the election that buried it? This was the trouble about all the goodwill which accompanied and followed the election: everyone could see that a lot of dirt could be hidden in a layer of goodwill three feet deep. Within three months of the election the idea that it had been rigged, at least in KZN and probably nationally, gained such wide currency that it became virtually the conventional wisdom.

Everyone had some interest in this notion. Whatever the ANC's formal acceptance of KZN result, the party found it emotionally impossible to accept that it might really have lost a fair fight to Buthelezi in KZN. Indeed, the local ANC prepared a lengthy submission with which to go to court in order to have KZN election set aside, and was only dissuaded from proceeding with this course of action by further strong pressure from the ANC leadership. But all the other parties had lost and they too assuaged their wounds by dismissing the results as fraudulent. The result was that as the election receded the question as to whether or not it had been truly free and fair, far from fading away, became sharper and more persistent.

Notes

I am indebted to a large number of people for their help in granting me interviews for this chapter. Some of my debts are recorded in the notes below but a number of other people helped me only on condition that their names were not mentioned.

1   *Citizen*, 4 and 5 May 1994, and *Natal Witness*, 3 May 1994.
2   Private communication.
3   *Citizen*, 6 May 1994.
4   Ibid.
5   Interview with Steve Collins, Durban, 24 Aug. 1994.
6   On 26 April the South African Police raided the IFP's training camp at Mlaba, in Umfolozi, and confiscated 76 G3 rifles, 49 shotguns, 5 rifle grenades, 26 hand grenades and 24 cases of ammunition. It was a tricky situation – the camp clearly enjoyed the benevolent neutrality of the KwaZulu Police (KZP) and several KZP members were present when the camp was raided. Nobody was arrested and the SAP announced that although the weapons were the property of the KwaZulu government, they were being taken in 'for ballistics testing'. *Natal on Saturday*, 30 April 1994.
7   Interview with Collins, 24 Aug. 1994.
8   Later Member of the Executive Council for Social Welfare in the KwaZulu-Natal regional government.
9   Interview with Collins, 24 Aug. 1994. Terry Bell, spokesman for the IEC, gave the figure of 13,000. Interview with Terry Bell, 23 Sept. 1994.
10 Interview with Collins, 24 Aug. 1994.
11 Interview with Terry Rosenberg, Durban, 1 Aug. 1994.
12 Two IEC commissioners were detailed to each of the nine regions. KZN, in recognition of its exceptional problems, had three – Gay McDougall, Charles Nupen and Dikgang Moseneke.
13 Interviews with Dave Durham, Durban, 4–5 Aug. 1994.
14 Interview with Collins, 24 Aug. 1994.
15 So widely diffused was this rumour within the IEC's own ranks that I had come to believe it myself until Charles Nupen set me right on this issue. I am deeply in his debt. Interview with Charles Nupen, 22 Sept. 1994.
16 Interview with Tony Wilson, 19 Aug. 1994.
17 Interviews with Durham, 4–5 Aug. 1994.
18 *Business Day*, 2 May 1994.
19 Interview with Guy Harris, 10 Aug. 1994.
20 Interview with Bheki Sibeiya, 25 Aug. 1994.
21 Interview with Tony Wilson, 19 Aug. 1994.
22 *Business Day*, 4 May 1994.
23 *Natal Witness*, 7 May 1994.
24 *Daily News*, 3 May 1994.
25 *Business Day*, 2 May 1994.
26 *The Star* (International Weekly Edition), 27 Oct.–2 Nov. 1994.
27 *Natal Witness*, 7 May 1994.

ELEVEN

The 1994 Election: Outcome and Analysis

R. W. Johnson

ALL TOLD, 19,726,610 votes were cast in the national contest and 19,633,571 in the regional contests. An initial query must exist over this difference for it was extremely rare, indeed virtually unheard of, for voters to walk out of the polling booth having exercised only half their franchise. Without doubt this difference is more to do with the differential invalidation by the IEC of votes in the two contests: in a sense, to have any significant difference at all was to admit that one or other total was wrong. The full import of this point is only grasped when one realises that the 93,039 vote difference is actually the product of far larger differences in the nine regions. Table 11.1 shows that the total variance – adding the pluses and minuses – was not 93,039 but 211,247.

These are not insignificant figures: it must be remembered that on a strict quota 49,317 votes was enough to win a seat in the National Assembly, and that to win a seat in one of the regional assemblies one needed, on average, only 46,197 votes. Moreover, just as the variance was greater than it appeared once one examined the regional figures, so it was still greater again once one broke down the regional figures into counting station figures. For example, the total variation in KZN is shown in the table as 93,320 but we have already seen that the difference between national and regional vote totals was 114,629 at the DEC counting station alone.[1] In a general sense the size of variation between these totals is a good, if somewhat rough, measure of how far the conduct of the election departed from reasonable norms. This is not to say that all variance was due to cheating or even to poor administration. Sometimes it was probably just a measure of the ferocity of partisan conflict and the success of parties in getting their opponents' votes invalidated. Sometimes such votes were rightly invalidated because of cheating, but quite possibly some votes were wrongly invalidated. The point remains: a high variance between the two vote totals requires extraneous explanation and is a warning signal that something was amiss.

Table 11.1   Votes cast in the regional as compared
to the national contest, by region

Eastern Cape	+47,012
Eastern Transvaal	+12,092
KwaZulu–Natal	−93,320
North-West	−16,961
Northern Cape	−1,936
Northern Transvaal	−3,792
Orange Free State	−18,447
Gauteng	−14,300
Western Cape	−3,387
Total variance	211,247

By this token, the election was clearly best administered and – as all observer accounts confirm – most free and fair in the Northern Cape and the Western Cape. To be sure, ANC supporters probably tipped the balance in the highly marginal Northern Cape by bussing in voters from the North-West region (where the ANC had votes to spare). But within the rules of the election anyone could vote where they wanted and this tactic was not illegal, even if some regarded it as unfair. Right across the Northern Cape the variance between regional and national votes was tiny, and it was almost as small in the Western Cape. The highest variance there was 0.62% of the 338,337 votes cast at the huge Wynberg counting station (with the difference in votes being expressed as a fraction of the higher of the two vote totals in each case). Even at the Mitchell's Plain counting station, where huge numbers of illiterate squatters voted, the variance was only 0.53%, and at nearby Goodwood, with 154,281 votes, it was only 0.12%.

In the North-West, variances were also acceptably low except at Potchefstroom, where variance reached a striking 6.56% our of 58,048 votes cast, and at Wolmaransstad (30,750 votes), where it reached 9.58%. Differences as large as this cannot be explained save by large-scale invalidation of votes and thus, presumably, irregularities on a significant scale. The Orange Free State had similarly low variances almost everywhere, but several striking exceptions – 4.08% at Odendaalrus, 4.14% in Qwa Qwa, 6.43% in Bethelehem and 8.16% at Botshabelo. The same pattern was visible in both the Eastern and Northern Transvaal, that is variance at 'acceptable' (low) levels in most areas with dramatic hiccups in a few areas, often in the former homelands where poor administration and corruption had become a way of life. In the Eastern Transvaal the largest variances were seen at Witbank (2.86%), Mkobola (3.92%), Moutse (5.35%), Eerstehoek (9.04%), Middleburg (15.79%) and Kamhlushwa (19.02%). In the Northern Transvaal there were notably deviant stations in Sekukhuneland (5.02%), Mhlala (5.03%), Sikgosese (10.46%), Mutale (18.01%) and, most remarkably of all, at the small (22,797 votes) station of Dzanani (34.35%).

The three worst areas from the point of view of variance – and thus the three areas which departed most sharply from acceptable electoral standards – were Gauteng, the Eastern Cape and KwaZulu-Natal. While the overall variance in Gauteng (14,300) seemed acceptably small, in fact this turned out to be the difference between two much larger numbers: analysis by counting station showed a total variance of 104,642 votes. This was, in turn, very largely a tale of two cities, with a variance of 44,821 (3.64%) at the gigantic Johannesburg counting station and 36,531 (5.28%) at Pretoria, with the third largest station, Benoni, showing a 4.6% variance.

The multitude of counting stations in the Eastern Cape, together with the poor quality of administration in much of the region, meant that a considerable number of stations showed above average variance: Lusikisiki (3.4%), Elliotdale (3.66%), Glen Grey (4.4%), Kentani (5.49%), Mt Fletcher (5.6%), Mqandulu (5.72%), St. Mark's (5.78%), Mdantsane (5.84%), Engcobo (6.25%), Butterworth (6.6%), Tsolo (6.79%), Qumbu (8.26%) and Port Elizabeth (8.32%). This variance of over 45,000 votes at Port Elizabeth is striking: there can be no good reason why it should be so high in that urban environment compared to East London (1.08%). Beyond that there was Victoria East (9.29%), Tabankulu (17.1%) and two tiny but truly aberrant stations, Steytlerville (32.4%) and Molteno (42.49%)! All told the total variance in the Eastern Cape was 119,758.

Finally there was KwaZulu-Natal with a total variance of 222,491 votes. Some of the most remarkable figures were in the IFP heartlands of Northern Natal – Nqutu (18.2%), Ubombo (40.3%) and Newcastle (47.62%), but there were also high figures in the violently contested squatter areas near Durban such as Inanda (25.24%), Mapumulo (18.38%) and the ANC stronghold of Camperdown (62.2%). It is quite staggering to record that the vast Indian suburb of Chatsworth (132,643 votes), an area of considerable literacy and sophistication, saw a variance of 43.89%. But most remarkable of all was the case of the tiny station at Mtunzini: 1,065 votes were counted there in the national election but none at all for the provincial contest. Since there were many times more than 1,065 potential voters in the district, it seems certain that many of the national votes, as well as all the provincial votes from this station, simply disappeared.

Who Voted?

In the absence of a voter's roll it is impossible to be certain of turnout, although it was indubitably very high. In his analysis Andrew Reynolds simply takes the national vote (less spoilt ballots) and expresses that as a percentage of the IEC estimates of potential voters in each region. This produces an average turnout figure of 86%, with a low of 80% in KZN and highs of 92% in the Eastern and Northern Cape.[2] While this is reasonable enough (although spoilt ballots should, of course, have been included), it is worth pointing out the discrepancies this method produces when set against the recall of turnout found in the IRI/MPD post-election survey carried out in August–September 1994 by Decision Surveys International.[3]

The figures (shown in table 11.2) do not match up: if the figure in the middle column is higher than that in the first column, the figure in the end column has to be higher than the overall average – and this is not always so. In the present state of knowledge it is not possible to reconcile this data. Very probably, more people recalled voting than actually did. But apart from differential turnout, there is a whole range of factors which could affect these figures: it may be that the census figures (and thus the IEC estimates) were wrong; that large numbers of people crossed regional boundaries to vote; or that the number of votes cast was, in some regions, artificially increased or reduced by fraud or wrongful invalidation.

Table 11.2 Potential voters, actual votes cast and post-election recall

Region	IEC–estimated potential voters (%)	Votes cast as % of total (national) vote	% turnout in DSI post-election survey	% turnout estimated by Reynolds
Gauteng	21.41	21.48	93.4	86
KZN	20.19	19.25	93.6	80
Eastern Cape	14.0	14.58	96.4	92
Western Cape	10.59	10.91	91.1	87
Northern Transvaal	10.07	9.82	97.0	84
North-West	7.77	8.15	94.2	89
Orange Free State	7.2	7.01	92.9	83
Eastern Transvaal	6.84	6.73	92.7	85
Northern Cape	1.93	2.07	96.6	92
Total	100.00	100.00	94.1	86

What is striking is that recalled turnout is 8% higher and considerably more uniform across the country than the Reynolds estimates suggest, and that Reynolds's method suggests that the Northern Transvaal (for example) had one of the lowest turnouts (84%), while actual voter recall put it, at 97%, as the highest of all. Similarly, Reynolds estimates the Western Cape as having an above average turnout while the IRI/MPD survey suggests that turnout was lowest of all there, a finding reinforced by the number of coloureds who say they abstained. Thus while the recall figures may be too high it seems likely that they are the best guide to differential turnout by region.

The IRI/MPD survey found the highest turnout among Xhosa-speakers (96.5%) and the lowest among Afrikaans-speakers (91.3%) – apparently an extraordinary inversion of the old order. However, many of these Afrikaans-speaking abstentionists were coloureds, who voted least of all (88.7%), doubtless as a result of the acute cross-pressures they felt. Pre-election surveys had suggested that the young were the most determined of all to vote, but in the end turnout was lowest among the 18–24s at 87.1%, 95.2% among the 25–34s, 95.5% among the 35–49s and 97.3% for the over-50s. The social group least likely to vote was farmworkers (90.7%) but in the big conurbations squatters were actually more likely (98.7%) to vote than those in formal housing (92.6%). While it must be remembered that the 'politically correct' answer was to say that one had voted, which may have pushed up all our figures, it is also tempting to see the squatter-camp figures as a testament to the power of community/shacklord boss pressures.

But one also has to be impressed by the way in which many of the normal rules of political sociology were stood on their head. One is well used to data showing that in most developed countries the old vote more than the young, the educated more than the uneducated, the middle class more than the working class, the urban rich more than the rural poor, and white more than black. In South Africa in 1994 the old, as we have seen, did vote more than the young, but those with either primary (96%) or no education (95%) outvoted those with high school (92.8%) or tertiary (94.8%) education, the unemployed (94.7%) voted more than the employed (94.3%), kraal-dwellers, typically the poorest of the rural poor, (96.6%) more than big city dwellers (93.5%) and Africans (95.1%) more than whites (92.7%) or Indians (91.8%). These figures reinforce again the sociological uniqueness of the election. It is likely to remain exceptional: as the normal laws of political sociology come into play one should expect dramatic falls in turnout among the less privileged groups.

When DSI asked respondents which party they supported, 3% refused to say and another 1% named parties which did not run in the election. Of those who said they supported a party, 100% of those who supported the Freedom Front claimed to have voted, compared to 73.8% of Conservative Party supporters, suggesting that right-wingers who voted had, by definition, to identify with the FF, the only rightist party to run. But the relatively high figure for CP supporters, despite their party's boycott, shows just how successfully the election pulled people in. Among supporters of the ANC 96.7% claimed to have voted, as did 98.3% of NP supporters, 98.1% of the IFP and 97.9% of the DP. PAC supporters reported a significantly lower (91.9%) turnout, confirming our impression of a relative demobilisation of this electorate in the latter stages of the campaign. For the PAC, bereft of funds and with only the most threadbare organisation, depended almost completely on its young militants to get out the vote – and in the course of the campaign many of these militants became disaffected by what they regarded as their leadership's electoral opportunism. Finally, 79.5% of the supporters of other parties said they had voted. Again, one must caution that some of the figures above may exaggerate the total turnout. None the less, they are evidence of a staggering degree of partisanship, with 96% identifying with one party or another, and an equally remarkable degree of electoral mobilisation. Again, these are the probably unrepeatable hallmarks of a 'founding election'.

Given the complexity of the ballot paper, the fact that most of the electorate were voting for the first time and that many were illiterate, the proportion of spoilt ballots (0.75% in the regional vote, 0.98% in the national vote) was so low as to make one wonder whether tbe IEC vote counters were not somewhat charitable in their interpretation of what 'spoilt' meant. It is also perhaps worth noting that the lowest rate of spoilt papers was in the one-party Eastern Cape (0.45% and 0.61%), only half the levels seen in hotly contested KZN (1.06% and 1.22%). One cannot help but wonder whether it mattered that usually the only party poll-watchers in the Eastern Cape were ANC, while in KZN all the major parties were in attendance – and in sharp contention. But the fact that spoilt ballots were highest of all in the relatively pacific North-West (1.19% and 1.23%) cannot be fitted into such a hypothesis.

Party Fortunes

Even those South Africans who had voted before had had little previous experience of 'split-ticket' voting and most did not avail themselves of it now. This was particularly true of ANC voters, who tended to vote their allegiance with almost no variation between the two contests. Others were less hegemonically party-minded. In general there was a tendency for those parties perceived as having a 'national' vocation – the ANC, NP and IFP – to do better on the national ballot, with significant minorities switching to the DP, FF or PAC at regional level.

Overall the most striking fact was the size and extent of the ANC sweep and the fact that its vote varied relatively little between the regional and national ballots. Undoubtedly, most of its voters saw a vote for the ANC as a matter of principle, even of ideology, though anecdotal evidence suggests that the ANC also benefited considerably from split-ticket voting by supporters of smaller parties, particularly the DP. In the end only the ANC could claim to be a truly national party, taking three-quarters or more of the vote in five regions, half in two more and a third of the vote even in the two regions it lost. So hegemonic were the ambitions of many ANC activists that even this was not wholly acceptable: the Western Cape result was treated as a deviant and somewhat scandalous outcome, explicable only by racist manipulation, while the KZN result was often regarded as simply fraudulent.

The National Party, by contrast, belied its name: its whole centre of gravity now lay in the Northern and Western Cape. Its historic dominance since 1948 has been rooted primarily in the Transvaal. But no more: even in the PWV it got only a quarter of the vote (23.88% and 27.58%). Its best national result after that was, surprisingly, in KZN, while in its old heartlands of the Northern, Eastern and Western Transvaal it was reduced to derisory proportions. It is tempting to see this as a reversal of the Great Trek: Afrikaner power, having expanded northwards from the Cape, is now collapsing back towards it. There is something to this: undoubtedly a steady trickle of white migration to the Cape is in train, reflected in soaring property prices there. But it is not much of an explanation for what is happening to the NP. The NP is becoming predominantly the party of coloureds in the Cape, of Indians in KZN (hence its strength there) and, to a somewhat lesser degree, of the beleaguered urban whites. The NP actually fared better among Indians and coloureds than among whites simply because among whites it suffered competition from the DP, FF, CP and even the IFP; among coloureds and Indians it did not.

The IFP surprised many by polling as strongly as it did – winning KZN and gaining over 10% nationally – with less than a week's campaign. But there was no doubt that the IFP was disappointed by its showing outside KZN. This was particularly true in Gauteng, where the IFP believed it had been robbed by large-scale election fraud: stories of polling stations gaily operating without IFP stickers were legion. But a party which had so obviously shot itself in the foot and, as some would see it, held the country to ransom for its own ends, gained scant sympathy for such complaints. More fundamental was the party's over-reliance on Zulu traditionalist support. Some whites had voted for the IFP as the force most strongly opposed to the ANC, but on the whole the IFP fared badly in that competition in comparison with the NP. More striking still was its failure to win the anti-ANC vote among coloureds and Indians. These communities found it difficult, after all, to vote for the NP, the party of apartheid, and should have been more receptive to a party which did not carry that burden, was not white-led and had a long anti-apartheid record. For the IFP none the less to lose that competition hands down was eloquent testimony to its failure to project itself as more than a Zulu nationalist movement.

Perhaps the most bitter disappointment was felt by the Democratic Party, whose 1.73% (2.76% in the regional elections) was scant reward for more than thirty years of often lonely anti-apartheid struggle. Its leader, Dr Zach de Beer, promptly resigned, thus pre-empting what would doubtless have been a searching inquest into the way he had led the party. Stronger leadership might have helped – many a wistful eye was cast in the direction of the lost leader, Dr Frederick Van Zyl Slabbert – but the DP's problem was more fundamental. It was the voice of liberalism in a conflict between two nationalisms which admitted of little middle ground. On the ground it was deserted by many of its left wing, who wanted to give one of their two votes 'to Mandela', and by far more who bolted towards de Klerk, a safe haven in the storm.

The Freedom Front had reason to be both pleased and disappointed about its result: on the one hand, despite being a new and untried party it gathered in most of the far right vote; on the other hand that bloc itself collapsed as its voters bolted towards the NP just like their DP counterparts, an effect particularly marked in the national ballot. At its peak, the right had commanded 30% of the white electorate and over half the Afrikaner vote, with the NP in 1989 taking around 50% and the DP 20%. But in 1994 the FF seldom achieved that 3:5 ratio with the NP vote. Indeed it did so only in the regional assembly ballots in areas where it might previously have run level with the NP or better – in the Orange Free State, the Northern and Eastern Transvaal and the North-West. In Gauteng, its peak region, where it took 6.17% in the regional ballot (and where more than 40% of the FF's total vote came from), it none the less ran behind the NP almost 4:1.

In the pre-election period almost as much anxiety had been expressed about the reactions of the far right as about the IFP, but in fact (as our pre-election surveys showed) the threat from the right diminished as the election approached. This was almost inevitable: the fire and passion of the right lay in threatening what they would do to prevent a transition to democracy and of promising their followers that they would somehow avert it. This entire posture depended on an unwillingness, often a sheer inability, to believe that the end of white rule was nigh. The closer the election got, the less credible these threats and promises became and the more their followers accepted the inevitable and turned their minds to managing their way through the transition.

The Regions

In general, voters tended to see the election as a two-horse race at national level – and the SABC had certainly helped this tendency by personalising the choice as one between Mandela and de Klerk, with these two alone enjoying the privilege of a US-style 'presidential debate'. Many voters had also failed to understand that a regime of pure PR meant that it was actually very difficult to waste one's vote; instead, many talked of how they should vote NP so as not to waste their vote. In the end such voters achieved their point in as much as they pushed the NP over the 20% line necessary to obtain one of the vice-presidencies. This logic applied less at regional level, so the general pattern of the regional elections was for the smaller parties to do better in these than in the same region's national vote.

During the election Judge Kriegler, chairman of the IEC, complained rather testily at one point that the IEC had relied heavily on census data, which had turned out to be anything but reliable. It is worth noting, however, that the advance allocation of National Assembly seats to the regions, based on that data, turned out to be accurate enough. If, in the light of the actual vote in the regions, one reallocated seats to achieve exact proportionality, the Eastern Transvaal, Orange Free State and KwaZulu-Natal would each have lost one seat, while the Eastern and Western Cape and the North-West would each have gained one.

Eastern Cape

The Eastern Cape delivered over 2.4 million ANC votes in both regional and national contests. This was only slightly less than the ANC received in (the far bigger) Gauteng; that is, the ANC's hope that the Eastern Cape would prove a vast vote bank, pushing its favourite son, Mandela, into office, proved fully justified. Given that Xhosa-speakers always showed up in surveys as the most radical and most enthusiastic ANC supporters, the only real surprise was that the ANC got a higher percentage of the vote in the Northern Transvaal than it did here.

The reasons for this were most apparent at regional level, where all the smaller parties (save the IFP) did better than in voting for the National Assembly. Although the ANC won Port Elizabeth (with 57% of the vote) and East London (with 62%), its position in these two conurbations, with over half a million votes between them, was considerably weaker than in the rest of the region outside them – where it gained 90.14%. The main reason why the ANC did better in the Northern Transvaal is that that region had no comparable conurbations, housing large numbers of whites and coloureds.

The second reason why the ANC did not do even better here was the PAC. In spite of internecine strife and a tendency for its vote to be squeezed by the 'wasted vote' argument, the PAC none the less achieved almost the same absolute vote here as it did in Gauteng, and this was the only province in which it ran third; indeed, in Butterworth, Glen Grey, Flagstaff, Elliotdale and a number of other small country towns, the PAC actually overtook the NP to run second. Like the ANC it did far less well in the two major conurbations, but if those are excluded its vote in the region increases from 1.39% to 2.3%. At the Butterworth, Glen Grey, Mdantsane, Umtata, Kentani and Engcobo counting stations the PAC got over 3% and at St Mark's it got its highest score in the country, 7.97%.

But these were mere blips on an ANC graph. Of the 56 seats in the regional assembly, the ANC won 48, the NP 6 and the DP and PAC one each. Raymond Mhlaba, veteran ANC activist and Robben Islander, became the region's premier.

Western Cape

The Western Cape result was a major disappointment for the ANC. For many young coloured ANC activists the outcome produced a major identity crisis: for years they had campaigned in the happy belief that they represented the feelings of their own community. It was a terrible blow to discover that they were actually quite atypical of the majority, which felt happier with Afrikaner than with African nationalism. In fact, our surveys had consistently forecast such a result. In both the national and regional contests the NP took over half the vote and the ANC a third.

The only place where the ANC ran ahead was at the giant Mitchell's Plain counting station where votes from the Khayelitsha squatter camps were counted, together with those from some of the neighbouring coloured townships. Given the clear 'ethnic census' aspect of the poll, ANC hopes for the whole region depended quite centrally on its vote in this, the only predominantly African area. But even there the result was extremely disappointing for the ANC, for less than 300,000 votes were cast in either contest, with the ANC taking 68.85% in the national and 68.73% in the regional contest. Yet estimates of Khayelitsha's population had generally been around the million mark – and there had been a spate of election rumours of extra busloads of African voters being brought into the area from the Eastern Cape in order to help swing the Western Cape vote. Even if one assumed 40% of the population was below voting age – and the number of single male emigrants there, sending back remittances to the Transkei or Ciskei, probably made that number too high – it should still produce 600,000 votes. Either the population was a lot less than estimated or else turnout had been unexpectedly low.

The poll was also a major disappointment for the PAC, which only scored 2.53% and 3.2% there. In the national contest there were 12,814 spoilt ballots at this station, compared to only 1,361 in the regional contest – and it was clear that virtually all these votes had been lopped off the ANC and PAC totals. A significant section of the PAC leadership had been drawn from the old Western Cape-based Unity Movement and they had, accordingly, nourished large hopes of the Western Cape – and were correspondingly crestfallen when these hopes so entirely failed to materialise. Both their reactions and, to a lesser extent, those of coloured ANC activists, illustrated how completely the years of disenfranchisement had allowed radicals to float free of any real sense of constituency. The final indignity for the PAC was to be overtaken by the African Christian Democratic Party (ACDP). The ACDP got less than a fifth of the PAC's vote at Mitchell's Plain where, as a black party, it might have expected to score best. But it ran comfortably ahead of the PAC in urban Cape Town, Bellville, Simonstown and Wynberg – all predominantly white areas, which suggests that the ACDP may have scooped a large number of domestic servants' votes.

The NP's vote was fairly evenly spread: while it did better among rural than urban coloureds it naturally fared worse in the Cape Pensinsula where Africans were concentrated, the two factors balancing out to some extent. The ANC was more heavily dependent on its vote in the Pensinsula, and particularly on just five of the region's 42 counting stations, Cape, Goodwood, Mitchell's Plain, Kuils River and Wynberg. On average, in the national vote, it scored 41.3% at these five stations, but only 26.5% at the other 37. Outside the Peninsula it did really well only at Knysna, with 38.63%.

The Western Cape was the DP's best region: it took 4.18% of the national vote and 6.64% of the regional vote. Both were miserable scores for a party that incarnated the now-triumphant Cape liberal tradition. Since the NP's score fell 3% between the two polls it seems clear that many regional DP voters voted for de Klerk at national level, but probably many more bolted towards the ANC or NP even at regional level. Mainly it was towards the latter: even in old DP areas like Simonstown and Wynberg, the NP outran the DP by 3:1 or 4:1. The FF experienced a similar fate: even in what had been its strongest areas such as Vredendaal and Oudtshoorn the NP outran it by 15:1 to 20:1 even at regional level.

The NP took 23 of the 42 seats in the regional assembly, the ANC 14, the DP 3, the FF and the ACDP one each, the NP's Hernus Kriel, the former Minister for Law and Order, becoming regional premier.

Northern Cape

The Northern Cape, by far the biggest and most sparsely populated of the nine regions, also witnessed the closest contest of all. It was also the nearest thing to a two-horse race, with the NP and ANC getting over 90% of the vote between them at both national and regional level. Given that the ANC ultimately won 15 of the 30 seats in the regional assembly, the NP 12, the FF 2 and the DP one, not a few politicians cursed the intervention of the PAC, IFP, ACDP and other small parties – but in fact the 1.94% of the vote they garnered between them would have made no difference to the distribution of seats. Both the IFP and PAC actually did worse at regional than national level here – a reversal of the usual pattern, and probably a sign that voters realised how close the local contest would be and did not want to 'waste' their votes in it.

The ANC's better performance here had been predictable enough from our surveys of the Western Cape, showing a much higher level of ANC support among rural coloureds there than among urban coloureds – this despite the stereotypical view that the cities are always move radical than the countryside. But unlike their peers in the Cape Peninsula, rural coloureds did not feel squeezed by a burgeoning African population: for them the spirit of 'liberation' from the Afrikaner farmer or policeman was both more keenly felt and a less nuanced concept. Undoubtedly, this held true among the rural coloureds of the Northern Cape as well and largely explained the result. Thus in a conservative rural area like Namaqualand, which includes virtually only whites and coloureds and no Africans, the ANC could rack up over 38% of the vote in both contests – and such scores were quite typical. But most of all the ANC owed its margin of victory to the mineworkers of Kimberley. Kimberley had a quarter of the voters of the entire region and the ANC scored over 60% in both contests there. It no doubt helped that Manne Dipico, the leader of the ANC list, was a former NUM organiser from Kimberley.

The NP ran ahead in 16 of the Northern Cape's 26 counting stations, winning comfortably in many of the small towns and rural areas. Its biggest vote came in Gordonia, its biggest majority (in percentage terms) in Calvinia – a town which had a Conservative Party mayor until not long ago. This was typical enough: although the FF held on to more of its vote here than anywhere else in the country, it was none the less greatly eroded by the NP's appeal in the crunch. The NP's losing margin in Kimberley of 31,381 votes nearly accounted for the whole ANC margin of victory of 37,387 votes in the entire region.

The DP managed to salvage a seat mainly because of its remaining pull in Kimberley and Namaqualand, As it turned out, the sole DP representative had a crucial vote for the regional premier. She (Ms Ethne Papenfus) did a deal with the ANC whereby she supported Dipico for regional premier, in return for which she obtained the speakership of the regional assembly.

Orange Free State

In the old white parliament the Orange Free State had been the Conservative Party's strongest area but there was little sign of this now, although there was a fair degree of ticket-splitting between the two ballots. In the national contest the FF got just 3.68%, in the regional one 6.03%, dwarfed by the NP (14.53% and 12.59% respectively), not to mention the ANC, which took over three-quarters of the vote in both contests. The pattern followed that seen elsewhere, with the NP and FF scoring mainly in the towns and the ANC swamping everyone in the rural areas. The bolt of right-wing voters towards the NP was so marked that even in the right-wing redoubt of Sasolburg (once captured by the ultra-right Herstigte (Purefied) National Party) the FF was outdistanced 3:2 by the NP in the regional contest and by 7:2 in the national one. All told, the NP received half of all its (national) votes (and the FF 41% of all its votes) in just three towns – Bloemfontein, Welkom and Sasolburg – even though they accounted for only 30% of the electorate. Even so, the ANC won all three towns handsomely. The Welkom results were particularly notable: in both the national and regional contests this was easily the PAC's strongest toe-hold in the OFS, just as it was also the IFP's. But, probably due to the mineworkers' union, this was also the ANC's strongest urban base – and it looks very much as if some voters split their votes between the NP and ANC.

The ANC did particularly well in the old homelands. In Thaba Nchu, the OFS outpost of Bophuthatswana, the ANC got 84.54% of the national vote. Sensationally – indeed, rather suspiciously – Thaba Nchu also rejoiced in the extraordinary fact of experiencing no spoiled ballots whatsoever in either contest: a highly improbable outcome in an education-poor rural area. Similarly, the ANC won 92.7% of the vote in the former Qwa Qwa homeland. This was the PAC's second best region but even so it represented a mere ripple next to the ANC's tidal wave.

The ANC won 24 of the 30 seats in the regional assembly, the NP 4 and the FF 2. The region's ANC forty-six-year-old premier, Patrick 'Terror' Lekota (the name won in a footballing, not a military career), quickly began to win over local white opinion, which was much impressed by his moderation and his championing of the interests of (white) OFS farmers.

North-West

The North-West region was a replica of the OFS, with an overwhelming ANC majority of over 83% in both ballots, the NP trailing at just over 10% in the national ballot and below the 10% line in the regional contest, with the Freedom Front coming in a distant third, though with 50% more votes in the regional ballot than in the national one. Before the election there had been much talk that President Lucas Mangope of Bophuthatswana (the former homeland which constituted most of the North-West region) might head a Christian Democratic party. In the event the coup which ended Mangope's rule shortly before the election also put paid to such notions. Mangope played no part in the election and the African Christian Democratic Party, which ran without his assistance, actually did worse in the North-West than in any other region. Similarly, one could have been forgiven for not realising that this western Transvaal region had once been a bastion of the Conservative Party. Thus the water simply closed over what was probably the second strongest homeland administration, with no visible traces or survivors even left floating on the surface.

The ANC won at every single counting station by very wide margins – at the biggest station, Odi, with 226,000 votes cast, it got over 95%. The FF everywhere trailed the NP, most narrowly in Potchefstroom. Of the NP's vote, 45% (and 55% of the FF vote) came in just three urban centres – Rustenburg, Potchefstroom and Klerksdorp, with the IFP and PAC also picking up several thousand votes apiece there.

The ANC took 26 of the 30 seats in the regional assembly, the NP 3 and the FF one. Popo Molefe, the former UDF activist, became the region's first premier at the age of forty-two.

Eastern Transvaal

Once again, the picture was very much as in the North-West and the OFS – an enormous ANC preponderance, the NP barely scraping 10% in the national ballot and the FF leaping from 1.3% in the national ballot to 5.66% in the regional one. In many counting stations the ANC majorities verged on unanimity – at Kamhlushwa, Mbibana and Nsikazi it got over 97%, and at Moutse, Mathanjana and Mdutjana over 96% of the national vote. The NP (and FF) vote was concentrated at Witbank, Middelburg, the steel town of Highveld Ridge and Nelspruit, while the IFP got 14.5% at Wakkerstroom and 20% at Piet Retief. Even so, these were disappointing results for the IFP given that 27% of the region's population is Zulu-speaking.

Only at Nelspruit did the ANC just fail (with 49.25%) to win a majority of the regional vote – and ironically Nelspruit was chosen as the new region's capital. The ANC gained 25 of the 30 regional assembly seats, the NP 3 and the FF 2, the ANC's youthful Mathews Phosa becoming premier.

Northern Transvaal

The Northern Transvaal, long the stronghold of the Conservative Party, saw the most one-sided election of all, with the ANC winning over 90% of the vote in both ballots. Given the pattern observed elsewhere of particularly huge ANC majorities in the old homelands, it was not surprising to find a vast ANC preponderance in Lebowa and Gazankulu: at Giyani, the old Gazankulu capital, the ANC won over 97% of the 131,000 votes cast in the national ballot, for example. Only in the small mining town of Phalaborwa was there a real contest, with the ANC taking 36% of the regional vote, the FF 30% and the NP 28%. The only other place where the FF ran ahead of the NP was at Ellisras: even in the old CP stamping grounds of Waterberg and Potgietersrus the NP ran ahead of the FF. The locally based Ximoko People's Party failed dismally, getting fewer than 5,000 of the nearly 2 million votes cast. But these were merely ticks on the side of the ANC elephant. More than anywhere else the Northern Transvaal confirmed the impression of the election as merely an 'ethnic census', for there was no doubt that the ANC owed its record scores here simply to the fact that this is the region with the largest (96%) African majority.

The ANC won 38 of the 40 seats in the regional assembly, the NP and FF taking one each. Ngoako Ramathlodi, the new premier, showed immediate sensitivity towards the conservative Afrikaners who had hitherto ruled the region, inviting an FF minister into the regional cabinet even though the NP would have had the better claim.

Gauteng

Gauteng, which produces 60% of South Africa's wealth and also has the largest population, saw a clear ANC win (57.6% of the regional poll, 59.1% of the national one) but a far more competitive political struggle than the rest of the former Transvaal. Not only did seven political parties gain representation in the regional assembly, but racial solidarity in voting was a little less pronounced here than elsewhere. The ANC's score was a good 10% below the level of the African proportion (69%) of Gauteng's population, and in fact the ANC must have gained many white and Indian votes too, so anything up a quarter of the African vote may have escaped the ANC here.[4]

As befits the most sophisticated region, there was a good deal of split-ticket voting, with the smaller parties gaining handily at regional level compared to their scores in the national poll. The DP went from 3% to 5.32%, the FF from 3.68% to 6.17% and the PAC from 1.25% to 1.46%. Only the IFP fell, from 4.13% to 3.66%. But all of these parties were none the less deeply unhappy with their results. The DP not only failed to break out of its white suburban rump but even failed to hold some of that electorate. The FF ran ahead of the NP only at the tiny Heidelberg voting station. Everywhere else it saw its redoubts fall by crushing majorities: even in Pretoria, where it had once held half the municipal council, it was beaten by a more than 2:1 margin by the NP. And the PAC, which had held high hopes of the large Black Consciousness and AZAPO presence in Johannesburg, was chagrined to find that it received under 16,000 votes even at the giant Johannesburg counting station.

The ANC tide reached its high point at the Vanderbijl Park station, where, even in the regional contest, it took 78.7%. But the ANC failed to win a majority at four stations – Germiston, where it was beaten 5:3 by the NP, Randburg (including many affluent suburbs), Roodepoort and Pretoria. This latter is worth remarking on in light of the controversy over the siting of the national capital. Some ANC MPs favoured moving the parliament from Cape Town to Pretoria partly because they disliked being in a town won by the NP. But it has to be pointed out that Pretoria is not ANC territory either – it got only 46% there, against the NP's 31.6%, the FF's 14.4% and the DP's 3.7%. Given the probability of lower African turnout in local elections, it may well be that municipal control of the capital will remain with the 'old white parties'.

The ANC took 50 of the 86 seats in the regional assembly, the NP 21, the FF and DP 5 each, the IFP 3, and the PAC and ACDP one each. The ANC's Tokyo Sexwale became the region's first premier.

KwaZulu–Natal

The KZN result was by far the most contested, the IFP taking 48.59% of the national vote and 50.32% of the regional one. There was, too, a considerable amount of split-ticket balloting, evident in the fact that 15.76% chose the NP at national level but that only 11.21% did so at regional level. Undoubtedly, the motivation of many voters was to choose the strongest anti-ANC force: nationally they conceived that to be the NP, locally the IFP. In addition, a good number of voters were so relieved by the IFP's late entry into the election that they wanted to reward the party with a good showing – and many more doubtless feared the consequences if the IFP lost. For while the ANC successfully positioned itself as the 'party of peace' at the national level, at the regional level many felt that the large number of irreconcilable traditionalists in the IFP camp posed the greatest danger to law and order if the IFP lost, and therefore an IFP vote was the way to vote for peace in KZN.

The ANC had always assumed that its way to victory lay in gaining a thunderous majority among the 49% of the region's population living in the Durban Functional Region (the DFR), and by capitalising on its strength in Pietermaritzburg. This urban vote, together with the bridge-heads the ANC had established down the South Coast, up the North Coast and in the Natal Midlands, would be sufficient to outweigh the IFP majority in Northern Natal. This strategy came apart badly.

First and most fundamentally, the sheer number of votes cast did not bear out the assumption that half the population lived in the DFR. Partly this was because more people voted in rural Natal and KwaZulu than had been expected, but partly it seemed that the DFR population had been over-estimated. Thus while it had been expected that around 1.8 million votes would be cast in the DFR, in the end under 1.25 million were. The large township of Umlazi to the south of Durban had been popularly reckoned to house a million people but in the wake of the election a hurried re-count suggested that 400,000 might be a more likely figure.

Second, the ANC's hegemony within its strongholds turned out to be far less complete than had been imagined. Within Durban the ANC got

only 46.93% of the vote, at Pinetown it got only 44.1%, and in the vast
squatter camps of Inanda, a presumed ANC fief, it was beaten 5:4 by the
IFP. And while it won a clear majority (53.1%) in Pietermaritzburg, this
was neither as large a victory as had been hoped, nor anything like
sufficient to outweigh the IFP majorities in the surrounding rural area.
Overall, of the total DFR vote (in the national contest) the ANC outran
the IFP only by 44.3% to 23.7%. The real area of ANC strength was
not the DFR so much as a narrower corridor between Durban and
Pietermaritzburg (including Camperdown and Pinetown). Of the 1.23
million votes cast in this corridor, the ANC won 50.7% to the IFP's
24.6%, but among the 2.53 million voters in the rest of Natal the IFP ran
ahead by 61.1% to 22.2%. The ANC won over 50% of the vote only in
Pietermaritzburg, Camperdown, Mt Currie, Richmond and Umbumbulu
and dead-heated with the IFP in Port Shepstone, the main South Coast
town.

Third, the IFP was able to rack up enormous majorities in its fiefs. Of
the 123,577 valid votes counted at the Mhlabathini station, for example,
122,304 (99%) were IFP. In the Zululand town of Eshowe the IFP led
the ANC by 78% to 17%; in the Midlands town of Estcourt by 63% to
20%; at the huge Hlabisa station (with 114,528 valid votes) it got 90%; at
Impendle it got 94%; and even in the bitterly contested Ixopo area it ran
ahead of the ANC by 61% to 33%.

Finally, the ANC's lingering hopes of a good showing among KZN's
900,000 Indians were thoroughly dashed. In the largest counting station
in an Indian area, at Chatsworth, the NP took 65.5% to the ANC's
25.5%.

All the figures above apply to the national vote. But, as we have seen,
there were large variations between the regional and national ballots in
KZN. Thus in Durban as a whole the NP won 29.6% on the national
ballot but only 18.8% on the regional one, while the DP increased from
4.3% to 5.4% and the IFP from 15.6% to 25%. In Chatsworth the NP fell
from 64.3% to 43.6% – with nearly 20,000 votes suddenly appearing for
Amichand Rajbansi's Minority Front on the regional ballot. (The extraordinary fact that 29,000 fewer votes were counted as valid in the latter
contest suggests that IEC officials believed that very extensive fraud had
taken place here.)

When one breaks down the KZN result by polling station one is struck
by the fact that in African areas the result was generally unanimous in one
direction or the other. Thus at the Lamontville polling station the ANC
led the IFP by 94% to 4%, and at the Glebelands polling station by 91%
to 7%. That is, much of the toughly contested region of KZN dissolves,
on closer examination, into a patchwork quilt of unchallengeable (and
thus virtually uncontested) territorial redoubts of the IFP or ANC.
Within such areas ticket-splitting was minimal as either side crashed out
a disciplined and identical vote on each ballot. It follows that ticket-

splitting was far more common in Indian areas (as we have seen above) and especially in white areas.

This indeed turns out to be the case if one examines the results by polling station (see table 11.3). While the primary social composition of each polling district has been annotated, it should be noted that at the least a smattering of African domestic servants voted in all the stations below – probably accounting for many of the ANC votes. The trends seem clear. The first three polling districts all previously had a DP majority. This vanished as voters bolted towards the NP on the national ballot and, often, towards the IFP on the regional ballot. Such figures make it clear that even had the old Westminster-style electoral system been retained, the DP would not have won a single seat – certainly not in KZN, perhaps not anywhere.

The Dirkie Uys district contains a large number of Afrikaans-speakers, while the Bellair district is more English-speaking, but it will be seen that this made little difference in 1994. In these lower-class white districts there was even less disposition to vote DP, a stronger tendency to vote

Table 11.3 National and regional results in selected Durban polling stations

	IFP (%)	ANC (%)	DP (%)	NP (%)
Norwegian Hall (Musgrave) (affluent white)				
National	15	10	20	51
Regional	40	10	23	24
Northlands Primary (Durban North) (middle-class white)				
National	16	10	19	51
Regional	33	5	26	30
Westville Civic Centre (Pinetown) (middle-class white and Indian)				
National	16	17	17	45
Regional	35	18	21	23
Dirkie Uys (Bluff) (lower-middle/working-class white)				
National	11	10	4	63
Regional	39	10	5	40
Bellair Primary (Umlazi) (lower-middle-class white)				
National	17	14	5	60
Regional	40	15	5	34

NP in the first place, and an even stronger disposition to switch to the IFP on the regional ballot.

The IFP won 41 of the 81 seats in the regional assembly – a majority it immediately lost through having to provide the Speaker. The ANC took 26 seats, the NP 9, the DP 2, the Minority Front, PAC and ACDP one each. The IFP's Dr Frank Mdlalose become the region's premier and a bitter quarrel immediately commenced as to whether the region's capital should lie in Pietermaritzburg or Ulundi. This was quickly followed by a great falling-out between King Goodwill and Chief Buthelezi, with the former edging towards the ANC. Although the levels of public violence in KZN fell back, the region's politics remained as complex and fractious as ever.

The New Political Sociology of South Africa

There are several ironies in the figures above. The ANC's enormous victory was founded less on the non-racialism that it preached than on the reverse, with the election constituting to a large extent a mere 'ethnic census', a worrying notion not only because of the persistence of such strong racial cleavages but because of the difficulties it presents for the development of a properly competitive multiparty system. Similarly, the fate of the DP, which had also preached non-racialism and a single South Africanism, shows that while this may have become the public rhetoric of the new system, that system's real social dynamics derive from quite different sources. The party which most successfully put together a cross-racial coalition was the NP, historically the party of apartheid – it won majorities of whites, Indians and coloureds and even a fringe of African support.

Second, it can be seen that social class continues to play an inverse role in South African voting behaviour. The ANC, which embodied a classic mix of African populist and socialist impulses, tended to phrase its appeal in terms of what could be achieved for the poorest and most underprivileged, while the IFP took a robustly capitalist approach and embodied far more conservative notions of tradition and hierarchy. Yet there was no doubt that ANC allegiance among Africans increased with education and urbanisation, and that the ANC most decisively won the key battle for the loyalty of rising African elites and the black middle class in general. The IFP electorate, on the other hand, was downwardly biased towards the less literate, more rural and often the poorest electors of all.

This tendency extended systematically into the minority groups as well. The fact that wealthier whites were more prone to liberal and reformist policies than were their lower-middle- and working-class peers has a long history in South Africa and continued to be true in 1994. More white

ANC supporters were to be found in Johannesburg's affluent northern suburbs than in the working-class suburbs to the south, and there was also a clear lower-class bias in support for the FF compared to that for the DP and NP. Within the Indian community the most solidly anti-ANC group was to be found among the working class: it is here that one found the peak vote for the NP (and a fringe for the IFP). Yet to read the Indian press was to get the impression that the Indian world was overwhelmingly pro-ANC, for the only vocally political members of the educated and wealthier Indian elite were the ANC supporters (those who support other parties tended to do so without much open declaration), such was the hegemonic position enjoyed by the ANC minority. Without doubt a good deal of money flowed to the ANC from wealthy Indian business-men, particularly from the Muslim community, and many of the most prominent Indian activists within the ANC were from the (more privi-leged) Muslim community.

A somewhat similar situation existed within the coloured community, with major community leaders such as Professor Jakes Gerwel and Dr Franklin Sonn siding very publicly with the ANC. Again, most of the coloured elite was so vocally pro-ANC that it was possible – just as it was within the Indian community – for ANC activists to believe right up to the election that they were politically representative of their communities. They were, in both cases, heavily disavowed by the vast mass of poorer and less privileged Indians and coloureds. If these communities are to prove politically effective in defending their interests in the new world of South African politics, it will be essential that this glaring gap between each community and its elite should be closed, or at least narrowed. As things stand, the majority within each community is poorly represented where it matters, while Indian and coloured leaders within the ANC are bound to be less effective now that their real lack of constituency has been made so painfully clear.

The leading question posed by the results of the 'founding election' of 1994 is, how can a more competitive party system develop? The answer can only be through a move away from the 'ethnic census' voting of 1994 towards a more non-racial pattern of political choice. In this respect one's attention is immediately caught by the 10% of Africans in the most sophisticated region, Gauteng, who did not vote en bloc along racial lines, and even more by the roughly 25% who did not vote for the ANC. One glimpses the possibility of a future evolution in which a monolithic ANC vote in the countryside remains impermeable, while the ANC vote in the metropolitan areas is subject to the more normal processes of attrition. Should this transpire it would constitute a major change in the movement's centre of gravity. It must be remembered that urban areas were inevitably more open and politically competitive than rural areas, most of which saw no real competitive political campaigning at all. In effect many rural Africans had the impression that there was only really one party to vote for. But in the urban areas far more people followed the election on television, more had access to newspapers, and more were almost inevitably exposed to the posturing and razzamatazz of multiparty electioneering, even though many townships and squatter camps in and around the cities were also no-go areas for most political parties.

The fact that the greatest deviation from straightforward racial voting within the African community took place within Gauteng is thus an encouraging sign – if South Africa is to make a success of its non-racial melting-pot, one must look towards an increasing electoral cross-over of the various racial groups. The fact that non-racial voting was highest in Gauteng, with its functional urbanisation rate of 99.6%, and that it was at its lowest in the Northern Transvaal, with its 12.1% functional urbanisation rate, is fairly striking, as is the fact that Gauteng Africans are the most literate, have the highest incomes and have by far the highest participation rate in the labour force. If South Africa's attempts at reconstruction and development succeed, one must expect more and more of its African population to share the same attributes as their Gauteng peers. That, together with a greater openness and greater political access to political information and competition, could well go a long way to loosening the racial cleavage in South Africa. Meanwhile, at the other end of the spectrum, it is equally striking to see up to 40% of lower-class whites in Durban[5] casting ballots for the IFP. The idea that such large numbers of poor (and even Afrikaans-speaking) whites can happily vote for a black party led by a Zulu chief is itself a remarkable sign of change. And, of course, the bulk of Indians and coloureds voted for parties led either by whites or Africans: Rajbansi's purely Indian appeal got short shrift and, despite much talk, the idea of a separate coloured party never got off the ground.

South Africa is a country of four large conurbations, Johannesburg, Pretoria, Cape Town and Durban. The overwhelming bulk of the country's wealth is produced there, the big companies, the trade unions, most universities and all media and communications are centralised there, and a large proportion of the population lives there. Yet the oddity is that Afrikaner nationalism never really established its hegemony in three of these four centres: in all save Pretoria, the more liberal English-speaking business world remained the dominant cultural (and usually the political) reality. Even after decades in power much of the strength of Afrikaner nationalism still derived from its rural and small-town roots.

To a rather lesser, though still significant, degree the same is true now. Nationally, the ANC won 62.65% of the vote but only in East London did it achieve such a figure (62%) in an urban environment. Even in Johannesburg, which most of the ANC elite consider to be their natural base, the party ran behind (with 58%) its average level. In Port Elizabeth it won 57%, and it was actually a minority in Durban (47%) and Pretoria (46%), while it lost in Cape Town so badly that many felt this was a reason to move parliament away. One should not overstress this point: these are still large percentages and the ANC is the largest single party in every city save Cape Town. And, of course, it may be that sheer demographic growth of the African population will be sufficient for even a somewhat eroded 'ethnic census' cleavage to ensure mountainous ANC majorities for years ahead. In the shorter term it remains the case that within the great conurbations the cultural predominance of the white and Indian commercial world remains almost unchallenged, whatever the election result.

All analysis of the results is, however, clouded by objections that the elections were so imperfectly managed and administered, and that cheating of one sort or another was so common, that the results may not reflect reality. Alas, even well after the tumult and euphoria of the founding election had died down, the great question that still remains is, how far were they really free and fair? It is to that question we now turn.

Notes

1   See table 10.1 in the previous chapter.
2   Andrew Reynolds (ed.), *Election '94 South Africa* (Cape Town: David Philip, 1994), p. 187.
3   'Tabular report of the findings of a study of social needs and attitudes in the post-election South Africa', 1994. This survey, carried out for the International Republican Institute in conjunction with the Institute for Multi-Party Democracy, had a large stratified probability sample of 4,003 voters. I have given its turnout figures to one decimal point but it should be realised that, even with such a large sample, such accuracy is tendentious. It is, none the less, the best we have.
4   Some of these African votes were cast for the IFP. It is a moot point as to whether this should count as racial voting too.
5   See table 11.3, p. 318.

TWELVE

How Free? How Fair?

R. W. Johnson

The ANC cheated, the IFP cheated. It was free and fair.
Resident of Imbali, Natal.

We expect that in some cases the numbers [of votes] will not balance. We are not running a fast food operation here.
Brian Gould, IEC International Commissioner.

For 'reasons of state' South Africans have been required to subscribe to the latest national myth, namely that the elections were 'substantially free and fair'. They were nothing of the kind and hardly any of the sanctimonious foreign observers who fell about themselves to declare it so would for one moment have accepted the validity of an election subject to such flaws in their own country.
Professor David Welsh, University of Cape Town.

THE GREAT QUESTION ABOUT the election remains that of how free and fair it really was. Clearly, there were many imperfections in the electoral process and a special question hung over the outcome in KwaZulu-Natal. Everywhere else in the country the final outcome was very close to that foreshadowed in our opinion surveys, but in the latter case it was radically different. Either our surveys were faulty; or there was a huge swing of opinion consequent on the IFP's entry into the election; or else the election there was fraudulent on a truly massive scale. Beyond even that, however, there was the question of how well or badly democracy in South Africa had been launched and what, in the light of the election, were the prospects for the continuing process of democratic transformation in South Africa.

The IEC Report

In October 1994 the IEC released its long-awaited report[1] on the elections amidst a rancorous dispute occasioned by the release by Judge Kriegler, Chairman of the IEC, of correspondence with the NP and DP.[2] Faced with voluminous reports of electoral fraud and their own disappointing scores, these parties had both concluded that they were being penalised by the large-scale 'manufacture' of fraudulent ballots (that is, by the ANC and IFP) which had the result of shrinking the proportionate share of all the smaller parties. Both parties based their claims on the failure of the IEC to reconcile ballot boxes with supporting paperwork from polling stations – a sensitive issue for Kriegler, for they were, in effect, claiming that his ruling against the need for such reconciliation had resulted in electoral fraud on such a scale as to jeopardise the overall freeness and fairness of the election. Indeed, the DP threatened court action if 1.47 million votes were not struck out as invalid. The NP made the same point but demanded the scrapping of 950,000 votes initially and then a further 723,000 to bring national and regional totals into line. The parties could make only rough estimates of the extent of the fraud they believed had occurred and thus suggested round number reductions of 100,000 votes here or 200,000 votes there. Interestingly, the DP and NP both agreed that there had been massive fraud in Transkei (where both suggested a 250,000 vote reduction) and in KaNgwane and KwaNdebele (where both asked for a 100,000 vote reduction), in Bophthatswana (where the DP wanted another 120,000 votes to be declared invalid, the NP only 100,000) and in Lebowa, Gazankulu and Venda (where the NP wanted to invalidate an extra 300,000 votes, the DP only 200,000). Both parties also agreed that there had been substantial fraud in Soweto, but the DP added Katlehong, Natalspruit, Atteridgeville and Soshanguve to their list as well. All these areas were ANC strongholds, so in effect both the NP and DP were alleging very large-scale cheating specifically by the ANC.

More striking was the fact that the DP also believed that substantial fraud had taken place in Mitchell's Plain/Khayelitsha (where they wanted a 100,000 vote reduction). Again, this meant pointing a finger at the ANC – but the NP, who as the ANC's chief rival in the Cape would presumably have been a major victim of such fraud, made no such claim. Similarly, the DP asked that 300,000 votes should be declared invalid in KwaZulu-Natal, but the NP made no mention of irregularities there. One can only conclude that the NP did not wish to affront the IFP by alleging fraud against it, and was happy enough to see the IFP win KZN anyway. For the NP was happy enough to allege fraud against the ANC everywhere else, but it could hardly make such allegations in KZN without pointing a finger at the IFP too.

Judge Kriegler obtained the backing of the IEC in resisting the DP and NP objections. Effectively, the IEC pushed ahead with the count and the two parties finally backed down rather than challenge the legitimacy of the entire election exercise. The strength of the DP/NP case was, however, implicitly admitted in the IEC report, particularly as regards the over-issue of temporary voters' cards (TVCs). All told, 3,557,727 of these were issued, of which nearly 1.5 million were issued in a virtually uncontrolled flood in the four days of 25–9 April when the IEC cut corners in its panic to ensure that no one should be disenfranchised. This led to large opportunities for fraud. As the IEC report commented, 'there can be little doubt that abuses of the system for the issuing of TVCs occurred on a substantial scale.' The report spoke of IEC data (not released) which indicated that abuses were particularly prevalent 'in remote areas of Transkei and KwaZulu where a single political party controlled the administrative structures'.[3] In effect this meant pointing the finger at both the IFP and ANC for fraudulent practices.

The weakness of the DP/NP case was, however, that they could not easily point to specific ballot papers or boxes which they believed to be fraudulent. This was why both parties phrased their demands not in a precise number of fraudulent boxes or ballot papers to be invalidated but in round-figure global estimates. Unsurprisingly, the IEC found such rough and ready estimates unacceptable. The DP and NP simply wanted *any* 250,000 votes subtracted in the Transkei, for example, without regard to whether this invalidation mixed valid and fraudulent votes: from their point of view any such reduction would be bound to push up their own percentage of the vote.

In the end the Commission found only one clear-cut case of electoral fraud, at Lady Frere in the Eastern Cape, where thirty ballot boxes had clearly been forcibly opened and tampered with. Although the IEC did not say so, this could only have been a fraud conducted in the interests of the ANC. Since the votes from these boxes had already been counted and there was no way of identifying them, the IEC decided simply to deduct 50,000 votes from both the regional and national vote totals in the Eastern Cape, the losses being spread among all parties proportionate to their vote. Since this left the relative party standings exactly as they were, it had no impact at all on the distribution of regional seats or on the region's share of the national seats. Even at the level of the 200-member national list this alteration was too small to effect any change. On the other hand, by making such a crude round-figure deduction in just the way the NP and DP had been urging, the IEC effectively undermined its own case against the corrective measures urged by these parties.

Judge Kriegler, in resisting the DP/NP proposals, angrily accused the NP of making 'improper' suggestions which would have been tantamount to vote tampering, and argued that to adjust the voting figures (in the way the IEC had already done) would be 'a perversion of the will of the electorate'. The parties reacted with fury: their proposals had been aimed at rectifying what they believed to be large-scale electoral fraud and yet now it was they who stood accused of attempted vote tampering. Once more – and this at a public press conference – Kriegler had to admit that he had acted with an entire lack of judgement and now had to swallow his words. The two parties, he now said, had acted in an 'astute' fashion and it would be quite wrong to say that they had been trying to pervert the result. He even averred that he had never spoken of 'tampering with the result' and nor had he changed his mind. When his letter with that phrase was read to him he had to admit that he had indeed changed his mind. Why had he called a press conference to repudiate the person who had leaked his correspondence with the DP and NP to the press, when in fact he was that person himself? And so it went on. The denouement was complete. Inevitably, Kriegler's appointment to the Constitutional Court was greeted with much cynical comment.

The row over the DP/NP proposals further strengthened the popular impression that the elections had been less than fully free and fair. The revelation that party bargaining had taken place over millions of votes was shocking enough and the fact that no bargain had actually been struck was lost in the mêlée caused when the IEC chairman, no less, flung around accusations of attempted vote tampering. The fact that the DP had thought that there were 1.47 million fraudulent votes threw the event into particularly sharp focus, for the DP's long record of principled opposition meant that it could hardly be accused of being a bad loser, and its reputation for fairness was widely accepted.

Such anxieties were hardly assuaged by the swift conclusion of the Commonwealth and Organization of African Unity (OAU) observer teams that the elections had been free and fair. Such conclusions carried more weight outside South Africa than within it, where it had always been assumed that this had been the preordained function of such groups anyway. Nor could the IEC report do much to still the cynicism of much popular reaction. After all, had not the IEC pumped out advance propaganda on television simply asserting that the election would be free and fair? How could it now be the body to sit in judgement as to whether it had really been free and fair – particularly since this involved passing a judgement on the role of the IEC itself? In any case, the IEC's advance publicity had repeatedly assured the electorate that all they had to do was roll up to vote: the IEC was fully prepared. 'We are ready: are you?' ran the TV ad. When this transpired to be anything but true, the effect was to spread distrust of whatever the IEC said, an impression hardly weakened by Kriegler's Reagan-like propensity to 'mis-speak'.

The overall conclusion of the IEC report was that, although various parties had lodged complaints, 'not a single voting irregularity which was material to the certification of the results of the elections was established. The IEC's certification of the voting process as substantially free and fair certainly corresponded with the sentiments of the electorate at large and was ultimately accepted by all major political parties.'[4] This was, however, a less impressive statement than it sounds. To say that the majority believed that the election was free and fair was to do little more than record that the ANC majority believed their victory was legitimate. More remarkable was the large number, including many of the country's educated opinion-makers, who retained persistent doubts as to the fairness of the electoral process. Similarly, the statement that no material voting irregularity was established was not only contradicted by the IEC's admission of the large-scale abuse of TVCs, but sat ill with the fact that the IEC Investigations and Prosecutions Department, charged with pursuing such irregularities, had collapsed completely well before the complaints of the various parties could be properly investigated.

Moreover, the report also admitted that 'at some voting stations in areas under the control of particular parties, intimidation, or at least vigorous persuasion, was present.' As the Commonwealth Observer Group (COG) pointed out, IEC officials were often intimidated themselves, especially when it came to issuing temporary voters' cards to hordes of 'obviously under-aged' youths who might well use violence if they didn't get them. COG observers approached IEC personnel they saw giving out clearly fraudulent TVCs and were told that IEC officials 'feared for their lives and property if they did not allow these youths to proceed'.[5]

This highly material fact was omitted from the IEC's own report, but even the admission that intimidation took place at some polling stations caused some eyebrows to be raised. After all, there were twenty-six IEC officials at every polling station with the ability to call on the army and police: they were there to prevent just such practices and to close the station if they could not. In practice, however, the IEC would have found this latter course politically impossible, which meant that they would, in the last analysis, tolerate intimidation. This political imperative worked at every level of the election: any irregularity was always more likely to be swept under the carpet in the interests of the greater need that 'the show must go on' or of 'national reconciliation'.

And, of course, each concession simply placed operations on a new plateau, where a fresh set of pressures would arise, requiring a new set of concessions. Thus, for example, the IEC gave way to ANC/Transkei pressure to set up no fewer than 2,612 polling stations in the Eastern Cape, a number far exceeding those indicated by demographics. This meant 'a late, sharp skewing in the national distribution of voting materials, leaving low-density population areas vastly over-supplied at the expense of higher density areas, which subsequently experienced acute shortages.'[6] This in turn forced all manner of other rule-breaking concessions in order to retain strained local good will in these 'high-density' areas. It also meant having to accept lower quality, one-party and untrained staff to man the extra Eastern Cape polling stations, which in turn resulted in more rule-breaking concessions to political bias, possible intimidation and the mechanics of counting. With so many of the home-lands outside the Eastern Cape now bereft of voting materials, an extra day's voting for six of these homelands had to be conceded, which thus broke the principle of a single national election. And so on and on.

A high poll among South Africans living overseas had been anticipated in the 187 polling stations abroad, but in fact only 96,268 voted out of an estimated émigré electorate of 428,461. More serious were the deficiencies in the 'special voting' on 26 April. The IEC had to admit that disorganisation had been so bad that many enfranchised voters were thereby deprived of the opportunity to vote – though it gratuitously added that 'there is no evidence to suggest that their disenfranchisement materially affected the outcome.' This was to take self-defence beyond the bounds of the acceptable, for it was quite impossible to say whether such votes might have had the 'material affect' of transferring seats from one party to another. But it was also an insensitive argument to make in a society which had for so long rested on disenfranchisement.

But the most dramatic impediment to free and fair elections was the fact that, as the HSRC had shown, there were no fewer than 165 no-go zones of exclusive one-party dominance, distributed all round the country save in the Northern Cape.[7] Since these zones included many populous townships and squatter camps, this actually meant that most political parties could not gain access to campaign freely among a very large proportion of the population. There were three main culprits: conserva-tive white farmers unwilling to allow 'agitators' (that is, ANC or PAC campaigners) on to their property to canvass their workforce; IFP chiefs and indunas who made much of rural KZN a one-party closed shop; and the ANC-aligned civics and street committees which set out with the publicly declared intention of preventing free campaigning in their areas. Since the ANC was the biggest party, with the largest geographical reach, this meant that its supporters were also the chief offenders in creating such no-go areas, a fact which infuriated its opponents when placed alongside the ANC's claim to be the party of liberation, the Freedom Charter and a 'human rights culture'.

To be sure, no party openly supported the prevention of free cam-paigning and all maintained 'deniability' on this issue. In practice they bore a degree of real responsibility for it, if only by their tolerance of such anti-democratic practices among their supporters. Thus, for example, Mr Dan Mofokeng of SANCO (the South African National Civics' Organ-isation), while running as an ANC candidate, openly declared that it was a SANCO objective to prevent free campaigning in areas under its control. Not only was Mr Mofokeng not disciplined by the ANC but he was promoted to the post of Minister for Housing in the Gauteng regional government. Similarly, the IFP and FF made no move to discipline party members who prevented canvassing by other parties in 'their' areas.

The existence of such numerous and extensive no-go zones was clearly the most serious challenge to free and fair elections and thus the greatest challenge to the IEC – which had, however, no means of enforcing its will in such areas. Of the 2,408 complaints received by the IEC Investigations Division relating to the campaign period, no less than two-thirds concerned the frustrated access to no-go areas for parties, monitors or voter educators, and a large proportion of the remainder concerned violence or intimidation occurring at public meetings when parties attempted to brave the no-go veto of locally dominant parties.

The IEC report took the view that it would have been 'unrealistic to expect wholly free and fair electioneering',[8] but wished, none the less, to insist that not only the election but even the campaign had been substantially free and fair. In order to do this, it argued that while the DP and NP had to stay out of black townships and homelands, the ANC had stayed away from white farms, and none of the three of them had tried to campaign in rural KwaZulu. In spite of this, it explained:

> it does not follow that such acceptance of the reality of no-go zones had any effect on the outcome of the elections. On the contrary, there is reason to believe that the political parties acted wisely in not wasting their efforts on lost causes. Political parties generally concentrate on persuading 'undecideds' and getting their faithful to the polls. Very few of either category are to be found for opposition parties in no-go zones.

Moreover, the report went on, the election had been pretty much an ethnic census. Given that voting had been so strictly along racial lines, 'It is highly questionable whether a greater degree of openness in electioneering would have had a significant effect on that broad pattern. Indeed, the two major competitors, the ANC and the NP, tended to concentrate their major efforts in areas where they enjoyed significant support.' This left the relatively minor fact, the report continued, that the DP, and to a lesser extent the NP, had performed less well than they had hoped among the non-white intelligentsia, and this may have been due to their 'inability adequately to reach [their] target areas'.[9]

While there was a certain crude realism to such sentiments, they shed no credit on the IEC – indeed, there is little doubt that they are quite incompatible with the development of a democratic political culture in South Africa. For the IEC to make such assumptions about the likely wishes of voters who were actually deprived of choice was not only beyond the proper competence and function of the IEC, but was uncomfortably reminiscent of the type of reasoning which became all too familiar to South Africans in the apartheid era. To reason that people who suffer a deprivation of political choice are anyway probably disposed in favour of those who deprive them of choice is precisely the type of *baaskap* logic which rightly infuriated critics of apartheid down the years. Similarly, to praise parties for acting 'wisely' for failing to campaign in no-go zones seems almost to make a virtue out of their intimidation.

It was also curious to see the IEC confidently asserting that there were very few opposition or undecided voters in the no-go zones. The whole point of such zones (as our own surveys here have again revealed) is that it was precisely in such areas that political choice was at its most constrained. It is impossible to treat the political opinions of those unfortunate enough to live in such areas as if their allegiance was the product of democratic choice; impossible, indeed, to know what these people's real and secret feelings might be. It was perhaps even more extraordinary to see the IEC calmly accepting the strength of the ethnic and racial cleavages as so fixed a reality as to make the prevention of free political activity an almost acceptably insignificant factor. Operation Access, the scheme through which the IEC sought to counteract no-go zones, was one of the most creative and worthwhile things the IEC did – and yet the arguments above can only undermine the weight attached to such initiatives.

Finally, the possibility remains – one must choose one's words with care – that the election result *was* to some extent the 'negotiated' result of popular report. After the election, rumours of such a negotiation were, as we have seen, rife in political circles and the Afrikaans Sunday paper *Rapport* went so far as to assert[10] that just before the election President de Klerk had assured another senior NP leader that an agreement had been reached in advance that the ANC would not get the two-thirds majority required for it to be able to amend the constitution unilaterally. It is difficult to imagine the terms of such an agreement, or between exactly which parties it might have been reached, but there is certainly no doubting the degree to which the NP's leaders and managers were preoccupied with the possibility of a two-thirds ANC majority and how, if it occurred, the NP should react to such an eventuality. As voting got under way, NP headquarters were deluged with reports of large-scale electoral fraud and of busloads of people driving around to polling stations where they could vote over and over again because of the breakdown of vote verification procedures. On the advice of its lawyers the NP gathered large numbers of affidavits attesting to such malpractice – sufficient, its lawyers believed, to substantiate a charge of large-scale fraud.

As the count began, the results from the cities, where the ANC was relatively weaker, tended to come in first; the longer the count went on, so the ANC's percentage mounted steadily as the rural vote came in. At this stage we must mention a report, stemming from high-level sources within the NP, which provides a coherent, though unsubstantiated, framework for the notion of a 'negotiated result'. When counting reached the half-way stage, NP officials approached Judge Kriegler with the demand that the irregularities they had documented should be rectified before a final result was declared: they felt confident that had the election been conducted rigorously by the rules the NP's vote would have been at least 25 per cent and that the election was being jeopardised by large-scale fraud. Kriegler reportedly said that he did not wish to rule on this but asked the NP to come to an accommodation with the ANC. The ANC secretary-general, Ramaphosa, then reportedly consulted with his party colleagues, but came back with a refusal to deal. As the ANC's percentage of the vote crept steadily up to over 65 per cent, further meetings took place. At this stage the NP made it clear to the ANC that it was not prepared to see an ANC two-thirds majority obtained by what it regarded as fraudulent means. Rather than accept that, it would go to court to secure an interdict declaring the election invalid in light of the multiple abuses detailed in its affidavits. The NP's officers, in making this threat, were reportedly well aware that to have the election thus set aside – or even to declare to its electorate that it regarded the result as illegitimate – would be likely to trigger large-scale violence, possibly even producing a descent into civil war.

The apparent result of this threat was to put the election count on hold: certainly it is true that at this stage there occurred an otherwise unexplained period of around forty-eight hours in which no further results were declared and the vote totals stood still. Then came the final result, with the ANC's percentage suddenly dropping to 62.65 per cent. In order to bring the party's total down to this level from the 65.5 per cent it had stood at previously must have involved a reduction of some 560,000 votes – or of over 785,000 votes had the ANC achieved the magic two-thirds figure towards which it had seemed to be heading. The final result, according to this account, was thus at least partially bargained, though the exact process by which this sudden fall in the ANC vote was achieved remains unexplained – presumably the answer lies in the large numbers of votes invalidated, which in turn account for the big differences we have noted between the national and regional vote totals.

Other accounts suggest that the bargaining of the result by the parties was made possible essentially by the very large numbers of disputed votes, especially in the Eastern Cape and in KwaZulu-Natal. Effectively, by either withdrawing or maintaining their demands for the invalidation of these votes the parties were able to move the vote totals up and down. It is clear from the calculations made above that very large numbers of votes indeed must have been in question so the margin of manipulation they allowed was quite broad. One of the greatest deficiencies of the IEC Report was its decision not to reveal how many votes had been invalidated – a decision which can only have been political and which has, as a result, only given greater currency to unofficial accounts such as the one above attributed to the NP. It is important to say that while the account above seems plausible – and would support both a number of phenomena that are otherwise difficult to explain and also the plethora of rumours of a 'deal' – the sources within the NP who disclosed this account were not willing to be named and it was not possible to corroborate their account with matching accounts from other sources.[11] This account throws an interesting light on President Mandela's immediate comment after the result that he was quite relieved that the ANC had not achieved a two-thirds majority. At the time this was taken as a comment on the fact that a two-thirds ANC majority might have had a panicking effect on racial minorities and possibly on Mandela's own greater vulnerability to pressure from the ANC's left in the absence of any need to take other parties into account. But it may also be that Mandela was reflecting on the nightmarish situation which would have ensued had the final results come under strong legal challenge.

Further – and somewhat damning – criticism of the electoral process came from the European Union's observer mission, the EU Election Unit. Although it had agreed a joint press statement with the other international observer missions saying it felt the elections had been free, the mission conspicuously refrained from saying the elections had been fair.[12] Although the EU Report was dated 27 May 1994, the European Commission apparently decided not to publish it, perhaps because of the embarrassment its strictures might have caused.[13] Word of its criticisms leaked out in South Africa only a year later, producing a clamour for copies which the EU refused.

Although the EU Election Unit was well aware of the practical difficulties faced by the IEC, it stated baldly that 'the organisation and management of the voting fell short of what South Africans as well as foreigners expected from a country respected for its efficiency'.[14] In part this was due to poor preparation: an EU survey in the final fortnight before the election found 9% of all voting stations unprepared, with the number rising to 13% in KZN, 15% in Gauteng and 16% in the OFS. More specifically,

- 19% of voting stations surveyed had no electricity, with the figure rising to 29% in KZN, 45% in the Eastern Cape and 57% in the Northern Transvaal;

- 24% of stations had no telephone, with the figure rising to 33% in KZN and the Northern Cape, 36% in the Northern Transvaal and 47% in the Eastern Cape;

- 7% had no toilets (an important consideration given the long voting queues), the figure rising to 14% in the Northern Transvaal and 15% in KZN;

- 38% had no medical services, the figure rising to 44% in the Northern Cape and the OFS, 51% in KZN and 71% in the Eastern Cape;

- 5% had not selected training officers (to train polling officials), the figure rising to 11% in the Northern Cape;

- 14% had not trained their voting officer, the figure rising to 21% in KZN, 28% in the Northern Cape and 36% in the OFS;

- in 20% party agents had not yet been appointed, the figure rising to 30% in the Eastern Cape and 65% in KZN.[15]

In addition, 6% of voting stations had not appointed monitors and 7% had not even trained them. The fact that KZN featured prominently in these figures was not surprising, given the last minute nature of its arrangements; elsewhere there was less excuse.

During the actual voting the EU Unit found that 8% of voting stations did not have sufficient voting equipment, including 14% in KZN, 16% in the Eastern Cape and 17% in the Northern Transvaal. 17% of voting stations surveyed suffered from a lack of voting materials (ballot papers, etc.) – the figure rising to 24% in KZN and 48% in the Northern Transvaal. 10% of voting stations did not respect official voting procedures (18% in KZN), and 28% failed to perform the required weapons check (including 41% in Gauteng and 34% in the Northern and Eastern Transvaal). The Unit then listed the problems experienced at voting stations, noting, somewhat drily, that 'the IEC's reaction to these problems was to change the rules'.[16]

But the EU Unit's strongest criticisms were reserved for the counting process. It found that in 17% of counting stations, staff and facilities were inadequate, the figure rising to 24% in the Eastern Cape (the UN's estimate here was 28%) and in the Northern Transvaal (UN: 26%). The Unit stressed the necessity of ballot boxes being reconciled and was dismayed that the IEC had allowed the reconciliation process to be abandoned after a single day. Overall, it found that 14% of voting stations (the UN said 17%) had not adhered to reconciliation procedures, the figure rising to 22% in the Eastern Cape (UN: 39%) and Western Cape (UN: 15%) and to 26% in KZN (UN: 41%).

The Unit also believed that it had been a major mistake not to count the votes either in the voting stations or at least as near as possible to them: a great deal of international experience suggested that this was desirable and yet 'this experience was not taken into account . . . there were major problems as a result. The larger a counting station was, the greater the chaos.'[17] The Unit observed that while many ballot boxes were improperly sealed with Inkatha stickers, such stickers had been sorely lacking during the voting itself.

There were harsh words for the 'unprofessional' conduct of the media, especially the SATV, which ruminated at length upon the results when almost no data were to hand, when the geographical origins of the votes cast were unknown, and when no serious analysis of trends was possible. This could well have had dire effects, the Unit warned, in raising or depressing the expectations of activists in an already overheated climate.[18] But the strongest criticism of all was reserved for the way the IEC controlled the counting process so as to make it completely impenetrable and opaque. The Unit clearly felt outraged that no international observers had been allowed to be present at the crucial stage of the count when party representatives negotiated over disputed ballots. In effect both the electorate and the world in general were simply left to guess at the way the final result was achieved, for the IEC published merely the gross results for the nine regions. Astonishingly, no break-down of the figures at any lower level was made available until many months after the election – and even then was available only to those who took special steps to secure them from the IEC. The EU Unit was reduced to guessing that 'the number of spoilt votes announced being extremely low, an agreement on recognising disputed votes must have been concluded'. It was informed by IEC officials that party officials had negotiated disputed ballots, but that was all it knew. Hence the Unit's damning final summary:

> Whilst the final results may be plausible, sheer plausibility is not satisfactory for observers. Since the election results have not yet been presented in sufficient detail it is not possible to assess to what extent the result is not only plausible but correct and thus fair.

> It is regrettable that an election, which was highly commendable as far as voter turnout and voter behaviour, should have been flawed first by inadequate logistics and then – even worse – by a non-transparent process of dispute settling . . .

> There is no doubt that the elections have been free. Due to the shortcomings of the voting and counting procedures, it cannot be ascertained whether they have been fair to all individual voters until the IEC publishes detailed results and, more importantly, explains the dispute settlement procedure . . .[19]

There was no doubting the force and validity of these criticisms. It is only with the publication of this volume that the detailed results are being made generally available. The way in which the final result was negotiated remains unexplained, and thus a subject for damaging rumour and speculation. In a country where social and political peace depends upon a respect for all substantial minorities, it was literally dangerous to life and limb to so shroud the electoral results in mystery that it was possible for one party to claim that the votes gained by others were so fraudulent that effectively they did not have constituencies which needed to be respected.

Such difficulties were perfectly foreseeable even at the time of the count. There seems little doubt that the final voting figures were at least to some extent negotiated; certainly they must be accepted as incorporating a degree of variance and perhaps even to be mere approximations. None the less, there seems little doubt that in a crude sense the election did represent the will of the people. For all the imperfections and irregularities in the ballot, it seems beyond dispute that the most popular party, the ANC, got the most votes; that the NP was truly the second most popular party; and that the IFP came a genuine third. And although the DP and PAC both made angry complaints of election irregularities, the stunned and somewhat subdued reaction of both parties left no doubt that they accepted the reality of their own poor performance. Moreover, with one exception, the results corresponded fairly closely to the opinion polls, and in the end all parties accepted the results. The exception was, once again, KwaZulu-Natal. Here the result diverged widely from our pre-election surveys, and although the KZN region of the ANC initially accepted the result, in the weeks following the election they found it impossible to maintain this stance and announced they were going to contest the election's validity in court.[20] Only extreme pressure from the ANC's national leadership finally led them to withdraw from legal action. Even so, the bitter conviction remained among many ANC activists in KZN that the election in the region had been stolen from them by IFP fraud on a colossal scale.

This was a unique claim. It was common ground that there had been considerable electoral fraud in, for example, the Eastern Cape and Gauteng – but no one believed that such irregularities would have overturned the large ANC victories there. And unhappy though ANC activists in the Western Cape were, they did not challenge the validity of the NP's victory there. But KwaZulu-Natal was different. In the weeks following the election a huge row developed over a land deal whereby, on the eve of the election, 1.2 million hectares – or 95 per cent of the old KwaZulu bantustan – were made over to a trust under King Goodwill Zwelethini. The *Weekly Mail* led the way in suggesting that this 'highly secretive deal' had been part of a corrupt bargain and quoted ANC leaders in KZN, the ANC Minister of Lands, Derek Hanekom, and the ANC Secretary-General, Cyril Ramaphosa, all expressing shock and indignation over the deal.[21]

In fact the land deal had been transacted by ANC, IFP and NP representatives and was the key to reassuring Zulu traditionalists that the old method of land allocation by the king could continue. Those who had brokered the deal were amazed by the fuss, since from the beginning it had been at the heart of negotiations to bring the IFP into the election.[22] Ramaphosa himself had been part of the negotiations, as had Joe Slovo and Mac Maharaj, and the deal as a whole had been accepted by Mandela. Immediately the cabinet met after the election Mandela accepted that there was nothing to query in the deal and the matter disappeared from view. The affair none the less strengthened the popular notion that the election in KZN had been part of a large and corrupt bargain.

But KwaZulu-Natal was unique in that the election outcome there was itself disputed. Given that the region contained almost a quarter of the total electorate and was the only place where ANC hegemony over the African vote was contested head-on, clearly the answer to the whole question of 'how free, how fair?' depends centrally on how one regards the KwaZulu-Natal result.

How Fair was the Result in KwaZulu-Natal?

All the parties made complaints about irregularities in KwaZulu-Natal, the DP asking, as we have seen, for the cancellation of 300,000 votes there. But the strongest, and politically most significant, claims came from the ANC and IFP.

The ANC case

The ANC had many heads of complaint. The first was simply the impossibility of free access to most of the KwaZulu rural areas. Of the 165 no-go zones the IEC delineated around the country (on data provided by the HSRC), 79 were in this region.[23] This meant that around half of the region's population were under the hegemonic control of the IFP and its chiefs and indunas. Several hundred IFP leaders and activists had been killed in a campaign of assassination generally assumed to be the work of ANC activists, and such hostilities were fully reciprocated. In the period before the IFP came into the election even voter educators – and even members of other parties – were risking their lives by going into such areas. Six voter education workers were killed at Ndwedwe, while thirteen youths preparing a session on voter education in the Creighton district of Southern Natal were also butchered. In both cases local IFP officials were arrested and charged with murder. Just a week before the election three ANC activists courageously went to canvass support in the KwaZulu capital of Ulundi. All three were butchered in full view of the police.[24]

Second, in the eyes of the ANC, the manning of polling stations by KwaZulu government officials and the reliance on the KwaZulu Police for security was unacceptable in itself. It reported incidents in which ANC party agents at polling stations, as also IEC monitors, were threatened, chased away or physically assaulted, leaving IFP-leaning officials in exclusive charge of the voting process.

Third, the ANC alleged, voting materials stored in KwaZulu government buildings had been tampered with. All told, it claimed, 140 ballot boxes containing 185,115 ballot papers either had broken seals or contained papers laid flat, not folded after voting. These ballot papers constituted 4.1 per cent of the total regional vote and, the ANC believed, most of them favoured the IFP.[25]

Fourth, because of multiple and under-age voting and the abuse of TVCs a number of Zululand rural polling stations recorded polls far in excess of the estimated number of voters resident there. Three such districts had turnouts of 300 per cent, and one had 800 per cent. At the same time the poll in the Durban townships was suspiciously low – due, the ANC alleged, to the disappearance of many ballot papers before they reached the counting station.[26] So bad were such abuses at Empangeni that four IEC officials there petitioned their superiors to declare the election in the whole KwaZulu-Natal region null and void. Their petition – which quickly found its way into ANC hands – formed one of the cornerstones of the aborted ANC court action after the election. Attached to their petition was a list of fifty-six 'pirate' voting stations, all in Northern Natal, and a long list of ballot boxes missing, unsealed or with votes piled flat in them.[27] Further complaints included the removal of ballot boxes from polling stations by IFP supporters or the KwaZulu Police; polling stations with the KZP providing the sole security and thus 'under IFP control'; the expulsion or exclusion of ANC party agents from many polling stations; and the use of threats and force against such agents.[28]

In light of such complaints the ANC's Southern Natal region appealed to the IEC on 6 May to 'treat Natal separately from the rest of South Africa' because 'the KwaZulu part of this province was the only part of this country where a political party and its police force (KZP) had a prominent and controlling role in the elections.'[29] The IEC, the ANC said, should not declare the result in KZN at the same time as the rest of the country but should first carry out a proper investigation; and it should then refuse to certify the elections and call for fresh elections in KZN only.

The IEC immediately asked for an enquiry into the 'pirate' stations from Professor M. Mchunu and Advocate L. Theron. They stated in their memorandum that 'There is no single report from any person who witnessed an unauthorised station in actual operation' and that 'the numbers and locations of (alleged) pirate stations has, since the voting began, been changing and thus throwing doubt on the list at hand. The information from various sources has not been very consistent.'[30] That is, while the rumours and hearsay relating to these pirate stations were voluminous, on examination they behaved very much as rumours often do: hard evidence was virtually impossible to come by.

In its report the IEC suggested that many of the allegations had arisen through sheer confusion.[31] Because of the last-minute nature of the whole voting process in KwaZulu, a full list of polling stations was only published in the government *Gazette* on 25 April, the day before the vote. Many party officials, who did not get copies of this *Gazette* until some time later and so had worked from outdated lists,[32] were horrified to find many stations in operation that they knew nothing about. This sometimes applied to IEC officials too: one IEC area co-ordinator for the Emolweni-Ngcolosi area told the author that he had entirely failed to notice one polling station, sited at the Ngcolosi Tribal Court, until two or three days into the election.[33] Second, this led to uncertainty about the precise name and location of some stations, which were occasionally misdescribed. Third, some of these stations proved unsuitable and were changed on the authority of the relevant IEC district election officer. Finally, the IEC found that the complaints about pirate stations were 'often vague, contradictory or speculative'.[34] In the end the IEC did not discover a single true 'pirate' station.

The ANC complaints about the role of KwaZulu government officials and the KZP were dismissed: having agreed to organise the election with their assistance the IEC could hardly turn round and decide they were illegitimate. The ANC was simply wrong when it argued that KwaZulu was 'the only part of this country where a political party and its police force had a prominent and controlling role in the elections'. The fact was that the local civil services and police forces were employed to similar effect in the other nine homelands and most of these were, if anything, biased in a pro-ANC direction: the only large-scale fraud leading to a mass annulment of votes by the IEC was, after all, in the Transkei, where the government and police were clearly in the ANC camp.

The super-high turnout seen in some areas and the unexpectedly low numbers voting in the Durban townships, so suspect in ANC eyes, were equally dismissed. This was inevitable in an election in which there was no electoral register and in which voters were free to vote at the polling station of their choice. Undoubtedly many voters voted away from home: some Zulus from the Reef came down to KZN to vote; a considerable number of Transkeians crossed into KZN to vote; and others, like the residents of the strife-torn Bhambayi squatter settlement who voted at Phoenix, north of Durban, did so because they feared trouble at their local polling station or because they believed their vote would be more secret if they did not vote under the threatening eye of the local warlord or area committee. And there were doubts about the accuracy of the census – it must be remembered that African squatter areas have often been 'enumerated' only by aerial photography.

No action seems to have been taken about the other ANC complaints. In effect the attitude taken to complaints about violence and intimidation was that they should result in individual prosecutions as necessary, but that no particular case could result in the invalidation of ballot papers unless direct cheating could be proved. From the IEC point of view everything came down to the question of whether particular ballot boxes should be regarded as valid or not: many of the complaints about intimidation, no-go zones and violence were probably true, but it was not clear, *post facto*, what the IEC was supposed to do about them. The same attitude was taken to the virtually identical IFP allegations under the same heads.

The IFP case

The IFP believed that it had been gravely wronged in KwaZulu-Natal; it believed that it should really have won by a far larger margin than the official result showed. A large (thirty-eight-page) dossier was compiled of IFP complaints,[35] most of which concerned KwaZulu-Natal. The most common – and to the IFP the most important – grievances were those of IFP stickers missing from ballot papers, the closure of polling stations at various periods and alleged pro-ANC bias by IEC officials. The IFP also believed that many of their supporters had been unable to vote because of the relative paucity of polling stations in KwaZulu: they claimed that for some of their supporters their nearest polling station was 25 km or more away and, in one case, 50 km.[36] Moreover, the IFP complained bitterly both that temporary voters' cards were only issued to those who could prove ANC allegiance and that many under-age ANC supporters obtained TVCs. The IFP had, too, its own list of allegations of violence and intimidation used against its supporters, very similar to the ANC's list. The IFP also believed that large-scale fraud had taken place in the major townships on the Reef, where it had been confident of a substantial hostel-dweller vote which entirely failed to materialise. In the end, the IFP claimed, the only votes they had got in Gauteng had been those cast by whites and African domestics in white areas. In addition, the IFP believed that many perfectly good IFP votes had been invalidated due to the persuasive powers of ANC agents at the count and the pro-ANC bias of IEC officials. IFP officials also complained that perhaps 100,000 to 200,000 Pondo tribesmen had crossed from the Transkei to vote in KZN as part of a deliberate ANC strategy to tip the election in KZN their way, just as similar cross-border movements had proved decisive in the Northern Cape.[37]

In effect the IEC dismissed all these allegations. The most important – the lack of IFP stickers and the relative paucity of polling stations in KwaZulu – were not things that could be retrospectively rectified. And at some level, no doubt, there must have been an understandable feeling that these were difficulties the IFP had brought on itself by its own off–on attitude to the election. The allegation concerning Pondos crossing into KZN to vote was dismissed, of course, since under the election rules this was perfectly allowable, and in any case there were grounds for believing that many had crossed over to vote simply because some Transkei polling stations were not working. On 30 April the IFP submitted a document detailing 490 complaints about electoral irregularities[38] and bitterly reproaching the IEC for partiality: when the ANC had alleged electoral fraud against the IFP, it noted, the IEC had issued a public statement lending legitimacy to such claims, while it had remained silent about the IFP's even more voluminous complaints.[39] Certainly there is no doubt that the ANC allegations gained far wider public currency than those of the IFP.

In his complaint the IFP campaign manager, Arthur Konigkramer, cited a *Sunday Times* report of a closed session of the IEC which 'resulted in the IFP being granted 250,000 votes (for papers without IFP stickers) but then having 250,000 votes subtracted (for "pirate voting stations")'.[40] When the author interviewed Mr Konigkramer he insisted that the IFP had been robbed of large numbers of votes by a crude 'allocation' of votes. Two months before the election, he said, he had carried out a 'thorough survey' of voting intentions, using IFP workers to question large groups of people in different areas. On this basis he had told Chief Buthelezi that the IFP would win 60 to 65 per cent of the vote in KZN (and 20 per cent nationally), a figure which gravely disappointed the IFP leader, who had been hoping for 80–90 per cent. 'The chief was very upset.' Konigkramer said. 'He insisted we would get a lot more.' Looking at the actual result – of 50 per cent – Konigkramer felt he had been right and that in reality the IFP had got over 60 per cent of the vote in KZN.[41] What had prevented the actual election figures reflecting this, alleged Konigkramer, was that the IEC, faced by the torrent of complaint over irregularities in Northern Natal/KwaZulu, had taken a crude decision simply to allocate the votes in that region on the same basis of 50 per cent to the IFP and 30 per cent to the ANC that had already emerged in the votes counted in the area south of the Tugela. In fact, argued Konigkramer, the IFP had racked up far larger majorities in the north and had been 'robbed'.[42]

The same theme was taken up by Chief Buthelezi. At the KwaZulu Day of Prayer and Thanksgiving held with church leaders at Ulundi on 15 May, he insisted that the IFP had finally accepted the result in KwaZulu-Natal with its tiny IFP majority merely for the sake of peace:

> There is no doubt in my mind that the IFP would have fared much better with proper vote-counting procedures in KwaZulu-Natal or with more than one week of political campaigning, or if the votes north of the Thukela were counted in a truly free and fair manner, rather than award-ing these votes in the same proportion as the votes already cast elsewhere in the province. With the full tally of the votes north of the Thukela the 50 per cent majority victory of the IFP would have risen to at least 60 per cent. These were some of the many concessions the IFP was prepared to make to ensure that the political process would continue and in order to avoid bloodshed.[43]

A further reference to this hypothesis was made by an IFP represen-tative on the IEC, Sipho Mzimela. Commenting on the DP and NP attempts to get votes annulled, Mr Mzimela claimed that the ANC had successfully lobbied the IEC to discount more than 20 per cent of the votes in KZN. In particular, he alleged, the IEC had reduced the IFP majority by discounting all votes cast in the IFP stronghold of Mhlabathini. The election result in KZN, he claimed, 'bore absolutely no relation to votes cast'.[44] He was supported by the NP's former executive director, Olaus van Zyl. The IEC had, he said, 'made corrections to the poll in Natal accounting for hundreds of thousands of votes'.[45] To some extent such allegations were echoed among a wider public by many who simply felt that the IEC 'decision' to declare an IFP one-seat majority in the regional legislature smacked of fine tuning of a deliberate kind, aimed at avoiding violent IFP resistance to any result save victory – but at the minimum political price.

There is no evidence for any of these claims. It is difficult even to understand how the notion of a crude 50:30 'allocation' of votes north of the Thukela can be made, given that the actual figures issued by the IEC bear no relation to such ratios but show the IFP racking up enormous majorities throughout that region. Not only do the figures not show the same proportions as those for Southern Natal but they also differ from place to place within Northern Natal-KwaZulu. And although it is known that the ANC successfully objected to the counting of any votes at Mhlabathini and several other Northern Natal centres, this simply meant they were counted elsewhere instead. And the IEC results certainly include figures for Mhlabathini – showing an enormous IFP majority. The only area where votes went missing or were disallowed on a huge scale in a likely IFP stronghold seems to have been Mtunzini.[46]

The author put the notion of such an 'allocation' of votes to two IEC commissioners. One said that it might have been just possible for some such 'fix' to have been performed but, if so, it had been kept from the commissioners at large – and that would have been very difficult. The other commissioner confessed ignorance of, and amazement at, the very existence of such a hypothesis.[47] One IEC investigator told the author that he believed the IFP allegation was preposterous. He had been called in to investigate a claim that 35,000 IFP voters in Paulpietersburg, on the Swazi border, had been prevented from voting by the failure of the relevant polling stations in the area to open. As a result a discussion had taken place in which suggestions had been made that the missing 35,000 could simply be 'allocated' to the IFP. In fact the case was summarily dismissed for lack of evidence and no such 'allocation' was made. None the less, it may have been this case which put into circulation the notion of 'allocation'.[48]

★

In the present state of knowledge it seems right to dismiss both the ANC and IFP central cases. That is, they were both doubtless correct to allege violence and intimidation against their own supporters, and both were right – as too was the DP – to allege large-scale fraud with temporary voters' cards, which was indeed admitted by the IEC. But just as there is no hard evidence for the ANC's 'pirate polling station' contention, so there is none for the IFP's 'allocation of votes' theory. On the basis of what we know, it makes more sense to see both these stories as examples of the phenomenon of adversarial rumour which has been rife in KZN for many years now. Such rumours are told of the other side with absolute conviction and are, indeed, widely believed, but often they merely express the loathing and distrust each side has for the other. In the quasi-civil war situation of KZN, belief in such rumours quickly hardens them into 'facts'. Indeed, there is a religious quality to the belief in each side's case. Not only are those who disbelieve such reports immediately alleged to be at best the willing dupes of the other side, but even those expressing doubts are accused of having a 'secret agenda'. It is very difficult in this environment to maintain a proper degree of secular and critical detachment. Anyone who has tried to retain an independent and critical distance from both the IFP and ANC during the last ten years in KZN knows how enormous are the pressures to seek the security of becoming a simple partisan of one side or the other, to say that one side is completely right and the other completely wrong.

But in the all-important matter of electoral fraud it would seem that both parties were wrong in their principal contentions. It must be remembered that such frauds would have been extremely difficult. To run even one pirate polling station would have required the complicity of the twenty-six IEC officials present at each polling station, not to mention any number of international observers, peace monitors and the like. To get away with a wholesale of reallocation votes in Northern Natal would have meant somehow squaring hundreds of officials and even opposing party agents involved at counting stations dotted right round that area. Moreover, the gap between the parties was, at the end, very wide. Even quite a large amount of cheating would not have changed the overall result. And, moreover, all parties *did accept the result*. Having done so their *locus standi* in returning to the fray with allegations they had already foresworn was, to say the least, problematic.

Surveys and the 'Lie Factor'

We had hardly anticipated, when conducting our opinion surveys in KwaZulu-Natal, that our surveys themselves would be treated as material evidence in judging whether the election in the province had been free and fair. This meant that re-examination of our results had much more than a merely academic significance.

If the two major charges of electoral fraud in Natal made by the ANC and IFP are discounted, one is left with the fraudulent use of TVCs and the unspecified but clearly large-scale invalidation of ballots by the IEC. If the IEC was even approximately competent at its job, these two factors should have been self-cancelling to some degree, and therefore the result as announced in KZN should have been crudely correct. In that case, we have the problem of explaining how our two KZN surveys which produced an ANC lead of 51 per cent to the IFP's 32.7 per cent in November–December 1993 and an even larger 50.3 per cent to 24.8 per cent lead in February 1994 could possibly have been consistent with an eventual IFP lead of 48.6 per cent to 31.6 per cent in the national ballot and a 50.3 per cent to 32.2 per cent victory in the regional ballot.

There are not many countries in the world where party support can swing to such an extent that one party's lead by a 5:3 or even 2:1 margin can be turned into a 3:5 margin the other way in the space of two months, and South Africa is emphatically not one of those countries. As Chris de Kock has shown[49] it did not take long in the new, post-1990 political world for the lines of racial, class and ethnic conflict to crystallise. This was particularly true in the wartorn context of KZN. Conditions there have long been so extreme that locals – of all political persuasions – speak of 'the lie factor' as a fact of life. Given the territorial nature of political power and the strong likelihood that belonging to the 'wrong' party will, in the wrong area, result in injury or death, many Africans have had to learn how to lie with complete plausibility even under conditions of extreme pressure.

Such mass dissimulation is not without historical precedents. Historians of the American Deep South have recorded how it became second nature for southern blacks to play the role of 'dumb nigger', replete with rolling eyes and Jim Crow attitudes: it was far safer to provide white supremacists with the image of blacks they felt comfortable with than to confront them with a more truthful assertion. Much the same survival techniques have been necessary in KZN. During our surveys we were cautioned both by ANC and IFP activists that they knew of areas in which their supporters all openly professed beliefs opposite to the ones they really held. Anyone who conducted surveys in such areas, they told us, would be systematically lied to on a large scale.

There are in fact considerable grounds for believing that the result in KZN was broadly correct and that our survey findings were distorted by a large lie factor, with very large numbers who eventually voted for the IFP either choosing to describe themselves to us as ANC or seeking refuge in a Won't say/Don't know response.

One must start by remembering that the ANC and IFP electorates in KZN have markedly different social profiles. When we carried out a regression analysis of African voters in our first Natal survey we found some interesting correlations with religious practice. There were strong clumps of IFP support among members of the Zionist, New Apostolic and Independent African churches, as also among the Congregationalists and Methodists. There were also slighter traces of a better than average IFP vote among Roman Catholics. The ANC did better among the Baptist and related churches (Assemblies of God, Apostolic Faith, Full Gospel) and among non-believers. Overall, the IFP vote was more homogeneously and actively Christian than its ANC counterpart.

However, similar regression analyses of both our KZN surveys showed much stronger differences along a rural–urban continuum. ANC support among Africans was positively correlated with urban (especially metropolitan) residence, with education, youth, with dwelling in formal houses or shack dwellings (as opposed to traditional huts) and with relatively higher incomes. IFP voting correlated significantly with the opposite categories. On our second survey we also found ANC support to be rather more male, though there was no significant bias of the IFP group towards one sex or the other. We then re-analysed those who had responded Won't say/Don't know to our second survey and found that their social profile was *even further along the urban–rural continuum than was that of the IFP supporters; that indeed they were sociologically 'more IFP than the IFP'* – and were thus the extreme opposite of ANC supporters. They were distinctively older, more rural, less educated, poorer and were more likely to be women.[50] Sociologically, there was no doubt that this group belonged in the IFP camp.

It must be remembered that rural Africans in Natal (that is, the IFP's key milieu) were much more scared and socially vulnerable than their urban counterparts – two-thirds of them confessed to being scared, while 58 per cent of their urban counterparts said they weren't scared of anyone.[51] Moreover, our survey findings – in common with those of other surveys over time – invariably found that both rural dwellers and IFP supporters were far more bullied and much more susceptible to political pressure than were ANC supporters. Even among the hard core to which the IFP had been reduced in our second survey, more than three times as many as among ANC supporters said they might have to vote against their own preferences in order to avoid conflict.[52] What this translated to on the ground was large numbers of the old and illiterate rural poor, especially women, being extremely frightened of young ANC 'comrades' and the ferocious pressure they could exert – and frightened too, no doubt, of the countervailing pressures exerted by the IFP chiefs and indunas. It looks very much as if the most scared and vulnerable – and the most archetypally IFP – section of the KZN rural electorate hid their political sympathies with noncommittal answers and then massively voted for the IFP.

If we reallocate all the non-committed voters in our first KZN survey to the IFP, the party takes a 51 per cent to 46 per cent lead over the ANC, and in our second survey a 53.3 per cent to 44.1 per cent lead, a variation well within the normal margin of error. That is to say, such an adjustment also provides us with a more believably stable picture of party preferences. However, this is still not enough to explain the ultimate result – a 5:3 IFP lead. To explain that we have also to assume that a large number of IFP voters went the further step of disguising themselves as ANC voters. If we put that figure at 10 per cent, we get an IFP lead of around 61 per cent to 36 per cent among Africans, which would approximate to the IFP's overall 5:3 lead.

There is no proof that this occurred, but it seems extremely likely that it did. The clue lies in the simulated ballot in our first survey. When we got African voters to cast an actual ballot, the number of the non-committed (pretty well all of whom were likely IFP voters) distributed themselves 3 per cent towards the (right-wing) Freedom Alliance, 12 per cent towards the ANC and 2 per cent to the ANC–SACP. Not one moved to the IFP, presumably because the whole point of their pretended non-committed status had been to hide that affiliation. Perhaps, in retrospect, we should have been alerted by the way in which these 'non-committed' voters fanned out in every direction but that of the IFP. On a purely random basis, after all, one would have expected around a third of them to move towards the IFP. When none at all did it was actually a signal that their strongest motive was not to give away their IFP loyalties, which they had previously dissembled in another way. It does not take a great leap of imagination to see that some others were likely to use the even better disguise of claiming to be ANC voters. In retrospect we should also have been alerted by the overly large proportion – 45 per cent – of Africans who said they needed assistance to fill in the ballot, that is, getting the interviewer to fill it in for them. On election day, judging by the small number of spoilt ballots, only a tiny fraction experienced such difficulties after all.[53] That is, many of those claiming they needed assistance to vote were not really in need of it: almost certainly many were actually just trying to hand over to our interviewers the responsibility of making a partisan choice for them. It must never be forgotten that, however valiantly they tried to be neutral, most of our interviewers had the classic ANC profile – they were young, urban, educated and somewhat better off than many of the really poor voters they interviewed. Respondents wishing to give the answers they thought the interviewer wanted would doubtless have said they were ANC.

Such hypotheses are not far-fetched. Even over the question of the possession of identity documents we found a substantial lie factor, and the relatively favourable attitude towards de Klerk and the NP among many Africans also suggests a large subterranean political consciousness not visible in simple questions of partisan choice. Moreover, the large numbers – in both urban and rural settings – who told us that it was difficult or impossible to live next to neighbours with different political views was, properly read, a clear suggestion that large numbers would have to lie about their allegiance for safety's sake. And there is little sign that those who were doing the lying were ANC. In all our surveys most ANC voters seemed to be quite happy, even proud, to state their allegiance. It must be remembered that our surveys showed the rural Africans of KZN splitting equally between IFP and ANC, whereas the official results show very few indeed voting ANC. It seems extremely likely that a very large proportion of the 'ANC' supporters we found in those areas were actually bogus. It seems likely, too, that there were a fair number of such voters in urban areas as well.

It is worth pointing out that Stanley Greenberg, President Clinton's private pollster who worked for the ANC during the election, had no doubt that the IFP victory in KZN was genuine – which could only be true if one endorsed the theory of a large 'lie factor'. 'I have no doubt that there was massive vote fraud,' said Greenberg, 'but it was not sufficient to account for the result, which showed a clear Inkatha victory.'[54]

Further light was shed by the IRI/MPD post-election survey of September 1994, which showed a picture of partisan choice in KZN virtually identical to that we had found in our February survey: the ANC at 51.8 per cent, the IFP at 25.2 per cent, the NP at 11.3 per cent and 8.5 per cent refusing to say. This time, however, we were able to check the 'lie factor'. We asked respondents whether people who defaulted on their mortgages should lose their houses or whether the state or community should pay for them, and similarly whether those who didn't pay their water, electricity and rates bills should have their services terminated or whether the state or community should pay those too. This turned out to be a strong differentiator of party choice: only 32 per cent of ANC voters but 59 per cent of IFP voters thought non-payers should lose their houses, and 39 per cent of ANC but 61 per cent of IFP voters took the 'tough' option over non-payment of service charges. Yet when we looked at the data by region, KwaZulu-Natal shone out as the only region where a 60 per cent majority took a tough line on both questions.[55] This would have been an impossible result if there were not a 'real' IFP majority among the region's African population.

This paradoxical picture of a hidden IFP majority which emerged briefly at the election and then slipped back into disguise on the morrow of the election was confirmed by extremely frustrated IFP organisers, who found that even in areas they had carried by large majorities they still could not set up branches or even get their supporters to identify themselves in the wake of the election.

> The problem we [the IFP] face is that you've got a whole bunch of reasonable, Christian-minded people who know that they want to vote for us, but who are not really active. What they want is a peaceful life and to be left alone, and God knows their lives are hard enough. But against that you've got a whole bunch of ANC activists whose life *is* the struggle. Often our people are leaderless because their leaders have been bumped off

by the activists. This absolutely terrorises them and so they stay invisible even to us.[56]

Even after one discounts the IFP gloss, there is here a substantive sociological reality. It is worth remembering the HSRC finding of an IFP lead over ANC of 37 per cent to 23 per cent in KZN in January–July 1992, as also the fact that the same polls showed the NP taking two-thirds and more of the Indian and coloured vote. In 1993 the picture changed, the ANC surged and both NP and IFP support fell back. In the end, however, Indian and coloured support 'homed' back towards its earlier levels. It looks as if something similar may have happened with the IFP vote, certainly in KZN, for the final 5:3 outcome was uncannily close to that 37:23 split of two years before.

The phenomenon of a large submerged IFP vote (and thus of a large lie factor) in KZN is, of course, a controversial finding. The obvious comparison is with the opposite phenomenon which we saw in the February 1994 survey in Gauteng, where both ANC and IFP support appeared to collapse because of a 'fear factor'.[57] We were particularly suspicious of the large fall in the ANC figure, especially when discussions with our interviewers revealed many anecdotes suggesting a near hysteria about 'the Zulus' and what they might do at election time. In light of these discussions we decided we must 'upgrade' many of the evasive responses we were getting back into probable ANC votes. We did not make a similar adjustment to the IFP vote there, for it appeared that most of the fear and intimidation had a one-way anti-ANC direction.

This turned out to be both right and wrong; that is, the ultimate result shows that we were right to adjust the expected ANC vote upwards in Gauteng, but also that we should have adjusted the IFP vote upwards as well – for clearly there had been a fear factor depressing the IFP vote there too. In the case of KZN we had our suspicions about both our surveys but there seemed no hard and clear reason to adjust the figures to hand. Accordingly, we released our surveys to the press, showing, on both occasions, large ANC leads over the IFP. Naturally, the IFP angrily criticised the survey results, while the ANC greeted them with pleasure – and later used them to bolster their argument that the results in KZN had been falsified against them. This sort of partisan reception of survey data is something all analysts of political behaviour have to face, but in retrospect, of course, it is a pity that we lacked the sorts of clue which would have enabled us to adjust our KZN data towards the IFP in the way that we had adjusted our Gauteng data towards the ANC. As it turned out, some of the IFP criticisms of our KZN findings appear to have been justified. The interesting point to notice is that the ANC majority in Gauteng were thoroughly frightened by the IFP minority there, in just the same way that the IFP majority in KZN was often similarly scared of what turned out to be an ANC minority there.

It would thus appear that, despite the many imperfections in the electoral process there, the KZN result was fair in the crucial sense that the IFP's lead over the ANC was genuine. Probably the greatest unfairness was that both the ANC and IFP manufactured many extra votes thanks to temporary voters' card abuses. This meant that both these parties probably got too many votes, which hurt the smaller parties like the NP and DP — whose complaints on this score were at least in some part justified.[58]

The Lessons for the Future

Although the IEC has come in for its share of criticism in our account above, there is no doubt that it played a crucial and valuable role. Our finding in relation to the KZN result bears out the IEC position even on this most difficult of cases, and in general it did manage — just — to deliver an election which passed muster and whose results have been accepted as crudely legitimate. There is no doubt that in a racially divided society such as South Africa there is a great and continuing need for a body such as the IEC, and that the main recommendation of its report — that no future election ever again be conducted without a proper voters' roll — would obviate a good deal of the abuses which did take place.

The great question mark over the IEC (or any similar replacement body) is not to do with the hard work or integrity of those who worked for it, but with the larger question of institution-building in the new South Africa. To work, new institutions need both to have legitimacy in the wider society and a credibility born of functional efficiency. Thus far it cannot be said that the track record is promising, for most of the new institutions created in the post-1990 'new South Africa' context have not worked well. The National Peace Keeping Force was a complete failure and had to be wound up, while the newly established South African National Defence Force has been racked by mutiny, absenteeism and other signs of disorder which bode extremely ill. The Independent Media Commission, set up to monitor the media during the election run-up, appeared to perform no useful function and was wound up in short order. After the election grave difficulties were experienced within the South African Police, with a rash of mutinies in January 1995 leading to the shooting of one police officer by other policemen engaged in putting down the mutiny. Worryingly, the indispensable hierarchies and disciplines of the force showed a tendency to fragment along racial lines. At the same time the government's plans for the democratisation of local government were placed in considerable difficulty by resistances experienced in many areas over the role of traditional chiefs: unless these difficulties could be resolved it was hard to see how the new institutions could work. And so on. Building new institutions — an essential prerequisite if the task of 'building the new nation' is to proceed – is simply a very difficult business.

Seen in that context, the IEC, for all its faults, was perhaps more effective than most. Even so, it was largely rescued by white business on the one hand, and the old white-led Defence Force on the other. The army provided 6,000 troops to perform crucial election duties and deployed many thousands of others in protection and reaction roles. In no fewer than 41 of the 46 subregions of country the army provided support and storage facilities, guards, escorts, transport for ballot boxes and the like. It and the South African Police also provisioned the IEC with everything from beds to electricity generators, while the army printed over 650,000 ballot papers itself. The South African Air Force was also quite crucial: it conducted 175 special missions during the election, provided airborne election observation, erected satellite dishes and communications networks around the country, flew in over 600 tons of ballot papers from Europe and repeatedly solved critical logistical problems by emergency flights.[59] During the election run-up many ANC and PAC militants had angrily demanded that the armed forces, as instruments of the hated apartheid state, be confined to barracks during the election. It may safely be said that had this occurred, the election would not have.

The contribution by the business community was no less crucial. As we have seen, the secondment of business expertise to help the IEC in KZN narrowly prevented the election and count there from collapsing completely. The same was true in many other regions. Without crucial help from businesses such as the Anglo-American Corporation, Engen, Shell, the Barlows Group, McCarthy Retail, Siemens, JCI and South African Breweries there would undoubtedly have been a complete and demoralising denouement. The count could not have taken place without the help of the banks and accountancy firms. The national telephone company, Telkom, also played a crucial role and without its help too, the IEC might have foundered.

In a way all this was magnificent. But it cannot be expected that business and the military will save the day again. Many of those who were seconded had the experience of a lifetime, but many more took a 'never again' attitude, or at least felt that if they were to be asked to save a desperate situation then it would be better to put them in charge from the start. There are large question marks over the organisation of future elections, and if the problems are not satisfactorily solved, they could fatally undermine the democratic process.

There were two miracles about the South African election. One was that it took place at all; the other was that it was relatively fair. But it cannot be said that it was really 'free'. The evidence we have accumulated in this study of the extent of intrusive and intimidating community pressures, of no-go zones, and of a degree of fear and insecurity sufficient to make large numbers of voters lie about their affiliations – all this suggests that South Africa has some way to go before properly open and competitive politics is established. The sight of the long queues of voters waiting patiently to vote, in good humour and multiracial harmony, remains a symbol almost all South Africans will treasure from the 1994 'founding election'. But democracy is not a castle to be captured in a day, or even a year. Democracy has indeed been launched, but this only means that the far longer process of building a democratic culture, of creating legitimate, stable and efficient institutions, of breaking down racial barriers so that voting becomes more than an 'ethnic census', and of instilling a new respect for civil rights, for the opinions of others and their right to organise and canvass for them, can now begin.

Notes

Epigraph sources: *Natal Witness*, 7 May 1994; *Natal Witness*, 30 Apr. 1994; Andrew Reynolds (ed.), *Election '94 South Africa* (Cape Town: George Philip, 1994), p. 113.

1　Report of the Independent Electoral Commission, *The South African Elections of April 1994* (hereafter *IEC Report*), (Johannesburg, October 1994).
2　*Sunday Times* (Johannesburg), 23 Oct. and 30 Oct. 1994.
3　*IEC Report*, p. 42.
4　Ibid., p. 62.
5　Commonwealth Observer Group, 'The end of apartheid', cited in *The Citizen*, 25 May 1994.
6　*IEC Report*, p. 37.
7　Ibid., p. 53.
8　Ibid.
9　Ibid., p. 54.
10　*Rapport*, 30 October 1994.
11　I am grateful to Hermann Giliomee, who conducted extensive post-election interviews with NP leaders, for his help with this section.
12　Press Release: 'International Observer Missions Issue Final Statement on South African Elections: Observer missions of the United Nations, Commonwealth, European Union and Organization of African Unity conclude that "the outcome of the elections reflects the will of the people of South Africa"'. (Roneo, Johannesburg), 6 May 1994.
13　'Observing South Africa's 1994 National and Provincial Elections', *Final Report to the European Commission from the European Election Unit* (Johannesburg), 27 May 1994, (hereafter referred to as *EU Unit Report*). This 134-page report was probably the most thorough of those prepared by the 458 organizations which monitored the election.
　　UNOMSA – the United Nations Observer Mission to South Africa – was the largest and most expensive electoral observation mission ever mounted by the UN, with 2,120 personnel in the field drawn from 120 countries. It is a moot point as to whether the UN got its money's worth since most UNOMSA personnel were sent home before the most crucial and controversial part of the election, the count, had been concluded. UNOMSA issued no report but its conclusions form the basis of the *Report of the Secretary-General on the Question of South Africa* to the UN Security Council, 16 June 1994.
　　This report found that the various deficiencies in the IEC's planning 'virtually guaranteed that a significant proportion of the electorate would experience some difficulty in voting'. Amazingly, UNOMSA reported of the count that 'it was unclear what mechanism was proposed by the IEC for the compilation and announcement

of the election results'. Their spot-check of 458 counting stations revealed that 16 per cent lacked sufficient staff and facilities, that in over 18 per cent proper counting procedures were not adhered to, and that in over 25 per cent there was no proper reconciliation of ballot papers. But UNOMSA was keen to avoid controversy: although noting that in a number of no-go areas officials issuing voting cards were subject to death threats or were prevented from carrying out their jobs, on the broader issue of alleged electoral fraud 'it was not possible for UNOMSA to make an independent judgement'.

14 *EU Unit Report*, p. 76.
15 Ibid., p. 74.
16 Ibid., p. 77.
17 Ibid.
18 Ibid., p. 78.
19 Ibid., p. 81.
20 *Natal Mercury*, 9 May 1994. The radical wing of the KwaZulu-Natal ANC, led by Harry Gwala, were determined not to accept the result, while the moderates, led by Jacob Zuma, were more susceptible to Shell House pressure to drop the matter.
21 *Weekly Mail*, 20–6 May 1994; see also *Natal Witness*, 23 and 24 May 1994.
22 The key intermediaries in this deal were Washington Okumu, the Kenyan 'freelance ambassador', and African Enterprise, a Christian body working for reconciliation, based in Pietermaritzburg and run by Michael Cassidy and Peter Kerton-Johnson. Cassidy and Kerton-Johnson were intimately involved with the negotiations and said that the main issue was always that of land tenure and the safeguarding of the traditional method of land allocation. Under the interim constitution, all the land and assets of KwaZulu were to be transferred to the central government, a fact which the IFP saw as a threat to the whole existing Zulu social system. Kerton-Johnson was emphatic that this was the main issue settled in negotiation, though the resulting Memorandum of Agreement did not mention land. Interview with Peter Kerton-Johnson, 4 Aug. 1994.
23 Paulus Zulu, 'South African elections: public opinion and party competition' (MS), p. 19.
24 Ibid., pp. 18–19.
25 Ibid., p. 21.
26 Ibid., pp. 21–2.
27 See IEC, 'Resolution by Empangeni sub-provincial office', 4 May 1994.
28 IEC, 'Resolution by Empangeni'; Reshaad Ismail (DCA Monitoring), confidential memo, 1 May 1994; 'Index to dossier on irregularities in elections in parts of KwaZulu-Natal', 29 Apr. 1994 (affidavit by M. S. Mhlungu).
29 ANC Southern Natal region, letter to the Chairperson, Independent Electoral Office, Johannesburg, 6 May 1994.
30 Professor M. Mchunu and Advocate L. Theron, 'Adjudication Secretariat memorandum to Advocate M. Gumbi: re: alleged informal voting stations, KwaZulu Natal', 3 May 1994.
31 *IEC Report*, p. 70.
32 Interview with IEC Commissioner Charles Nupen, 22 Sept. 1994.
33 Interview with Guy Harris, 10 Aug. 1994. Harris told me, however, that while the opportunity for fraud had been large at the unmonitored station, only a few under-age voters seemed to have taken advantage of it.
34 *IEC Report*, p. 70.
35 Inkatha Freedom Party (National Campaign Office), 'A synopsis of electoral irregularities reported to the National Campaign Office during the course of the April 1994 election', 30 Apr. 1994.
36 Arthur Konigkramer, IFP Campaign Manager, fax of 16 May 1994 to Advocate Nicholas Tee, National Co-ordinator, IEC Investigations, 'Polling stations and TVC problems for the IFP'.
37 Interview with Gavin Woods, Director of the Inkatha Institute, 28 July 1994.
38 Arthur Konigkramer, IFP Campaign Manager, fax of 26 Apr. 1994 to Mr Justice

Kriegler, Chairman IEC, 'Polling stations – general problems'.

39   Konigkramer, fax of 16 May 1994, pp. 1–2.

40   Ibid.

41   Interview with Arthur Konigkramer, 29 July 1994.

42   Ibid.

43   'Testimony by Mangosuthu Buthelezi, President of Inkatha Freedom Party', KwaZulu Day of Prayer and Thanksgiving, Ulundi, 15 May 1994.

44   *Natal Mercury*, 24 Oct. 1994.

45   Ibid.

46   For Mtunzini see chapter 11, p. 303.

47   Private communications.

48   Private communication.

49   See chapter 3 above, esp. pp. 59–60.

50   I am grateful to Bill Hunt of Research International Ltd (Durban) for his crucial assistance in this part of the analysis.

51   See chapter 7 above on Natal opinion, pp. 193–4, 209.

52   See ibid., esp. tables 7.7 and 7.8.

53   See ibid., pp. 191–2.

54   *Business Day*, 17 June 1994. Greenberg stopped the ANC campaigning, as it had wanted to, on the slogan 'Now is the time . . .', which he found to have threatening connotations beyond the ANC's hard core. Instead, he successfully insisted on the blander but more widely appealing 'A better future for all'. None the less, he was unable to stop the earlier slogan being used to some extent – which may have cost the ANC the vital votes needed for a two-thirds majority.

55   Design Surveys International, 'Tabular report of the findings of a study of social needs and attitudes in post-election South Africa', study prepared for IRI/MPD based on a randomly stratified sample of 4,003 voters, Oct. 1994.

56   Interview of 5 Aug. 1994 with Dave Durham, IFP organiser for Northern Natal and now an IFP MP in the regional assembly.

57   See above, pp. 250–53.

58   This was, for example, the opinion of Bheki Sibeiya, who oversaw the Durban count. Interview of 25 Aug. 1994.

59   *Business Day*, 2 May 1994. The contribution of business was soon lost sight of, but the IEC's image deteriorated further with the publication in June 1995 of the *Report of the Auditor-General on the Financial Statements of the IEC for the period 12 December 1993 to 30 September 1994 and Related Matters*. The A-G found multiple 'examples of double and overpayments, fruitless, unauthorised and avoidable expenditure', 'no fixed asset register', that inadequate control existed over the physical existence and location of assets . . . , and that 'uncertainty exists as to the amount of losses suffered by the IEC'. The A-G was thus damningly 'unable to express an audit opinion on the financial statements'. Among the items detailed by the A-G were: salary payments to non-authorised personnel; failure to deduct tax; no documentation for payments exceeding R300,000 (R3.60 = \$1); salaries paid in excess of scale; double salaries for some; overpayment of seconded staff by over R1 million; unaccounted advances of R949,106 to other employees; deposit of voting officers' cheques into a private bank account of one particular officer and his family members; the impossibility of reconciling 62,884 voting officers' cheques amounting to R62.8 million; incorrect tax deductions resulting in penalties of R258,676; losses of R5 million worth of computers, R2 million in vehicles and R1.2 million in radios; unverifiable payments of R7.5 million for meal allowances; over R6.4 million lost due to fraud; uncontrolled use of taxis in the Eastern Cape costing R3.8 million; R6.2 million unaccounted for in IEC expenditure in Gauteng; write-offs of R998,827 due to petty cash irregularities; fruitless extra insurance of R26 million when insurance was already carried; a report from a printing company that it had paid R770,000 in 'commission' to an IEC agent for work given to it. And so on and so on. Much of the damage had been caused, the A-G stated, as a result of 'the lack of qualified and competent staff'. The Report caused a major row in Parliament with MPs demanding restitution, but only paltry amounts were recovered.

THIRTEEN

Into the Brave New World: Post-Election South Africa

R.W. Johnson and Lawrence Schlemmer

WITH THE ELECTION RESULT universally accepted and the triumphal inauguration of President Mandela on 10 May 1994 (with Thabo Mbeki and F. W. de Klerk as his two vice-presidents), South Africa moved peacefully, almost miraculously it seemed, into a new post-election world. The images of the SAAF jets and helicopter gunships dipping in salute to their new black president, the tears and joy of a long struggle triumphantly concluded, and President Mandela's repeated and heartfelt insistence on the need for national reconciliation – all contributed to colouring the months after the election with a degree of public euphoria which was certainly historically unique in South Africa. Among the young militants of the ANC the rejoicing and excitement reached states of near delirium. Wordsworth's famous greeting of the French Revolution

> Bliss was it in that dawn to be alive
> But to be young was very heaven

seemed perfectly appropriate to the virtually universal spirit of release and goodwill which characterised the immediate post-election period. The installation of a coalition government of national unity, in which erstwhile enemies from the ANC and NP sat together with the IFP, solidified this new spirit of national unity. The government's ambitious Reconstruction and Development Programme, which foresaw an immense and wide-ranging effort in the fields of education, housing, health and economic development, found virtually unanimous political support.

While this unique period of political euphoria continued, normal politics were, so to speak, suspended. But at the same time increasing attention fastened on the problem (as many saw it) of the dramatically heightened expectations which liberation had brought. We decided to probe the situation with two post-election surveys. The first of these – which was the largest in scope and also in its nationwide sample of

4,003 voters – was carried out in September 1994 by Decision Surveys International for the International Republican Institute and the Institute for Multi-Party Democracy, while the second survey of 2,200 voters was carried out by the HSRC's opinion-polling centre, MarkData. Both surveys were of random stratified samples. At the time of writing (February 1995) only the African results of the latter survey were available and it is these that are referred to in this chapter.

September 1994: The Honeymoon Goes On

The September sample showed post-election euphoria continuing to dominate the South African political climate at a general level, affording the government of national unity a quite unprecedented measure of popular support. The government's honeymoon with the voters was reflected in a staggering 82% to 15% majority believing that 'things in general in this country are going in the right direction'. A clear majority of every racial group shared this optimism, though most narrowly among whites, Indians and coloureds. Africans were optimists by 91% to 7% (95% to 2% among Xhosa-speakers), with IFP supporters only slightly less optimistic at 84% to 14%. Only among the Freedom Front and Conservative Party electorates were pessimists in the majority. When the pessimists were asked to specify their reasons, no consensus existed: lack of jobs, violence, crime, the lack of economic progress, broken promises and a lack of personal progress were all mentioned by over 10%, with resentment over affirmative action, housing problems, government mis-spending and general mismanagement all being mentioned by 4% or more.

Only 8% of voters thought their lives had got worse since the election (including 16% of Indians and 26% of whites), as against 36% who said it had got better and 56% who said it had stayed the same. Only 3% of Africans said 'worse' compared with 47% 'better', with Xhosa-speakers again the most euphoric – 54% 'better' and 2% 'worse'. These are staggering figures given that the survey was conducted too soon for there to have been any real improvement in material conditions. That is, this extraordinary euphoria must be seen not as a reflection of real material gains but as a continuation of the 'uhuru' mood noted in MPD–HSRC surveys in the pre-election period.

1995: The Honeymoon Begins to Wane

The results of the second survey suggested, however, that by the end of 1994 this euphoria was on the wane. When African voters were asked 'How has the government performed over the past three months?' while

26% thought it had performed 'better than expected', no less than 46% felt it had performed 'not as well as expected'. Predictably, ANC supporters were close to the average, with 44% feeling that the government had not lived up to expectations. The proportions feeling disillusioned were higher among PAC and IFP supporters at 71% and 56% respectively. Surprisingly, NP supporters were similar to ANC supporters in their responses.

Among some categories of African voters there were actual majorities who said the government had disappointed them. Most notably, these included rural Africans (52% disappointed), voters in KwaZulu-Natal (50%), the Eastern Transvaal (55%) and the North-West (57%). A negative response might have been expected in IFP-ruled KwaZulu-Natal but not in these massively pro-ANC areas. Similarly, the 51% majorities of disappointed voters among lower professionals and blue-collar workers suggested an early degree of disaffection among key ANC constituencies. This is, however, to put it too strongly: such majorities would be perfectly normal in most countries much of the time – and in this case the voters were still signalling their allegiance to the ANC.

MarkData followed up by asking 'What good things has the government already done?' No less than 36% of African voters responded with a resounding 'nothing', with even higher numbers of negative responses among those with less than a Std 3 education (42%), among PAC supporters (47%), those with no political allegiance (48%), among members of the smaller African tribal groups (50% or more), among migrant workers (50%) and lower salaried professions (51%), and those living in the Eastern Transvaal (50%) or in the Orange Free State (63%). It may not be an accident that Patrick Lekota, the impressively able ANC premier of the OFS, had at the time of our survey just lost his position as ANC Secretary-General for the OFS after lively criticism of his administration for having been overly concerned with the task of reconciliation with the region's whites.

We also asked the open-ended question, 'What has disappointed you or made you angry?' Of African voters, 53% said they had a grievance of one kind or another, with above average levels of disappointment being voiced by Africans in the Western Cape and the Northern Transvaal, the unemployed who were seeking work, those with no incomes, and among PAC, IFP and NP supporters and those who refused to reveal their political allegiance.

The most telling results, however, were given in response to the earlier question about the good things the government had done. In general the achievements recognised were not associated with issues of greatest importance to voters but usually reflected lower-order priorities. The government was praised by 24% for its health care initiatives, by 20% for improving transport – though this had never emerged as either a popular or a governmental priority – and by 15% for reducing violence, which had subsided of its own accord after the election. Only 6% mentioned the indubitably important area of housing – an extremely low level when one considers the enormous and favourable publicity which the late Minister of Housing, Joe Slovo, had gained for his housing policies.

In all, these responses among Africans suggested that a mere eight months after the election the sense of victory and excitement had been quite profoundly tempered. While the ANC (and even more so its leader) remained popular, there had been a significant recession of sentiment among many of its key constituencies – often among the poorest and most dispossessed.

When voters were probed on how they would respond to delays in the delivery of change and reforms, however, certain contradictions emerged – and there may also have been a shift of mood in responses to such questions between September and the end of 1994. When voters in the September DSI survey were asked how they would feel if they had to wait several years for any real change to occur, African voters almost wholly refused to use negative adjectives in describing their reactions, with 64% saying 'hopeful', 17% 'patient' and 6% 'satisfied': only 6% said they would be angry, impatient, discouraged or frustrated. Again, Xhosa-speakers were the extreme case, with only 3% finding it in themselves to use such negative adjectives. Even when we gave respondents a second chance to say how they would feel if their hopes of early change were disappointed, this failed to elicit any negative opinion from a staggering 85% of our African respondents. These figures were truly remarkable, particularly in a context where over half of all Africans said they felt that their lives had stayed the same or got worse since the election. In effect such respondents seemed to be saying that they were so delighted with the symbolic achievement of the transition that, irrespective of material changes, they could hardly conceive of themselves ever feeling disappointed.

It was, of course, impossible to imagine that such a mood could persist indefinitely and it was no surprise to find that it had already eroded to some degree by the time of our MarkData survey. When Africans were asked when they expected to experience the benefits that they felt should be delivered by government, 46% replied 'immediately' and 90% felt that they should gain such benefits within a year. It is a moot point whether the ANC should have felt encouraged or discouraged by the finding that the most impatient voters were usually (with the exception of a tiny group of PAC supporters) to be found among those who were most sympathetic to the ANC and most closely linked to its structures, while the least impatient were found in groupings which tended generally to feel most alienated from the ANC – the smaller African language groups, informal sector traders, and Africans living in white non-metropolitan areas, mainly small-town domestic servants. On the one hand this situation guaranteed that the ANC leadership would come under sharp pressure from its supporters; on the other hand it suggested that those pressures might be contained, that impatience over reform and committed support for the ANC can co-exist. This could provide the government of national unity with a 'cushion' of voter commitment, at least for a while.

The effect of this 'cushion' was evident in the MarkData survey when we asked African voters what the 'main cause' would be if the changes they expected did not materialise: many were willing to see reasons which would exculpate the ANC-dominated government from responsibility – a shortage of money, too high a level of demand, and so on. However, roughly a quarter of African voters said that such a failure would be due to government 'neglect', 'ignorance' of popular needs, or unwillingness to assist ordinary people. If indeed the government finds it difficult to deliver on its promises, this quarter of the African electorate is clearly a potential node of dissent which could grow into protest or even opposition over time.

But this was to anticipate a situation which, as at the end of 1994, had certainly not arrived. Indeed, contrary to much of what was said about the government having to run scared in front of sky-high expectations, and notwithstanding the evidence of growing impatience, the government still enjoyed such enormous goodwill that it had a fair amount of leeway. Certainly, the government had every reason to be pleased with its September 1994 ratings. Of all voters, 54% said they had 'a great deal of confidence' in the government and another 34% said they had 'some confidence'. Xhosa-speakers were the most emphatic, with 79% having a great deal and 18% some confidence – a staggering 97% in total. ANC supporters were almost equally unanimous, but nearly two-thirds of NP voters (and 80% of DP voters) said they had at least some confidence, as did a third of the far right. Of IFP voters, 45% had a 'great deal' and 46% some confidence. Furthermore, even in the December 1994 MarkData study, and even among impatient and disaffected African voters, virtually only the ANC was perceived as having the commitment, the authority and the legitimacy to restructure society. Even NP supporters tended to identify the ANC as being the party most likely to deliver tangible reforms to the masses of the population.

The Key Issues

Once we moved away from our findings relating to patience/confidence, we found that the more detailed findings of our larger September survey were merely echoed in a more general way by our MarkData survey. Accordingly, in the remainder of this chapter we rely exclusively on the former study.

There was, we found, a high degree of consensus across all racial and party groupings as to which were the most important problems before the new government: 30% named unemployment and jobs, 20% lack of housing, 10% lack of water, 8% education, 7% low wages, 5% crime and 5% peace and political stability – the startling relegation of this latter issue was itself a large comment on the new era we were now in. The unemployment issue received particularly prominent mention among the unemployed (51%), among PAC supporters (44%), in Gauteng (38%), among squatters (37%) and among coloureds (35%). Strikingly, the IFP and ANC electorates were as one on this issue, as on many others. The pressure on the government over unemployment was particularly great when one took into account the particular sensitivity of the ANC elite to African opinion in the towns and metropolitan areas, particularly in Gauteng: Gauteng is far larger, richer and more sophisticated than other areas, and politically it 'belongs' to the ANC more than Cape Town or Durban do. Across all the urban and metropolitan areas 35% of respondents put jobs as the top issue – almost twice as many as mentioned housing – and in Gauteng the figure rose to 38%. Those dwelling on farms and in kraals accorded the job issue a considerably lower priority: the top issue for kraal dwellers (30%) was lack of water, an issue mentioned by twice as many women as men, reflecting the feminine predominance in these bone-poor (and bone-dry) rural backwaters.

Given the way that housing had dominated the political stage since the election it was somewhat surprising that it did not rate higher. This was, again, partly due to the rural–urban divide, with kraal dwellers notably less concerned by the housing shortage. When, however, respondents were allowed to mention the three most important problems before the government, housing got almost as many total mentions (55%) as did unemployment (60%). Education also leapt in importance (34%), followed by lack of water (25%), low wages (17%), crime (17%) and electrification (12%). It was a matter of some surprise that only 1% mentioned health and medical services as their top issue and that even when three mentions were allowed it was still cited by only 9%. Even more striking was the scant interest in 'reducing the gap between rich and poor', land reform, ensuring individual rights, improving services or dealing with labour unrest: only 2% of respondents mentioned these among their three top issues, while pension levels and birth control were mentioned by only 1%. On this evidence the more radical and redistributive policies being urged by the ANC left had little popular backing. Thus, despite the rhetorical heat generated by the topic of land redistribution, it looked as if the government would suffer only minimal political damage if, for example, it jettisoned its land reform programme.

The primacy of the economy was even more pronounced when respondents were asked what they would regard as most important to them a year hence in determining whether the country was heading in the right direction: 32% mentioned better access to jobs, another 11% general economic improvement and 8% higher wages, while improved access to housing was mentioned by only 15%. Whites and Indians were particularly likely to mention the economy, and they were also more likely to stress peace and political stability. Among Africans, IFP supporters were most likely to mention peace and less violence. This concentration on the economy was not reflected, however, by familiarity with the ANC's Reconstruction and Development Plan. Just over a third of respondents said they were somewhat or very familiar with the RDP. Those least familiar with it were women, Sotho-speakers, the elderly and the least educated. The ironic result was that those who were supposed to benefit most from the RDP knew least about it, while the best informed were whites, specially DP supporters. Of all Africans, 41% said they were 'not familiar at all' with the RDP. Even among ANC supporters nearly two-thirds said they were either not very familiar or not familiar at all with the RDP, though the ANC also contained the largest (13%) group who claimed to be 'very familiar' with it.

A real problem for the government was that the electorate as a whole, and ANC supporters in particular, had a very demand-orientated view of the economy. That is to say, there was an overwhelming demand for what a healthy economy could deliver (jobs, housing, education, welfare, etc.) but relatively little interest in what was required to produce that healthy economy. This emerged clearly when respondents were asked to rate the relative importance of the problem areas the government should give priority to over the next few years: 53% of respondents (and 60% of ANC supporters) gave either top or second top priority to 'community needs such as water and housing'. Using the same top two priorities as a measure, the 47% (51% of ANC voters) who thought the top priority was 'social needs such as health and education' were followed by the 42% (45% of ANC voters) who gave priority to 'workers' needs such as skills training and fair wages'. Concern for 'economic factors such as stable prices and taxes' was dramatically less at 22% (and only 13% among ANC voters), and lower still for 'business needs such as attracting foreign investment' (20% and 15% respectively). Right at the bottom came priority for 'political factors such as racial equality and democracy' (15% for ANC voters and all voters, with only IFP voters (22%) showing stronger concern). Again, one found little resonance with the radical cry that 'the struggle goes on': the voters had clearly decided that 'the Struggle' was yesterday's battle.

The Leviathan and the Entitlement Culture

Given that job creation was overwhelmingly the top demand, it is striking that voters believed massively that this was government's responsibility: 69% of all voters plumped for this, including 75% of ANC voters. A much smaller 17% (15% of ANC voters) thought companies should take the lead, while the other alternatives — trade unions/small business start-ups/involvement of everybody — drew only derisory support. A mirror image of this was achieved by emphasising that all South Africans had to participate in improving their country and then asking which issues were most important in that context. Only in the provision of basic housing (where millions of South Africans have helped build their own houses) did a majority (61%) see a role for the public. Generally speaking, the sense of public efficacy was low. The only other issue where public involvement was substantially thought to be relevant was 'reducing crime and violence', and even that was prioritised by less than half (46%) of all voters. Even when it came to 'increasing political co-operation and tolerance' only 20% saw this as a matter for participation by the public, and only 28% saw the formation of small businesses in that light.

Such responses showed how difficult the government's job would be. On the one hand, a culture of entitlement existed in terms of which many goods and services (jobs, housing, water, education, higher wages, elec-trification, etc.) were passionately sought. On the other, the government was thought by respondents to be centrally responsible for providing all such things. The same hegemonic spirit which viewed the government with complete confidence also tended to see government as virtually omnipotent, a Hobbesian Leviathan. There was great consciousness of the poverty and weakness of the masses and the power of government above them, but very little sense of a significant or empowered civil society working at an intermediate level: hence the low levels of public self-efficacy noted above. There was, too, a far greater popular awareness of the demand side of progress — the social, community and workers' needs the electorate wished to see met — than there was of the requirements of the economic machine which provided the supply side of the equation. It is, for example, uncontroversially true that most popular needs can only be met through rapid economic growth, and that such growth has never been achieved in South Africa without substantial foreign investment. Yet public consciousness of this linkage was extremely weak, and it was weakest of all among the ANC's own supporters, only 7% of whom put attracting foreign investment as their top priority.

So, in order to achieve progress towards the goals which its supporters want, the ANC will need to give priority to objectives which its voters little understand or support — and which are far more the concern of whites and Indians. Thus while only 13% of ANC voters gave top or second top priority to 'economic needs', 53% of whites and 31% of Indians did so. That is, in order to achieve progress, the government, particularly its ANC component, may have to work to change the way its supporters think and, in particular, to combat the 'entitlement culture' which it has hitherto encouraged. Already, in the field of housing, the responsible ministers have had to work to reduce expectations (to one-roomed houses, by cutting housing targets by 30%, etc.) while emphasising anti-entitlement objectives (an end to land seizures, the necessity of paying for rent and services, etc.). The implication of our survey was that most other ministers faced much the same task.

The Disempowered Citizenry

Respondents were then asked which were the most important criteria for good government. While 36% gave priority to 'honest and clean government', 25% to the keeping of campaign promises and 23% to the protection of citizens' rights, only 13% emphasised government listening to voters and trying to help them. Doubtless this partly reflected the fact that most South Africans were unused to thinking of government as responsive, attentive or helpful: its job was primarily to be strong and effective. But there was also a sense in which voters did not seem to mind this lack of responsiveness and accountability provided government was honest and effective. Whites, coloureds and Indians, as also IFP voters, placed particularly high stress on 'honest and clean government', perhaps a reflection of suspicions aroused by the government 'gravy train'.

We then tested opinion about the two key areas where we had anticipated a large sense of public involvement, asking what was the best way to reduce crime and to increase political tolerance and co-operation. Again, the results emphatically showed how little voters saw even these areas as appropriate for citizen involvement. The best ways to reduce crime were to create jobs (54%), to increase the number of police (34%), to increase fines and sentences (30%) and to improve the economy (13%): all measures seen as essentially the province of government. Only 7% mentioned 'the community working together with the police and reporting crimes', and among the minority communities even fewer were likely to mention this at all. Similarly, the most popular way of increasing tolerance (with total mentions of 30%) was for political leaders and parties to meet and talk – that is, something requiring no public involvement.

Other prominent methods cited were similarly top-down: the holding of joint rallies (11%), leaders teaching or controlling their supporters (7%), a one-party state (6%). One of the alternatives provided was 'the involvement of the community in political decisions' but only 1% chose this option. It was striking that both ANC supporters and Africans as a whole were notably more leadership-centred than were the minority groups or other parties: thus, for example, while 38% of ANC supporters (and 31% of IFP voters) put their faith in political leaders talking together, only 17% of Indians and coloureds and 7% of whites did. One is forced to the conclusion that the long, bitter and violent political struggle in South Africa has been a trauma which has left people of all groups nervously conscious of the risks of political participation. They would far, far rather leave tricky issues to their leaders than stick out their own necks. There has been a certain amount of rhetoric about mass participatory democracy in the new South Africa but everything suggests that the electorate is currently quite particularly unsuited to it.

Concern over crime and violence often centres on the number of illegal weapons in circulation. When we asked how their number could be reduced, 52% opted for a simple increase in punishment for having such weapons and 35% for more roadblocks at which weapons could be confiscated. That is, suggestions were retributive and technical on the whole: only 4% said 'increase the police force' and 2% mentioned community policing, for there was little confidence in such institutions.

Getting and Spending

Respondents were then asked how money should be raised to pay for (the overwhelmingly popular) provision of health, housing and education. There was a striking lack of consensus, even when respondents were allowed to mention two forms of revenue raising. This lack of consensus doubtless reflected not merely the sheerly uncomfortable subject of taxation but also the lack of connectedness in many minds between government spending and revenue raising. But there were also sharp differences between groups. Of all respondents, 30% suggested that money be saved (that is, and taxation thus avoided) by cutting government expenditure elsewhere, particularly on the 'gravy train'. But while over half of whites and nearly half of coloureds and Indians mentioned this method, only 22% of Africans did. Interestingly, there was a relative consensus between IFP and ANC voters on this and other economic issues.

For African voters, the leading (24%) option was to increase company taxes, with 20% suggesting higher personal taxes on the richest citizens – both options clearly assumed to hit only whites. Another 14% of Africans (again with an ANC–IFP consensus) wanted to 'increase' personal taxes in general, doubtless with the same assumption in mind. In general African opinion clearly felt that no more revenue could be raised from its own ranks – only 3% said even that individuals or the community should pay more for extra services. On the other hand, while this pushed African respondents towards redistributive options, these were favoured by strikingly fewer than might have been expected. There was, after all, nothing to prevent Africans opting 100% for higher company taxes: it was notable that, even with two available mentions, only 24% did. Moreover, the second most popular (21% of all respondents) option – higher taxes on luxuries such as alcohol and cigarettes – was bound to hit African consumers heavily. Women were more in favour (24%) of this measure than men (18%), doubtless because they drink and smoke less. Only 6% said government should borrow more.

We then tested the same question negatively by asking which revenue-raising methods should not be used. African voters (with considerable non-African support) believed that price increases in basic foodstuffs must be avoided, followed by VAT increases. Whites (with some support from other groups) were overwhelmingly against personal tax increases, but no racial group thought that avoiding higher luxury taxes or company taxation was a high priority – suggesting that they may be sitting ducks for any finance minister looking around for extra revenue sources.

The crunch question was simply whether respondents would be willing to pay higher taxes to help everyone have better health, housing and education services. Whites, Indians and coloureds were heavily and predictably unwilling to be taxed more. Africans were unwilling by a thin 44% to 40% majority and ANC voters were similarly (42% to 40%) divided. Oddly, opinion in favour of higher taxes was overwhelming in just one area, the (extremely poor) Northern Transvaal. Overall, however, if such data are taken into account the government will find it difficult to raise taxes. Both NP and IFP voters were against, as were the educated and metropolitan African elites, and all such groups could point to World Bank studies showing South Africa to be already somewhat overtaxed. But in that case the government faced a conundrum. The electorate clearly wanted dramatically higher standards of provision of jobs, housing and education and it expected government to provide them. But it was not willing to pay for them and did not seem keen to borrow.

This unwillingness to borrow was, however, somewhat fragile. This emerged when the lack of consensus over revenue-raising options was confirmed by a further question which probed the trade-offs for each option. Opinion was evenly split as to whether or not it was a good idea to borrow funds for development spending, even if that meant higher taxes to pay off a higher debt. However, while the minority groups were heavily against borrowing, Africans (and ANC voters) favoured it by 2:1. Clearly, if the ANC listens to its own electorate, it will borrow. Strikingly, a two-thirds majority thought that trade and investment should be increased to secure economic growth, even if that meant less funds available for social services. Given the enormous public demand for those services, this was an impressive reflection of the priority attached to job creation via economic growth.

A small majority of Africans and ANC voters wanted to increase wages fast even if it resulted in inflation, but opinion in the minority groups was sufficiently strongly against this to make it an unpopular option overall. Opinion was evenly divided on the obverse question of whether prices should be held stable even if that meant holding wages down, though large African and ANC majorities were hostile to such a notion. Clearly, the government will have great difficulty in preaching wage moderation to its supporters, particularly since it was noticeable that Xhosa-speakers, always the ANC's keenest supporters, took the hardest line on all these issues. Although English-speakers were split on the issue, all other groups thought that it was more important to prevent price rises by raising interest rates rather than the reverse. Almost certainly this reflects the fact that most African voters have never been in a position to borrow money and are not (yet) interest rate sensitive.

In general African voters were heavily in favour of tax-and-spend policies: 74% thought 'more should be spent on health, education and housing even if that means extra taxes for everyone' – a sentiment shared by coloured and Indian majorities but opposed by 57% of whites. On the other hand, most Indians agreed with whites (and coloureds were evenly divided) that 'taxes should be kept down, even if it means fewer services will be provided.' A majority (64%) of both ANC and IFP voters disagreed, as did Africans as a whole.

There was comfort for ANC radicals in such figures, for while African opinion was not positive about redistributive measures *per se*, it wanted more taxes and more spending and yet did not want its own tax burden increased. In effect it would like to see the extra tax burden shifted on to corporate and, presumptively, non-African shoulders. That is, African opinion did not explicitly favour redistributive measures, but it did so implicitly, perhaps even unconsciously.

The Overloaded Government

We then asked a series of questions as to who (of government, business, individuals or trade unions) was primarily responsible for achieving a variety of desirable economic objectives – increasing economic growth, improving living standards, increasing exports of South African goods, preventing inflation, reducing unemployment, improving the growth of existing private companies, developing new companies and attracting foreign investment to South Africa. In the first five cases a steady majority of 73% to 78% saw government as primarily responsible: even when it came to 'improving your standard of living' only 14% of Africans (but half of whites and a third of coloureds and Indians) thought the individual in question had primary responsibility. Even when it came to 'improving the growth of existing companies' 74% of Africans (and thus 63% of all voters) thought this primarily a government responsibility rather than that of the companies themselves. Even when it came to the development of new companies, 76% of Africans took this view. 84% of all voters took the same view about the attracting of foreign investors to South Africa. The idea that individual or corporate initiative, or entrepreneurship in general, had much to do with securing these economic objectives seemed almost wholly lacking.

Many ANC ministers, perhaps conscious of the enormity of the tasks ahead, have suggested that the implementation of the RDP is not just government's task but everybody's. This had not been accepted by the electorate, who by a 2:1 majority thought that it was the government's responsibility. Ironically, the Xhosa-speaking ANC loyalists rejected the notion that it was everybody's task most strongly of all (78% to 18%). Derisory percentages believed that others – civics, labour, business or regional premiers – had anything to do with it. Whether the government likes it or not, it will be judged quite centrally now on whether or not it implements the RDP successfully – and it cannot lay off its risk much in any direction.

When respondents were asked about the achievement of social objectives – ensuring racial and gender equality, improving access to education and training, and improving access to housing – even stronger identifications emerged of government as carrying primary responsibility. For each of these social objectives, majorities of all voters of 81%, 92% and 93% respectively took this view. Typically, business was seen as the second most responsible agency in securing all these objectives, but it should be remembered that for most respondents business was almost as remote an entity as government.

It was not the point of this survey to suggest where primary responsibility for such questions *ought* to lie, but it must be pointed out that in most other societies there would be a far smaller tendency to attribute virtually all social and economic responsibility to government. To some extent one is here measuring the degree to which apartheid prevented the development of a participant civic culture: most South Africans feel they are subjects, not citizens. That is, their statist approach is partly a measure of their own extremely weak sense of civic efficacy. The attribution of all responsibility to government is not the sign of a healthy democratic political culture, but then South Africa has not been a democracy and such a culture has had scant chance to grow.

This statist approach was, doubtless, also a reflection of the fact that the electorate was in the first place the (largely unwilling) object of a government social engineering operation which created ten new states, uprooted populations, held 80% of the population in a state of subjugation, and so on. The same electorate then saw the ship of state under F.W. de Klerk navigate a 180-degree turn and create the wholly new present situation. After such a performance there is a tendency to believe that the state can do almost anything; to see government not as an emanation of its citizenry but a Behemoth, a true Leviathan. There is little consciousness in South Africa of the debates which have racked Western states in the 1980s about 'government overload', of how difficult it is for governments to effect change, and of how reduced the scope is for autarchic national strategies. It goes without saying that such acceptance of governmental omnipotence is pregnant with undemocratic possibilities. But it is also a double-edged situation for government. On the one hand, its authority is absolute; on the other hand, if it fails to deliver on its promises it will not be able to escape blame.

The Politicised Society

This awed attitude towards the state went hand in hand in our survey with very high levels of politicisation: 79% of all respondents considered themselves supporters of a political party. Even the 'low' (63%) party identification of English-speakers would be a high figure in many democracies; the high of 92% seen among Xhosa-speakers was a staggering figure in a democracy. Such levels of party identification have typically been seen only in the context of extreme racial/tribal mobilisation or in the inflated party support levels which used to be reported from the East European People's Democracies. However, there are grounds for believing that party support may have been inflated in South Africa too: when we asked respondents to describe their support, 27% said either that they were 'not really' party supporters or that they were not interested in politics at all, although our earlier question had revealed only 21% non-supporters.

Even so, levels of party activism – 13% of all respondents – were high (22% among Xhosa-speakers, 18% among Sotho-speakers, a staggering 40% among hostel dwellers). The distribution of activists among parties was very unequal: an amazing 19% of ANC voters identified themselves as activists, as did 17% of IFP voters. The white right had a 14–15% level of activism, but among DP voters the figure was 8% and among the NP 4%. (Even these levels are high: a normal figure for Britain or the USA would be 1–2%.) These very unequal levels of activism meant that the effective party balance within civil society was even more lop-sided than the election results suggested, for the strength of the parties on the ground – in the streets, to be exact – was directly proportional to the numbers of their activists. The ideal type portrait of an activist was that of a young African male living in a squatter camp. Men were more than twice as likely as women to be activists, the 18–34 age group was twice as likely to be activist as the over-50s, and squatters in metropolitan areas were twice as likely to be activists as those living in formal houses. Without doubt many of these activists will be unemployed youngsters with little education and a lot of time on their hands.

This sense of overpoliticisation was strengthened by the fact that two-thirds of all respondents could not or would not name their 'second favourite party'. Of all Africans 75% fitted into this category, as did over 70% of both ANC and IFP voters, whereas a majority of other party followers could name a second favourite. Worryingly high proportions of

Africans (54% of Xhosa-speakers, for example) said that 'my party is the only one for me and I cannot support another party.' If the beginning of political tolerance is the realisation that politics is about compromise, many South Africans have not yet realised it.

We then asked voters how they would respond to the possibility that their party might let them down. Over 40% of FF, IFP and ANC voters were so unconditional in their partisanship that they replied that 'my party is the only one for me and I cannot support another party'; 48% of ANC, 36% of NP and 34% of IFP voters were a little more conditional and said that they would 'give it time to achieve results'. But while a quarter of NP and DP voters said they would switch loyalties if their party did not deliver on its promises in a year or two, among the ANC there were only 11% of such 'floaters', and among the IFP 20%. In one sense the ANC figure was worryingly low: democracy depends on political leaders believing that they must respond to their followers' needs or lose them. But one should not overstress this danger. One must remember that our survey was conducted in the heat of post-election euphoria and a quite unreal degree of confidence in the government. In that context a figure of only 11% ANC 'floaters' was perhaps not so surprising.

We then asked respondents to tell us which were the most important values and ideas they shared with their party. Women's rights was mentioned by 8% of all voters and 14% of women. This was a particularly important issue for African women, especially those living in kraals and especially in the Northern Transvaal, where an amazing 17% of voters cited this as the most important value shared with their party. Racial equality was chosen as the most important value by 10% of all voters (13% of Xhosa-speakers), while peace and reconciliation was mentioned by 21% of voters – evenly spread across all social and racial groups, but most important of all to those without education (27%) and IFP supporters (30%).

Community development was mentioned by 12% and was particularly espoused by ANC and IFP supporters and, especially, by hostel dwellers (21%). Only 3% mentioned 'more powers for provinces and local areas' and 2% 'protecting traditional customs'. Religious values were mentioned by 9%, mainly by Afrikaans-speakers (25%), especially supporters of the far right. 'Improving the economy' was mentioned by 19%, with men (22%) and English-speakers (31%) particularly prominent. The fact that whites (29%) were twice as likely as Africans (16%) to mention this factor confirmed the lesser levels of African interest in the economy apparent in many other responses: it was as if the attribution of omnipotence to government has made the government, not the economy, the crucial source of the extra jobs so fervently desired.

'Reducing inequalities between rich and poor' was mentioned as the most important shared value by only 8% (13% of Xhosa-speakers, 11% of

ANC supporters), confirming again that direct redistributive sentiment was far less significant at mass level than among the elite. And only 9% mentioned 'individual rights and freedoms'. This value was most important to Indians (13%), English-speakers (16%) and, especially, DP voters (22%). Such findings suggested that individualism was a notably weak force in South Africa, but at least a latent individualism was apparent when voters were asked who influenced their political opinions, with the largest single group (42%) saying 'nobody/myself', compared to 20% who cited political leaders, 16% friends and family, and 16% the media. Whites, coloureds and Indians were particularly prone to deny being influenced, but all Africans (IFP, ANC and PAC) were more leadership-centred. There was, though, a staggering contrast between Zulu-speakers, 52% of whom insisted they were not influenced by anyone, and Xhosa-speakers, only 19% of whom did so.

The New Politics and the Distant Government

The respectful confidence in which government was held by respondents did not imply the same attitude towards MPs. Fully 45% of voters said that they thought MPs didn't know what voters' priorities were. Majorities of whites, coloureds and Indians expressed this negative perception and even among the ANC-loyalist Xhosa-speakers 30% echoed this view, as did 47% of Sotho-speakers and 38% of ANC voters, as well as 40% of IFP and 61% of NP voters. At the very least this suggested that the decision to do away with constituency representation has had a strongly disempowering effect on voters. It also means that with MPs unable to take much, if any, of the strain of popular demands and frustrations, all the pressure is directly on government.

This sense of distance was only increased when voters were asked how they would make their concerns known to their leaders. In effect, most voters have no direct means of doing this: a third of whites, coloureds and Indians said they would write a letter, but less than one African in six said they would do this; 25% of Africans would approach a local civic organisation, 23% would go to a political rally and 11% would go to their party. Only 4% said they would bother to go to see an MP, confirming how little MPs were seen to matter even as conduits to the leadership. One cannot but be struck that all the major means mentioned offered no certainty of direct access at all – and only 7% said they would go to see their leaders in person. The sense of a disempowered electorate without usable points of access to those they take to be in authority was very strong. This is, of course, what black South Africans were used to under the ancien régime.

It is tempting to see a further sign of this sense of disempowerment in the fact that only two-thirds of our respondents believed that the April

1994 election had been 'very free and fair'. Less than half of Indians and coloureds believed it had been very free and fair and only one white in six did: these were worrying figures indeed for an election which was supposed to represent a triumph of democratisation. Complete disbelief in the fairness of the election was particularly strong on the far right and among Afrikaners as a whole (24%). Less than three-fifths of IFP voters believed the election to have been completely free and fair, and among NP and DP voters less than a quarter did. Partisanship among losers could only explain part of this disaffection. On the other hand, the ANC in KwaZulu-Natal would not be pleased to know that 84% of ANC voters thought the elections were 'very free and fair'. When we asked those who objected why they did so, there was little consensus: 56% of Zulu objectors mentioned intimidation, but many others mentioned the theft of ballot papers and interference with ballot boxes.

We then asked how free voters now felt to express their views. One in eight (and 20% of Zulus) said that 'people put pressure on me to hold particular views.' IFP and FF voters were most likely to report such pressures, but so did 9% of ANC voters. In the Orange Free State 22% of voters and 20% of KwaZulu-Natal residents reported such pressures. These were high figures when one considered that voters do not like reporting direct pressures which diminish their sense of individual autonomy. Typically, far more voters experience such pressures than are actually willing to report them.

There was a large (77%) consensus among all races and parties that traditional leaders should keep their traditional powers and elected leaders and chiefs should co-operate and share power. There was a somewhat smaller but still majority consensus that the power of such traditional leaders should be exercised particularly in rural areas. The crux of such power was clearly the power to exercise judgement in tribal courts, assented to by a much narrower majority, with Xhosa-speakers the only group to be (narrowly) against. Only a large IFP majority (77%) carried the day here.

We then tested more radical assumptions about the chieftaincy. Only 23% of all voters thought it should it be ended altogether, 31% of Sotho-speakers favouring abolition, together with 23% of Xhosas, but only 18% of Zulus. But perhaps the chieftaincy should be retired into a form of constitutional monarchy? African opinion was divided almost down the middle on this, with 47% favouring it and 53% wanting to retain a traditional (that is, more powerful) chieftaincy. The real surprise here was that IFP voters were the most anti-traditional, 54% wanting traditional leaders who would 'only appear in ceremonies but have no other powers'. Only 48% of ANC voters agreed with this view and 54% of the electorate disagreed entirely. Yet IFP voters were also by far the most emphatic (91%) that the system of traditional leaders must be maintained. The only way to make sense of this was that the post-election quarrel between King Goodwill and Chief Buthelezi had left IFP loyalists as much in favour of the chieftaincy as ever but keen that the king should step back into a strictly constitutional role and thus end the conflict.

Economic Insecurities

Affirmative action recruitment policies have been both generally applied and hotly resented in the new South Africa. Of all voters, 61% felt that 'even if some people do not make progress, it is necessary that people compete for jobs based on their qualification and skill', and only 38% believed that 'it is necessary for people oppressed by apartheid to get special treatment, even if some businesses and offices will be less efficient until people are trained.' Clearly, the principle of affirmative action is often put a great deal more bluntly than that, so the negative reaction even to our 'softer' formulation should be seen as highly significant. The only group (heavily) in favour of affirmative action were Xhosas-speakers. In party terms only the PAC was in favour of such appointments even if they reduced business efficiency. All other groups, including ANC voters, were against such discrimination and in favour of appointments on merit. All racial groups showed majorities against affirmative action hiring policies, with Africans against by 52% to 48%. Yet affirmative action is a dramatic and daily fact of life. One can only conclude that the minority within the African community is currently getting its way on this question (and affirmative action can only benefit a minority). If so, caution would be advisable. A majority of all racial groups was against affirmative action, with coloureds, Indians and whites feeling very strongly: the backlash potential is considerable.

Before the elections many people of all races told interviewers that they could well leave the country. By September 1994, however, only 8% said that circumstances existed which made them consider leaving: 4% of Africans, 5% of coloureds, 12% of Indians and 28% of whites, with male English-speakers living in Gauteng and the Western Cape being the most likely emigrants. Of NP voters, 13% said they might consider leaving, as did a staggering 49% of DP voters. This was the hidden side of post-election euphoria: President Mandela's repeated assurances to whites had not been enough to allay their fears. Those who said they might leave gave violence and crime (48%) as their main reason (though this was far truer of African would-be emigrants than of others), followed by less job opportunity (17%) and the 'unstable economy' (14%); 4% worried about anti-white discrimination and another 4% about a declining quality of education for their children, but only 3% mentioned 'civil war' and 2% political instability.

There was, we have seen, an overwhelming concern with unemployment – but also a strong wish for higher wages. We tested these against one another by asking whether trade unions 'should work for better wages, even if it means more people will be unemployed'. Only 29% agreed, while 70% thought the opposite. Feeling about low wages ran deepest among farmworkers, who took the same view but by a narrower 59% to 36% margin. The implications for trade union activism were clearly unpromising, a fact emphasised when we asked what role trade unions should play in improving the economy: 25% said trade unions should 'stop inciting workers to strike', against only 12% who wanted to see them 'fight for better wages'. All told, only 22% of respondents wanted the unions to fight for better wages and conditions or defend rights. Almost all other responses emphasised that trade union demands should be moderated, that the unions should strive for better industrial relations, and so forth. These priorities were shared by all groups, including ANC voters.

Thus while COSATU may have a privileged position with the ANC at an organisational level, labour militancy had, by September 1994, become decidedly unpopular with the ANC rank and file – and even more so with the rest of the electorate. The post-election strike wave had doubtless taken its toll, but it may also be that the position of the unions was undergoing a downward revision among the African public now that unions are not the main carriers of grievances and that their actions can be seen as undermining a government which Africans have taken to their heart. Attitudes towards business were less divided: 37% of respondents wanted to see business expand, develop and create more jobs, while only 10% put the emphasis on the payment of better wages. Notions that business must disburse itself in a redistributive direction were weak (although respondents had been happy to suggest higher company tax). Only 2%, even among ANC supporters, thought that business ought to 'donate funds to the government to improve the economy', and only 1% thought it should offer more loans, bursaries or benefits.

Paying for Services and Housing

Both Joe Slovo, the late Minister for Housing, and many others within the government had made it plain that there could be no way ahead towards solving the housing problem unless the culture of non-payment of rent/mortgage bonds/service charges ceased. One of the difficulties cited by building societies is that township residents often believe that those who default on their bond payments should keep their houses anyway. And this indeed turned out to be true of two-thirds of all ANC voters. Only a third of ANC voters believed that those who defaulted should lose their houses, which should then be sold on to other people. By contrast, 29% thought that the government should pay the bond for them 'even if it means the government has less money to build houses for others', and 37% believed that 'the community, including my family and me, should share costs even if it means everyone will pay a little more.' The ANC electorate was exactly representative of Africans as a whole on each of these choices, but a 59% majority of IFP voters believed that those who defaulted should lose their houses. That is, the extraordinarily strong 'entitlement' attitudes displayed here turned out to be an unexpectedly good differentiator of party allegiance. Mr Slovo's successors will thus have to turn round the views primarily of their own voters – and it looks as though the task will be difficult. It is not clear whether those who believe that the community or the government should bail out loan defaulters have realised that this is bound to lead to almost universal defaulting, and that this is thus a demand for free housing.

One reason why the government's task will be so difficult in this respect was that the township 'entitlement' options had significant support elsewhere as well – a staggering 72% of coloureds, 47% of Indians and 16% of whites agreed that defaulting housebuyers should keep their houses. Indeed, surprisingly large groups within the NP (35%), DP (26%) and even the FF (25%) also supported the 'entitlement' view. For the government to convince Africans unused to paying for housing that their 'boycott' must now cease will not be made any easier by the fact that even a quarter of the Freedom Front electorate were willing for house buyers to keep their houses without paying for them. Only in Gauteng (51%) and KwaZulu-Natal (60%) did clear majorities insist that defaulters should lose their houses.

The same attitudes existed in only slightly weaker form when it came to payment for services such as water, electricity and garbage collection: 41% of Africans (39% of ANC voters but 61% of IFP voters) believed that those who didn't pay should not receive the services, and the same significant minorities in the NP, DP and FF agreed with them. One of the many oddities of these figures was that the large majorities who believed that unpaid bonds and service payments should be borne by government or the community were also among those who strongly rejected extra taxation. To some extent this was probably because government has seemed so remote that the connection between 'the government pays' and 'more taxes' is not made by some. But this cannot be the principal reason, for 3:2 majorities in both cases suggested that the community, including themselves, should pay – that is, voluntary extra taxation.

One could only conclude that this subject elicits extremely strong emotions among South Africans and that it also acts as a focus for strong communitarian feelings. Perhaps the most bitterly resented aspect of apartheid was that it meant that a majority of the population felt they lacked a secure home in the part of the country where they wanted to be. This elemental and long-thwarted human need is now expressed in terms which could, sadly, jeopardise the attempts to satisfy it at last.

One obvious solution to the housing problem would be high-rise flats – denser and cheaper than houses. But 74% of Africans said they would prefer to live in a single-storey free-standing house, even it cost them more, rather than a cheaper flat of the same size. These views were almost exactly mirrored by other races, but it was possible that the fact that whites and Indians have preferred houses to flats may have created an ideological preference for 'a proper house' (like others have). It was difficult, otherwise, to understand why 35% of IFP voters but only 27% of ANC voters would choose the flat. The only glimmer of light for hard-pressed housing administrators was that preference for flats rose with youth, so that 35% of the 18–24 group would opt for them, and that 46% of hostel dwellers would also plump for a flat.

Another major controversy was whether resources should go into building fewer, more expensive four-room township houses; into much smaller, cheaper and more numerous one- or two-room units which people can add on to; or whether minimal site and service schemes should be chosen, the cheapest alternative and the one allowing most people to be helped quickly. It is to some extent an ideological choice – building 'proper houses' was a matter of radical principle for some. Thus 36% of Xhosa-speakers – always the most hard-line ANC group – insisted on 'complete houses even if they cost people more' and only 22% would accept site and service. Among Sotho-speakers, also an ANC-inclined group but notably more pragmatic in its response to many questions, the comparable figures were the obverse, 23% and 38%. Overall, only 29% of Africans insisted on 'complete houses', 44% plumped for two-room houses, and 26% for site and service, with the three minority groups chosing these same less ambitious options. Site and service was the preferred option only in the Northern Transvaal, although a third of kraal dwellers and 27% of farm dwellers opted for it too. But the option of two-room houses was the most popular choice everywhere: all told, 71% of Africans opted for something less than 'complete houses' – indicating that the regional premiers who had so indignantly rejected any solution short of 'complete houses' were almost certainly out of touch with their voters.

A similar scale of priorities was visible in connection with housing subsidies. Only 16% of Africans thought that the government should give a subsidy of R12,500 (the most frequently mentioned figure) to all poor people, but two-thirds thought that 'much less than R12,500 should be offered so that more people could be helped sooner', and 18% opted for assistance in paying off a mortgage rather than for any subsidy at all. Typically enough, more than twice as many Xhosa-speakers as other Africans insisted on the full R12,500 subsidy – but even there a majority favoured smaller subsidies. The message was, again, that the high-subsidy, high-quality housing demanded on principle by activists was not really a representative cry. It will doubtless bring some comfort to the government to know that the electorate's demands are in this respect more moderate and reasonable than those of many of their own activists.

Education – the Toughest Issue

Much more difficult to handle was the fact that 69% of all Africans insisted on 'equal education right away, even if some school standards fall', an opinion shared quite equally by IFP, PAC and ANC voters, and almost equally heavily by coloured voters. Yet 88% of whites (with Indians equally divided) believed that 'high standards must be maintained even if it means some inequality now.' Two-thirds of those with higher education wanted standards maintained, but only a quarter of those with no formal education did. Nowhere else was such a dramatic racial divide found as on this question: people were far more uncompromising about their children's education than they were about their own conditions. On the one hand, the Minister of Education's inability to provide equal education right away, or even soon, is going to be bitterly unpopular with the party's own supporters; on the other hand, for many white respondents a decline in the quality of their children's education was an emigration issue.

Conclusion

Overall, government must be thankful that only in the area of education did such racially divisive choices present themselves in acute form. Elsewhere there was reason for optimism. Despite what is often said, much of the electorate was willing to be patient and, despite some waning of the post-election honeymoon, there was still almost unbounded faith and optimism about the new government. Almost nowhere did African voters insist on the sort of brutally redistributive policies which would divide the country and result in the emigration of badly needed skilled manpower. True, many demands existed which could implicitly push the government in that direction, but it was not clear that the public would persist with such options once their implications became clear. There was almost no public clamour for land reform and it would seem possible for South Africa to avoid some of the traumas Zimbabwe has undergone over this issue. The overpoliticisation of society, the tendency to citizen disempowerment, the entitlement culture and the attribution of far too much to the state were all disturbing aspects of the new South Africa, but these are early days: one cannot expect a full-blown democratic political culture to spring into existence right away in a society traumatised by decades of repression and violence. On the crucial issue of housing, public opinion was actually more moderate and reasonable than many had feared.

Above all the public was quite united in its emphasis on the need for economic growth and development and a consequent reduction in unemployment. Whites, Africans, Indians and coloureds will be equally delighted if this can be achieved. Many hoped that this would also produce a reduction in violence: the third most popular option (out of 24) when the public faced the problem of illegal weapons was 'improve the economy so crime won't be so tempting.' Without doubt many of the other difficulties visible in our survey would be ameliorated, or in some cases dissolve away altogether, if only sustained economic growth could be achieved. This requirement is so overwhelming for the government that the real question is how far it will wish to push any other policies at all which may detract from that single goal. If the government could achieve sustained and dynamic growth, almost anything else it failed in would be forgiven – and the national unity it craves would be all but guaranteed.

★

South Africa had, by 1995, come a long way since the process of democratisation was launched just five years before. Although many had died in political violence in those years, the process of change, the dismantling of apartheid and the installation of a democratic new order had all been achieved with far less bloodshed than had usually been imagined, and altogether more rationally and smoothly than anyone would have predicted. There was no doubt that South Africa was lucky to have had two such exceptional leaders as Nelson Mandela and F. W. de Klerk to guide this process through, a fact recognised when they were jointly awarded the Nobel Peace Prize. But the history of democratisation in other polities suggests that a great deal more than luck such as this is required if a rocky ride is to be avoided. Typically, first democratic governments fail, as indeed do second such governments. Often the mass frustrations and yearnings so long suppressed under the preceding non-democratic regime burst forth in ways that make the job of government far more difficult in an already overstressed situation. All too frequently new elites attempt to consolidate their wealth and power in ways uncomfortably reminiscent of the ancien régime. These are all among the challenges that lie ahead for South Africa. A liberal democracy has been born, against all the odds, but it will be many years before this achievement is secure. For that to occur a new culture of tolerance, of independent civic association and action, of democratic alternation in power, and of the rule of law will all have to grow and become entrenched. This will not happen in a day or even in a mere few years. The present volume is a record of the foundation of the fledgling new South Africa and, as such, is intended as a contribution towards the continuing effort to build that secure and mature democracy.

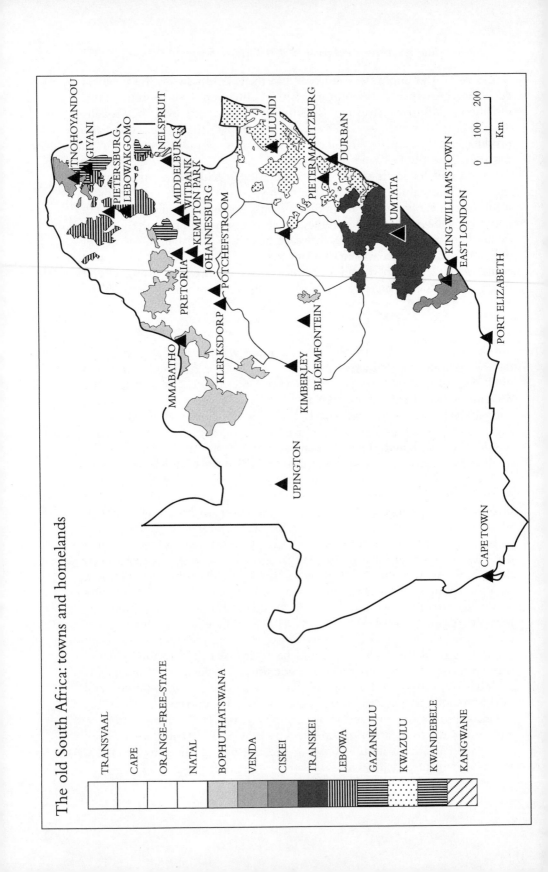

The old South Africa: towns and homelands

TRANSVAAL
CAPE
ORANGE-FREE-STATE
NATAL
BOPHUTHATSWANA
VENDA
CISKEI
TRANSKEI
LEBOWA
GAZANKULU
KWAZULU
KWANDEBELE
KANGWANE

0   100   200
Km

TNOHOYANDOU
GIYANI
NELSPRUIT
PIETERSBURG,
LEBOWAKGOMO
MIDDELBURG
WITBANK
KEMPTON PARK
PRETORIA
JOHANNESBURG
POTCHEFSTROOM
KLERKSDORP
MMABATHO
KIMBERLEY
BLOEMFONTEIN
UPINGTON
ULUNDI
PIETERMARITZBURG
DURBAN
UMTATA
KING WILLIAM'S TOWN
EAST LONDON
PORT ELIZABETH
CAPE TOWN

Full Results of the 1994 Election

Political Parties with a Share of the Vote

Africa Muslim Party
African Christian Democratic Party
African Democratic Movement
African Moderates Congress Party
African National Congress
Democratic Party
Dikwankwetla Party of South Africa
Federal Party
Freedom Front (was AVF; appears in tables as FF/VF or VFFF)
Green Party
Inkatha Freedom Party
Islamic Party
Keep it Straight and Simple Party
Luso-South African Party
Merit Party
Minority Front
National Party
Pan Africanist Congress of Azania
Right Party
South African Women's Party
Sport Organisation for Collective Contributions and Equal Rights
United People's Front
Wes-Kaap Federaliste Party
Women's Right Peace Party
Workers International to Rebuild the Fourth International (SA)
Workers' List Party
Ximoko Progressive Party

National result by province

	IFP	PAC	SOCCER	KISS	FF/VF	WRPP	WLP	XPP	AMP	ACDP	ADM	AMCP	ANC	DP	DPSA	FP	Luso	Min. Fr.	NP	Spoilt	Total
Eastern Cape	6 798	56 891	918	900	18 656	524	374	574	1 235	10 879	1 869	4 919	2 411 695	35 435	1 098	750	263	981	302 951	17 432	2 875 142
Eastern Transvaal	20 872	17 800	636	415	45 964	311	309	416	906	4 474	611	2 625	1 072 518	5 492	834	527	269	503	134 511	16 614	1 326 607
KwaZulu-Natal	1 822 385	23 098	2 311	1 010	17 092	955	1 193	1 501	6 790	17 122	3 819	3 305	1 185 669	60 499	1 927	3 347	961	6 410	591 212	46 407	3 797 013
North-West	7 155	24 233	959	548	49 175	568	331	578	1 386	3 901	701	3 244	1 325 559	5 826	2 088	500	252	772	160 479	19 822	1 608 077
Northern Cape	1 902	3 941	245	293	17 480	151	167	113	320	1 294	189	864	201 515	5 235	415	162	138	494	169 661	4 663	409 242
Northern Transvaal	2 938	20 295	666	365	29 000	273	259	1 354	437	5 042	597	3 168	1 780 177	3 402	722	310	253	662	69 870	17 964	1 937 754
Orange Free State	8 446	23 310	857	403	50 386	398	258	683	324	4 523	553	2 644	1 059 313	7 365	8 796	519	203	490	198 780	14 748	1 382 999
Gauteng	173 903	52 557	2 953	1 107	154 878	1 850	554	828	7 413	20 329	1 062	5 635	2 486 938	126 368	2 424	6 844	490	1 575	1 160 593	29 632	4 237 933
Western Cape	13 895	21 353	1 030	875	41 924	1 404	724	273	15 655	20 540	485	1 286	714 271	88 804	1 147	4 704	464	1 546	1 195 633	25 830	2 151 843
Grand total	2 058 294	243 478	10 575	5 916	424 555	6 434	4 169	6 320	34 466	88 104	9 886	27 690	12 237 655	338 426	19 451	17 663	3 293	13 433	3 983 690	193 112	19 726 610

Source: All appendix tables give figures from the Independent Electoral Commission's Election Administration Directorate.

National result by province (per cent)

Province	IFP	PAC	FF	ACDP	ANC	DP	NP	Other
Eastern Cape	0.24	1.99	0.65	0.38	84.4	1.24	10.6	0.50
Eastern Transvaal	1.59	1.36	1.30	0.34	81.87	0.42	10.27	2.85
KwaZulu-Natal	48.59	0.61	0.45	0.46	31.61	1.61	15.76	0.91
North-West	0.45	1.52	3.1	0.25	83.46	0.37	10.10	0.50
Northern Cape	0.47	0.97	4.32	0.32	49.81	1.29	41.93	0.89
Northern Transvaal	0.15	1.06	1.51	0.26	92.73	0.18	3.64	0.47
Orange Free State	0.62	1.70	3.68	0.33	77.42	0.54	14.53	1.18
Gauteng	4.13	1.25	3.68	0.48	59.1	3.00	27.58	0.78
Western Cape	0.65	1.00	1.97	0.97	33.6	4.18	56.24	1.39
Total	10.54	1.25	2.17	0.45	62.65	1.68	20.04	1.22

National result: Eastern Cape by district

	IFP	PAC	SOCCER	KISS	FF/VF	WRPP	WLP	XPP	AMP	ACDP	ADM	AMCP	ANC	DP	DPSA	FP	Luso	Min. Fr.	NP	Spoilt	Total
Aberdeen	31	30	0	1	155	3	0	1	1	12	0	3	1304	112	3	5	2	7	2096	34	3800
Adelaide	12	86	2	1	103	0	1	1	0	18	2	15	6896	166	3	2	2	1	878	63	8252
Albany	235	734	22	17	298	31	16	4	24	327	15	74	34847	2258	24	43	3	13	6657	328	45970
Albert	14	241	2	2	217	1	1	3	1	9	4	32	6728	94	6	2	3	3	1788	96	9247
Alexandria	54	91	2	4	289	2	1	4	3	71	7	39	11802	157	10	4	4	6	1202	151	13901
Aliwal-North	25	211	3	3	124	2	2	3	1	20	5	40	10335	52	15	1	0	4	1196	126	12170
Barkly East	9	130	2	5	180	1	0	3	1	14	3	14	4778	63	6	2	1	2	1010	93	6317
Bathurst	179	160	11	9	284	7	1	3	0	188	8	51	15607	1165	12	24	2	10	3337	203	21261
Bedford	22	89	1	5	32	0	2	3	3	23	2	11	4388	129	2	1	0	3	1298	53	6067
Bizana	119	958	15	23	53	17	12	20	9	68	20	161	87281	83	24	6	9	16	203	646	89743
Butterworth	29	1621	12	7	12	6	5	9	3	53	14	61	47489	67	14	2	6	9	323	444	50186
Cathcart	23	157	3	1	59	4	1	0	0	62	3	17	6533	265	13	7	0	0	601	67	7806
Cradock	52	154	4	3	429	5	3	6	5	62	7	53	15410	176	18	7	4	12	4707	250	21367
East London	1386	1766	47	110	2371	38	11	8	80	3048	64	293	100154	8757	54	129	6	39	40910	1212	160483
Elliot	17	162	3	0	153	2	3	1	1	9	6	27	6836	86	4	1	2	3	631	114	8061
Elliotdale	13	403	7	9	14	3	4	7	2	25	12	85	32135	48	9	6	3	4	65	269	33121
Engcobo	34	2515	50	47	68	12	18	36	14	60	33	173	68803	109	26	10	19	39	165	477	72708
Flagstaff	17	422	72	14	13	4	6	16	5	21	22	101	43464	93	5	7	4	1	72	274	44634
Fort Beaufort	19	367	3	8	127	5	0	2	2	43	6	28	11724	142	4	5	1	4	1807	99	14396
Glen Grey	30	2783	23	13	21	7	7	12	4	44	28	93	67939	55	18	4	4	17	304	153	71559
Graaff-Reinet	171	198	12	13	456	9	6	6	7	175	4	18	8721	736	18	22	3	25	7005	171	17776
Hankey	48	120	3	8	250	0	3	3	1	71	2	23	7622	89	11	8	0	17	5441	90	13810
Herschel	14	903	15	11	15	5	5	7	6	15	14	74	40482	35	10	2	2	8	174	323	42120
Hewu	6	1319	4	3	2	0	0	0	3	10	32	49	25118	20	6	2	0	2	109	182	26867
Hofmeyr	9	47	0	1	82	1	2	2	0	5	1	10	2005	5	1	0	1	2	449	21	2642
Humansdorp	188	251	15	18	1479	6	4	7	8	422	8	60	12330	879	39	43	8	37	12864	274	28940
Idutywa	48	1073	11	6	13	3	6	9	2	9	4	66	41044	31	7	2	0	7	49	299	42689
Indwe	6	186	1	2	67	0	1	2	0	19	2	11	3920	27	5	0	0	2	299	74	4624
Jansenville	29	57	6	5	113	1	3	2	3	37	1	12	2907	49	10	1	2	18	2059	64	5379
Joubertina	54	96	11	6	316	1	2	5	5	14	3	18	3105	44	7	4	11	14	4067	83	7866
Keiskammahoek	7	555	4	7	9	0	3	2	1	16	74	41	20125	30	8	2	6	2	84	186	21162
Kentani	16	1610	20	14	25	6	4	10	2	21	15	71	39536	48	6	0	2	11	78	273	41768
King Williams Town	135	492	5	5	342	7	7	3	54	312	56	25	13560	679	13	7	0	9	6006	199	21916
Kirkwood	51	291	11	18	340	4	5	7	5	133	7	64	14922	139	7	2	1	5	3236	226	19474
Komga	39	219	1	2	110	1	1	0	1	71	3	23	5322	214	7	2	1	2	872	57	6948
Lady Grey	8	360	5	4	75	1	0	4	1	26	4	35	10670	57	92	11	1	1	666	157	12178
Libode	14	1047	32	18	30	35	10	23	10	28	140	86	56633	70	19	4	3	13	198	265	58678

Lusikisiki	74	1 563	48	42	80	20	11	50	19	76	59	237	111 334	174	51	11	10	29	412	0	114 300
Maclear	27	228	6	6	158	4	1	5	3	25	5	35	10 457	79	6	6	1	7	910	149	12 118
Mdantsane	13	3 294	16	12	11	15	11	10	4	52	113	167	104 415	89	33	3	6	9	311	430	109 014
Middelburg (E. Cape)	39	88	4	6	321	1	2	3	7	81	3	23	5 675	108	6	4	2	10	4 679	129	11 191
Middledrift	3	387	2	2	6	0	1	4	2	10	33	33	15 878	11	1	0	0	2	48	119	16 542
Molteno	2	183	0	0	15	0	0	0	1	0	0	4	2 208	7	0	0	0	0	61	11	2 492
Mount Ayliff	14	367	8	14	16	3	6	3	3	15	9	43	27 690	30	8	2	2	4	62	195	28 494
Mount Fletcher	23	934	22	24	23	8	9	15	9	54	20	100	42 350	66	24	2	2	21	153	143	44 002
Mount Frere	30	810	18	24	31	6	7	12	9	27	8	71	52 291	52	11	4	3	22	191	289	53 916
Mqanduli	15	1 096	17	12	41	8	10	8	4	24	40	103	51 672	65	11	3	3	11	104	154	53 401
Ngqeleni	25	1 049	27	16	48	0	3	19	5	43	17	100	53 089	82	23	0	4	16	219	47	54 832
Nqamakwe	6	776	9	19	16	5	5	20	3	26	8	37	29 007	32	11	2	2	7	80	0	30 071
Pearston	8	5	0	0	32	0	0	0	0	9	2	6	1 311	15	1	0	1	3	1 256	17	2 668
Peddie	8	515	6	7	14	4	3	2	2	12	38	85	32 308	38	4	0	22	9	131	8	33 216
Port Elizabeth	2 236	3 229	74	79	4 691	106	45	25	733	3 496	54	363	211 932	13 991	117	247	27	96	127 496	2 628	371 665
Port St Johns	15	447	5	11	15	8	6	3	3	20	3	90	26 434	47	8	1	2	11	141	255	27 525
Queenstown	101	962	6	9	305	12	7	6	9	181	20	92	38 745	782	23	6	0	10	6 359	395	48 030
Qumbu	34	1 085	19	8	3	3	5	10	6	24	16	65	50 012	34	7	3	3	11	110	204	51 662
Somerset-East	37	202	5	11	386	1	2	1	4	32	12	41	10 904	181	24	4	1	14	4 075	144	16 077
St Marks	6	2 624	13	0	8	0	3	7	2	4	3	5	32 517	15	6	1	0	4	37	106	35 373
Sterkstroom	12	77	1	1	82	1	0	1	0	9	0	8	3 512	55	2	1	0	0	313	55	4 130
Steynsburg	13	67	0	0	147	0	1	2	1	15	0	10	3 451	37	4	2	2	2	918	44	4 717
Steyderville	5	7	0	0	55	0	2	0	1	4	1	6	870	19	1	1	3	3	778	15	1 771
Stockenstrom	0	255	0	0	0	0	1	0	0	0	22	8	7 642	12	0	0	0	0	108	0	8 048
Stutterheim	39	372	7	1	175	4	1	7	3	139	13	66	17 478	331	7	8	1	3	1 378	227	20 260
Tabankulu	22	738	25	25	62	14	15	15	6	60	38	225	46 719	124	8	4	5	18	122	0	48 245
Tarka	16	75	1	0	94	1	0	1	1	35	0	10	3 246	116	4	2	0	0	706	30	4 338
Tsolo	10	666	10	9	25	2	7	5	8	16	7	41	31 609	35	5	1	4	5	57	0	32 522
Tsomo	17	563	9	3	21	2	2	9	4	10	5	26	27 328	26	8	3	5	1	65	289	28 396
Uitenhage	271	1 351	15	27	2 494	17	9	17	71	442	10	120	66 066	771	45	22	10	40	31 204	710	103 712
Umtata	95	3 359	39	38	80	17	22	29	27	144	47	131	115 941	283	22	17	11	50	1 927	924	123 203
Umzimkulu	215	695	17	8	26	8	5	15	2	66	29	81	73 206	64	22	2	5	8	209	511	75 194
Venterstad	23	30	0	4	109	2	2	0	1	5	0	10	1 459	25	3	1	1	7	967	34	2 681
Victoria East	9	583	6	1	9	2	2	8	0	14	79	62	30 938	39	6	6	0	6	227	177	32 169
Willowmore	23	29	4	0	103	1	1	2	0	16	4	7	2 075	42	1	1	0	7	2 913	51	5 282
Willowvale	63	1 021	15	20	31	6	6	14	5	26	14	127	44 005	79	26	0	4	13	77	0	45 554
Wodehouse	9	203	0	1	166	1	2	1	3	8	7	34	5 747	104	3	2	0	3	534	78	6 904
Xalanga	10	1 309	10	14	9	4	0	2	2	12	6	51	21 846	35	4	1	3	9	105	183	23 615
Zwelitsha	67	3 743	14	16	22	7	7	9	4	86	492	139	105 853	111	22	3	3	141	602	585	111 926
Total:	6 798	56 891	918	900	18 656	524	374	574	1 235	10 879	1 869	4 919	2 411 695	35 435	1 098	750	263	981	302 951	17 432	2 875 142

National result: Eastern Transvaal by district

	IFP	PAC	SOCCER	KISS	FF/VF	WRPP	WLP	XPP	AMP	ACDP	ADM	AMCP	ANC	DP	DPSA	FP	Luso	Min. Fr.	NP	Spoilt	Total
Amersfoort	527	296	17	13	357	6	23	4	9	41	17	68	12440	47	21	8	10	13	956	300	15173
Balfour	255	288	12	8	901	7	7	11	36	36	10	57	15896	62	24	9	3	10	2566	272	20470
Barberton	344	534	26	17	1853	8	7	13	19	233	11	74	26418	202	34	24	8	21	5490	505	35841
Belfast	127	273	14	10	1012	3	9	12	13	55	8	70	12044	122	14	16	8	13	2144	265	16232
Bethal	344	586	18	17	1609	10	10	15	23	122	18	290	21733	73	24	10	3	13	3392	498	28808
Carolina	109	237	14	9	1034	12	8	12	34	42	8	29	11344	57	26	10	2	15	1657	281	14940
Delmas	245	401	10	9	1494	5	1	8	10	76	7	37	18923	128	17	19	5	10	3493	324	25222
Eerstehoek	1335	803	36	15	68	16	9	14	10	107	34	113	56900	96	36	11	7	25	1816	835	62286
Ermelo	1258	1125	28	29	3442	15	21	30	51	233	41	136	46472	179	44	15	7	45	8335	993	62499
Groblersdal	76	340	15	10	1987	3	7	10	6	50	16	79	18494	70	27	16	7	23	3220	393	24849
Highveld Ridge	1716	995	30	15	5912	13	11	14	72	588	22	85	54681	409	49	46	12	28	17590	633	82921
Kamhlushwa	80	835	15	6	44	14	14	12	12	139	19	165	77313	102	33	10	12	29	799	946	80603
Kriel	620	232	6	5	1384	3	3	6	5	223	2	25	10709	129	7	15	5	4	4074	239	17696
Lydenburg	114	355	20	8	2506	4	3	1	33	84	19	116	18095	110	32	12	34	17	3234	435	25232
Mathanjana	12	439	13	13	10	15	4	8	2	54	6	50	36756	65	25	6	4	6	625	301	38414
Mbibana	18	244	9	7	11	6	4	0	4	16	15	44	22452	31	9	3	0	3	227	253	23356
Mdutjana 1 + 2 + 3	83	894	82	15	27	16	20	16	9	48	21	72	59219	56	19	11	8	24	691	646	61977
Middelburg (E. Tvl)	958	970	38	20	6555	12	15	27	166	241	40	119	50265	411	25	35	35	3	15513	609	76057
Mkobola	275	1617	39	21	40	25	18	21	19	212	117	176	117484	173	47	10	19	23	2117	2006	124459
Moutse 1 + 2	82	779	15	16	38	14	9	9	12	64	14	94	51046	124	20	3	9	29	475	525	53377
Nelspruit	524	318	9	11	3344	15	13	10	94	282	11	67	15954	744	19	45	4	18	10913	447	32842
Nsikazi	180	1465	25	21	28	15	23	34	25	217	24	182	134653	107	51	6	7	22	1001	1262	139349
Piet Retief (E. Tvl)	5820	401	23	14	1094	3	10	13	37	224	37	63	18433	93	22	6	7	18	3505	375	30198
Pilgrim's Rest 1 + 2	135	161	8	4	834	3	3	3	8	84	7	26	7558	372	17	34	2	4	3174	117	12554
Standerton	697	661	19	40	2482	9	16	13	74	113	14	79	31106	124	49	15	4	24	6078	601	42222
Volksrust	708	277	17	10	1011	6	7	7	22	115	9	33	11856	77	32	9	4	15	3093	228	17536
Wakkerstroom	2346	326	27	15	286	3	12	21	25	58	25	48	11709	57	17	9	8	18	1172	2	16184
Waterval Boven	47	39	1	0	259	4	2	0	2	15	3	3	2797	26	4	3	1	0	668	66	3940
White River	282	226	11	7	1493	9	9	18	8	262	9	57	17123	423	19	58	15	6	4601	313	24949
Witbank	1555	1683	39	30	4849	37	11	54	66	440	27	168	82645	823	71	53	14	24	21892	1944	116421
Total:	20872	17800	636	415	45964	311	309	416	906	4474	611	2625	1072518	5492	834	527	269	503	134511	16614	1326607

	IFP	PAC	SOCCER	KISS	FF/VF	WRPP	WLP	XPP	AMP	ACDP	ADM	AMCP	ANC	DP	DPSA	FP	Luso	Min. Fr.	NP	Spoilt	Total
Alfred	29 488	530	77	38	56	12	39	70	48	222	95	82	17 376	105	70	25	59	109	1 993	0	50 494
Bergville	34 596	204	56	10	170	11	28	24	21	147	49	28	5 370	173	39	43	24	53	2 283	759	44 088
Camperdown	15 852	872	37	30	162	21	30	41	38	241	57	147	67 434	467	73	56	26	56	3 076	0	88 712
Chatsworth	5 245	462	41	38	92	41	20	19	1 041	936	23	79	33 194	1 887	50	38	14	1 745	85 247	2 419	132 643
Dannhauser	21 456	315	54	6	303	4	26	23	58	87	45	31	6 549	35	25	17	15	50	3 895	745	33 738
Dundee	29 327	195	40	9	376	5	18	27	94	117	36	29	7 241	225	22	27	61	35	5 120	4 258	47 216
Durban	85 787	3 631	248	176	4 079	228	119	105	2 198	3 802	258	495	255 545	23 250	182	682	25	995	162 643	4 114	548 598
Eshowe	65 550	398	63	16	86	5	32	54	12	199	94	41	14 560	261	30	30	32	37	2 599	1 053	85 145
Estcourt	37 872	366	65	20	274	16	26	42	194	265	70	46	12 237	713	47	62	11	77	7 451	1 011	60 886
Glencoe	3 540	83	14	1	276	0	2	5	36	24	9	12	2 647	95	4	6	11	18	3 148	204	10 125
Hlabisa	103 034	197	55	5	395	16	19	24	16	215	55	28	7 458	173	37	32	18	50	2 708	1 129	115 657
Impendle	55 445	107	36	6	4	11	10	19	34	52	34	10	2 587	24	15	4	25	25	529	601	59 571
Inanda	54 899	997	87	35	235	38	64	76	536	699	1 104	174	44 174	2 608	130	83	40	630	49 233	1 360	157 198
Ixopo	42 939	486	76	25	69	0	29	45	30	250	81	104	23 042	282	44	40	36	92	2 711	1 606	71 991
Kliprivier	30 773	928	86	53	632	27	40	64	395	383	85	93	39 849	718	52	52	28	159	12 603	1 428	88 448
Lions River	25 956	610	74	15	370	14	20	46	70	502	65	80	26 983	2 309	49	236	21	52	7 743	1 036	66 251
Lower Tugela	12 326	620	42	30	178	14	20	33	338	490	65	64	23 861	1 063	36	36	13	384	34 134	1 609	75 356
Lower Umfolozi	75 773	381	55	21	1 542	21	25	41	42	727	60	61	19 898	1 048	39	77	13	78	16 984	1 505	118 391
Mapumulo	18 493	96	20	5	13	4	13	5	3	34	19	12	3 537	10	12	4	9	6	275	236	22 806
Mhlabatini	122 304	68	8	4	3	3	3	3	1	13	30	5	887	24	3	6	4	4	206	583	124 160
Mount Currie	383	1 236	35	45	259	14	22	29	25	330	30	163	48 371	961	60	29	10	33	4 942	774	57 751
Mtonjaneni	20 790	33	13	1	107	4	9	4	6	46	11	9	1 157	71	5	15	7	14	711	270	23 283
Mtunzini	252	4	1	0	2	0	8	7	2	1	0	0	782	0	0	0	12	0	13	0	1 065
Ndwedwe	34 229	306	37	18	18	17	25	38	11	62	85	50	15 576	60	20	14	25	30	862	1 174	52 644
New Hanover	57 617	642	63	17	354	17	32	52	51	432	94	78	24 995	502	52	92	47	81	6 211	123	91 530
Newcastle	63 221	1 427	112	72	268	48	88	93	54	397	139	145	38 660	413	116	72	0	84	9 682	2 922	118 060
Ngotshe	10 725	34	5	2	156	1	4	2	0	23	10	7	719	32	9	2	6	3	793	160	12 684
Nkandhla	66 819	33	12	0	1	4	0	5	1	19	10	7	1 120	9	6	6	2	8	278	445	68 789
Nongoma	82 031	44	12	2	0	16	5	3	4	19	5	78	1 422	9	10	6	14	16	260	908	84 849
Nqutu	22 000	66	17	2	9	3	8	7	2	20	11	9	2 941	11	6	3	9	11	432	356	25 919
Paulpietersberg	47 748	192	38	7	199	3	20	28	8	114	44	25	5 271	37	6	6	14	21	1 575	717	56 114
Piet Retief (Natal)	71 973	114	26	3	361	5	5	12	4	88	32	18	2 325	40	29	19	9	16	1 508	188	76 758
Pietermaritzburg	69 521	2 019	159	64	1 423	126	64	62	731	2 217	124	323	182 817	10 246	125	8	44	404	71 840	955	344 070
Pinetown	81 328	1 739	81	28	840	70	60	47	166	1 881	250	156	101 500	7 586	91	806	23	182	33 871	1 561	231 729
Polela	19 496	211	44	8	31	10	15	33	10	77	30	43	8 285	85	28	18	20	44	694	576	29 758
Port Shepstone	43 000	888	99	34	1 268	34	58	83	235	870	140	174	43 245	2 500	115	269	50	367	22 339	1 835	117 458
Richmond (Natal)	10 831	491	21	12	146	13	14	27	18	173	39	63	22 588	541	40	124	10	65	3 608	0	38 742
Ubombo	99 370	387	98	42	153	16	56	60	19	185	159	87	11 282	134	59	42	106	99	1 557	3 432	117 345
Umbumbulu	16 361	428	41	9	13	10	21	29	8	59	64	48	22 375	50	37	44	22	27	1 249	803	41 664
Umzinto	63 268	845	106	58	395	36	62	81	185	391	125	154	24 771	1 139	88	10	46	204	14 016	2 006	108 055
Underberg	4 930	145	23	12	68	5	11	12	3	79	20	16	3 265	315	18	79	8	13	1 120	130	10 278
Utrecht	10 284	104	9	4	448	2	6	7	3	45	12	8	2 056	33	5	85	6	8	1 938	273	15 258
Vryheid	41 531	147	22	27	1 177	6	24	21	21	166	40	23	5 017	227	24	7	18	25	6 667	1 004	56 223
Weenen	14 022	17	3	0	81	1	1	0	20	23	11	3	700	28	2	36	1	0	465	130	15 513
Total:	1 822 385	23 098	2 311	1 010	17 092	955	1 193	1 501	6 790	17 122	3 819	3 305	1 185 669	60 499	1 927	3 347	961	6 410	591 212	46 407	3 797 013

National result: North-West by district

	IFP	PAC	SOCCER	KISS	FF/VF	WRPP	WLP	XPP	AMP	ACDP	ADM	AMCP	ANC	DP	DPSA	FP	Luso	Min. Fr.	NP	Spoilt	Total
Bafokeng	163	1 035	27	16	70	22	14	16	13	133	39	123	76 420	125	69	7	6	21	1 787	1 023	81 129
Bloemhof	16	128	10	5	441	1	2	6	6	21	4	25	7 390	27	12	1	1	4	812	338	9 250
Brits	617	876	39	21	6 054	24	13	37	105	329	26	168	41 377	727	59	77	5	26	14 230	0	64 810
Christiana	22	121	7	6	629	1	3	4	1	14	2	19	6 492	27	14	2	3	5	1 500	144	9 016
Coligny	19	106	3	3	454	2	5	5	2	8	7	43	7 503	22	20	2	1	5	993	180	9 383
Delareyville	39	274	67	23	1 430	10	13	18	8	68	24	127	17 906	105	52	13	9	29	2 074	635	22 924
Ditsobotla	71	1 229	52	26	36	36	10	25	13	115	40	113	67 184	107	90	22	16	27	1 804	563	71 579
Ganyesa	76	404	16	16	27	10	12	23	10	45	14	64	23 794	77	44	8	5	28	2 411	416	27 503
Klerksdorp	2 530	2 964	77	49	13 082	69	33	61	222	643	54	350	176 949	1 177	175	82	33	63	45 073	3 811	247 497
Koster	79	235	14	5	1 111	3	7	10	8	19	13	29	9 465	37	21	3	1	17	1 881	283	13 241
Lehurutshe	62	987	45	20	46	14	14	16	7	114	25	131	40 078	104	76	5	10	39	2 675	559	45 027
Lichtenburg	162	516	25	21	3 167	8	10	10	91	109	21	123	26 490	178	67	18	10	19	6 922	339	38 306
Madikwe	16	632	8	9	20	11	8	13	5	54	9	81	32 344	51	33	6	2	32	1 147	0	34 481
Mankwe	260	1 067	37	25	92	22	19	15	24	125	25	156	68 729	241	78	14	17	47	2 802	756	74 551
Marico 1 + 2	130	374	16	11	1 963	8	6	11	95	50	18	63	12 334	124	35	17	2	14	3 987	451	19 709
Molopo (Mafeking)	149	2 100	95	40	66	63	13	43	110	188	41	219	91 338	325	197	18	17	51	6 328	1 180	102 581
Moretele	89	1 186	37	16	40	29	34	34	11	150	49	209	98 349	159	99	10	15	20	1 809	974	103 292
Odi 1 + 2	403	3 423	87	39	62	99	22	62	44	350	68	348	213 320	318	132	23	16	52	5 070	2 068	226 006
Potchefstroom	719	793	25	13	5 586	16	6	17	32	267	14	71	34 492	347	315	25	5	12	14 563	730	58 048
Rustenburg 1 + 2	890	909	36	27	7 481	13	7	16	396	526	27	119	56 531	757	64	74	9	26	19 359	715	87 982
Schweizer-Reneke	41	296	8	12	1 065	7	1	14	14	35	13	73	18 018	44	30	5	9	16	1 455	290	21 435
Swartruggens	28	105	6	7	660	4	3	2	9	12	5	12	5 931	29	21	4	2	6	1 335	19	8 200
Taung	128	1 672	84	30	62	38	32	36	32	187	45	149	70 475	199	100	21	12	49	2 429	1 209	76 989
Thlaping-Thlaro + Kuruman	71	1 098	47	48	59	22	21	41	25	126	34	89	46 994	179	57	16	11	56	3 746	659	53 399
Ventersdorp	50	425	29	12	1 127	7	8	11	16	22	13	52	12 842	59	38	2	9	19	1 719	905	17 365
Vryburg	249	847	44	36	2 599	22	32	32	72	150	57	199	37 691	225	148	18	20	73	10 063	1 047	53 624
Wolmaransstad	76	431	15	12	1 746	7	10	11	15	41	14	89	25 123	56	42	7	6	16	2 505	528	30 750
Total:	7 155	24 233	959	548	49 175	568	331	578	1 386	3 901	701	3 244	1 325 559	5 826	2 088	500	252	772	160 479	19 822	1 608 077

National result: Northern Cape by district

	IFP	PAC	SOCCER	KISS	FF/VF	WRPP	WLP	XPP	AMP	ACDP	ADM	AMCP	ANC	DP	DPSA	FP	Luso	Min. Fr.	NP	Spoilt	Total
Barkly West	58	287	12	22	580	9	7	7	12	54	18	76	17 801	158	22	9	6	15	3 520	359	23 032
Bristown	15	18	0	0	138	0	0	0	1	21	1	1	976	10	4	0	0	1	2 199	19	3 404
Calvinia	44	24	7	8	768	2	1	1	2	25	7	4	1 602	123	2	4	11	27	7 599	95	10 356
Carnarvon	23	14	3	5	180	3	2	0	1	6	0	6	1 186	31	4	1	2	18	3 526	184	5 195
Colesberg	19	144	5	4	173	1	2	1	1	19	9	30	5 725	69	4	0	1	3	2 478	74	8 762
De Aar	54	112	5	13	476	3	6	0	8	29	2	13	5 985	61	12	7	5	18	7 574	135	14 518
Fraserburg	23	5	0	1	95	1	2	0	0	3	0	0	138	12	2	0	0	8	1 920	16	2 226
Gordonia	230	361	47	49	3 014	27	61	25	35	134	21	324	29 000	488	74	29	28	81	31 091	571	65 690
Hanover	12	39	2	4	69	1	3	0	2	12	3	7	1 173	38	2	2	0	8	998	62	2 437
Hartswater	64	233	14	7	1 205	4	7	8	7	36	16	60	10 718	85	34	5	3	28	4 344	284	17 162
Hay	35	31	4	5	243	2	3	1	2	11	2	5	2 134	26	4	2	1	15	2 790	59	5 375
Herbert	90	109	12	26	718	10	11	9	8	46	10	31	6 054	146	31	8	13	48	5 325	280	12 985
Hopetown	41	30	8	12	294	1	2	2	8	26	1	13	1 767	86	7	2	6	21	3 999	61	6 387
Kenhardt	14	7	1	1	238	0	0	0	0	14	0	2	1 276	72	6	3	3	3	2 852	0	4 490
Kimberley	614	1 489	37	40	3 088	46	16	17	179	495	40	115	61 422	2 177	90	47	19	51	31 258	1 046	102 286
Kuruman	79	129	17	8	1 132	6	3	4	1	67	12	27	7 257	63	14	2	6	15	6 335	187	15 364
Namaqualand	185	247	42	31	1 258	20	16	11	31	79	18	39	13 872	1 058	37	27	16	41	19 081	326	36 435
Noupoort	10	38	0	2	116	0	1	0	0	11	2	9	2 224	12	1	1	0	3	1 803	48	4 281
Philipstown	18	38	0	2	384	0	0	0	0	8	1	2	1 501	17	1	1	0	5	2 891	35	4 904
Postmasburg	127	242	11	8	1 717	7	6	3	4	90	6	48	15 267	215	27	3	7	20	11 351	271	29 430
Prieska	40	37	6	15	339	2	9	10	6	63	4	9	3 055	69	10	1	1	19	5 654	129	9 478
Richmond (N. Cape)	11	18	1	4	125	1	1	0	3	2	1	2	1 023	55	3	1	2	8	1 748	20	3 028
Sutherland	10	3	2	4	154	0	0	0	0	3	0	0	148	13	0	1	0	12	1 532	18	1 900
Victoria-West	35	30	1	7	239	0	2	2	1	23	4	0	1 107	84	2	0	8	13	4 170	52	5 780
Warrenton	41	248	8	13	656	5	6	6	4	17	10	40	8 562	44	18	5	1	10	2 182	317	12 197
Williston	10	8	0	2	81	1	0	2	4	0	1	1	542	23	4	1	1	3	1 441	15	2 140
Total:	1 902	3 941	245	293	17 480	151	167	113	320	1 294	189	864	201 515	5 235	415	162	138	494	169 661	4 663	409 242

National result: Northern Transvaal by district

	IFP	PAC	SOCCER	KISS	FF/VF	WRPP	WLP	XPP	AMP	ACDP	ADM	AMCP	ANC	DP	DPSA	FP	Luso	Min. Fr.	NP	Spoilt	Total
Bochum	22	447	24	7	20	6	5	16	7	119	26	89	60 011	55	22	4	9	42	392	536	61 860
Bolebedu	12	467	22	3	11	5	1	19	1	96	16	124	76 727	57	14	6	6	11	248	669	78 518
Dzanani 1 + 2	5	138	3	0	7	1	1	0	0	13	2	10	14 424	10	1	0	0	3	282	67	14 967
Ellisras	597	438	16	10	4 670	5	4	10	4	188	21	94	47 167	180	21	18	6	18	6 510	701	60 678
Giyani	61	802	44	28	306	19	11	333	7	355	20	170	127 242	141	25	10	9	38	1 112	846	131 579
(Hlanganani)																					
Letaba (Lulekani)	10	107	2	0	14	1	3	92	1	35	5	22	10 652	21	3	1	1	2	171	93	11 236
Letaba 1	210	404	11	7	2 887	2	6	32	10	216	15	79	18 057	221	25	26	11	18	5 314	452	28 003
Malamulele	25	341	16	9	12	6	4	149	1	133	15	85	64 236	48	23	3	5	10	420	300	65 841
Messina	62	257	11	4	704	0	4	11	5	63	12	24	9 677	48	15	4	5	6	1 899	110	12 921
Mhala	34	1 044	20	16	21	10	11	89	8	108	17	70	85 237	53	15	5	3	17	423	766	87 967
Mutale	13	246	1	6	3	0	2	6	3	12	5	14	28 509	20	2	0	0	6	288	154	29 291
Namakgale	20	224	1	4	8	1	1	12	1	71	6	30	23 051	23	5	1	2	3	351	292	24 106
Naphuno 2	32	634	17	15	50	7	9	21	2	109	14	96	57 719	49	16	10	7	26	362	603	59 798
Nebo	67	1 669	58	16	56	20	12	35	16	188	42	447	141 057	172	52	14	12	53	969	1 530	146 485
Phalaborwa	261	93	10	4	2 924	6	6	26	3	100	5	24	5 773	268	88	14	1	7	5 947	168	15 642
Pietersburg	693	1 351	44	48	8 527	18	27	59	235	1 025	38	178	78 988	682	64	64	76	68	21 680	1 585	115 473
Pietersburg	34	792	13	12	27	10	10	29	4	144	31	105	61 759	49	25	9	6	31	485	717	64 292
(Mapulaneng)																					
Potgietersrus	287	1 865	75	39	4 152	35	36	60	31	438	88	354	164 467	312	99	36	25	86	7 653	2 243	182 381
Ritavi 1	21	469	15	6	22	3	5	138	10	172	7	32	35 039	53	11	5	5	18	341	174	36 546
Ritavi 2	14	243	7	1	5	2	9	68	3	94	4	49	23 136	36	6	1	1	4	225	276	24 184
Sekgosese 1 + 2	19	508	24	5	19	3	6	15	6	83	11	72	44 193	52	11	4	5	16	373	376	45 801
Sekhukhuneland	52	1 481	43	20	73	10	17	20	3	275	47	233	145 558	126	42	7	15	36	715	1 013	149 786
Seshego	49	1 307	41	31	47	26	20	26	33	275	45	203	95 947	143	51	12	16	46	1 884	999	101 201
Sibasa	46	1 296	52	15	103	12	10	9	5	105	24	101	121 348	99	21	3	1	19	1 328	602	125 199
(Tthohoyandou)																					
Thabamoopa	61	2 302	57	30	87	47	28	46	19	358	58	263	130 963	209	76	18	10	50	2 244	1 527	138 453
Tshitale	5	217	7	3	3	1	1	7	4	51	4	30	23 627	21	6	1	2	3	268	187	24 448
Vuvani	15	458	14	5	14	1	3	8	1	29	4	60	45 813	45	14	1	5	7	409	293	47 199
Waterberg	211	695	18	21	4 228	16	6	18	14	187	15	110	39 800	209	29	33	9	18	7 577	685	53 899
Total:	2 938	20 295	666	365	29 000	273	259	1 354	437	5 042	597	3 168	1 780 177	3 402	722	310	253	662	69 870	17 964	1 937 754

National result: Orange Free State by district

	IFP	PAC	SOCCER	KISS	FF/VF	WRPP	WLP	XPP	AMP	ACDP	ADM	AMCP	ANC	DP	DPSA	FP	Luso	Min. Fr.	NP	Spoilt	Total
Bethlehem	288	714	29	19	2006	16	6	7	7	222	19	92	25998	297	111	19	8	52	7624	424	37958
Bethulie	39	82	2		271	1		5	1	16	2	12	4195	34	6	7	0	7	1493	108	6285
Bloemfontein	1497	2518	102	45	12966	61	32	31	57	1334	43	253	136214	2269	822	125	36	60	61006	1897	221368
Boshof	44	145	7	8	999	5	0	6	3	65	7	52	10948	55	19	4	4	5	2157	268	14801
Bothaville	42	386	12	7	1152	13	2	7	6	45	13	63	23035	44	33	5	5	6	1969	301	27146
Botshabelo	53	1782	41	8	19	24	12	8	11	149	22	121	75258	198	1886	8	5	11	991	298	80905
Brandfort	54	241	9	8	803	4	1	7	1	37	7	43	9488	60	20	6	4	4	1962	168	12927
Bultfontein	29	312	11	6	585	3	5	10	3	32	10	47	11430	33	13	1	3	6	1456	173	14167
Clocolan	18	204	3	6	333	2	11	6	4	18	4	28	7598	42	29	7	3	3	1294	151	9764
Dewetsdorp	13	113	6	2	335	1	0	6	0	14	3	22	4652	19	7	3	2	3	882	88	6170
Edenburg	14	44	6	2	192	0	1	1	1	3	1	8	2639	10	9	2	1	0	968	63	3965
Excelsior	26	142	8	5	216	3	2	5	2	5	1	21	5966	68	50	3	2	1	755	116	7397
Fauresmith	36	59	4	7	334	2	1	6	4	18	1	20	2910	36	4	5	1	2	1442	65	4957
Ficksburg	81	498	22	18	742	9	15	12	4	116	4	62	17807	147	38	16	6	10	2452	330	22389
Fouriesburg	34	179	6	5	250	9	3	8	8	42	15	35	7896	57	30	4	3	8	872	212	9676
Frankfort	130	340	13	7	1123	3	12	15	9	56	19	70	19139	57	52	7	8	13	2516	298	23887
Harrismith	615	460	31	13	1173	5	9	15	7	152	14	64	25364	293	121	20	8	26	5329	463	34182
Heilbron	69	301	3	5	1061	4	2	6	3	51	6	48	14964	31	54	3	2	4	2385	227	19227
Hennenman	110	189	9	3	650	3	2	5	3	51	4	13	12381	29	12	5	2	4	1984	168	15629
Hoopstad	23	213	6	4	485	1	3	5	7	58	9	26	7811	29	23	3	2	0	1001	0	9710
Jacobsdal	26	59	5	3	347	1	2	0	2	53	1	8	2976	15	17	5	1	6	1057	45	4629
Jagersfontein	13	73	2	2	123	1	0	0	0	10	3	6	2691	12	3	1	0	1	818	51	3808
Koffiefontein	22	145	2	0	287	4	4	7	2	35	2	12	4200	24	14	3	1	3	1415	83	6267
Koppies	16	167	9	3	414	3	5	5	3	24	8	32	9009	27	28	0	2	5	834	137	10731
Kroonstad	271	1082	32	21	2787	24	13	13	12	151	19	87	45827	192	57	24	4	17	9774	701	61108
Ladybrand	60	431	12	6	440	7	3	11	2	47	6	39	10805	121	96	6	3	10	2731	180	15016
Lindley	65	703	11	10	981	3	2	8	52	53	11	71	16744	43	23	3	3	15	1683	328	20812
Marquard	21	209	11	3	238	0	1	0	1	22	3	20	6032	61	11	3	3	3	606	84	7332

National result: Orange Free State by district (*Continued*)

	IFP	PAC	SOCCER	KISS	FF/VF	WRPP	WLP	XPP	AMP	ACDP	ADM	AMCP	ANC	DP	DPSA	FP	Luso	Min. Fr.	NP	Spoilt	Total
Odendaalsrus	460	872	32	7	1083	12	3	13	7	38	10	56	44901	67	55	5	5	12	4892	574	53104
Parys	131	387	25	3	1816	9	5	4	3	94	7	43	19644	88	21	14	0	6	4348	301	26949
Petrusburg	12	108	7	2	331	0	2	4	0	10	1	13	3323	20	13	0	3	4	796	67	4716
Philippolis	26	19	1	0	240	0	0	0	0	26	3	5	1756	18	4	4	0	2	1347	0	3451
Qwa Qwa	279	1875	143	32	54	29	12	40	17	123	34	274	121570	806	4051	20	7	46	1784	1216	132412
Reddersburg	14	85	3	2	284	2	1	1	0	5	0	12	2702	22	10	1	1	2	818	53	4018
Reitz	73	293	13	4	573	7	10	9	2	50	9	56	10057	39	23	5	12	15	2089	295	13634
Rouxville	9	172	2	0	276	1	1	1	3	12	1	21	4475	14	4	4	0	4	906	64	5970
Sasolburg	619	985	13	5	3960	12	11	311	10	109	105	83	33459	365	47	35	2	6	13972	604	54713
Senekal	57	335	17	14	789	10	5	7	1	43	8	36	14004	61	410	5	1	7	2253	230	18295
Smithfield	13	135	1	1	160	0	1	1	1	15	1	12	2489	22	10	1	0	3	610	47	3523
Thaba Nchu	95	635	38	16	66	35	7	15	10	89	16	39	30642	203	73	8	6	23	3538	0	35554
Theunissen	201	335	7	1	558	5	4	4	1	24	4	38	17375	30	33	2	4	6	1452	308	20392
Trompsburg	13	47	4	2	164	0	1	0	1	14	1	7	1988	6	0	0	0	1	748	41	3038
Ventersburg	17	110	1	3	260	5	1	1	2	13	3	17	5369	22	11	2	2	3	681	91	6611
Viljoenskroon	295	417	15	8	738	3	2	9	4	46	5	69	25789	120	27	5	2	3	1288	323	29168
Virginia	424	743	30	13	1390	10	13	12	5	125	16	71	33754	165	34	22	5	10	7522	743	45107
Vrede	186	205	9	5	771	6	4	3	7	42	9	45	13418	54	28	6	7	7	2054	230	17096
Vredefort	18	136	6	3	402	3	0	4	1	46	5	17	6399	14	12	1	1	1	703	104	7876
Welkom	1701	2687	43	25	3717	22	13	19	28	624	35	244	109686	792	267	72	14	29	23666	1443	145127
Wepener	25	195	10	13	220	4	2	2	1	31	2	20	5718	40	17	6	1	6	1059	142	7510
Wesselsbron	25	329	7	6	575	3	4	0	0	13	9	51	12635	30	29	1	2	3	985	212	14919
Winburg	25	144	7	1	352	4	0	3	3	14	5	23	7349	21	15	1	2	6	988	104	9067
Zastron	19	270	9	9	295	3	5	5	3	38	7	17	6834	43	14	3	1	7	825	129	8536
Total:	8446	23310	857	403	50386	398	258	683	324	4523	553	2644	1059313	7365	8796	519	203	490	198780	14748	1382999

National result: Gauteng by district

	IFP	PAC	SOCCER	KISS	FF/VF	WRPP	WLP	XPP	AMP	ACDP	ADM	AMCP	ANC	DP	DPSA	FP	Luso	Min. Fr.	NP	Spoilt	Total
Alberton	8 687	2 471	72	22	3 271	56	23	37	24	1 011	35	198	131 864	1 372	104	118	18	30	28 247	4 293	181 953
Benoni	8 968	2 364	104	81	4 434	82	33	42	370	697	59	138	122 047	5 312	110	245	18	49	39 863	1 532	186 548
Boksburg	6 899	1 271	43	23	4 208	36	7	27	86	681	27	99	63 155	1 553	69	118	11	97	32 919	447	111 776
Brakpan	1 969	858	38	17	5 024	17	6	8	114	333	19	61	50 612	1 251	29	70	9	26	26 316	0	86 777
Germiston	8 793	914	64	31	7 010	43	16	21	21	999	24	79	40 336	8 435	73	456	31	45	69 280	930	137 601
Heidelberg (PWV)	2 048	720	18	12	2 570	6	7	8	47	144	19	53	25 811	191	32	27	4	9	7 411	227	39 364
Johannesburg	78 858	13 200	851	243	13 076	811	228	265	3 989	3 445	286	1 614	732 310	47 399	642	2 088	177	386	322 241	8 243	1 230 352
Kempton Park	5 515	3 524	52	37	7 354	67	15	39	29	1 019	41	198	149 116	3 071	107	188	19	25	45 853	1 348	217 617
Krugersdorp	3 213	2 554	60	32	7 401	44	22	26	216	383	29	618	81 232	1 945	99	151	23	29	31 541	1 298	130 916
Nigel	770	733	18	200	2 370	7	5	14	55	154	10	60	36 383	291	35	23	5	17	10 739	359	52 248
Oberholzer	5 438	1 673	42	23	3 023	25	13	37	15	152	48	120	69 164	381	73	41	10	29	13 502	1 661	95 470
Pretoria (PWV)	9 541	6 066	1 060	196	55 964	236	61	109	1 143	6 621	266	1 377	313 764	16 601	323	1 082	69	576	240 330	0	655 385
Randburg	12 120	2 539	178	50	3 146	151	25	52	106	1 466	41	215	121 499	25 434	148	1 345	15	42	77 131	2 018	247 721
Randfontein	1 135	1 011	22	14	4 329	17	6	15	128	130	17	64	39 398	442	64	32	10	21	17 684	871	65 296
Roodepoort	5 811	1 347	95	26	9 309	71	12	17	128	1 237	25	145	81 742	7 640	119	528	10	35	72 269	939	181 505
Springs	3 221	1 461	42	21	5 028	31	13	28	80	336	17	95	73 906	1 630	59	107	11	41	28 406	0	114 533
Vanderbijlpark	2 150	4 809	65	30	6 221	69	18	33	34	637	31	236	186 716	856	124	61	20	31	32 143	1 550	235 834
Vereeniging	4 091	3 736	91	26	9 500	58	23	14	673	725	36	178	113 826	2 111	155	145	23	52	51 029	2 748	189 240
Westonaria	4 676	1 306	38	23	1 640	23	21	36	269	159	32	87	54 057	453	59	19	7	35	13 689	1 168	77 797
Total:	173 903	52 557	2 953	1 107	154 878	1 850	554	828	7 413	20 329	1 062	5 635	2 486 938	126 368	2 424	6 844	490	1 575	1 160 593	29 632	4 723 933

National result: Western Cape by district

	IFP	PAC	SOCCER	KISS	FF/VF	WRPP	WLP	XPP	AMP	ACDP	ADM	AMCP	ANC	DP	DPSA	FP	Luso	Min. Fr.	NP	Spoilt	Total
Beaufort-West	69	178	13	16	667	4	7	9	6	77	6	9	4967	297	15	12	18	28	10994	193	17585
Bellville	1275	419	28	36	5801	50	44	5	604	2833	14	35	27470	4747	35	324	23	65	120337	795	164940
Bredasdorp	82	43	3	7	778	10	2	3	10	117	2	11	2332	1110	8	12	7	16	8717	112	13382
Caledon	212	379	19	43	1007	22	21	10	50	265	19	56	13400	2108	36	58	26	42	26927	400	45100
Calitzdorp	34	22	6	7	174	0	7	1	1	4	1	2	516	35	4	1	6	13	2909	66	3809
Cape	1597	1193	62	30	1470	142	46	6	1674	1345	35	47	36087	11016	44	582	16	43	70286	806	126527
Ceres	87	273	16	15	409	7	5	8	14	91	7	24	7695	237	20	17	18	50	16610	180	25783
Clanwilliam	71	55	12	8	532	5	3	2	5	87	6	7	3942	199	15	9	6	34	10324	109	15431
George	546	589	124	36	2091	26	23	7	23	708	18	29	21621	1705	38	99	20	55	32037	385	60180
Goodwood	828	2002	30	33	1674	60	52	6	1029	1443	20	85	46789	4458	45	236	14	74	94402	1001	154281
Heidelberg (W. Cape)	35	29	0	7	271	2	3	1	2	26	2	4	1343	144	7	3	0	16	4053	49	5997
Hermanus	162	152	7	6	804	4	3	2	8	172	1	15	4222	974	7	40	5	7	11090	164	17845
Hopefield	34	16	3	4	239	8	0	0	11	74	2	1	852	186	0	11	0	7	4378	49	5875
Knysna	519	433	19	14	926	55	12	15	17	452	9	28	14281	2540	32	122	10	35	17475	305	37299
Kuils River	458	1239	29	38	2591	48	55	12	249	1249	37	68	47682	1584	56	58	21	58	68432	779	124743
Ladismith	26	32	5	1	272	2	1	4	4	58	5	6	1813	136	14	6	1	11	4569	44	7013
Laingsburg	21	15	1	3	166	1	2	0	1	53	1	0	545	40	2	1	0	8	2611	20	3491
Malmesbury	364	233	27	25	1370	28	11	12	120	463	16	21	13048	1026	166	74	31	75	43223	435	60768
Mitchell's Plain	238	7127	103	32	63	68	67	21	2510	948	48	274	194255	1829	90	68	8	63	74338	12814	294964
Montagu	77	141	6	13	357	1	3	4	4	120	4	13	3388	834	1	19	7	19	8023	121	13158
Moorreesburg	30	18	2	5	458	2	4	4	3	28	1	8	953	51	1	4	5	12	4647	69	6305
Mossel Bay	249	270	9	10	1944	5	12	6	22	359	7	28	10745	529	17	27	10	31	19177	186	33643
Murraysburg	9	9	2	1	73	2	0	1	1	14	2	2	874	34	2	1	1	6	1585	27	2645
Oudtshoorn	168	217	15	30	1377	14	11	9	9	90	12	26	10123	416	34	15	21	61	23813	370	36831
Paarl	298	784	37	54	1623	20	22	16	472	433	14	61	32106	1574	74	75	27	94	47617	624	86025
Piquetberg	100	123	15	21	886	8	4	6	14	70	5	17	4026	203	18	17	8	42	14499	167	20249
Prince Albert	26	6	0	4	190	0	1	0	0	9	0	4	655	70	1	2	1	5	3872	59	4905
Riversdale	98	33	5	6	918	8	9	8	3	94	5	7	2015	199	11	30	1	26	11000	117	14577
Robertson	114	219	10	26	488	13	25	5	8	79	7	15	4324	307	16	20	14	43	11559	212	17491
Simonstown	1135	310	65	26	714	103	14	4	466	1461	4	17	12439	7071	13	573	8	17	37019	332	61803
Somerset West	546	310	12	12	1026	14	23	4	83	676	6	25	12422	3209	20	136	14	58	24518	208	43252
Stellenbosch	389	383	43	35	1525	31	23	12	128	739	12	37	13908	2571	24	187	15	58	30911	432	51463
Strand	284	141	9	30	1613	10	4	3	174	479	7	11	8473	855	11	45	7	13	19692	176	32011
Swellendam	104	145	14	27	657	6	6	5	6	105	8	26	5030	660	26	16	4	33	9823	155	16856
Tulbagh	52	115	7	14	315	3	1	5	10	46	8	9	4290	177	14	11	10	21	8593	129	13830
Uniondale	22	37	0	4	164	1	0	5	2	8	1	12	1221	31	0	8	1	10	2559	43	4125
Van Rhynsdorp	46	48	5	13	367	3	6	4	4	24	4	6	1628	47	14	4	1	19	5735	125	8103
Vredenburg	109	117	6	8	657	3	3	3	33	163	5	10	7125	320	17	14	5	19	14868	154	23639
Vredendal	481	235	30	35	1298	98	26	7	127	269	12	17	10261	4802	17	109	15	37	28169	182	46227
Wellington	99	95	13	9	613	15	13	3	68	168	4	9	5281	580	19	15	8	39	15701	207	22959
Worcester	235	585	27	29	1656	16	11	18	174	517	16	61	23304	852	52	24	15	80	40102	622	68396
Wynberg	2566	2583	191	128	1700	486	171	28	7506	4124	93	143	96820	29041	105	1619	40	147	188439	2407	338337
Total:	13895	21353	1030	875	41924	1404	724	273	15655	20540	485	1286	714271	88804	1147	4704	464	1546	1195633	25830	2151843

Provincial result by province and grand total

	PAC	SAWP	UPF	XPP	GRP	FF/VF	WKFP	WI	AMP	ACDP	WRPP	ADM	ANC	DP	DPSA	FP	Luso	IP	NP	IFP	MP	RP	MF	Spoilt	Total
Eastern Cape	59 475	0	0	0	0	23 167	0	0	0	14 908	0	4 815	2 453 790	59 644	0	0	0	0	286 029	5 050	2 028	0	0	13 248	2 922 154
Eastern Transvaal	21 679	0	0	0	0	75 120	0	0	0	6 339	0	5 062	1 070 052	7 437	0	0	0	0	119 311	20 147	0	921	0	12 631	1 338 699
KwaZulu-Natal	26 601	0	0	0	0	18 625	0	4 626	17 931	24 690	0	8 092	1 181 118	78 910	0	0	0	0	410 710	1 844 070	0	0	48 951	39 369	3 703 693
North-West	27 274	0	0	0	0	72 821	0	0	0	5 570	0	3 569	1 310 080	7 894	0	0	0	0	138 986	5 948	0	0	0	18 974	1 591 116
Northern Cape	3 765	0	0	0	0	24 117	0	0	0	1 610	0	734	200 839	7 567	0	0	0	0	163 452	1 688	0	0	0	3 534	407 306
Northern Transvaal	24 360	0	10 123	4 963	0	41 193	0	0	0	7 363	0	3 662	1 759 597	4 021	0	0	0	0	62 745	2 233	0	0	0	13 702	1 933 962
Orange Free State	24 451	0	0	0	0	81 662	0	0	0	6 072	0	2 008	1 037 998	7 664	17 024	0	0	0	170 452	6 935	0	0	0	10 286	1 364 552
Gauteng	61 512	0	0	3 275	0	258 935	0	0	12 888	25 542	7 279	4 352	2 418 257	223 548	4 853	16 279	5 423	0	1 002 540	153 567	0	0	0	25 383	4 223 633
Western Cape	22 676	2 641	0	0	2 611	44 003	6 337	855	20 954	25 731	0	1 939	705 576	141 970	0	0	0	16 762	1 138 242	7 445	0	0	0	10 714	2 148 456
Grand total	271 793	2 641	10 123	8 238	2 611	639 643	6 337	5 481	51 773	117 825	7 279	34 233	12 137 307	538 655	21 877	16 279	5 423	16 762	3 492 467	2 047 083	2 028	921	48 951	147 841	19 633 571

Provincial result: Eastern Cape by district

District	PAC	SAWP	UPF	XPP	GRP	FF/VF	WKFP	WI	AMP	ACDP	WRPP	ADM	ANC	DP	DPSA	FP	Luso	IP	NP	IFP	MP	RP	MF	Spoilt	Total
Aberdeen	29	0	0	0	0	190	0	0	0	12	0	5	1308	127	0	0	0	0	2063	22	13	0	0	25	3794
Adelaide	85	0	0	0	0	97	0	0	0	16	0	10	6922	201	0	0	0	0	849	9	5	0	0	54	8248
Albany	800	0	0	0	0	311	0	0	0	401	0	54	34819	3437	0	0	0	0	5605	141	25	0	0	240	45833
Albert	246	0	0	0	0	242	0	0	0	21	0	16	6699	98	0	0	0	0	1787	12	11	0	0	84	9216
Alexandria	80	0	0	0	0	312	0	0	0	64	0	28	11856	270	0	0	0	0	1924	36	9	0	0	113	14692
Aliwal-North	210	0	0	0	0	127	0	0	0	28	0	24	10388	50	0	0	0	0	1202	16	10	0	0	79	12134
Barkly East	130	0	0	0	0	186	0	0	0	13	0		4793	78	0	0	0	0	999	9	6	0	0	68	6291
Bathurst	168	0	0	0	0	284	0	0	0	225	0	36	15621	1889	0	0	0	0	2692	93	10	0	0	163	21181
Bedford	89	0	0	0	0	40	0	0	0	24	0	8	4408	154	0	0	0	0	1282	16	8	0	0	36	6065
Bizana	1037	0	0	0	0	39	0	0	0	84	0	98	87566	104	0	0	0	0	439	137	11	0	0	521	90036
Butterworth	1591	0	0	0	0	14	0	0	0	78	0	54	44465	72	0	0	0	0	324	29	12	0	0	234	46873
Cathcart	157	0	0	0	0	50	0	0	0	83	0	13	6522	301	0	0	0	0	559	14	5	5	0	63	7768
Cradock	173	0	0	0	0	514	0	0	0	70	0	43	15470	215	0	0	0	0	4621	31	40	0	0	139	21316
East London	1692	0	0	0	0	2825	0	0	0	4356	0	233	98651	11017	0	0	0	0	38124	830	166	0	0	859	158753
Elliot	181	0	0	0	0	165	0	0	0	17	0	17	6831	90	0	0	0	0	603	12	8	0	0	66	7990
Elliotdale	381	0	0	0	0	18	0	0	0	29	0	43	31079	40	0	0	0	0	74	14		0	0	232	31910
Engcobo	2435	0	0	0	0	70	0	0	0	107	0	111	73933	85	0	0	0	0	202	19	25	0	0	570	77557
Flagstaff	479	0	0	0	0	19	0	0	0	30	0	60	44350	70	0	0	0	0	114	24	12	0	0	232	45390
Fort Beaufort	355	0	0	0	0	123	0	0	0	50	0	68	11758	213	0	0	0	0	1759	17	11	0	0	63	14373
Glen Grey	2731	0	0	0	0	21	0	0	0	60	0	27	76613	50	0	0	0	0	225	55	16	0	0	104	79900
Graaff-Reinet	190	0	0	0	0	531	0	0	0	209	0	21	7574	898	0	0	0	0	6780	31	48	0	0	164	13639
Hankey	117	0	0	0	0	315	0	0	0	96	0	49	39917	183	0	0	0	0	5231	16	4	0	0	67	41373
Herschel	919	0	0	0	0	20	0	0	0	30	0	52	25161	26	0	0	0	0	193	4	8	0	0	195	26856
Hewu	1363	0	0	0	0	7	0	0	0	13	0			18	0	0	0	0	120	6	8	0	0	110	
Hofmeyr	48	0	0	0	0	89	0	0	0	4	0	5	2012	18	0	0	0	0	438	6	3	0	0	16	2639
Humansdorp	261	0	0	0	0	1762	0	0	0	489	0	36	12402	1366	0	0	0	0	12118	154	70	0	0	206	28864
Idutywa	1087	0	0	0	0	41	0	0	0	35	0	64	41056	61	0	0	0	0	114	14	16	0	0	218	42706
Indwe	190	0	0	0	0	60	0	0	0	25	0	16	3932	33	0	0	0	0	300	8	1	0	0	41	4606
Jansenville	61	0	0	0	0	128	0	0	0	42	0	14	2879	91	0	0	0	0	2011	31	41	0	0	42	5340
Joubertina	94	0	0	0	0	350	0	0	0	22	0	18	3110	91	0	0	0	0	4011	46	37	0	0	78	7857
Keiskammahoek	560	0	0	0	0	6	0	0	0	21	0	101	20127	27	0	0	0	0	97	8	6	0	0	127	21080
Kentani	1743	0	0	0	0	16	0	0	0	38	0	54	42027	63	0	0	0	0	99	18	7	0	0	130	44195
King Williams Town	515	0	0	0	0	355	0	0	0	404	0	101	13529	799	0	0	0	0	5819	114	18	0	0	191	21845
Kirkwood	270	0	0	0	0	395	0	0	0	147	0	24	14998	207	0	0	0	0	3110	41	33	0	0	184	19409
Komga	215	0	0	0	0	112	0	0	0	92	0	11	5334	250	0	0	0	0	829	29	3	0	0	69	6944
Lady Grey	399	0	0	0	0	88	0	0	0	39	0	18	10683	68	0	0	0	0	659	12		0	0	118	12084
Libode	1088	0	0	0	0	38	0	0	0	36	0	71	58707	129	0	0	0	0	244	22	18	0	0	205	60558
Lusikisiki	1849	0	0	0	0	73	0	0	0	149	0	214	115225	188	0	0	0	0	456	91	72	0	0	0	118317

	1	2	3	4	5	6	7	8	9	10	11	12	13	14	15	16	17	18	19	20	21	22	23	24	25	26	27	28	29	30	31	32	33	34
Maclear	257	0	0	0	0	0	0	0	0	152	0	0	0	0	0	0	0	40	0	0	0	0	31	10410	89	0	0	0	919	11	12	0	132	12053
Mdantsane	3273	0	0	0	0	0	0	0	0	18	0	0	0	0	0	0	0	69	0	0	0	0	190	98377	80	0	0	0	312	20	22	0	287	102648
Middelburg (E. Cape)	104	0	0	0	0	0	0	0	0	362	0	0	0	0	0	0	0	95	0	0	0	0	15	5681	157	0	0	0	4576	34	49	0	103	11176
Middeldrift	396	0	0	0	0	0	0	0	0	4	0	0	0	0	0	0	0	0	0	0	0	0	49	15913	18	0	0	0	51	5	0	0	85	16521
Molteno	166	0	0	0	0	0	0	0	0	99	0	0	0	0	0	0	0	10	0	0	0	0	5	3541	57	0	0	0	435	0	7	0	13	4333
Mount Ayliff	391	0	0	0	0	0	0	0	0	14	0	0	0	0	0	0	0	23	0	0	0	0	38	27368	28	0	0	0	68	18	7	0	110	28065
Mount Fletcher	907	0	0	0	0	0	0	0	0	33	0	0	0	0	0	0	0	57	0	0	0	0	62	40079	73	0	0	0	208	29	17	0	73	41538
Mount Frere	551	0	0	0	0	0	0	0	0	37	0	0	0	0	0	0	0	49	0	0	0	0	69	50825	55	0	0	0	207	25	25	0	142	51985
Mqanduli	1281	0	0	0	0	0	0	0	0	38	0	0	0	0	0	0	0	33	0	0	0	0	54	48607	61	0	0	0	113	21	5	0	136	50349
Mgqeleni	1210	0	0	0	0	0	0	0	0	40	0	0	0	0	0	0	0	64	0	0	0	0	102	53954	71	0	0	0	229	26	20	0	66	55782
Nqamakwe	801	0	0	0	0	0	0	0	0	26	0	0	0	0	0	0	0	39	0	0	0	0	46	29211	26	0	0	0	96	12	17	0	0	30274
Pearston	9	0	0	0	0	0	0	0	0	38	0	0	0	0	0	0	0	8	0	0	0	0	1	1310	21	0	0	0	1232	7	8	0	20	2654
Peddie	555	0	0	0	0	0	0	0	0	11	0	0	0	0	0	0	0	16	0	0	0	0	102	31586	46	0	0	0	115	9	9	0	1	32452
Port Elizabeth	4196	0	0	0	0	0	0	0	0	6000	0	0	0	0	0	0	0	4872	0	0	0	0	349	248231	31026	0	0	0	117714	1646	581	0	2199	416814
Port St Johns	457	0	0	0	0	0	0	0	0	14	0	0	0	0	0	0	0	28	0	0	0	0	36	26462	53	0	0	0	152	22	10	0	126	27360
Queenstown	1053	0	0	0	0	0	0	0	0	342	0	0	0	0	0	0	0	240	0	0	0	0	76	38705	1125	0	0	0	6026	54	0	0	287	47908
Qumbu	1024	0	0	0	0	0	0	0	0	19	0	0	0	0	0	0	0	41	0	0	0	0	68	45796	61	0	0	0	164	21	8	0	193	47395
Somerset-East	178	0	0	0	0	0	0	0	0	459	0	0	0	0	0	0	0	44	0	0	0	0	21	11011	249	0	0	0	3942	32	13	0	139	16075
St Marks	2981	0	0	0	0	0	0	0	0	23	0	0	0	0	0	0	0	36	0	0	0	0	36	34203	29	0	0	0	90	12	1	0	120	37543
Sterkstroom	82	0	0	0	0	0	0	0	0	91	0	0	0	0	0	0	0	11	0	0	0	0	8	3503	76	0	0	0	301	7	9	0	46	4126
Steynsburg	59	0	0	0	0	0	0	0	0	191	0	0	0	0	0	0	0	20	0	0	0	0	8	3453	52	0	0	0	865	13	4	0	39	4709
Steytlerville	11	0	0	0	0	0	0	0	0	146	0	0	0	0	0	0	0	13	0	0	0	0	7	1025	67	0	0	0	1318	9	1	0	20	2620
Stockenstrom	336	0	0	0	0	0	0	0	0	3	0	0	0	0	0	0	0	1	0	0	0	0	31	7541	4	0	0	0	121	5	6	0	0	8043
Stutterheim	386	0	0	0	0	0	0	0	0	184	0	0	0	0	0	0	0	172	0	0	0	0	34	17594	381	0	0	0	1308	25	17	0	161	20251
Tabankulu	591	0	0	0	0	0	0	0	0	35	0	0	0	0	0	0	0	78	0	0	0	0	108	53554	86	0	0	0	124	51	2	0	0	54644
Tarka	78	0	0	0	0	0	0	0	0	96	0	0	0	0	0	0	0	30	0	0	0	0	6	3249	146	0	0	0	687	13	14	0	16	4319
Tsolo	815	0	0	0	0	0	0	0	0	29	0	0	0	0	0	0	0	27	0	0	0	0	45	32316	47	0	0	0	102	12	11	0	199	33607
Tsomo	521	0	0	0	0	0	0	0	0	13	0	0	0	0	0	0	0	18	0	0	0	0	21	25257	21	0	0	0	60	199	146	0	181	26115
Uitenhage	1303	0	0	0	0	0	0	0	0	3999	0	0	0	0	0	0	0	553	0	0	0	0	82	65870	1487	0	0	0	28890	122	32	0	517	103046
Umtata	3994	0	0	0	0	0	0	0	0	89	0	0	0	0	0	0	0	228	0	0	0	0	234	116907	372	0	0	0	2012	279	0	0	721	124711
Umzimkulu	752	0	0	0	0	0	0	0	0	26	0	0	0	0	0	0	0	98	0	0	0	0	83	72933	71	0	0	0	297	19	12	0	299	74838
Venterstad	25	0	0	0	0	0	0	0	0	119	0	0	0	0	0	0	0	6	0	0	0	0	3	1429	28	0	0	0	894	6	3	0	26	2561
Victoria East	573	0	0	0	0	0	0	0	0	10	0	0	0	0	0	0	0	27	0	0	0	0	88	28061	35	0	0	0	242	15	20	0	136	29181
Willowmore	26	0	0	0	0	0	0	0	0	118	0	0	0	0	0	0	0	19	0	0	0	0	12	2072	49	0	0	0	2910	19	15	0	33	5274
Willowvale	1195	0	0	0	0	0	0	0	0	38	0	0	0	0	0	0	0	51	0	0	0	0	73	43860	76	0	0	0	124	4	5	0	0	45451
Wodehouse	212	0	0	0	0	0	0	0	0	178	0	0	0	0	0	0	0	11	0	0	0	0	7	5782	117	0	0	0	510	14	9	0	0	6826
Xalanga	1266	0	0	0	0	0	0	0	0	10	0	0	0	0	0	0	0	29	0	0	0	0	33	21903	30	0	0	0	138	14	9	0	125	23557
Zwelitsha	3442	0	0	0	0	0	0	0	0	30	0	0	0	0	0	0	0	93	0	0	0	0	732	104769	97	0	0	0	401	30	114	0	391	110099
Total:	59475	0	0	0	0	0	0	0	0	23167	0	0	0	0	0	0	0	14908	0	0	0	0	4815	2453790	59644	0	0	0	286029	5050	2028	0	13248	2922154

Provincial result: Eastern Transvaal by district

	PAC	SAWP	UPF	XPP	GRP	FF/VF	WKFP	WI	AMP	ACDP	WRPP	ADM	ANC	DP	DPSA	FP	Luso	IP	NP	IFP	MP	RP	MF	Spoilt	Total
Amersfoort	315	0	0	0	0	484	0	0	0	72	0	59	12363	41	0	0	0	0	922	562	0	15	0	237	15070
Balfour	266	0	0	0	0	1267	0	0	0	51	0	63	14712	73	0	0	0	0	2308	234	0	111	0	185	19270
Barberton	597	0	0	0	0	2556	0	0	0	313	0	614	25393	583	0	0	0	0	4341	269	0	273	0	387	35326
Belfast	257	0	0	0	0	1350	0	0	0	78	0	62	11922	157	0	0	0	0	1979	109	0	14	0	7	15935
Bethal	734	0	0	0	0	2373	0	0	0	141	0	82	21815	93	0	0	0	0	2880	257	0	20	0	332	28727
Carolina	274	0	0	0	0	1304	0	0	0	65	0	42	11370	72	0	0	0	0	1465	106	0	15	0	211	14924
Delmas	482	0	0	0	0	2196	0	0	0	112	0	47	17970	138	0	0	0	0	2931	188	0	16	0	271	24351
Eerstehoek	910	0	0	0	0	130	0	0	0	170	0	134	63227	103	0	0	0	0	1959	1273	0	24	0	545	68475
Ermelo	1242	0	0	0	0	5068	0	0	0	316	0	173	46740	239	0	0	0	0	7436	1177	0	33	0	766	63190
Groblersdal	400	0	0	0	0	2660	0	0	0	81	0	99	18361	88	0	0	0	0	2714	76	0	15	0	266	24760
Highveld Ridge	1053	0	0	0	0	10081	0	0	0	664	0	103	53323	432	0	0	0	0	12070	1380	0	17	0	406	79529
Kamhlushwa	885	0	0	0	0	66	0	0	0	194	0	267	62008	123	0	0	0	0	899	103	0	8	0	719	65272
Kriel	234	0	0	0	0	2362	0	0	0	270	0	47	10624	143	0	0	0	0	3191	581	0	11	0	257	17720
Lydenburg	449	0	0	0	0	3402	0	0	0	108	0	70	17897	126	0	0	0	0	2532	70	0	16	0	376	25046
Mathanjana	531	0	0	0	0	22	0	0	0	87	0	49	36147	99	0	0	0	0	788	27	0	10	0	242	38002
Mbibana	338	0	0	0	0	16	0	0	0	36	0	43	22366	29	0	0	0	0	341	21	0	8	0	134	23332
Mdutjana 1 + 2 + 3	1085	0	0	0	0	48	0	0	0	104	0	141	58639	143	0	0	0	0	817	165	0	20	0	500	61662
Middelburg (E. Tvl)	1394	0	0	0	0	12158	0	0	0	479	0	190	58295	610	0	0	0	0	15111	1036	0	63	0	987	90323
Mkobola	2220	0	0	0	0	70	0	0	0	368	0	273	122101	208	0	0	0	0	2869	336	0	25	0	1071	129541
Moutse 1 + 2	917	0	0	0	0	74	0	0	0	135	0	109	53997	151	0	0	0	0	615	90	0	24	0	280	56392
Nelspruit	460	0	0	0	0	5162	0	0	0	350	0	90	16691	970	0	0	0	0	9249	340	0	12	0	430	33754
Nsikazi	1816	0	0	0	0	63	0	0	0	311	0	280	135733	197	0	0	0	0	1357	225	0	33	0	849	140864
Piet Retief (E. Tvl)	490	0	0	0	0	1511	0	0	0	275	0	117	18107	116	0	0	0	0	3257	5967	0	9	0	356	30205
Pilgrim's Rest 1 + 2	194	0	0	0	0	1282	0	0	0	127	0	33	7372	486	0	0	0	0	2711	105	0	9	0	182	12501
Standerton	796	0	0	0	0	3970	0	0	0	152	0	78	30693	163	0	0	0	0	4917	636	0	15	0	461	41881
Volksrust	322	0	0	0	0	1536	0	0	0	155	0	39	11720	104	0	0	0	0	2680	742	0	23	0	197	17518
Wakkerstroom	356	0	0	0	0	401	0	0	0	95	0	83	11475	79	0	0	0	0	1238	2375	0	28	0	258	16388
Waterval Boven	47	0	0	0	0	365	0	0	0	19	0	6	2775	43	0	0	0	0	582	39	0	1	0	54	3931
White River	278	0	0	0	0	2152	0	0	0	356	0	67	17241	528	0	0	0	0	3877	195	0	13	0	254	24961
Witbank	2337	0	0	0	0	10991	0	0	0	655	0	1602	78975	1100	0	0	0	0	21275	1463	0	40	0	1411	119849
Total:	21679	0	0	0	0	75120	0	0	0	6339	0	5062	1070052	7437	0	0	0	0	119311	20147	0	921	0	12631	1338699

Provincial result: KwaZulu/Natal by district

	PAC	SAWP	UPF	XPP	GRP	FF/VF	WKFP	WI	AMP	ACDP	WRPP	ADM	ANC	DP	DPSA	FP	Luso	IP	NP	IFP	MP	RP	MF	Spoilt	Total
Alfred	607	0	0	0	0	92	0	55	71	332	0	254	17067	148	0	0	0	0	2030	29640	0	0	141	0	50437
Bergville	262	0	0	0	0	221	0	56	41	216	0	104	5987	249	0	0	0	0	2976	38689	0	0	129	820	49750
Camperdown	892	0	0	0	0	127	0	50	347	68	0	275	59055	485	0	0	0	0	1750	11193	0	0	82	0	74324
Chatsworth	371	0	0	0	0	70	0	89	3171	2451	0	81	22880	2574	0	0	0	0	4529	4982	0	0	19895	730	102423
Dannhauser	320	0	0	0	0	393	0	41	127	121	0	77	6125	137	0	0	0	0	3496	22160	0	0	215	499	33711
Dundee	194	0	0	0	0	366	0	26	59	129	0	65	6218	236	0	0	0	0	4144	28167	0	0	126	3394	43124
Durban	4092	0	0	0	0	3909	0	248	5402	5680	0	1184	258331	30409	0	0	0	0	108134	145706	0	0	7997	3710	574802
Eshowe	385	0	0	0	0	124	0	65	14	267	0	161	12306	277	0	0	0	0	1978	61916	0	0	41	725	78259
Estcourt	391	0	0	0	0	264	0	55	382	363	0	12	12047	732	0	0	0	0	5748	39406	0	0	586	794	60910
Glencoe	96	0	0	0	0	307	0	6	61	46	0	24	2506	111	0	0	0	0	2383	4269	0	0	160	147	10116
Hlabisa	225	0	0	0	0	277	0	71	30	265	0	149	6870	171	0	0	0	0	1814	104372	0	0	47	1098	115389
Impendle	126	0	0	0	0	13	0	38	35	78	0	47	2310	52	0	0	0	0	546	53452	0	0	29	476	57202
Inanda	971	0	0	0	0	126	0	95	1662	1089	0	313	45172	1905	0	0	0	0	28498	30745	0	0	6341	601	117518
Ixopo	662	0	0	0	0	108	0	85	68	353	0	238	21072	372	0	0	0	0	2841	43083	0	0	110	1191	70183
Kliprivier	940	0	0	0	0	724	0	89	792	530	0	192	38080	904	0	0	0	0	9865	32706	0	0	771	1105	86698
Lions River	640	0	0	0	0	277	0	44	162	594	0	180	26404	2500	0	0	0	0	5319	31096	0	0	340	781	68337
Lower Tugela	1027	0	0	0	0	209	0	78	608	671	0	348	35430	1140	0	0	0	0	12421	26981	0	0	1976	1470	82359
Lower Umfolozi	457	0	0	0	0	1266	0	79	69	767	0	177	19494	838	0	0	0	0	8055	86916	0	0	284	1143	119545
Mapumulo	138	0	0	0	0	14	0	12	2	44	0	69	3811	223	0	0	0	0	472	22865	0	0	13	278	27941
Mhlabatini	96	0	0	0	0	8	0	8	5	17	0	22	1107	18	0	0	0	0	176	127418	0	0	6	538	129419
Mount Currie	1344	0	0	0	0	206	0	43	36	375	0	174	48145	1359	0	0	0	0	4024	1344	0	0	54	559	57663
Mtonjaneni	37	0	0	0	0	59	0	22	9	48	0	26	1069	67	0	0	0	0	393	21304	0	0	19	243	23296
Mtunzini	0	0	0	0	0	0	0	0	0	0	0	0	0	0	0	0	0	0	0	0	0	0	0	0	0
Ndwedwe	147	0	0	0	0	36	0	24	23	129	0	147	13625	75	0	0	0	0	1025	33952	0	0	63	1225	50741
New Hanover	666	0	0	0	0	318	0	46	88	547	0	241	24584	617	0	0	0	0	5244	59728	0	0	432	3	92514
Newcastle	1590	0	0	0	0	3059	0	133	491	1000	0	299	36328	1071	0	0	0	0	17772	36254	0	0	1077	1558	100632
Ngotshe	30	0	0	0	0	98	0	6	1	33	0	21	596	25	0	0	0	0	579	11124	0	0	3	152	12668
Nkandhla	48	0	0	0	0	2	0	7	0	35	0	25	1082	14	0	0	0	0	224	65156	0	0	6	422	67021
Nongoma	51	0	0	0	0	20	0	4	2	40	0	14	1234	13	0	0	0	0	239	76085	0	0	20	3789	81511
Nqutu	110	0	0	0	0	15	0	11	4	42	0	20	2148	5	0	0	0	0	573	18054	0	0	12	207	21201
Paulpietersberg	245	0	0	0	0	206	0	34	17	151	0	85	5000	49	0	0	0	0	1420	48455	0	0	23	570	56255
Piet Retief (Natal)	132	0	0	0	0	356	0	22	6	100	0	75	2226	49	0	0	0	0	1184	70698	0	0	20	557	75425
Pietermaritzburg	2237	0	0	0	0	1183	0	2278	2085	2749	0	535	180824	11958	0	0	0	0	49632	90621	0	0	2657	740	347499
Pinetown	2339	0	0	0	0	867	0	134	1130	2591	0	519	122081	14621	0	0	0	0	31656	53480	0	0	2681	2047	234146
Polela	253	0	0	0	0	47	0	41	16	100	0	114	8097	110	0	0	0	0	791	20159	0	0	69	481	30278
Port Shepstone	1113	0	0	0	0	992	0	118	368	1037	0	438	41721	2577	0	0	0	0	12969	51480	0	0	717	1408	114938
Richmond (Natal)	634	0	0	0	0	138	0	48	38	272	0	183	24594	648	0	0	0	0	2556	13910	0	0	308	0	43329
Ubombo	391	0	0	0	0	113	0	160	45	199	0	318	9474	155	0	0	0	0	1516	85772	0	0	108	2631	100882
Umbumbulu	502	0	0	0	0	34	0	53	23	155	0	192	21672	74	0	0	0	0	694	16511	0	0	52	608	40570
Umzinto	1090	0	0	0	0	344	0	93	363	650	0	356	24223	1280	0	0	0	0	9626	66741	0	0	1262	1511	107539
Underberg	160	0	0	0	0	55	0	18	15	103	0	69	3068	389	0	0	0	0	961	5272	0	0	25	110	10245
Utrecht	125	0	0	0	0	482	0	10	8	53	0	30	1975	30	0	0	0	0	1514	10686	0	0	15	216	15144
Vryheid	169	0	0	0	0	1040	0	29	25	174	0	93	4444	197	0	0	0	0	4181	41144	0	0	30	757	52283
Weenen	26	0	0	0	0	60	0	2	30	26	0	16	636	46	0	0	0	0	14162	3780	0	0	9	75	15466
Total:	26601	0	0	0	0	18625	0	4626	17931	24690	0	8092	1181118	78910	0	0	0	0	410710	1844070	0	0	48951	39369	3703693

Provincial result: North-West by district

	PAC	SAWP	UPF	XPP	GRP	FF/VF	WKFP	WI	AMP	ACDP	WRPP	ADM	ANC	DP	DPSA	FP	Luso	IP	NP	IFP	MP	RP	MF	Spoilt	Total
Bafokeng	1254	0	0	0	0	135	0	0	0	274	0	165	74783	185	0	0	0	0	2287	142	0	0	0	728	79953
Bloemhof	152	0	0	0	0	590	0	0	0	30	0	35	7163	25	0	0	0	0	663	10	0	0	0	551	9219
Brits	843	0	0	0	0	9405	0	0	0	376	0	145	39209	961	0	0	0	0	11371	431	0	0	0	681	63422
Christiana	130	0	0	0	0	866	0	0	0	23	0	8	6542	43	0	0	0	0	1273	22	0	0	0	98	9005
Coligny	91	0	0	0	0	639	0	0	0	15	0	22	7388	26	0	0	0	0	840	16	0	0	0	158	9195
Delareyville	316	0	0	0	0	1765	0	0	0	99	0	85	15726	93	0	0	0	0	1890	56	0	0	0	470	20500
Ditsobotla	1466	0	0	0	0	76	0	0	0	207	0	211	66692	194	0	0	0	0	2015	102	0	0	0	782	71745
Ganyesa	464	0	0	0	0	63	0	0	0	76	0	93	23713	124	0	0	0	0	2415	82	0	0	0	330	27360
Klerksdorp	3108	0	0	0	0	22789	0	0	0	796	0	300	173692	2118	0	0	0	0	36902	2030	0	0	0	2810	244545
Koster	236	0	0	0	0	1415	0	0	0	34	0	39	9372	54	0	0	0	0	1628	64	0	0	0	234	13076
Lehurutshe	1113	0	0	0	0	87	0	0	0	146	0	143	39681	177	0	0	0	0	2782	66	0	0	0	470	44665
Lichtenburg	517	0	0	0	0	4609	0	0	0	132	0	85	26856	191	0	0	0	0	5713	103	0	0	0	1974	40180
Madikwe	742	0	0	0	0	45	0	0	0	118	0	81	31092	69	0	0	0	0	1095	32	0	0	0	71	33345
Mankwe	1305	0	0	0	0	154	0	0	0	255	0	180	67867	374	0	0	0	0	2881	216	0	0	0	332	73564
Marico 1 + 2	378	0	0	0	0	2768	0	0	0	72	0	69	12360	147	0	0	0	0	3260	96	0	0	0	352	19502
Molopo (Mafeking)	2753	0	0	0	0	238	0	0	0	360	0	310	89666	459	0	0	0	0	7004	194	0	0	0	1064	102048
Moretele	1510	0	0	0	0	21	0	0	0	304	0	213	97284	221	0	0	0	0	2279	99	0	0	0	812	102743
Odi 1 + 2	4027	0	0	0	0	129	0	0	0	676	0	389	211481	528	0	0	0	0	5938	469	0	0	0	2228	225865
Potchefstroom	832	0	0	0	0	7931	0	0	0	238	0	64	34013	275	0	0	0	0	9843	561	0	0	0	481	54238
Rustenburg 1 + 2	768	0	0	0	0	10045	0	0	0	448	0	131	59702	533	0	0	0	0	15253	531	0	0	0	662	88073
Schweizer-Reneke	335	0	0	0	0	1473	0	0	0	44	0	58	18132	69	0	0	0	0	1268	27	0	0	0	207	21613
Swartruggens	97	0	0	0	0	901	0	0	0	31	0	21	5947	34	0	0	0	0	1149	24	0	0	0	137	8341
Taung	1909	0	0	0	0	123	0	0	0	272	0	243	70528	273	0	0	0	0	2607	148	0	0	0	807	76910
Thlaping-Thlaro + Kuruman	1181	0	0	0	0	105	0	0	0	242	0	123	46982	267	0	0	0	0	3838	122	0	0	0	595	53455
Ventersdorp	406	0	0	0	0	1434	0	0	0	42	0	56	12965	65	0	0	0	0	1526	36	0	0	0	769	17299
Vryburg	927	0	0	0	0	3384	0	0	0	209	0	220	37857	314	0	0	0	0	9536	220	0	0	0	784	53451
Wolmaranstad	414	0	0	0	0	1631	0	0	0	51	0	80	23387	75	0	0	0	0	1730	49	0	0	0	387	27804
Total:	27274	0	0	0	0	72821	0	0	0	5570	0	3569	1310080	7894	0	0	0	0	138986	5948	0	0	0	18974	1591116

Provincial result: Northern Cape by district

	PAC	SAWP	UPF	XPP	GRP	FF/VF	WKFP	WI	AMP	ACDP	WRPP	ADM	ANC	DP	DPSA	FP	LUSO	IP	NP	IFP	MP	RP	MF	Spoilt	Total
Barkly West	277	0	0	0	0	785	0	0	0	75	0	66	17618	211	0	0	0	0	3316	51	0	0	0	283	22682
Britstown	14	0	0	0	0	157	0	0	0	21	0	2	979	14	0	0	0	0	2178	12	0	0	0	19	3396
Calvinia	21	0	0	0	0	921	0	0	0	25	0	11	1635	172	0	0	0	0	7369	44	0	0	0	54	10252
Carnarvon	15	0	0	0	0	239	0	0	0	8	0	5	1202	56	0	0	0	0	3580	24	0	0	0	44	5173
Colesberg	149	0	0	0	0	229	0	0	0	17	0	26	5725	60	0	0	0	0	2459	15	0	0	0	67	8747
De Aar	123	0	0	0	0	614	0	0	0	31	0	18	5992	104	0	0	0	0	7452	48	0	0	0	115	14497
Fraserburg	6	0	0	0	0	118	0	0	0	5	0	1	129	22	0	0	0	0	1839	18	0	0	0	14	2152
Gordonia	357	0	0	0	0	3865	0	0	0	183	0	85	29482	726	0	0	0	0	31078	240	0	0	0	543	66559
Hanover	37	0	0	0	0	107	0	0	0	13	0	9	1191	39	0	0	0	0	983	12	0	0	0	39	2430
Hartswater	215	0	0	0	0	1592	0	0	0	49	0	45	10771	107	0	0	0	0	4002	64	0	0	0	219	17064
Hay	21	0	0	0	0	316	0	0	0	17	0	9	2122	30	0	0	0	0	2711	30	0	0	0	47	5303
Herbert	110	0	0	0	0	923	0	0	0	58	0	32	6060	266	0	0	0	0	5185	95	0	0	0	235	12964
Hopetown	33	0	0	0	0	385	0	0	0	25	0	17	1750	125	0	0	0	0	3946	22	0	0	0	33	6336
Kenhardt	6	0	0	0	0	296	0	0	0	10	0	6	1265	67	0	0	0	0	2783	11	0	0	0	16	4460
Kimberley	1434	0	0	0	0	4792	0	0	0	592	0	184	60446	3282	0	0	0	0	29065	549	0	0	0	763	101107
Kuruman	134	0	0	0	0	1772	0	0	0	85	0	36	7246	75	0	0	0	0	5728	54	0	0	0	154	15284
Namaqualand	174	0	0	0	0	1762	0	0	0	128	0	62	13892	1540	0	0	0	0	18499	130	0	0	0	254	36441
Noupoort	33	0	0	0	0	152	0	0	0	12	0	2	2243	10	0	0	0	0	1781	8	0	0	0	39	4280
Philipstown	44	0	0	0	0	431	0	0	0	11	0	7	1460	22	0	0	0	0	2699	11	0	0	0	33	4718
Postmasburg	228	0	0	0	0	2686	0	0	0	116	0	42	15143	282	0	0	0	0	10400	106	0	0	0	202	29205
Prieska	40	0	0	0	0	430	0	0	0	66	0	12	3037	89	0	0	0	0	5573	42	0	0	0	99	9388
Richmond (N. Cape)	17	0	0	0	0	138	0	0	0	3	0	7	1016	60	0	0	0	0	1756	11	0	0	0	18	3026
Sutherland	3	0	0	0	0	194	0	0	0	5	0	1	144	21	0	0	0	0	1509	12	0	0	0	12	1901
Victoria-West	24	0	0	0	0	269	0	0	0	23	0	5	1096	102	0	0	0	0	4095	37	0	0	0	35	5686
Warrenton	243	0	0	0	0	850	0	0	0	30	0	41	8665	61	0	0	0	0	2031	34	0	0	0	184	12139
Williston	7	0	0	0	0	94	0	0	0	2	0	3	530	24	0	0	0	0	1435	8	0	0	0	13	2116
Total:	3765	0	0	0	0	24117	0	0	0	1610	0	734	200839	7567	0	0	0	0	163452	1688	0	0	0	3534	407306

Provincial result: Northern Transvaal by district

	PAC	SAWP	UPF	XPP	GRP	FF/VF	WKFP	WI	AMP	ACDP	WRPP	ADM	ANC	DP	DPSA	FP	LUSO	IP	NP	IFP	MP	RP	MF	Spoilt	Total
Bochum	543	0	351	24	0	44	0	0	0	162	0	102	59 311	92	0	0	0	0	498	22	0	0	0	391	61 540
Bolebedu	681	0	404	49	0	15	0	0	0	194	0	111	74 926	56	0	0	0	0	309	14	0	0	0	372	77 131
Dzanani 1 + 2	199	0	5	1	0	7	0	0	0	16	0	15	22 142	10	0	0	0	0	317	6	0	0	0	79	22 797
Ellisras	485	0	111	51	0	6 653	0	0	0	231	0	128	46 766	168	0	0	0	0	4 648	524	0	0	0	694	60 459
Giyani (Hlanganani)	945	0	51	1 522	0	269	0	0	0	465	0	166	124 809	145	0	0	0	0	1 084	60	0	0	0	613	130 129
Letaba (Lulekani)	115	0	11	263	0	20	0	0	0	47	0	25	10 471	20	0	0	0	0	157	15	0	0	0	35	11 179
Letaba 1	433	0	186	131	0	3 942	0	0	0	314	0	105	17 645	185	0	0	0	0	4 429	132	0	0	0	440	27 942
Malamulele	362	0	20	422	0	18	0	0	0	191	0	81	63 783	65	0	0	0	0	470	26	0	0	0	273	65 711
Messina	281	0	44	24	0	1 029	0	0	0	73	0	29	9 599	50	0	0	0	0	1 669	39	0	0	0	73	12 910
Mhala	1 191	0	24	522	0	34	0	0	0	182	0	121	89 260	99	0	0	0	0	520	49	0	0	0	628	92 630
Mutale	324	0	4	7	0	11	0	0	0	17	0	20	23 142	30	0	0	0	0	332	11	0	0	0	117	24 015
Namakgale	233	0	133	98	0	9	0	0	0	94	0	44	21 571	28	0	0	0	0	351	12	0	0	0	201	22 774
Naphuno 2	693	0	775	63	0	57	0	0	0	176	0	120	56 291	85	0	0	0	0	469	35	0	0	0	214	58 978
Nebo	2 087	0	552	56	0	110	0	0	0	292	0	422	137 841	195	0	0	0	0	1 351	86	0	0	0	1 096	144 088
Phalaborwa	109	0	53	117	0	4 692	0	0	0	128	0	30	5 566	235	0	0	0	0	4 372	140	0	0	0	124	15 566
Pietersburg	1 573	0	803	252	0	12 389	0	0	0	1 374	0	224	77 832	1 004	0	0	0	0	18 719	302	0	0	0	1 271	115 743
Pietersburg (Mapulaneng)	871	0	254	110	0	40	0	0	0	246	0	105	60 962	75	0	0	0	0	643	37	0	0	0	490	63 833
Potgietersrus	2 269	0	1 846	165	0	5 590	0	0	0	669	0	487	162 812	350	0	0	0	0	6 874	228	0	0	0	1 646	182 937
Ritavi 1	542	0	42	430	0	36	0	0	0	255	0	79	34 765	48	0	0	0	0	369	19	0	0	0	268	36 853
Ritavi 2	227	0	25	229	0	14	0	0	0	138	0	47	23 000	25	0	0	0	0	255	13	0	0	0	182	24 155
Sekgosese 1 + 2	784	0	235	34	0	44	0	0	0	127	0	75	48 994	65	0	0	0	0	512	18	0	0	0	265	51 153
Sekhukhuneland	1 638	0	585	50	0	106	0	0	0	357	0	230	137 477	67	0	0	0	0	828	65	0	0	0	865	142 268
Seshego	1 512	0	1 520	99	0	86	0	0	0	462	0	246	93 086	216	0	0	0	0	2 302	71	0	0	0	901	100 501
Sibasa (Thohoyandou)	1 673	0	36	37	0	134	0	0	0	175	0	112	120 638	136	0	0	0	0	1 555	61	0	0	0	459	125 016
Thabamoopa	3 028	0	1 931	125	0	130	0	0	0	614	0	367	127 274	291	0	0	0	0	2 886	78	0	0	0	1 214	137 938
Tshitale	296	0	11	19	0	12	0	0	0	71	0	36	23 702	33	0	0	0	0	316	5	0	0	0	143	24 644
Vuvani	527	0	6	26	0	15	0	0	0	52	0	31	45 841	61	0	0	0	0	464	17	0	0	0	145	47 185
Waterberg	739	0	105	37	0	5 686	0	0	0	241	0	104	40 091	187	0	0	0	0	6 046	148	0	0	0	503	53 887
Total:	24 360	0	10 123	4 963	0	41 193	0	0	0	7 363	0	3 662	1 759 597	4 021	0	0	0	0	62 745	2 233	0	0	0	13 702	1 933 962

	PAC	SAWP	UPF	XPP	GRP	FF/VF	WKFP	WI	AMP	ACDP	WRPP	ADM	ANC	DP	DPSA	FP	Luso	IP	NP	IFP	MP	RP	MF	Spoilt	Total
Bethlehem	747	0	0	0	0	2744	0	0	0	242	0	50	25120	205	383	0	0	0	5755	188	0	0	0	84	35518
Bethulie	87	0	0	0	0	405	0	0	0	16	0	14	4168	45	17	0	0	0	1375	49	0	0	0	104	6280
Bloemfontein	2706	0	0	0	0	22154	0	0	0	1662	0	183	131251	2665	2179	0	0	0	53108	1023	0	0	0	1474	218405
Boshof	122	0	0	0	0	1277	0	0	0	65	0	27	10924	42	31	0	0	0	1902	38	0	0	0	209	14637
Bothaville	440	0	0	0	0	1613	0	0	0	50	0	62	23048	44	41	0	0	0	1612	28	0	0	0	207	27145
Botshabelo	1622	0	0	0	0	43	0	0	0	158	0	70	68858	101	2017	0	0	0	1200	63	0	0	0	170	74302
Brandfort	236	0	0	0	0	1066	0	0	0	52	0	19	9471	59	41	0	0	0	1792	35	0	0	0	134	12905
Bultfontein	322	0	0	0	0	822	0	0	0	42	0	32	11355	44	36	0	0	0	1286	22	0	0	0	123	14084
Clocolan	238	0	0	0	0	470	0	0	0	27	0	25	7538	58	64	0	0	0	1196	17	0	0	0	101	9734
Dewetsdorp	107	0	0	0	0	424	0	0	0	21	0	11	4564	26	14	0	0	0	824	9	0	0	0	86	6086
Edenburg	49	0	0	0	0	273	0	0	0	4	0	9	2735	17	14	0	0	0	799	20	0	0	0	44	3964
Excelsior	136	0	0	0	0	277	0	0	0	19	0	17	5862	86	72	0	0	0	733	18	0	0	0	83	7303
Fauresmith	52	0	0	0	0	422	0	0	0	27	0	9	2872	43	10	0	0	0	1387	42	0	0	0	46	4910
Ficksburg	551	0	0	0	0	1028	0	0	0	171	0	45	17638	202	97	0	0	0	2284	56	0	0	0	264	22336
Fouriesburg	217	0	0	0	0	354	0	0	0	43	0	30	7867	75	47	0	0	0	837	39	0	0	0	145	9654
Frankfort	360	0	0	0	0	1535	0	0	0	75	0	49	19015	79	99	0	0	0	2144	109	0	0	0	194	23659
Harrismith	446	0	0	0	0	1831	0	0	0	195	0	62	25229	314	366	0	0	0	4933	572	0	0	0	327	34275
Heilbron	337	0	0	0	0	1404	0	0	0	54	0	23	14828	46	81	0	0	0	2104	63	0	0	0	248	19188
Hennenman	172	0	0	0	0	1074	0	0	0	55	0	7	12337	39	31	0	0	0	1567	94	0	0	0	110	15486
Hoopstad	168	0	0	0	0	617	0	0	0	64	0	28	7608	25	31	0	0	0	840	20	0	0	0	0	9401
Jacobsdal	48	0	0	0	0	467	0	0	0	51	0	6	2976	26	15	0	0	0	974	18	0	0	0	35	4616
Jagersfontein	75	0	0	0	0	184	0	0	0	11	0	5	2669	15	11	0	0	0	783	8	0	0	0	44	3805
Koffiefontein	131	0	0	0	0	414	0	0	0	39	0	8	4214	45	18	0	0	0	1298	16	0	0	0	58	6241
Koppies	170	0	0	0	0	594	0	0	0	32	0	35	8297	18	35	0	0	0	691	16	0	0	0	129	10017
Kroonstad	1241	0	0	0	0	4630	0	0	0	222	0	79	46816	206	151	0	0	0	8222	220	0	0	0	501	62288
Ladybrand	441	0	0	0	0	598	0	0	0	68	0	21	10789	139	138	0	0	0	2611	56	0	0	0	83	14944
Lindley	491	0	0	0	0	1388	0	0	0	69	0	36	16675	53	71	0	0	0	1593	45	0	0	0	260	20681
Marquard	198	0	0	0	0	304	0	0	0	32	0	8	6026	63	34	0	0	0	576	15	0	0	0	66	7322
Odendaalsrus	929	0	0	0	0	2358	0	0	0	99	0	67	42776	109	169	0	0	0	3725	361	0	0	0	344	50937
Parys	443	0	0	0	0	2879	0	0	0	102	0	40	19551	109	44	0	0	0	3444	89	0	0	0	208	26909
Petrusburg	96	0	0	0	0	487	0	0	0	17	0	14	3268	24	12	0	0	0	673	12	0	0	0	53	4656
Philippolis	19	0	0	0	0	367	0	0	0	26	0	3	1724	13	9	0	0	0	1229	26	0	0	0	0	3416
Qwa Qwa	2300	0	0	0	0	126	0	0	0	222	0	189	112089	254	8711	0	0	0	1915	284	0	0	0	844	126934
Reddersburg	67	0	0	0	0	399	0	0	0	9	0	8	2715	18	11	0	0	0	727	17	0	0	0	39	4010
Reitz	301	0	0	0	0	708	0	0	0	218	0	32	9988	61	77	0	0	0	1927	85	0	0	0	155	13552
Rouxville	175	0	0	0	0	400	0	0	0	10	0	10	4505	18	10	0	0	0	802	8	0	0	0	36	5974
Sasolburg	1143	0	0	0	0	7571	0	0	0	265	0	103	33120	402	131	0	0	0	10698	440	0	0	0	390	54263
Senekal	340	0	0	0	0	1035	0	0	0	54	0	37	13995	60	494	0	0	0	2009	36	0	0	0	206	18266
Smithfield	130	0	0	0	0	212	0	0	0	13	0	4	2497	19	15	0	0	0	565	10	0	0	0	41	3506
Thaba Nchu	845	0	0	0	0	129	0	0	0	152	0	71	30078	315	130	0	0	0	3753	104	0	0	0	0	35577
Theunissen	308	0	0	0	0	880	0	0	0	31	0	26	17366	44	22	0	0	0	1211	188	0	0	0	228	20304
Trompsburg	47	0	0	0	0	234	0	0	0	17	0	8	1957	10	4	0	0	0	678	7	0	0	0	23	2985
Ventersburg	123	0	0	0	0	394	0	0	0	15	0	10	5241	22	20	0	0	0	571	16	0	0	0	67	6479
Viljoenskroon	416	0	0	0	0	1021	0	0	0	48	0	42	25873	130	47	0	0	0	1072	286	0	0	0	196	29131
Virginia	799	0	0	0	0	3012	0	0	0	167	0	57	33711	211	118	0	0	0	6108	317	0	0	0	524	45024
Vrede	215	0	0	0	0	1042	0	0	0	52	0	36	13743	58	57	0	0	0	1963	167	0	0	0	116	17449
Vredefort	149	0	0	0	0	567	0	0	0	41	0	20	6408	16	18	0	0	0	574	18	0	0	0	61	7872
Welkom	2794	0	0	0	0	7426	0	0	0	808	0	191	114007	843	672	0	0	0	18948	1489	0	0	0	1000	148178
Wepener	194	0	0	0	0	322	0	0	0	39	0	11	5748	56	11	0	0	0	994	20	0	0	0	106	7501
Wesselsbron	306	0	0	0	0	798	0	0	0	20	0	29	12707	29	35	0	0	0	844	26	0	0	0	133	14927
Winburg	143	0	0	0	0	503	0	0	0	20	0	16	7347	25	27	0	0	0	818	17	0	0	0	84	9000
Zastron	259	0	0	0	0	380	0	0	0	61	0	14	6834	38	36	0	0	0	778	13	0	0	0	103	8516
Total:	24451	0	0	0	0	81662	0	0	0	6072	0	2008	1037998	7664	17024	0	0	0	170452	6935	0	0	0	10286	1364552

Provincial result: Gauteng by district

	PAC	SAWP	UPF	XPP	GRP	FF/VF	WKFP	WI	AMP	ACDP	WRPP	ADM	ANC	DP	DPSA	FP	Luso	IP	NP	IFP	MP	RP	MF	Spoilt	Total
Alberton	2791	0	0	138	0	5469	0	0	84	600	200	202	135417	2416	262	244	55	0	26730	8200	0	0	0	1470	184278
Benoni	2751	0	0	113	0	6779	0	0	725	967	293	206	111858	8789	199	576	77	0	35543	7931	0	0	0	1161	177968
Boksburg	1505	0	0	98	0	6948	0	0	107	900	148	86	60765	2959	138	233	67	0	31101	6517	0	0	0	388	111960
Brakpan	1034	0	0	40	0	8240	0	0	175	468	88	93	49567	1960	59	164	34	0	23384	1800	0	0	0	512	87618
Germiston	945	0	0	108	0	11070	0	0	31	1225	187	102	38534	15552	165	1073	209	0	58738	7090	0	0	0	825	135854
Heidelberg (PWV)	783	0	0	25	0	6009	0	0	52	146	24	72	23695	419	82	54	16	0	5940	1854	0	0	0	369	39540
Johannesburg	15904	0	0	1228	0	17903	0	0	6657	4660	2977	1171	686955	88046	1479	5213	3931	0	270419	71743	0	0	0	7245	1185531
Kempton Park	4469	0	0	190	0	11223	0	0	40	1275	241	202	147844	5158	197	413	67	0	41419	4784	0	0	0	1072	218594
Krugersdorp	2875	0	0	95	0	11241	0	0	349	533	173	174	82168	2923	281	368	60	0	25988	3518	0	0	0	665	131411
Nigel	808	0	0	16	0	3910	0	0	77	175	27	14	35684	499	63	54	21	0	9392	646	0	0	0	445	51831
Oberholzer	1522	0	0	96	0	5571	0	0	26	172	76	135	68798	541	123	60	33	0	11272	5191	0	0	0	1101	94717
Pretoria (PWV)	7488	0	0	393	0	99238	0	0	2245	8345	749	669	317208	25546	533	2397	437	0	217422	6185	0	0	0	3061	691916
Randburg	2822	0	0	295	0	4158	0	0	177	1937	623	280	116674	46687	314	3369	99	0	58780	9613	0	0	0	1649	247477
Randfontein	1023	0	0	44	0	7402	0	0	43	167	76	76	38696	665	80	90	45	0	14888	1056	0	0	0	628	64979
Roodepoort	1575	0	0	83	0	15996	0	0	257	1584	263	172	80645	12988	209	1248	84	0	61801	4830	0	0	0	1921	183656
Springs	1756	0	0	73	0	8168	0	0	106	473	131	111	71807	2647	137	227	38	0	25363	2883	0	0	0	0	113920
Vanderbijlpark	5757	0	0	59	0	11185	0	0	66	800	246	223	182926	1266	221	142	62	0	27825	1731	0	0	0	1346	233855
Vereeniging	4468	0	0	100	0	15190	0	0	1092	882	669	257	113876	3630	227	290	60	0	44607	3538	0	0	0	767	189653
Westonaria	1236	0	0	81	0	3235	0	0	579	233	88	107	55140	857	84	64	28	0	11928	4457	0	0	0	758	78875
Total:	61512	0	0	3275	0	258935	0	0	12888	25542	7279	4352	2418257	223548	4853	16279	5423	0	1002540	153567	0	0	0	25383	4223633

Provincial result: Western Cape by district

	PAC	SAWP	UPF	XPP	GRP	FF/VF	WKFP	WI	AMP	ACDP	WRPP	ADM	AN	DP	DPSA	FP	Luso	IP	NP	IFP	MP	RP	MF	Spoilt	Total
Beaufort-West	169	10	0	0	10	765	65	10	18	90	0	25	4983	389	0	0	0	20	10825	66	0	0	0	154	17599
Bellville	404	159	0	0	135	5663	400	58	650	3321	0	51	26470	8105	0	0	0	704	117413	500	0	0	0	547	164580
Bredasdorp	34	10	0	0	9	817	44	6	10	133	0	12	2337	1330	0	0	0	12	8492	42	0	0	0	77	13365
Caledon	346	51	0	0	39	1039	230	20	77	329	0	79	13203	2834	0	0	0	53	26294	167	0	0	0	306	45067
Calitzdorp	24	6	0	0	8	182	6	3	4	6	0	2	520	50	0	0	0	8	2918	25	0	0	0	50	3812
Cape	1222	213	0	0	297	1560	219	49	2195	1702	0	68	34227	18107	0	0	0	1619	63709	641	0	0	0	490	126318
Ceres	252	18	0	0	16	420	76	5	25	101	0	38	7666	374	0	0	0	30	16526	72	0	0	0	129	25748
Clanwilliam	43	14	0	0	5	654	85	5	10	100	0	27	3899	287	0	0	0	14	10146	68	0	0	0	64	15421
George	620	67	0	0	54	2200	179	23	36	886	0	64	21402	2571	0	0	0	44	31238	318	0	0	0	268	59970
Goodwood	2028	173	0	0	145	1883	368	63	1414	1844	0	105	45874	7754	0	0	0	1101	90219	391	0	0	0	739	154101
Heidelberg (W. Cape)	23	3	0	0	4	270	24	2	3	23	0	10	1341	171	0	0	0	6	4034	26	0	0	0	42	5982
Hermanus	149	12	0	0	30	655	65	1	9	204	0	15	4172	1393	0	0	0	4	10318	83	0	0	0	123	17233
Hopefield	14	0	0	0	8	259	0	0	15	74	0	5	1316	369	0	0	0	0	4230	32	0	0	0	33	6355
Knysna	368	69	0	0	72	993	137	14	33	525	0	46	14067	3863	0	0	0	15	16490	240	0	0	0	325	37257
Kuils River	1159	115	0	0	59	3072	461	48	282	1514	0	138	46658	3054	0	0	0	255	66742	287	0	0	0	595	124439
Ladismith	28	7	0	0	2	261	32	2	8	62	0	12	1795	168	0	0	0	2	4570	25	0	0	0	32	7006
Laingsburg	13	10	0	0	2	185	23	1	1	51	0	3	538	61	0	0	0	8	2546	13	0	0	0	15	3470
Malmesbury	206	59	0	0	48	1519	241	20	164	563	0	60	12751	1941	0	0	0	103	42148	202	0	0	0	350	60375
Mitchell's Plain	9323	202	0	0	46	144	436	81	3918	1702	0	262	200703	4555	0	0	0	3670	66640	337	0	0	0	1361	293380
Montagu	143	9	0	0	11	353	215	7	7	146	0	15	3329	937	0	0	0	8	7840	46	0	0	0	79	13145
Mooreesburg	16	7	0	0	3	469	21	3	4	39	0	5	955	101	0	0	0	11	4616	30	0	0	0	43	6323
Mossel Bay	257	22	0	0	26	2243	92	13	32	453	0	27	10725	782	0	0	0	37	18576	132	0	0	0	161	33578
Murraysburg	8	1	0	0	1	78	3	0	4	14	0	9	872	40	0	0	0	1	1581	6	0	0	0	19	2637
Oudtshoorn	171	33	0	0	20	1575	83	10	24	119	0	75	10139	557	0	0	0	38	23528	156	0	0	0	205	36733
Paarl	687	83	0	0	54	1745	357	34	486	468	0	54	31779	2432	0	0	0	205	46869	212	0	0	0	477	85942
Piquetberg	55	20	0	0	14	976	132	7	24	96	0	20	4002	343	0	0	0	25	14279	54	0	0	0	101	20148
Prince Albert	6	2	0	0	3	202	41	0	2	13	0	2	649	89	0	0	0	2	3792	20	0	0	0	48	4871
Riversdale	34	11	0	0	8	897	37	2	1	116	0	11	2006	289	0	0	0	7	11011	48	0	0	0	84	14562
Robertson	206	12	0	0	30	538	111	13	13	89	0	26	4273	456	0	0	0	25	11412	98	0	0	0	171	17473
Simonstown	286	141	0	0	213	658	165	23	655	1793	0	39	11767	11269	0	0	0	428	33533	378	0	0	0	253	61601
Somerset West	283	25	0	0	65	921	131	10	145	805	0	38	12161	4847	0	0	0	55	23325	189	0	0	0	243	43243
Stellenbosch	321	55	0	0	96	1349	236	26	205	863	0	71	13552	3982	0	0	0	100	30000	196	0	0	0	315	51367
Strand	133	21	0	0	25	1578	98	1	309	544	0	29	8186	1407	0	0	0	187	19179	105	0	0	0	139	31941
Swellendam	125	7	0	0	3	633	49	9	14	107	0	30	4980	803	0	0	0	12	9808	82	0	0	0	140	16802
Tulbagh	106	14	0	0	11	351	61	7	26	63	0	19	4221	252	0	0	0	16	8514	48	0	0	0	114	13823
Uniondale	35	4	0	0	6	183	39	2	0	17	0	7	1159	51	0	0	0	5	2548	26	0	0	0	42	4124
Van Rhynsdorp	37	5	0	0	10	451	53	3	7	22	0	14	1645	74	0	0	0	10	5657	35	0	0	0	80	8103
Vredenburg	111	9	0	0	7	721	99	7	27	196	0	20	7098	483	0	0	0	23	14617	73	0	0	0	2	23493
Vredendal	206	153	0	0	234	1479	166	41	124	299	0	31	10844	7041	0	0	0	123	28494	251	0	0	0	159	49645
Wellington	78	23	0	0	14	614	114	8	85	184	0	19	5179	846	0	0	0	49	15433	87	0	0	0	162	22895
Worcester	546	45	0	0	29	1726	257	25	218	538	0	76	23190	1307	0	0	0	134	39520	195	0	0	0	459	68265
Wynberg	2401	741	0	0	719	1722	686	193	9670	5517	0	280	88943	46206	0	0	0	7593	168612	1443	0	0	0	1518	336244
Total:	22676	2641	0	0	2611	44003	6337	855	20954	25731	0	1939	705576	141970	0	0	0	16762	1138242	7445	0	0	0	10714	2148456

National and provincial results: Spoilt ballots by province (per cent)

Province	National	Regional
Eastern Cape	0.61	0.45
Eastern Transvaal	1.25	0.94
KwaZulu-Natal	1.22	1.06
North-West	1.23	1.19
Northern Cape	1.14	0.87
Northern Transvaal	0.93	0.71
Orange Free State	1.07	0.75
Gauteng	0.70	0.60
Western Cape	1.20	0.50
Total	0.98	0.75

Index